NEW MEXICO GEOLOGICAL SOCIETY

Guidebook
of the
ALBUQUERQUE COUNTRY
Edited by
Stuart A. Northrop

TWELFTH FIELD CONFERENCE
October 6, 7, and 8, 1961

NEW MEXICO GEOLOGICAL SOCIETY ◆ TWELFTH FIELD CONFERENCE

CONTENTS

President's Message 3

Executive and Field Conference Committees 4

Publications of the New Mexico Geological Society 5

Schedule 5

A Few Words from the Editor 6

Physiographic Setting 7

Photo mosaic maps of Sandia, Lucero, and Jemez areas, central New Mexico .... Lowell E. Bogart 8

ROAD LOGS

Sandia Mountains and vicinity
    First day, Friday, October 6 .... Vincent C. Kelley and Charles B. Read 14

West of Albuquerque in the Rio Puerco, Rio San Jose, and Lucero areas
    Second day, Saturday, October 7 .... V. C. Kelley and C. B. Read 33

Jemez Mountains and vicinity
    Third day, Sunday, October 8 .... V. C. Kelley, E. H. Baltz, Jr., and R. A. Bailey 47

PAPERS

Physiography, climate, and vegetation of the Albuquerque region	Roger Y. Anderson	63
Sandia Cave	Frank C. Hibben	72
Indians, ancient and modern, in the Albuquerque country	Sidney R. Ash	75
History of the Albuquerque region	Frank D. Reeve	82
Chronological resume of some early geologists in the Albuquerque country	Stuart A. Northrop	85
Absolute geologic time scale		89
Precambrian rocks of the Albuquerque country	J. Paul Fitzsimmons	90
Pennsylvanian rocks in north-central New Mexico	Frank E. Kottlowski	97
Mississippian and Pennsylvanian fossils of the Albuquerque country	Stuart A. Northrop	105
Permian strata of central New Mexico	D. L. Baars	113
Triassic and Jurassic rocks of the Albuquerque area	Clay T. Smith	121
Cretaceous rocks of the Albuquerque country		129
Late Cenozoic sediments of the lower Jemez River region	Zane Spiegel	132
Outline of the geology of the Jemez Mountains, New Mexico	C. S. Ross, R. L. Smith, and R. A. Bailey	139
Structural problems of the Rio Grande trough in the Albuquerque country	Anonymous	144
The Rio Grande trough near Albuquerque, New Mexico	H. R. Joesting, J. E. Case, and L. E. Cordell	148
Earthquakes of central New Mexico	Stuart A. Northrop	151
Earthquake research at New Mexico Institute of Mining and Technology	A. R. Sanford and C. R. Holmes	153
The new U. S. Coast and Geodetic Survey Seismological Laboratory at Albuquerque		154
Mineral resources of Bernalillo, Sandoval, and Santa Fe Counties, New Mexico (exclusive of oil and gas)	Wolfgang E. Elston	155
Mineralogical notes on the uranium deposits of the Grants and Laguna districts	Abraham Rosenzweig	168
Check lists of minerals for mining districts and other localities near Albuquerque	Stuart A. Northrop	172
Petroleum exploration in a part of north-central New Mexico	Edward C. Beaumont	175
Ground-water geology of the Rio Grande trough in north-central New Mexico, with sections on the Jemez caldera and the Lucero uplift	Frank B. Titus, Jr.	186
Abstracts of technical papers		193

IN POCKET

Geologic map of the Albuquerque country
by
Stuart A. Northrop and Arlette Hill

Tectonic map of a part of the upper Rio Grande area, New Mexico
by
V. C. Kelley

PRESIDENT'S MESSAGE

THE BROAD VIEW

— — is important to all geologists, regardless of their status within the science, and regardless of their degree of professional specialization. To provide this view is the distinct privilege of the only non-affiliated Geological Society serving New Mexico. We take this seriously enough to consider it a duty.

The Twelfth Field Conference of the New Mexico Geological Society brings us back from far-flung and comprehensive forays into the far corners of the State—and some adjacent areas—back to the environs of the great population center, Albuquerque. Here, through the efforts of professional and student geologists, a wide variety of geologic, mineralogic, paleontologic, and physiographic information is continually updated and expanded. In every direction, new data add to a better understanding of familiar geologic features and of their interrelated importance.

Under the able guidance of Charles B. Read of the United States Geological Survey, 5th president of the Society, as general chairman of the Conference, and of Stuart A. Northrop of the Geology Department at the University of New Mexico, 3rd president of the Society, as editor of the Guidebook, we will have an authoritative look at a variety of features at the very heart of New Mexico geology. The trip leaders and the guidebook authors are outstanding students of their phases of geologic interest and of their areas of investigation.

To every geologist in New Mexico, and in the surrounding territory, this Conference will be a valuable experience in re-orientation, and the guidebook will be an indispensable addition to his professional library.

The committee's ingenuity in operating this Conference from Albuquerque as a hub, with a return to the city each evening, works to the advantage of all participants. Scheduling on a week end permits more of our friends to whom geology is an avocation to come "rock-hounding" with us. This is an ideal field trip in many respects. We express our gratitude to the many committee members, authors, and trip leaders whose efforts make it so. Much work was done, also, by members who shared the serious responsibilities of the Society, but whose names do not appear in these formal listings.

These conscientious workers find their reward in your enthusiastic attendance, and your appreciative acceptance and use of the guidebook. They gain, also, in ability and effectiveness in their own field of endeavor through the experience of this cooperative effort. This is the way an effective scientific society works, and this is the reason it is effective.

The members of the executive committee welcome you. We know you will enjoy the comradeship and discussions with friends of mutual interest. We believe you will be inspired by inspection of geologic phenomena from Precambrian to Recent, and from stratigraphic and structural to igneous and mineralized. We hope you will be stimulated by the invigorating climate from warm, low deserts to cool, majestic pine-clad mountains.

Join us, too, next May at our Technical Meeting in Albuquerque. And plan ahead for our next Field Conference. Our delayed plans with the Arizona Geological Society should develop, and will take us into the "Tonto Rim" country from westernmost-central New Mexico into east-central Arizona.

Richard D. Holt, President
New Mexico Geological Society

EXECUTIVE COMMITTEE

Richard D. Holt	President	Humble Oil and Refining Co.
Elmer H. Baltz, Jr.	Vice-President	U. S. Geological Survey, Water Resources Division
Frank B. Titus, Jr.	Secretary	U. S. Geological Survey, Water Resources Division
Wolfgang E. Elston	Treasurer	Department of Geology, University of New Mexico
Frank E. Kottlowski	Past President	New Mexico Bureau of Mines and Mineral Resources

FIELD CONFERENCE COMMITTEES

Charles B. Read	General Chairman	U. S. Geological Survey, Paleontology and Stratigraphy Branch

Guidebook Committee

Stuart A. Northrop	Editor	Department of Geology, University of New Mexico

Road Logging Committee

Vincent C. Kelley	Chairman	Department of Geology, University of New Mexico
Roy A. Bailey		U. S. Geological Survey
Elmer H. Baltz, Jr.		U. S. Geological Survey, Water Resources Division

Registration Committee

Frederick J. Kuellmer	Chairman	New Mexico Bureau of Mines and Mineral Resources

Caravan Committee

Frank E. Kottlowski	Co-Chairman	New Mexico Bureau of Mines and Mineral Resources
Sam Thompson, III	Co-Chairman	Humble Oil and Refining Co.

Advertising Committee

James L. Albright	Chairman	Pubco Petroleum Corp.

Finance Committee

Wolfgang E. Elston		Department of Geology, University of New Mexico

Catering Committee

S. Eugene Buell	Chairman	U. S. Geological Survey, Water Resources Division

PUBLICATIONS OF THE NEW MEXICO GEOLOGICAL SOCIETY

1. Guidebook of the San Juan Basin [covering north and east sides], New Mexico and Colorado; First Field Conference, 1950; edited by Vincent C. Kelley and others; 153 pages, 40 illustrations. (Out of print)
2. Guidebook of the south and west sides of the San Juan Basin, New Mexico and Arizona; Second Field Conference, 1951; edited by Clay T. Smith and Caswell Silver; 163 pages, 69 illustrations. (Out of print)
3. Guidebook of the Rio Grande country, central New Mexico; Third Field Conference, 1952; edited by Ross B. Johnson and Charles B. Read; 126 pages, 51 illustrations. (Out of print)
4. Guidebook of southwestern New Mexico; Fourth Field Conference, 1953; edited by Frank E. Kottlowski and others; 165 pages, 67 illustrations. $5.00
5. Guidebook of southeastern New Mexico; Fifth Field Conference, 1954; edited by T. F. Stipp; 213 pages, 83 illustrations. $5.00
6. Guidebook of south-central New Mexico; Sixth Field Conference, 1955; edited by J. Paul Fitzsimmons; 193 pages, 70 illustrations. Prepared with the cooperation of the Roswell Geological Society. $7.00 (Only a few copies left)
7. Guidebook of southeastern Sangre de Cristo Mountains, New Mexico (Raton Basin); Seventh Field Conference, 1956; edited by A. Rosenzweig; 154 pages, 61 illustrations. $7.00
8. Guidebook of southwestern San Juan Mountains, Colorado (Four Corners Area); Eighth Field Conference, 1957; edited by Frank E. Kottlowski; 258 pages, 109 illustrations. $7.00
9. Guidebook of the Black Mesa Basin, northeast Arizona; Ninth Field Conference, 1958; edited by Roger Y. Anderson and John W. Harshbarger; 205 pages, 105 illustrations, hard binding. Prepared in cooperation with the Arizona Geological Society. $8.50
10. Guidebook of west-central New Mexico; Tenth Field Conference, 1959; edited by James E. Weir, Jr. and Elmer H. Baltz, Jr.; 162 pages, 83 illustrations, hard binding. $8.50
11. Guidebook of Rio Chama country [New Mexico and Colorado]; Eleventh Field Conference, 1960; edited by Edward C. Beaumont and Charles B. Read; 129 pages, 35 illustrations, hard binding. $8.50
12. Guidebook of the Albuquerque country [New Mexico]; Twelfth Field Conference; edited by Stuart A. Northrop; hard binding. $9.50.

These publications are available by mail (please add 25¢ for handling and postage) from the New Mexico Bureau of Mines and Mineral Resources, Campus Station, Socorro, New Mexico. Also over-the-counter sales at either the Bureau of Mines or the Department of Geology, University of New Mexico, Albuquerque. Checks should be made payable to the New Mexico Geological Society. Geologic maps accompanying certain guidebooks are available by mail or over the counter at the Bureau of Mines, Socorro, as follows:

(a) Geologic map of the Sierra County region, New Mexico; compiled by Vincent C. Kelley; accompanies Guidebook of the Sixth Field Conference. $1.00
(b) Geologic map of the Rio Chama country; compiled by Clay T. Smith and William R. Muehlberger; accompanies Guidebook of the Eleventh Field Conference. $0.50
(c) Geologic map of the Albuquerque country; compiled by Stuart A. Northrop and Arlette Hill; accompanies Guidebook of the Twelfth Field Conference. $1.00

———O———

SCHEDULE

Thursday, October 5
5:00 - 10:00 p.m. — Registration, New Mexico Union, University of New Mexico Campus, Albuquerque, New Mexico.

Friday, October 6
7:30 a.m. — Caravan assembles on East Central (U. S. 66-East) at Juan Tabo Road.

Saturday, October 7
7:30 a.m. — Caravan assembles on West Central (U. S. 66-West), 3 miles west of Rio Grande bridge.

Sunday, October 8
7:30 a.m. — Caravan assembles on San Mateo Blvd., N.E., at Montgomery Road.

? — Field Conference ends near Santa Fe.

———O———

A FEW WORDS FROM THE EDITOR

A glance at the accompanying geologic map (in pocket) will reveal that Albuquerque is not at the geographic center of the map-area. One of the chief reasons for this is that the U. S. Geological Survey's revised map of the northeastern quarter of the State has not yet been published. The map from which the Guidebook map was compiled is Dane and Bachman's (1957) "Preliminary geologic map of the northwestern part of New Mexico" (U. S. Geol. Survey Misc. Geol. Inv. Map I-224), which distinguishes more than 78 stratigraphic units. It seemed to some of us that a map designed for use on a field conference, in conjunction with a road log, should be kept as simple as possible. Thus, the Guidebook map employs only 10 stratigraphic units. (In the planning stages, we referred to our map as a "60-mile-an-hour map.")

It has not been possible to cover all aspects of the geology of the Albuquerque country in this Guidebook. The Guidebook does not pretend to be a compendium of all that is known of the geology of the area. Many significant facets are described in one or more chapters, but several short articles might have been prepared to deal with certain other aspects. The geologic literature is voluminous and many important published papers are neither cited in the text nor even included in the several lists of references. At one time we thought of compiling a complete bibliography—a sort of master bibliography—for the Guidebook, but this would have entailed so much repetition that we abandoned the idea.

Geographic Names.—Map-makers seem to delight in changing geographic names in the Southwest. Note the following changes in names of certain features in the area on U. S. G. S. maps from 1928 to 1960.

Darton's Geologic Map (1928)	New Mexico Base Map (1960)
Ladron Pk	Ladron Mts
Mesa Chivato	Cebolleta Mts
Nacimiento Mts	Sierra Nacimiento
San Pedro Mtn (near Cuba)	San Pedro Mountains [error]
San Pedro Mts (near Golden)	[not named]
Valle Mts	Jemez Mountains

The Ladron Mountains, just south of the south edge of the Guidebook map, have also been referred to as Sierra Ladron and Sierra Ladrones. The Jemez Mountains have been called the Sierra de los Valles; the latter term is properly applied to only a part of the mountains surmounting the Jemez Plateau. The great depression at the summit of the Jemez Plateau has been called Jemez crater, Jemez caldera, Valles crater, Valles caldera, and is often referred to by many local people as the Valle Grande. Actually, Valle Grande is simply one of several valleys occupying the caldera, as pointed out by Ross, Smith, and Bailey in their article in the Guidebook.

Editorial Policy.—Editorial policies and practices change continually. In some of the Society's guidebooks, the editors have given contributors a free hand, especially in the format of citing references. In view of the commendable attempts in recent years to standardize the order of citation in bibliographic lists (see "Suggestions to authors of the reports of the U. S. Geological Survey," 5th ed., p. 107) and also to standardize the abbreviations used in citations (ibid., p. 111-118), your editor has made a valiant attempt to achieve some degree of uniformity in this Guidebook. He apologizes to certain authors for making extensive alterations in format, especially in their lists of references. Practically every reference has been checked for the name of the author, the date, the title, the source (periodical, series, etc.), the volume number, and pages. The bibliographies are thus believed to be relatively free of errors.

Incidentally, the editor has not followed Geological Survey style in every particular. For example, he prefers "New Mexico" to the Survey's familiar abbreviation "N. Mex." He does not care for the Survey's use of "N. Mex. Univ.", but prefers "Univ. New Mexico" (partly because the institution near Las Cruces now calls itself "New Mexico State University"). He has generally shortened "New Mexico Institute of Mining and Technology State Bureau of Mines and Mineral Resources" to "New Mexico Bur. Mines and Mineral Res." The editor has a distinct aversion to the recently adopted capitalization of stratigraphic terms, such as system, group, and formation, in "Permian System," "Santa Fe Group," "Madera Limestone." Again, the editor sees no necessity for the hyphen in such color terms as "light gray" or "reddish brown" when used as modifiers before the noun. On the other hand, he has retained the hyphen in such terms as "olive-green" and "chocolate-brown." (The reader will find some inconsistencies in hyphening of color terms between chapters edited early and those edited late.) Writers have been allowed individual preference in some cases; some prefer "Abo Pass" and others, "Abo pass;" some prefer "Sandia Crest" and others, "Sandia crest." Some prefer "aligned" and others, "alined."

The Geological Survey has long frowned on citation of theses and dissertations on the grounds that "unpublished theses generally are not conveniently available." However, such material is now becoming available in microfilm form. In this Guidebook frequent citation of unpublished theses is made. We believe that such a great storehouse of information should not go unmentioned.

Every paper submitted for the Guidebook has been read by Charles B. Read, and the editor has profited greatly by his long experience with field conferences and guidebooks.

Stuart A. Northrop

PHYSIOGRAPHIC SETTING

According to the well-known Fenneman map, "Physical Divisions of the United States" (U. S. Geol. Survey, 1930), within a radius of 90 miles of Albuquerque there are three major physiographic divisions, four provinces, and seven sections, as follows:

INTERIOR PLAINS major division
    Great Plains province
        Raton section (13g)
        Pecos Valley section (13h)
ROCKY MOUNTAIN SYSTEM major division
    Southern Rocky Mountains province (16)
    (not subdivided into sections)
INTERMONTANE PLATEAUS major division
    Colorado Plateaus province
        Navajo section (21d)
        Datil section (21f)
    Basin and Range province
        Mexican Highland section (22d)
        Sacramento section (22e)

Characteristics of the sections are as follows:

Raton section: trenched peneplain surmounted by dissected lava-capped plateaus and buttes.

Pecos Valley section: late mature to old plain.

Southern Rocky Mountains province: complex mountains of various types; intermont basins.

Navajo section: young plateaus; smaller relief than the Canyon Lands section (21c) of Colorado and Utah.

Datil section: lava flows entire or in remnants; volcanic necks.

Mexican Highland section: isolated ranges (largely dissected block mountains) separated by aggraded desert plains.

Sacramento section: mature block mountains of gently tilted strata; block plateaus; bolsons.

The only section well represented in the State that does not approach to within 90 miles of Albuquerque is the High Plains (13d), about 150 miles east of Albuquerque. The Canyon Lands section (21c) barely enters the State at the northwest corner; this is about 175 miles from Albuquerque.

Note that the Rocky Mountains terminate between Santa Fe and Las Vegas, despite a National Geographic Society map that shows them extending clear across New Mexico and terminating in West Texas. (It is reliably reported that the reason for this was that the Society had many members residing in Texas who liked to think that their State included a bit of the Rockies! These people still invade New Mexico and Colorado to fish.) Of course, it all depends on the point of view. Structurally, the Sandia-Manzano Range may partake of some of the characteristics of the Southern Rocky Mountains province, but Fenneman's classification stresses physiography, and the Rio Grande depression, the Sandia-Manzano Range, and the Estancia bolson certainly resemble Basin and Range physiography—with "isolated ranges (largely dissected block mountains) separated by aggraded desert plains."

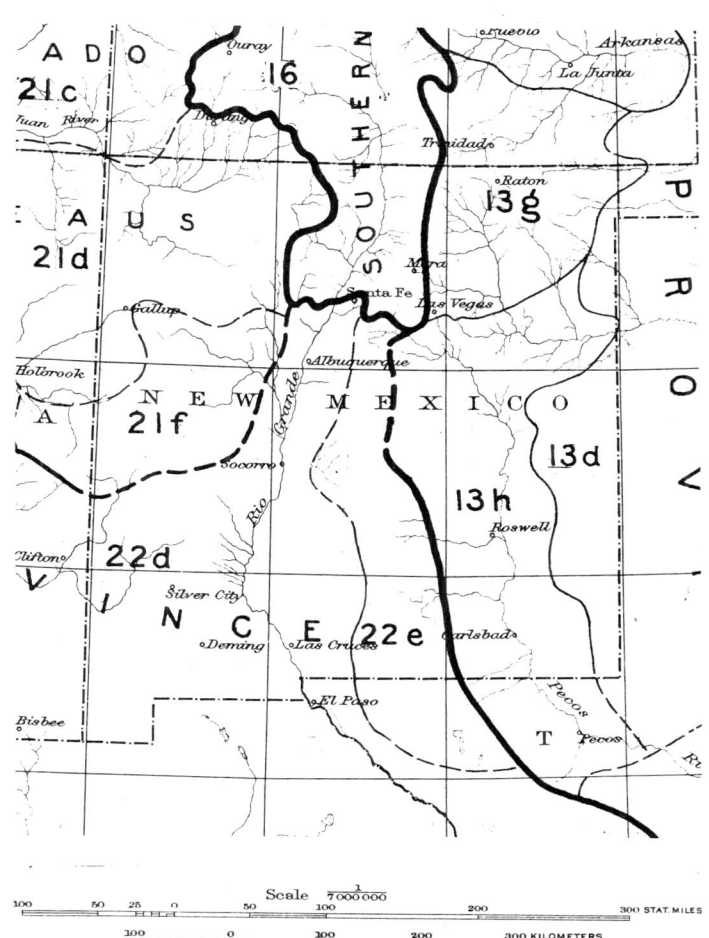

Physiographic divisions of New Mexico. Adapted from Fenneman (1930).

PHOTO MOSAIC MAPS OF SANDIA, LUCERO, AND JEMEZ AREAS, CENTRAL NEW MEXICO

LOWELL E. BOGART
Bogart and Wilson, Photogeologists, Albuquerque

INTRODUCTION

This paper is intended to demonstrate use of mosaics in reconnaissance mapping of land form, rock type, and regional structure. The photo map provides an excellent base for compilation of geologic data. All the qualities of a map are combined with the infinite detail of a photograph to present geologic data in a completeness unapproachable with line drawing.

Three maps are presented, one for each trip of the three-day conference. They are: Figure 1, Sandia Mountains-Hagan Basin Area; Figure 2, Lucero Area; and Figure 3, Jemez Area. Where possible, the route traversed and stops are shown.

Each map delineates land forms that are clearly expressed by reason of rock type, elevation, or structure. Lithologic type and stratigraphic position are shown only in the broadest sense. Structural grain is mapped in a detail dependent upon degree of expression visible on aerial photographs.

It must be emphasized that all data presented here result from mosaic interpretation without benefit of stereoscopic study. Accordingly, the position, or even presence, of some data on the maps may precipitate controversy. With this pleasant thought, we plunge into the three areas.

ACKNOWLEDGMENTS

Thanks are due Sinclair Oil and Gas Company and the Ground Water Branch of the U. S. Geological Survey for loan of mosaics. Gratitude is extended Charles de Sutter for aid in geologic annotation and Gene D. Wilson for critical review of the paper.

SANDIA MOUNTAINS-HAGAN BASIN AREA

Figure 1, bounded by 35°00', 35°30' N. Lat. and 106°00', 106°30' W. Long., includes the Sandia-San Pedro-Ortiz Mountains chain and bordering basins. Rocks ranging in age from Precambrian to Recent crop out.

Geomorphology

The Sandia Mountains trend N-S along the western side of the map. Precambrian granite occupies the western face of the mountains and is partially buried by alluvial fans to the west. Granite terrane is characteristically jointed. Dendritic drainage erodes granite into a texture of spines and pinnacles. Superposed upon the granite and dipping eastward into the Tijeras and Hagan coal basins is a sedimentary sequence from Pennsylvanian to Cretaceous in age. The Pennsylvanian limestone that forms the dip slope of the Sandia Mountains supports dense tree cover.

The South Mountain-San Pedro Mountains-Ortiz Mountains-Cerrillos Hills chain forms an intrusive belt. Note the distinctive texture of these areas. All of the peaks except Cerrillos Hills, at the north end, have coarse, rugged texture and dendritic drainage. Cerrillos Hills are low, partially obscured and exhibit fine texture on photos. The well-exposed geomorphology and structure of the porphyry belt is bounded on the east by the featureless Estancia Valley.

The barren lowland between Ortiz Mountains and Sandia Mountains is a synclinal area called the Hagan coal basin. Strata in the basin are partially covered by pediment gravel on the eastern side and faulted against Tertiary Santa Fe beds on the western side. Note the dendritic, sharp texture of the drainage pattern on the Santa Fe formation. This type of drainage pattern occurs on shales and unconsolidated fine clastics. Predominant lithology of Santa Fe beds is sandstone and siltstone which are poorly consolidated.

Characteristic of semi-arid climates, all the uplift areas are surrounded and partially obscured by alluvial aprons of their own erosional debris.

Structure

The Sandia Mountain-Hagan basin area clearly exhibits several major structural features. Tijeras fault is one of major proportion trending NE-SW through Tijeras Canyon. It appears to have large vertical and horizontal displacement. Along its trace the fault forms the boundary of several features: an area of metamorphic terrane, the Tijeras coal basin, and a Precambrian block northeast of San Antonito.

The Hagan fault forms the western boundary of the Hagan basin and terminates the north end of the Sandia Mountains. Santa Fe beds on the west are faulted against Cretaceous and older strata to the east.

The La Bajada fault extends northward from the west side of the Ortiz Mountains. Its throw accounts for the same Cretaceous beds on both sides of the fault, dipping steeply eastward but separated by several miles. Northward, the fault scarp rises to form a prominent physiographic feature.

There appears to be a major fault zone along the topographic saddle occupied by San Antonito and extending southeastward into the Estancia Valley. The Tijeras coal basin appears downfaulted two miles south of a Precambrian block. To the southeast, the Pennsylvanian outcrop terminates along this line.

The Tijeras coal basin is a folded wedge of Cretaceous rocks lying between two major faults. Throw on the Tijeras fault must be great because Precambrian basement is several thousand feet below the coal basin whereas basement is upthrown to 10,000 feet above sea level in the Sandia Mountains a few miles west.

The South Mountain-Ortiz Mountains-Cerrillos Hills form a belt of intrusive porphyry trending NNE-SSW. Surrounding the intrusives is a radial dike swarm. The porphyry belt is cut by the Tijeras fault zone at an angle near 30°.

LUCERO AREA

Figure 2, bounded by 34°30', 35°00' N. Lat. and 107°15', 107°45' W. Long., illustrates the Lucero uplift and adjacent basalt-capped mesas. The uplift has monoclinal west dip and is bordered on the east by a major thrust fault, Comanche fault.

Geomorphology

The Lucero uplift is dominated by a NE-trending scarp of Permian beds which plunges northward under basalt-capped Mesa Lucero. To the east the scarp rapidly descends into an open, low relief valley of Permian and Penn-

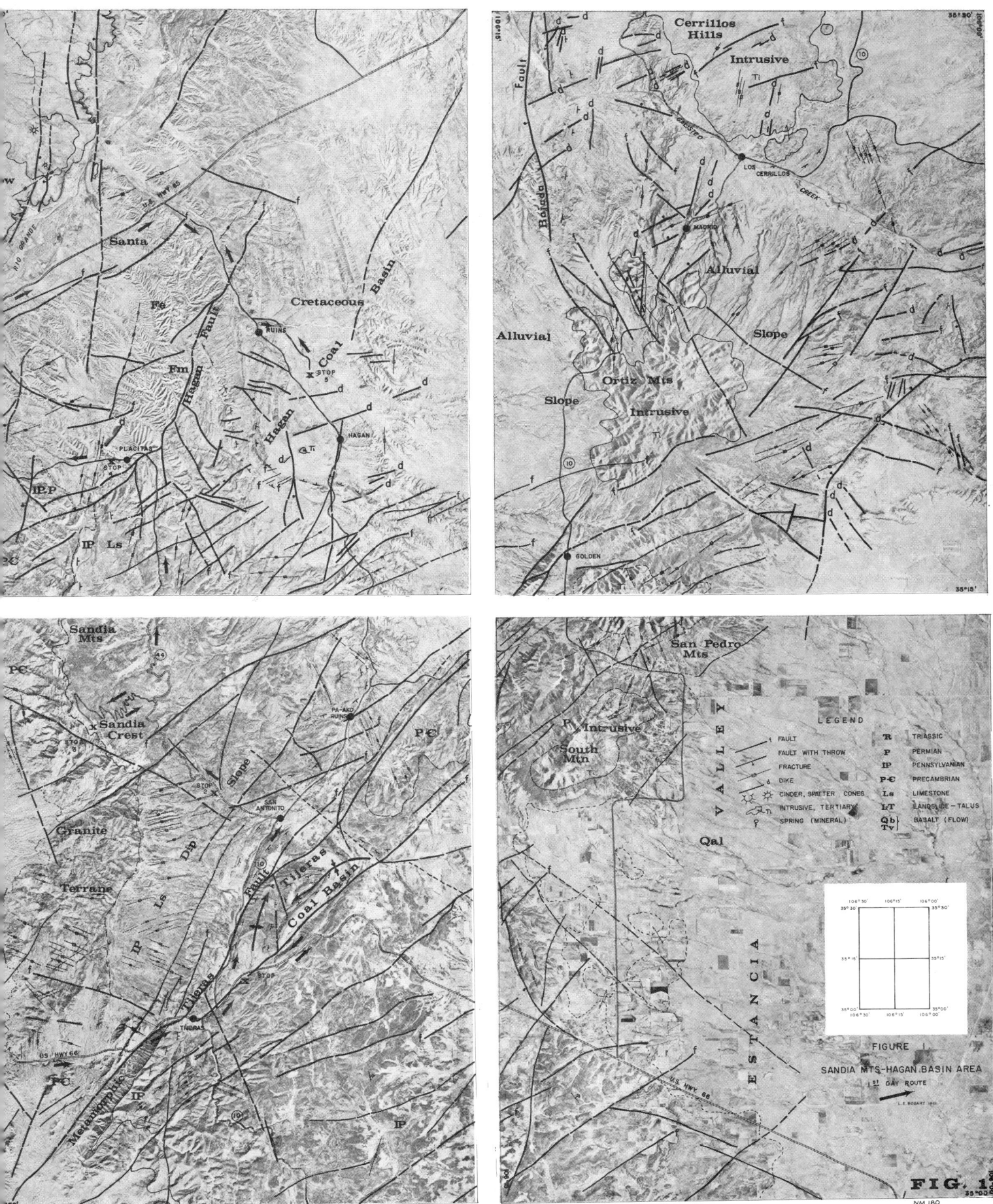

FIGURE 1
SANDIA MTS-HAGAN BASIN AREA
1ST DAY ROUTE

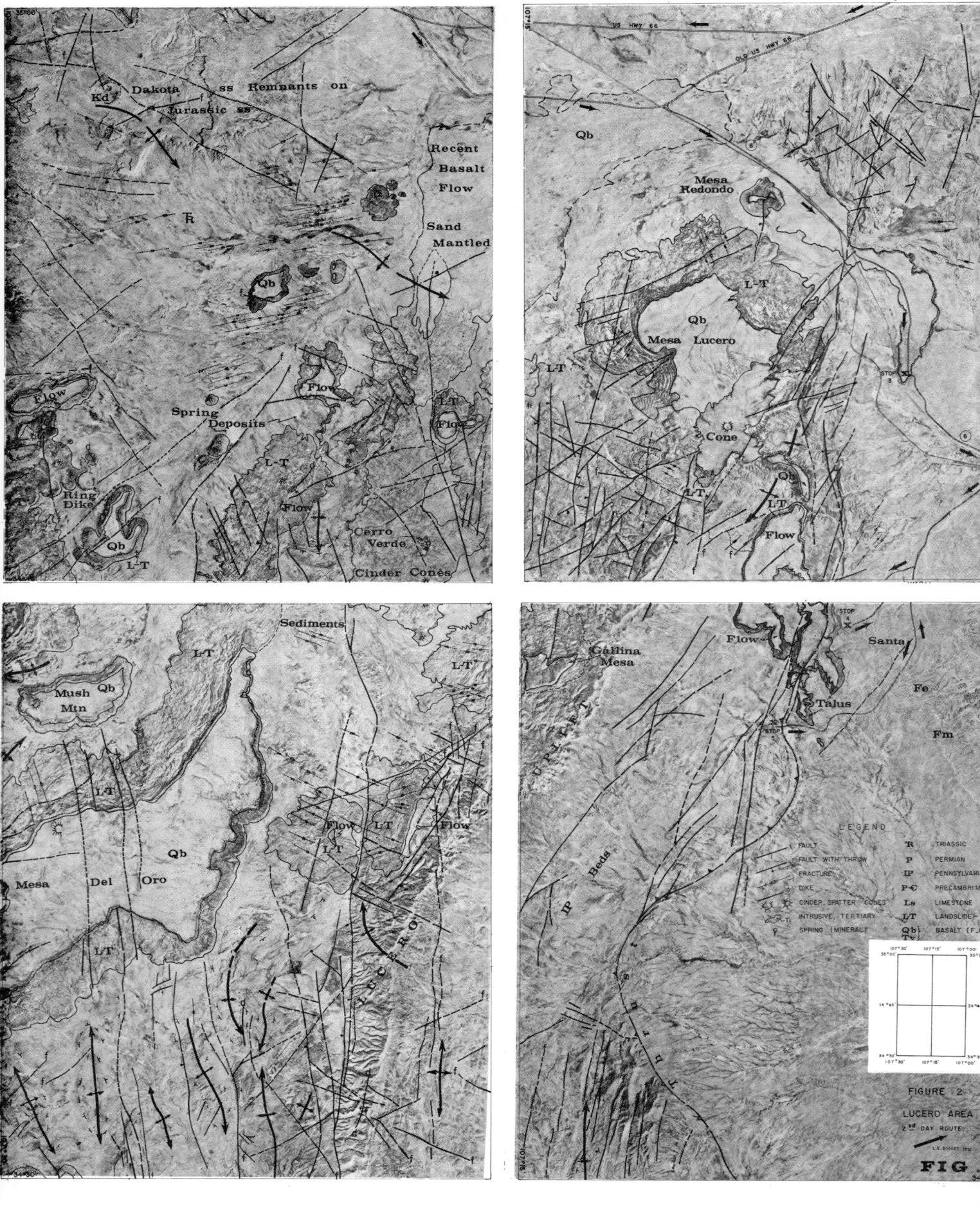

sylvanian rocks. The dip slope on Permian rocks is westerly and northwesterly.

The western portion of the map shows several prominent mesas that are capped with basalt. A very distinctive geomorphic feature of this area is the halo of landslide talus peripheral to each flow. Where flows cap incompetent Triassic Chinle shale, the talus forms stair steps of concentric landslide blocks. The talus apron is usually wider on the western side of flows because of the angle of divergence between flow surfaces and underlying beds. Note this condition surrounding Mesa del Oro. Sediments and lava converge at the northern tip of the mesa where local dip of strata is south. In areas where basalt flows occur updip and lie on Permian sandstones, the apron of landslide is missing.

The open valley, between Cerro Verde and the Jurassic cliffs in the northwest corner of the map, is formed on Triassic shale. The ENE-WSW lineations in the center of the valley suggest fracturing but may be merely the result of sand which is aligned by prevailing winds through wind gaps. The marked lineation, however, suggests structural origin.

Structure

Forces that elevated Lucero uplift, and folded and ruptured the rocks, appear to be essentially E-W compression. This compression thrust Pennsylvanian rocks toward the east and aligned fold axes in a N-S direction. Major faulting and folding is generally N-S in the southern part of the area. To the north this direction is complemented by NE- and NW-trending faults. The area between Mesa Lucero and Gallina Mesa is complexly faulted in a pattern suggesting shear. Elsewhere, the pattern suggests normal faulting of small magnitude.

Along the southern edge of the map, several N-S anticlines are well exposed. Conspicuously absent are well-defined synclines separating the anticlines. This suggests that folds are denuded only slightly into the amplitude of folding, so that synclines are sharp and narrow in extent compared to anticlines. In some cases it appears that this condition results in two anticlines being separated merely by a fault. The anticlines have steep limbs, narrow linear trend, and small area of closure. In most cases, plunge is north. Because of shape and size of these folds, they are not attractive as exploration targets for petroleum. Much greater importance can be attached to the broad structural highs that are suggested in several places by open, semicircular amphitheaters eroded in cliff-formers.

JEMEZ AREA

Figure 3, bounded by 35°30′, 36°00′ N. Lat. and 106°00′, 107°00′ W. Long., includes the prominent Jemez caldera bordered on the west by the Nacimiento uplift and on the east by the Rio Grande graben.

Geomorphology

The Jemez caldera, one of the three largest extinct volcanoes known, is a feature of great impact when viewed on aerial photographs. It has a circular rim, approximately 12 miles in diameter, which represents the central collapsed portion of the volcano. Within the rim are numerous younger cones resulting from renewed activity. Redondo Peak is the largest of these. Valle Grande is an elongated, open valley in the southeastern part of the caldera. The volcano is centered over the western fault boundary of the Rio Grande graben. This boundary fault zone no doubt provided an avenue for the escape of extrusives.

Completely surrounding the caldera is the main sloping body of the volcano which has been deeply dissected by drainage. This slope, from rim to base, is an average distance of 14 miles. Thus, the entire volcano has an approximate diameter of 40 miles.

Along the west side of Jemez volcano is Nacimiento Mountains, a fault block uplifted and partially thrust over sediments of the San Juan Baisn. The west front of the Nacimiento Mountains is a prominent geomorphic as well as structural feature. It is mainly a high-angle reverse fault but forms a thrust in places. The fault is a strikingly linear boundary between granite terrane on the east and the steeply dipping hogback on the west.

Two areas of basaltic extrusion occur near the base of Jemez volcano. Santa Ana Mesa, composed of flows and cinder cones, is located due south of Jemez caldera. Only the northernmost portion of Santa Ana Mesa is shown. Cerros del Rio is located southeast of Jemez caldera and is composed of flows and a large mass of cinder cones. The La Bajada scarp forms the western border of Cerros del Rio.

Most of the area south and east of Jemez volcano, with the exception of the two areas of extrusives, is covered by Santa Fe beds of Tertiary age. The Santa Fe formation contains a variety of unconsolidated sands and silts which erode into a finely dendritic drainage pattern very similar to that formed on shale. Note the area of parallel drainage southwest of Pojoaque which contrasts with surrounding textures. Although on one flank of a drainage divide, it may have a structural rather than a geomorphic origin.

Structure

Nacimiento uplift, with associated faulting, dominates the structural grain of Figure 3. Nacimiento fault, separating basin from uplift, is long and linear. Intersecting this fault at approximately 45° is a complex set of NE- and NW-trending faults. They appear to be tear faults while faults trending N-S are normal. One prominent NE-trending fault zone bisects Sierra Nacimiento and extends southwestward into the Basin. The entire southwest flank of Jemez Mountains is complexly faulted.

Another area of complex faulting is Cerros del Rio. NE-trending faults appear to terminate against La Bajada fault. Note the linear course of Rio Grande parallel to these faults. Therefore, this portion of the river may be fault controlled but there is no direct evidence visible on photographs. Similarly, this portion of the river is parallel to the margin of the Rio Grande graben.

Several faults are shown on the dissected volcanic slope of Jemez Mountains. Some exhibit fair evidence while others are conjectural.

Just west of San Ysidro is a normal fault of large throw that elevates Red Mesa. The mesa plunges south under Rio Salado valley and its edges are upturned by faults both on the east and west.

Along the west side of Nacimiento fault there are several folds plunging northwestward into the San Juan Basin. They diverge from Nacimiento fault at an angle of 15°. They appear, therefore, to be drag folds associated with a major wrench fault—the Nacimiento fault.

Several hot springs occur parallel to Nacimiento fault but some distance west. They indicate that the major frontal fault is, in actuality, a zone of rupture that extends somewhat west of the surface trace.

SUMMARY

Aerial mosaics are uniquely descriptive in presentation of geomorphic and structural data. Figure 1 shows the fault-block Sandia Mountains, the northeastward-extending belt of porphyry intrusions, and intervening basins. Figure 2 illustrates the monoclinal west dip of the Lucero uplift and numerous basalt-capped mesas. Figure 3 is dominated by the very large Jemez volcano and the fault-block Nacimiento Mountains bordering the San Juan Basin.

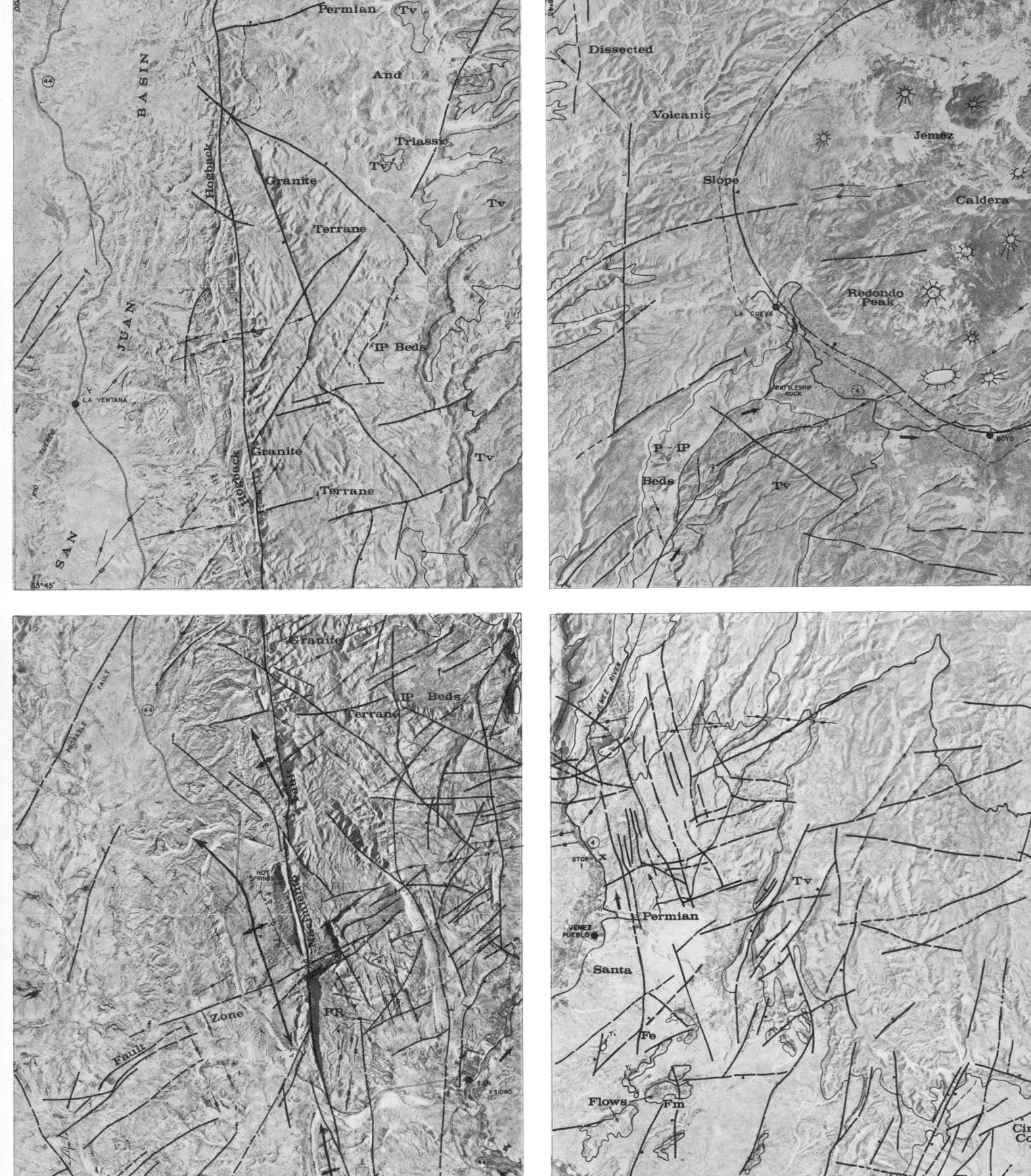

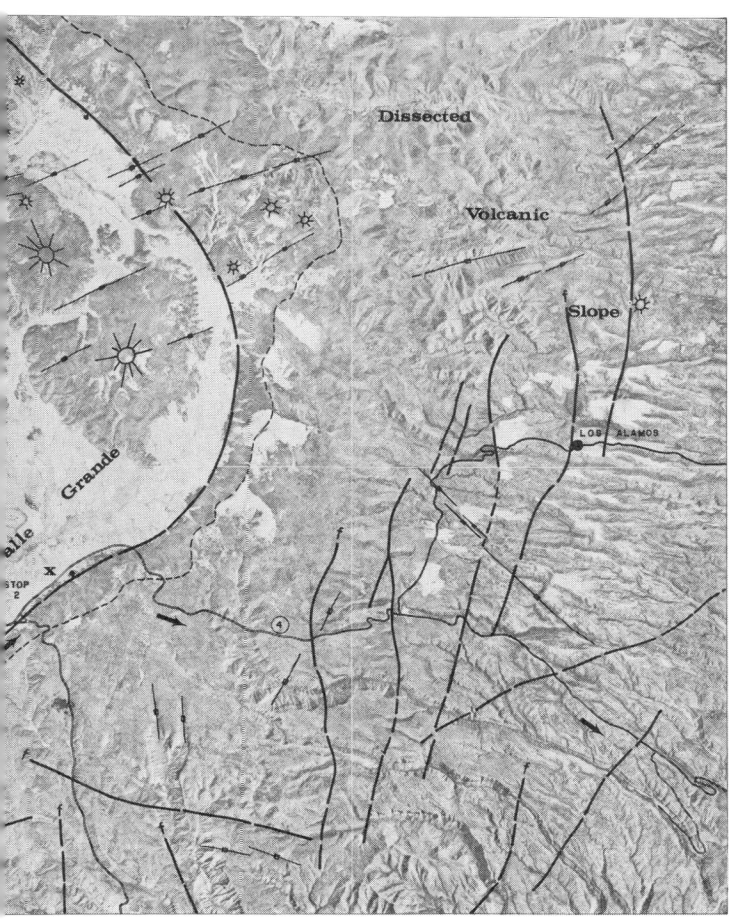
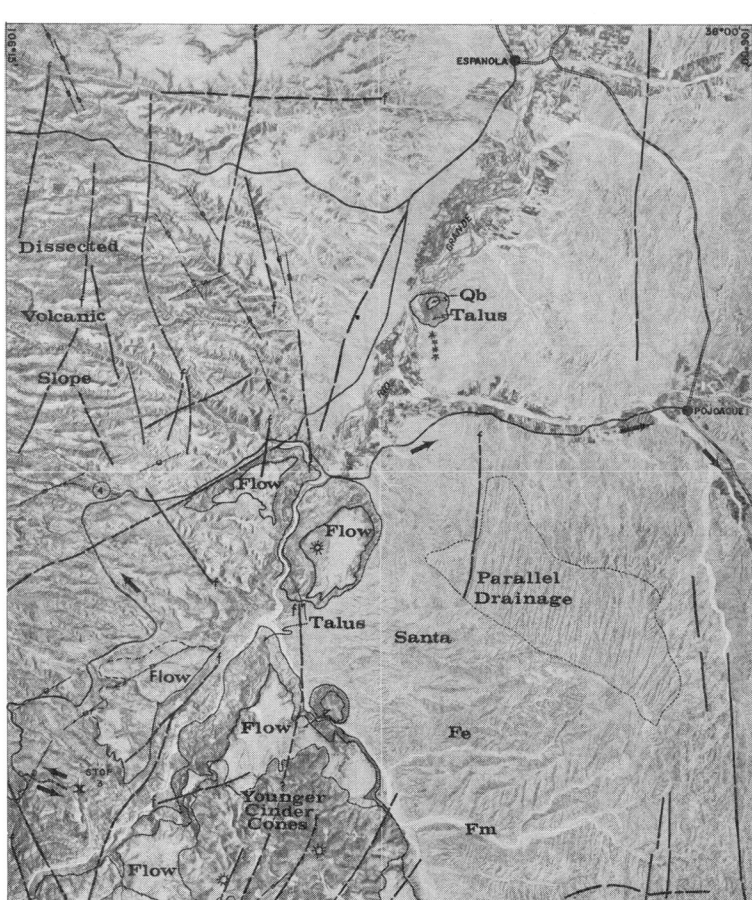

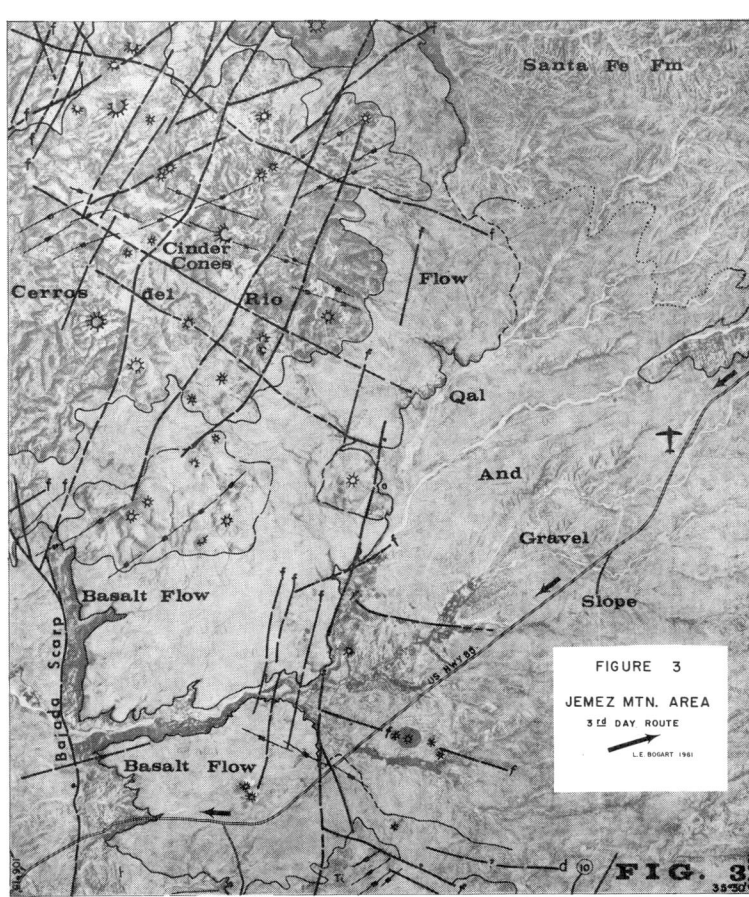

FIGURE 3
JEMEZ MTN. AREA
3rd DAY ROUTE
L.E. BOGART 1961

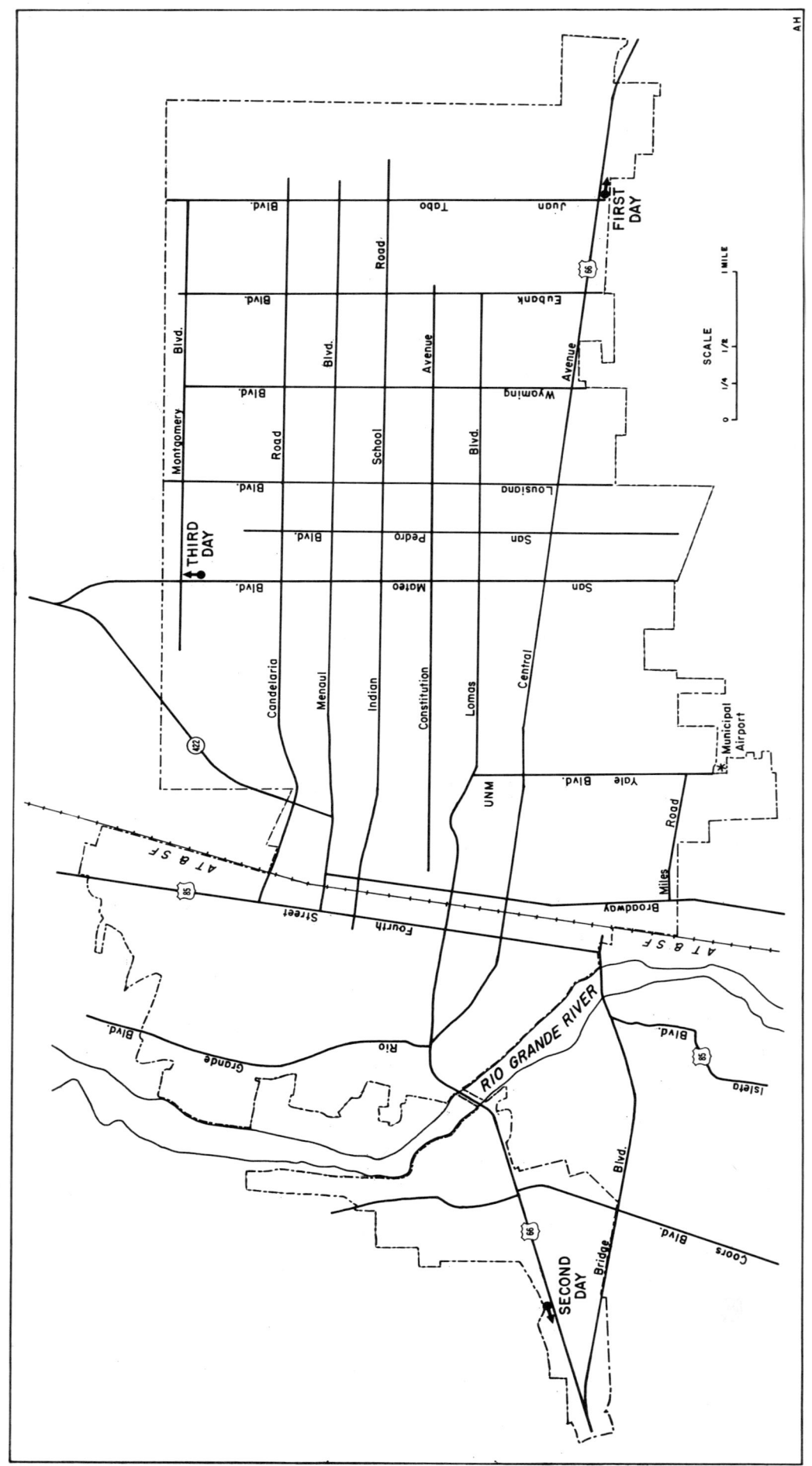

Figure 1. — Road index of Albuquerque showing assembly points for the three field trips.

ROAD LOG: SANDIA MOUNTAINS AND VICINITY

FIRST DAY, FRIDAY, OCTOBER 6, 1961
Vincent C. Kelley and Charles B. Read

Distance of Travel: 101.2 miles (logging odometer 4% low).
Starting Time: 7:30 a.m.
Assembly Point: East Central (U. S. Highway 66) at Juan Tabo Road. See Figure 1 for location of assembly point.

GEOLOGIC SUMMARY

This trip enters the Sandia Mountains through Tijeras Canyon. It traverses the Tijeras graben and back-slope structures to the east of the range with a side trip to the crest of the range for a regional view of the surrounding areas. It then descends the northern end of the uplift and goes into the adjoining Hagan basin where the younger stratigraphy from Jurassic to Eocene will be seen.

The Sandia Mountains are an eastward-tilted north-south uplift about 20 miles long bounding the Rio Grande depression on the east. Several subsidiary high-angle faults modify the back slope, and the diagonal Tijeras wrench fault together with the Gutierrez branch fault drop Cretaceous rocks into a wedge-shaped graben at the eastern base of the uplift. The complicated coordinate sets of faults through which the uplift descends at its north end will be seen.

The following is a brief outline of the formations of the Sandia Mountains.

Precambrian Rocks:
  Gneiss of Tijeras Canyon: pinkish, leucocratic, fine- to medium-grained granite gneiss.
  Quartzites: gray, white, and reddish quartzite in and with gneiss, greenstone, schist, and granite.
  Schists: mica, chlorite, hornblende, and sillimanite schists separately and with greenstones, quartzites, and gneisses.
  Greenstone of Tijeras Canyon: dark green, fine- to medium-grained chlorite and hornblende rocks derived by low-grade metamorphism of andesitic flows and tuffs, diabases, and basalts.
  Sandia granite: light gray to reddish granite with variable quantities of micas, mostly biotite.
Tererro formation: 0-60'; of Mississippian age and probably equivalent to the Leadville limestone of southwestern Colorado; lies on a surface of low relief cut in the Precambrian; consists of gray to dark gray crystalline and locally oolitic cherty limestone; bedding massive; base conglomeratic; characterized by a karst surface of pre-Pennsylvanian age at upper limit.
Sandia formation: 50'-270'; basal part of the Magdalena group of Pennsylvanian age; lies on undulating but low-relief Precambrian surface; consists of varying proportions of black shale, conglomerate, sandstone, and marine limestone with local coal seams a few inches thick; transitional upward into the Madera.
Madera formation: 1,000'-1,300'; upper part of Magdalena group; lower one-half (lower gray limestone) consists of prominent limestone ledges with intercalated shale and some sandstone; marine; upper one-half (arkosic member and Red Tanks or Bursum transitional member) consists of limestone, arkose, and feldspathic conglomerate, micaceous sandstone, and reddish, grayish, and greenish shales; marine.
Abo formation: 800'-1,000'; Permian; reddish brown mudstone and sandstone with some purplish mudstone, limestone pellet beds, and buff sandstone.
Yeso formation: 400'-500'; Permian; massive resistant tan-brown sandstone, 75'-100', at base termed Meseta Blanca; and soft upper part, 300'-400', consisting of fine-grained tan sandstone with some limestone, termed San Ysidro.
Glorieta sandstone: 50'-150'; Permian; white to light buff, massive sandstone.
San Andres limestone: 100'-200'; Permian; includes beds in upper part mapped elsewhere as Bernal; lower limestone, 30'-100', and upper unit, 75'-150', of sandstones like Yeso and Glorieta and some limestone.
Santa Rosa sandstone: 600'-800'; Upper Triassic; reddish brown and purplish sandstone, conglomerate, and mudstone with some limestone pellet beds.
Chinle formation: 1,000'-1,500'; Upper Triassic; purplish and reddish mudstone in lower part and brick-brown mudstone in upper part; thin sandstone ledges throughout and commonly at the top; several limestone pellet beds.
Entrada sandstone: 100'-150'; Jurassic; reddish brown sandstone in lower part and white in upper part.
Todilto formation: 5'-250'; Jurassic; papery limestone unit at base, 5'-10'; and white gypsum in upper part; mostly absent in the Sandia and Tijeras area but usually present in the Hagan basin area.
Morrison formation: 500'-1,000'; Jurassic; buff to light gray sandstone, variegated mudstones, and some thin limestones; sandstones locally conglomeratic in upper part.
Dakota formation: 100'-150'; Cretaceous; gray to buff sandstone, locally conglomeratic, with thick dark shale intervals; sandstone ledges variable in thickness and prominence laterally.
Mancos shale: 1,500'-2,000'; Upper Cretaceous; dominantly dark shale but with numerous siltstones and sandstones especially in the upper part where some coal is present.
Mesaverde formation: 2,200'-2,600'; Upper Cretaceous; dark shale and buff to brown sandstone; several repeated units with some poor coal at several intervals.
Galisteo formation: 2,400'; Paleocene(?) to Eocene; massive white, buff, and reddish sandstone with prominent intervals of reddish, purplish, brownish, and drab mudstones; large petrified logs in many of the sandstones which are commonly conglomeratic.
Santa Fe group: up to several thousand feet; Pliocene; buff and pinkish sandstone, mudstone, gravel, and fanglomerate.
Terrace gravel: 0-100'; Quaternary; forms several levels as river terraces and fans, often with very large blocks.

Note.—Users of the road log should bear in mind that the cumulative mileages are approximate. Variations can be expected due to differences in individual odometers and to errors on the part of those preparing the log. Check points such as bridges and road intersections in the log permit ready correction.

Cumulative Mileage

0.0 **East Central Ave. (U. S. 66) at Juan Tabo Rd.**
Caravan assembles along highway east of the intersection headed east with the lead car at the U. S. 66 road sign.

0.5

0.5 Four Hills Country Club golf course at 2:00 o'clock to south of Tijeras Arroyo which runs westward across the mesa in a barranca-type canyon, about 80 feet deep here.

0.3

0.8 From here to the mountains scattered obscure outcrops of granite may be found on the mesa, and the surface, especially north of the highway, is essentially a rock fan (elev. about 5,700') with only a thin veneer of granitic alluvium. Several low granite knobs, such as the cone-shaped Supper Rock near the "U", rise above the pediment.

0.15

0.95 **Western Skies Hotel** on right.

0.15

1.1 Lomas Blvd. intersection. Lomas is alternate route to Menaul Blvd., 2.5 miles to north, which one may take to avoid traffic through Albuquerque business area. Road down canyon to the south is to the Four Hills Country Club residential addition. Tijeras Arroyo may be seen at the bottom. The eastern side of the small canyon is Precambrian gneissic granite; the western side is Pliocene Santa Fe sand and gravel. A westward-dipping exhumed fault surface with remnants of the gravel stuck to the granite may be found along the eastern bank of the small canyon near the junction with Tijeras Arroyo. Divided highway ahead on U. S. 66.

0.4

1.5 Outcrops of Precambrian Sandia granite (about 1,350 m.y. old by K-A, Rb-Sr) in gullies along both sides of the highway.

0.2

1.7 Cuts, as road descends from canyon shoulders of the mesa surface into Tijeras Canyon. Terrace remnants of the mesa level may be noticed along the canyon sides for the next several miles. Numerous steep fractures in the cuts strike N. 15° E. to N. 40° W. Many are marked by dip-slip slickensides.

0.3

2. Road cut on left along curve has prominent north-trending joints which are dominant in this part of the uplift. Note also sets that dip 20°-40° eastward which are displaced by the vertical set in places and displace (reversely) the vertical set in other places.

0.4

2.4 In the high small canyons at about 9:30 a lamprophyric dike may be seen along the north-trending joints. At about 10:00 a small pegmatite body (white) may be seen on a high spur. Note the profusion of large residually weathered granite boulders in the next mile or so. The rock is a biotite porphyritic granite which contains numerous inclusions, some mafic and some felsic. These together with the phenocrysts of orthoclase give a rough, lumpy appearance to the boulders. In addition, the generally leucocratic granite locally has outcrops of as much as an acre or so of abundant concentrations of biotite. These melanocratic facies are commonly marked by considerable epidotization.

0.2

2.6 **Santo Nino** church on right.

0.4

3.0 **Tijeras Creek** on right. Note dissection of Recent alluvium and terraces cut on granite about at road level along next one-half mile.

0.3

3.3 **Village of Carnuel** on right.

0.3

3.6 High road cut on left exposes fresh granite. Note, near the top of the cut, the transition from angular joint blocks into rounded residually weathered "boulders."

0.2

3.8 At 10:00 south end (elev. about 8,600') of South Sandia Peak. Pennsylvanian Magdalena beds cap the ridge. From 12:00 to 3:00 is the ridge known as Cerro Pelon (elev. about 7,200'). It is similarly capped, but the underlying Precambrian rocks are greenstone and quartzite. The near pinkish hills at about 1:00 are granite gneiss.

0.15

3.95 Dirt road to right crosses Tijeras Canyon, leads up the broad valley and across the low saddle to the south and down into Coyote Canyon (about 11 miles away), but ends now at a locked gate at a military reservation.

0.4
4.35 Beginning in the small road cut on the right, behind the "One Way" sign, is the transitional contact zone between the Sandia granite and the Sevilleta (?) granite gneiss. This contact trends northeasterly and crosses the saddle north of the peak which stands at about 11:00. The gradational zone, in which it is questionable as to whether the rock is granite or gneiss, is usually 50-100 feet wide. Toward the gneiss the rock becomes gradually more foliated, less coarse grained, and weathers reddish rather than gray. Farther away from the granite the large orthoclase crystals become augen. At about 4.65 near the western end of the high road cut on the left, the irregular coarse gneissic foliation gives way eastward to more evenly banded gneiss and schist of greenish gray cast. The foliation in this belt dips 45°-60° northwesterly into the Sandia granite contact which appears to be steep. The gradation described above is clearly a granitization effect upon metasediment and possibly metarhyolite.

0.55
4.9 Quartzite beds, 20-30 feet thick, form crest of ridge across canyon on right and small knob above road on left. They dip northwesterly in conformance with the gneiss above and below, which here steepens in the gneiss below (?) the quartzite to about 55°-65°. The gneiss underlying the quartzite is coarse grained like that nearer the granite contact near 4.35.

0.15
5.05 Note the marked shear zones dipping about 50° to the N. 70° W. near the center of the deep cut. The rocks in the cut are progressively more sheared and shattered toward the eastern end and the Tijeras fault.

0.15
5.2 Historic Marker sign on right. This is about over the original natural Tijeras Creek channel, a new channel having been cut through terrace gravel to the right of the filled roadbed. Note the old road in hillside cut to left. The road curves northeastward and follows the northern side of the canyon and roughly the trace of the Tijeras fault which has entered the canyon from across the low saddle to the southwest (about 4:30). The fault is presumably between the Precambrian Tijeras greenstone that forms the southeast walls of the canyon, beneath the Pennsylvanian Magdalena limestone, and the gneiss which forms the northwestern slopes of the canyon. The greenstone is a foliated hornblende and chlorite metavolcanic sequence apparently derived from andesitic and basaltic flows and some intrusive plugs and sills. The foliation generally dips steeply to the southeast. The foliation and shearing become more marked near the faulted gneiss contact. Recall that the gneiss series dips northwesterly.

0.3
5.5 "East Bound" sign on right. Ahead and to right of highway note greenstone outcrops capped thinly by light-colored terrace gravel. The fault trace here follows the highway closely.

0.1
5.6 Note the quartzite unit, seen at 4.9, in the canyons and ridges to the left.

0.15
5.75 The terrace on the gravel exposed in these cuts was probably once continuous with the mesa level at the entrance to the mountains.

0.05
5.8 Tijeras greenstone in road cuts on left. The Tijeras fault lies only a short distance back of the cuts. The Tijeras fault continues northeastward on the left of the road and across the back of the flat shoulder on the skyline ridge just above and to the left of the green house that is on line with the highway. The Tijeras fault displaces the Paleozoic rocks along this ridge and, several miles northeastward, strata of Cretaceous age. Althought it has post-Cretaceous movement of considerable magnitude, owing to the more marked effects in the Precambrian rocks than in the Paleozoic rocks along Tijeras Canyon, it is thought to have been first active in late Precambrian time.

On ridge to right, the small "soft" slope between the greenstone and the Pennsylvanian Madera limestone ledges above is composed of Pennsylvanian Sandia formation consisting of shale, conglomerate, limestone, and sandstone.

0.4
6.2 **Tijeras Canyon Historic Marker.** It reads: "This pass between the Sandia and Manzano (Manzanita portion) Mountains was used for centuries by Indians, Spanish explorers, traders, 49'ers. Both mountain ranges top 10,600 feet. Canyons crossing at Tijeras resemble opened scissors which gave village (farther along) its name."

Note sharp contact between thick stratified alluvium and greenstone. This thick alluvial fill suggests a considerable period of aggradation in an old valley following an earlier time of canyon cutting. Note foliation of greenstone in this and succeeding cuts.

0.1
6.3 Across canyon to the right Magdalena limestone beds dipping 25° east lie nonconformably upon Precambrian greenstone.

0.1
6.4 Note quartzite and gneiss up canyon to left.

	0.2
6.6	Road cut on left is limestone and shale of Madera limestone of Magdalena group. The beds are disrupted by small faults and dip about 35° in a N. 45° E. direction near the western end of the cut; 50° in a N. 75° E. direction in the middle part; and 30° in a N. 45° E. direction in the eastern part. Similar variation exists south of the canyon, and the general lack of conformity between the two canyon walls has led to the supposition of a small fault along the canyon bottom. Jules Marcou was here in October 1853 collecting fossils!
	0.2
6.8	Road cut on left is in limestone and gray, green, and maroon shale of the upper part (arkosic member) of the Madera limestone.
	0.1
6.9	Tijeras fault follows the base of the ridge on skyline at 9:00. Immediate hills to left of highway are red beds of the Permian Abo formation, here overlain and obscured by alluvial material consisting of Madera limestone debris lying on an elevated terrace.
	0.1
7.0	Dirt road up hills to left leads to Carlito Springs (private) which issue along the Tijeras fault.
	0.2
7.2	Across valley 2:00-3:00 are the silos and buildings of the new Ideal Cement Co. plant.
	0.05
7.25	Road cuts on left are in Permian Abo sandstone and siltstone. Note small normal faults. Most of the tree-covered terrain to the south (right) is underlain by low-dipping Pennsylvanian Madera limestone. The village of Tijeras lies in the valley 1:00-3:00.
	0.25
7.5	Junction of U. S. 66 and N. M. 10 South. Continue on 66. N. M. 10 South follows a winding course up Cedro Canyon for many miles and leads into Estancia Valley east of the Manzanita and Manzano Mountains. Tilted sandstone ledges across valley at about 12:00 are also Permian Abo strata. Manzano Mountains Historic Marker sign reads: "Overlooking ruins of the 'cities that died of fear', seven once populous Indian towns. All were abandoned in fear of Apache raiders. One, Gran Quivira, now a National Monument, has been dug over in search of treasure reportedly buried by a priest during the Indian Rebellion of 1680."
	0.2
7.7	Road cuts in Abo. Gray hogback up valley on left beyond road cut at about 10:30 is Cretaceous Mesaverde sandstone. A large fault (Gutierrez) which split from Tijeras fault near Carlito Springs brings the Abo and Mesaverde into juxtaposition here with a throw of some 5,000 feet.
	0.1
7.8	Tijeras fault lies along base of aligned spurs seen up valley at 9:00 (back of green-roofed cabin).

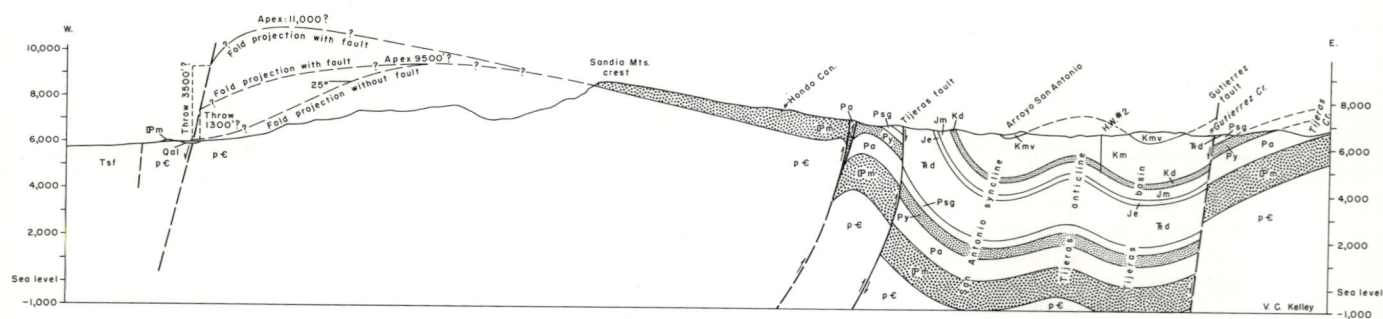

Figure 2. -- Structure section across the southern part of the Sandia Mountains and the Tijeras basin. Horizontal scale equals vertical. See figure 3 for explanation of symbols.

	0.25
8.05	Junction N. M. 10 North. Continue on 66. Gutierrez fault crosses N. M. 10, trending easterly about 300 yards north of the junction. Cedro Peak (elev. 7,767') at 3:00 on skyline, with microwave and beacon towers, is visible from Albuquerque.
	Sandia Loop Drive, Historic Marker Sign reads (westside): "Magnificent scenic drive through Cibola (See-bowla) National Forest to Sandia Crest, elevation 10,678 feet, overlooking Rio Grande Valley and 15,000 square miles of the Land of Enchantment. Camping and picnic facilities in cool forest areas. Route continues to Albuquerque over 'The Turquoise Trail.' (To the "Crest" from Albuquerque is about 70 miles round trip); (east-side) Ancient home of Sandia Man, among the earliest of cave-dwelling humans known on this continent. Cibola National Forest has heavily timbered picnic areas, (Madera) ski-run, deer, bear, wild turkey, mountain goats (sheep). Nearby are picturesque adobe villages and churches, ghost towns, mines worked since prehistoric times."

0.25
8.3 End of divided highway. Note along road cut ahead the change from red-brown strata of the Abo to the tan-brown of the Meseta Blanca member of the Permian Yeso formation. The Abo beds here are high in the section and the overlying Meseta Blanca sandstone beds crop out back of the cuts. Near the white and yellow road signs ahead a small fault brings the Meseta Blanca down into the road cut.
0.3
8.6 Road cut on left reveals Meseta Blanca beds.
0.1
8.7 Junction left of old abandoned U. S. 66. Continue ahead.
0.05
8.75 Highway crosses Tijeras Creek.
0.45
9.2 **STOP NO. 1.** Near concrete table. This point offers a good view of the back slope of the tilted Sandia uplift. The eastern dip slope, visible to the northwest, is surfaced by the Sandia and Madera formations. These formations on the back slope dip 15°-20° as may be seen toward the northern end of the slope that is visible from here. This dip terminates in a small buckle near the lower part of the slope, and in the part visible from here the buckle adjoins the Tijeras fault.

Turning to the foreground geology, the rocks along this side of the Tijeras valley are Permian Abo red beds of siltstone and sandstone. They strike nearly parallel to the highway and dip generally northward. The north side of the valley is rimmed by a semicircular outcrop of Upper Cretaceous Mesaverde sandstone. The outcrops in the valley below the rim are Cretaceous Mancos shale. The obvious fold is the Tijeras anticline, the east limb of which dips 30°-45° and the west limb about 22°.

The view from here toward the high part of the rim is almost directly along the trace of the axis of the anticline. The anticline is terminated on the south against the Gutierrez fault which crosses the valley floor from near the small red house at the base of the eastern end of the hogback. The fault trace is about at the old highway a hundred yards or so north of the barracks buildings. To the west the trace is at the end of the western limb of the Mesaverde hogback just back of the house. The stratigraphic throw on the Gutierrez fault along the anticline ranges from 3,000 to 4,000 feet.

Two wells have been drilled on the Tijeras anticline in the east-central part of the valley. They are the L. O. Hickerson Wright Nos. 1 and 2, drilled in 1947 and 1948 to 1,121 and 1,510 feet, respectively. The second well reached the top of the Dakota sandstone at 1,295 feet; the top of the Morrison at 1,360 feet. Both wells were drilled within a few tens of feet of each other near a dike about 700 feet east of the crest of the anticline. From the asymmetry of the fold it may be noted that at the Dakota level the distance from the crest may have been greater.

Turning again to the east it may be noted that the Mesaverde rim at its southeastern end swings around to an easterly strike and forms a small syncline. This is the southern end of the Tijeras syncline which forms the major part of what is known as the Tijeras (Cretaceous) coal basin. The syncline is double plunging and much larger than the anticline, although it does not appear so from here where the view is along the end of the northeastward-plunging axis. Only about 1,500 feet of Mesaverde beds are preserved from erosion in the center of the basin, about that much more having been removed. The coal beds in the basin are generally no more than 1-2 feet thick. The Tijeras coal basin comprises the major part of a wedge-shaped graben between the Tijeras and Gutierrez faults.

The Precambrian structural top in the Sandia uplift to the west is about 10,000 feet above sea level. In the bottom of the Tijeras syncline it is about 2,000 feet below sea level. Traversing southward over the ridge to the south of this stop, one may go down section through the Abo and Magdalena and into Precambrian schist in a smaller inlier exposed along Cedro Canyon about 3 miles south of Tijeras village.
0.2
9.4 Reddish brown Abo shale in road cut on right.
0.3
9.7 Meseta Blanca sandstone beds in old road cut across valley at 9:00 intruded by two hornblende andesite dikes.
0.2
9.9 Gutierrez Canyon, 9:00 Mesaverde up canyon across Gutierrez fault north of Abo red beds in foreground.
0.45
10.35 Light tan to buff Abo sandstones on right in entrance to side canyon. Highway follows strike valley in Abo shale. Valley is also followed by a longitudinal fault which is downthrown on the north by about 100 feet thus omitting some of the Abo section. High Abo sandstone forms ridge across valley on left.
0.55
10.9 Zuzax Indian-Mexican mart on left. Note chair lift to ridge for tourist view, not skiing.
0.5
11.4 **Keep left for sharp turn onto dirt Zamora Rd.** The road cut ahead on left is the upper Madera transition (Red Tanks or Bursum) zone into the Abo. Note the purplish shale alternating with marine limestone. The base of the Abo is about at the Zamora Rd. signpost as you make the hairpin turn at 11.6.

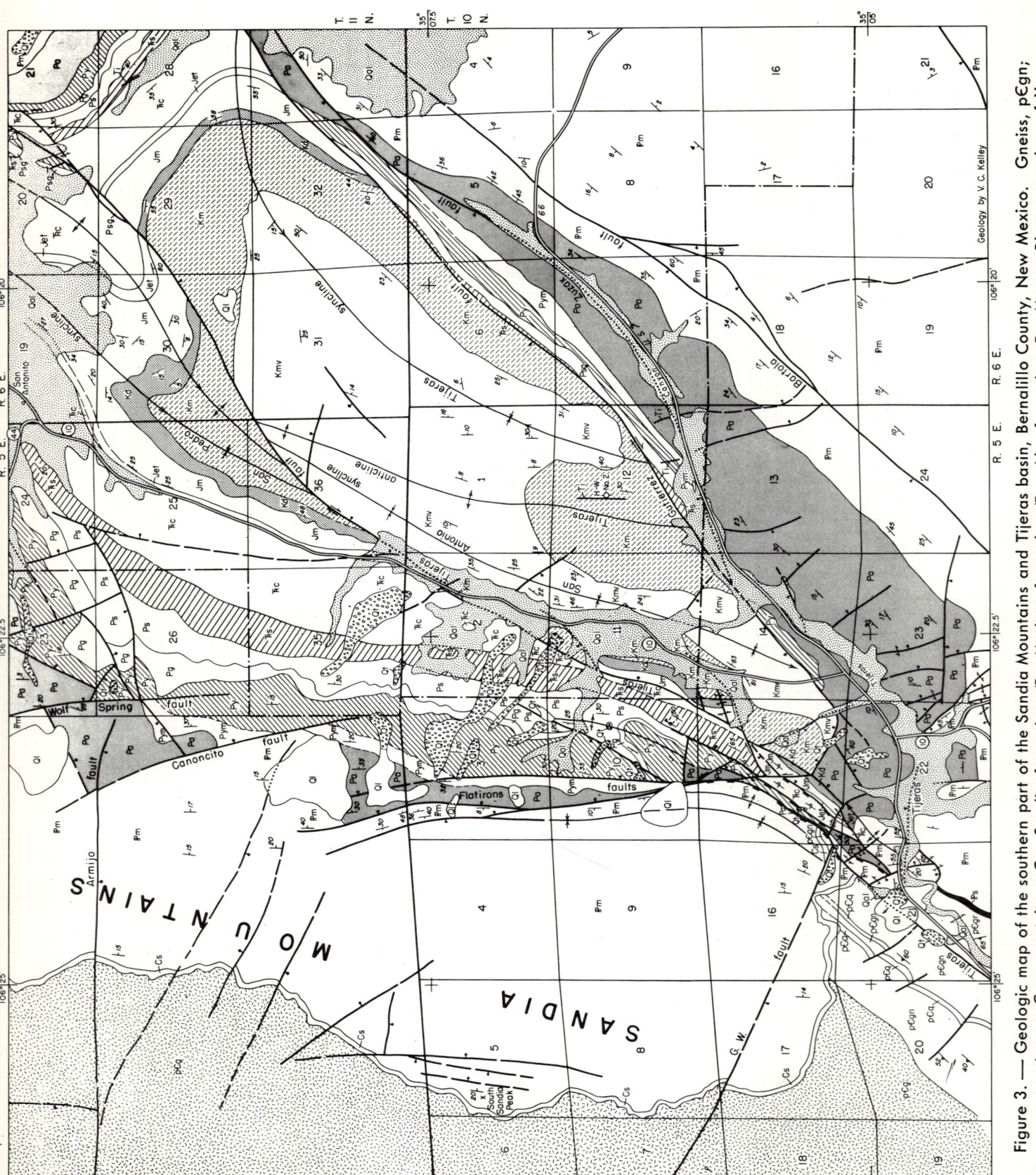

Figure 3. — Geologic map of the southern part of the Sandia Mountains and Tijeras basin, Bernalillo County, New Mexico. Gneiss, pЄgn; greenstone, pЄgr; quartzite, pЄq; Sandia formation, ℔s; Madera formation, ℔m; Meseta Blanca member of Yeso formation, Pym; Yeso formation, Py; Glorieta sandstone, Pg; San Andres formation, Ps; Santa Rosa formation, ⟍Rs; Chinle formation,

	0.3
11.7	Typical buff sandstones and purplish and reddish brown shales of the lowermost Abo.
	0.5
12.2	Passing under chair lift. This road is the old U. S. 66 which was used prior to about 1945 when the new road across valley was built. Cedro Peak with microwave tower at 10:30 is high Madera limestone. The base of the restored Abo might be at about the top of the tower. The base of the Abo here is along the ridge south of Tijeras valley.
	1.1
13.3	Small bridge and side road right up Gutierrez Canyon. Continue ahead. Abo shale and sandstone in road cut, and ahead behind old house are Meseta Blanca beds; hence Abo-Yeso contact crosses road at about 13.4.
	0.2
13.5	Good phenocrysts of hornblende can be collected from the dikes in the cut on right.
	0.3
13.8	Quaternary gravel in cuts.
	0.35
14.15	Side road right. Road here crosses trace of the Gutierrez fault which drops the Cretaceous of the Tijeras anticline to the north.
	0.25
14.4	Road recrosses trace of Gutierrez fault.
	0.2
14.6	**Stop sign, continue west on U. S. 66.**
	0.7
15.3	**Junction N. M. 10 (north) Turn right.** Abo mudstone and sandstone in road cut on left.
	0.15
15.45	Cross Gutierrez fault; Mesaverde beds downthrown on north side. Lowermost Mesaverde sandstone beds form hogback ahead from 10:00 to 12:00.
	0.15
15.6	Road cut on left exposes Mesaverde sandstone and shale.
	0.3
15.9	Vertical Mesaverde sandstone at 12:00.
	0.05
15.95	Side road left to Hobbie's. At 9:00 light-colored Magdalena beds along top of prominent ridge are upthrust upon steeply dipping brick-colored Yeso beds. Near hogback from 9:00 to 10:00 is Dakota sandstone. Mancos beds underlie valley to left of road.
	0.15
16.1	Red exposures in left road cuts are alluvium derived from Triassic and Permian beds up canyons. Note Mancos shale in gullies on right.
	0.2
16.3	Mesaverde beds at 12:00 are west limb of Tijeras anticline.
	0.1
16.4	**Village of San Antonio.** Dakota forms hogback to left.
	0.2
16.6	**Cedar Crest post office.**
	0.35
16.95	Side road left to mountain homes.
	0.35
17.3	East-dipping Mesaverde beds to right are west limb of a narrow syncline paralleling the Tijeras anticline. Ridges to left are gravel capped. These gravel beds are a correlative of the Ortiz gravels north of the Sandia Mountains.
	0.15
17.45	**Forest Park.**
	0.15
17.6	Red exposures to left are Triassic Chinle shale. Trace of Tijeras fault passes in field to left of road. N. M. 10 is on Mancos shale.
	0.2
17.8	Mancos shale in road cut on left. Tijeras fault trace is just west of this exposure.
	0.05
17.85	Cross trace of Tijeras fault. Road to Sierra Vista real estate subdivision on right.
	0.35
18.2	Triassic Chinle shale forms hill to left; Mesaverde beds form ridges to right.
	0.15
18.35	Small fault in road cut on right separates red Chinle shale and light-colored Morrison beds.

	0.15
18.5	Tijeras fault runs up valley to right between Mesaverde hogback ridge and Morrison-Dakota hogback at 12:30.
	0.1
18.6	Excellent view of eastern dip slope of Sandia Mountains from 9:00 to 10:30.
	0.1
18.7	Ideal Cement Company's quarry in Jurassic Todilto gypsum. The gypsum in the Todilto is local as it pinches out a few tens of yards north of the quarry. Side road left to village of Canoncito and to Cole Springs. Good exposures of Santa Rosa, San Andres, and Yeso beds may be seen going to Cole Springs recreation area.
	0.05
18.75	Entrada sandstone below culvert on right.
	0.15
18.9	Road is in Chinle shale valley. Hogback on left is formed by Santa Rosa sandstone.
	0.9
19.8	Divide between Tijeras Creek drainage to south and San Pedro Creek which drains northward around the Sandia Mountains. Exposures along road for next 0.8 mile are Chinle. Ridge to right is held up by Morrison and Dakota sandstone.
	1.1
20.9	**Junction N. M. 44. Turn left on Sandia Crest road.** Wide valley here is largely in Chinle shale. Village at this junction is San Antonito.
	0.4
21.3	Near ridge to right is held up by Permian Glorieta sandstone.
	0.45
21.75	**Junction, continue right on N. M. 44.** Paved road on left is old Sandia Crest route. Dirt road left past Tilton's store goes to Cienega Canyon recreation area. Red beds in hill to right and road cuts ahead are Permian Abo formation.
	0.65
22.4	Crossing contact from Abo into Magdalena. Abo is downfaulted some. In road cuts along curve ahead are excellent Magdalena exposures. Note thin coal seam at about 22.75.
	0.45
22.85	Nonconformity between Pennsylvanian Magdalena and Precambrian Sandia granite. A 1.5-foot bed of arkosic grit at the base is about the only bed here that is distinctive of the Sandia formation. Immediately above this there is a gray crystalline fossiliferous limestone containing scattered quartz pebbles. Fossils are mostly brachiopod and crinoid fragments.
	0.10
22.95	**STOP NO. 2, Doc Long's picnic grounds.** This picnic and recreation grounds is at the junction of Tejano Canyon, leading west, and Barro Canyon, leading north. Barro Canyon follows the Barro fault which tilts a small block upward on the east some 1,500 feet and thereby exposes the Precambrian basement. Other details of the geology will be pointed out, and the group will be led to the exposures of the basal Magdalena beds down the road and to the complicated road-cut exposures up the road.
	0.35
23.3	**Begin hairpin curve left.** Small pink granite dikes in granite road cuts on right are displaced southward by several small low-angle reverse faults.
23.5	Road cut on right exposed complicated and enigmatic relations between granitic rocks and Magdalena beds. Tongues of granite appear to invade the sediments, but it is difficult to believe that this could indicate that the Sandia granite is post-Pennsylvanian, on the basis of the regional relations. Perhaps the complications can be passed off as the effects of subsidiary or later small displacements adjacent to the Barro fault which in general appears to downthrow to the west the Precambrian contact exposed in the hillside to the east of the road by nearly 1,500 feet. It should be noted that no steep north-trending fault is exposed in this cut at the granite, and the beds immediately in contact with the granite are identical to those found in basal contact elsewhere. In view of this it is believed that the main Barro fault is west of these beds and more or less parallels the cut just east of the purplish mudstones and crosses the road diagonally about through the culvert on the inside of the road. The red beds and associated limestones are probably the uppermost Magdalena and equivalent to the Red Tanks or Bursum members.
	0.1
23.6	**Sharp right curve.** Road now descends the Magdalena section as it goes up Tejano Canyon. Although the section is beautifully exposed in the road cuts for the next 0.6 mile, it is broken by longitudinal faults which duplicate and omit some of the section. The positions of these principal north-trending faults are at 23.95 and 24.0. Note dike at 24.2 which also may be on a fault.
	0.7
24.3	**Hairpin curve left** switches to west of Tejano Canyon.
	0.2
24.5	Note southward dips in road cuts on right. The beds exposed in the cuts of the switchbacks are all of the lower part of the Madera.

Figure 4. — Contact between weathered Precambrian granite and basal Sandia beds. Note residual granite boulder. View in old road cut above point 25.35.

0.75

25.25   Contact of Madera and Sandia in road cuts on curve.

0.1

25.35   Base of Magdalena in road cuts on left. Note granite and Magdalena contact across canyon.

0.35

25.7   Landslide debris in cut on left.

0.2

25.9   Note westerly dip of Magdalena beds of a narrow fault slice between two north-trending faults.

0.3

26.2   Road cut on left shows regular easterly dip of back slope of the range. Note small fault at western end of cut with drag on northwestern side. A fault along this canyon extends over the crest of the mountains where it displaces the Precambrian contact about 250 feet on the northern side.

0.15

26.35   Red beds on left are in lower part of the arkosic member of the Madera limestone. They are not Abo.

0.25

26.6   **Tree Spring winter sports area.** In 1956 unusually fine mastodon molar teeth were found by Nicky Durrie in the soil about ¼ mile northwest of Tree Spring. According to J. L. Harbour, this find from a Pleistocene or Recent American mastodon at an altitude of 8,470 feet may be a record.

0.4

27.0   View northeast into Hagan basin. Upper Madera limestones and shales in road cuts ahead.

0.2

27.2   Typical buff-colored arkosic sandstone of upper part of Madera limestone just beneath purplish shale beds with striking cut-and-fill crossbedding. Ortiz Mountains formed of porphyry laccolithic intrusives at 12:30. San Pedro Mountains, at about 1:00. Local white outcrop in Hagan basin is Entrada sandstone. Note thin Todilto limestone at its top and just beneath the dissected cap of drab Ortiz gravels. Do you need glasses?

0.5

27.7   **Side road to La Madera ski area.**

0.1

27.8   Disturbed beds in old cuts at 12:00 are part of a large dip-slope landslide that occupies the head of La Madera Canyon and the ski basin.

0.2

28.0   From left to right between about 1:00 and 2:00 are the San Pedro and South Mountain laccolithic centers. In the foreground to South Mountain and extending some to the right is the Monte Largo uplift which exposes Precambrian gneiss, schist, and quartzite. It is bounded along its western base by the Tijeras fault. Note N. M. 10 in San Pedro valley.

0.1

28.1   At 3:00 across canyon, spur is Precambrian granite capped by basal Sandia formation. Just to the left of this spur a large fault drops the upper Madera beds into juxtaposition.

0.15

28.25   **Pavement ends. Turn left up dirt road to Sandia Crest.** The next 5.5 miles to the crest is a series of eight switchbacks through pine and aspen forest and up a dip slope which does not change stratigraphically by more than about 50 feet and is mostly in the upper part of the lower Madera. At the top the beds are still about 500 feet above the base of the Magdalena.

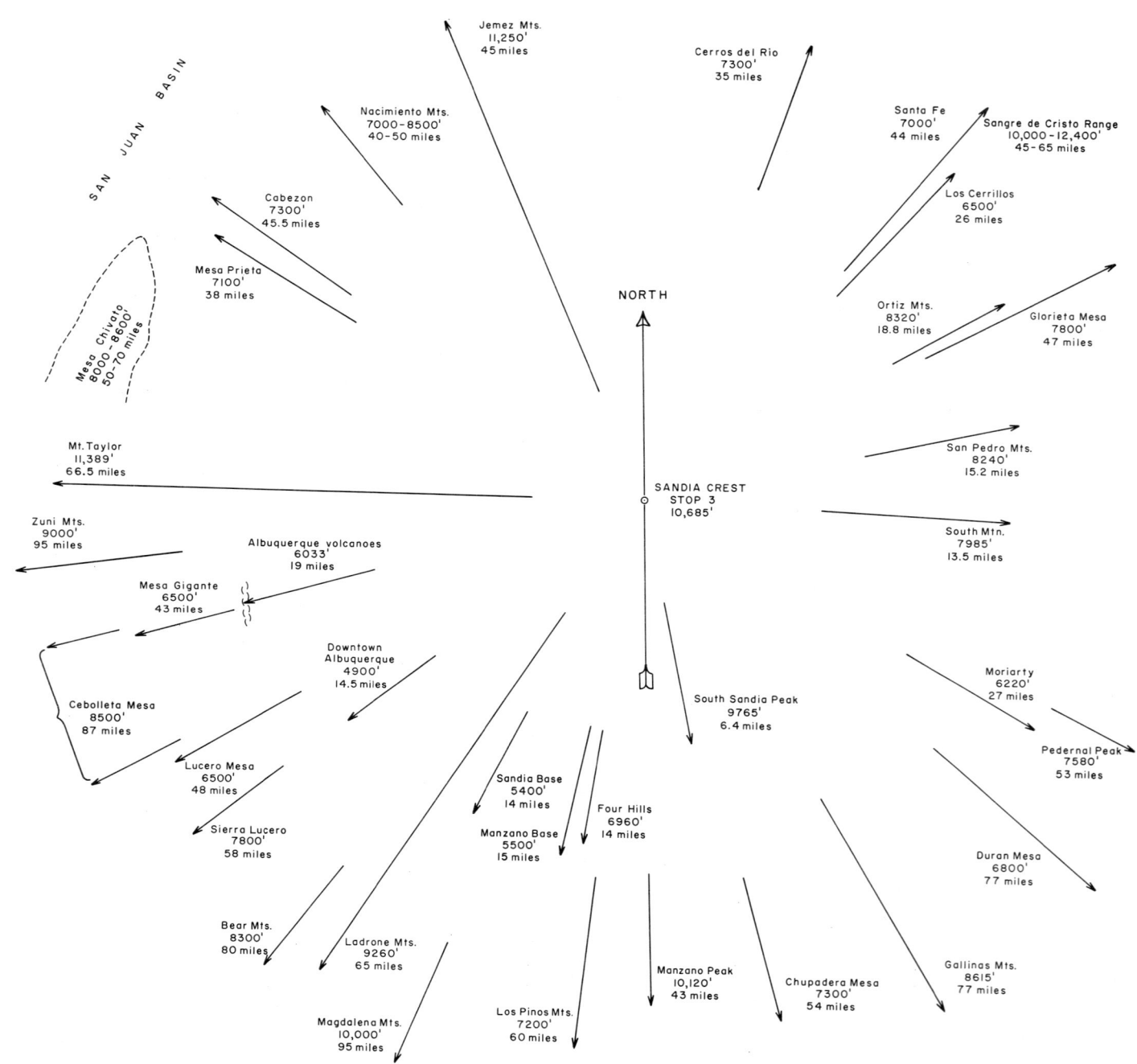

Figure 5. -- Panoramic index of features seen from Sandia crest.

	0.65
28.9	Capulin picnic ground and side road right.
	5.0
33.9	Left fork to Kiwanis Point 0.7 mile, keep straight ahead to crest.

Figure 6. — Air view along Sandia crest; faulted lava-capped mesas in Rio Grande valley beyond; Jemez Mountains on skyline. Precambrian, pЄg; Sandia formation, Cs; lower Madera formation, IPml. Photo by Dick Kent Photography, Albuquerque.

	0.05
33.95	**CREST — STOP NO. 3.**

We had an easier climb than Marcou in October 1853! From the Sandia crest one may recognize on a clear day landscape features nearly 100 miles away. To the west is the Rio Grande valley, a structural trough which in this latitude is some 30 miles wide from the Sandia-Manzano escarpments on the east to the Lucero and Rio Puerco fault zones on the west. The latter lie just this side of Mesas Lucero and Gigante (see Panoramic Index).

To the east of the mountains is the broad Estancia Valley, a downwarp between the Sandia-Manzano uplifts and the subdued Precambrian-cored Pedernal Hills. This valley was occupied by a lake whose northern end was about at Moriarty during Pleistocene. Additional features of the geology will be described during the conference.

Return to N. M. 44.

	5.55
39.5	**Junction N. M. 44, Turn left.**
	0.2
39.7	Road cut on left, shale and limestone of lower part of lower Madera.
	0.3
40.0	Capulin Peak at 8:30.
	0.3
40.3	Shaft at roadside on vein at fault between Precambrian quartzite and Sandia formation reportedly contained some scheelite.
	0.15
40.45	Palomas Peak at 12:00. Lower Madera limestone ledges.
	0.45
40.9	Precambrian granite on left.
	0.1
41.0	Basal Sandia formation sandstones on left.
	0.15
41.15	Palomas Peak at 12:30. Unusual development of Sandia sandstones on left in road cuts.
	0.15
41.3	**Slow, sharp left turn.** Sandia sandstones in cut. View down Las Huertas (Gardens) Canyon to right, and west up dip slope of range to television towers at crest. Cross fault around turn, with Sandia granite faulted up against Sandia sandstone beds. Much decomposed granite exposed in cuts for next 0.5 mile.
	0.6
41.9	Landslide in road cuts on left. Side road left.

		0.1
42.0	Decomposed granite in cuts on left.	
		0.1
42.1	Ellis Ranch road on left.	
		0.2
42.3	Decomposed granite in road cuts on right for next mile.	
		0.7
43.0	**Las Huertas picnic ground** road on left. The Las Huertas fault follows this canyon northward. It is downthrown on the west several hundred feet.	
		0.55
43.55	Note granite along both sides of canyon.	
		0.45
44.0	Sandia formation on right.	
		0.5
44.5	Sandia Cave and other caves on cliffs at 2:00. These caves have yielded remains of Folsom (8,000-9,000 years ago) and Sandia (26,000 years ago, late Pleistocene) cultures. See Hibben article in this Guidebook.	
		0.1
44.6	Road down canyon ascends the Madera section for the next 1.5 miles.	
		1.6
46.2	Stream deposits on right.	
		0.6
46.8	**Paved road begins.** Montezuma Ridge from 12:00 to 2:00. Beds in slopes to left are high in the upper Madera whereas Precambrian rocks are exposed in the base of Montezuma Ridge. The throw on the Las Huertas fault here is more than 1,000 feet.	
		0.2
47.0	Basal beds of Abo formation in road cut on left and in small hill at 12:30. Road very nearly follows the Magdalena-Abo contact for the next 0.8 mile.	
		0.9
47.9	Abo purplish mudstones in road cut on left.	
		0.1
48.0	Note Abo red beds faulted down at base of Montezuma Ridge. Several closely spaced faults lie between the Abo beds and the first visible Magdalena ledges and in these slices are Precambrian schist, Sandia beds, and a pre-Sandia limestone (Tererro) that has been thought to be Mississippian in age. Small veins along these faults have been prospected.	
		0.35
48.35	Abo beds on both sides of road.	
		0.15
48.5	**Side road right.** Hogback at 3:30 is held up by San Andres formation. Crude oil pipeline of the Texas-New Mexico Pipelines Co. is just to the right of the road. This 16-inch line transports oil and some LPG products from the Aneth field in southeastern Utah. Continue on paved N. M. 44.	
		0.1
48.6	Yeso beds in lower slopes at 3:00; Pliocene Santa Fe caps this hill. Magdalena at 9:00 and dip slope of north end of Sandia Mountains at 9:30. Village of Placitas at 11:00-12:00.	
		0.5
49.1	**STOP NO. 4.** Mesaverde beds at 3:30. The valley around Placitas is underlain by beds from Permian to late Cretaceous and the geology is complicated and considerably obscured by pediment gravel and alluvium. In general the terminus of the Sandia uplift as seen to the south of the road is a much-faulted nose. The faults are of two principal sets: north-trending and east-trending. In general, the north-trending set steps down westward and the east-trending set steps down northward.	
		0.2
49.3	Mesa from 12:00 to 2:00 is largely Santa Fe formation.	
		0.2
49.5	Dakota sandstone forms low ridge about 100 yards to left of road.	
		0.15
49.65	Green mudstone of Morrison formation beneath thin Dakota sandstone.	
		0.2
49.85	Morrison variegated beds in cut on left.	
		0.05
49.9	Todilto limestone in cut on left.	
		0.1
50.0	Triassic Chinle in hills at 9:00.	
		0.6
50.6	Pediment gravels underlie surfaces on left; Santa Fe in hills to right.	
		0.45
51.05	Mesaverde beds on left.	

Figure 9. — View southeastward from Jemez River valley, showing dip slope and western escarpment of the Sandia Mountains. Albuquerque to right and edge of Santa Ana Mesa to left. Photo by Walter Lissiuk.

	0.15
51.2	Mancos shale valley. Note Cabezon volcanic neck at 2:00 on skyline and faulted lava-capped surface of Santa Ana Mesa at 3:00. Prominent granite shields of the great western facade of the Sandias capped by the Magdalena rim are coming into view from 9:00 to 9:30.
	0.45
51.65	Mancos shale and sandstone in cut on left.
	0.25
51.9	Red Triassic Chinle shale in valleys on left.
	0.05
51.95	Contact between Santa Fe gravel and Mancos shale in road cut on right.
	0.3
52.25	Santa Fe gravel in road cuts here dips about 4° eastward or away from the axis of the Rio Grande depression ahead.
	0.35
52.6	Road descends along a pediment cut on slightly deformed Santa Fe beds from here nearly to the Rio Grande floodplain. Note again the eastward-tilted and faulted lava sheets on Santa Ana Mesa from 1:00 to 2:00. Nacimiento Mountains from 12:30 to 1:00 and Jemez caldera rim 2:00-3:00 on distant skyline.
	1.6
54.2	At 1:30 on the opposite side of the floodplain may be seen the low dissected remains of a diatreme and caldron sink (Canjilon Hill).
	0.9
55.1	Road descends dissected slopes from mesa to inner Rio Grande valley.
	0.3
55.4	Approaching overpass over N. M. 422. **Turn Right before overpass** onto N. M. 422 toward Santa Fe.
	0.3
55.7	Merge with main highway N. M. 422 and Interstate 25.
	0.8
56.5	Canjilon Hill across Rio Grande valley at 10:00. This cliffy hill with irregular basaltic intrusives is an explosive diatreme that has sunk around several coalescing funnels. The bedded explosion breccias, which make up the over-all caldron sink, are several hundreds of feet thick and consist of fanglomerate-like material with much incorporated basaltic debris. This bedded material is intruded by numerous dikes, sills, small plugs, cone sheets, and small breccia pipes. The caldron sink is oval-shaped, about 2,000 by 3,700 feet, and intruded into Santa Fe beds.
	0.5
57.0	Santa Ana Mesa from 10:00 to 11:30. The large basaltic lava field appears to have erupted from San Felipe cone, the lighter colored round hill on top at about 11:00. The lava field, which rests on a pediment cut on Santa Fe beds, is much broken by high-angle north-trending faults whose throws range up to nearly 200 feet. They are downthrown east and west in general, but one or two are pivotal, yielding scissor faults. Just to the right of Canjilon Hill one may see a graben in the faulting; this has been termed the San Felipe fault zone and is step-faulted down on both sides. Also one may note an over-all eastward tilt to the field which must have occurred after the eruption (perhaps even after the faulting) as the western part of the field is higher than the source at San Felipe cone. This tilt attests to the late and possibly still-occurring downwarp of the Rio Grande depression in this area about along an axis followed by the river.
	0.6
57.6	The considerable gravels in the Santa Fe beds in the low hills to the right and ahead have been referred to by Bryan as "axial" gravels deposited by the ancestral, through-flowing Rio Grande. These gravels are well rounded and in the form of lenticular bodies in several beds through a vertical range of 200-300 feet. They are not easily separable from the main Santa Fe, nor are they continuously traceable for great distance in the Rio Grande. However, this is not a necessary requisite to support this plausible concept. The principal point is that they are well known only in the uppermost Santa Fe and hence one can not as yet be sure that such a through-flowing ancestral Rio Grande existed during the greater part of Santa Fe time. Furthermore, there is a strong possibility that some or all of these gravels are younger insets in juxtaposition to the Santa Fe beds, as the result of late (Pleistocene) cutting and filling along the Rio Grande.
	1.65
59.25	Road rises onto one of the numerous low river terraces cut by the Rio Grande. Note that it was cut after the faulting that dislocated the basalt caps across the valley, 9:00-9:30, as fault scarps are not present on this surface.
	0.55
59.8	Bridge.
	0.2
60.0	Note the well-rounded river gravels in road cuts.
	0.3
60.3	Side road left to Algodones. Road is descending onto present valley bottom.
	1.4
61.7	R. E. A. power plant on left.

	0.8
62.5	Note Santa Fe outcrops up valley, 2:00-2:30, that are tilted northward, about 10°.
	0.4
62.9	End of N. M. 422; from here north, road is designated U. S. 85.
	0.2
63.1	The northward-tilted basalt flows in the Santa Fe beds at 10:00 are not part of the basalt cap across the river. They are older, but nevertheless may have come from earlier eruptions from the San Felipe center. It is noteworthy also that some gravel veneers occur on the San Felipe basalt cap across the river above the road and elsewhere.
	0.25
63.35	Bridge.
	0.8
64.15	Note axial gravels in road cuts from here to top of hill, some with northward tilt related to that mentioned above.
	0.45
64.6	Rusty gravels on left due to ground water or spring action. Note beautiful foresetting, channeling, and small reverse faults in the road cut.
	0.7
65.3	Descending into Tonque Arroyo, prepare for **right turn.**
	0.2
65.5	**Turn right** on dirt road up Tonque Arroyo. Road to left leads to San Felipe Indian Pueblo on Rio Grande.
	0.6
66.1	Note white volcanic "ash" beds in Santa Fe, 3:00.
	0.1
66.2	Road is on old railroad bed built to the Mesaverde coal up Tonque Arroyo. It was never finished as the coal proved inferior.
	1.1
67.3	Hogback on skyline at 11:00 is formed by Morrison sandstone.
	0.4
67.7	Road crosses Tonque Arroyo.
	0.4
68.1	Westward-tilted Santa Fe beds, 2:00-2:30.
	0.6
68.7	The Santa Fe here is near the eastern structural boundary of the Rio Grande depression and it appears to be faulted down against Jurassic Entrada near 68.9. However, the fanglomerate on the left may be a Quaternary inset or terrace remnant of a type that is probably very common along the Rio Grande and proximate tributaries. The bounding fault to the depression is here referred to as the Hagan. It is a northern extension of the Sandia fault zone on which the Sandia uplift rose (see 1:00-2:00). Cliff ahead on left is Todilto limestone and gypsum overlying white and red Entrada in steep slope. Top of underlying Triassic Chinle is about at road level.
	0.3
69.0	Triassic Chinle sandstone along arroyo at 3:00.

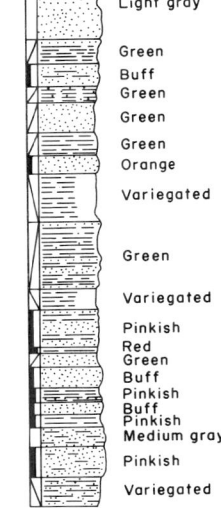

Figure 8. — Graphic section of Morrison formation in Tonque Arroyo. Modified from Earl Harrison (1949).

	0.1
69.1	Note fine exposure of "papery"-bedded Todilto limestone in side arroyo left; gypsum hill behind. The gypsum here is more than 200 feet thick (possibly by flowage) and contains several 1-6-inch limestone beds in its upper part. Also the upper gypsum is often pale pinkish from iron oxide and disseminated red jasper grains.
	0.15
69.25	Morrison sandstone and variegated mudstone form the slopes and top of the hills on the left. This is a thick and well-exposed section (Fig. 8).

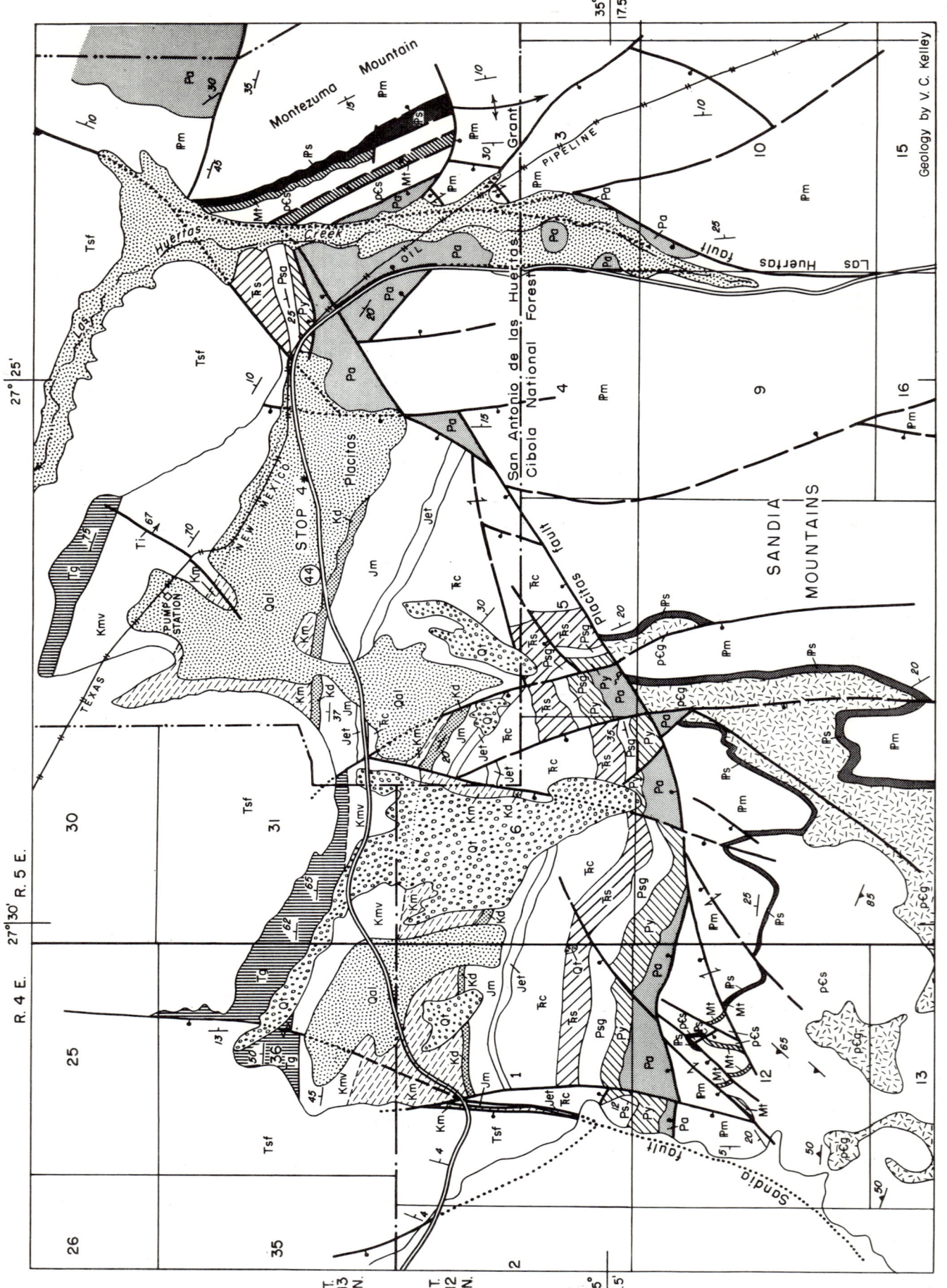

Figure 7. — Geologic map of the Placitas area, Sandoval County, New Mexico. See Figure 3 for explanation of symbols except Mississippian(?) Tererro formation, Mt; and Pre-cambrian schist, pЄs.

	0.35
69.6	Todilto gypsum across valley on right. Re-exposure of underlying Todilto limestone and light buff Entrada on this, the dip-slope side of the ridge, is caused by a longitudinal fault whose trace position may be mapped just the other side of the dark ledge of the Todilto limestone.
	0.2
69.8	Massive sandstone of the Morrison formation in cliff on left.
	0.1
69.9	Note variegated Morrison mudstones and white sandstone across arroyo, 10:00-10:30.
	0.25
70.15	Cattle guard. Diamond Tail ranch ahead. Road leaves Tonque Arroyo and ascends onto terrace cut on soft Mancos shale. Note thin Dakota beds in low knobs at 8:00 at eastern base of Morrison hogback.
	0.4
70.55	Prominent even ridge on near skyline from 2:00 to 4:00 is held up by Triassic Santa Rosa sandstone, San Andres limestone, and Glorieta sandstone. The broad valley between here and this ridge is underlain largely by Triassic on the far side, but by Mancos on this side. The normally resistant Morrison and Dakota have been strongly beveled by the Tonque regimen and only small knobs of this Dakota sandstone may be made out up the valley toward about 2:00.
	0.6
71.15	Side road left to Diamond Tail ranch headquarters; continue ahead. Three prominent porphyry laccolithic centers may be seen on skyline: Ortiz, 10:30-11:00; San Pedro, 11:45; and South Mountain, 12:00-12:15. Ridge forming skyline to left from 7:30 to 10:30 is Espinaso Ridge, type locality for the Oligocene(?) or Miocene(?) volcanic fanglomerate. The type section, if there is one, is in the crossing canyon at the notch, 9:00.
	0.45
71.6	Ruins of old village of Coyote on left. South Mountain, 12:00; lower and to right, about 12:15, is Monte Largo, an uplift of Precambrian rocks. Note fine view of the back slope of the Sandias, 2:00-3:00. Road here is on surface cut on lower Mesaverde formation.
	0.1
71.7	Mesaverde sandstone and shale on left. As the curve ahead is approached, the sandstones which are picked in this locality as the base of the Mesaverde may be seen down the arroyo at the base of a small knob at about 2:00.
	0.2
71.9	Note coal prospects in Mesaverde at 9:00.
	0.1
72.0	Crossing ledges of prominent sandstone unit in the Mesaverde.
	0.05
72.05	Crossing shale member in valley to 72.2.
	0.2
72.25	Road turns south to follow strike of the formation.
	0.2
72.45	White sandstone along low ridge to left is basal sandstone of Eocene Galisteo formation.
	0.3
72.75	Side road left, continue ahead.
	0.1
72.85	**STOP NO. 5.** Examination of upper Mesaverde and lowermost Galisteo beds. The contact and lithologies used in drawing the Cretaceous-Tertiary boundary will be pointed out. The Mesaverde formation here is more than 2,000 feet thick and the overlying Galisteo is some 2,400 feet thick. The Espinaso formation which overlies the Galisteo forms a prominent ridge to the east.
	0.25
	Return to U. S. 85.
73.1	At 12:00, contact between Galisteo and Mesaverde.
	1.2
74.3	Jemez Mountains across the Rio Grande valley form skyline, 12:00-1:30.
	2.2
76.5	At 12:15 note lavender basal mudstone of Morrison in contact with underlying Todilto gypsum with its thin intercalated limestone seams. A red jasper bed 5-6 inches thick may be found at the contact.
	4.0
80.5	U. S. 85. Cross over to south lane and turn left for return to Albuquerque.
	2.5
83.0	**Junction N. M. 422, bear left** along new divided highway. The road straight ahead to Algodones is the old highway.
	0.7
83.7	Note striking profile of Sandia uplift, 10:30, and the small uplifted block on its back and the prominent projection westward of the Precambrian Rincon Ridge which is due to westward offsetting of the structural front in the northern part. This will be seen more clearly near the end of the trip.

	6.5
90.2	**Exit** for junction with N. M. 44 to Cuba, **continue ahead.**
	0.2
90.4	Das Overunderpassen.
	0.1
90.5	Merger from right. Excellent exposures of Santa Fe formation for next 3.5 miles in road cuts and ravines.
	1.2
91.7	**Exit to Bernalillo** in valley bottom at 3:00.
	2.1
93.8	The prominent mountain at 9:00 is known as the Rincon Ridge. It stands out in front of the main Sandia uplift and consists of quartz-mica schists, and micaceous quartzites. Note the striking sets of aplite and pegmatite dikes.
	3.5
97.3	From here south, N. M. 422 traverses the East Mesa surface from which excellent views of the Sandia escarpment may be had. The valley between the Rincon Ridge and the main escarpment is referred to as the Juan Tabo area. The deep embayment in the range, south of the high crest with the television towers is occupied by Pino and Bear Canyons. The two canyons in the southern facade, west of South Sandia Peak are Embudito and Embudo Canyons.
	0.7
98.0	**Exit to 2nd and 4th St. approaches to downtown Albuquerque.** Continue ahead.
	0.5
98.5	Coronado Airport.
	1.6
100.1	Overpass.
	0.3
100.4	American Gypsum Co. plant and the New Mexico Public Service Co.'s power plant at 3:00. Albuquerque volcanoes on skyline at 2:30.
	0.8
101.2	First day's field trip ends here. Those wishing to go to downtown areas continue straight ahead on N. M. 422; those wishing to go to East Central or Heights areas take the San Mateo Exit ahead. End of Road Log for First Day.

ROAD LOG: WEST OF ALBUQUERQUE IN THE RIO PUERCO, RIO SAN JOSE, AND LUCERO AREAS

SECOND DAY, SATURDAY, OCTOBER 7, 1961
V. C. Kelley and C. B. Read

Distance of Travel: 123.4 miles (logging odometer 4% low).
Starting time: 7:30 a.m.
Assembly Point: U. S. Highway 66, 3 miles west of Rio Grande bridge. **See Figure 1, first day's log, for location.**

RESUME

The route of the second day's conference leads west from Albuquerque across the faulted margin of the Rio Grande trough and then into the southeastern part of the San Juan Basin, one of the larger subprovinces of the Colorado Plateau. As the caravan traverses the Puerco fault zone, Mesozoic and some Cenozoic rocks will be seen in the various fault blocks.

The first stop is in the vicinity of Mesa Gigante where the pre-Cretaceous Mesozoic stratigraphy will be seen and discussed. Still farther west on U.S. 66 the route crosses the broad valley of Rio San Jose to a stop at the Laguna Indian village of Mesita where the conferees will see fine exposures of the Entrada, Todilto, and at least a part of the Morrison sequences of Jurassic age.

From Mesita the caravan will travel to the southeast along old U. S. 66 to the vicinity of Correo and then follow N. M. Route 6 for a short distance. A stop will be made along the northern front of Lucero uplift where late Tertiary normal faulting is superimposed along earlier thrust faulting.

At Puerco siding the caravan will leave N. M. 6 and follow a ranch road south along the front of the Lucero uplift. At Carrizo Arroyo a stop will be made to examine in detail the structural relationships of this complex area. There are sharp conflicts of opinion regarding the geologic structure in this vicinity, some individuals preferring low-angle thrusting from west to east. Others, however, are of the opinion that the apparent thrusting is due to gravity gliding from the uplifted blocks along normal faults. Both points of view will be taken into account in the discussion.

From Carrizo Arroyo the route next leads to Comanche Canyon where Pennsylvanian and Permian sequences will again be examined and additional observations will be made on the faulted front of the Lucero uplift.

The caravan will then return to N. M. 6 and drive southeast to the interesting old settlement of Los Lunas. Many fine vistas of the magnificent western fronts of the Manzano, Manzanito, and Sandia Mountains will be seen. From Los Lunas the caravan will drive north along the valley of the Rio Grande and return to Albuquerque for the night.

Note. Users of the road log should bear in mind that the cumulative mileages are approximate. Variations can be expected due to differences in individual odometers and to errors on the part of those preparing the log. Check points such as bridges and road intersections in the log permit ready correction.

Cumulative Mileage

0.0 West abutment of bridge over Rio Grande on U. S. Highway 66.
   0.65
0.65 Begin ascent from Rio Grande valley bottom onto a low river terrace referred to as West Albuquerque, West Mesa, or Lavaland. It is about 40 feet above the Rio Grande floodplain and extends from about 1 mile south of the highway to about 4 miles north. It has been termed by Bryan (1938) the Segundo Alto surface.
   0.25
0.9 Coors Road to left.
   0.3
1.2 Segundo Alto surface.
   0.95
2.15 **Turn right onto frontage** road parallel to U. S. 66. **Caravan forms here.**
   0.55
2.7 Lead car of caravan parks here.
   0.9
3.6 Merge left onto U. S. 66 West.
   0.9
4.5 Begin ascent of Nine-Mile Hill (distance from Albuquerque) to high mesa.
   0.95
5.45 Top of Nine-Mile Hill, edge of a surface referred to as Llano de Albuquerque. This eastern white rim of caliche has been termed Cejita Blanca (little white eyebrow). This surface was presumably cut on Santa Fe beds in Pleistocene time. It is capped by pediment sand and gravel perhaps as much as 20-30 feet thick and surmounted by eolian material, soil, and caliche. The Llano is some 50 miles long and about 5 miles wide and is a youthful flat-topped divide between the Rio Grande and the Rio Puerco. At the northern end the Llano is about 6,000 feet; at the southern end 5,400 feet. Over-all slopes on it, however, are diagonal to the southeast.
   0.25
5.7 On the horizons are Isleta volcano, 8:30; Los Lunas volcano, 9:00; Isleta cinder cones, 9:30; Ladron Peak, 10:00; and Sierra Lucero, 11:00.

	1.4
7.1	At 1:00 may be seen the extinct volcano, Mt. Taylor, elev. 11,389 feet.
	0.8
7.9	About 200 feet north of the highway are the abandoned mud pits of the F. H. Carpenter-Atrisco Grant No. 1 well drilled in 1948 to 6,652 feet. Well bottomed in sand and silt of the Pliocene(?) Santa Fe formation and encountered five basalt intervals 20 to 130 feet in thickness. The total drilling time was less than five days.
	1.9
9.8	West rim of the Llano, termed Ceja del Rio Puerco. Begin descent into the wide valley of the Rio Puerco.
	0.3
10.1	Mesa Lucero at 11:00 and higher flat-topped Cimarron Mesa (on Sierra Lucero) beyond.
	0.1
10.2	Cerro Colorado, at 11:00 about 0.5 mile away, is a complex acidic plugdome (H. E. Wright's (1943) non-basaltic volcano) intruded into Santa Fe and overlapped by upper Santa Fe beds.
	0.3
10.5	Mt. Taylor at 1:00. The high level that extends northward from Mt. Taylor is Mesa Chivato. It is capped by basaltic flows and studded by numerous cones. Mesa Prieta, 3:00, is similarly capped and it has been commonly thought to be an outlier of Mesa Chivato. However, Mesa Prieta is somewhat lower and was probably either formed later or on a lower, not coextensive surface. Note volcanic neck in the Puerco Valley between these two mesas. This is La Senora Peak.
	2.4
12.9	From 12:30 to 2:00 local basalt sheet in tilted Santa Fe beds, Mesa de la Negra.
	1.0
13.9	**Rio Puerco bridge.**
	0.2
14.1	Side road right up Puerco valley.
	0.45
14.55	Upper Cretaceous Mesaverde sandstone and shale on right.
	0.85
15.4	Dark gray Mesaverde mudstone forms soft rounded hills on right.
	0.3
15.7	Santa Fe pediment gravel on Mesaverde.
	0.7
16.4	Tertiary (Santa Fe?) sand and gravel. These are thought to be in a narrow graben (Apache) of the Puerco fault zone (Wright, 1946).
	0.65
17.05	Arched Santa Fe beds, within the Apache graben at 10:30.
	0.35
17.4	Bridge.
	0.4
17.8	Santa Fe(?) sand and gravel in road cuts on left.
	0.8
18.6	Road cuts in tilted Santa Fe sand and gravel. Note fault and highly deformed Santa Fe on left side. Note apparent unconformities on right side.
	0.4
19.0	Approximate western margin of Apache graben. To the west the Puerco fault zone is largely in Mesaverde beds, but this area is subdued and extensively covered by thin pediment materials. Note large Mesaverde sandstone concretions to right of highway.
	3.1
22.1	Valencia County line.
	0.3
22.4	Gallup sandstone outlier, 3:00, one-quarter mile away.
	0.3
22.7	**Canoncito Exit.** Continue on U. S. 66.
	0.1
22.8	Overpass. Note Santa Fe(?) or Quaternary(?) sands in road cuts and gully just beyond.
	0.6
23.4	Begin long road cut in Dakota(?) sandstone.
	0.3
23.7	Dakota hogback, 9:00; Gallup sandstone hogback, 8:00; pyramid-shaped Suwanee Peak at 10:00; table-shaped Redonda Mesa beyond and just to left; and Lucero Mesa beyond forming far skyline.
	0.2
23.9	Gate in fence on right. Pink and white Entrada is capped by thin "line" of Todilto limestone at 2:30. Westernmost fault of Rio Puerco fault zone passes northward through this valley between the Entrada and Dakota outcrops.

0.7
24.6 Dakota knobs 200-300 yards south at 9:00. Broad valley of the Rio Colorado eroded in Triassic Chinle shale spread out to west. On curve ahead is where the old U. S. 66, built in 1936 and now abandoned, took off to southwest toward the distant overpass over the Santa Fe railroad.
1.2
25.8 Type locality of Correo sandstone member of Chinle shale in bluff at 3:00. Note toreva block of Correo sandstone at 12:30-1:00 near road.
1.2
27.0 Overpass.
0.1
27.1 **N. M. 6 Exit to Los Lunas**; continue on U. S. 66.

Figure 1. — View north from Stop No. 1 of south face of Mesa Gigante. Entrada sandstone, Je; Todilto formation, Jt; buff shale, Js; brown-buff sandstone, Jb; white sandstone, Jw; variegated shale, Jv; and Dakota sandstone, Kd.

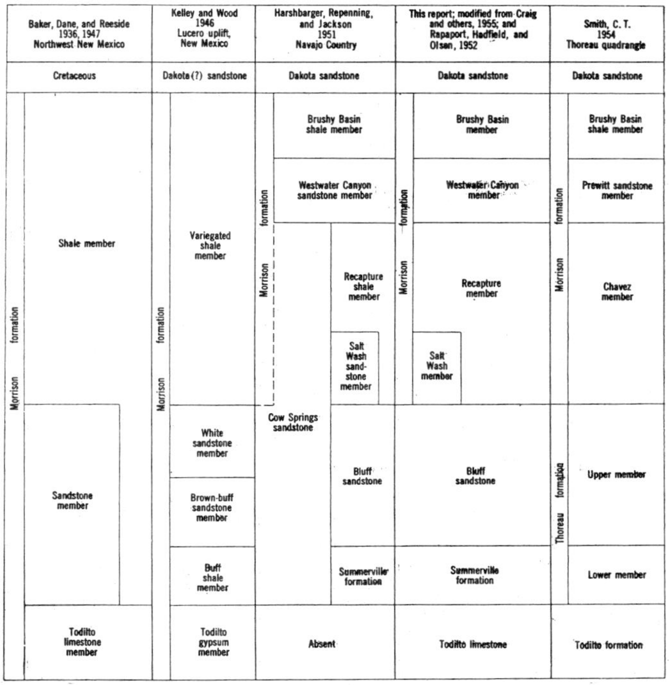

Figure 2. — Nomenclature of the Morrison formation in northwestern New Mexico, according to Freeman and Hilpert (1956).

2.7
29.8 **STOP NO. 1.** Discussion of stratigraphy and structure of Rio Colorado and Rio San Jose Valleys and their surroundings. Mesa Gigante from 2:00 to 4:30. Lead car, 29.9, at culvert.
The broad valley to the south is largely eroded in soft Triassic Chinle shale. The northern part of the valley is drained from west to east by Rio San Jose. The southern part is drained by the Rio Colorado which joins Rio San Jose near Mesa Redonda. The floors of both valleys are veneered by basalt flows. The regional dip here is northward at about 2° away from the Lucero uplift and along the eastern side of the Acoma embayment.
The Morrison and adjacent beds are unusually well exposed in the southern slope of Mesa Gigante and the problems of the terminology and correlations of the Morrison formation will be discussed (See Figs. 1-3).
1.8
31.6 Bluff on right is composed of Correo beds.
0.2
31.8 **Overpass** over Santa Fe railroad. Mesa Encantada at 12:00. Village of Mesita up tracks at 1:30.
1.5
33.3 Bridge over San Jose Creek.
0.4
33.7 Correo sandstone outlier forms small knob to right of curve.
0.5
34.2 Pass under overpass.
0.5
34.7 Note recent eolian deposits in low road cuts, and small pink and white butte of Entrada with thin Todilto limestone cap at 10:30. Mesita, one of the villages of Laguna Indian Pueblo, and excellent exposures of Todilto gypsum and brown-buff sandstone member at 1:30.
0.9
35.6 **SLOW. Mesita Exit. Turn right.**

Figure 4. — View of mesa at Stop No. 2 near Mesita village, showing from bottom up: Todilto gypsum, buff shale, and brown-buff sandstone.

	0.2
35.8	**Stop sign. Turn right.**
	0.5
36.3	**Cattle guard,** continue straight on road to Mesita.
	0.3
36.6	Rising onto Quaternary basalt flow which followed old Rio San Jose channel from centers in the Zuni Mountains and Grants area some 35 miles to the west.
	0.1
36.7	Turn sharp left to parking area.
	0.1
36.8	**STOP NO. 2.** Unusually good exposures of the Entrada sandstone, Todilto limestone and gypsum, buff shale, and brown-buff sandstone are seen in close view at this stop and the regional distribution and correlation of these units will be discussed.
	After stop, return to paved road.
	0.6
37.4	**Turn left** before cattle guard.
	1.6
39.0	**SLOW,** approaching overpass at 39.1. At overpass, El Paso Natural Gas Co. compressor station at 1:30. Light buff sandstone in hills beyond the station is Entrada that is bleached and more resistant to erosion owing to diabase sills intruded into and adjacent to the overlying Todilto. Dark band at base of Entrada is Correo sandstone, which horizon you are also on here!
	0.2
39.2	Turn left onto old U. S. 66 leading to Correo and Los Lunas.
	2.8
42.0	Sandstone cuesta in Chinle shale at 9:30 near road; basaltic cone at 3:00; Lucero Mesa, 12:00-12:30. Cimarron Mesa of Sierra Lucero, 1:30; on far horizon is old, high-level basalt cap on westward-tilted and truncated lower Chinle shale. Roundish soft hill a couple of miles toward 2:00 appears to be Chinle, but we haven't been there.
	0.7
42.7	Bridge; Suwanee Peak at 12:00; Mesa Redonda, 12:45. Note basalt fragments along ditch bank to right of road indicating presence of Recent basalt flow which probably extends through here from Mesita. At 43.7 is a hummock on this flow that has not been completely buried by valley alluvium or eolian debris.
	0.25
42.95	Crossing El Paso Natural Gas Co. pipeline.
	1.4
44.35	Bridge.

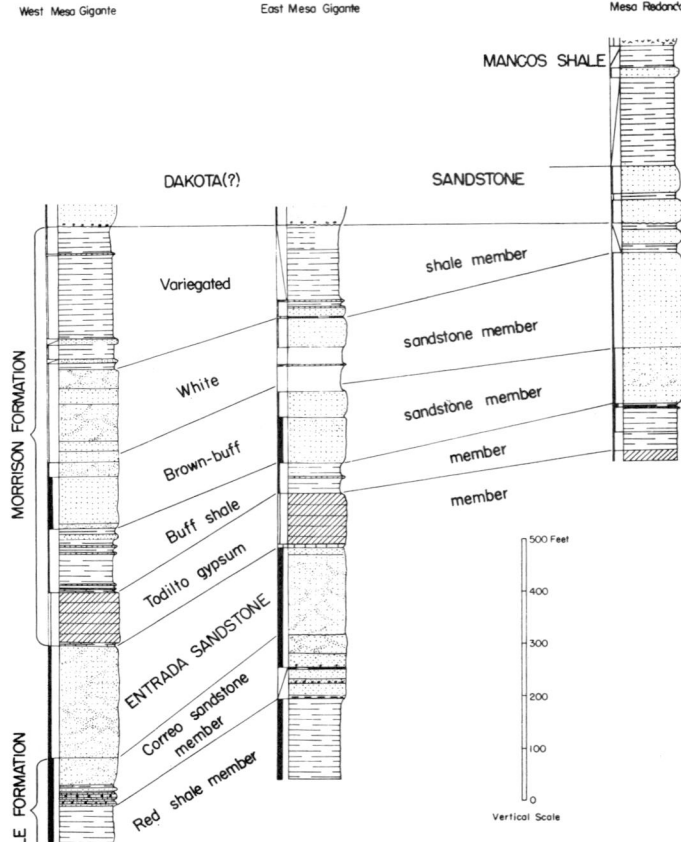

Graphic sections of Mesozoic strata, Mesa Gigante to Mesa Redonda

Numbers refer to localities given in list.
7. Mesa Redonda: Antonio Sedillo Grant.
8. East Mesa Gigante: begins in sec. 27, T. 9 N., R. 3 W., and ends in sec. 9, T. 9 N., R. 3 W.
9. West Mesa Gigante: begins in sec. 24, T. 9 N., R. 4 W., and ends in sec. 1, T. 9 N., R. 4 W.

Figure 3. — Graphic sections of Mesozoic strata, Mesa Gigante to Mesa Redonda. From Kelley and Wood, (1946).

45.55	**1.2** Side road right leads many miles south to ranches in the Cerro Colorado area and eventually to Puertecito. Still on the basalt flow which continues east between Suwanee Peak and Mesa Redonda after coalescing with one which probably came from Cerro Verde cone at 3:30 on skyline.
46.45	**0.9** Old Correo store, post office, and motel units.
46.8	**0.35** **Overpass.** Santa Fe railroad.
47.	**0.2** **Stop Sign.** N. M. 6 to Los Lunas, **Turn right.** Road left leads back to new U. S. 66. Old 66 was straight ahead. It dead-ends now!
48.8	**1.8** Mesa Lucero 2:00-3:00.
49.	**0.2** Note small gorge in basalt ahead on left.
49.3	**0.3** Suwanee Peak at 9:00. Massively bedded rusty sandstone near base is white sandstone member; variegated shale member forms slope; brown-stained first ledge of the Dakota forms main bench which is stripped on a shale break above. The pyramid-shaped peak is a remnant of the main Dakota ledge; it is capped here by about 20 feet of Quaternary(?) travertine. Compare the double ledging of the Suwanee Dakota with that in the western end of Mesa Redonda at 10:30. Also note higher, lighter colored sandstone in the Mancos slope. This may be Gallup. See Figure 5.
49.7	**0.4** Suwanee station on right. Mesa Redonda beyond is a faulted syncline truncated and capped by basalt which may be an outlier of Lucero Mesa, although if so it is sufficiently lower as to suggest late faulting between the two mesas. Note the Recent landslide that came out of the soft beds in the trough. The mesa cap in this bite is only about 50 feet across on top. The syncline appears to be broken by two faults which are just east of the axial plane of the syncline. Also note the exposures locally of a thinner sandstone ledge above the Gallup(?) sandstone.
51.1	**1.4** The lowest massively bedded sandstone in Mesa Redonda, 2:00-3:00, is the brown-buff sandstone member. Note the white sandstone member above it and the very thin variegated shale member above. Compare the much thicker variegated shale member in the beds at 9:00. This agrees with the regional southward overstepping by the Dakota. Here the split between the two Dakota sandstone ledges is about 3 feet thick.
51.5	**0.4** The basalt flow is to the left of the road. In the rise ahead and in the adjoining railroad cuts, Entrada and overlying Todilto limestone are exposed. As you top out on this rise note the Todilto gypsum in the mesa base at 3:00-4:00 and the gypsum mounds at 2:30. Weathered gypsum underlies much of the flats to the south of the railroad and it has been stripped and mined in the mounds at 2:30. This operation was in 1952 and 1954 by the Suwanee Gypsum Products Corp. and the White Eagle Gypsum Co. probably for agricultural use (Weber and Kottlowski, 1959).
53.35	**1.85** Cattle guard. Note cliffs in banded brown-buff sandstone member at 9:00 and slopes in more rounded and crossbedded white sandstone member above. The small hogbacks from 2:00 to 3:00 are Dakota in separate fault slices.
53.5	**0.15** Rio San Jose basalt flow capping inner mesa from 10:00 to 11:00. Note entrenched meandering course of Rio San Jose as it runs easterly to a junction with the tree-lined Rio Puerco in the center of the valley. Ceja del Rio Puerco forms eastern middle skyline with Manzano Mountains as a backdrop. There are a few isolated Todilto limestone exposures just beneath the basalt flow at about 53.6.
54.0	**0.5** Side road to South Garcia station which is on the sinuous, gentler, upgrade track of the Santa Fe, south of the low Dakota sandstone hill across the downgrade track.
54.2	**0.2** The northern end of the Santa Fe fault zone is exposed intermittently in the hills at 3:00. Landslides and numerous travertine spring deposits much obscure the bedrock.
54.9	**0.7** We are riding on the mesa-capping terminal lobe of the San Jose lava flow.
56.5	**1.6** Note descent onto a lower flow layer.
56.9	**0.4** Along here from 2:00 to 4:00 there is an excellent view of the complicated covering of the northern end of the Santa Fe fault zone by numerous small terraces at different levels and by slopes and banks of lighter colored younger springs. It is from this travertine that the All American Marble Co. is getting much of its product that is currently marketed in New Mexico and elsewhere. Near the southern end of the Lucero uplift travertine terraces, as much as 100 feet thick and 1 mile wide, stretch for several miles along the base of the uplift in a volume of nearly 200 million tons. All these deposits appear to have resulted from carbonate waters issuing along or near the fault zones of the Lucero uplift. See Figure 7.

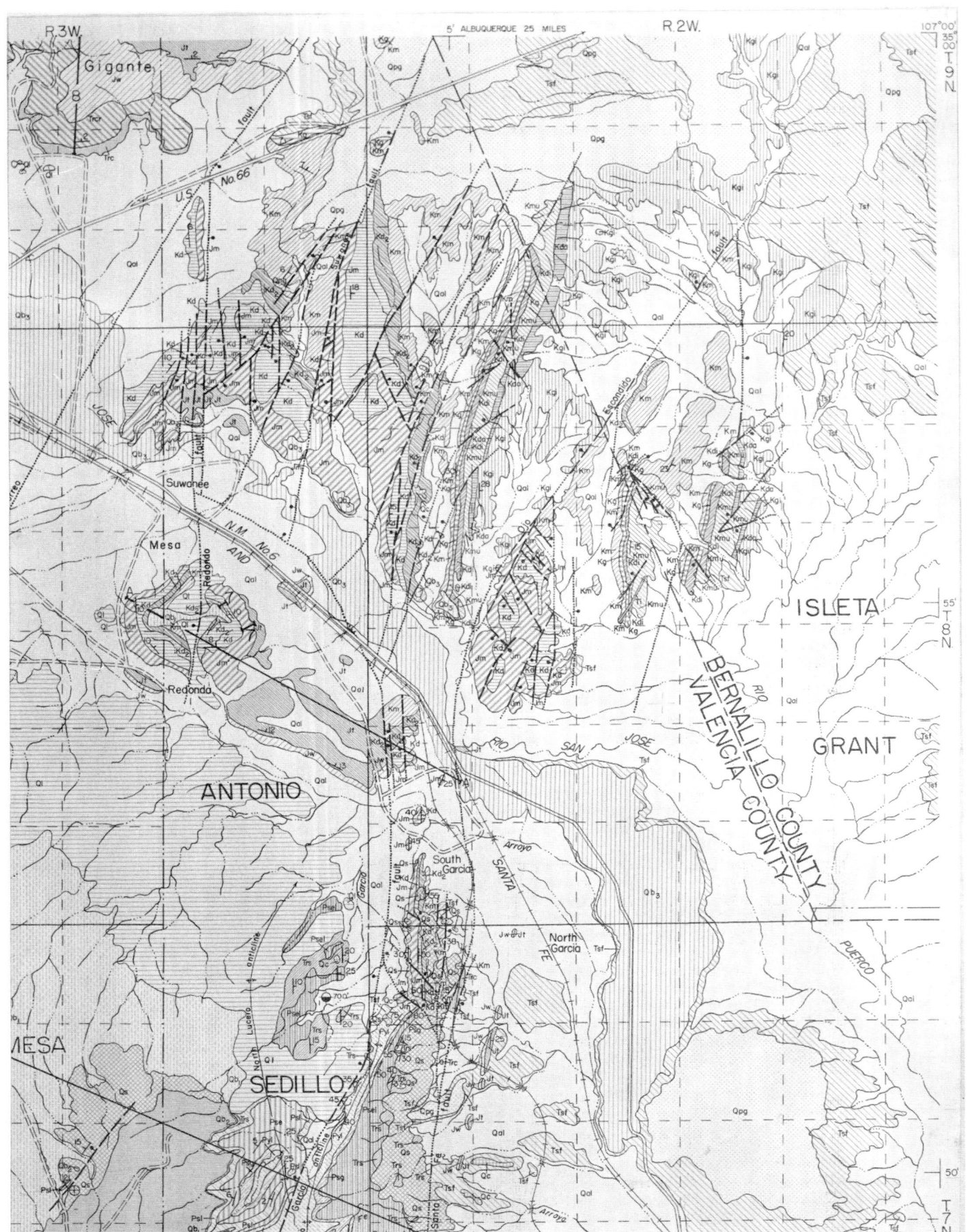

Figure 5. — Geologic map of the Suwanee Peak area and the northern end of the Lucero uplift. See Figure 6 for explanation of symbols. From Kelley and Wood (1946).

Figure 6. — Explanation of the formations shown on Figures 5 and 8.

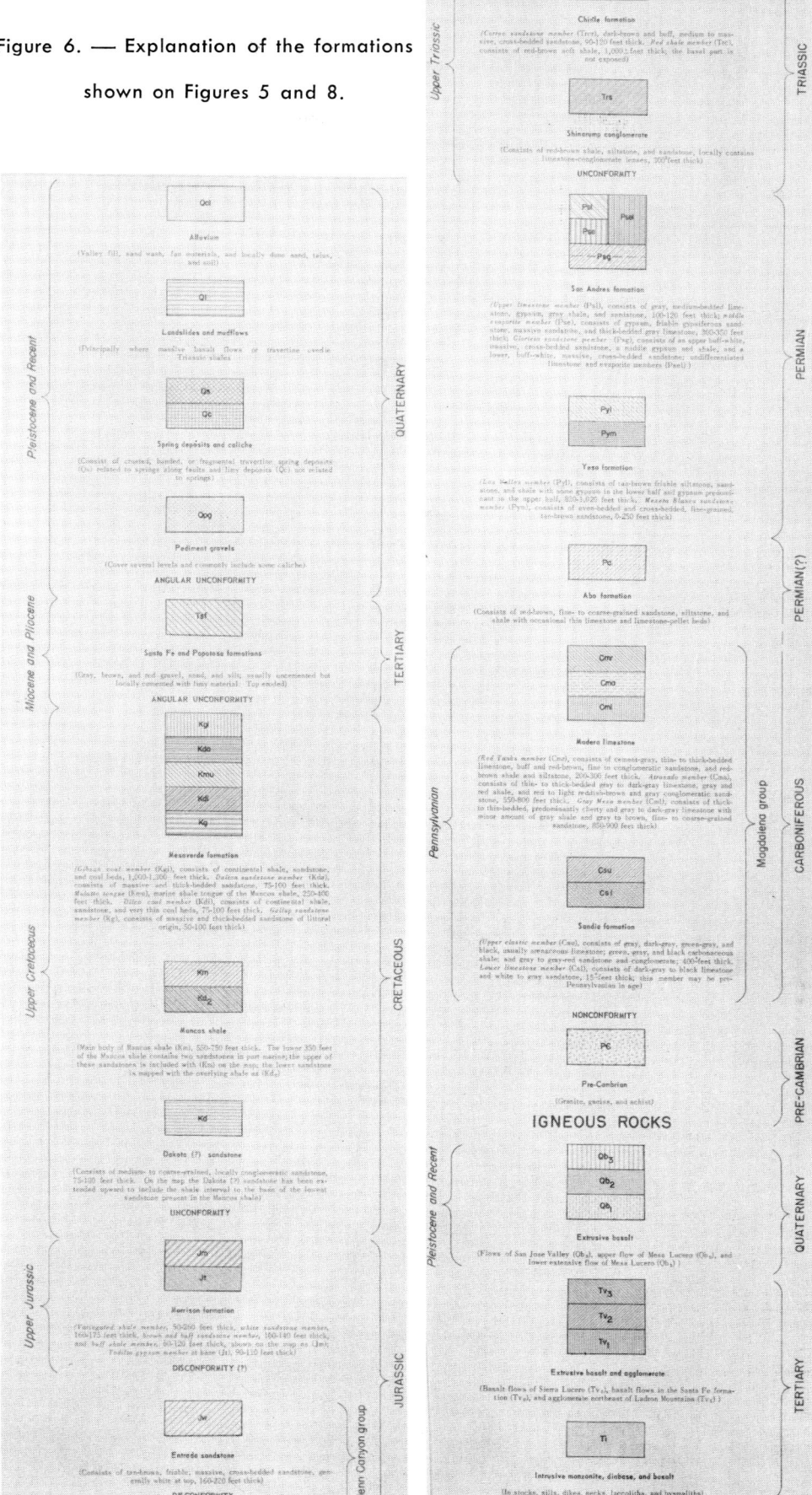

40 NEW MEXICO GEOLOGICAL SOCIETY ⬥ TWELFTH FIELD CONFERENCE

0.5
57.4   Ladron Peak, 9,260 feet, at 12:00. Flat-topped Bobo Butte, at 12:30, is formed by a caliche-cemented gravel cap across tilted Santa Fe beds. It appears to be an outlier of an extensive surface that may have been once coextensive with the Llano forming the level beneath the Sierra Ladron, the Ceja, 9:00-10:00, and the Lucero Mesa, 1:00-3:00. If so, there probably has been some dropping of Bobo Butte with respect to the Lucero surface along the Comanche fault zone. The scalloped hogback from 1:30 to 3:00 appearing beneath Lucero Mesa is formed by eastward-dipping San Andres limestone of the eastern limb of the Lucero anticline.

Figure 7. — Vertical air view of the area around Stop No. 3. Note the thin Todilto hogback crossing the (western) curving railroad track. Pliocene Santa Fe beds are turned up to vertical immediately east of the Todilto, as may be seen in a cut along the railroad. The scalloped ridge in the western part of the photo is formed by Glorieta sandstone and San Andres limestone. Note the dark landslide apron that adjoins the basalt-capped Lucero Mesa along the left edge of the photo. See Figure 6 for symbols.

	0.6
58.0	**STOP NO. 3.** The northern end of the Lucero uplift west of this stop consists of a north-plunging anticline whose axial trace is about at the edge of the basalt-capped mesa (Fig. 7). West of here and just beyond the first ridge the diagonal Garcia fault breaks through the eastern limb, upthrowing the eastern side. Along eastern base of ridge is the Santa Fe fault zone on which in this latitude the Rio Grande trough is dropped. Thus, the ridge that is seen about 2 miles west of this stop is a horst about 1 mile wide lying between the Garcia and Santa Fe faults. Consulting Figures 5 and 7, it may be noted that this horst together with the North and South Lucero anticlines characterize the northern structure of the uplift north of the Comanche zone of thrusting.
	The chaotic disposition of the travertine spring deposits along the slopes of the horst ridge is partly due to dispersion of the spring orifices, the existence of several terrace levels, and landsliding of these deposits on the weak Triassic Chinle mudstones.
	0.2
58.02	**Sharp left turn** as road descends end of San Jose basalt flow. Note how thin it is as you go through the road cut, especially in view of its length. It must have been about 10-20 weight! Note the far west-going Santa Fe track and the near east-going one.
	0.9
59.1	Side road right leads to Lucero front.
	0.3
59.4	At 3:00 quarry of All American Marble Co. in canyon.
	1.6
61.	Flat-lying Pliocene Santa Fe sand, gravel, and tan beds in hills at 9:00. Mohinos Hills at 1:00-2:00 consist of sills, dikes, and plugs in deformed Santa Fe beds.
	1.8
62.8	**Puerco siding road. Turn right.**
	0.1
62.9	Cross double Santa Fe tracks, plus one extra for cattle siding! **Hold the trains!!**
	0.5
63.4	Fork in road, turn right. Left fork leads to Humble No. 1, Santa Fe & Pacific well.
	0.7
64.1	Gate.
	0.35
64.45	Crossing gas pipeline of El Paso Natural Gas Co.
	0.85
65.3	Cattle guard, Santa Fe gravel on right.
	1.7
67.2	**Side road; turn right up Carrizo Arroyo.** Carrizo Canyon enters the uplift between Bobo Butte and the first Glorieta-capped knob to the south. The geology of the Lucero front here is dominated by two north-trending faults, one behind or west of the Glorieta-capped buttes, and one in front or to the east. The western one is high-angle and elevates upper Madera beds against Yeso (see between the buttes). The eastern one (Comanche) upthrusts Yeso against Triassic beds (see at the base of the buttes). The red beds up Carrizo Arroyo are Abo and the paler red beds in the distance just beneath the basalt cap of Lucero Mesa are Meseta Blanca beds.
	0.55
67.75	**Gate; pass through and continue ahead on left fork.**
	0.8
68.55	**Gate; do not pass through but bear right along fence.**
	0.3
68.85	**STOP NO. 4.** The structure of the front of the Lucero uplift here is complicated. It has been interpreted in part as a low-angle thrust, as a high-angle thrust, and as a normal fault modified by landslides. Some of the details and problems of this most controversial part of the uplift will be pointed out on a walking trip along the base of the uplift.
	After the stop return to the Comanche road.
	2.1
70.95	Comanche road, **turn right.**
	0.65
71.6	Windmill, 9:00.
	9.5
72.1	Consolidated Santa Fe sand and gravel forms butte at 1:30. The Comanche fault zone passes beneath the Lucero basalt at about 2:30 but reappears to the south. The road ahead traverses gently dipping and dissected Santa Fe sand and gravel for the next 2 miles.
	0.9
73.	From 2:00 to 3:00 Yeso, Glorieta, San Andres form the front of the uplift with Madera limestone to the west of the faults just beneath the basalt.

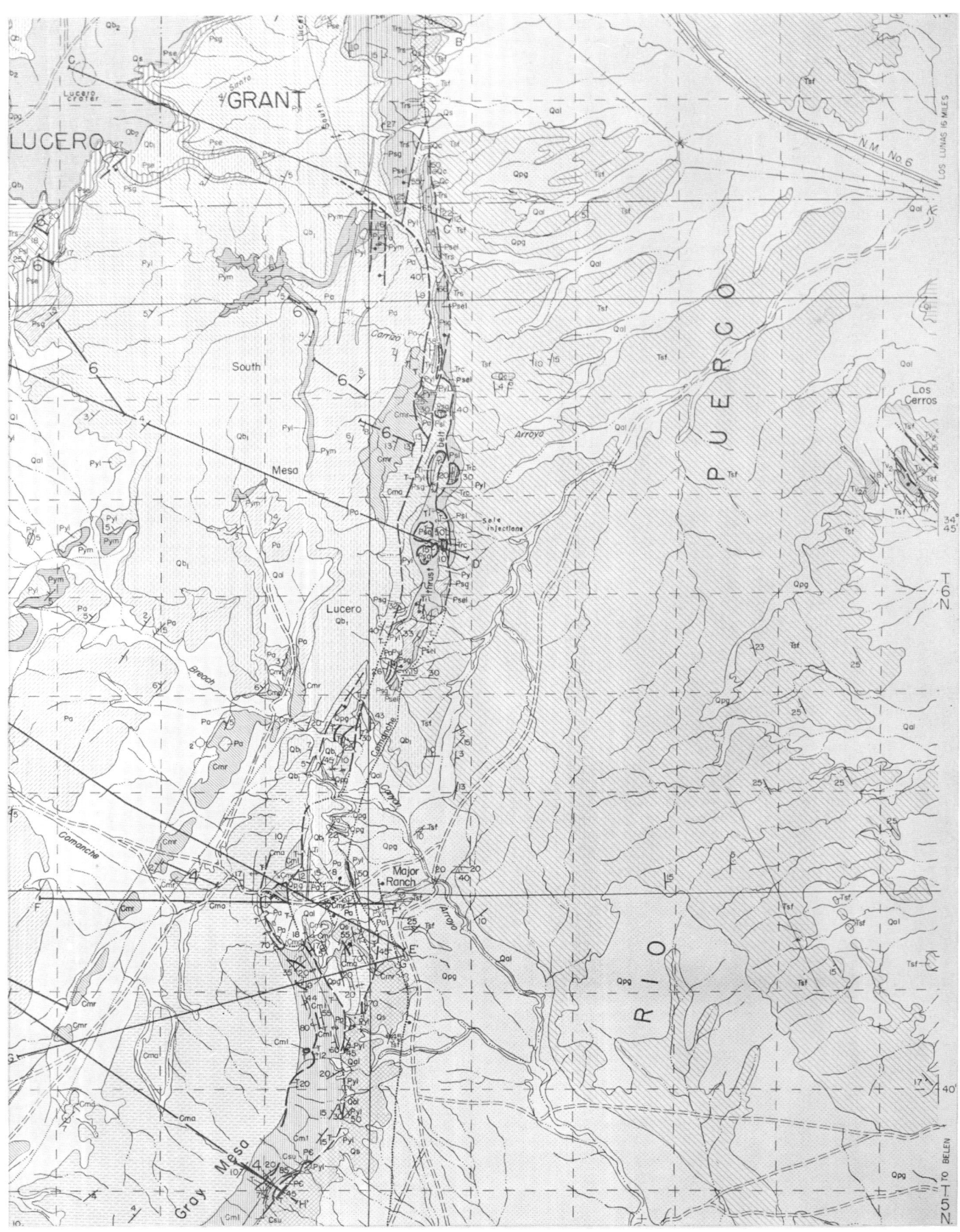

Figure 8. — Geologic map of the east-central part of the Lucero uplift. See Figure 6 for explanation of symbols. From Kelley and Wood (1946).

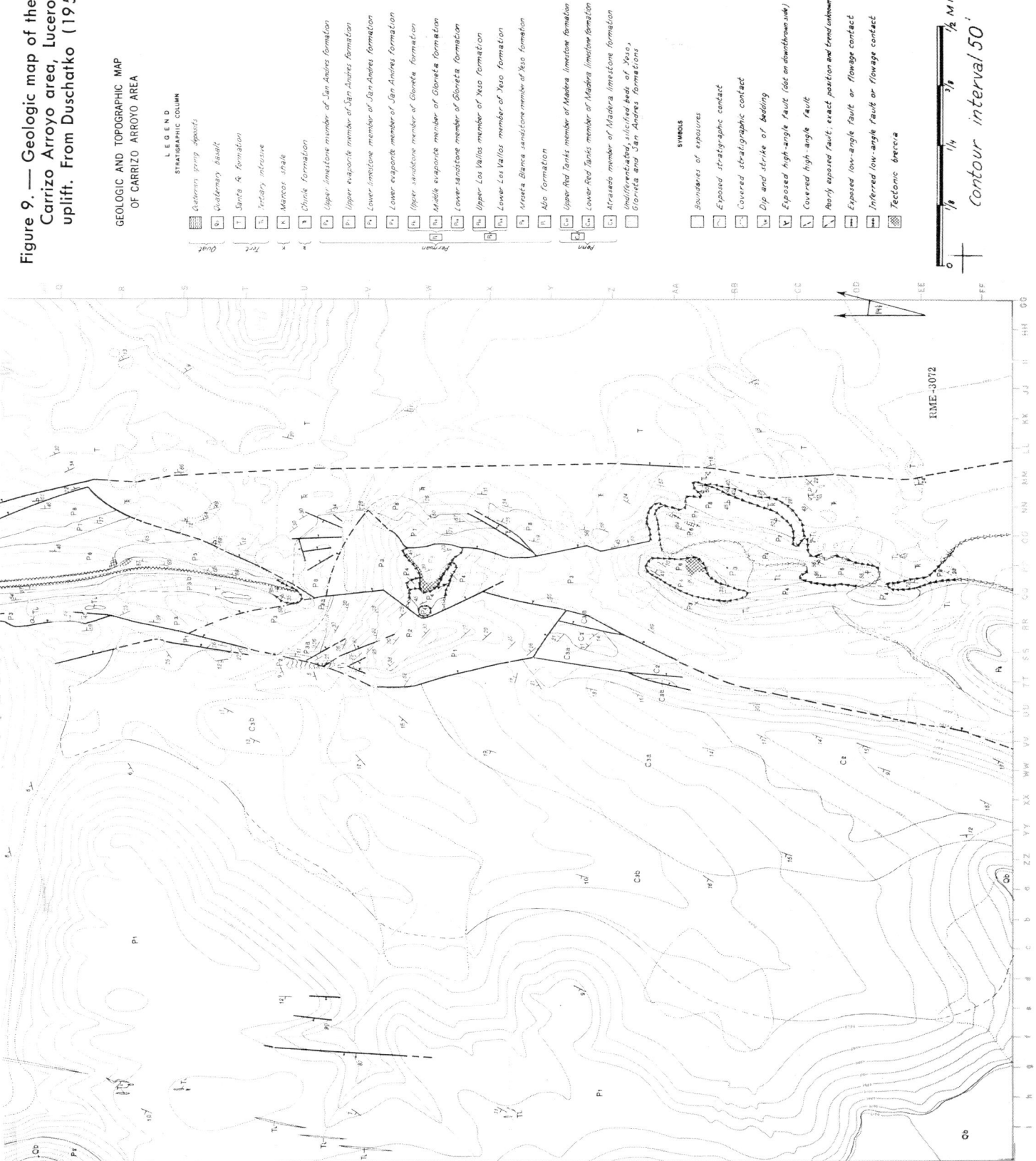

Figure 9. — Geologic map of the Carrizo Arroyo area, Lucero uplift. From Duschatko (1953).

		1.7
74.7	Divide.	
		0.05
74.75	Cattle guard.	
		0.05
74.8	**Turn right. Side road** to Comanche Canyon.	
		0.6
75.4	Gate.	
		1.1
76.5	Yeso in small hill to left; Abo ahead and in basalt-capped mesa to right. Gray Mesa, 11:00-12:00, consists of Madera limestone.	
		0.2
76.7	Lowermost Abo sandstone, mudstone, and pellet conglomerate.	
		0.3
77.	Vertical basalt dike in lower Abo beds in creek bottom at 3:00.	
		0.2
77.2	Madera limestone thrust upon Abo in hill 2:00-3:00. Terrace gravel on Abo at 9:00.	
		0.3
77.5	**STOP NO. 5.** Here in Comanche Canyon the Comanche fault swings westward about five-eighths of a mile between the southern end of Lucero Mesa and Gray Mesa. This is the Major embayment of Kelley and Wood (1946). Lower Madera beds are upthrust against Abo beds. Some of the details and problems of the structure will be considered. See Figure 8. Turn around and retrace route to N. M. 6.	
		0.5
78.	Note hogback of upturned Yeso beds just east of Comanche fault zone and large white travertine spring mound at 1:00.	
		11.0
89.	**New Mexico 6. Turn right.**	
		0.2
89.2	**Bridge over Rio Puerco.**	
		2.4
91.6	Los Pinos Mountains, 2:00; Manzano Mountains, 11:30-1:30; Ladron Mountains, 3:30. Driving in Santa Fe beds. Humble No. 1, Santa Fe & Pacific well located just behind low basalt-strewn hills of Santa Fe at 4:00. Located on Gabaldon anticline in Santa Fe beds. This well was drilled in 1953 to a depth of 12,691 feet. It bottomed in Cretaceous after drilling some 9,000 feet of Tertiary sediments.	
		2.0
93.6	Bridge.	
		0.6
94.2	Road rises onto the Llano de Albuquerque; Los Lunas volcanic centers, 1:00; Isleta cinder cones and lava flow on Llano 10:00-11:00.	
		1.8
96.0	Dalies Station at 2:30 is junction point of main line of Santa Fe railroad through Albuquerque with southern route from Clovis through Abo pass and Belen. Santa Fe railroad has three wells, 750, 1,100, and 1,225 feet deep, capable of large yields of good water. Numerous deeper tests for oil have been drilled in the area between here and Los Lunas. See Beaumont article.	
		0.9
96.9	Cinder cones at 9:00 are southern ones of a nearly north-south line of 15 cones in a field of basaltic lava. The flat basaltic mound at 9:30 is not one of the line of cinder cones.	
		1.4
98.3	Overpass, main line Santa Fe railroad.	
		0.35
98.65	**Side road to Dalies Station, straight ahead.**	
		0.85
99.5	Leaving Llano surface. Note soil profile in caliche cap and white caliche nodules at intervals in the bedded sand and silt below.	
		1.0
100.5	Side road right. The Los Lunas volcanic center is a complicated basaltic intrusion into and on the Santa Fe. It has domed and broken the Santa Fe in places and the uptilting of these beds may be seen at 3:00 west of the basaltic centers. Isleta volcanic center at 10:30.	
		1.2
101.7	Manzano Mountains from 12:00 to 2:00 are a tilted fault block which bounds the Rio Grande depression on the east. In the northern part of the uplift Pennsylvanian Magdalena beds rest nearly flat upon a Precambrian complex. In the southern part the Magdalena is stripped from the top, and the entire western escarpment is Precambrian. From 10:30 to 12:00 is the relatively low Manzanita uplift in which gently dipping Magdalena beds lie much lower on the Precambrian.	

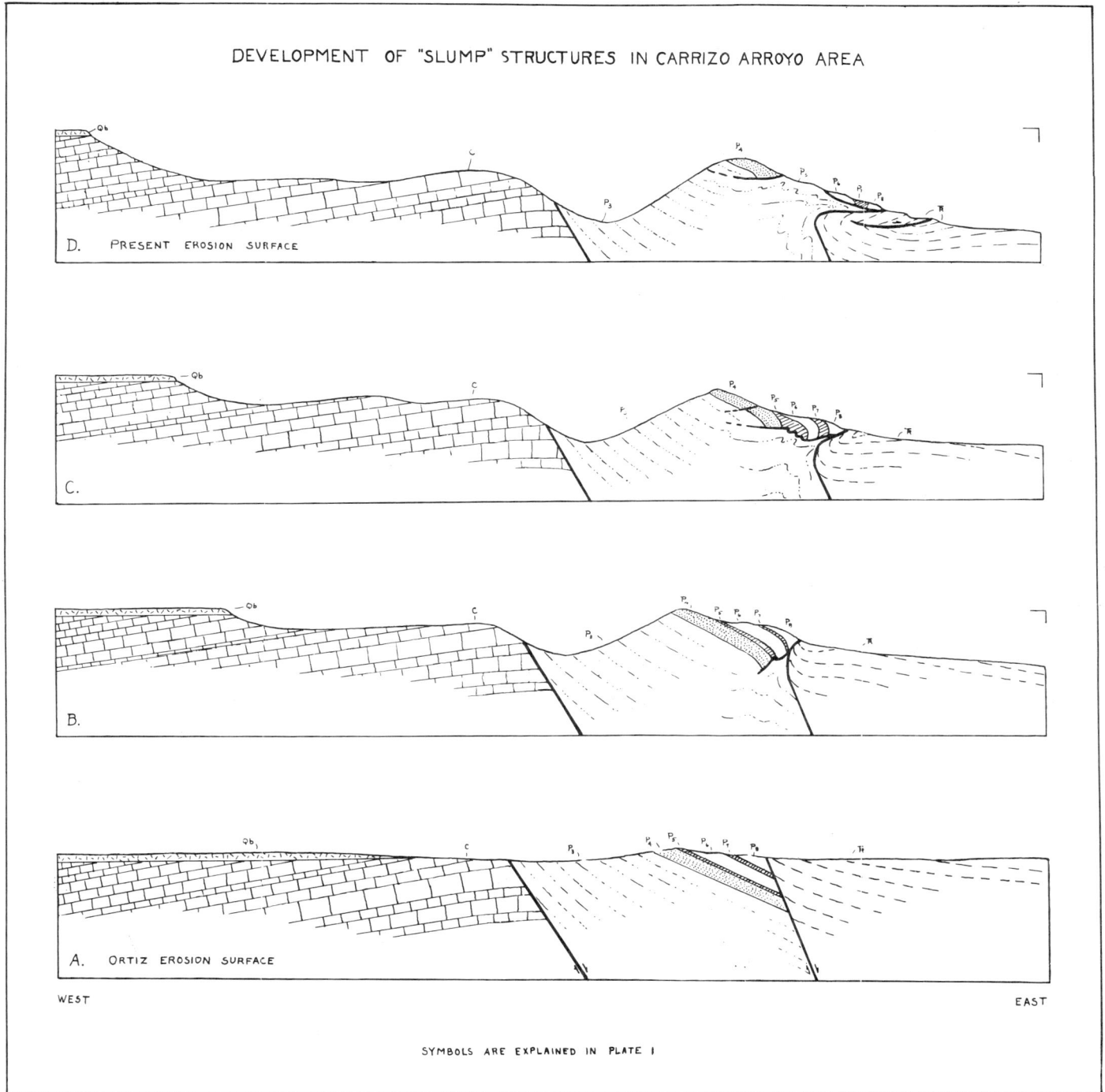

Figure 10. — Evolution of the Carrizo Arroyo structures. From Duschatko (1953).

	0.7
102.4	At 11:00 in the floodplain of the Rio Grande is the rounded Tome basaltic center. Scattered patches of gravel are present on top of it, suggesting that it was at one time buried by Santa Fe beds. Note that its top is higher than the mesa level to the east.
	1.9
104.3	Descending onto the plain of the inner valley of the Rio Grande and entering Los Lunas, county seat of Valencia County. At 3:00 a.m., April 7, 1893, many persons were awakened by an earthquake. "The frame depot shook and swayed to such an extent that the agent fled in terror."
	0.5
104.8	**Junction U. S. 85. Turn left.**
	2.7
107.5	Santa Fe at 10.30; at 3:00 on skyline Bosque Peak (southern), 9,630', and Mosca Peak (northern), 9,490'.
	1.1
108.6	County line.
	0.6
109.2	Swamps on right and left are ground-water levels of Rio Grande.
	0.6
109.8	Sandia Mountains at 12:00.
	1.15
110.95	Overpass.
	0.25
111.2	**Junction. Continue straight ahead on 45.**
	0.5
111.7	Basalt and cinders in road cut derived from Isleta center at 9:30.
	0.4
112.1	Intra-Santa Fe basalt. Note overlying gravels on left.
	0.3
112.4	Descending bluff, held up by flow, to Rio Grande floodplain.
	0.3
112.7	Note irregular pre-basalt surface at 9:00; another intra-Santa Fe basalt also occurs at a lower level.
	1.1
114.9	Santa Fe right and left.
	8.2
122.	Road rises to Segundo Alto surface. View of city to right.
	1.4
123.4	U. S. 66. End of second day's trip.

ROAD LOG: JEMEZ MOUNTAINS AND VICINITY

THIRD DAY, OCTOBER 8, 1961
V. C. Kelley, E. H. Baltz, Jr., and R. A. Bailey

Mileage Traveled: 176.6 miles (logging odometer 2.5% high).
Starting Time: 7:30 a. m.
Assembly Point: San Mateo Blvd. at Montgomery Road, northeastern Albuquerque. **See Figure 1, first day's log for location.**

RESUME

The third day's trip is northward into the Jemez Mountains along the western margin of the Rio Grande depression. Fine exposures of the Jurassic Entrada and Todilto formations will be seen near San Ysidro, and the type localities of the Meseta Blanca and San Ysidro members of the Permian Yeso formation will be observed along the route up Jemez Canyon. Farther up the canyon exposures of the Pleistocene Bandelier tuff rise in spectacular cliffs above Permian and Pennsylvanian rocks.

The middle part of the trip passes through the Jemez (Valles) caldera with its beautiful forested mountain scenery. The problems and history of this great area of volcanic activity will be pointed out. To the east of the caldera in the dissected Pajarito Plateau around Los Alamos the interrelationships of the Jemez volcanics, the basaltic eruptions from the Cerros del Rio area, and the Santa Fe group will be seen, along with their influence upon the course of the Rio Grande in White Rock Canyon.

The later part of the trip will be southward along the Rio Grande depression through Santa Fe. The type area of the Santa Fe group will be seen. In addition the deformation of these beds, the associated basaltic eruptions, and the several extensive erosion surfaces will be observed.

Note. Users of the road log should bear in mind that the cumulative mileages are approximate. Variations can be expected due to differences in individual odometers and to errors on the part of those preparing the log. Check points such as bridges and road intersections in the log permit ready correction.

Cumulative Mileage

0.0 San Mateo and Montgomery. City limits. The lead car parks at intersection headed north. City water storage tanks are lined up parallel to Montgomery toward the mountains. Sandia Mountains from 1:30 to 4:30; Albuquerque volcanoes are at 9:00-9:30 on horizon. These are aligned north-south as though along a fissure. West Mesa terrace across the Rio Grande floodplain from 7:30 to 9:30.
   1.0

1.0 Nacimiento Peak at 11:00 on skyline; Jemez volcanic plateau at 11:45-12:30; Redondo Peak, 11,252 feet, at 12:00.
   0.5

1.5 **Road junction: TURN RIGHT to junction with N. M. 422.**
   0.3

1.8 Bear right onto N. M. 422 (Interstate 25) and proceed north.
   0.9

2.7 At 9:00 American Gypsum Co. plant (red, white, and blue); processes gypsum from Jurassic Todilto formation near San Ysidro. Farther west, Reeves power plant of Public Service Co. of New Mexico. On terrace west of the Rio is Paradise Hills country club.
   0.4

3.1 Overpass.
   0.7

3.8 At 3:00 is Bear Canyon erosional reentrant in the Sandias between North and South Sandia Peaks.
   1.2

5.0 Coronado Airport at 3:00.
   0.1

5.1 **Alameda Exit.** Continue on N. M. 422.
   0.9

6.0 At 9:30 are good exposures of pinkish Santa Fe beds across the valley. Road is also on the Santa Fe.
   2.6

8.6 Rincon Ridge at 3:00 in front of the Sandias is a resistant mass of Precambrian metamorphic rocks west of the main granitic escarpment. Note north-trending foliation of quartz mica schist cut by numerous narrow aplite and pegmatite dikes.
   1.1

9.7 Bridge. Numerous good exposures of Santa Fe sand, silt, and gravel in road cuts and ravines for next 4 miles.
   2.35

12.05 **Bernalillo Exit. Continue ahead** on N. M. 422. Village of Bernalillo on floodplain at 9:30.
   1.65

13.7 **Placitas Exit. Continue ahead** under overpass and prepare to **turn right.**
   0.15

13.85 **TURN RIGHT** onto N. M. 44 to Bernalillo and Cuba.

	0.15
14.0	Cross overpass and continue west.
	0.4
14.4	Descending into valley bottom of Rio Grande.
	0.3
14.7	**STOP SIGN** at junction with U. S. 85. **Continue ahead** on N. M. 44.
	0.7
15.4	East end of bridge over Rio Grande.
	0.35
15.75	Road to Coronado State Monument (Kuaua) on right.
	0.35
16.1	Side road right leads to Jemez Dam. Continue ahead on N. M. 44.
	0.4
16.5	At 3:00 below skyline are contorted and tilted breccias of Canjilon diatreme and caldron sink. San Felipe cone and basaltic lava field. Santa Ana Mesa beyond. Road ascends dissected slope in Santa Fe beds.
	4.6
21.1	From 9:00 to 10:30 vista of badlands in the Santa Fe. At 11:00 is Nacimiento Peak near southern end of Nacimiento Range. At 12:00 lower on the skyline is the Jemez Plateau capped by Bandelier tuff. At 12:15, the tilted lava-capped mesa is Chamisa Mesa. Redondo Peak and rim of Jemez (Valles) caldera at 1:00. From 2:00 to 3:00 is Santa Ana Mesa formed of Santa Fe capped by Pliocene (?) basalt. The basalt is tilted on the east and broken by numerous north-trending faults.
	2.2
23.3	At 10:00-11:00 bouldery outcrops are strongly cemented sandstone along a fault in the Santa Fe.
	0.2
23.5	Bridge. **Sharp curve ahead**, side road right.
	1.2
24.7	Santa Ana Pueblo at 3:00. Sign reads "On the plaza of this ancient pueblo stands the church of Santa Ana de Alamillo which was constructed by General Don Diego de Vargas following the reoccupation of New Mexico in 1692. The original mission erected shortly after 1600 was destroyed by fire in 1687." For the next 11 miles the highway traverses Santa Fe and alluvium derived from the Santa Fe. The valley north of the road is the lower part of Jemez Creek. When the Jemez Dam (farther downstream) is full, water backs up in the valley past Santa Ana.
	8.1
32.8	Road to right leads to Zia Indian Pueblo on low terrace north of Jemez Creek. Sign reads "visited by Francisco Vasquez Coronado in 1540-41. The ancient Indian sun symbol of Zia Pueblo is used as the design for the New Mexico State Flag." The New Mexico Geological Society emblem also utilizes this symbol (see cover of guidebook).
	1.4
34.2	At 12:00 is White Mesa. The dark band near the top is Jurassic Todilto limestone resting on white and pink Entrada. Limestone is capped by white Todilto gypsum which is being mined by American Gypsum Co. Olive-drab shale on lower part of hill is Cretaceous Mancos shale brought up against the Entrada along the Sierrita fault. See Figure 1.
	1.3
35.5	At 10:00-11:00 are variegated shale and sandstone of the Morrison formation capped by Dakota sandstone.
	0.4
35.9	At 9:00 the north end of Llano de Albuquerque surface cut on Santa Fe beds. The Sierrita fault runs up this valley and passes beneath the Santa Fe which laps onto Jurassic and Cretaceous rocks. Crude oil pipeline, Texas-New Mexico Pipeline Co., on left.
	1.15
37.05	At 9:00 fault contact between Mancos shale and Todilto gypsum. At 9:30 note sharp base of Todilto formation on white upper part of Entrada. Base of Entrada is below brown cliff-forming bed. Lower slope is underlain by shale of the Triassic Chinle formation. At 10:00-12:00 the flat-bottomed La Sierrita syncline is surfaced by the Agua Zarca sandstone member of the Chinle. The high west limb is Red Mesa and the east limb is referred to as Mesa Cuchilla. Precambrian granite of Nacimiento Peak beyond the syncline is faulted up against these beds (Fig. 1).
	0.75
37.8	Southern end of bridge across Rio Salado.
	0.8
38.6	**SAN YSIDRO. Junction N. M. 4 and 44. BEAR RIGHT** on N. M. 4 toward Jemez Springs. Jemez fault at 10:30 throws Cretaceous Mancos shale against Chinle formation.
	0.5
39.1	Hogback in Permian rocks at 9:30. See Figure 2.
	1.0
40.1	Outcrops to right are Santa Fe.

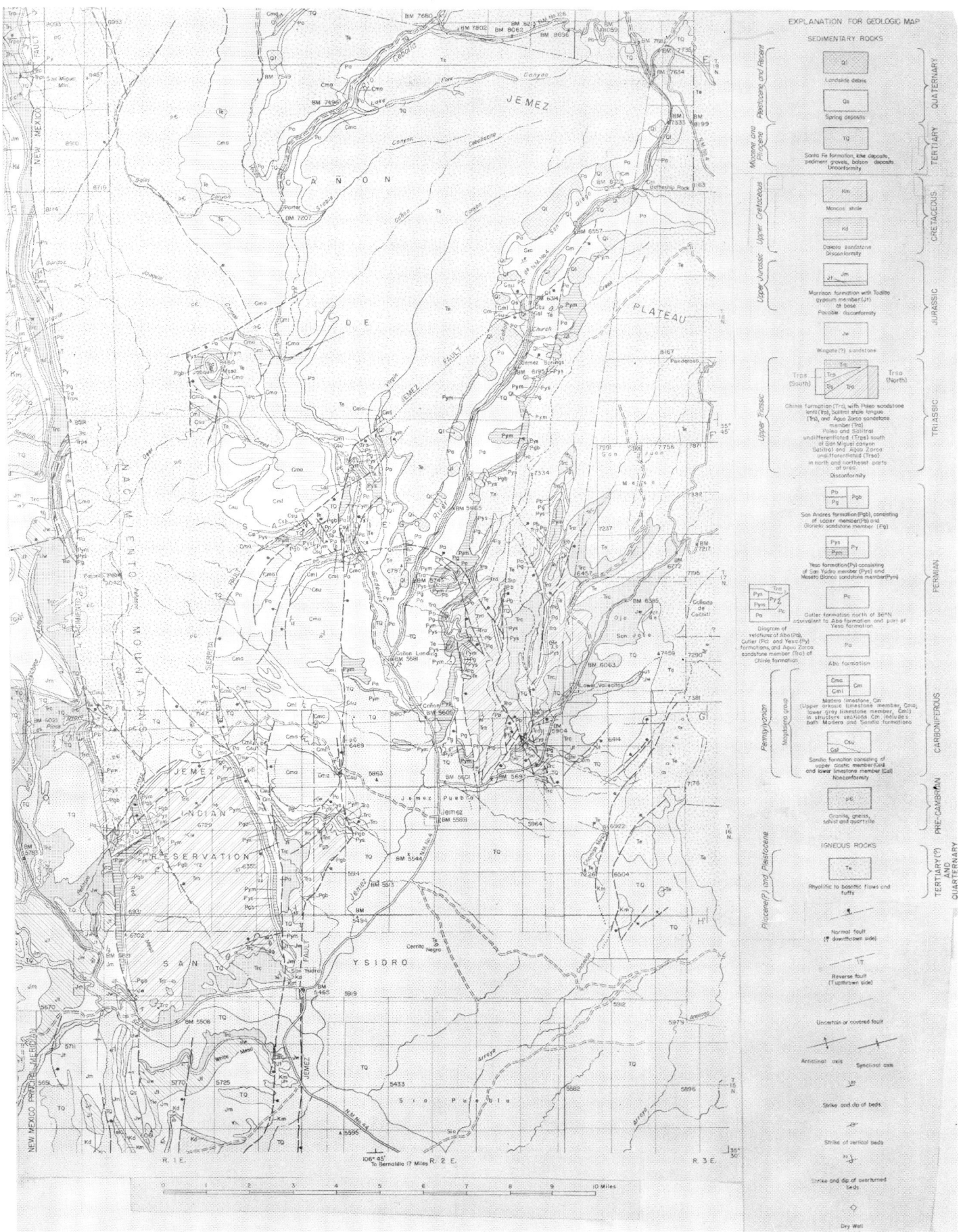

Figure 1. — Geologic map of the Nacimiento Mountains and adjacent plateaus, Sandoval County. Modified from Wood and Northrop (1946).

Figure 2. — View of eastern face of Mesa Cuchilla. Triassic Agua Zarca sandstone, TRa; Permian, Glorieta sandstone, Pg; San Ysidro member of Yeso formation, Pys; Meseta Blanca member of Yeso, Pym; Abo formation, Pa.

Figure 4. — View of stratigraphy at prominent spur between Guadalupe and San Diego Canyons. Bandelier tuff, Qbt; Meseta Blanca, Pym; and Abo formation, Pa. Note slide.

	0.5
40.6	Bridge.
	0.35
40.95	Agua Zarca caps mesa, 8:30-9:00, and forms open anticline. Santa Fe faulted down at base of mesa.
	0.95
41.9	Cross meadow at lower end of side creek.
	0.75
42.65	White Santa Fe sand in road cut; at 10:00 similar beds are dropped against older rocks along Jemez fault. Note pediment gravel cap on truncated white Santa Fe (lacustrine?) sand beds. Some of the white Santa Fe is tuff.
	1.35
44.	Jemez Pueblo. Sign reads: "This pueblo was established around 1700. The last survivors of the pueblo of Pecos moved here in 1838. It is the only surviving pueblo at which the Towa language is spoken. The people are noted for their unique style of basket-weaving."
	0.8
44.8	Santa Fe in road cuts.
	0.15
44.95	Bridge over Vallecito Creek.
	0.1
45.05	Side road right, to Vallecito and Paliza camp ground; ahead is another hill of white Santa Fe capped by Quaternary boulder beds.
	1.25
46.3	**STOP NO. 1.** Type locality of Meseta Blanca member of the Yeso. The lighter red, more massive and cross-bedded sandstone is Meseta Blanca member of the Yeso formation. (Does it remind you of Canyon de Chelly? See paper by Baars.) It is overlain by darker red thinner beds of the San Ysidro member seen along rim at 3:00. Road ahead follows crest of open southward-plunging anticline. The stratigraphy and regional relations will be discussed here.
	0.75
47.05	**Canyon.** Beds around this valley are Permian Abo. At 3:00 note Meseta Blanca, overlain by San Ysidro, with Glorieta capping mesa. Highest part of mesa has a Pleistocene Bandelier tuff outlier.
	1.45
48.	Canyon Landing, side road to Guadalupe Canyon of the Rio de las Vacas. Note junction of the Vacas and Jemez Creeks at 10:00. Road continues in Abo. Continue ahead.
	0.75
49.25	At 10:00 note sharp contact of Bandelier tuff on Meseta Blanca.
	0.6
49.85	At 12:00 on high cliffs note channel fill of Bandelier tuff in orange-colored Meseta Blanca. The filled channel appears to parallel the slope and the present canyon. As you round curve ahead note that erosional contact descends east wall of canyon also. Perhaps the old canyon was as much as one-half as deep as the present one.

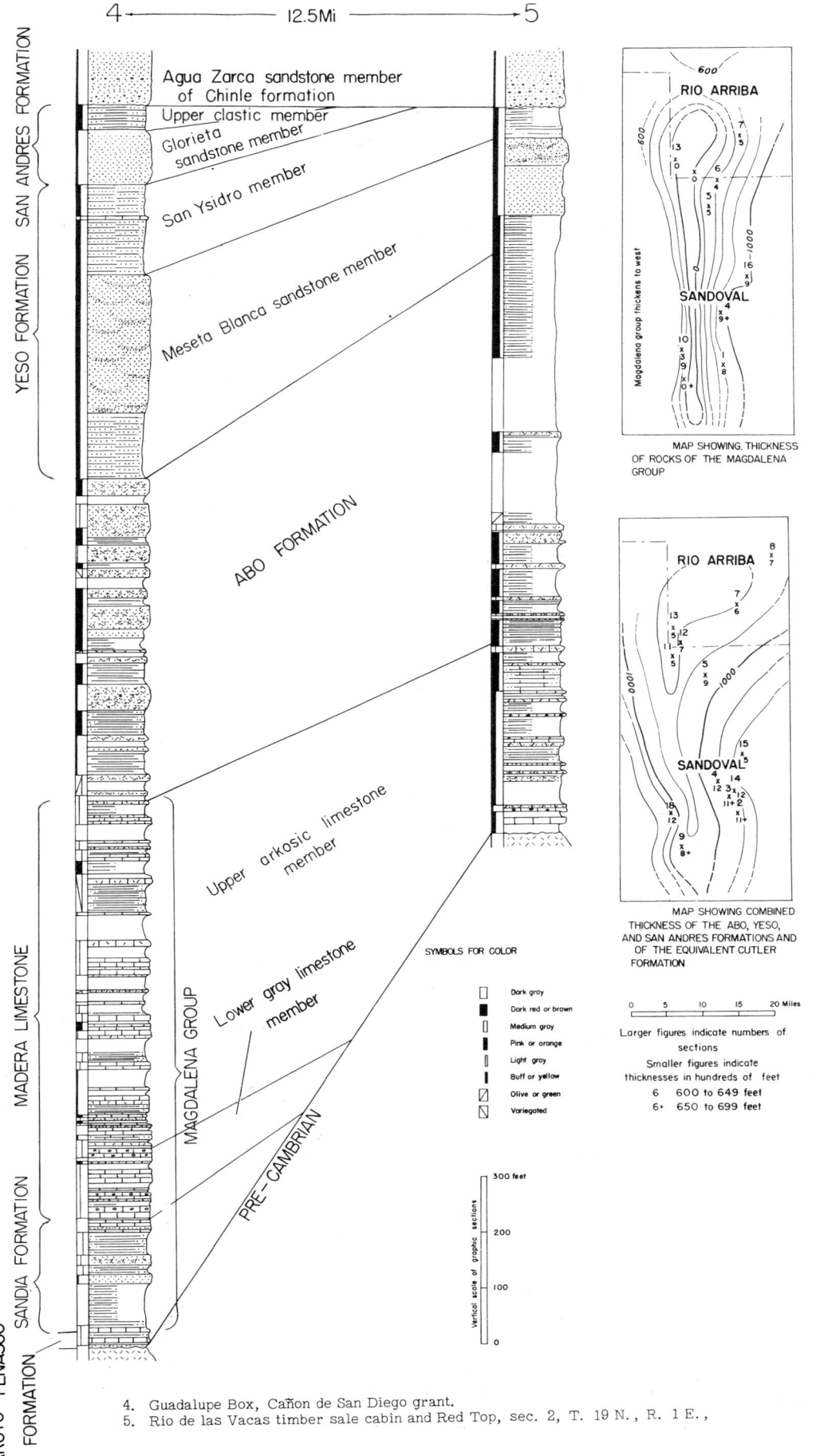

Figure 3. — Graphic sections and isopachous maps of Permian and Carboniferous rocks. Adapted from Wood and Northrop (1946).

		2.4
52.25	Note dissected talus and sliderock, 10:30-11:00.
		1.3
53.55	At 2:00 note portals of old Spanish Queen copper mine low on hillside. This is a red-beds copper deposit consisting of chalcocite, malachite, and azurite in buff sandstone and carbonaceous shale 1-4 feet thick that run as much as 8 percent copper in places. The carbonaceous shale also contains as much as 0.1 percent uranium. Fossil plants and vertebrates in the shale indicate that this part of the Abo formation is lower Permian or Wolfcamp in age (floral zone 13 of Read and Mamay, 1960). Romer collected amphibians and reptiles here in 1931, including the type of **Sphenacodon ferocior**, 8-9 feet long and 285 pounds in weight, "the most powerful carnivore of its day and age in New Mexico."
		0.3
53.85	At 9:00-12:00 the Bandelier tuff consists of two members. The base of the upper member is marked by a thin ash-fall bed just below the orange ledge about one-third of the way below the top of the mesa.
		1.5
55.35	Note prominent, massive, orange Meseta Blanca cliffs at 1:00 high on east canyon wall.
		0.9
55.25	Approaching Jemez Springs village.
		0.45
56.7	**Jemez Springs post office** on left. According to Clyde Kelly and E. V. Anspach (Univ. New Mexico Bull. 71, chem. ser., v. 1, no. 1, 1913, p. 7), "these springs are located geographically in two groups. At each group are built comfortable bath houses and sweating rooms. A daily stage runs between the springs and Albuquerque. The springs are known throughout America and in Europe and occasionally one meets a foreigner here." Water temperatures range from 119° to 155° F.
		0.45
57.15	Large landslide across river; red beds in low slopes on right contain fossiliferous nodular and massive limestone beds. This is uppermost Madera limestone or transition zone similar to the Red Tanks or Bursum of elsewhere.
		0.3
57.45	Ranger Station on right.
		0.1
57.55	**Jemez State Monument**, sign reads: "This monument contains ruins of the ancient Indian Pueblo of Guisewa and of the Franciscan Mission which was founded between 1617 and 1621-22. The pueblo was first visited by Coronado in 1541, was abandoned between 1680 and 1694."
		0.1
57.65	Road cut on right in Madera formation.
		0.5
58.15	Bridge over Jemez Creek. Note Madera in lower slopes at 3:00. Cross fault that brings up Precambrian pink gneiss at 58.25.
		0.4
58.55	**Soda Dam.** This spectacular spring deposit of travertine has been built from carbonated waters issuing from along a fault crossing the canyon. The main fault brings pinkish Precambrian gneiss up against Magdalena beds. Travertine-building waters have issued in this area for a long time; there are deposits several hundred feet above the canyon bottom on the west side apparently aligned along subsidiary faults. Also note the prominent travertine cones across the canyon north of the Soda Dam. Note by Editor.—In 1902 there were 22 springs flowing along the dam; by 1912, only 11 springs; now only 2 or 3. High on the west wall of the canyon, 900 feet above present creek level, are remains of older "dams," formed before Jemez Creek had cut to present level. Rounded pebbles, cobbles, and boulders are imbedded in the basal part of these high-level travertine deposits. Oolites and pisolites ranging up to 45 mm in diameter occur in the spring conduits — the first discovery of pisolites in a spring deposit in North America (Northrop, 1932; 1934).
		0.7
59.25	Note top of Magdalena several hundred feet up eastern side of canyon.
		1.55
60.8	Upper Madera in slopes at 9:30; Bandelier tuff forms upper canyon walls.
		0.65
61.45	Note dark cliffs of andesite below Bandelier at 9:30-10:00; part of lower Pliocene volcanic series.
		0.45
61.9	White travertine deposits of recent springs below road on right and ahead in road and on left. Whew!
		0.55
62.45	Madera in hill at 12:00. Battleship Rock at 2:00 is a Pleistocene rhyolite welded tuff and breccia. This poured down San Diego Canyon from El Cajete center to the northeast near the southern base of Redondo Mountain.
		0.15
62.6	Cattle guard. Confluence of North and East Forks of the Jemez.
		0.5
63.1	Madera across creek at 2:00 in trees; Abo on west side of creek. Fault?

	0.2
63.3	Landslide blocks of older andesite flow breccias of pre-Bandelier volcanics at left of road.
	0.35
63.65	Abo in hillside on left above fossiliferous Madera at road level.
	0.25
63.9	Typical Abo red beds in cuts on left; Battleship Rock welded tuff forms cliffs high on right canyon wall.
	0.5
64.4	Abo in left road cut.
	0.6
65.0	Black vitrophyre of Banco Bonito flow exposed in cliff wall on right and ahead. This is post-Bandelier rhyolite and fills canyons that were cut in Battleship Rock welded tuff. See Figure 5.
	0.9
65.9	Cattle guard.
	0.1
	LUNCH STOP
66.0	La Cueva Forest Camp.
	0.05
65.05	Bridge over San Antonio Creek; Battleship Rock welded tuff forms cliffs.
	0.5
66.1	**Road junction**, N. M. 126, **straight ahead** on N. M. 4 to Los Alamos.

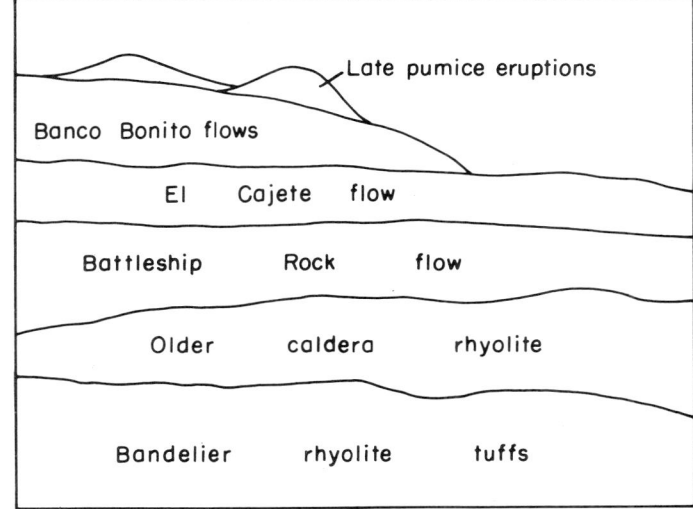

Figure 5. — Diagram of the stratigraphic relations of the principal rhyolitic eruptions in the western part of the Jemez caldera.

	0.7
66.8	Perlitic rhyolite on both sides of road. This is post-Bandelier and pre-Battleship Rock tuff. Perlitic rhyolite was derived from nearby post-caldera centers.
	0.15
66.95	Side road left to Sulfur Springs up La Cueva Creek. Continue ahead. Redondo Mountain, 1:00, hills at 12:00 are Redondo Border consisting of tilted blocks of Bandelier tuff. West slopes are dip slopes; east slopes are fault scarps.

Brief note on Jemez Sulfur Springs: It is not feasible for the caravan to visit this group of springs, but if you haven't seen them you should return some day. These springs were visited by several of the early Spanish explorers. Don Juan de Onate was here in 1598 and in a letter to the viceroy mentioned "the mountains of brimstone, of which there is a greater quantity than in any other province." There are several mineral and thermal springs, fumaroles, and solfataras. Excellent crystals of sulfur have been found. Around the turn of the century an attempt to mine sulfur was made. Later, bath houses (of a crude sort) were erected. The springs have been given fanciful names, such as the sour spring, alum spring, seltzer spring, and electric spring; the mud of a so-called mud geyser has been recommended as a beauty mud; one spring has been reputed to remove corns. Renick (1931) concluded that the waters of the Sulfur Springs are chiefly volcanic (juvenile); that the waters of San Ysidro Springs, a few miles west of San Ysidro, are a mixture of original volcanic and meteoric waters; and that the waters at Soda Dam are largely meteoric waters that were heated by circulating in proximity to uncooled masses of igneous rock.—Ed.

	0.15
67.1	At 9:30 in timbered ridge, to right of light-colored bluffs of perlitic rhyolite, are reddish alluvial deposits derived from the caldera walls and containing blocks of fossiliferous Madera limestone and Abo sandstone.

	0.4
67.5	Cut on right exposes float of buff and red-brown sandstone in tuffaceous sand caldera fill.
	0.05
67.55	Pumice of the Battleship Rock welded tuff.
	0.85
68.4	Road is on surface of glass flow of Banco Bonito. Ridges are primary flow structures. Dark boulders and outcrops are rhyolite vitrophyre admixed with pumiceous rhyolite. These flows appear to come from a low crater called El Cajete at the southern base of Redondo Mountain. In some places the black glass displays a bluish iridescence.
	0.25
68.65	Cattle guard, Baca Location fence.
	0.75
69.4	Road curves left and descends the margin of the glass flow of Banco Bonito.
	0.75
70.15	Banco Bonito picnic grounds on right. Road is on surface of an older post-caldera rhyolite flow. Scarp at left is margin of Banco Bonito flow.
	0.6
70.75	Cattle guard, more vitrophyric obsidian along road and in cliffs to left. Canyon to right is East Fork of Jemez Creek, which we saw back at Battleship Rock.
	0.1
70.85	Pumice bed on left lies between Banco Bonito flow and older, post-caldera flow.
	0.15
71.0	**Bear right across bridge.**
	0.4
71.4	Pumice beds in road cuts were erupted from El Cajete center to north after extrusion of Bandelier and caldera collapse.
	0.4
71.8	Pumiceous rhyolite blocks on left are weathered older, post-caldera flow.
	0.2
72.0	Side road right to Jemez Falls recreation area.
	0.3
72.3	Redondo Mountain at 11:30; high central dome of caldera consists of Bandelier rhyolite tuff.
	0.3
72.6	Ridge from 12:00 to 1:00 is Los Griegos ridge, part of the Sierra de los Valles; south rim of the caldera. These are pre-caldera, pre-Bandelier andesites.
	0.1
72.7	Side road right to Ponderosa and Bernalillo, continue ahead.
	1.7
74.4	Crudely bedded air-fall in road cut on left was erupted from El Cajete center to the west.
	0.8
75.2	Cattle guard.
	0.4
75.6	Older, post-caldera rhyolite flow, pre-Banco Bonito and El Cajete.
	0.25
75.85	Cattle guard; entering upper valley of East Fork of Jemez Creek.
	0.15
76.0	To the left, edge of post-Bandelier rhyolite flow that dammed Valle Grande, which is to the east. To the right is the south wall of the caldera composed of pre-Bandelier andesite.
	0.4
76.4	Outcrop of pre-Bandelier andesite.
	0.1
76.5	Las Conchas forest camp.
	1.2
77.7	El Cajete pumice deposits on left.
	0.6
78.3	View to the northeast into the beautiful Valle Grande.
	0.85
79.15	**Road Junction, take left fork.**
	1.25
80.4	**STOP NO. 2.** Discussion of Jemez caldera. Lake at 12:00 is approximately N. High flat-topped ridge from 10:00 to 11:00 is Redondo, highest part of the late structural dome in center of caldera. High knob and lower ridge to the east is all part of central structural dome. The structural dome is underlain by Bandelier rhyolite tuff dipping generally to the south. The caldera rim extends from 9:00 (Los Griegos peaks) behind observer (6:00) and along the grass-covered peaks at 4:00 and red talus-covered mountain at 3:00. Rim continues behind forested domes from 2:00 to 3:00 and is visible again at 1:00 (grass-covered slopes on sky-

line). Rhyolite domes that are peripheral to Redondo structural dome at 10:00 (Cerro la Jara), including small knob just west of lake, and heavily forested mountains 1:00-2:00 (Cerro del Medio, Cerro de Abrigo, and Cerro des Trasquillar). See article by Ross, Smith, and Bailey in this Guidebook.

1.7

82.1 Road cut on right is talus from caldera wall.

1.1

83.3 Saddle in rim of caldera and Sierra de los Valles; rocks are pre-Bandelier dacites.

0.4

83.6 Crossing obscured contact from pre-Bandelier volcanics into Pleistocene Bandelier tuff. This is now outside the caldera and in the upper part of Frijoles Canyon drainage. The Bandelier tuff here fills an older canyon cut into the "Chicoma" (H. T. U. Smith, 1938) rocks. The Chicoma or Tschoma rocks were described by Ross (1931) as all the older andesitic to latitic flows and breccias, including some basalt and rhyolite. Owing to the variety of types and terranes, the term is unlikely to prove useful in the future. The Bandelier down the canyon a short distance is as much as 1,000 feet thick. Road is on flat surface or shoulder of Bandelier for about one mile.

1.2

84.8 Hairpin curve right and road goes back into pre-Bandelier dacite. Contact of Bandelier and pre-Bandelier dacite follows the bottom of the canyon at the right.

0.4

85.2 Bench is on Bandelier again.

1.2

86.4 Profile of tilted Sandia Mountain uplift in distance at 12:00. Deep canyon of the Frijoles on right is all in Bandelier tuff. The Cochiti Range from 1:00 to 2:30 is composed of pre-Bandelier volcanics consisting largely of andesite and rhyolite. Pre-Bandelier dacite in road cuts on left.

0.35

86.75 Road curves left. Note St. Peter's Dome and lookout at 2:00 in the near distance. The dome is part of the San Miguel Mountains which are andesite rocks ("Chicoma" group), nearly surrounded by Bandelier. Ortiz, San Pedro, and South Mountains on skyline east of the Sandias are laccolithic porphyry centers. Road cut on left is typical porphyritic dacite which, in weathered outcrops, superficially resembles welded upper part of the Bandelier.

0.3

87.05 Cattle guard. Enter Los Alamos County. Road cuts are in "Chicoma" rocks.

0.35

87.4 Road cut is in well-bedded pumice gravel which may be younger than Bandelier. Bandelier is in outcrops ahead.

0.15

87.55 Road cut in pre-Bandelier dacite. Flat bench ahead is on top of Bandelier.

1.35

88.9 Road cuts in Bandelier rhyolite tuff.

0.45

89.35 Welded tuff of Bandelier.

0.25

89.6 Sharp curve left. Sangre de Cristo Mountains from 10:30 to 1:00 on skyline. Pajarito Plateau is the broad surface below this escarpment. Cerros del Rio from 1:00 to 2:00 east of White Rock Canyon of the Rio Grande. As the road curves to the left, Los Alamos and its technical areas may be observed to the north and northeast on the Pajarito Plateau which is capped by Bandelier tuff. Road descends the scarp of the Pajarito fault along which the Bandelier tuff was downthrown 400-500 feet in Quaternary time.

0.5

90.1 Outcrop of pumice gravel in road cut to the right. This seems to be the same pumice observed on the Bandelier west of the Pajarito fault.

0.2

90.3 **Road junction. CONTINUE STRAIGHT AHEAD ON N. M. 4 toward Bandelier National Monument.** Road to left leads to Los Alamos. Although the Pajarito Plateau appears to be a continuous bench it is dissected by numerous eastward-draining canyons which cut deeply into the Bandelier and underlying Santa Fe and basaltic rocks. The narrow, intervening mesa segments are known as "potreros".

0.9

91.2 Road is on welded rhyolite tuff of the upper member of the Bandelier, and on remnants of pumice gravel resting on Bandelier.

0.2

91.4 Road cut in welded tuff of the upper member of the Bandelier. The Bandelier is an apron of explosive rhyolite debris which nearly surrounds the eroded older "Chicoma" volcanics. The basal member of the Bandelier is pumice and pumice gravel locally known as the "Santa Clara pumice bed" and locally more than 100 feet thick. The medial member consisting of pumiceous tuff, tuff breccia, and pumice is from a few feet to 220 feet thick. The upper member, composed of crystal tuff and tuff breccia, ranges in thickness from about 200 feet on the east to about 1,000 feet in upper Frijoles Canyon.

	1.2	
92.6		View to left into Water Canyon, almost 300 feet deep at this point. Note the topographic expression of hard and soft units in the upper member of the Bandelier. Six distinct persistent units occur in the upper member with slight erosional unconformities between several units. Part of the tuff is of ashfall origin, and part was laid down probably as "nuee ardente" — incandescent gas, ash, and breccia which flowed rapidly down the slopes from the west. Although the Pajarito Plateau has been deeply incised by canyons the general upper surface is close to that of the original top of the Bandelier at many places. Numerous Indian ruins dot the mesas of the plateau and cliff dwellings occur in nearly all of the major canyons. The ruins range from one or two rooms to large pueblos. The earliest Pueblo Indian ruins may date from A.D. 1150 to 1200, and the Pajarito Plateau is believed to have been mainly abandoned before the coming of Coronado in 1540. The ancient Pajarito people were the ancestors of the people of the present Rio Grande pueblos of Santa Clara, San Ildefonso, and Cochiti, and perhaps others, according to tradition. Some of the cliff dwellings were reoccupied briefly after the coming of the Spanish. Sankewi'i (gap of the sharp round cactus), a large mesa-top ruin at the east edge of the plateau, may have been occupied from about 1150 to the 18th century.
	3.8	
96.4		Entrance to Bandelier National Monument. **CONTINUE STRAIGHT AHEAD.** The people of present Cochiti and San Felipe Pueblos claim that their ancestors built some of the cliff dwellings and surface ruins in Frijoles Canyon. According to tradition, these people were driven out by Tewa people from the northern part of the Pajarito Plateau. The Navajos (spelling "Navahos" preferred by anthropologists and historians) also raided in this area, and the name Navajo (Navaho) appears to have come from the Tewa word "Navahu'u" meaning "arroyo of cultivatable fields," or "large area of cultivated lands" or "Apache who cultivated fields." (Kluckhohn states that in Spanish it means a knife or razor or a large, more or less worthless, flat piece of land.—Ed.) The Navajo were said by Fray Alonso de Benavides in 1630 to be great farmers. At 12:00-1:30 are the basaltic eruptive centers of the Cerros del Rio (hills of the river) east of White Rock Canyon of the Rio Grande. Road is on the upper member of the Bandelier.
	0.8	
97.2		View to the left into Ancho Canyon. Note individual bedded units of the upper Bandelier.
	0.4	
97.6		At 3:00 the reddish hill is a basalt cone nearly buried in Bandelier tuff.
	0.6	
98.2		Road descends into Ancho Canyon on upper member of the Bandelier.

Figure 6. — View to north across Ancho Canyon. Cliffs are upper member of the Bandelier tuff. Thin-bedded tuff below the lower cliff rests on white pumice which is at the base of the upper member. The pumice exposed in scars above the road rests unconformably on gray pumiceous tuff of the middle member of the Bandelier.

	0.4	
98.6		Curve in Ancho Canyon. Note cliff dwellings in lower part of the upper member of the Bandelier.
	0.1	
98.7		At 12:00 the well-bedded lower part of the upper member rests with erosional unconformity on pumice and pumiceous tuff of the middle member of the Bandelier.

	0.7
99.4	Road cut on hill exposes orange-colored beds of the lower part of the upper member. This unit is a persistent marker resting unconformably on the middle member.
	0.2
99.6	At 2:30 down Ancho Canyon note the basalt ledge in the middle ground. To the east the middle member of the Bandelier fills a deep narrow canyon cut in basalt.
	0.9
100.5	View to the northwest of the eastern rim of the Jemez caldera. The high peaks are composed mainly of dacite flows and several latite domes. Dacites are overlain at places on the rim and west of the rim by the upper member of the Bandelier, which laps onto the flanks of the older volcanics and fills deep canyons eroded prior to the Bandelier eruptions. Road cuts continue to be in upper Bandelier.
	0.9
101.4	Orange cliffs at 11:00 are basal part of the upper member of the Bandelier. Pre-Bandelier basalt at right.
	0.2
101.6	Road cut on the right is in pre-Bandelier basalt which flowed westward from centers in the Cerros del Rio. Some of these flows stood as hills during the Bandelier eruptions and all three members of the Bandelier thin onto the basalt. Note the slight westward tilt of the upper member ahead. This tilt may be the result of compaction of buried pre-Bandelier Puye gravel which lies in the subsurface between the basalt and the "Chicoma" volcanics (see Fig. 7), or the result of cooling shrinkage of the thicker Bandelier to the west, or the result of post-Bandelier structural adjustments, or a combination of these factors.
	1.4
103.0	Basalt in road cuts overlain by thin pumice of the middle member of the Bandelier, overlain by orange tuff-breccia of the upper member. The mesa to the east is soil-capped basalt surmounted by erosional remnants of the Bandelier. **Slow for sharp right turn** onto dirt road.
	0.4
103.4	**TURN SHARP RIGHT** onto dirt road leading southeastward to edge of White Rock Canyon. Road is on soil on basalt.
	0.2
103.6	Passing onto middle member of the Bandelier resting on basalt. **Watch for high centers.**
	0.9
104.5	To the south is Potrillo Canyon. At the confluence of Potrillo and Water Canyons at about 2:30 (not visible from here) is a deep pre-Bandelier canyon cut in basalt and filled by the middle member of the Bandelier. This was part of a deep, narrow, meandering, but generally southwestward-trending canyon. Other parts of this canyon can be observed in lower Ancho and Frijoles Canyons.
	0.5
105.0	**SLOW — ROCKY ROAD** descending hill from Bandelier onto soil-capped basalt.
	0.1
105.1	Cross deep arroyo. Road is on soil on basalt.

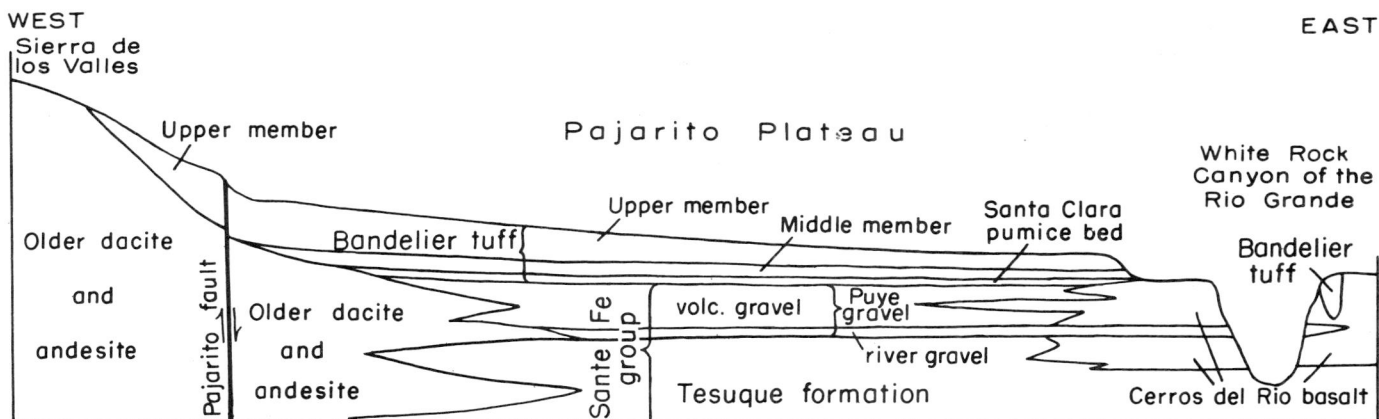

Figure 7. — Diagram showing stratigraphic relations of the Santa Fe group and volcanic rocks of the Jemez Mountains and Rio Grande area.

	0.55
105.65	**STOP NO. 3.** Rim of White Rock Canyon. **Park as directed by flagman.** Approximately 30 minutes will be devoted to observing and discussing the volcanic geology of White Rock Canyon and the Pajarito Plateau. White Rock Canyon is noted for its rattlesnakes!
	To the east is an excellent view of the northern part of the Cerros del Rio and the east wall of White Rock Canyon of the Rio Grande. The canyon is about 870 feet deep here, and was cut through a complex

sequence of basalt, andesitic basalt, and interflow sediments, all about 1,300 feet in maximum thickness south of here. The Tesuque formation (of the Santa Fe group) is exposed in the lower part of the gorge. At places canyons were eroded in the basalt between periods of eruption, and basalt-filled channels may be observed to the southeast of the viewing point. Almost directly across the canyon is a remnant of a meander of a pre-Bandelier canyon cut in basalt and filled with white and light gray tuff of the middle and upper members of the Bandelier.

On the basis of fossil mammals collected near San Ildefonso and farther north by Cope in 1874 and by Frick in the 1920's and 30's, the Tesuque formation of the Santa Fe group is probably middle Miocene to middle Pliocene age. The Childs Frick (1937) collections of horned ruminants alone number hundreds of specimens. The lowest basalt flows here intertongue with the Tesuque formation, may be of late Pliocene age. The youngest flows are probably Pleistocene. At exposures to the north, and in the subsurface of the Pajarito Plateau the basalt flows intertongue with the Pliocene(?) Puye gravel of H. T. U. Smith (1938). This gravel consists largely of fragments of the "Chicoma" formation, and seems to intertongue with "Chicoma" flows in the subsurface. The youngest basalts overlap the Puye and may be of Pleistocene age. The basalts are probably equivalent, or at least partly equivalent, to the extensive basalts of the Taos Plateau to the north, and may be equivalent to the Hinsdale basalts of the San Juan Mountains and northern Rio Grande trough.

Retrace route to N. M. 4.

        2.25

107.9   **TURN RIGHT onto N. M. 4 and proceed north.** Road is on basalt.

        0.5

108.4   At 12:00 are cliffs held up by the upper member of the Bandelier tuff.

        1.15

109.55   Cattle guard. Road crosses "Santa Clara pumice bed" and middle member of the Bandelier.

        0.1

109.65   Enter Santa Fe County, leave Los Alamos County. Orange and brown beds of the basal part of the upper member of the Bandelier are exposed west of the road.

        0.2

109.85   Cross arroyo. At 3:00 the area of pavement and telephone poles marks the site of White Rock, formerly a contractor's town. The site is on basalt from the Cerros del Rio centers.

        0.4

110.25   In the road cut are exposures of gray pumiceous tuff of the middle member of the Bandelier overlain by the upper member. Individual units within the upper member thicken gradually westward, and several erosional unconformities occur between units of tuff-breccia and crystal-fragment tuff.

        1.95

112.2   Entering Otowi section of Bandelier National Monument. Cross cattle guard. Note cliff dwellings at 2:00-3:00. Otowi ruin, several miles to the north, may have been the home of the ancestors of the present San Ildefonso people.

        0.25

112.45   **Road junction. CONTINUE STRAIGHT AHEAD on N. M. 4.** Road to left leads up Sandia Canyon to Los Alamos. Sankewi'i ruins on the mesa at 1:00. Note cliff dwellings near the base of the upper member of the Bandelier on the high mesas left of the road. Light gray pumiceous tuff and tuff-breccia of the middle member of the Bandelier form the talus-strewn slope.

        1.4

113.85   **Stop sign. BEAR RIGHT on N. M. 4** down Los Alamos Canyon. Road to left is main highway to Los Alamos. Slope at 11:00 is cut on light tan to pinkish white pumiceous tuff and tuff-breccia of the middle member of the Bandelier. The sharp unconformable contact between the middle and upper members is at the top of the silt beds at the base of the steep cliff. The contact of the middle member and the underlying basal Santa Clara pumice bed of the Bandelier is near the level of the telephone lines. Here the gravel-size pumice fragments of the Santa Clara bed rest on the Puye gravel. North of here especially on Santa Clara Mesa the Santa Clara pumice is much mined for light-weight aggregate and the manufacture of pumice blocks. On Santa Clara Mesa the overlying members of the Bandelier have been stripped and extensive blankets several tens of feet thick of the Santa Clara pumice member cap mesas held up by the underlying resistant Puye gravel of the Santa Fe group.

MEASURED SECTION OF BANDELIER RHYOLITE TUFF.
(Point 113.85)

No.	Description	Thickness (feet)
	(Top eroded)	
	Upper Member:	
9.	Massive, pink, pumiceous rhyolite tuff with lithic and crystal fragments (upper pink cliff)	35
8.	Massive, gray, lithic rhyolite tuff with some pumice fragments and coarser fragments than in the underlying bed (middle cliff)	75
7.	Massive, pinkish, sandy, pumiceous rhyolite tuff, pocked with many weathering holes in lower part (lower cliff)	108

Middle Member:

No.	Description	Thickness
6.	Coarse, even-bedded, light gray, angular rhyolite pumice breccia	1
5.	Pinkish, sandy, pumiceous rhyolite tuff	4
4.	Like no. 6	1
3.	White, slope-forming, pumiceous rhyolite tuff-breccia, much fine pumice powder (pumicite)	140
2.	Stratified (water-laid) rhyolite pumice tuff; sandy in lower part, coarser in upper part	5
1.	**Santa Clara pumice bed** (Qbs): Unstratified, light gray to white breccia and sand-size fragments	35
	Total	404

(Basalt flow)

0.15
114.0 Road cut in pumice gravel of the Santa Clara bed. Outcrops in the canyon to the right are basalt flows from the Cerros del Rio centers.

0.45
114.45 At 12:00 in the road cut the Santa Clara pumice rests on basalt.

0.15
114.6 In outcrops to the left note greenish clays mixed with basalt. Pillow lavas with tachylite selvages in clay are exposed in road cuts ahead. The clay beds probably are lacustrine deposits in a valley or canyon dammed by basalt farther south. The basalt in these roads cuts flowed northward into the lake to a point about ¼ mile north of the highway.

0.3
114.9 At 9:00 are thin-bedded gravel, sand, silt, and clay with interbedded chilled subaqueous basalt flow-breccia. At 2:00 across the road bend are brown clays overlain by rusty gravel and sand and green clays, all surmounted by tilted landslide blocks of Bandelier tuff.

MEASURED SECTION OF CULEBRA LAKE CLAY (KELLEY, 1952)
(Point 115.25)

No.	Description	Thickness (feet)
5.	Greenish gray, plastic clay	27
4.	Rusty buff conglomeratic sandstone	11
3.	Conglomerate of well-rounded pebbles and cobbles	7
2.	Light buff, fine-grained, evenly stratified sandstone with thin clay partings	40
1.	Light gray, laminated, plastic clay	20
	Total	105

0.1
115.0 At 9:00 note the erratic basalt mass partially enclosed in sand and gravel. This mass may be the contorted end of a flow pushed into soft sediments, and later slumped into its present position. Note the reverse fault in gravel and clay at 12:00 in road cut.

0.25
115.25 At the left is brown clay resting on volcanic boulder beds of the Puye gravel. The Puye consists mainly of "Chicoma" detritus and is partly of laharic (mudflow) origin. In the subsurface to the west the Puye is more than 700 feet thick and contains latitic to rhyolite tuff more than 300 feet thick.

0.45
115.7 Totavi quarry at left is in stream-channel gravel of the lowest part of the Puye. The gravel is mostly Precambrian granite and metamorphic detritus, and is interpreted by some workers as being the deposit of the Pliocene or early Pleistocene Rio Grande.

0.1
115.8 To the north and south, brown and tan silt and sand of the Tesuque formation rest beneath the Puye. The total thickness of the Tesuque here is not known. A well west of here penetrated more than 3,000 feet of Tesuque sediments without reaching the base of the formation.

0.4
116.2 Pink and tan sand and silt of the upper part of the Tesuque in the slopes north and south.

1.0
117.2 Road crosses spillway at the mouth of Guaje Canyon.

0.5
117.7 **Road junction. CONTINUE STRAIGHT AHEAD on N.M. 4.** Road to left leads to Espanola. Road is on upper beds of the Tesuque formation.

0.7
118.4 At 2:00 on the skyline is a Quaternary basalt cone younger than the flow capping "Mesita Mesa". Note the basalt-filled canyon in Tesuque sediments north of the cone.

0.4
118.8 Western end of Otowi Bridge across the Rio Grande. This has been the starting point for boating expeditions down White Rock Canyon. Several people have been drowned riding the rapids in the spring runoff.

	1.5	
120.3		**Side road left to San Ildefonso Indian Pueblo. CONTINUE AHEAD on N. M. 4.** Sign reads: "Ancestors of the San Ildefonso Indians once lived in the cliffs rising west of here but had moved to the present site by the time the first Spanish colonists arrived. The modern pueblo is noted for its black and red pottery. It is the home of Maria Martinez, perhaps the best-known of Pueblo Indian potters."

To the west from 7:30 to 10:00 is the Puye escarpment at the eastern edge of the Pajarito Plateau. The highest mesas along the escarpment are capped by Bandelier resting on Puye gravel. Note white pumice strip-pits on Santa Clara Mesa. Santa Clara Mesa is surfaced by the Santa Clara pumice bed of the Bandelier.

0.9

121.1   San Ildefonso Butte at 8:30 is basalt-capped and contains its own feeder. Basalt rests on the Tesuque formation of the Santa Fe group. Indian legend says that a monster dwells in caves and tunnels in this butte.

2.3

123.5   At 9:00 are westward-tilted sand and silt beds of the Tesuque formation. The structurally deepest part of the Rio Grande trough in this latitude lies to the west, possibly in the vicinity of Los Alamos. The depositional axis in late Pliocene and early Pleistocene was probably near the eastern edge of the Pajarito Plateau where the main part of the Puye (derived from the pre-Bandelier "Chicoma" volcanics to the west) interfingers with the Cerros del Rio basalts, and with sediments derived from the east and north. Some northward-tilting of the Cerros del Rio basalts may have occurred as recently as Pleistocene time. The Bandelier may also have been tilted eastward slightly.

2.2

125.7   Western end of bridge across Tesuque Creek. **Divided highway, keep right.**

0.7

126.4   **Road junction. BEAR RIGHT and merge with southbound lane of U. S. 64-84-285 toward Santa Fe.** Settlement to the left is Pojoaque.

0.8

127.2   Pumice mill at left processes pumice from the Santa Clara bed of the Bandelier of the Pajarito Plateau.

0.7

127.9   Note the northwestward dip of the Tesuque formation. Farther east the Tesuque formation dips steeply westward at the edge of the Sangre de Cristo Mountains where it is in fault contact with uplifted Precambrian rocks at most places.

The Sangre de Cristos are carved from a long, narrow, northward-trending Laramide uplift which extends about 115 miles in New Mexico, and 120 miles in Colorado. At most places the western, structurally highest part of the uplift consists of Precambrian rocks uplifted and thrust eastward along high- to low-angle thrust faults. The central part of the range is mainly Pennsylvanian sedimentary rocks. At the western margin of the range are numerous high-angle normal faults along which the Rio Grande trough subsided in Miocene, Pliocene, and Pleistocene time. At places along the edge of the uplift the Santa Fe group rests on volcanic rocks of the Picuris tuff and Espinaso formation which may be correlated and of Oligocene or Miocene age. The Picuris rests on red beds which may correlate with the Galisteo formation of Eocene age.

2.2

130.1   At 9:00 are white to light gray tuff and tuffaceous sand beds in the Tesuque formation of the Santa Fe group.

1.4

131.5   At the right is Camel Rock, a well-known landmark carved from the Tesuque formation. Tesuque Creek is marked by scattered cottonwoods to the west.

1.4

132.9   Tesuque Pueblo on the right. **Continue ahead toward Santa Fe.** At 3:30-5:30 is a general view of the Jemez Mountains and Pajarito Plateau.

2.3

135.2   Bridge across Tesuque Creek.

0.8

136.0   At 8:00-9:00 note the northward tilt of the Tesuque formation into the Espanola basin of the Rio Grande trough. At 7:00 is a westward-sloping pediment cut on the Tesuque. High pediments cut on the Tesuque can be seen also to the south and west.

3.55

139.55   Divide between Tesuque Creek and Santa Fe Creek drainage. Historic marker at right reads "Santa Fe. Founded 1610, elevation 7,000. Oldest capital city in America. Established as seat of Spanish colonial government for area extending from Mississippi River to Pacific Ocean. The palace where Spanish governors ruled for 212 years still stands in the historic old plaza and now serves as a state museum.

"The Spaniards were driven out of Santa Fe in the Pueblo Indian uprising of 1680. Don Diego de Vargas took the city in a bloodless reconquest in 1692, an event celebrated annually by the Santa Fe Fiesta. In the 19th century traders brought caravans into the plaza here after their arduous journey over the Santa Fe Trail."

0.45

140.0   At 12:00 on the skyline are the Ortiz Mountains. At 12:30, below the skyline Cerrillos Hills (the little hills); at 12:30 on the skyline the Sandia Mountains.

	1.2
141.2	To the left note the southward dip of the Tesuque formation.
	0.6
141.8	Entering Santa Fe. Capitol building at 12:30; U. S. National (military) Cemetery at 8:00.
	0.6
142.4	**Stop light. CONTINUE STRAIGHT AHEAD.**
	0.1
142.5	**Stop light. TURN LEFT and proceed ½ block; then TURN RIGHT onto U. S. 85 and cross bridge over Santa Fe Creek. Proceed south.**
	0.2
142.7	**Stop light. CONTINUE STRAIGHT AHEAD.**
	0.15
142.85	**Merging traffic. BEAR RIGHT and continue south on U. S. 85 toward Albuquerque.**
	0.75
143.6	On the right is New Mexico School for the Blind. Farther southwest is the U. S. Indian School. **Continue southwest** through the southwestern part of Santa Fe.
	2.7
146.3	At 1:00-2:30 are the Cerros del Rio. At 2:30-3:00 on the horizon are the Jemez Mountains; Redondo Peak in the caldera is at about 2:30. The road is on the Airport pediment surface cut on the Tesuque formation. This surface probably correlates with the Ortiz surface in the distance beyond Cerrillos Hills.
	1.7
148.0	Road to airport at right. **BEAR LEFT and continue on U. S. 85.**
	0.8
148.8	Ortiz Mountains at 11:45; Cerrillos Hills at 12:00-12:30.
	0.8
149.6	Southwestern end of the Sangre de Cristo Mountains at 9:00.
	2.1
151.7	Road to village of Cerrillos on left.
	3.3
155.0	Conical hill at 11:00 is Calvary Butte formed of limburgite; bouldery hills left of the butte are monzonite porphyry outliers of the porphyry centers of Cerrillos Hills.
	0.9
155.9	Grassy valleys with cottonwoods crossing the road in this vicinity are due to the spill of perched ground water from beds of the Santa Fe group. The water is perched on Mancos shale at shallow depth and discharges into arroyos and stream valleys which have been eroded to the water table.
	0.8
156.7	**Side road right to La Cienega. CONTINUE AHEAD on U. S. 85.**
	0.8
157.5	At 2:45 is La Tetilla Peak.
	1.3
158.8	At 9:00-9:30 is one of the monzonite porphyry stocks of Cerrillos Hills. These stocks may have been feeders for the volcanics of the Espinaso formation, and thus of possible Oligocene or Miocene age.
	0.3
159.1	Edge of basalt flow at 12:00-2:30. Central vent for this flow was the cone right of the highway.
	1.6
160.7	Basalt cone at 3:00-4:00; Ortiz Mountains porphyry centers at 9:00. The extensive gently sloping erosional surface west of the Ortiz Mountains is Kirk Bryan's Ortiz surface and Ogilvie's (1905) conoplain. It appears that the surface on which the basalts were erupted (in the vicinity of U. S. 85) was continuous with the Ortiz surface prior to the cutting of the valley of Rio Galisteo which lies several miles south of the highway.
	1.4
162.1	Descending La Bajada; note the thin pediment gravel below basalt and resting on Mancos shale. Note landslide block of basalt at 2:00.
	1.1
163.2	Sandstone in lower Mancos in road cut to left.
	0.1
163.3	Bright red beds in valley on right are Eocene Galisteo formation; drab rounded hills beyond them are Oligocene or Miocene Espinaso volcanic breccias.
	0.05
163.35	Galisteo and Espinaso in road cut at right are faulted down against Mancos shale.
	0.15
163.5	Road cuts are in Galisteo formation.
	0.4
163.9	At 9:00 is Dakota sandstone. The Dakota is thin in this region, and locally rests on sandstone of the upper Morrison.

	1.0
164.9	Buff and reddish alluvium probably is Pleistocene outwash from the Galisteo on La Bajada fault scarp. Alluvium covers down-faulted Ortiz or La Bajada surface.
	0.2
165.1	At 9:00 is buff Entrada sandstone overlain by Todilto limestone and gypsum, and in flank of hill at 8:30 lavender Morrison mudstones are capped by Morrison sandstone.
	0.1
165.2	**Side road right to Cochiti.** Side road to Kaiser Gypsum Co.'s Rosario plant. **CONTINUE AHEAD on U. S. 85.**
	0.15
165.35	Overpass, Santa Fe railroad.
	0.35
165.7	Bridge across Rio Galisteo. Rosario gypsum quarry at 9:15. Gypsum is the Todilto.
	2.5
168.2	Road is on a pediment surface slightly lower than the Ortiz surface to the southeast. This pediment surface probably is slightly younger than the surface beneath the basalt east of La Bajada fault scarp (seen at 3:30-5:30). The pediment probably was dropped several hundred feet along the west side of the La Bajada fault.
	1.6
169.8	**Junction with N. M. 22 at the right. CONTINUE STRAIGHT AHEAD on U. S. 85.** Santo Domingo Indian Pueblo 4 miles to north. Sign reads: "Santo Domingo is the largest of the Rio Grande Keres Pueblos and one of the least changed Indian villages in New Mexico. The Santo Domingans harvest abundant crops each year, and are noted for the excellence of their pottery making."
	2.1
171.9	At 9:30 is Espinaso Ridge, the type area of the Espinaso volcanic breccia. The Galisteo formation lies under the Espinaso south of the ridge. North of the ridge are tilted lower beds of the Santa Fe group that are nearly conformable with the Espinaso.
	0.8
172.7	At 9:00 note hogbacks of Eocene Galisteo sandstone southwest of Espinaso Ridge.
	0.2
172.9	At right is monument erected by Church of the Latter Day Saints to the Mormon Battalion of General Kearny's Army which passed through here in 1847 during the Mexican War.
	0.8
173.7	At 11:30 the cut in the long ridge marks the route of the old Santa Fe-Albuquerque road.
	1.0
174.7	Bridge.
	0.3
175.0	Outcrops of Santa Fe group in road cut. At 2:30 is the San Felipe volcano. At 9:00 is the Hagan basin.
	1.4
176.4	Bridge over Tonque Arroyo.
	0.2
176.6	Side road right leads to San Felipe Pueblo. Side road right leads up Tonque Arroyo (see First Day's log). CONTINUE STRAIGHT AHEAD to Albuquerque.

End of Third Day's log. For points of interest between here and Albuquerque see First Day's log (mileage 80.5 to 101.2).

———O———

PHYSIOGRAPHY, CLIMATE, AND VEGETATION OF THE ALBUQUERQUE REGION

ROGER Y. ANDERSON
University of New Mexico

INTRODUCTION

Varied physiographic features, a 6,800-foot difference in elevation, several sources of atmospheric moisture and directions of air mass movement combine to make the climate, vegetation, and topography of the Albuquerque region interesting and complex. One can observe, first-hand, the intimate relationship between physiography, precipitation, temperature, and vegetation and use the region as a model for geomorphic and geologic interpretation.

PHYSIOGRAPHIC AREAS IN THE ALBUQUERQUE REGION

A photographic copy of the Army Map Service plastic relief maps of the Albuquerque region gives an excellent over-all view of the major physiographic features (Fig. 2). For convenience, the region is divided into a number of structural-physiographic units (Fig. 1, modified from Kelley, 1952) and specific points of interest are designated by numbers (i.e., 23). In the area covered by the photographs, elevations range from 11,389 feet at Mount Taylor Peak (39), 11,252 feet at Redondo Peak (3) in the Valles caldera, 10,685 feet at Sandia crest (17), and 10,120 feet at Manzano Peak (23) to about 4,800 feet at Belen in the southern part of the Belen-Albuquerque-Santo Domingo Basin. Elevations rise to about 6,000 feet at the northern end of this basin (8, 11, 14) and elevations of about 7,000-9,000 feet are found on some of the higher mesas and cuestas of the Colorado Plateau and San Juan Basin areas (1, 42).

CLIMATE

Temperature and precipitation in the Albuquerque region are determined largely by local topography and air mass movements from regions outside the State. The mean annual temperature ranges from 57°F at the Albuquerque Airport to 38°F at Sandia crest (17); the difference in elevation is 5,365 feet. This gradient of about 1°F for each 200-300-foot rise in elevation is the principal controlling factor in the distribution of precipitation and vegetation, and, indirectly, in the physical appearance of the landforms. The mountain tops would be even colder were it not for the increase of wind velocity with elevation which tends to displace the normally cold air with warmer air. The gradient is moderated somewhat in the deeper parts of the basins as the heavier cool air drains and settles at night after daytime convection stops. Low temperatures in the Rio Grande valley are normally 8-10 degrees cooler than for the pediments and mesas, a few hundred feet higher in elevation. The climate is decidedly continental with diurnal changes of 40°F. being common.

Air masses invade the Albuquerque region from five principal source areas as follows (Thornthwaite and others, 1942; Dorroh, 1946):

(1) Cold, dry Polar Continental from Canada and northward
(2) Cool, moist Polar Pacific from the north Pacific Ocean
(3) Hot, dry Tropical Continental from Mexico and extreme southwest United States
(4) Warm, moist Tropical Gulf from the Gulf of Mexico and the Caribbean
(5) Warm, moist Tropical Pacific from the southern Pacific Ocean.

So many directions of air movement make weather prediction in Albuquerque extremely difficult. Most of our winter and spring moisture comes from the north Pacific (type 2) although the source is so remote and so many mountain barriers intervene that only a little more than 20 percent of the annual total is from this source. These air movements (storms) result in high-level moisture that forms snow on the mountains, a little rain or snow at intermediate elevations, and blowing dust at the lower elevations, particularly in the spring. About 65-70 percent of the annual total precipitation comes in the warm season (April-September) from the Gulf of Mexico (type 4) in the form of wandering convectional thunderstorms and orographic thunderstorm buildups over the mountains. Both the North Pacific and the summer orographic storms release most of their moisture in the mountains so that there is a direct increase in precipitation with elevation, and a precipitation map (Fig. 3) of the region is very nearly a topographic map as well.

Movements of moist air from the Tropical Pacific (type 5) add little to the annual rainfall although on rare occasions some of our longest and heaviest rains have come from that source. Interpretations of Pleistocene climate and terrace formation are made difficult because of the unknown influence of this moisture source. Tropical Continental (type 3) air usually results in warm dry weather while in the winter months Polar Continental (type 1) air sweeps down the east side of the State, resulting in extended cold periods and some snow if warm moist air is displaced. Tijeras Canyon presents the Albuquerque area with a local problem as the heavy, cold air, held back by the Sandia-Manzano Mountains, finds access to the basin and literally pours through the canyon and spreads out on the "mesa" and valley below in gusts up to 50 miles per hour.

VEGETATION

Early naturalists in the Southwest soon recognized the remarkable correlation between vegetation and elevation and realized that under the influence of temperature and moisture availability the vertical changes corresponded, in an approximate way, with latitudinal changes. Each 1,000-foot increase in elevation is about equivalent to a 200-mile northward shift of latitude so that the type of plants found in Canada, such as spruce and fir, occur above 8,000 feet on mountains while plants typical of Mexico, such as mesquite and creosote bush, have extended their range up the Rio Grande valley as far north as the Rio Salado. This resulted in the formulation of the concept of **life zones** by Merriam (1890) and the naming of zones such as the Hudsonian, Canadian, and Sonoran based on the vertical distribution of plant and animal life but using geographic terms to impart the idea of a relationship to latitude. Later, ecologists found it necessary to refine the concept of life zones and classify character-

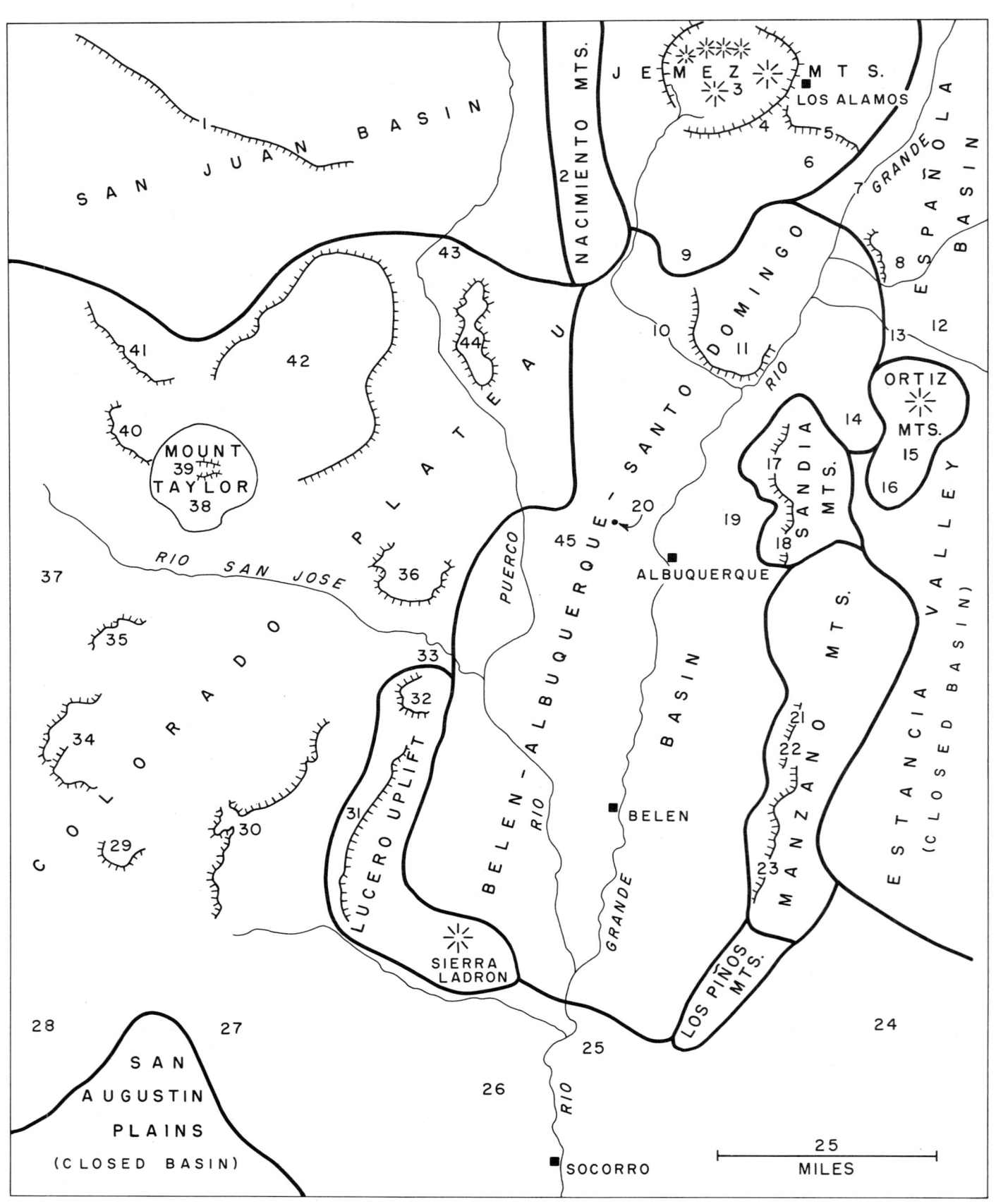

Figure 1. Structural-physiographic areas and physiographic features in the Albuquerque region, New Mexico (modified from Kelley, 1952).

PHYSIOGRAPHIC FEATURES IN THE ALBUQUERQUE REGION

1. Chacra Mesa (elev. circa 7,000 feet)
2. Pajarito Peak in Nacimiento Mts. (elev. circa 9,000 feet)
3. Redondo Peak in Valles caldera (elev. 11,252 feet)
4. Sierra de Los Valles (elev. circa 10,000 feet)
5. Pajarito Plateau or Jemez shield, cut here by Frijoles Canyon—1,000 feet deep
6. San Miguel Mts. (elev. circa 8,000 feet)
7. White Rock Canyon, about 1,000 feet deep below rim at circa 6,500 feet
8. La Bajada Mesa (elev. circa 6,200 feet)
9. Borrego Mesa (elev. circa 7,500 feet)
10. Jemez River, breaching the Valles caldera and flowing southward through Canon de San Diego, 1,800 feet deep
11. Santa Ana Mesa—basalt capped (elev. circa 6,000 feet)
12. Los Cerrillos—mainly stock-like intrusions (elev. circa 7,000 feet)
13. Galisteo Creek
14. Hagan structural embayment (elev. circa 6,000 feet)
15. San Pedro Mts. (elev. 8,240 feet)
16. South Mtn. (elev. 7,985 feet)
17. Sandia crest (elev. 10,685 feet)
18. South Sandia Mtn. (elev. 9,765 feet)
19. Sandia (East) Mesa, opposite Bear Canyon (elev. circa 6,000 feet)
20. Albuquerque volcanoes, mainly on Segundo Alto terrace (elev. of volcanoes, 6,033 feet; elev. of terrace circa 5,600-5,800 feet)
21. Mosca Peak (elev. 9,490 feet)
22. Bosque Peak (elev. 9,630 feet)
23. Manzano Peak (elev. 10,120 feet)
24. Chupadera structural platform (elev. circa 6,500 feet)
25. San Acacia structural constriction (elev. of Rio Grande is circa 4,600 feet in this area)
26. Socorro structural uplift
27. Gallinas Mts. (elev. 8,730 feet)
28. Datil Mts. (elev. 9,585 feet)
29. Cachow Mesa (elev. circa 8,300 feet)
30. Mesa del Oro (elev. circa 7,500 feet)
31. Gallina Mesa (elev. 7,840 feet)
32. Lucero Mesa (elev. circa 6,500 feet)
33. Mesa Redonda (elev. 5,420 feet)
34. Cebolleta Mesa (elev. circa 8,500 feet)
35. Putney Mesa (elev. 8,165 feet)
36. Mesa Gigante (elev. circa 6,500 feet)
37. Lava beds (elev. circa 7,000 feet)
38. San Mateo Mts. (elev. circa 9,000 feet)
39. Mount Taylor Peak (elev. 11,389 feet—highest point in Fig. 2)
40. La Jara Mesa (elev. 8,560 feet)
41. San Mateo Mesa (elev. circa 8,100 feet)
42. Mesa Chivato (elev. circa 8,500-9,000 feet)
43. Cabezon Peak—volcanic neck (elev. circa 7,500 feet)
44. Mesa Prieta (elev. circa 7,200 feet)
45. Llano de Albuquerque—Ortiz surface (elev. circa 6,000 feet)

Explanation for Figure 1.

istic plant and animal associations into biotic communities. The elevation tolerances for these **biomes** are as restrictive as those of life zones. Hoff (1959) has suggested elevation ranges for the plant and animal associations in New Mexico and has related them to life zones (Fig. 5).

The Arctic zone or Alpine Tundra association does not occur on Mount Taylor, the Jemez Mountains, or the Sandia-Manzano Range although it does cap the highest peaks in the Sangre de Cristos. The Desert Plains association or Lower Sonoran life zone barely extends into the southern part of the Albuquerque-Belen basin.

The three main types of vegetative cover are grassland, shrub, and forest. Grass is of the short semi-desert type in the lowlands and of the taller mountain grass and meadow type when associated with forest cover at the higher elevations. Shrubs are mainly sagebrush, salt-bush, grease-wood, catclaw, rabbit-brush, and creosote-bush. The pinyon-juniper forest association is the most extensive vegetative cover in the region (5,470,000 acres in the upper Rio Grande basin, as compared to 2,883,000 acres for semi-arid grassland and 2,163,000 acres for ponderosa pine; Dortignac, 1956). Other forest types are ponderosa pine, spruce, fir, and aspen. A map of these vegetative types (Fig. 4) approximates a topographic map and a precipitation map.

The extreme dryness, occasional summer thunderstorm, little runoff, and sparse vegetation of the lowlands are in sharp contrast to the wetness, periodic rainfall and snowfall, high spring runoff, and thick vegetative cover of the uplands. Also, it is now known that moisture and temperature changes were considerable in the Pleistocene. Life zones were lowered several thousand feet, the lowlands were covered with woodland, and the closed basins contained large lakes. In some way, these complex factors are responsible for the typically "arid" aspect of the topography expressed in steep canyons, the break in slope at mountain bases, the steep retreating slopes of the mesas and terraces, and the lingering closed basins.

CHARACTER OF STRUCTURAL-PHYSIOGRAPHIC AREAS IN THE ALBUQUERQUE REGION

Nacimiento Mountains and San Juan Basin

Structurally, these are the oldest features in the region, with the initial folding and faulting beginning near the end of the Cretaceous and continuing intermittently through the Tertiary. Cuestas (1) dip into the basin along the southern margin and outcrops of the Mesozoic formations swing sharply to the north and become hogbacks along the eastern side of the basin adjacent to the Nacimiento uplift. The Nacimiento Mountains are an asymmetrical domal anticline about 50 miles long with a core of gneissic granite flanked by patches of upper Paleozoic sediments except along the steep west side where the granite is exposed.

Bryan and McCann (1936) and Church and Hack (1939) believed that the flat summit of San Pedro Mountain (just north of Fig. 1) in the Nacimientos represented an old erosion surface, possibly of early-middle Tertiary age. Bryan and McCann also believed that they could trace remnants of the younger Ortiz surface into the area and recognized four other surfaces in the upper Rio Puerco drainage (Fig. 5).

Spruce, fir, and aspen are found on San Pedro Mountain and ponderosa pine covers most of the range. Most of the San Juan Basin is covered with the pinyon-juniper association and large patches of sagebrush (**Artemesia tridentata**) are found east of Cuba. Salt-bush and greasewood are found along the Rio Puerco.

Jemez Mountains

The Jemez Mountains consist of a high central caldera (reported to be the largest in the world) flanked by a broad shield of volcanic flows and pyroclastics. Several high peaks such as Redondo Peak (3, elev. 11,252 feet) occupy the crater. The bordering Valles Mountains (4) on the southeast attain elevations of over 10,000 feet and even higher elevations are found on the northern rim, north of Figure 1. Many large streams have dissected the shield or plateau around the caldera forming a radial pattern of steep-walled canyons more than 1,000 feet deep. Jemez River (10), flowing through one of these (Canon de San Diego), has breached the caldera rim on its southwest side.

The history of the volcanic center can be summarized from Ross (1931) as follows:

1. Even-bedded and chaotic flows of andesite, latite, and some basalt and rhyolite, from a center not far removed from the present caldera, accumulated on a mid-Tertiary erosion surface sloping upward to San Pedro Mountain.
2. Profound erosion, and then a series of basalt eruptions from local centers.
3. Erosion, followed by explosive rhyolitic eruptions on a tremendous scale during which the great caldera was blasted out of the older volcanics and extensive tuff beds were deposited on the flanks.
4. Some erosion, followed by more rhyolitic volcanic activity and the building up of secondary cones 2,000-3,000 feet above the floor of the caldera.
5. Erosion, and caldera-filling with alluvial and lacustrine deposits (the lake persisted long enough to allow wave-cut terraces to form on the sides of the peaks). Finally, deep erosion of the flanks and breaching of the rim. Many hot-spring deposits were formed during this last phase.

None of the high peaks in the Jemez Mountains reaches timberline but the trees are dwarfed on northeast slopes and a few Hudsonian plants are found. Spruce, fir, and aspen represent the Canadian life zone and the large park-like valleys of the caldera (e.g., Valle Grande) are grass covered. Ponderosa pine and Gambel oak mark the Transition zone with pinyon pine, juniper, and live oak in the Upper Sonoran zone at the lower elevations. In 1913, Bailey stated that elk and mountain sheep had disappeared and few if any grizzlies remained. Black bear, mule deer, mountain lions, bobcats, coyotes, foxes, badgers, porcupines, prairie dogs, squirrels, and chipmunks remain.

Sandia-Manzano and Ortiz Mountains

The Sandia-Manzano Ranges are easterly tilted fault blocks with a western slope and core of Precambrian granitic and metamorphic rocks and a crest and east flank of Pennsylvanian limestone. Sandia Mesa (19) and the east mesa of the Manzanos are treeless pediment slopes merging with the alluvium of the basin at some unknown distance from the break in slope at the base of the mountains. The dip slope, if projected to the probable area of greatest faulting 2-5 miles from the crest would suggest a hypothetical elevation for the Precambrian surface

Figure 2. Physiography of the Albuquerque region, New Mexico.

of about 11,000 feet (Kelley, 1959). Kelley also believes that as much as 15,000 feet of Tertiary deposits may occupy the deeper parts of the Albuquerque-Belen basin. This would mean a total vertical displacement in excess of 20,000 feet. If the thickness of the Paleozoic and Mesozoic section is added (probably present prior to faulting), a displacement of more than five miles is likely. Fossils from the associated deposits in the basin indicate that most of the tilting and faulting took place in late Miocene and Pliocene time, perhaps coincident with the early volcanic activity at Mount Taylor and in the Jemez Mountains.

The Ortiz Mountains, San Pedro Mountains (15), South Mountain (16), and Los Cerrillos (12) are a complex cluster of sills and stock-like and laccolithic intrusions of monzonite and latite-andesite into volcanics and early Tertiary sediments. Intrusive activity pre-dates the faulting and tilting of the Sandia-Manzano Mountains (late Eocene, Stearns, 1953; McRae, 1958). Equivalents of the pediment surface (Ortiz surface) surrounding the Ortiz Mountains (Ogilvie's conoplain) have been traced over the entire region and beyond.

The Sandia and Manzano Mountains have narrow crests of the Canadian life zone extending down to about 8,000 feet on the colder slopes. Elements of this forest include white fir, blue spruce, Douglas fir, limber pine, and Rocky Mountain maple, with ash, alders, and willows along the streams (Bailey, 1913). The Canadian patches are surrounded by a continuous Transition zone (7,000-8,000 feet on cold slopes and 8,000-9,000 feet on warm slopes) of ponderosa pine forest and scattered oaks. The

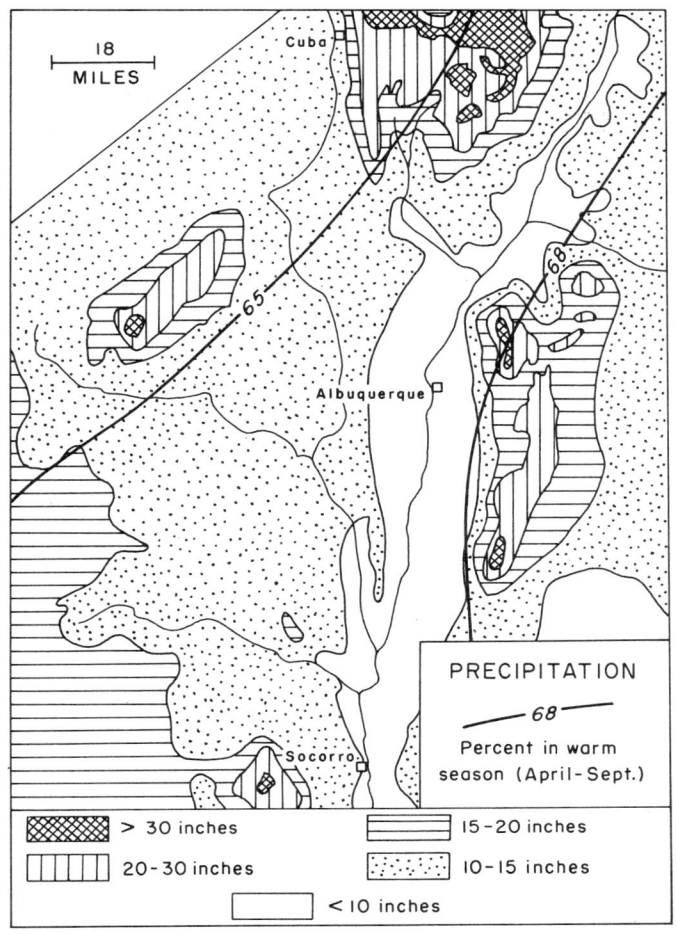

Figure 3. Mean annual precipitation in the Albuquerque region, New Mexico (from Dortignac, 1956).

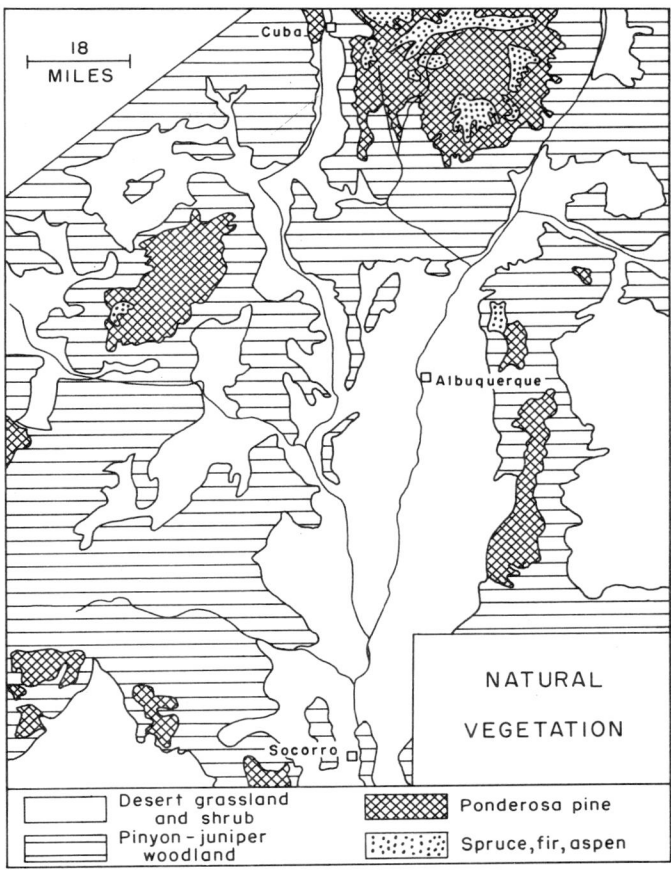

Figure 4. Vegetation in the Albuquerque region, New Mexico (after Dortignac, 1956).

Upper Sonoran zone occupies the foothills and surrounding higher valleys. A few ponderosa pine are found on top of the Ortiz Mountains. Mule deer and black bear are found in the mountains and mountain sheep have been doing well since their re-introduction (one estimate places the present total near 600 in the Sandia Mountains).

Mount Taylor and the Colorado Plateau

The group of mountains around Mount Taylor include the high lava plateaus of Mesa Chivato (42), La Jara Mesa (40), several smaller mesas, and the flanking San Mateo Mountains (38) on the south side of the peak. The main cone is the oldest volcanic feature in the area and consists of rhyolitic tuff, flows of porphyritic latite and trachyte, and porphyritic andesite, in that approximate order of formation (Hunt, 1936). At the peak of the cone is a large amphitheater-like depression surrounded by a high arcuate ridge (Mount Taylor Peak (39), 11,389 feet, is the highest point on this rim) and containing a steep secondary cone about 1,000 feet high. The high mesa country surrounding the cone and to the northeast is held up by later flows of basalt and andesite. The largest mesa (Mesa Chivato, 42) covers about 400 square miles and is about 2,000 feet above the general drainage level. The lava on Mesa Prieta (44), the large outlier to the northeast, was once part of the same series of flows. Several volcanic necks such as Cabezon Peak (43) occupy the valley between the mesas and apparently were the feeders for the flows on the mesas. The eruptions that formed Mount Taylor proper probably began in the Miocene with continuing subsidiary activity (Hunt, 1938). Some of the younger flows on the mesas overlie correlatives of the Ortiz surface which may be as young as early mid-Pleistocene (discussed later).

Structurally, the Colorado Plateau adjacent to the Albuquerque-Belen basin is divided into the Lucero uplift on the south and the Rio Puerco fault zone on the north marking the transition from the Rio Grande trough to the plateau. The Acoma structural embayment lies west of these two units and Mount Taylor is in the northwest corner along the axis of the largest structural feature, the McCartys syncline. This entire area contains remnants of an old erosion surface (probably Ortiz) that was once graded to the Albuquerque-Belen basin. The surface is preserved under the lava caps on the mesas around Mount Taylor, smaller outlying mesas, and on the higher parts of the Lucero uplift (Fitzsimmons, 1959). Present river level is 1,000 to 1,500 feet below the old surface but successively lower and younger surfaces are poorly preserved if present. Some of the isolated lava-capped mesas may have preserved younger stages in the stripping of the area but this would be difficult to demonstrate. Younger surfaces seem to persist mainly along the main drainage of the Rio Grande and Rio Puerco and up Jemez River as far as San Ysidro. Several basalt flows (37) in the Rio San Jose drainage are found at the present river level (McCartys flow near Grants) or just a few feet above the present

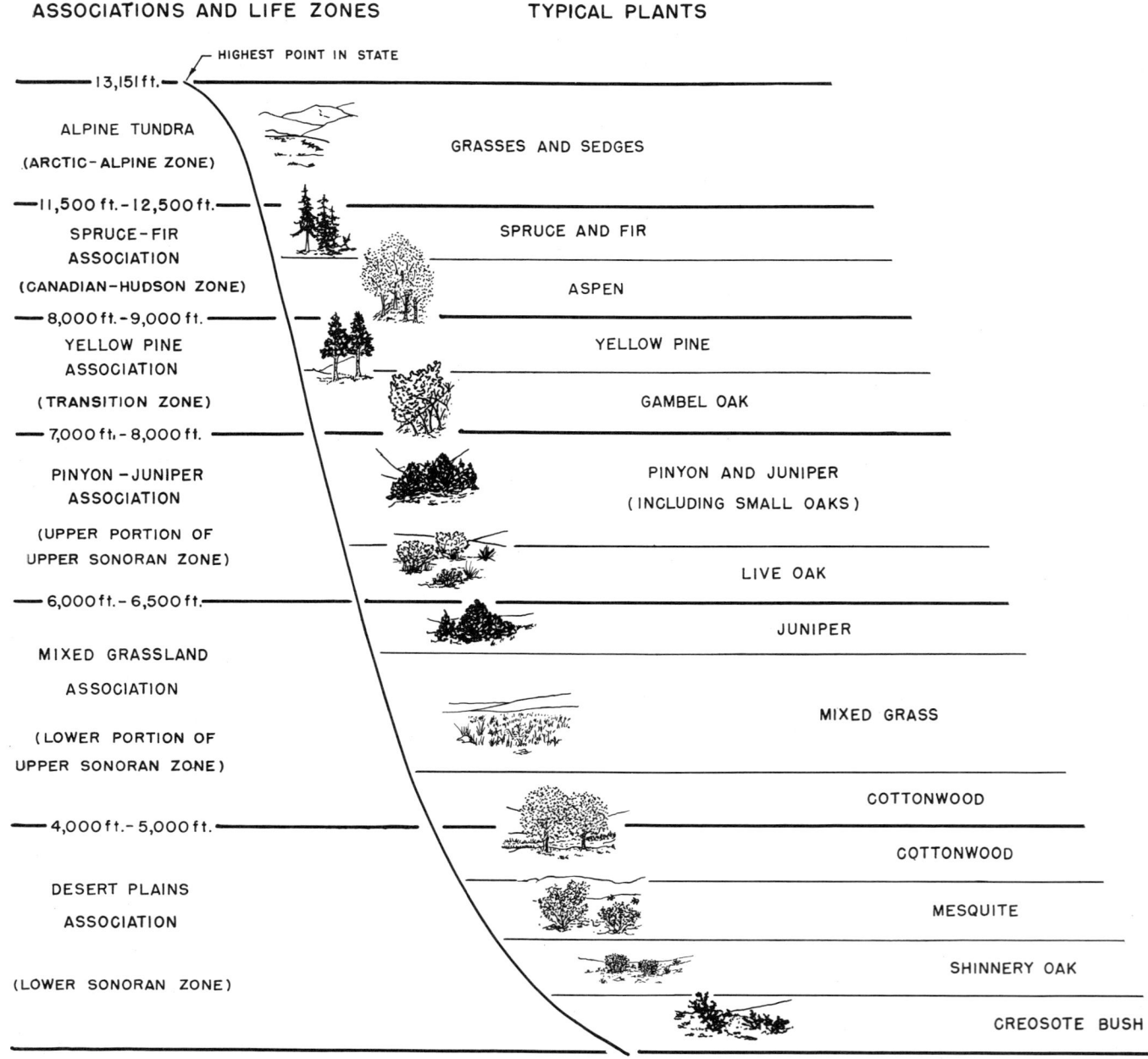

Figure 5. The altitudinal distribution of community types (designated as "associations" and the conspicuous plants at various elevations. The chart pertains chiefly to the central and north-central parts of New Mexico. (Drawing by Bettie Brockman. Reprinted from **The ecology and distribution of the pseudoscorpions of north-central New Mexico** [Univ. New Mexico Pub. in Biology No. 8], by C. Clayton Hoff, Albuquerque, 1959, by permission of the University of New Mexico Press.)

level where recent arroyo cutting has taken place.

The upper part of the crater of Mount Taylor is forested with spruce, fir, and aspen and the lower inner part with mountain grassland. The Canadian zone, however, lacks many of the typical members of the spruce-fir association (Bailey, 1913), perhaps because of the small size of the high mountain mass. The outer slopes and high mesa tops of the plateaus have scattered stands of ponderosa pine and Gambel oak. Semi-desert grassland and shrub consisting mainly of salt-bush and grease-wood occupy most of the river bottoms of the Rio Puerco and Rio San Jose and virtually all the mesas are covered with juniper and pinyon-juniper woodland.

The Canadian zone on Mount Taylor has black bear, mule deer, porcupines, meadow mice, and shrews. The outer slopes and mesa tops have gray squirrels, chipmunks, Colorado wood rats, pocket gophers, Rocky Mountain cottontails, and raccoons.

Belen-Albuquerque-Santo Domingo Basin

This basin is one of the largest in a series of north-trending basins in the Rio Grande trough. It is widest in the vicinity of Albuquerque and constricted to the south by the San Acacia channel and to the north by a structural narrowing formed by the continuation of the Cerrillos (12) trend (La Bajada constriction, Kelley, 1952). Coincident with the large-scale faulting, deepening of the basin, and tilting of the adjacent mountain blocks in late Miocene time, detritus from the highlands was washed into the basin and now comprises a complex sequence of gravel, sand, silt, clay, and caliche deposits collectively known as the Santa Fe formation. At first, deposition must have been in a series of isolated closed basins but by mid-Pleistocene time the Rio Grande had established itself and begun the stripping that is now so evident. Nothing is known of the sediments under the deeper parts of the basin; presumably they are Cretaceous and older although some early Tertiary deposits may also be present. Where the basin narrows and shallows in the Santo Domingo area, the early Tertiary Galisteo formation and Espinaso volcanics are exposed.

The basinal deposits are very complex although a three-fold classification has been made by Bryan and McCann (1937) and clarified by Baldwin (1956). The lower gray member includes the Abiquiu tuff to the north and the Abiquiu (?) formation overlying the Espinaso volcanics and the Galisteo formation in the Santo Domingo basin. The middle red member constitutes the main body of the Santa Fe formation and is a thick sequence of fanglomerates representing the main subsidence. Faunal evidence for the age of the formation has come from this member which is considered to be in the Miocene-Pliocene transition zone (Baldwin, 1956). Confusion enters at this point. In places there is an unconformity between the middle red and upper buff members. The upper member contains well-sorted gravels that have been referred to as the Tuerto gravel, Ancha formation, and Puye gravel in different parts of the Santo Domingo basin and northward. Apparently, these few hundred feet of sediments represent axial gravels interfingered with basalt flows and pediment material from the sides of the basin that were deposited after the Rio Grande had begun integrating its drainage.

A persistent geomorphic surface (Ortiz) is found in the Albuquerque region and beyond. The gradient when projected to the Rio Grande near the type area of the Ortiz Mountains reaches the river at about 500 feet above the floodplain. The surface is found on the conoplain around the Ortiz Mountains, under the basalt cap on Santa Ana Mesa? (11), and on the Llano de Albuquerque (45, the divide between the Rio Puerco and Rio Grande). West of the Albuquerque-Belen basin it is preserved under basalt caps in the plateau area. Southward, correlatives of the Ortiz (Jornada-La Mesa surface) can be traced to Chihuahua, Mexico. The western correlative (Zuni surface) can be traced to the Chuska Mountains and into Black Mesa, Arizona (Fitzsimmons, 1959). The truncation of pre-Tertiary units in regions outside the basin and the local truncation of deformed beds in the Santa Fe formation has led to the belief that the Ortiz surface, and correlatives, is an erosion surface (Bryan and McCann, 1938). However, a surface of such wide areal extent at such a high elevation would be easier to conceive if it were a combined erosional-depositional surface graded to playa basins rather than an integrated erosional system (assuming that a longer stable period can be maintained in a closed system). The problem of the type of surface centers around the relationship of the Ortiz to the axial gravels of the ancestral Rio Grande. Baldwin (1956) has already pointed out that the surfaces above and below the gravels were referred to indiscriminately as "Ortiz" by Bryan. A recent statistical study of the surface gravels in the Santo Domingo basin by Blagbrough (1961) has demonstrated that the Ortiz surface is entirely on pediment material whereas the next younger La Bajada surface is cut on both pediment and axial material. The La Bajada surface, then, is younger than the axial gravels and the axial-pediment-gravel relations of the Ortiz surface are still partly undemonstrated.

The recent discovery of fossil mammals under the Jornada-La Mesa surface in southern New Mexico allows a more precise determination for the probable age of the Ortiz surface. Hibbard identified a Kansan mammalian fauna indicating that the surface is no older than early mid-Pleistocene (Ruhe, 1960). Ruhe also concluded that integration did not take place until after the formation of the surface. If this is the case, the Albuquerque-Belen basin remained closed until the mid-Pleistocene and the axial gravels postdate that time.

Terraces below the Ortiz surface have been cut on both the main body of the Santa Fe formation and on the axial gravels and are a prominent feature in the Rio Grande and Rio Puerco drainage. These surfaces have been assigned many local names because correlation is difficult and complicated by basinward tilting and faulting. A compilation (Fig. 6) shows little agreement in terrace levels with the possible exception of the prominent surface about 75 feet above river level. The information in Figure 6 was taken from Bryan (1938), Bryan and McCann (1936, 1938), Cabot (1938), Denny (1941), Wright (1946), and Miller and Wendorf (1958). The elevations are the number of feet of the projected grade above the present floodplain.

The terraces are in various stages of preservation along the sides of the valley owing to local differences in drainage and dissection. For example, in the Albuquerque vicinity, the flat, level Ortiz surface can be seen on the western skyline (45), the Segundo Alto terrace is under the basalt flows associated with the Albuquerque volcanoes (20), and the two lower terraces can also be seen on the west side of the river. On the eastern Sandia Mesa (19), however, there is one long, continuous sloping plain from Bear Canyon, the large re-entrant in the Sandias, to the Rio Grande terrace near the river.

The surfaces represent successive intervals of stabilization in the downcutting and stripping of the Rio Grande and Rio Puerco drainage systems. There is little agreement on the mechanisms of stabilization and causes of downcutting, and apparently either climatic-vegetative changes or tectonic instability or both can be invoked although climatic control has gained more acceptance. Life zones in the region may have been lowered by as much as 4,000 feet during glacial intervals in the Pleistocene (Antevs, 1954), and even if half of that estimate is accepted, pinyon-juniper woodland would have covered most of the Rio Grande valley and ponderosa pine forests would have clothed the higher mesas and terraces. The maximum of the last such lowering in the region took place about 30,000 years ago (Clisby and others, 1957). At the same time, a large lake 150 to 200 feet deep, and requiring a rainfall of 30 inches per year to support its high lake levels, occupied the closed Estancia basin (Harbour, 1958).

If one accepts the revised estimates for the length of the Pleistocene (Kummell, 1961), the time involved in the cutting of the terraces and deepening of the valley is on the order of 200,000 years. Miller and Wendorf

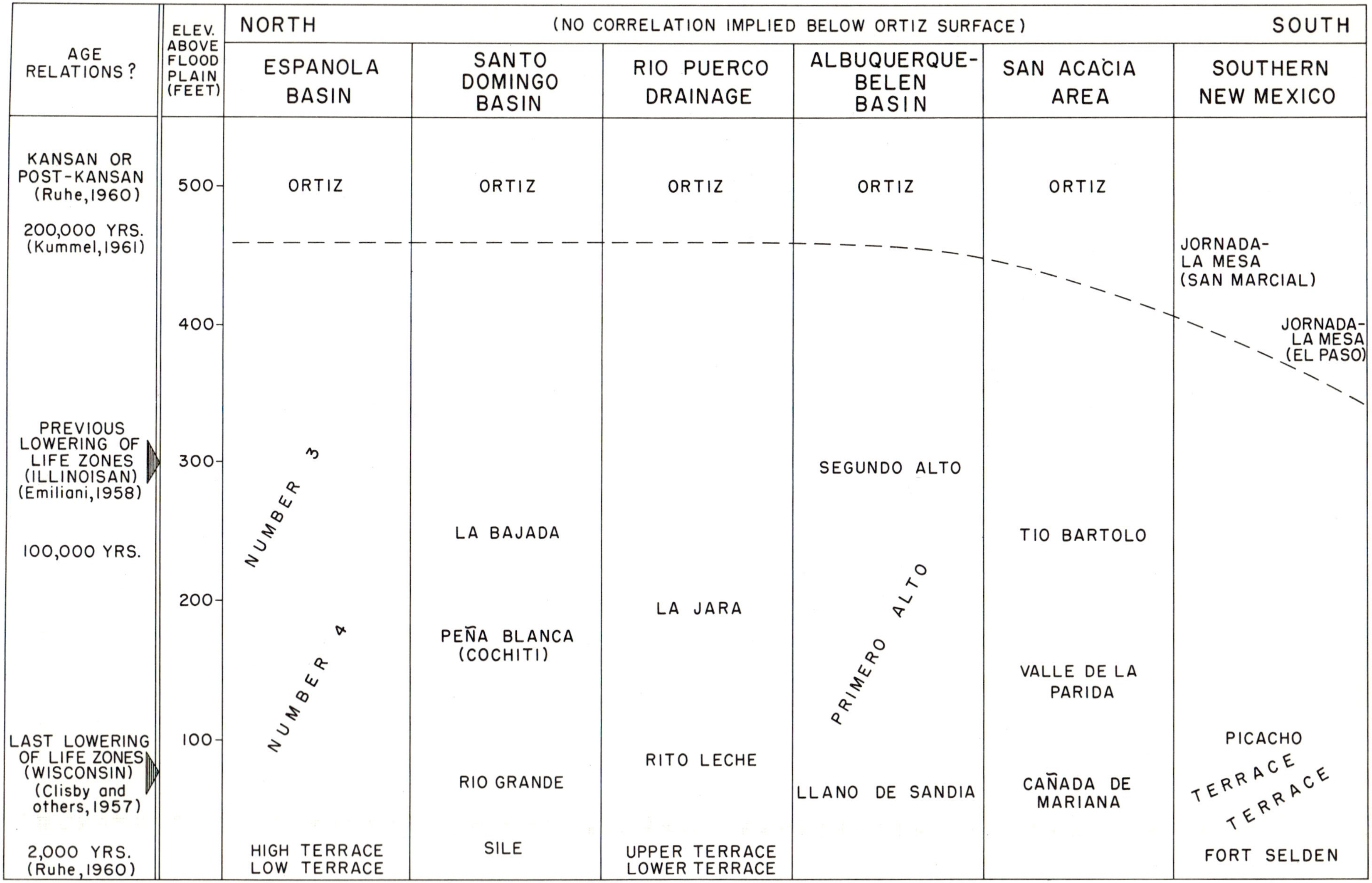

AGE RELATIONS?	ELEV. ABOVE FLOOD PLAIN (FEET)	NORTH				SOUTH	
		ESPANOLA BASIN	SANTO DOMINGO BASIN	RIO PUERCO DRAINAGE	ALBUQUERQUE-BELEN BASIN	SAN ACACIA AREA	SOUTHERN NEW MEXICO
		(NO CORRELATION IMPLIED BELOW ORTIZ SURFACE)					
KANSAN OR POST-KANSAN (Ruhe, 1960)	500	ORTIZ	ORTIZ	ORTIZ	ORTIZ	ORTIZ	JORNADA-LA MESA (SAN MARCIAL)
200,000 YRS. (Kummel, 1961)	400						JORNADA-LA MESA (EL PASO)
PREVIOUS LOWERING OF LIFE ZONES (ILLINOISAN) (Emiliani, 1958)	300	NUMBER 3	LA BAJADA		SEGUNDO ALTO	TIO BARTOLO	
100,000 YRS.	200	NUMBER 4	PEÑA BLANCA (COCHITI)	LA JARA	PRIMERO ALTO	VALLE DE LA PARIDA	PICACHO TERRACE
LAST LOWERING OF LIFE ZONES (WISCONSIN) (Clisby and others, 1957)	100		RIO GRANDE	RITO LECHE	LLANO DE SANDIA	CAÑADA DE MARIANA	TERRACE
2,000 YRS. (Ruhe, 1960)		HIGH TERRACE LOW TERRACE	SILE	UPPER TERRACE LOWER TERRACE			FORT SELDEN

Figure 6. Geomorphic surfaces along the Rio Grande in New Mexico.

(1958) have determined that the upper (18-20 feet above stream level) young terrace in the Espanola basin was formed after A.D. 1200 and the youngest terrace (Fort Selden) in southern New Mexico is less than 2,600 years old (Ruhe, 1960). This means that the precipitation changes and life-zone shifting of two glacials and interglacials is involved in the formation of the complex of terraces between the lowest bench and the Ortiz surface (Fig. 6; the chronology is only suggestive and no correlation in either time or terrace levels in the space between the Ortiz and Fort Selden surfaces is implied).

Present vegetation in the Belen-Albuquerque-Santo Domingo basin consists mainly of desert shrubs (catclaw, salt-bush, white sage, rabbit-brush, mesquite, and creosote-bush), cacti, and short grasses. Several plants from the Old World, such as Russian olive and tamarix, are found along many watercourses in addition to the native Rio Grande cottonwood. One introduced plant, Russian thistle (tumbleweed), has been most successful, particularly in areas disturbed by man. An Indian name characterizes it as the "white man's plant". Common mammals are the kangaroo rat, mice, ground squirrels, prairie dogs, and rabbits.

REFERENCES

Antevs, E. V., 1954, Climate of New Mexico during the last glaciopluvial: Jour. Geology, v. 62, p. 182-191.

Bailey, Vernon, 1913, Life zones and crop zones of New Mexico: U. S. Dept. Agri. Bur. Biol. Survey North Am. Fauna, No. 35, p. 1-100.

Baldwin, Brewster, 1956, The Santa Fe group of north-central New Mexico, in New Mexico Geol. Soc. Guidebook of southeastern Sangre de Cristo Mountains, New Mexico, 7th Field Conf.: p. 115-121.

Blagbrough, J. W., 1961, Statistical study of terrace gravels in the Santo Domingo basin, New Mexico: Univ. New Mexico unpub. rept. Dept. Geology.

Bryan, Kirk, 1938, Geology and ground-water conditions of the Rio Grande depression in Colorado and New Mexico, in Regional planning; Pt. 6, The Rio Grande joint investigation in the upper Rio Grande basin in Colorado, New Mexico, and Texas, 1936-1937: [U. S.] National Resources Committee, v. 1, pt. 2, sec. 1, p. 197-225.

Bryan, Kirk, and McCann, F. T., 1936, Successive pediments and terraces of the upper Rio Puerco in New Mexico: Jour. Geology, v. 44, p. 145-172.

──────────, 1937, The Ceja del Rio Puerco, a border feature of the Basin and Range province in New Mexico; Pt. 1, Stratigraphy and structure: Jour. Geology, v. 45, p. 801-828.

──────────, 1938, The Ceja del Rio Puerco, a border feature of the Basin and Range province in New Mexico; Pt. 2, Geomorphology: Jour. Geology, v. 46, p. 1-16.

Cabot, E. C., 1938, Fault border of the Sangre de Cristo Mountains north of Santa Fe, New Mexico: Jour. Geology, v. 46, p. 88-105.

Church, F. S., and Hack, J. T., 1939, An exhumed erosion surface in the Jemez Mountains, New Mexico: Jour. Geology, v. 47, p. 613-629.

Clisby, K. H., Foreman, Frederick, and Sears, P. B., 1957, Pleistocene climatic changes in New Mexico, U. S. A.: Trans. Fourth International Session of the Botanical Quaternary, from Geobot. Inst. Rubel, v. 34, p. 21-26.

Denny, C. S., 1941, Quaternary geology of the San Acacia area, New Mexico: Jour. Geology, v. 49, p. 225-260.

Dorroh, J. H., Jr., 1946, Certain hydrologic and climatic characteristics of the Southwest: Univ. New Mexico Pub. in Eng. No. 1, 64 p.

Dortignac, E. J., 1956, Watershed resources and problems of the upper Rio Grande basin: U. S. Dept. Agri. Rocky Mountain Forest and Range Experiment Station, Fort Collins, Colorado, 107 p.

Emiliani, Cesare, 1958, Paleotemperature anaylsis of core 280 and Pleistocene correlations: Jour. Geology, v. 66, p. 264-275.

Fitzsimmons, J. P., 1959, The structure and geomorphology of west-central New Mexico, in New Mexico Geol. Soc. Guidebook of west-central New Mexico, 10th Field Conf.: p. 112-116.

Harbour, Jerry, 1958, Microstratigraphic and sedimentational studies of an Early Man site near Lucy, New Mexico: Univ. New Mexico unpub. master's thesis, 111 p.

Hoff, C. C., 1959, The ecology and distribution of the pseudoscorpions of north-central New Mexico: Univ. New Mexico Pub. in Biol. No. 8, 68 p.

Hunt, C. B., 1936, Geology and fuel resources of the southern part of the San Juan Basin, New Mexico; Pt. 2, The Mount Taylor coal field: U. S. Geol. Survey Bull. 860-B, p. 31-80.

──────────, 1938, Igneous geology and structure of the Mount Taylor volcanic field, New Mexico: U. S. Geol. Survey Prof. Paper 189-B, p. 51-80.

Kelley, V. C., 1952, Tectonics of the Rio Grande depression of central New Mexico, in New Mexico Geol. Soc. Guidebook of the Rio Grande country, Santa Fe, New Mexico, 3d Field Conf.: p. 93-105.

──────────, 1959, Log of preconference field trip to Tijeras Canyon, Sandia Mountains, New Mexico: Program, 9th Ann. Mtg. Rocky Mountain Section Am. Assoc. Petroleum Geologists, Albuquerque, New Mexico, p. 31-41.

Kummell, Bernhard, 1961, History of the earth: San Francisco, W. H. Freeman, 610 p.

McRae, O. M., 1958, Geology of the northern part of the Ortiz Mountains, Santa Fe County, New Mexico: Univ. New Mexico unpub. master's thesis, 112 p.

Merriam, C. H., 1890, Results of a biological survey of the San Francisco Mountain region and desert of the Little Colorado in Arizona: U. S. Dept. Agri. Bur. Biol. Survey North Am. Fauna, No. 3.

Miller, J. P., and Wendorf, Fred, 1958, Alluvial chronology of the Tesuque Valley, New Mexico: Jour. Geology, v. 66, p. 177-194.

Ross, C. S., 1931, The Valles Mountains volcanic center of New Mexico [abs.]: Am. Geophys. Union. Trans. 12th Ann. Mtg., p. 185-186.

Ruhe, R. V., 1960, Age of the Rio Grande valley in southern New Mexico [abs.]: Geol. Soc. America Bull., v. 71, p. 1962-1963.

Stearns, C. E, 1953, Tertiary geology of the Galisteo-Tonque area, New Mexico: Geol. Soc. America Bull., v. 64, p. 459-507.

Thornthwaite, C. W., and others, 1942, Climate and accelerated erosion in the arid and semi-arid Southwest, with special reference to the Polacca Wash drainage basin: U. S. Dept. Agri. Tech. Bull. 808.

Wright, H. E., Jr., 1946, Tertiary and Quaternary geology of the lower Rio Puerco area, New Mexico: Geol. Soc. America Bull., v. 57, p. 383-456.

SANDIA CAVE

FRANK C. HIBBEN[1]
University of New Mexico

During the seasons of 1936, 1937, 1938, 1939, and terminating in 1940, the University of New Mexico excavated a cave known as Sandia Cave, in Las Huertas Canyon in the northern end of the Sandia Mountains northeast of Albuquerque, New Mexico. In addition, Davis Cave and Guano Cave, two other cavities of the Sandia group, were partially excavated.

The findings in Sandia Cave are of major importance. The cave fill was stratified with definite cultural objects in various strata, some of which could be identified as paralleling certain other known culture horizons. In the mouth of the cave modern material was present in the form of potsherds. These are of black-on-white types of the Pueblo III period and late Glaze wares such as occur at Pueblo IV and Pueblo V sites in the Rio Grande valley and in the Galisteo district. Other recent accumulation was represented by deposits of guano and pack-rat debris, diminishing toward the rear of the cave. Beneath this modern deposit extended a sheet of cave travertine or calcium carbonate representing a wet period preceding the Recent. This calcium carbonate crust seems to represent the end of the Pleistocene. Beneath this cave crust lies the uppermost of the two main cultural horizons. This one is termed the Folsom occupation because of included artifacts. It is characterized by loose debris cemented into a breccia by calcium-charged waters percolating from above. Below the Folsom floor is a sterile laminated stratum of yellow ochre representing another and earlier wet phase. Below the yellow ochre is the Sandia layer, the earliest cultural stratum of the site. The Sandia layer is less consolidated than the Folsom and contains fire areas or hearths. Below the Sandia occupation, between the Sandia and bedrock, lies an intermittent layer of disintegrated limestone of claylike consistency.

Artifacts of the Folsom layer comprise a series of tools and implements, including Folsom points and other objects considered typical of Folsom times. Classic Folsom points are represented by two whole points and two bases. Three unchanneled Folsom-shaped points are present, as well as one lanceolate Southern Plains type. Five large blades, six gravers, seven snub-nosed scrapers, four side scrapers, ten flake knives, one ivory shaft, and two worked splinters of bone make up the rest of the Folsom series.

The Sandia layer is equally distinctive. Sandia points are generally larger than typical Folsoms, and not so well chipped. These earlier points are distinguished by a side shoulder or notch suggestive of Solutrean points, although no contemporaneity or connection between them and the Old World forms is necessarily implied by such comparison. The Sandia points are further divided into two subtypes, both possessing the side-shouldered feature. Type I is lanceolate and rounded in outline. Type 2 is straight-shafted with paralleling sides. Type I is apparently slightly older than type 2. The rest of the Sandia collection comprises three snub-nosed scrapers, one side scraper, numerous flakes which may or may not have been used as knives, and two bone points.

[1]Professor of Anthropology, Curator of the Museum of Anthropology.

Twelve species of animals are present in all the strata of Sandia Cave. In the recent layer, only the ground sloth is an extinct member. Sloth remains were found only in the lowermost portions of the recent deposit and in the rear of the cave. The Folsom layer is distinguished by horse, camel, bison, mammoth, ground sloth, and wolf. The Sandia stratum includes in its faunal assemblage horse, bison, camel, mastodon, and mammoth. The paleontological grouping of Sandia Cave is chiefly valuable as contributing to knowledge of late Pleistocene and early Recent times. None of the species is particularly distinctive nor are the associations new. The sloth is again indicated as one of the last survivors of the many large Pleistocene mammals which become extinct at the end of that period and in the beginning of the Recent.

In this region and perhaps with validity applicable to a much larger area, a sequence has been erected. This is especially important as it involves the famous Folsom culture, now firmly dated by C-14 dating in the range 9,000-8,000 years before the present. The various components of the sequence occur in the following order:

Recent Pueblo occupation
Considerable time interval
Wet period .... End of Pleistocene
Folsom .... Late Pleistocene or early Recent
Wet Period .... Late Pleistocene
Sandia .... Late Pleistocene

This sequence involving an earlier-than-Folsom culture again brings to the fore the question of Old World connections. This problem is rendered the more pressing by reason of the remarkable resemblance between the Sandia points and certain Solutrean examples from the Old World. It has already been pointed out by many of those interested (McCown, 1939), that Solutrean cultural relationship is not to be suggested in the case of Folsom man because of the remoteness of true Solutrean (almost entirely within continental Europe) and the complete lack of demonstrable connection between Solutrean regions and the New World across the as yet unknown reaches of Asia. The perhaps fortuitous circumstance that the Sandia projectile points even more closely resemble certain Solutrean examples bring this question even more prominently to the fore. It is well known by those who have studied Solutrean collections in Europe that the bulk of the material is not distinguished by fine ripple flaking and delicately made points. Indeed, European Solutrean is much closer to the Sandia than to the Folsom, especially as the Folsom is distinguished by a specialized facial channel as yet unparalleled in European or Asiatic horizons. However, it is fruitless to discuss Solutrean connection or contemporaneity until Asiatic gaps of awe-inspiring magnitude have been bridged, a possibility at the present time extremely remote.

Folsom and Sandia have been definitely associated with extinct mammal forms and with climatic changes coincident with the last phases of the Wisconsin glaciation. There is no reason to deny these New World cultures an antiquity comparable with European and Asiatic cultural phenomena occurring under similar climatic circumstances and accompanying a like fauna. There is no need for correlations with definite European cultures especially by

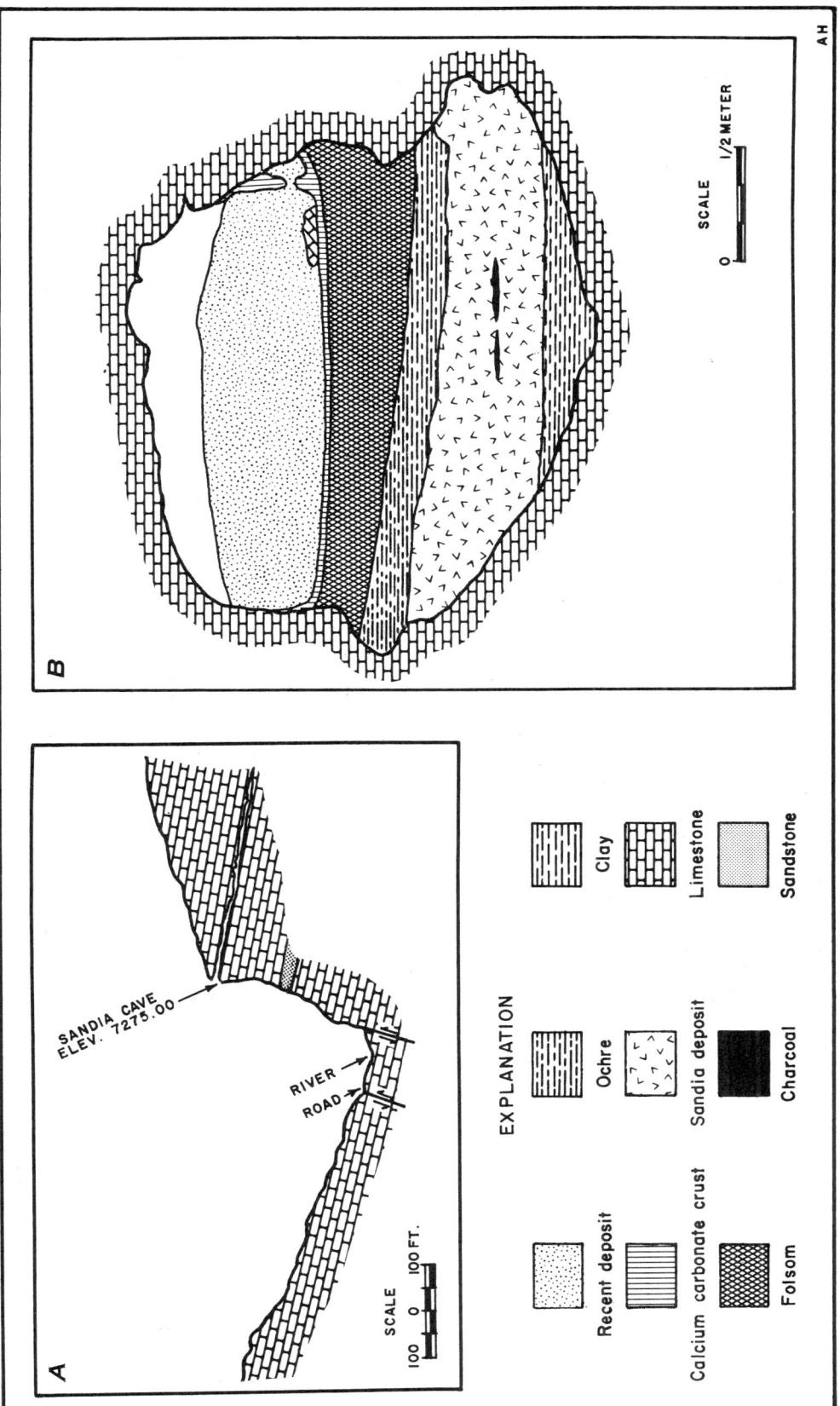

Figure 1. Cross-sections of Sandia Cave. (Adapted from Hibben, 1941, figs. 5 and 7.)
A. Longitudinal east-west cross-section, showing general location of the cave in Las Huertas Canyon, Sandia Mountains.
B. Transverse cross-section of the cave, 15 meters from the entrance, showing stratigraphy of the cave deposits.

name, or even Asiatic ones. Horizons roughly corresponding to Folsom and Sandia have been described from southern and eastern, but not as yet northeastern, Siberia. These are usually lumped under an "Upper Paleolithic" category which is descriptive of a cultural status and time rather than of a European connection by name, although the blade industries of the European levels and the Near East are also represented in Asia (elaborations and variations of Aurignacian, Aurignacian-Magdalenian, and Gravettian). There seems little need to connect New World cultures, whether Sandia, Folsom, or any other, with Asiatic or European cultures when intervening areas, i.e., eastern and northeastern Siberia, are not known. Even Alaska is comparatively untouched as far as the question of the Paleo-Indian is concerned. The Sandia culture has been tentatively dated by radioactive carbon samples of mammoth ivory as 26,000 years before the present.

It is becoming more apparent, as a cultural sequence is being evolved for North America, that the first hunting groups of the New World arrived here in times corresponding to the Upper Paleolithic of Europe and Asia and with a tradition of flint chipping comparable with Siberian centers of the same age. The famous facial channel that distinguishes the Folsom point is but a refinement of a blademaking technique that is, after all, the real basis of differentiation of some of the Old World Upper Paleolithic movements and changes. The Folsom graver is an instrument comparable to a burin although lacking the burin stroke. Refinements of basal technique, such as the striking off of blades, would logically differ in application in widely separated locales especially if contact with the points of origin had long been lost. We may postulate on this basis with fair certainty that the first comers to this continent came armed with a knowledge of blade making and a rudimentary idea of pressure flaking as well. Sandia and Folsom types of flint work represent some of the first variations on these basic techniques of the New World. If the Solutrean was a European outgrowth of this development in one direction, the New World manifestations may be logically suggested as an outgrowth in another, with no direct connection with or knowledge of the Solutrean implied. Climatic and faunal considerations all argue for a similar age. Indeed, it is becoming more evident that both Lower and Upper Paleolithic horizons in Europe, Africa, and Asia represent variant manifestations of the development of a few basic forms, such as the fist ax, the side scraper, and the blade.

In all considerations, the Sandia and Folsom aspects manifest themselves as Upper Paleolithic in character, but with no connection with Asiatic or European phases of specific nature beyond a common sharing of some basic ideas.

REFERENCES

Hibben, F. C., 1941, Evidences of early occupation in Sandia Cave, New Mexico, and other sites in the Sandia-Manzano region: Smithsonian Inst. Misc. Coll., v. 99, no. 23, Pub. 3636, 64 p., illus.; with appendix on Correlation of the deposits of Sandia Cave, New Mexico, with the glacial chronology, by Kirk Bryan, p. 45-64.

McCown, T. D., 1939, The magic word, Solutrean: Am. Antiquity, v. 5, p. 150-152.

INDIANS, ANCIENT AND MODERN, IN THE ALBUQUERQUE COUNTRY

SIDNEY R. ASH

INTRODUCTION

The Albuquerque country has been occupied by Indians more or less continuously for the last 26,000 years as shown by the many campsites, ruins, and modern pueblos found here. This area was in the past, as it is now, an attractive place for man to live and during much of this time it has probably been one of the most densely populated parts of New Mexico. There has been considerable interest in the Indians of this area and, as a result, the literature about them is voluminous and is scattered in many technical and popular journals, books, and magazines. In this paper only some of the more important and interesting high lights of the history of the Indians of the Albuquerque country are summarized. The articles listed in the bibliography contain detailed information and interested readers are referred to them for information in depth.

Figure 1 shows the location of the sites and pueblos mentioned in this paper.

HISTORICAL SUMMARY

The Indians of the Albuquerque country were not completely isolated from other people in the southwestern part of what is now the United States. There was contact between the various inhabited regions and exchange of ideas and material items. At times there were actual emigrations of people from one area to another and there were periods when certain parts of the Southwest were practically abandoned by the Indians.

Apparently man first entered this area 26,000 or more years ago. These were the Sandia people who probably were nomadic hunters. They were succeeded about 10,000 years ago by the Folsom people who may or may not have been descendants of the Sandia. The Folsom people probably were also hunters and for several thousand years continued with their way of life, following the bison, horse, camel, and other animals that they hunted. Evidences of both of these two cultures have been found northeast of Albuquerque in Sandia Cave.

At least 3,000 years ago and possibly before then some of the people in this area began to depend almost entirely on the gathering of wild plants, particularly seeds, for food and only supplemented their diet with small game. These were the Cochise people or others with a similar type of culture. Undoubtedly, however, there were other groups that continued to hunt animals for their livelihood. The Atrisco and Santa Ana early-man sites in the Albuquerque country contain evidence of the gatherers in this part of New Mexico.

It has been possible to devise a relative chronology for the Indians who lived in the Southwest after the time of Christ, through the use of tree-ring data and diagnostic pottery types. A number of periods have been recognized; however, there were actually no sharp breaks between them and the dates used are only of general value. The following table, modified from Martin, Quimby, and Collier (1947, p. 103) and Wormington (1947), shows the names, sequence, and dates of the various periods as they are now understood.

The Indians of this area apparently had limited contact with the Basketmakers of the Four Corners area early in the Christian Era, as typical Basketmaker implements have been found with local cultural material in Jemez Cave. At about A. D. 300 the Indians here began to build relatively permanent dwelling places. One type was the pit-house which was made by digging a pit to the desired depth and then either roofing it over or building walls of mud, stone, or wood to hold the roof. The jacal was another type; it was made of upright poles and brush which sometimes were plastered with mud. Around A. D. 500 or possibly earlier the Indians learned to make pottery, which was comparatively crude at first but became highly refined as time passed. Close to the present pueblos of Zia and Santa Ana, four pit-houses have been excavated. One pit-house was occupied by Indians about the end of the Modified Basketmaker period. The other three pit-houses were in use later in the Developmental-Pueblo period.

During the Great-Pueblo period the justly famous communal dwellings were built at Mesa Verde, in Chaco Canyon, and at other places on the Colorado Plateau. The Indians in the Albuquerque country did not build comparable structures although a few small pueblos of this period are known. Toward the end of the 13th century the Colorado Plateau was abandoned by most of the Indians who had lived there. This abandonment is usually attributed to an extensive drought which occurred at about the same time.

The Regressive-Pueblo period is marked in the Albuquerque country by the construction of many large communal dwellings. Abandoned examples of these dwellings are found in Frijoles Canyon and at Paa-ko and Unshagi. Some of the modern pueblos in the Albuquerque country were originally built during this period also. It is thought that some of the Indians from the Colorado Plateau emigrated into the Rio Grande valley and were more or less responsible for the large communal dwellings built here during this period.

When the Spanish entered this area during the middle part of the Regressive-Pueblo period there were at least 70 pueblos here that were occupied. They eventually established limited control over the land and its inhabitants although the Indians successfully withstood most of the Spanish influences and maintained their own culture during the following 150 years. In 1680 the Pueblo Indians united and succeeded in driving all of the Spanish from New Mexico except those that they were able to catch and kill. Eventually this union of the Indians broke apart and the Spanish completed their reconquest of New Mexico in 1692.

The Reconquest marks the beginning of the Historic-Pueblo period because after that time the Indians no longer were able to withstand the Spanish culture as they had previously. Beginning early in the 18th century whole villages were abandoned as the result of disease and war and the Indians were concentrated into fewer and fewer pueblos; eventually they were reduced in number to the 18 now found in the Rio Grande valley.

Today there are 11 pueblos that are still inhabited in the Albuquerque country. Although the Indians have accepted many outside traits they still maintain certain of their old customs and ideals. The Pueblos are nominal Roman Catholics and each village has a chapel or a church, although nearby are kivas in which they continue to practice the old rites and ceremonies. Many of the houses have galvanized-iron roofs and glass windows, but the basic architecture of the dwellings is the same as it was in much of the past.

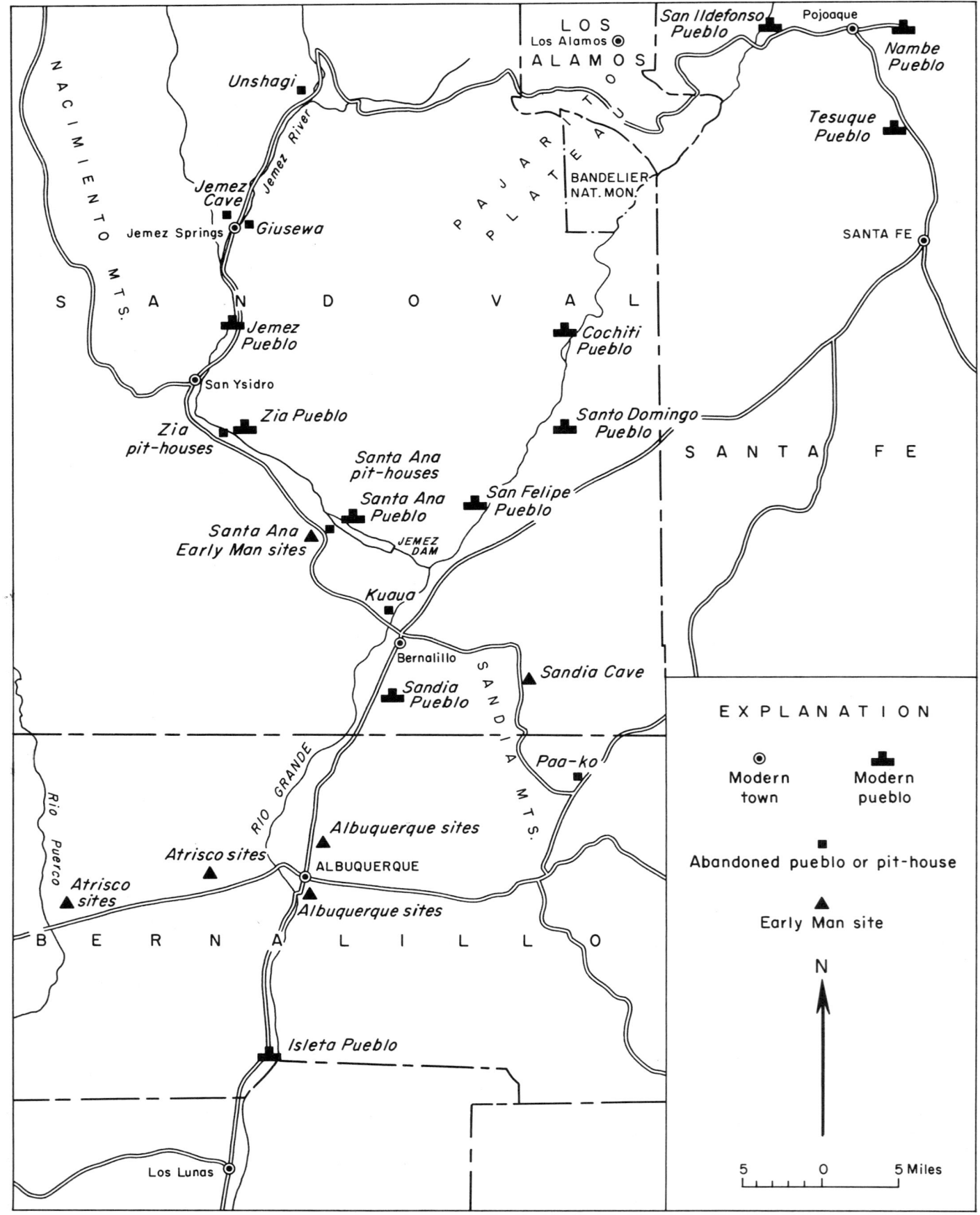

Figure 1. — Index map showing the location of the modern pueblos and certain abandoned pueblos, pit-houses, and early-man sites in the Albuquerque country.

Estimated date	Period
A.D.1700 - to date	Pueblo V or Historic-Pueblo
A.D.1300-A.D.1700	Pueblo IV or Regressive-Pueblo
A.D.1050-A.D.1300	Pueblo III or Great-Pueblo
A.D.900-A.D.1050	Pueblo II)
A.D.700-A.D.900	Pueblo I) or Developmental-Pueblo
A.D.500-A.D.700	Basketmaker III or Modified Basketmaker
A.D.1-A.D.500	Basketmaker II or Basketmaker

TABLE 1.

EARLY-MAN SITES

The term early man, as used in this paper, refers to those people who lived or visited in the Albuquerque country prior to A.D. 1. It is assumed but not proven that early man was of the Mongoloid race to which the modern Indians belong.

The various early-man cultures in North America are characterized by the artifacts, particularly the projectile points, they used. In North America it is now possible to outline a relative chronological sequence of the various early-man cultures and their particular point types. For a number of reasons however it is not possible to rely entirely on the points as "index fossils" and it is necessary in most cases to study the whole artifact "assemblage" before a definite conclusion can be reached. In a few cases it has been possible to date some of the cultures by radiocarbon analyses.

Sandia Cave

Sandia Cave is probably the most famous early-man site in New Mexico if not in the entire New World. This cave, located on the east side of Las Huertas Canyon near the north end of the Sandia Mountains, contained artifacts that are probably the oldest known in the New World. It was excavated by the University of New Mexico during the years 1936-1940 and a detailed report on the cave was published by Hibben in 1941. He has recently summarized and evaluated his findings for this Guidebook in the article entitled "Sandia Cave". Therefore only brief mention of it is made here.

The deposits in Sandia Cave are stratified and contain three distinct occupation levels. The uppermost is relatively young and contains Indian pottery. The middle level contains points typical of the Folsom early-man culture which elsewhere has generally been dated at about 9,000-8,000 years before the present by the use of the radiocarbon-dating technique. A Folsom point from Sandia Cave is sketched in Figure 2-A. The lowest occupation level is characterized by "Sandia" points (Fig. 2-B, C). In the accompanying article, Hibben suggests that Sandia Cave was occupied by man using Sandia points as early as 26,000 years ago.

Santa Ana Early-Man Sites

At present radiocarbon dates are available for one group of early-man terrace sites in the area. These dates were obtained from charcoal taken from hearths that occur on and within the terraces across Jemez River from Santa Ana Pueblo. Only 6 of the more than 150 hearths found were sampled for dating. The buried hearths range in age from 3,000 ± 700 years to 3,100 ± 500 years, while the surface hearths range from 2,180 ± 250 to 2600 ± 300 years (Agogino and Hibben, 1958, p. 423-424). Associated with the hearths are manos, metates, blades, points, choppers, drills, and unidentified bones. Among the points are some that resemble points found in Texas and others found in sites of the San Pedro stage of the Cochise culture in southern Arizona (Agogino and Hester, 1953). Apparently early man, who in this case was both a hunter and a gatherer, occupied the area of the Santa Ana sites intermittently for about 1,000 years or more.

Atrisco Sites

The river terraces west of Albuquerque, which are related to the Rio Grande and Rio Puerco, also contain early-man sites. These are generally referred to as the Atrisco sites because they were originally found on the Atrisco land grant. Several hundred Atrisco sites have been found here. They consist of hearths and fired areas with which are associated artifacts of various types, including points, blades, manos, metates, scrapers, choppers, and drills. The point types include, as in the Santa Ana sites, some that are similar to points found in Texas and others, termed Atrisco points, that look like those found in the San Pedro stage of the Cochise culture (Campbell and Ellis, 1952, p. 211-221). Judging by the point types, the Atrisco sites and the Santa Ana sites may be about the same age.

Albuquerque Sites

The river terraces on the east side of the Rio Grande in the vicinity of Albuquerque contain several early-man sites too. These have been uncovered in gravel pits on both the southern and northern edges of Albuquerque.

The gravel pits on the southern edge of Albuquerque contain hearths with which were associated artifacts and bones of various types. Artifacts found are crudely made and include scrapers, knives, and a milling stone. No points have been reported from this site. Bones of mammoth, bison, horse, camel, and other animals were found directly or closely associated with the artifacts (Hibben, 1951, p. 41-43). The gravel pits on the northern edge

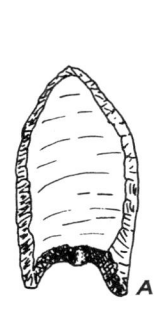

Figure 2.—Sketches of artifacts from Sandia Cave about x ¾
A. Folsom point from Folsom occupation level
B. Sandia Point, type 1, from Sandia occupation level
C. Sandia point, type 2, from Sandia occupation level

of Albuquerque have yielded a large quantity of mammal bones including those of elephant, horse, and a human skull. However, because the skull was not found in place it is not possible to determine if it actually belonged to early man.

Hibben suggests that the artifacts in the southern group of gravel pits are Cochise and it is probable that the material in the northern group is of about the same age as both groups of sites occur in gravels which have the same approximate stratigraphic position.

PREHISTORIC INDIAN SITES

Prehistoric Indian sites, as used here, are those sites that were occupied between A. D. 1 and A. D. 1700 and have since been abandoned.

Zia Pit-Houses

Two round pit-houses southwest of the modern pueblo of Zia have been recently excavated. One was occupied near the end of Modified Basketmaker period or during the early part of the Developmental-Pueblo period and the other was in use during the Developmental-Pueblo period. In the older pit-house the skeletal remains of a young adult, a burned basket and cradle board, pottery, and chipped- and ground-stone artifacts were found. Material recovered from the younger pit-house included pottery, chipped- and ground-stone artifacts, turquoise, shell, and bone artifacts (Vytlacil and Brody, 1958).

Santa Ana Pit-Houses

Southwest of the modern pueblo of Santa Ana two round pit-houses have been excavated by Allen and Mc-Nutt (1955) of the University of New Mexico. Associated with the houses were pottery of several different types and a number of chipped- and ground-stone artifacts. It is apparent that these people had had contact with the cultural areas in what is now eastern Arizona and southern and northern New Mexico. These pit-houses were in use during Developmental-Pueblo period or possibly a little earlier in Modified Basketmaker period.

Jemez Cave

In the west wall of Jemez Canyon, about a mile north of Jemez Springs, is a cave which is of considerable interest for it contained the naturally mummified remains of an Indian child and a large quantity of perishable cultural material, such as feather-string blankets and sandals.

This cave, about 100 feet vertically above Soda Dam, was excavated by the University of New Mexico during 1934. It occurs in a breccia of calcareous tufa similar to the present Soda Dam and may have been developed in a similar manner to the caves now being formed beneath the Dam. In addition to the blankets and sandals, arrow shafts, planting sticks, a fragment of bison-hair blanket, pottery of various types, bone, projectile points, knives, scrapers, drills, corncobs, and much other cultural material were found in the cave. The strata of the occupation levels had been mixed somewhat both by the Indians who used the cave and by the pot-hunters who originally discovered the mummy. However, a study of the cultural remains shows that the Basketmakers must have occasionally visited the cave before it was briefly occupied by Pueblo Indians during the Great-Pueblo period. It has been visited occasionally since that time by other Indians (Alexander and Reiter, 1935).

Rio Puerco Pueblo Site

A small pueblo ruin in the Rio Puerco valley northwest of Albuquerque contains evidence supporting the theory that one of the routes used by emigrants from Mesa Verde after the drought of the late 13th century was down this valley. The ruin which is built on the top of a small butte has been tested recently (Davis and Winkler, 1959). Ready access to the butte-top is by a single path that goes through a narrow crevice. The site consists of about 60 rooms built of sandstone slabs. Some of the excavated rooms had a floor of gray clay while others had only a bare stone floor. Cultural remains were rare except for pottery, and the types represented at the site are some that appear to be identical with a type found at Mesa Verde.

Reportedly the Laguna Indians in the San Jose valley a few miles to the south of the ruin, have a tradition that their ancestors once lived on a high butte-top accessible by only one path. Possibly this butte was a refuge for the Lagunas on their emigration south during the Regressive-Pueblo period from Mesa Verde to their present pueblo.

Paa-ko

About one mile north of the village of San Antonito in the valley between the Sandia and San Pedro Mountains is the ruin of a large pueblo named Paa-ko. The ruin has been only partially excavated (Lambert, 1954).

The main pueblo was originally started near the close of the 13th century during the Regressive-Pueblo period, although evidence was found of an earlier occupation in the immediate area during Developmental-Pueblo time. Paa-ko was abandoned about A. D. 1425 and then reoccupied during the Regressive-Pueblo period. It was finally abandoned in about 1670, 10 years before the Pueblo Revolt. Lambert (1954, p. 177) believes the scarcity of cultural material in the second occupation zone indicates that final abandonment was planned and was not hastily completed. It is thought that descendants of the population of Paa-ko are now living in the present pueblo of Santo Domingo, about 35 miles northwest of the ruin.

Kuaua

During Coronado's exploration of the Southwest in 1540 he maintained headquarters in a pueblo on the west side of the Rio Grande northwest of the present city of Albuquerque. In an attempt to determine the exact site of that pueblo the ruins of Kuaua, about two miles west of Bernalillo, were excavated during the late 1930's. Although nothing was unearthed to either confirm or disprove the theory that Kuaua was the site of Coronado's headquarters, the site remains as a graphic illustration of how the people in the Rio Grande valley lived during the time of Coronado's entrada.

The pueblo was built around the beginning of the 14th century during the Regressive-pueblo period and continually occupied until it was abandoned about the end of the 16th century. The entire pueblo was not occupied at the same time. The southern section was slowly abandoned and allowed to fall into ruin as new dwellings were built to the north. After its abandonment the survivors moved in with their linguistic kinsmen at Sandia Pueblo a few miles to the southeast.

In the excavations it was found that the pueblo consisted of more than 1,200 rooms, 2 main plazas and 6 kivas. Approximately 600 skeletons were unearthed as well as pottery, tools, weapons, pieces of fabric, seeds, and baskets. However the most important find was the so-called Painted Kiva.

The walls of the Painted Kiva were found to be covered with seventeen layers of frescoes, which were moved to the University of New Mexico for study. The

Kiva has been restored and one set of the murals has been reproduced on the walls. Other exhibits including material from the excavations at the site are housed in a museum at the ruin.

Giusewa

The Jemez country contains the ruins of many pueblos that were occupied by the Jemez Indians. One of the most widely known ruins attributed to the Jemez people is that of Giusewa on the northern edge of the modern settlement of Jemez Springs. The classic name for the ruin is Giusewatowa, which means "pueblo at the hot place", according to Harrington (1916, p. 393). It was partially excavated in the 1920's but only a few notes concerning the findings have been published (Reiter, 1938, p. 87-91).

Apparently there was a large pueblo here when the Spanish arrived in the area. A mission was founded during the fall of 1621 or the winter of 1621-22. The pueblo was abandoned in 1680 and one of the Franciscan missionaries stationed there was killed during the Pueblo Indian revolt of that year. In 1694 these Indians submitted to the Spanish and returned to their pueblo. However, in 1696 they once again revolted, killing their missionary, and abandoning their home forever. They then fled to the Navajo country where they remained until 1709 when all the Jemez Indians banded together at the site of the present pueblo of Jemez (Hewett, 1943, p. 175-182; 1947, p. 120).

During the excavation of the mission, fragments of Spanish murals were found on the walls. Copies of these are in the State Museum, Santa Fe, and are one of the few authentic examples of the mural decoration used by Spanish in the Southwest during the 17th century.

The mission was repaired and stabilized in the late 1930's and is now one of the popular tourist attractions of the Jemez country.

Unshagi

Another ruin in the Jemez area which has been excavated is about half a mile below Battleship Rock near surfur springs in Jemez Canyon. Unshagi, or "place where the one-seeded juniper trees are" (Harrington, 1916, p. 393), was a rather large pueblo. Remains of at least 150 rooms were found and considering that there may have been second and third stories in places, it may have contained a total of 250 or more rooms. Unshagi, judging by the pottery and tree-ring dates, was probably founded late in the 14th century near the end of the Great-Pueblo period. It was abandoned early in the 17th century during the Regressive-Pueblo Period, the population moving to Giusewa or to another pueblo near the site of the present pueblo of Jemez, or both.

Pajarito Plateau

Pajarito Plateau is the term applied to the tuff-capped plateau between the Rio Grande and the Valle Grande. Indians in the past built hundreds of large and small pueblos in this area. Most of the dwellings were of conventional pueblo design while others were made by using natural or artificial caves in the tuff for some of the rooms. Apparently, it was deserted as a place to live within the first half of the Regressive-Pueblo period, because of a change in climate on the plateau. The survivors apparently founded some of the pueblos in the Rio Grande valley. Because of the abundance of Indian ruins in this plateau area a portion of it was set aside as Bandelier National Monument. Adolf Bandelier, after whom the Monument is named, was a Swiss ethnologist who did considerable work in the Southwest, particularly in the Pajarito Plateau, for the Archaeological Institute of America during the last part of the 19th century.

The Canyon of El Rito de los Frijoles is the central feature of the Monument. It contains several types of dwellings, including a circular pueblo on the floor of the canyon, a cave which was large enough to contain a small village, and cliff dwellings. These latter consist of terraced houses of from two to four stories built against the northern tuff wall of the canyon into which back rooms were excavated. Also within the Monument boundaries are many conventional small pueblos, a number of cliff dwellings, a cave on whose walls have been painted many Indian designs and symbols, and a possible Indian hunting shrine. This shrine consists of two figures, representing crouching mountain lions, carved out of the tuff. The bodies of the lions are about four feet long and lie with heads pointing to the east and tails extending to the west. It is still visited by Indians from many parts of New Mexico who leave offerings at the shrine.

North of the Monument proper is a small section of the plateau which has also been set aside as a part of the Bandelier National Monument. This is the Otowi section and within it are the remains of pueblo of about 700 rooms, several cliff dwellings, and a unique village in which the dwelling places were carved into eroded cones of tuff, called tent-rocks. From a distance this village has the appearance of a cluster of beehives.

One other group of ruins on the Pajarito Plateau is of some interest. It is the Puye Mesa group which lies a few miles north of Bandelier. It includes both cliff dwellings similar to those found in the Monument and the ruins of a large pueblo on the mesa top above the cliff dwellings. The pueblo has been partially excavated and probably at one time consisted of more than a thousand rooms, built of blocks of tuff laid in adobe mud. This group of ruins is in the Santa Clara Pueblo Indian Reservation. Tourists are allowed to visit the ruins for a small charge and view the Indian ceremonies occasionally held there.

MODERN PUEBLOS

Cochiti

Thirty miles southwest of Santa Fe is the pueblo of Cochiti. Apparently it was founded about the middle of the 13th century and the members claim that their ancestral home was in El Rito de los Frijoles. During the Reconquest the pueblo was destroyed but was soon rebuilt. Cochiti has a population of about 327. It is famous for its drums made of cottonwood logs and also for cream-colored pottery. Like the other pueblos in the area, Cochiti holds an annual Corn Dance.

Isleta

The pueblo of Isleta is on the west bank of the Rio Grande about 13 miles south of Albuquerque. Apparently the village was originally founded here in the early part of the 16th century although it was abandoned during the Revolt. More than 500 captives from here were taken by the Spanish during their retreat to El Paso. Some of the captive Indians settled near El Paso at Isleta del Sur where their descendants still live. The pueblo was refounded after the Reconquest in 1692. Agriculture and the care of livestock is the leading occupation. Isleta had a population of about 1,830 in 1960.

Jemez

The present pueblo of Jemez is located about 20 miles northwest of Bernalillo on the east side of the Jemez River. The date of its founding is unknown but was probably some time prior to 1620. The pueblo was abandoned during the Revolt of 1680 and the inhabitants retreated onto the high mesas to the north. Apparently in 1695, after years of fighting with the Spanish, Utes, and other Indians, all of the Jemez Indians, including those which had occupied the other pueblos in the area, returned to the present site of Jemez Pueblo. Shortly thereafter they revolted, killing their missionary, and once again retreated to the high mesa country. It was not until 1703 that the Spanish finally succeeded in bringing the rebels back to this pueblo, where they have since remained. In 1838 the pueblo of Pecos, southeast of Santa Fe, was abandoned and the seventeen survivors moved to Jemez where they took up residence with their linguistic kinsmen. In 1940 nearly one-third of the population of Jemez claimed to be descendants of Pecos mothers. This pueblo is famous for two of its ceremonies, the Buffalo Dance which is held in the winter, and its Corn Dances held in the fall. Some baskets and pottery are made, poster-paint ware being the most popular among tourists. Stock raising and farming are important sources of livelihood. Today Jemez has a population of about 1,065.

Nambe

Nambe, one of the smallest pueblos in New Mexico, is located about 16 miles north of Santa Fe. It has been occupied since 1300 and was originally much larger, judging by the many room outlines that can be seen in the ground near the present dwellings. Today the pueblo looks much like another Mexican village in the area and it will probably lose most of its distinguishing characteristics in the not-too-distant future (Stubbs, 1950, p. 54). The population of Nambe is about 127.

Sandia

Sandia Pueblo is on the east side of the Rio Grande, 14 miles north of Albuquerque. It apparently was founded about 1300 and visited by Coronado in 1540. The pueblo has been occupied almost continuously since then, although it was nearly completely abandoned during the Pueblo Revolt. At that time most of the inhabitants fled to the Hopi country in Arizona and did not return to their pueblo until 1742. A ruined pueblo on the Second Hopi Mesa has the same Hopi name as is applied to the modern pueblo of Sandia. According to tradition, the ruin was originally built by Indian refugees from the Rio Grande area during the Revolt. Today Sandia has a population of about 122.

San Felipe

The pueblo of San Felipe is on the west side of the Rio Grande, about 30 miles north of Albuquerque. The present pueblo was built early in the 18th century although the San Felipe Indians lived in the area as early as the middle of the 16th century. San Felipe is one of the most conservative pueblos in the area. It is particularly famous for its Green Corn Dance, given on May 1 each year. The principal occupation of the San Felipe Indians is farming. The pueblo had a population of 976 in 1960.

San Ildefonso

The pueblo of San Ildefonso is on the east side of the Rio Grande 20 miles northwest of Santa Fe. It has been occupied since about 1300 although there have been several shifts of the center of population from one part of the village to another. The pueblo is noted for its artisans, especially the potters. According to Stubbs (1950, p. 50), "the work of one potter, Maria Martinez, has made San Ildefonso pottery perhaps the most widely known of all modern pueblo styles." Her style has a matte-black design on polished black ware and is copied by other potters in the village as well as in other pueblos. San Idlefonso now has a population of about 216.

Two miles north of the pueblo is Black Mesa, a butte capped by lava. To the Indians it is a sacred mountain, which they still visit and worship on. During the past it was also a place of refuge from the Spanish who laid seige to it several times.

Santa Ana

On the north bank of the Jemez River, eight miles northwest of Bernalillo, is Santa Ana Pueblo. This is one of the youngest pueblos, having been founded after the Revolt, in about 1700. The location of the original older pueblo is unknown. Nowadays most of these Indians live in small villages a few miles north of Bernalillo where they can farm. However they gather periodically at the pueblo for dances and ceremonies. The population of Santa Ana is about 350.

Santo Domingo

The most conservative of the pueblos is Santo Domingo, on the east side of the Rio Grande about 30 miles southwest of Santa Fe. This pueblo was originally built at the present site after the Reconquest but it has since been nearly destroyed by flood three times. The Pueblo is famous for its pottery and the annual Green Corn Ceremony held on August 4. Santo Domingo has a population of about 1,375.

Tesuque

Tesuque Pueblo is about ten miles north of Santa Fe. It is one of the smaller of the New Mexico pueblos and was built near the beginning of the 14th century. The pueblo is now particularly noted for its gaudy poster-paint pottery. This ware is characterized by being decorated with tempera water colors in bright shades of pink, purple, green, blue, and other colors Even though the colors will rub or wash off, tourist demand for this modern type of pottery remains high. Tesuque has a population of about 136.

Zia

The pueblo of Zia is on the north bank of the Jemez River 16 miles northwest of Bernalillo at a site that has been occupied since about 1300. In 1582 it was reported to be prosperous and to consist of over a thousand houses, three or four stories high, but it was reduced considerably in size during the Pueblo Revolt. Because the pueblo capitulated early in the Revolt, after suffering extremely high losses to the Spanish, the Zia people have been held as more or less social outcasts by other Pueblo Indians. The Zia lack adequate farm land, so their pueblo has remained small since the Revolt. Pottery made in the pueblo is of such high quality that it is purchased and used by other Pueblo Indians. Currently this pueblo together with several other pueblos in the area have land-claim suits pending against the Federal government. If the claims are settled in favor of the Indians then the Zia may become prosperous once more. The pueblo had a population of about 334 people in 1960.

To summarize, we have seen how the Indian cultures in this area have developed from quite primitive nomadic hunting and gathering cultures to sedentary groups living in pueblos. What of the future? Should the Indians of this area remain as objects of curiosity frozen in a number of anthropological museum-like reservations so that in the future the white man can say "Here they are, just as they were a hundred years ago"? Or should they be encouraged to assimilate with the white man and his culture and turn their backs on their ancestral home and way of life and become full-fledged Americans?

BIBLIOGRAPHY
Early Man

Agogino, George, and Hester, Jim, 1953, The Santa Ana pre-Ceramic sites: El Palacio, v. 60, p. 131-140, 5 figs.

Agogino, George, and Hibben, F. C., 1958, Central New Mexico paleo-Indian cultures: Am. Antiquity, v. 23, p. 422-425.

Campbell, J. M., and Ellis, F. H., 1952, The Atrisco sites: Cochise manifestations in the middle Rio Grande valley: Am. Antiquity, v. 17, p. 211-221, figs. 70-75.

Hibben, F. C., 1941, Evidences of early occupation in Sandia Cave, New Mexico, and other sites in the Sandia-Manzano region: Smithsonian Inst. Misc. Coll., v. 99, no. 23, Pub. 3636, 64 p., illus.; with appendix on Correlation of the deposits of Sandia Cave, New Mexico, with the glacial chronology, by Kirk Bryan, p. 45-64.

............, 1951a, Sites of the paleo-Indian in the middle Rio Grande valley: Am. Antiquity, v. 17, p. 41-46, pl. 1, figs. 28-32.

............, 1951b, A survey of the sites of the paleo-Indian in the middle Rio Grande valley, New Mexico: Texas Jour. Sci., v. 3, p. 362-367.

Martin, P. S., Quimby, G. I., and Collier, Donald, 1947, Indians before Columbus: Chicago, Univ. Chicago Press, 582 p., 18 charts, 121 figs.

Sellards, E. H., 1952, Early man in America, a study in prehistory: Austin, Univ. Texas Press, 211 p., 47 figs.

Wormington, H. M., 1957, Ancient man in North America, 4th ed.: Denver Mus. Nat. Hist. Pop. Ser. No. 4, 322 p., 72 figs.

Prehistoric Indians

Alexander, H. G., and Reiter, Paul, 1935, Report on the excavation of Jemez Cave, New Mexico: Univ. New Mexico and School Am. Research Mon. 4, 71 p., 20 pls.

Allen, J. W., and McNutt, 1955, A pit house site near Santa Ana Pueblo, New Mexico: Am. Antiquity, v. 20, p. 241-255, figs. 69-74.

Amsden, C. A., 1949, Prehistoric southwesterners from Basketmaker to Pueblo: Los Angeles, Southwest Museum, 163 p., 2 maps, 46 figs.

Hendron, J. W., 1946, Frijoles, a hidden valley in the New World: Santa Fe, Rydal Press, 92 p., illus.

Hewett, E. L., 1947, Landmarks of New Mexico, 2d ed.: Albuquerque, Univ. New Mexico Press, 204 p., illus.

............, 1953, Pajarito Plateau and its ancient people: Albuquerque, Univ. New Mexico Press, 174 p., 15 pls., 84 figs.

Hewett, E. L., and Fisher, R. G., 1943, Mission monuments of New Mexico: Albuquerque, Univ. New Mexico Press, 269 p., illus.

Lambert, M. F., 1954, Paa-ko, archaeological chronicle of an Indian village in north central New Mexico: School Am. Research Mon. 19, 183 p., 39 pls., 54 figs., 13 tables.

Reiter, Paul, 1938, The Jemez Pueblo of Unshagi, New Mexico, with notes on the earlier excavations at "Amoxiumqua" and Giusewa: Univ. New Mexico Mon., v. 1, no. 4, 211 p., 23 pls., 9 figs.

Sinclair, J. L., 1951, The story of the pueblo of Kuaua: El Palacio, v. 58, no. 7.

Underhill, R. M., 1946, First penthouse dwellers of America: Santa Fe, Lab. Anthropology, 161 p.

Vytlacil, Natalie, and Brody, J. J., 1958, Two pit houses near Zia Pueblo: El Palacio, v. 65, p. 174-184, 4 figs.

Wormington, H. M., 1947, Prehistoric Indians of the Southwest: Denver, Colorado Mus. Nat. Hist., Pop. Ser. No. 7, 191 p., 58 figs.

Modern Pueblos

Aberle, S. D., 1948, The Pueblo Indians of New Mexico, their land, economy and civil organization: Am. Anthropol. Assoc. Mem. 70, 93 p., 13 tables, 1 map, 1 chart.

Harrington, J. P., 1916, The ethnogeography of the Tewa Indians: Bur. Am. Ethnol. 29th Ann. Rept., p. 29-618, 21 pls., 31 maps.

Lange, C. H., 1959, Cochiti, a New Mexico pueblo, past and present: Univ. Texas Press, 618 p., 28 pls., 35 figs., 2 maps.

Robbins, W. W., Harrington, J. P., and Freire-Marreco, Barbara, 1916, Ethnobotany of the Tewa Indians: Bur. Am. Ethnol. Bull. 55, 124 p.

Stevenson, M. C., 1894, The Sia: Bur. Am. Ethnol. 11th Ann. Rept., p. 3-157, 35 pls., 20 figs.

Stubbs, S. A., 1950, Birds-eye view of the pueblos: Norman, Univ. Oklahoma Press, 122 p., 25 pls., 27 figs.

White, L. A., 1932, The pueblo of San Felipe: Am. Anthropol. Assoc. Mem. 38, 69 p., 3 pls., 17 figs.

............, 1935, The pueblo of Santo Domingo, New Mexico: Am. Anthropol. Assoc. Mem. 43, 210 p., 8 pls., 53 figs.

............, 1942, The pueblo of Santa Ana, New Mexico: Am. Anthropol. Assoc. Mem. 60, 360 p., 7 pls., 54 figs.

HISTORY OF THE ALBUQUERQUE REGION

FRANK D. REEVE[1]
University of New Mexico

People have lived in the Albuquerque region for an unknown number of centuries. When the first Spanish arrived in 1540 they found about twenty villages, or **pueblos**, extending from Acoma on the west to the Piros of the Manzano Mountains, and along the Province of Tiguex (Tee-way) from the neighborhood of present Bernalillo to the pueblo of Isleta.

Don Francisco Vasquez de Coronado, governor of New Galicia and commander of His Majesty's forces in search of wealth and territory for the glory of God, the King, and himself, established headquarters in the flourishing pueblo of Alcanfor, now the ruins that constitute the Coronado State Monument on the right bank of the Rio Grande across from Bernalillo. Don Francisco's search was fruitless, but two Franciscan missionaries laid down their lives for The Cross and became the first martyrs in the history of New Mexico: Fray Juan de Padilla and Fray Luis Escalona.

Don Juan de Onate, Governor, Captain General and Adelantado, made the first settlement in 1598 north of Santa Fe. In the course of time, the Albuquerque region became known as the Rio Abajo, or down river from Santa Fe, where settlers located on small ranches during the seventeenth century. The Camino Real ran parallel to the Rio Grande, bearing the traveler to Chihuahua on the south or Santa Fe to the north. The road to the west lay past the mouth of Jemez Canyon while on the east an Indian trail snaked its way through Tijeras Canyon, or Carnue as it was originally named.

The missionaries soon established The Cross in the various pueblos of the region; the oldest physical monuments to their labors are the church of St. Augustine at Isleta and St. Stephen at Acoma, dating back probably to 1618. Fray Alonso Peinado began spreading the gospel in 1613 among the folks at the pueblo of Chilili where the church was dedicated to La Navidad de Nuestra Senora. The mission of San Gregorio was established at Abo about 1622, some ten miles west of present Mountainair; San Isidro at Gran Quivira seven years later, twenty miles to the south as the crow flies; and Nuestra Senora de la Concepcion at Quarai, a few miles to the east. Another mission might have been located at Tajique as early as 1629.

During the seventeenth century, the settlers and Pueblos were occasionally harassed by Indians from the east and west, Apache and Navaho; and friction developed between the Pueblos and Spanish to the point where the former rebelled against their masters in 1680, driving them southward to El Paso. Some of the Isleta folk migrated with the Spanish and established the pueblo of Isleta del Sur downstream from El Paso (Juarez), Mexico.

Don Diego Jose de Vargas Zapata y Lujan Ponce de Leon Contreras, scion of an illustrious Spanish family, ventured into New Mexico in 1692 with a small troop of soldiers and made a peaceful reconnaissance of Puebloland. The following year he returned with settlers and reoccupied Santa Fe. Others located in the Bernalillo area by 1695. Since the frontier folks were still hostile, Don Diego was forced to fight them, and while on a punitive campaign toward Abo Pass in 1704, he fell ill and returned to Bernalillo where he soon died.

Along the western frontier of New Mexico, the Spanish took official recognition in 1699 of some Pueblos who had settled at the Laguna near the south end of Cebolleta Mountain. The mission was dedicated to San Jose; the name also came to be applied to the stream that flows eastward through the village to join the Rio Puerco of the East. The Navahos frequented Laguna and Jemez Pueblos, sometimes for peaceful trading and occasionally as enemies. Since the Pueblos were intimately interlocked with the Spanish, it was impossible for the frontier foe to draw any clear line between the two groups, so both suffered from their attacks.

The Navahos had a fortified stronghold on Big Bead mesa, an elongation on the north end of Cebolleta Mountain. When Captain Rocque de Madrid campaigned in 1706, he pursued them southward from the San Juan region to this site but was unable to surmount the difficulties of the terrain and failed to punish the foe. Several campaigns were launched against this western enemy during the first two decades of the century, setting forth from Sia Pueblo or farther north via the Chama Valley.

Peace reigned between the Navahos and Spanish-Pueblos for a half century, beginning about 1720. Missionaries moved into Navaholand in the San Juan country in 1744 and eventually persuaded a group to move southward in 1748 to form a settlement at Cebolleta Canyon which drains from the southeastern side of Cebolleta Mountain. Another mission was established a few miles to the west at Encinal for other Navahos, but both of these ventures were shortlived. These folks were not habituated to a settled way of life, and the acquisition of livestock from the Spanish, especially sheep, turned them into a seminomadic people.

Beginning in 1753, the Governors of New Mexico granted sizeable tracts of land to various and sundry New Mexicans that soon encircled Cebolleta Mountain. These

Albuquerque. 1891. July. Gold Ave. - looking east. This photo was probably taken from the San Felipe Hotel (Elk's Club) (5th and Gold). The Central Bank and the Whiting Bldg. can be clearly distinguished in the background (2nd and Gold). Note boardwalk. (U.N.M. Library collection)

---

[1] Professor of History, Editor of the **New Mexico Historical Review**.

were an outlet for the expanding population and livestock in the Rio Abajo. The grants were always made with the proviso that the rights of the Navahos should not be violated; that is, the authorities recognized the Indians' usufructuary to the land, and were even willing to grant titles in fee simple. However, relations between these near neighbors finally led to hostilities because of competing needs for land and water. The New Mexican's contempt for the Indian was met by pride and a rebellious spirit against the intruders.

Increasing population led to settlements elsewhere in the Albuquerque region during the eighteenth century. Governor Francisco Cuervo Valdes founded Albuquerque in 1706, naming it in honor of Don Francisco Fernandez de la Cueva Enriquez, Duque de Alburquerque, one-time viceroy of New Spain. The site had been known in the previous century as the Bosque Grande de San Francisco Xavier, so the name of this Saint was attached to the church in the new village. However, in deference to King Philip V of Spain, San Felipe de Neri was soon substituted officially, although the change in local usage came about slowly. The church building on the north side of the plaza was erected in 1793.

Other small settlements came into existence in the years following the founding of Albuquerque. On the south side lay Atrisco with a name derived from the Aztec word Atlixco, the name of a valley near Puebla, Mexico. Farther along the placita of San Isidro de Pajarito developed on the land granted to Captain Antonio Baca; then came Los Padillas, established about 1718. A group of genizaro families who were hispanicised Plains Indians settled in 1740 at Valencia, the site of the seventeenth century ranch of Captain Francisco Valencia, and at Tome where Captain Dominguez de Mendoza, distinguished military leader of the latter part of the same century once held title to the land. Governor Don Tomas Veles Cachupin responded favorably to a petition for land in 1764 for the village of San Gabriel de las Nutrias, south of Tome, and other settlers moved onto the land across the river at Belen.

Northward from the Duke City, New Mexicans spread along the valley to Alameda where Francisco Montes Vigil, corporal in the presidial troop of Santa Fe, was a pioneer land owner. The nearby pueblo of Sandia, abandoned in the rebellion of 1680, was resettled in 1748 by refugees induced to return from Hopiland by Franciscan missionaries. The church was dedicated to Nuestra Senora de los Dolores y San Antonio. The site of Las Huertas, east of Bernalillo, better known today as Placitas, was occupied by settlers in 1767, and about mid-century a few settlers were located at Los Corrales west of the Rio Grande. Some time past mid-century, a few families located at San Isidro near the mouth of Jemez Canyon and also north of Bernalillo at the sites of Algodones and Angostura. Vallecito in the Jemez Mountains was occupied in 1768 with the folks looking to Santo Toribio as their patron Saint.

To the east of Albuquerque, Governor Cachupin granted permission in 1763 for settlers to locate in Carnue (Tijeras) Canyon. However, the site was too exposed to attacks by Apaches and was abandoned in 1770. One more attempt was made the following year, but an overnight stay convinced the men that they should not remain. Their predicament was illustrated more sharply about 1774 when the Navahos erupted on the western frontier and drove away the land grant folks. Las Nutrias to the south and Las Huertas to the north were also abandoned.

Upper Photo — Los Griegos, about 1885.
Lower Photo — Albuquerque, 1885. View westward toward Rio Grande. Large building is San Felipe Hotel, later the Elk's Club. (U.N.M. Library collection)

All told, from October of 1774 to March of 1775 there were five invasions by Comanches from the east, eight by Gila Apaches from the southwest and three actions by Navahos. Consequently, for the remainder of the century the New Mexicans remained crowded within the confines of the Rio Abajo.

Further expansion of settlements began with the opening of the nineteenth century. Los Lunas became the jumping off point for a road to the west from the Rio Abajo. Settlers reoccupied the site of Cebolleta and managed to retain possession under pressure from the government to do so in spite of Navaho attacks. The village of Cubero was established in 1834, much to the annoyance of the Laguna folks who claimed the land.

Southward from Belen the placitas of Los Gabaldones, Los Chaves, and Sausal appeared. Casa Colorado was established in 1823 on the abandoned site of Las Nutrias. Carnue (Tijeras) Canyon again lured the people to take up choice bits of land at San Miguel in 1816. Three years later they received a formal grant which extended from the mouth of the canyon to about Sedillo Hill and northward to San Antonio del Carnue which today lies astride State Highway 10. The site of San Antonito, a few miles north of San Antonio, was reserved as a campsite for travelers heading for the Santa Fe trail by way of the Galisteo Valley. Many years later, Andres Nuanes, age 85, recalled the establishment of San Miguel because "at that time I was coming along with a cart load of wood & my oxen's got scared on seeing so many people in the canon & upset the cart & the people assisted me in fixing my cart."

Gold was found in 1828 in the Sierra Obscura or Ortiz Mountain, giving rise to the mining camp of El Real de Dolores, more commonly known as the Placer (Old Placers mining district). About a decade later another strike created the New Placer or Placer del Tuerto, also known as Real de San Francisco, but finally by the prosaic nome of Golden (New Placers mining district, San Pedro Mountains). The boom brought in a population estimated at 4,000 persons.

Southward from Carnue (Tijeras) Canyon, settlers moved into the Manzano Mountains as early as 1816. They established a fortified plaza at Manzano and constituted a frontier outpost in that area until the Apaches were placed on reservations and cattlemen could move onto the plains area stretching away to the south and east. The settlers were willing to move away in the 1830's because of their dangerous location, but the authorities did not permit them to do so. In subsequent years they both profited and suffered from the Jicarilla and Mescalero Apaches who traded powder and lead when in a good mood, or stole sheep and occasionally killed a shepherd when in a bad mood. The village of Chilili strengthened the frontier when settlers moved in about 1824, receiving a formal grant of land some fifteen years later.

When General Stephen W. Kearny proclaimed the sovereignty of the United States over New Mexico on August 18, 1846, the responsibility for subduing the Indians was transferred from provincial New Mexican authorities to the United States Government. The picture did not change, however, until the white men had a little war of their own. In its course, the Confederate forces under Brigadier General H. H. Sibley defeated the Federal troops under Colonel E. R. S. Canby at Valverde and moved up the valley, taking possession of Albuquerque and the capital. The high tide of success was ended with their defeat in Glorieta Pass. The last firing occurred at Peralta, fifteen miles south of Albuquerque, when a small force of Confederates, having missed the ford across the Rio Grande, engaged in a brief skirmish with Canby's troops. Then the war fever subsided and New Mexicans turned their energies toward building a new commonwealth.

The new departmental commander, General James H. Carleton, compelled the bulk of the Navahos to migrate to the Pecos Valley by way of Albuquerque, Tijeras Canyon, and San Antonito during the years 1863-1866, but two years later the Navaho leaders persuaded the Government to move them home to the mountains, so a sepentine line of men, women, and children wended their way across the Rio Grande about the time when patriotic Americans were holding their annual Independence Day celebration.

With the Navahos subdued, settlers returned to the farm land in the valley of the Rio Puerco northward and southward from El Cabezon, but overgrazing and soil erosion doomed them in the twentieth century. From San Ignacio on the south to La Tijera on the north the people moved away. El Cabezon (or La Posta) managed to survive until the 1950's, so it is the most tangible example of a ghost town created by man's abuse of the land. The development of the highway from Bernalillo to the San Juan Valley boomed the village of Cuba (formerly Nacimiento), now the most prominent settlement on the northern side of the Albuquerque region.

Transportation was essential for the development of New Mexico, and the dreams of those who wanted to join the Orient and Occident in bonds of trade soon brought the railroad to the Rio Abajo. The Atchison, Topeka and Santa Fe Railroad won the contest to serve the region, and the first train rolled into Albuquerque on April 5, 1880. Swinging southward and then westward to take advantage of the easy gradient extending westward from Los Lunas, new towns were born along the way, among them Grants, now the capital of the uranium industry.

Albuquerque boomed and the population increased during the 1880's from 2,600 to 6,100 in round numbers. "Progress was evident . . . as early as 1882 in the graded streets with good sidewalks, three miles of street car line in operation, a telephone exchange with twenty-five miles of wire connecting all parts of the town [the telegraph arrived in 1876], gas lighting on the streets and in residences and business places, blocks of business houses with iron and glass fronts, two banks, two daily newspapers, the **Morning Journal** and the **Evening Review**, five churches, and hotels, stores, and offices necessary to accommodate the public"[2] and about ten houses of prostitution along with the ubiquitous saloon.

The railroad era witnessed the continued rise of population in New Mexico, and the appearance of various institutions that, in addition to church and school, were common to the American scene. The original Grant Opera House served the public in Albuquerque from 1883 until its destruction by fire in 1898. The University of New Mexico opened its doors in the summer of 1892, and gradually became a center of regional studies dealing with the rich and varied cultural heritage of the Southwest. An early symptom appeared when the pueblo style of architecture was adopted for the University in 1906.

The development of the automobile, and highway improvement following World War I, made U. S. Highway 66 a main east-west route and Albuquerque became a crossroads for the region which helped to continue its status as a trade center for the surrounding country. World War II ushered in the Atomic Age and a marked increase of population. Albuquerque alone grew from 35,000 to 200,000 between 1940 and 1960 with the big increase occurring after the War. The great stimulus came from the expenditure of Federal money with the establishment of Sandia Base, Manzano Base, and the Special Weapons center, to the discomfiture of jackrabbits and patrons of Lovers' Lane.

With jet-powered war planes patrolling the skies to ward off a surprise attack from an enemy, the Albuquerque region has experienced a revolution in appearance from the days when Spanish soldiers with sword and breastplate stormed the walls of sun-dried mud in the face of flying arrows tipped with a hard rock—from the age of stone weapons and animal power to the atomic bomb and a new power scarcely yet harnessed for civilian use.

[2]The **Journal**, June 16, 1882, quoted in Lucille Boyle, 1948, **The economic history of Albuquerque, 1880-1893**: Univ. New Mexico unpub. master's thesis, p. 14.

CHRONOLOGICAL RESUME OF SOME EARLY GEOLOGISTS IN THE ALBUQUERQUE COUNTRY

STUART A. NORTHROP
University of New Mexico

To avoid much repetition, no bibliography is appended to this resume. The interested reader can find most of the sources by consulting the annual bibliographies compiled by the U. S. Geological Survey or the summary ones compiled by the New Mexico Bureau of Mines and Mineral Resources.

Prehistoric inhabitants of the area exploited minerals and rocks but left no record of "geologic" observations. The first recorded observations, beginning in 1540, are to be found in the chronicles and narratives of early Spanish expeditions. The Spaniards were particularly interested in gold, turquois, copper, sulfur, and salt.

1807.—Lieut. Zebulon M. Pike made a few observations after he had been arrested and was being escorted to Santa Fe and southward to Mexico.

1828.—Placer gold discovered in Ortiz Mountains (Old Placers)—the first important discovery of gold west of the Mississippi River.

1833.—Gold-quartz veins discovered near the Old Placers.

1839.—New Placers discovered in San Pedro Mountains.

1841.—Thomas Falconer, a Fellow of the Geological Society of London, was arrested while a member of the Texan-Santa Fe expedition. His field notes and mineral collection were seized. Our first real geologist was off to a good start!

1844.—Josiah Gregg, most famous of all the early Santa Fe traders, wrote a chapter on the mines of New Mexico for his book, "Commerce of the Prairies." He noted gold mines, salt at Estancia, use of selenite for windowpanes, and the large petrified logs near Cerrillos (first mention of fossils?).

1846.—A notable year—geologic observations made by three men: Dr. F. A. Wislizenus, Lieut. W. H. Emory, and Lieut. J. W. Abert. The last-named saw the "immense petrified trees" near Cerrillos, and in the valley of the Rio Puerco he found "shark teeth, fish bones, fragments of large ammonites, and pieces of inoceramus." (The shark teeth were illustrated by lithograph.)

1849.—Lieut. J. H. Simpson found "beautiful specimens of petrified wood" near Cabezon; illustrated in color.

1853.—During the period 1853-1856 geologic reconnaissance for railroad routes across New Mexico was carried on by several geologists. Jules Marcou, a French-Swiss geologist, accompanied Lieut. A. W. Whipple on his exploration of the 35th parallel. Marcou's field notes in French, together with a translation by W. P. Blake (in parallel columns), were published in 1856. In 1858 Marcou published in Zurich his modestly entitled book, "Geology of North America," in which is a chapter, "Geology of New ·Mexico." He visited Pecos and Tijeras, collecting Pennsylvanian fossils which he described and illustrated. At Tijeras he collected the types of **Spirifer rockymontanus**. Then, on October 8, 1853, he wrote:

"I started with my friend Dr. John Bigelow, the botanist of the expedition, to ascend the highest peak' of the Sierra de Sandia *** The ascent of one of the most elevated summits of the Rocky Mountains,—which after all is not a very easy matter, considering the wilderness, the difficulty of the roads and the fear of the Apache Indians—was effected by Dr. Bigelow and myself the 10th of October 1853. We chose the most elevated point of the Sierra de Sandia seen from Albuquerque, which attains the height of 12,000 feet above the level of the sea." (Heat waves may have introduced this error in their triangulation. Anyway it wasn't important in the selection of a route for the railroad!) Marcou prepared a colored geologic map of a strip across New Mexico.

1857.—Prof. John Strong Newberry accompanied Lieut. J. C. Ives in 1857-58 (published 1861) and Capt. J. N. Macomb in 1859 (not published until 1876).

1870.—Collections made during the 1870's by parties of the U. S. Geological Surveys West of the 100th Meridian under Lieut. G. M. Wheeler were studied by mineralogists and both invertebrate and vertebrate paleontologists.

1880.—Gen. U. S. Grant visited the New Placers district. Benjamin Silliman, Jr. was in New Mexico looking at gold placers.

1881.—Several prizes of $100 each were offered at the Territorial Fair in Albuquerque, Oct. 3-8, for collections of minerals and ores. This year an attempt was made to pipe water from the Sandias to the New Placers.

1884.—Capt. Clarence E. Dutton, of the Ordnance Corps, was supposed to study the volcanics of the Cascade Range in 1884, but the topographic mapping had been delayed. Meanwhile, topographers mapping northwestern New Mexico had brought back such glowing accounts of the volcanic necks of the Rio Puerco valley that

"the Director was of the opinion that a single season could be spent with advantage in studying them. The Cascade business was therefore postponed for a year, and I was ordered to New Mexico to see what was there."

Thus Dutton came to New Mexico and that great classic, "Mount Taylor and the Zuni plateau,"[1] resulted from a single summer's work. I have not checked the weather records, but it must have been hot. "At the town of Albuquerque," Dutton saw "the Zandia Range, a large and rather imposing mountain ridge." He did not tarry long, however, because

"In the immediate valley of the Rio Grande the climate is temperate in winter and insufferable in summer; higher up the summers are temperate and the winters barely sufferable *** Even the sagebrush, the ashy bloom of the desert elsewhere, resents the

---
[1] Dutton, C. E., 1885, U. S. Geol. Survey 6th Ann. Rept., p. 105-198, illus.

Air view of Cabezon Peak and other volcanic
necks in the valley of the Rio Puerco.
Dick Kent Photography, Albuquerque.

scorching summer and refuses to stay, and the cacti, vengeful and repellant everywhere, here assume a still more cruel and misanthropic mien."

So Dutton hurried westward to the plateau country—the Zuni Plateau and Mount Taylor. His report contains an interesting disquisition on topographic terms borrowed from the Spanish.

"And by the way, what is a mesa? What is the special significance of this term? And why is it used instead of good Anglo-Saxon? I will answer these questions by asking another. Did it ever occur to the reader how poverty stricken the (I will not say English exactly, but) Anglo-American language is in sharp, crisp, definite topographic terms? *** But the Spanish—or Mexican, if you prefer—is rich in topographic terms which are delightfully expressive and definite. There is scarcely a feature of the land which repeats itself with similar characteristics that has not a pat name. And these terms are euphonious as well as precise; they designate things objective as happily and concisely as the Saxon designates things subjective. Therefore we use them. There are no others adapted to the purpose."

He notes that it is not necessary that the high tabular surface should be completely encircled by a cliff to be called a mesa. Thus rock terraces, even sloping pediment surfaces, have come to be called mesas. (Many years ago I received an inquiry as to the definition of the term "arroyo." This correspondence led me to write a squib, "Terms from the Spanish," eventually published in AMERICAN SPEECH, v. 12, p. 79-81, 1937. In addition to mesa, arroyo, and canon [with tilde], other geomorphic terms from the Spanish include bajada, barranca, bolson, canada, ceja, cienega, cordillera, cuesta, playa, rincon, rio, and sierra.)

Dutton was far more interested in the volcanic necks and lava flows than in Mount Taylor, which he described as

"a large conical pile, planted upon a lofty

Copy (X ½) of Kirk Bryan's (1909) geologic map of the Albuquerque area. Note how most of the city lay west of the railroad; the small rectangle northwest of Powder House Hill is the campus of the University of New Mexico.

The original map, printed in five colors by Rand, McNally & Co., Chicago, accompanied Bryan's paper, "Geology of the vicinity of Albuquerque," Univ. New Mexico Bull. 51, geol. ser., v. 3, no. 1, 24 p., 7 figs., map, 1909. Kirk Bryan was the second geology major to receive the B. A. degree from U. N. M. (1909). In those days a senior thesis was required. The paper deals with the Tertiary and Quaternary geology. Units discussed include the Rio Grande beds, Rio Grande gravels, University beds, Recent deposits, basalt, and the Albuquerque marl.

mesa. It has no neighbors of its own kith and kin.*** Of Mount Taylor itself there is little to be said, and the description may be very brief. Its structure and composition have nothing of novelty.*** If the cone of Mount Taylor were all that this locality has to present for study it would hardly have repaid the trouble of a visit. But the volcanic district of which it is the culminating point presents matter of great interest and instruction when viewed as a whole, for it discloses clearly the origin of the great lava caps which form such a conspicuous feature in many parts of the West, and offers a wide range of information concerning the modes of accumulation of lavas in the basic group."

"If we stand upon the eastern brink of the Mount Taylor mesa we shall overlook the broad valley of the Puerco (East). The spectacle is a fine one and in some respects extraordinary. The edge of the mesa suddenly descends by a succession of ledges and slopes nearly 2,000 feet into the rugged and highly diversified valley-plain below. The country beneath is a medley of low cliffs or bluffs, showing the light browns and pale yellows of the lower and middle Cretaceous sandstones and shales. Out of this confused patchwork of bright colors rise several objects of remarkable aspect. They are apparently inaccessible eyries of black rock, and at a rough guess, by comparison with the known altitudes of surrounding objects, their heights above the mean level of the adjoining plain may range from 800 to 1,500 feet. The blackness of their shade may be exaggerated by contrast with the brilliant colors of the rocks and soil out of which they rise, but their forms are even more striking. *** These black rocks are technically called 'necks'."

Dutton describes a number of the larger necks and gives excellent illustrations, photographed on wood. Ironically, he was unable to visit the highest (2,000 feet) and most impressive, Cabezon. He wrote: "I had already been long away from my base of supplies and a tedious journey of nearly a hundred miles was necessary in order to reach it."

Another excellent account is Douglas Johnson's "Volcanic necks of the Mount Taylor region, New Mexico" (1907). And a generation later came C. B. Hunt's "Igneous geology and structure of the Mount Taylor volcanic field, New Mexico" (1938). This seems to be the finest display of volcanic necks in the United States. Hunt thought that there might be about fifty of them, but Dutton (1885, p. 168) wrote that there are "scores *** and perhaps *** several hundreds of them. *** Thus nature has wonderfully dissected out for us the structure of these volcanoes and has dug away the earth from their roots. There is every gradation in the amount of exhumation and in the amount of destruction." Dutton's style is as unique as the necks about which he wrote. One can read what he wrote with pleasure.

1885.—Many geologists have lived and worked in the Albuquerque country since Dutton. Around the turn of the century, that most prolific writer, Charles Rollin Keyes, came to New Mexico and the New Mexico School of Mines; our stratigraphic nomenclature abounds with many names from his pen. Two of the early presidents of the University of New Mexico, Clarence Luther Herrick (first professor of geology and second president) and William George Tight, were geologists. Certain U. N. M. alumni later attained fame: Douglas Johnson, 1901; Kirk Bryan, 1909; Walter Frank Gouin, 1916; and John Walter Gruner, 1917. Johnson did the geology of the Cerrillos Hills for his Ph.D. at Columbia under Prof. Kemp (and Lobeck was Johnson's first graduate student).

Many readers may be surprised to learn that a national meeting of the Geological Society of America was held in Albuquerque in December 1907. Only 28 Fellows attended—the smallest national meeting since the one held at Columbus, Ohio in 1891, with only 23 attending. But at the first meeting of the Society, held at Ithaca, New York, 1888, the attendance was only 13.

ABSOLUTE GEOLOGIC TIME SCALE

One of the most fascinating questions—to the professional geologist as well as the layman—is: how old is it? Early age determinations were based almost wholly on the uranium / lead and thorium / lead ratios. More recently, other methods have been used, such as the lead / alpha-particle ratio, the potassium / argon ratio, and the rubidium / strontium ratio. For the uppermost end of the time table—the last few thousand years (of more interest to the archeologist)—the carbon-14 or radiocarbon method is suitable.

For several decades the uranium / lead and thorium / lead determinations gave the following approximate dates, widely cited in various textbooks:

Cenozoic Era
    60-70 million years ago
Mesozoic Era
    200 million years ago
Paleozoic Era
    500 million years ago
Precambrian (Cryptozoic) Eon
    3,000 million years ago

Within the last few years a great deal of research has been accomplished and a more reliable time scale seems to be emerging. The beginning of the Paleozoic Era has been pushed back about a hundred million years. The recent work is ably summarized by J. L. Kulp (1961), and the new scale, together with certain stratigraphic units of the Albuquerque country, is given below.

REFERENCE

Kulp, J. L., 1961, Geologic time scale: Science, v. 133, p. 1105-1114 [April 14, 1961].

Era	Period	Key Formations	Millions of Years Ago
CENOZOIC			
	Quaternary (Pleistocene)	Several fms.	
			1
	Tertiary	Several fms. Santa Fe group San Jose formation Nacimiento formation	
			65
MESOZOIC			
	Cretaceous	Many stratigraphic units	
			135
	Jurassic	Morrison Todilto Entrada	
			180
	Triassic	Chinle and Dockum	
			230
PALEOZOIC			
	Permian	San Andres, etc. Yeso Abo	
			280
	Pennsylvanian	Madera Sandia	
			310
	Mississippian	Arroyo Penasco and Tererro	
			345
	Devonian	(missing?)	405
	Silurian	(missing)	425
	Ordovician	(missing)	500
	Cambrian	(missing)	600
PRECAMBRIAN (CRYPTOZOIC) EON			
		Sandia granite	1,350
		Older sedimentary and igneous rocks	?

PRECAMBRIAN ROCKS OF THE ALBUQUERQUE COUNTRY

J. PAUL FITZSIMMONS
University of New Mexico

ABSTRACT

Precambrian rocks are found in the cores of the mountain ranges of the Albuquerque country. Medium-grade regionally metamorphosed rocks, including quartzite, quartz-mica schist, greenstone, and metarhyolite, generally with northeast trend and steep dip, are the country rocks in which microcline granite and more or less related dike rocks (pegmatites, aplites, lamprophyres) have been emplaced. Quartz-feldspar gneiss is present in many localities, contiguous to the granite. Both gneiss and granite have been modified by potash metasomatism. Radioactive measurements indicate an age of 1,350 million years for the granite and suggest that the Precambrian rocks of the Albuquerque country were deformed, metamorphosed, and invaded by granite during the Mazatzal revolution.

INTRODUCTION

Of Paleozoic and younger rocks one may ask, for any specified area: are they present? For Precambrian rocks, this question is superfluous. Precambrian rocks are everywhere present. The question is rather: are they exposed? Rocks of other ages may be missing entirely, having never been deposited or having been eroded away after deposition, but one needs merely to probe deeply enough, if the rocks are not at the surface, to be sure of encountering Precambrian formations. The pre-eminence attained by this world-wide distribution, however, is offset by extensive burial beneath some or all of the representatives of later ages. Probing, theoretically very neat and tidy, is expensive and time consuming, and it is not comparable with a full view of the rocks. One does not gain full enjoyment or understanding of a symphony by hearing three isolated measures from widely spaced parts of the composition. At best he may get some notion of the key, the tempo, the constituents of the orchestra; but keys may change between measures, tempos may increase or decrease, and all instruments do not play incessantly. Similarly, a few probes will not give complete information about the basement rocks. No system of indirect observation can substitute for good outcrops.

In the Albuquerque country, Precambrian rocks crop out on the steep western slopes of the faulted Sandia, Manzanita, and Manzano Mountains, in smaller masses in faulted zones within these ranges, on the steep western slopes and along the crest of the faulted Nacimiento and San Pedro Mountains, in a few small faulted zones east of the main mass of Precambrian rock in these mountains, on the steep eastern slope of the Lucero uplift (in one small area), and in the core of the domal Zuni Mountains.

ROCKS

This Precambrian terrane is represented chiefly by a sequence of regionally metamorphosed rocks, clastic sedimentary and volcanic, in which large volumes of granitic rocks have been emplaced. Locally there is moot evidence of thermal metamorphism and of retrogressive metamorphism, but the dominant process has been regional.

Quartzite is one of the most abundant metamorphic rock types, particularly in the Sandia-Manzano zone. In places it consists almost exclusively of quartz, but much of it exhibits some admixture—sericite, biotite, kyanite (rare), apatite, magnetite, hematite, feldspar; the contacts are commonly gradational into quartz-feldspar gneiss or into quartz-mica schist. The gradational zones to quartz-feldspar gneiss may be due to original increase of feldspar in the clastic sediments, to produce arkosic sandstone, or they may be due to feldspathization during or attendant upon regional metamorphism. The gradations to quartz-mica schist are probably due to gradual increase of original clay admixture. That the quartzite is metamorphosed sandstone there can be no doubt: cross-lamination has been observed in many places. But a clastic source for the feldspar has not been established beyond question.

Foliation in the quartzite is displayed by streakings of the admixtures: stringers of sericite, lenses and bands of hematite flakes, and zones of discoloration too nebulous to define microscopically. The color of the quartzite ranges from white through light gray to dark gray. Locally, greenish and reddish zones are observed, but these are minor.

The quartzite is generally resistant and forms prominent ridges. It forms the backbone of the ridge crossing U. S. Highway 66 at "Dead-man's curve" in Tijeras Canyon. It also forms the constriction at Abo Pass on U. S. Highway 60 at the south end of the Manzano Mountains.

Quartz-mica schists, ranging from micaceous quartzites to rocks with mica predominating, are widespread constituents of the Precambrian terrane. They are the dominant rock at the north end of the Sandia Mountains, are present in Tijeras Canyon, and are found at many places in the Manzanita and Manzano Mountains (as well as in the Los Pinos Mountains farther to the south). Mica-rich varieties are not abundant. Both biotite and muscovite may be present, the former very rarely occurring without the latter. The grain size in some of these rocks is so fine that it were better to call the rocks phyllites. They commonly display a sheen, a crumpled or crenulated surface, and few megascopically identifiable minerals; the microscope shows the principal minerals to be quartz and sericite. Accessories are generally oligoclase-andesine, biotite, epidote, garnet, chlorite, magnetite, and rare apatite and zircon.

Colors of the schist range from pinkish gray through silvery gray (particularly the phyllitic rocks) to dark gray. Many are stained brown or yellowish brown on weathering surfaces. Exposures are generally poor because of rapid disintegration along foliation planes and secondary fractures.

Quartz-feldspar gneisses are found in Tijeras Canyon and are very abundant in the Nacimiento Mountains. Banded gneisses are not common. Most of the gneisses are lenticular, with undulatory planes of foliation; augen gneisses are characteristic. The augen are mostly pink microcline. Oligoclase-andesine is an abundant feldspar in these rocks, exceeding the microcline in many places, but it occurs in finer grains and is more uniformly spread throughout the rock. The quartz shows moderate straining and has sutured borders. Accessories are biotite, less hornblende and epidote, and occasional sphene, apatite, zircon, and magnetite. The predominant color is pink, but may be anything from pinkish gray to bright red.

In Tijeras Canyon this rock has a composition remarkably similar to that of the contiguous "Sandia granite," except that microcline is not so abundant and does not show the sieve structure so characteristic of this mineral in the granite. Also the plagioclase in the gneiss is cleaner, less altered, than in the granite.

Some quartz-feldspar gneiss consists almost exclusively of these two minerals (or three, for two kinds of feldspar are invariably present), with only minor amounts of other minerals. In some varieties, however, biotite forms up to ten percent of the rock. In none of these rocks does hornblende form the dominant mafic constituent.

Lodewick (1960) found rounded (eroded) zircons in the gneiss in Tijeras Canyon and, on this basis, postulated a metasedimentary origin. This is a significant position in view of the similarity of mineral composition of the gneiss to composition of the adjacent granite.

Erosional forms on the gneiss greatly resemble granitic terrain: moderately resistant rounded knolls and undulating uplands. Such landscape is typical in the Nacimiento Mountains.

Greenstone is a term used to designate a rather diverse assemblage of rocks, most of which are more or less metamorphosed flows, sills, dikes, and tuffs of the basaltic or basalt-andesitic kindred. Clastic rocks may be included, but more by virtue of propinquity than of consanguinity. The greenstone consists mostly of foliates, though in places the foliation is feeble and inconspicuous; chlorite schists and epidote amphibolites are perhaps the most typical members. Locally one may find, on microscopic examination, some traces of the character of the original rocks—saussuritized plagioclase, and altered, but not wholly obscured, pyroxene—but generally, though the grade of metamorphism is moderate, relict textures have been destroyed. Commonly, where one might expect to find amphibolite, he finds hornblende schist, that is, a rock containing quartz and little or no feldspar. Some of the rocks of Tijeras Canyon contain both plagioclase and quartz, though the former is generally more abundant than the latter. Intercalated rocks of rather insignificant volume include metasilts and metashales, which have now the structures and compositions of quartz phyllites and slates.

The general hue of the greenstone is very dark green. Local zones are somewhat lighter, especially among the chlorite schists, but the deviation from dark green is not marked. Small localized zones of greenstone are found among other types of metamorphic rocks, but there are also large continuous masses, one of the largest forming much of the south side of Tijeras Canyon, below the ledge of Madera limestone, and extending southward into the Manzanita Mountains. The units of the greenstone are not generally resistant, decomposing readily and eroding easily. Where exposed on slopes they are protected by more resistant cap rock.

Metarhyolite has been reported from a number of places in the Precambrian terrane of the Albuquerque country. The evidence for calling some of this rock metarhyolite is flimsy: perhaps nothing more than fine grain size and general composition. But there appears to be sufficient evidence (of relict structures and of enduring minerals) that metarhyolite is present in considerable volume, apart from the doubtful masses. A characteristic feature of the varieties of this rock is a rather high content of quartz, generally 50 to 80 percent, a rather curious phenomenon when it is recalled that high quartz content in such rocks as gneiss is frequently considered a criterion for sedimentary origin. Quartz in excess of 50 percent is not typical of rhyolites.

However, many investigators have reported considerable thicknesses of metarhyolite in the Albuquerque region: Reiche (1949) in the North Manzano Mountains, Stark (1956) in the South Manzano Mountains, and Bruns (1959) in Tijeras Canyon. Harbour (1960) has indicated over a thousand feet of such rock in the Franklin Mountains, far to the south, and Just (1937), Montgomery (1953), Barker (1958), and Muehlberger (1960) have mapped similar rocks in the Petaca and Picuris region in northern New Mexico. Metarhyolite is also an important constituent of possibly correlative rocks in central Arizona (Wilson, 1939). Flawn (1956) has reported a great northeast-trending belt of rhyolitic and related rocks (Panhandle volcanic terrane) in the covered basement of eastern New Mexico and the Texas panhandle, but he has stated that these rocks are virtually free of metamorphic effects.

In weathering characteristics, the metarhyolite is somewhere between the schists and the gneisses. Indeed, the rock is fundamentally a schistose to gneissose quartz-feldspar rock with varying, but generally minor, proportions of muscovite and biotite.

Granite is perhaps the most abundant type of Precambrian rock in the Albuquerque country, at least in surface exposures. There are undoubtedly many individual bodies of granitic rock, but the compositional variations are not great. The rock is generally rather coarse grained, though fine-grained varieties are locally present. Much of it is porphyritic, or, what is more likely, porphyroblastic. Large insets of microcline, ranging up to three inches across, are fairly common and abundant. All weathered granite takes on brownish or yellowish brown hues, but in fresh cuts the granite of the region ranges from a medium gray to red. Some areas consist almost exclusively of gray granite. In this variety the microcline, as might be expected, is gray. Quartz is commonly blue. Elsewhere the granite is pink or red, chiefly because of coloration in the microcline. The relation of one variety of granite to the other is not everywhere systematic, but some generalizations may be drawn. In the Sandia Mountains the rock immediately underlying the late Paleozoic strata along the crest of the range is characteristically red. Downslope the granite becomes pinker in hue, not so deeply colored, and at the base gray granite is typical. There are no sharp contacts marking these as distinct units, and the gradation is not persistent or invariable. Furthermore, red granite may be found in localized zones in the midst of gray granite. Mineralogically there is little difference between megascopic color varieties. One feature alone seems rather systematic. Secondary epidote is widely present throughout the other outcrop areas of Precambrian granite in the Albuquerque country. It is much more abundant, however, in the red granite. Or, perhaps it would be nearer the truth to say that red granite that is localized in predominantly gray granite is almost always accompanied by abundant epidote. Microcline is generally the dominant feldspar. It appears to engulf minerals, or to invade them, or to occupy interstitial zones that resemble late filling less than late invasion or late replacement. Except in definitely weathered specimens, it appears to be fresh everywhere in the rock. Albite or albite-oligoclase is invariably present, usually in lesser amounts than the microcline. It always appears cloudy or dirty by virtue of alteration to clay or other secondary minerals. Quartz is abundant, commonly forming 30 to 35 percent of the rock, and is characteristically strained. Extinction in this mineral is not merely undulatory, but aggregate-undulatory; that is, what appears in plain light to be a large quartz grain proves to be an aggregate of many small units, each with its particular undulatory pattern. The composite picture is one of extremely uneven extinction. Biotite is the common mafic mineral and is present everywhere, but the content is generally less than 10 percent, mostly less than 5 percent. Hornblende is rarely present, though there is some indication locally that the biotite is secondary after hornblende. Sphene is ubiquitous as an accessory, usually occurring in reddish brown euhedral wedge-shaped crystals. Apatite also is almost universally present. Magnetite is the common opaque mineral, though ilmenite is also present, and, at least in Tijeras Canyon, pyrite also. The fairly recent road cuts of Tijeras Canyon have exposed rocks fresher than can generally be found in other Precambrian areas of the Albuquerque country. It is in these fresh rocks that pyrite may be seen. It is never found in rocks long exposed at the surface, because of its great susceptibility to weathering. It may very well be that pyrite is present in most of the granite of the Albuquerque country, but that it eludes our scrutiny because it remains only in fresh rock below the surface.

Statistical work on a number of orogenic zones about the world, particularly in Fennoscandia, Greenland, Canada, and Sierra Leone, indicates that different phases of granitic rocks are associated with stages of orogenic development. Early kinematic, late kinematic, and post-kinematic granitic rocks have been distinguished. The synkinematic rocks are generally granodioritic or dioritic in composition, predominantly gray in color, and mostly gneissic. Post-kinematic rocks are more frequently pink or reddish, have more potash than soda, and are generally directionless.

It is not easy to fit the granitic masses of the Albuquerque country into this scheme. The first question is: are there two (or more) granites? or is there but one? And if there is but one, to which stage does it belong? More detailed work needs to be done to bring the full illuminating light of understanding into focus on this problem, but present data appear to indicate but a single granitic phase, at least in respect to the orogenic classification outlined above. Firstly, the mineral content, while not perfectly homogeneous, does not vary greatly; it attests to a single process of petrogenesis. Secondly, the color variation, however suggestive it may appear, does not permit any profound orogenic interpretation at this time. In its relation to the crest of the mountain, that is, toward the ancient erosion surface, it suggests an association with weathering or some other surface phenomenon, though I am not prepared to say that this is so. A knowledge of what the color is, where it lies, what causes it is imperative before any decision can be made on this matter. It is not yet clear whether the color is due to staining, to primary incorporation of matter, or whether it is due to cooling history or crystallization history (and thus not directly related to chemistry in the sense normally suspected).

Some have suggested that the local zones of red granite in the gray granite are actually late intrusions, whether immediately later or much later. This may be true, but it appears strange that both the gray granite and the red granite contain similar inclusions—xenoliths—of metamorphic country rock. If the red granite invaded a zone of gray granite, what happened to the gray granite? If the later rock digested the earlier rock, either by piecemeal stoping or by replacement, where did the inclusions come from? And why are there no inclusions of gray granite—merely of the metamorphic rock? The red granite appears to be due to a later process than the initial emplacement of the gray granite, but it would seem that this process may have been a milder one than the emplacement of a completely new rock.

No dogmatism will be displayed here regarding the origin of these granitic masses. It is doubtful that sufficient data are yet at hand to permit such presumption. Lodewick (1960) found euhedral zircons in the granite and, because of this, proposed that the Sandia granite is igneous. The conclusion may be valid, but not solely from this evidence. It is known that zircons will form in a metamorphic environment if the physicochemical conditions are suitable. Rounded zircons may present a very cogent argument for sedimentary origin, but euhedral zircons, however suggestive their presence, do not uniquely define igneous origin. There is, on the opposite side, evidence that metasomatic replacement has occurred on a rather grand scale, within the granite, within inclusions, and within some of the contiguous foliated rocks. But it will still be contended, with justification, that the demonstration of metasomatic replacement in contact zones, or even throughout an entire granitic mass, does not constitute proof that the granite as a whole is a metasomatic body. And there, for the moment, the matter lies. The most obvious metasomatic phenomenon in the Precambrian rocks of the Albuquerque area is the growth of microcline porphyroblasts. Large crystals of microcline, precisely like those in the granite proper, are found scattered through xenoliths of schist; indeed, in places they may actually pierce the contact, extending into both the granite and the xenolith. With no great strain to the mind, even the unimaginative mind, one may fancy that he sees these porphyroblasts caught in the process of growing. Even within the granite, with no reference to the relation of the microcline to xenoliths or to country rock, one may observe peculiarities in this mineral that attest to a "birth date" later than the formation of the rest of the rock. These peculiarities include sieve structure (numerous inclusions of quartz and altered plagioclase), invading stringers and embayments into both quartz and plagioclase, and interstitial positions much more suggestive of invasion than of passive filling (that is, the interstices are "open," not "closed"; linear, not confined; continuous, not isolated).

If the above-indicated observations reflect actual historical events, and if but one granitic phase is present (despite the titillating enigma of the red coloration), the process of granite emplacement was probably synkinematic. Without the secondary microcline the rock would be granodioritic or tonalitic, and hence, if the scheme is valid, synkinematic. Many feldspathized (microcline) synkinematic granites have been noted in other orogenic zones, and this possibility for the Sandia granite is thus an acceptable one to many students of the problem.

Xenoliths in the granite offer a tantalizing challenge to the curious. In the Sandia Mountains these are observed in most parts of the granitic mass, though they are more abundant in some zones than in others. The zones of greater abundance, however, cannot yet be related to any systematic distribution of country rock, contacts, erosion surfaces, or to any other known point of reference.

The xenoliths are of several kinds, obviously reflecting the country rock from which they came, but correlations on this evidence cannot be made. The xenoliths are not numerous enough, and continuations of the xenolithic zones into the country rock cannot be followed, because of lack of outcrops (truncation by fault zones or by covers of younger rocks). The xenoliths range in size from minute to two or three feet in length, and, exceptionally, to six or eight feet in length. A black, mildly schistose rock is very common as an inclusion. It consists of quartz, biotite, andesine, abundant hornblende, and porphyroblasts of microcline. Epidote is generally present. Quartzite xenoliths are also found, though not in such abundance. They too contain porphyroblasts of microcline and abundant epidote.

The xenoliths are generally flattened and elongate, but nearly spherical forms are not rare. In most places one needs to exert his imaginative faculties to discern any pattern of orientation of the xenoliths, but in a few zones a definte pattern may be observed over distances up to one hundred feet and more, and here the plane of the xenoliths appears to be horizontal.

In the South Manzano Mountains, Dorman (Stark, 1956) noted inclusions somewhat similar to those found in the Sandia Mountains, but exhibiting more systematic orientation. Dorman was able to measure strikes and dips on a number of these inclusions, and his observations indicate that the strike of the xenoliths diverges about 20° from the strike of the foliation in the country rock. His solution to this discrepancy is that "the granite was emplaced by injection and that its inclusions and schlieren are fragments of the country rock carried along in the flowing mass." It is not easy to see why flow lines, if they occur, should diverge appreciably from the contact (and the contact appears to parallel the foliation in the area indicated). Even more uncongenial to my mind is the attempted resolution of this view with any concept of emplacement of granitic masses. If the granite be magmatic and flow into an open chamber, then there might be current for orientation of inclusions torn from the sides of the chamber. Or, if the magma forcibly thrust the country rock aside, the movement might occur at some appreciable rate and produce flow orientation. But if piecemeal stoping be the mode of emplacement (and there is no evidence that the country rocks have been pushed aside to make room for the granite mass, nor, certainly, any evidence that a cavity was excavated first), how great a current can be postulated for invading magma? Piecemeal stoping entails downward movement of stoped blocks, a movement contrary to any possible current of invasion. The question may be asked here: if the granite is magmatic, what mechanism of emplacement would produce sufficient current, at an angle of 20° to the contact, to orient included blocks? It would seem, on investigating trends among the foliated rocks, that a divergence of 20° is no greater than frequently measured between members of a foliated sequence where no problem of separate origin (because of divergence) could possibly arise. Trends among schists and gneisses are not uniform and consistent, and I think, in view of the still meager data, that we should not ignore the possibility that the indicated trend of xenoliths may be relict trends of the rocks that occupied the site before the granite was emplaced.

The granite weathers in typical fashion, producing spheroidally weathered boulders, which clutter the surface, form tor-like hummocks, or stand poised on "tiny feet," tempting man and nature alike to thrust them from their pedestals. The xenoliths are, as a rule, more resistant than the host granite, and stand out as knobs on the weathered surfaces.

Dike rocks in the Precambrian terrane may be assigned to one of three types: pegmatite, aplite, and lamprophyre. Spatially they have little relation to each other. Aplites appear to be most widespread of this group. Pegmatites are localized, but are very abundant in a few areas. Lamprophyres tend to be somewhat localized and somewhat uncommon, but a few dikes persist over distances greater than any of the pegmatites or aplites.

Pegmatites are very abundant in the rincon, or outer prong, in the Juan Tabo area at the north end of the Sandia Mountains. A few occur in Tijeras Canyon and others are to be found wherever granitic masses occur. They are not confined to the granite. In fact, in the Juan Tabo area they are much more abundant in the metamorphic rocks adjacent to the granite, though some are completely within the granite, and some cut across the contact. Most are merely aggregates of quartz and feldspar, commonly intergrown in graphic structure. Microcline is the dominant feldspar, but oligoclase is generally present. Muscovite is practically absent in some pegmatites, but may constitute up to eight percent of the mass, locally forming books up to one inch across. Schorlite is generally absent, but is present in some pegmatites in amounts up to three or four percent. Other constituents are rare: ilmenite, magnetite, and garnet.

The pegmatites are mostly pinkish white, pink microcline and white quartz being intimately intergrown in parts of the mass, occurring in segregated zones in other parts. The longest pegmatite dike observed is about half a mile long (in the Juan Tabo area of the Sandia Mountains). Most are but a few feet long (up to a hundred feet) and are rather irregular in outline. In the Juan Tabo area the largest number of pegmatite bodies have a northwesterly trend, at right angles to the foliation of the metamorphic rocks. A few pegmatites, especially in the northern part of the Juan Tabo area, parallel the foliation.

Aplites are mostly pink dike rocks, consisting almost exclusively of quartz and feldspar, with very minor muscovite or, less commonly, biotite, and generally exhibiting sharp straight contacts. Quartz-feldspar dikes might be better terminology, because many do not have typical aplitic, or sugary-grained, texture. The grain size may vary markedly within short distances, or it may be fairly uniform and persistent. Some dikes have coarse-grained or medium-grained margins and fine-grained interiors. Many cut across xenoliths. The width of the dikes ranges from a fraction of an inch to several inches, rarely to as much as one foot.

Aplites appear to be confined to granitic terrane. In Tijeras Canyon most trend approximately east, though other trends may also be observed.

Lamprophyres are not abundant, but a few of them persist for considerable distances. One, a spessartite (euhedral hornblende with minor oligoclase-andesine and diopsidic pyroxene), may be traced from south of Tijeras Creek, near the entrance to Tijeras Canyon, northward across U. S. Highway 66, over the ridge into Embudo Canyon and beyond, a distance of over two miles. The width of this dike is variable; in places it practically pinches out, elsewhere swells to twenty feet and more. Grain size is very erratic, displaying no particular relation to contact or interior. Coarse-grained zones alternate with fine-grained zones, suggesting a streaming action of multiple or spasmodic intrusion. The rock in this dike is very fresh, but it is found only in Precambrian granite and, for this reason, has been assigned to the Precambrian. Another type of lamprophyre in Tijeras Canyon may be referred to as mica trap (possibly a minette or kersantite). It weathers so readily that fresh samples are practically unattainable, but the shiny biotite phenocrysts, however altered, are readily visible and diagnostic. The age of this rock is uncertain. It has been considered Precambrian in Tijeras Canyon, where it cuts only Precambrian rock, but a very similar dike rock may be seen on the Sandia Crest road, just above Doc Long's picnic area, cutting the Pennsylvanian Madera limestone.

Carbonate rocks are conspicuously absent in the Precambrian terrane of the Albuquerque country. Calcite is present in several rocks as a secondary mineral and there are a few small localizations of calcite that may be primary, but marbles or lime-silicate rocks are virtually absent.

STRUCTURAL FEATURES AND METAMORPHISM

The foliated metamorphic rocks of the Sandia-Manzanita-Manzano zone have a general northeasterly trend; that is, the foliation has this trend. A similar trend has been observed in the Nacimiento Mountains, but fewer details on this area are available. Bedding, where it may be observed, may diverge from the foliation, but not greatly. Dips are mostly steep, and may be either to the northwest or to the southeast, in places changing within short distances. In Tijeras Canyon the foliation of the greenstone complex on the south side of the canyon dips uniformly to the southeast; the foliation in the gneiss and associated rocks on the north side of the Tijeras fault dips to the northwest. Drag folds may be observed in places and larger fold structures within the Precambrian foliates have been observed, but exposures along the strike are of insufficient length to permit delineation of regional Precambrian structures. The general northeasterly trend, however, is a fact of great significance. A similar trend has been observed in possibly correlative Precambrian rocks in Arizona (in the Grand Canyon, in central and southern Arizona, and elsewhere). It is probable that sediments accumulated in Precambrian time in a geosynclinal zone continuous into what is now Arizona, indeed occupying much of the territory that is now New Mexico and Arizona, and that these sediments were deformed and metamorphosed in a single major event, the concomitant forces acting at right angles to this general northeasterly trend.

There is no clear-cut evidence for more than one episode of metamorphism involving the Precambrian rocks. This, of course, does not mean that such evidence may not yet be found. And it is not meant to imply that local processes of contact metamorphism were not effective. But major transformation by contact metamorphism about the borders of the large granitic masses, if it occurred, can hardly be said to represent a separate episode, since the granitic rocks were surely begotten by the rogenesis that produced the regional metamorphism.

Regional metamorphism (dynamothermal) of the Precambrian rocks was generally low to medium grade, although local zones of higher grade are indicated by the presence of sillimanite. Potash feldspar is generally considered an index of high grade in progressive metamorphism of argillaceous sediments, but there is evidence that the microcline in the quartz-feldspar gneiss is due to potash metasomatism (in association with the adjacent granitic masses) and, as such, is not proof that these rocks attained high-grade dynamothermal metamorphism. There is ample proof that such feldspathization may occur in mesozonal (medium-grade) environments. The assignment of metamorphic grade in the Albuquerque country is thus not a simple task. Chlorite schists in the greenstone complex suggest low-grade metamorphism. Epidote in schists and amphibolites marks medium grade. Chlorite tends to disappear in medium-grade rocks, and epidote disappears in high-grade rocks. The relation of low-grade to medium-grade rocks is not yet sufficiently clear to designate isograds or to discover any other systematic pattern in the trend of metamorphism. Faulting has been responsible for some juxtaposition of rocks of different grade, but it is not certain that all such anomalous associations can be explained in this way. Some mineral changes are related to the contact zone of the granitic masses. Such changes have been called contact metamorphism by some, but in view of the metasomatism known to occur in the contact zone, the changes that are spatially related to this contact may indicate advancing fronts of metasomatism. Fronts of this kind may, of course, result from contact metamorphism. But, until the granitic rocks can be definitely proved to be magmatic, it may be presumptuous to designate the mineral changes as contact effects.

The disregard of some prismatic and platy minerals for foliation planes, as observed for some sillimanite and mica, has been considered by a number of investigators to be indication of an episode of thermal metamorphism superimposed on earlier dynamothermal metamorphism (whether the thermal metamorphism be contact metamorphism or something else). This seems hardly justifiable. Foliation in metamorphic rocks is due to dynamothermal processes, the combined effects of shearing and elevated temperatures, and it strains the imagination to suppose that both effects cease at precisely the same "geologic instant." Shearing movements and the influx of heat are seldom so nicely adjusted that they rise and fall with the same phase of the moon. It is customary for one to outlast the other. If shearing outlasts heat inflow, then foliated rocks should display some cataclastic features unhealed by recrystallization (since this process is contingent upon the heat). If temperatures remain high after shearing has ceased, then minerals tend to grow with little or no regard for foliation, and unoriented minerals are formed. These are but natural consequences of the dying stages of dynamothermal metamorphism, and should not be interpreted as separate events.

GEOLOGIC HISTORY

The Precambrian history of the Albuquerque country remains to be written. What we now know represents but a few isolated scenes from a pageant that stretched across a temporal interval at least five times the length of all remaining geologic time. There are too many gaps in the record of that remote era.

The story (what story there is) is in the rocks, but how many rocks there are, how many episodes of accumulation, how many intervals of erosion—these are questions easy to ask and hard to answer.

Stratigraphers have their problems with correlation among the fossiliferous or potentially fossiliferous strata, but the Precambrian geologist, deprived at the start of any hope of correlation by fossils, both through the dearth or absence of life in the Precambrian seas and through the obliterating effects of metamorphism, and faced with the task of comparing isolated masses of rock that formed great distances apart and have since been modified by various degrees of metamorphism and unknown degrees of metasomatism, is presented with a labor that Hercules was fortunate in being spared.

In areas of continuous outcrops, such as continental shields, rock units may be traced for some distance, through various changes in lithology, though even here exposures are not always good and the picture at best is but two dimensional. In the southwestern part of the United States, which is no shield area, where Precambrian outcrops are isolated in the cores of mountains, tracing is out of the question (though, with more data from well samples of basement rock, where such information is available, we may approximate this technique), and it is necessary to resort to other means. The most promising is radioactive dating. However, this is a statistical method, and one or two measurements hardly suffice to outline the events of two or three billion years.

One age determination (really a dual determination—1,300 million years by the K-A method and 1,340 million years by the Rb-Sr method) of the Sandia granite indicates an age on the order of 1,300-1,350 million years (Aldrich and others, 1957). This age is in agreement with determinations for Precambrian rocks in the Sangre de Cristo Mountains (near Mora and near Dixon) as well as for Precambrian rocks of similar occurrence in Colorado (Aldrich and others, 1957). It is also comparable with the age determined for rocks in the Vishnu schist at the bottom of the Grand Canyon and for other primitive Precambrian rocks of southern Arizona (Giletti and Damon, 1961).

If the value 1,350 million years is valid for the Sandia granite, the metamorphic rocks that are hosts for the granite are yet older. If the granite is synkinematic the metamorphic rocks are not much older, and all the Precambrian rocks may be on the order of 1,350 million years old (though it must be remembered that sedimentary rocks may accumulate for many millions of years before they are metamorphosed). If the granite is post-orogenic, then the metamorphic rocks may be considerably older than the granite, but they still belong to the same orogenic cycle. The date 1,350 million years probably more or less fixes the orogenic movements of the southwestern part of the United States and is the age of the Mazatzal revolution.

The Mazatzal revolution, however, represents something of a midpoint in our history of the Precambrian. Sediments and volcanic rocks accumulated for countless ages before, the record of which is partially and dimly preserved in the rocks, and erosion acted for perhaps a billion years after (before deposition of the Paleozoic sedimentary rocks now observed on top of them), the record of which has been irrevocably removed.

Of published reports, Reiche's (1949) postulates the greatest number of Precambrian events in the Albuquerque country. His study of the Manzanita and North Manzano Mountains led him to propose the following sequence of events: accumulation of several thousand feet of basic to intermediate tuffs and lavas, with intercalated clays and silts; accumulation of clays, silts, and fine well-sorted sands (at least 7,500 feet thick); moderate deformation and subsequent erosion; renewed subsidence and accumulation of more clastics, rather more quartzose than previous deposits (a total of more than 4,000 feet); accumulation of more than 5,000 feet of predominantly rhyolitic lavas and ash; emplacement of dikes and granitic bodies, and strong deformation with attendant metamorphism, changing the basic lavas and tuffs to greenstones and chloritic schists, the quartz sandstones to quartzite, the clays and silts to phyllites, schistose grits, and schists, and the rhyolite to a moderately schistose quartz-feldspar mass; and erosion, lasting well into the Paleozoic, until Mississippian and Pennsylvanian rocks were deposited on the deeply weathered surface.

It may be said, in regard to this chronicle, that the evidence for assigning the greatest age to the parent rocks of the greenstone is insubstantial. Reiche assumed that the sedimentary sequence indicated in the above list was deposited on the basic lavas and tuffs, but he admitted that this relationship could not be verified. At another place he stated that all observed contacts of the greenstone complex are either intrusive or faulted, a statement somewhat at variance with his view that the greenstone is derived from flows and tuffs. There is also some doubt concerning the existence of two separate sequences of clastic rocks, separated, as indicated, by an unconformity. A variance of trends is observed, but faulting and folding may be responsible for this. The remaining events are rather well established and conform to the record of neighboring areas. Stark (1956), for instance, outlined the geologic history of the South Manzano Mountains in the following form: deposition in a marine environment of approximately 7,000 feet of sands (now the Sais quartzite), shales and siltstones (now the Blue Springs schist), and more sands (now the White Ridge quartzite); emergence, tilting to the east, and erosion; extrusion of the Sevillita rhyolite (about 5,000 feet); intrusion of basic igneous sills; folding and metamorphism; intrusion of granite (Monte Largo stock); invasion of vein quartz and development of quartz reefs; cross folding, faulting, and development of regional schistosity; intrusion of Priest granite; erosion.

Stark finds no traces of the earliest events recorded by Reiche. This by no means signifies that such events did not take place. But, since the evidence is much less than overpowering, it is well to set our beliefs accordingly. Some of the later events chronicled by Stark are also supported by little evidence in adjoining areas. Again this does not disprove their validity, but it does urge caution in using them as keys to unlock the history of every Precambrian exposure.

We may take it as established, then, that there was a period of accumulation of clastic sediments, markedly quartzose, preceded by or possibly accompanied by accumulations of basic to intermediate igneous rocks, and followed by accumulation of rhyolitic rocks. This period of accumulation was followed by deformation, metamorphism, and emplacement of granitic masses and associated rocks (aplites, pegmatites, and, possibly, lamprophyres). Erosion followed. Erosional intervals probably occurred locally at various times and places within the zones of accumulation, but there is no evidence that the entire region was raised and lowered to produce widespread traceable unconformities. Basic dikes and related hypabyssal masses were injected at various times.

The kinds of rocks and the sequence of events here depicted correspond fairly well with the rocks and events of central Arizona (Wilson, 1939). In Arizona, however, there followed, after a period of erosion, another period of accumulation (coarse and fine clastics and limestone). In the Albuquerque country there are no known rocks that record any comparable event. Nor, so far as known, is there any record northward in New Mexico of extensive deposits of Precambrian sediments after the orogeny that produced the deformation and metamorphism and prepared the scene for the emplacement of granitic rocks.

REFERENCES

Aldrich, L. T., Wetherill, G. W., and Davis, G. L., 1957, Occurrence of 1,350 million-year-old granitic rocks in western United States: Geol. Soc. America Bull., v. 68, p. 655-656.

Barker, Fred, 1958, Precambrian and Tertiary geology of the Las Tablas quadrangle, New Mexico: New Mexico Bur. Mines and Mineral Res. Bull. 45, 104 p.

Bruns, J. L., 1959, Petrology of the Tijeras greenstone: Univ. New Mexico unpub. master's thesis, 119 p.

Ellis, R. W., 1922, Geology of the Sandia Mountains: Univ. New Mexico Bull. 108, geol. ser., v. 3, no. 4, 45 p.

Flawn, P. T., 1956, Basement rocks of Texas and southeast New Mexico: Univ. Texas Pub. 5605, 261 p.

Giletti, B. J., and Damon, P. E., 1961, Rubidium-strontium ages of some basement rocks from Arizona and northwestern Mexico: Geol. Soc. America Bull., v. 72, p. 639-644.

Harbour, R. L., 1960, Precambrian rocks at North Franklin Mountain, Texas: Am. Assoc. Petroleum Geologists Bull., v. 44, p. 1785-1792.

Hayes, P. T., 1951, Geology of the Precambrian rocks of the northern end of the Sandia Mountains, Bernalillo and Sandoval Counties, New Mexico: Univ. New Mexico unpub. master's thesis, 54 p.

Just, Evan, 1937, Geology and economic features of the pegmatites of Taos and Rio Arriba Counties, New Mexico: New Mexico Bur. Mines and Mineral Res. Bull. 13, p. 44.

Lambert, P. W., 1961, Petrology of the Precambrian rocks of part of the Monte Largo area, New Mexico: Univ. New Mexico unpub. master's thesis, 108 p.

Lodewick, R. B., 1960, Geology and petrology of the Tijeras gneiss, Bernalillo County, New Mexico: Univ. New Mexico unpub. master's thesis, 63 p.

Montgomery, Arthur, 1953, Precambrian geology of the Picuris Range, north-central New Mexico: New Mexico Bur. Mines and Mineral Res. Bull. 30, 89 p.

Muehlberger, W. R., 1960, Precambrian rocks of the Tusas Mountains, Rio Arriba County, New Mexico, in New Mexico Geol. Soc. Guidebook of Rio Chama country, 11th Field Conf.: p. 45-47.

Reiche, Parry, 1949, Geology of the Manzanita and North Manzano Mountains, New Mexico: Geol. Soc. America Bull., v. 60, p. 1183-1212.

Stark, J. T., 1956, Geology of the South Manzano Mountains, New Mexico: New Mexico Bur. Mines and Mineral Res. Bull. 34, 49 p.

Stark, J. T., and Dapples, E. C., 1946, Geology of the Los Pinos Mountains, New Mexico; Geol. Soc. America Bull., v. 57, p. 1121-1172.

Wilson, E. D., 1939, Precambrian Mazatzal revolution in central Arizona: Geol. Soc. America Bull., v. 50, p. 1113-1164.

PENNSYLVANIAN ROCKS IN NORTH-CENTRAL NEW MEXICO

FRANK E. KOTTLOWSKI
State Bureau of Mines and Mineral Resources Division of New Mexico
Institute of Mining and Technology

For untold centuries the Mississippian limestones had lain exposed to the sun. Then tongues of the early Pennsylvanian seas invaded the karsted lowlands. Chert, limestone pebbles, and reddish clay from the Mississippian beds and quartz, feldspar, and mica from the Precambrian-rock hills where the Mississippian had been completely removed—these mingled to form the clastic member of the early Pennsylvanian Sandia formation in what is now north-central New Mexico. Local coal swamps developed on lowlands bordering debris-choked bays. By middle Pennsylvanian, Desmoinesian time, much of the region was covered by shallow seas teeming with invertebrate life and only high parts of the positive areas were exposed to local erosion—the Zuni dome to the southwest, the Pedernal mountain range to the southeast, and the Penasco-Santa Fe (Uncompahgre-San Luis) mountainous islands and shoals to the north. To the northeast, thick argillaceous sediments filled the Mora basin, contrasting with the "normal" marine bioclastic (recrystallized drewite?) limestones of the Desmoinesian seas and the local biohermal masses near atolls and islands.

Late Pennsylvanian time, Missourian and Virgilian, was marked by increasing tectonism. Parts of the Zuni dome may have been awash, but the Pedernal mountains and Penasco-Santa Fe-Uncompahgre ranges towered above the arkose-encumbered seas; thickest, coarse-grained sediments were deposited in the Mora, Estancia, Lucero, and San Juan basin areas. The results are shown in the arkosic limestone member of the Madera limestone and the lower beds of the arkosic red-bed Sangre de Cristo formation. This pulsating active orogeny extended at least into Wolfcampian time as recorded by the middle Sangre de Cristo formation, Bursum formation, and lower and middle Abo and Cutler formation red beds. In most places, the end of the Pennsylvanian period is now registered only by an obscure bedding plane within red beds or within intercalated marine limestones and terrestrial deposits.

PREVIOUS GEOLOGIC STUDIES

The type localities of the Sandia and Madera formations of the Magdalena group are in the Sandia Mountains east of Albuquerque and they have been mapped in some detail within most of the mountain ranges of north-central New Mexico. Herrick (1900) proposed the term Sandia series for the lower part of the "Coal Measures" of the Sandia Mountains. Keyes (1903) named the upper limestones of the Upper Carboniferous the Madera limestone, for the village of La Madera in the eastern foothills of the Sandia Mountains. Gordon (1907) labeled the strata between the Mississippian Kelly limestone below and the Abo red-bed formation above as the Magdalena group in the Magdalena Mountains and other areas of central New Mexico, and used the Sandia and Madera formations as the two main divisions of the group. Darton (1928) described the gross characteristics of the Magdalena group, noting its thinness or absence in the Zuni, Pedernal, and Nacimiento Mountains. He commented that the plane of division between the Sandia and Madera formations appears not to be constant, and that the transitions from one formation to the other differ in different localities. Renick (1931) described the Magdalena group in the western Nacimiento Mountains and western San Pedro Mountain, showing that locally the Abo red beds rest directly on Precambrian rocks, and suggesting that the absence and thinness of the Pennsylvanian strata at the northwest corner of the Nacimiento uplift was due to post-Pennsylvanian uplift and erosion prior to deposition of the Abo formation.

Melton (1925) and Ver Wiebe (1930) outlined the southern parts of the Uncompahgre-San Luis uplift which they considered as extensions of the late Paleozoic Ancestral Rockies from Colorado into north-central New Mexico. Needham (1937) described scattered collections of Pennsylvanian fusulinids from the region, and gave (Needham, 1940) generalized correlations based on the faunas.

Thompson (1942) believed the typical Sandia formation to be confined to the general region in and near the Sandia Mountains, and listed faunal correlations of Pennsylvanian units in north-central New Mexico with his faunal-stratigraphic sequence for the south-central part of the State. He described overlapping relationships of Pennsylvanian and Permian beds onto Precambrian rocks in the Pedernal Hills, Zuni Mountains, and Nacimiento Mountains. The Sandia formation of the Sandia Mountains area was correlated, by fusulinid studies, with the early Desmoinesian Elephant Butte formation. The thick argillaceous Desmoinesian of the eastern Sangre de Cristo Mountains, east of Figure 1, in the area of the Rowe-Mora basin (Read and Wood, 1947) was noted.

During the middle 1940's geologic maps compiled by members of the U. S. Geological Survey and the University of New Mexico, covering much of the Pennsylvanian outcrop area of north-central New Mexico, were published (Read and others, 1944; Henbest and Read, 1944; Northrop and Wood, 1946; Kelley and Wood, 1946; Wilpolt and others, 1946) and the Pennsylvanian stratigraphy synthesized by Read and Wood (1947). Read and others (1944) mapped the area of Figure 1 east of Albuquerque and south of Santa Fe, and measured many sections in the Manzano, Manzanita, Sandia, and Sangre de Cristo Mountains. They compiled an isopach map showing the combined thickness of the Pennsylvanian strata and Abo-Sangre de Cristo formations; some Mississippian (Armstrong, 1955) and possible Devonian(?) (Baltz and Read, 1960) rocks were included in the basal Sandia formation. The Madera limestone was shown grading upward into the red-bed Sangre de Cristo formation in the southern Sangre de Cristo Mountains, but locally the red beds rest on Precambrian rocks.

Henbest and Read (1944) listed the stratigraphic distribution of Pennsylvanian fusulinids from measured sections in the Nacimiento Mountains, concurring with and proving Thompson's (1942) suggestion that the northwestern part of the range was a granite ridge early in Pennsylvanian time and subsequently was progressively overlapped northward by younger and younger Pennsylvanian and Permian sediments. They noted the local presence of possible Mississippian beds between the basal Pennsylvanian strata and the Precambrian rocks, as veri-

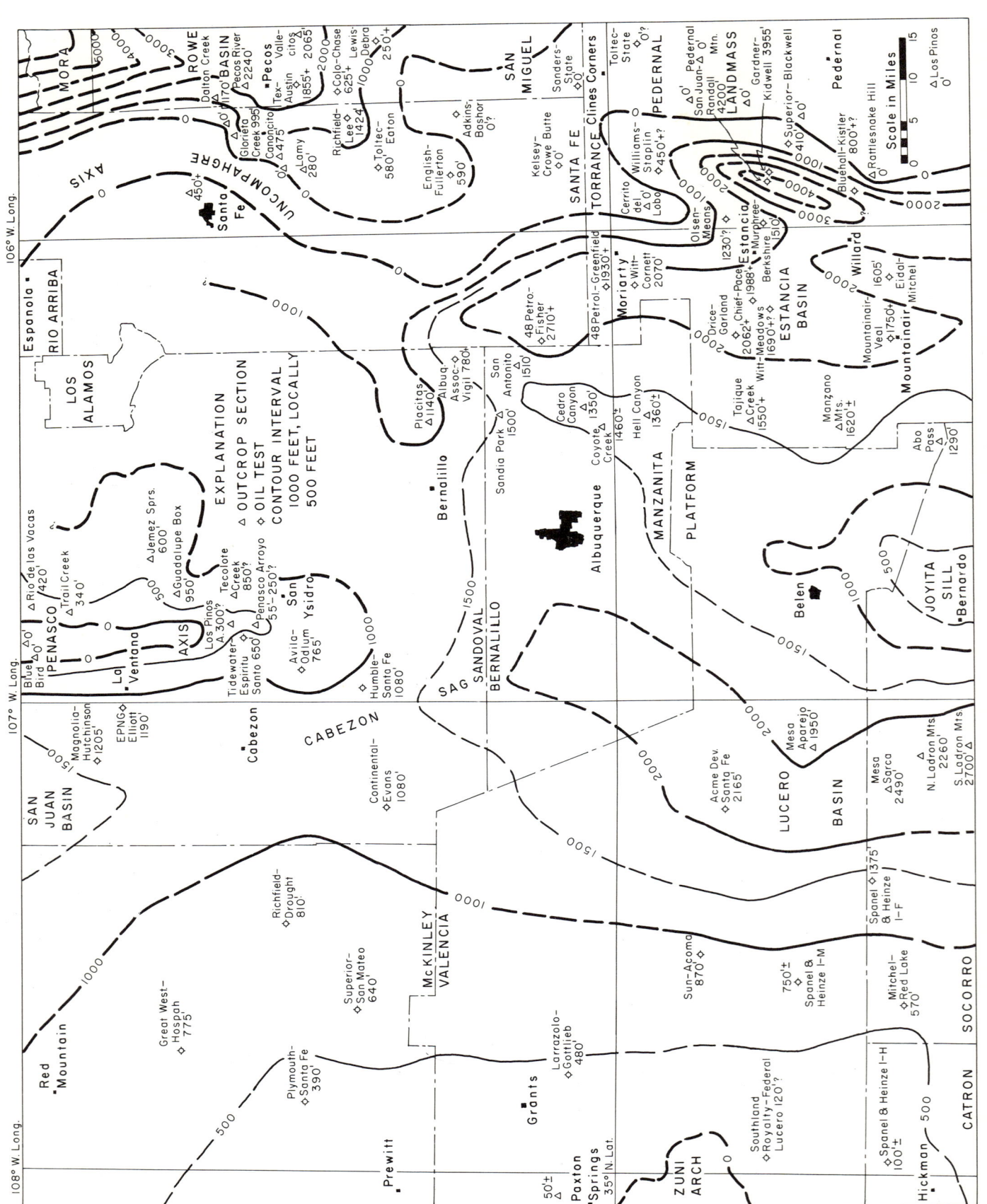

FIGURE 1—ISOPACH MAP OF PENNSYLVANIAN ROCKS IN NORTH-CENTRAL NEW MEXICO

fied by faunal studies (Armstrong, 1955, 1958; Fitzsimmons, Armstrong, and Gordon, 1956). Mapping of the Nacimiento Mountains and San Pedro Mountain by Northrop and Wood (1946) outlined a narrow north-south positive area (as shown by an isopach map) that was exposed to erosion during most of Pennsylvanian time, and was bordered on the west and east by Pennsylvanian-Permian-age sedimentary basins. Five faunal zones, based on both megafossils and fusulinids, were recognized in the Pennsylvanian sequence. The San Pedro-Nacimiento landmass was termed the Penasco axis by Read and Wood (1947).

The thick, dominantly marine Pennsylvanian section of the Lucero uplift area was mapped by Kelley and Wood (1946), and key sections were measured to describe the rocks of the Pennsylvanian-age Lucero-area sedimentary basin. Wilpolt and others (1946) mapped the Abo Pass area near the junction of Socorro, Valencia, and Torrance Counties; their stratigraphic studies indicated a Pennsylvanian positive area, called the Joyita axis, that was suggested as a southern continuation of the Penasco axis.

The distribution and correlation of the Pennsylvanian rocks in northern New Mexico was summarized by Read and Wood (1947) based upon the above-mentioned mapping and stratigraphic investigations. They presented an isopach and facies map of the Pennsylvanian rocks showing the location of the basins and positive features, as well as the ratio of clastic to calcareous sediments—one of the earlier maps of this type. The Pennsylvanian-early Permian sedimentary cycle was noted as consisting of two phases, an older marine one, and a younger continental phase. The marine phase was listed as (1) a suite of transgressive sediments, the upper clastic member of the Sandia formation, (2) evenly and widely distributed marine sediments that were deposited during maximum transgression, the lower gray limestone member of the Madera limestone and part of the upper arkosic member, and (3) unevenly distributed and restricted alternating marine and continental sediments that represent a period of offlap or marine regression, part of the upper arkosic member and Red Tanks member of the Madera limestone, and the Bursum formation. This marine phase is encompassed within the Magdalena group. The overlying continental phase is the Abo red beds and arkoses of central New Mexico, the Sangre de Cristo formation of the Sangre de Cristo Mountains, and the lower part of the Cutler formation of the San Pedro Mountain area.

Bradish and Mills (1950) suggested correlations between the Magdalena group and the Pennsylvanian units of the Paradox basin region. Cheetham (1950) collected and identified (as collaborated by Arthur L. Bowsher) bryozoans and brachiopods of Desmoinesian and Missourian aspect from limestone lenses within basal red beds of the Zuni Mountains. These rocks appear to have been shoreline deposits on the edge of the Zuni arch. McKee (1951) drew an isopach map of the Pennsylvanian of New Mexico and Arizona with the New Mexico part based chiefly on above-listed studies. Brill (1952) made lithologic and isopach studies in the Sangre de Cristo Mountains region.

Foster (1957) reviewed the occurrence of the Pennsylvanian in west-central New Mexico and included interpretations of the subsurface data. Smith and others (1958, 1959) mapped and briefly described lenses of Pennsylvanian limestones lying on the Precambrian rocks of the northwestern and southeastern Zuni Mountains. Wengerd (1959) and Kottlowski (1959) discussed the Pennsylvanian of the region from the Zuni Mountains eastward to the Manzano Mountains, each drawing isopach maps that show some differences in interpretation. Wengerd's paper, along with a previous one (Wengerd, 1958b), was directed at the petroleum possibilities of the Lucero basin region. He (1958a) summarized the habitat of oil in the Pennsylvanian of the San Juan Basin, and with Matheny (Wengerd and Matheny, 1958) made a detailed analysis of the Pennsylvanian outcrop and subsurface data for the Four Corners region, including the northwestern part of Figure 1. Fetzner (1960) described the Pennsylvanian in about the same region and his interpretations of paleotectonics, thickness, and sand-shale ratios for north-central New Mexico differ but slightly from earlier published studies. Kottlowski's (1960) summary of Pennsylvanian sections in southwestern New Mexico barely reaches the south edge of Figure 1 but most of New Mexico is covered by a regional paleogeographic sketch map (ibid., pl. 10). Several quadrangles in the southwestern Sangre de Cristo Mountains near Santa Fe were mapped by the writer (Kottlowski, in Spiegel and Baldwin, 1956) and the Pennsylvanian rocks examined in an area that was near the southern termination of the Uncompahgre-San Luis axis.

AREAL DESCRIPTIONS OF THE PENNSYLVANIAN ROCKS

The Pennsylvanian outcrops and the Pennsylvanian beds reached in oil tests throughout north-central New Mexico fall naturally into seven geographic areas: the Zuni Mountains, Ladron Mountains-Lucero Mesa, Manzano-Manzanita-Sandia Mountains, Estancia Basin-Pedernal Hills, southwestern Sangre de Cristo Mountains, San Pedro-Nacimiento Mountains, and the southeastern San Juan Basin.

Zuni Mountains

Local limestone lenses occur sporadically in the lower part of the Abo red beds of the Zuni Mountains. Most of the fossils reported (Cheetham, 1950) from these scattered marine deposits are of Pennsylvanian age. As much as 125 feet of the basal red beds may be various parts of the Pennsylvanian and Desmoinesian, Missourian, and Virgilian probably present locally. The Pennsylvanian-Permian boundary must vary within short distances from hillock to valley on the pre-red bed surface, and probably only some of the basal noncalcareous beds are of Pennsylvanian age. Whereas the present area of the Zuni Mountains appears to have been near the shoreline during most of Pennsylvanian time, the higher part of the Pennsylvanian-age Zuni uplift was probably to the southwest.

On the eastern flanks of the Zuni Mountains, in the southern San Juan Basin, Acoma area, and North Plains-Mesa del Oro area, a few scattered oil tests have been drilled through the Pennsylvanian and into the underlying Precambrian rocks. These wells record a gradual thickening toward the northeast (Plymouth-Santa Fe, Superior-San Mateo, Richfield-Drought, Continental-Evans, Great Western-Hospah) into the southeastern San Juan Basin, and a somewhat more abrupt thickening toward the southeast (Larrazolo-Gottlieb, Sun-Acoma, Spanel Heinze 1-M, Mitchel-Red Lake) into the Lucero basin (Wengerd, 1958b). Southward, as shown (Southland Royalty-Federal Lucero, Spanel Heinze 1-H) along the southwest border of Figure 1, the Pennsylvanian is thin, and is dominantly a shoreline facies. A large region between Grants and Albuquerque is untested, so that a possible northern extension of the Lucero basin to the 3-corners area at the junction of Bernalillo, Sandoval, and Valencia Counties is hypothetical.

Ladron Mountains-Lucero Mesa

One of the thicker sections is at the southern edge of the Ladron Mountains where the Pennsylvanian is probably about 2,700 feet thick. Derryan and Desmoinesian strata are well exposed along the western backslope of the range, but Missourian and Virgilian beds are scattered on the western dip slope in low ridges amid blanketing sheets of Cenozoic gravels and travertine. A section measured by Cheetham (1950), as checked and modified by the writer, shows many fine-grained clastic rocks in the Derryan, unusually numerous sandstone and shale beds in the Desmoinesian, and a large percentage of shale and much arenaceous calcarenite in the upper Pennsylvanian. Northward in the Ladron Mountains, Mesa Sarca, Mesa Aparejo, and the Acme Development Co.-Santa Fe oil test, the Pennsylvanian thins to about 2,000 feet and contains a larger amount of argillaceous detritus. Some of the variation in thickness is in the lower sandy beds (probably mainly of Derryan age) which are 695 to 450 feet thick in the southern Ladron Mountains and in the Acme-Santa Fe oil test, but only about 400 feet thick in the intervening sections.

Wengerd (1959) noted that during Pennsylvanian time this Ladron Mountains-Lucero Mesa area was a broad, westward-projecting sag-like shelf off the basinal axis of the Cabezon-Lucero-San Mateo-Orogrande marine accessway which joined the Paradox basin on the north to the Sonoran geosyncline on the south. He suggested that the Pennsylvanian sediments vary from gray limy shale and shaly limestone near the axis of the accessway to massive carbonate rocks, possibly of reef origin, westward across the break-in-slope toward the Zuni positive area.

As mapped by Kelley and Wood (1946), the Pennsylvanian from Lucero Mesa southward into the northern Ladron Mountains was divided into the Sandia formation and Madera limestone of the Magdalena group. The lower limestone member of the Sandia is of Mississippian age (Noble, 1950; Armstrong, 1958). The upper clastic member of the Sandia formation was reported to thin toward the north, west, and northeast. The Madera limestone was divided into the lower Gray Mesa member, the middle Atrasado member, and the upper Red Tanks member. The Gray Mesa member is dominantly gray to dark-gray cherty limestone with several biostromal beds (Fig. 2) that form persistent thick cliffs; the member is about 800 to 890 feet thick. The Atrasado member thins northward from 760 feet in the northern Ladron Mountains to about 555 feet on Mesa Sarca (Monte de Belen) and Mesa Aparejo (Gray Mesa), and becomes more shaly in the northern sections. This member contains more clastic beds than the Gray Mesa member, and some of the clastic rocks are red shales and arkosic sandstones. The Red Tanks member is 200-230 feet thick and consists of interbedded reddish and buff sandstone, siltstone, and shale, limestone pebble-conglomerate, thin-bedded gray limestone, gray shale, and gray arkosic sandstone. The member appears to be essentially conformable with the underlying Pennsylvanian strata and the overlying Abo red-beds formation. The Pennsylvanian-Permian boundary may occur somewhere within the Red Tanks member.

Figure 2. Cliff of biostromal limestone near top of Mesa Sarca.

Manzano-Manzanita-Sandia Mountains

No oil tests have penetrated as deep as the Pennsylvanian rocks in the Albuquerque-Belen basin (Kelley, 1954) or graben of the Rio Grande structural depression. The Cenozoic sediments alone may be 1 to 3 miles thick in this complex graben, suggesting that the top of the Pennsylvanian may be 2 to 5 miles below the surface. To the east, however, the Magdalena group crops out over much of the crest and eastern dip slopes of the Los Pinos, Manzano, Manzanita, and Sandia Mountains. As mapped by Read and others (1944) and Wilpolt and others (1946), the group was divided into the clastic member of the Sandia formation, the lower limestone member of the Madera limestone, and the upper arkosic limestone member of the Madera limestone. Near Abo Pass the early Permian Bursum formation is relatively conformable on the Madera limestone, whereas northward the Abo formation rests on the Madera. Thin local erosional remnants of Mississippian limestones occur between the Pennsylvanian strata and Precambrian rocks in the Sandia and Manzano Mountains. These Mississippian rocks are essentially continuous in the northern Sandia Mountains from the Tecolote Peak area northward.

In the Manzano Mountains, Read and others (1944) measured about 160-250 feet of the upper clastic member of the Sandia formation, 430-705 feet of the lower limestone member of the Madera, and more than 950 feet of the upper arkosic limestone member. Whereas the clastic ratio (0.6) is slightly lower than that for the Mesa Sarca outcrops to the west, the sand-shale ratio (0.8) is much higher than that for sections to the west, west of the Rio Grande, indicating relative nearness to the Pedernal landmass to the east. The clastic member of the Sandia formation consists mainly of greenish to blackish shaly siltstones and sandstones, with thin beds of shale and limestone as well as several ledge-forming beds of limestone-chert-quartz pebble-conglomerate. The lower member of the Madera is dominantly cherty limestone, with some nodular shaly beds and scattered thin lenses of white sandstone. The upper member of the Madera limestone is composed of cherty limestone, gray shale, feldspathic calcarenite, and arkosic sandstone. Reddish siltstone and reddish arkosic sandstone occur as interbeds near the top, a gradational facies from the marine Pennsylvanian into the Abo red beds. Some gypsiferous shales were described by Stark and Dapples (1946) near Abo Pass in the upper Pennsylvanian beds.

The Magdalena group is somewhat thinner (1,350 -1,450 feet) in the northern Manzano and in the Manzanita Mountains owing chiefly to thinning of the lower limestone member of the Madera limestone. In the Sandia Mountains (Fig. 3), the Magdalena group, exclusive of the local remnant Mississippian strata, is about 1,500 feet thick and thins northward to the Placitas area—apparently owing to loss of upper beds of the upper arkosic limestone member of the Madera limestone. A 50-foot-thick buff sandstone at the base of the arkosic limestone member appears to be a prominent unit near San Antonito. Thin coal seams occur in the Sandia formation and locally in the arkosic limestone member.

Figure 3. — Cliffs and ledges of Madera limestone at Sandia Crest.

Wengerd (1959) noted thinning of the Pennsylvanian marine section in the Manzano and Manzanita Mountains as compared with the Lucero-area sections to the west, and suggested the existence of a north-south-trending platform separating the Lucero basin from the Estancia basin to the east; he called this postulated submarine platform the "Manzanita platform." Small bioherms of **Chaetetes** corals were found by Wengerd (1959) in the Madera limestone of the Manzano and Sandia Mountains and were believed to indicate shallow-water break-in-slope areas favorable to organic reef development.

Estancia Basin-Pedernal Hills

Many oil and gas tests have been drilled in the southern part of the Estancia Basin in southern Torrance County, and a small carbon dioxide gas field was developed on the Wilcox dome northwest of Estancia. Pennsylvanian and Permian rocks dip gently eastward from the Manzano and Manzanita Mountains into the Estancia Basin but pinch out against the Precambrian-rock core of the Pedernal Hills to the east where the Pennsylvanian strata are overlapped by the Permian beds. Numerous shows of oil and gas have been reported, mainly from the bituminous black shales and porous sandstones of the lower Pennsylvanian. Comparison of the Pennsylvanian rocks penetrated in the various oil tests suggests that they were deposited on the west flank of a landmass that was supplying eroded detritus more or less continuously throughout the period. Except for brief localized floods of clastic sediments, however, a relatively small amount of debris accumulated in the Estancia depositional basin until near the end of Pennsylvanian time; then thick red beds and arkoses were derived from abrupt uplift of the Pedernal "Mountains" in a tectonic interval that was concluded by deposition of the lower Permian continental Abo red beds.

The Pennsylvanian-age Estancia basin appears to have contained two troughs, (Fig. 1), both bordering the west side of islands or peninsulas. The southeastern trough lay just east of the present location of Laguna de Perro, apparently terminating northward in a bay between Cerrito del Lobo and the northwestern part of the Pedernal Hills. Any northeastward connection to the Rowe-Mora trough (Read and Wood, 1947) must have been a shallow narrow strait as the marine Pennsylvanian section is absent or thin in the Toltec-State, Kelsey-Crowe Butte, and Sanders-State oil tests of the southeastern Santa Fe- southwestern San Miguel Counties area. In the "Perro" trough there is abrupt thickening of the Pennsylvanian westward from the Pedernal landmass. The Yeso formation is unconformable on Precambrian rocks (Fig. 4) 4 miles east of the Superior-Blackwell oil test; in this well red beds and coarse-grained arkoses dominate but the lower 400 feet, above Precambrian granite and schist, include interbeds of gray limestone, black shale, and gray to greenish calcareous shale of probable Pennsylvanian age.

Figure 4. — Basal Yeso conglomerate unconformable on Precambrian quartzite (beneath hammer head) in Pedernal Hills.

Just 4-5 miles to the northwest, two oil tests, the Gardner-Kidwell and the San Juan-Randall No. 2, encountered about 4,000 feet of probable Pennsylvanian strata. The lower Sandia formation unit is 530-1,000 feet thick and consists of arkose, sandstone, and shale, whereas the Madera unit (3,432-3,280 feet thick ?) is of dark-gray to tan limestone, shaly limestone, and black to greenish shale. In the Gardner-Kidwell test, there are many interbeds of green to pale-red sandstone, quartzose to arkosic. About 5 miles farther to the west in the Murphree-Berkshire oil test the possible Pennsylvanian strata, including many upper interbeds of red shales and siltstones, is only about 1,510 feet thick. To the south, however, in the Bluehall-Kistler oil test, at least 800 feet of Pennsylvanian rocks were encountered, with the well bottoming in the upper part of the Madera limestone. This latter well is only 4 miles northwest of the Precambrian outcrops on Rattlesnake Hill, and suggests a southern continuation of the thick Pennsylvanian section in the Gardner-Kidwell oil test, a thick section deposited on an abrupt edge of the Pedernal landmass. As this paper was written, however, the Abernathy and Jones-Dean oil test, being drilled (sec. 28, T. 3 N., R. 9 E.) about 9 miles south and 1 mile east of Willard, was yielding cuttings, at depths below 4,150 feet, of sericite-garnet schist (from bedrock, or from pebbles?) after penetrating less than a thousand feet of marine Pennsylvanian rocks.

The western "trough" may extend from south of Mountainair (southward under Chupadera Mesa?) northward to north of Edgewood and Moriarty as outlined by a series of oil tests which drilled incomplete Pennsylvanian sections ranging from 2,000 to 2,700 feet in thickness. Near Mountainair, the Mountainair-Veal oil test penetrated at least 1,750 of the Pennsylvanian and apparently had not reached the Sandia formation. The Drice-Garland and Chief-Pace wells, drilled west of Estancia, went through 1,988-2,062 feet of Pennsylvanian rocks but were abandoned in the Sandia formation. West of Moriarty, the Witt-Cornett and Forty-Eight Petrol.-Greenfield oil tests spudded in upper Madera limestones and encountered 1,930-2,069 feet of Pennsylvanian beds. Farther north and west, in southwestern Santa Fe County, the Forty-Eight Petrol.-Fisher well began in the arkosic member of the Madera and went through 2,710 feet of Pennsylvanian before encountering Precambrian schist and granite. About 5 miles northwest of this latter oil test, Read and others (1944) measured only 1,510 feet of a complete Pennsylvanian section on the back slope of the Sandia Mountains.

Along the east side of the northern part of this "Moriarty" trough is Cerrito del Lobo, a gently domed knob of Precambrian rocks overlapped by upper Permian and Triassic strata. This positive area extends northward into southeastern Santa Fe County to tie onto the northern end of the Pedernal Hills uplift; it probably extends northward to join the Uncompahgre axis of Read and Wood (1947) although there is no oil test nor outcrop data in west-central and northern Santa Fe County to verify or disprove its existence.

Southwestern Sangre de Cristo Mountains

Read and others (1944) and Read and Andrews (1944) mapped the southwestern Sangre de Cristo Mountains from T. 16 N. southward. Brill (1952) measured some sections in the upper Pecos River area and described the relationships of late Paleozoic lands and seas extending from north-central New Mexico northward into Colorado. Baltz and Bachman (1956) described the Pennsylvanian rocks of the southeastern Sangre de Cristo Mountains, providing control for the northeast border of the region shown on Figure 1.

The Pennsylvanian is more than 2,240 feet thick (Read and others, 1944) near Pecos, as part of the Sangre de Cristo formation red beds that overlie the Madera limestone is probably of late Pennsylvanian age. The Sandia formation, about 375 feet thick, rests unconformably on karsted cherty Mississippian limestone (Baltz and Read, 1960; Armstrong, 1958), and consists of gray to brown sandstone, shale, and thin limestone with local conglomerate beds. The lower gray member of the Madera limestone is about 635 feet thick, and is chiefly dark-gray cherty limestone with considerable dark-gray shale in the upper part, and pebbly sandstone in the lower beds. The arkosic member of the Madera limestone is about 1,230 feet thick and consists of gray to light-gray arkose and arkosic limestone with some interbedded shale. Arkoses near the top of the member are reddish, the gradational contact with the overlying Sangre de Cristo formation being picked at the top of the highest limestone.

Southeastward toward Vallecitos, the Pennsylvanian rocks are similar in lithology and thickness to those of the Pecos area. The southwestern end of the Rowe-Mora Basin appears to be in east-central Santa Fe County, southwest of Pecos, as shown by the absence(?) of marine Pennsylvanian rocks in the Adkins-Bashor oil test, the thin (580-590 feet, sections of the English-Fullerton and Toltec-Eaton wells, and the relatively thick (1,425 feet) marine Pennsylvanian beds of the Richfield-Lee oil test. To the northeast—north and east of the northeast corner of Figure 1—the thick clastic deposits of the Mora basin total 7,000-8,500 feet in thickness (Baltz and Bachman, 1956).

West of Pecos, the marine Pennsylvanian strata thin to about 995 feet near Glorieta and to only 475 feet of intercalated red siltstones, gray argoses, and thin gray limestones near Canoncito. Part of this thinning is due to intertonguing with and equivalent replacement of the upper part of the Pennsylvanian by the Sangre de Cristo formation, but along Apache Canyon near Lamy the Magdalena group (restricted) is only 280 feet thick. A few miles west of Canoncito, and in the area north of Glorieta, Read and others (1944) found the Sangre de Cristo formation unconformable on Precambrian rocks, marking a southeast edge of the Uncompahgre-San Luis landmass.

Except for a few isolated fault blocks of Pennsylvanian rocks near Santa Fe, there is no outcrop nor well-data control for the large area of northwestern and northern Santa Fe County, Los Alamos County, southern Rio Arriba County, and northeastern Sandoval County. The thick clastic Pennsylvanian of the upper Pecos River valley and the Rowe-Mora basin must have been derived at least in part from a Precambrian landmass rock source in northeastern Santa Fe County, to judge from the amount and angularity of the fresh feldspar grains in the arkoses and arkosic limestones. One wonders if there was a deep sedimentational trough west of this southern Uncompahgre prong, a thick buried Pennsylvanian section in western Santa Fe County, saved from erosion during post-Pennsylvanian time, and downdropped in the Rio Grande structural depression.

East of Santa Fe in the foothills of the southwesternmost Sangre de Cristo Mountains a few square miles of Pennsylvanian rocks have been mapped by the writer (in Spiegel and Baldwin, 1956) in the Santa Fe and Seton Village quadrangles. Locally as much as 50 feet of the Mississippian cherty limestone and underlying Mississippian or Devonian limestone, sandstone, and shale occur beneath the Sandia formation but in most places the basal Pennsylvanian rests on deeply and thoroughly weathered Precambrian rocks. Irregularities are common along the basal contact with as much as 150 feet of local relief noted; in places depressions in the pre-Pennsylvanian surface were filled by carbonaceous shales and shaly coal beds. In most of the mapped area, the Pennsylvanian is overlain unconformably by the Tertiary Santa Fe formation but locally a thin remnant of the red-bed Sangre de Cristo formation gradationally overlies the arkosic member of the Madera. The complete marine Pennsylvanian does not exceed 500 feet in thickness and resembles the Magdalena group section near Lamy except in having a considerable thickness of cliff-forming cherty limestone in the limestone member of the Madera, and in showing nonred-bed arkose and limestone of the arkosic member.

The lithologies and thicknesses suggest that these outcrops were on the west side of the southern Uncompahgre-San Luis prong.

Nacimiento Mountains and San Pedro Mountain

As noted by Henbest and Read (1944) and Northrop and Wood (1946), the lower limestone member of the Sandia formation, of Mississippian age, is extremely discontinuous, the Pennsylvanian in most places in these mountain ranges resting on Precambrian rocks. Armstrong (1955) and Fitzsimmons, Armstrong, and Gordon (1956) collected Mississippian fossils from these lower discontinuous limestones and placed them in the Arroyo Penasco formation of Meramec age. The clastic member of the Sandia, or actually the restricted Sandia formation, consists of dark-brown, grayish-brown, and brownish-green sandstone and impure arenaceous limestone, with minor coal lenses, underclays, and siltstones. Thickness is reported (Northrop and Wood, 1946) to vary considerably because of the unevenness of the surface on which the unit was deposited. The formation is absent in the central and northern part of the Nacimiento Mountains, where the Madera limestone or Abo-Cutler red beds overlie the Precambrian rocks.

The lower gray limestone member of the Madera limestone consists of dark-gray limestone interbedded with gray shale and a few sandstones. In the center of the Nacimiento Mountains, this member rests on the Precambrian rocks but northward it too is absent, either by non-deposition or by a facies change into the upper Madera. The upper arkosic member of the Madera limestone is made up of gray limestone, arkosic limestone, gray and red shale, and arkose, and rests on the lower Madera member in the south but on the Precambrian rocks to the north. Northrop and Wood (1946) noted that its thickness and age vary considerably as a result of overlap relations. Gradationally above the Madera are terrestrial clastic beds assigned to the Abo in the south and to the Cutler formation in the north; in the northwestern Nacimiento Mountains and southwestern San Pedro Mountain the Abo-Cutler strata unconformably overlie Precambrian rocks—this is the real core of the Penasco axis. The relations near Los Pinos and Penasco Arroyos in the southwestern Nacimiento Mountains are complex. Locally, as mapped by Northrop and Wood (146), the arkosic member of the Madera is on the Precambrian, whereas in nearby areas Armstrong (1955) found early Pennsylvanian beds between the Madera limestone and the Mississippian Arroyo Penasco formation. He called these ferruginous red shales, sandstones, and conglomerates the Log Springs formation and found evidence of post-Log Springs, pre-Madera faulting. Such tectonic activity is what one would expect near the south end of an active positive area.

There is no well-data control to the east of these ranges. Was the Penasco axis an isolated island lying amid deeps west of the Uncompahgre-San Luis axis? Certainly there is no abrupt eastward thickening shown in the outcrops; a deep trough may have existed between the Penasco axis and the Uncompahgre axis but more likely the area was covered by a shallow "shelf" sea, a wide southward-facing bay, in which less than 2,000 feet of Pennsylvanian beds were deposited.

Southeastern San Juan Basin

To the west and southwest of the Nacimiento Mountains is the area of the Cabezon sag of Wengerd and Matheny (1958), a shallow marine accessway between the Pennsylvanian-age San Juan basin to the northwest and the Lucero-San Mateo-Orogrande chain of basin-like features to the south. Directly westward from the Nacimiento Mountains, the Pennsylvanian thickens in 6 miles from a knife-edge on the margin of the Penasco axis to about 1,190 feet in the El Paso Nat. Gas Co.-Elliott oil test near La Ventana. The Magnolia-Jicarilla 1-A and Skelly-Crittenden wells, 25-30 miles to the north, penetrated about 1,860-1,990 feet of marine Pennsylvanian strata, suggesting that a Pennsylvanian-age sedimentation basin bordered the west margin of the San Pedro-Nacimiento Mountains region. To the south-southwest of the Penasco axis, the Pennsylvanian rocks increase gradually in thickness from 650-765 feet in the Tidewater-Espiritu Santo and Avila-Odlum wells to about 1,080 feet in the Humble-Santa Fe and Continental-Evans oil tests of southwestern Sandoval County. These latter two oil tests lie athwart Wengerd and Matheny's (1958) Cabezon sag or strait, a saddlelike paleogeographic feature also shown on Read and Wood's (1947) isopach and facies map of northern New Mexico.

Near Bernardo, close to the center of the southern border of Figure 1, was the site of the Joyita axis of Read and Wood (1947) and Wilpolt and others (1946), postulated as a small north-south-trending positive area. As this local axis is directly south (about 85 miles) of the southern end (as far as is known) of the Penasco axis, there has been much speculation that the two are part of a discontinuous north-south positive area (Read and Wood, 1947), perhaps the west flank of Wengerd's (1959) submarine "Manzanita platform." The hypothetical axis is now deeply buried in the Rio Grande depression, but clues may be found in the sediments to the east in the Manzano-Sandia Mountains, or to the west in the Ladron-Lucero area.

CONCLUSIONS

As pointed out previously by many geologists, the Pennsylvanian rocks of north-central New Mexico reflect complex paleogeographic relationships. Source areas were the Zuni landmass to the southwest, the Pedernal mountains to the southeast, the Uncompahgre-San Luis-Cerrito del Lobo axis on the east and northeast, and the Penasco axis or island in northern Sandoval and southern Rio Arriba Counties. Thick sections, rich in clastic rocks, were deposited in the Rowe-Mora basin, Estancia basin, Lucero basin, and southeastern San Juan basin. The rest of the area, from the ancient shorelines to the edges of the stagnant deeps, spawned the prolific invertebrate life recorded in the Sandia and Madera formations, and may have been the natural habitat of oil.

REFERENCES CITED

Armstrong, A. K., 1955, Preliminary observations on the Mississippian system of northern New Mexico: New Mexico Bur. Mines and Mineral Res. Circ. 39, 42 p.

..................., 1958, The Mississippian of west-central New Mexico: New Mexico Bur. Mines and Mineral Res. Mem. 5, 34 p.

Baltz, E. H., Jr., and Bachman, G. O., 1956, Notes on the geology of the southeastern Sangre de Cristo Mountains, New Mexico, in New Mexico Geol. Soc. Guidebook of southeastern Sangre de Cristo Mountains, New Mexico, 7th Field Conf.: p. 96-108.

Baltz, E. H., Jr., and Read, C. B., 1960, Rocks of Mississippian and probable Devonian age in Sangre de Cristo Mountains, New Mexico: Am. Assoc. Petroleum Geologists Bull., v. 44, p. 1749-1774.

Bradish, B. B., and Mills, N. K., 1950, Pennsylvanian rocks of the San Juan Basin, in New Mexico Geol. Soc. Guidebook of the San Juan Basin, New Mexico and Colorado, 1st Field Conf.: p. 58-61.

Brill, K. G., Jr., 1952, Stratigraphy in the Permo-Pennsylvanian zeugogeosyncline of Colorado and northern New Mexico: Geol. Soc. America Bull., v. 63, p. 809-880.

Cheetham, A. H., 1950, Preliminary survey of some New Mexico Bryozoa: New Mexico School of Mines unpub. senior thesis, 107 p.

Darton, N. H., 1928, "Red beds" and associated formations in New Mexico: U. S. Geol. Survey Bull. 794, 356 p. (1929).

Fetzner, R. W., 1960, Pennsylvanian paleotectonics of Colorado Plateau: Am. Assoc. Petroleum Geologists Bull., v. 44, p. 1371-1413.

Fitzsimmons, J. P., Armstrong, A. K., and Gordon, M., Jr., 1956, Arroyo Penasco formation, Mississippian, north-central New Mexico: Am. Assoc. Petroleum Geologists Bull., v. 40, p. 1935-1944.

Foster, R. W., 1957, Stratigraphy of west-central New Mexico, in Four Corners Geol. Soc. (Guidebook) Geology of southwestern San Juan Basin, 2d Field Conf.: p. 62-72.

Gordon, C. H., 1907, Notes on the Pennsylvanian formations in the Rio Grande valley, New Mexico: Jour. Geology, v. 15, p. 805-816.

Henbest, L. G., and Read, C. B., 1944, Stratigraphic distribution of the Pennsylvanian Fusulinidae in a part of the Sierra Nacimiento of Sandoval and Rio Arriba Counties, New Mexico: U. S. Geol. Survey Oil and Gas Inv. Prelim. Chart 2.

Herrick, C. L., 1900, The geology of the White Sands of New Mexico: Jour. Geology, v. 8, p. 112-128; Univ. New Mexico Bull., v. 2, fascicle 3, 17 p.

Kelley, V. C., 1954, Tectonic map of a part of the upper Rio Grande area, New Mexico: U. S. Geol. Survey Oil and Gas Inv. Map OM-157.

Kelley, V. C., and Wood, G. H., Jr., 1946, Lucero uplift, Valencia, Socorro, and Bernalillo Counties, New Mexico: U. S. Geol. Survey Oil and Gas Inv. Prelim. Map 47.

Keyes, C. R., 1903, Geological sketches of New Mexico: Ores and Metals, v. 12, p. 48.

Kottlowski, F. E., 1959, Pennsylvanian rocks on the northeast edge of the Datil plateau, in New Mexico Geol. Soc. Guidebook of west-central New Mexico, 10th Field Conf.: p. 57-62.

..................., 1960, Summary of Pennsylvanian sections in southwestern New Mexico and southeastern Arizona: New Mexico Bur. Mines and Mineral Res. Bull. 66, 187 p.

McKee, E. D., 1951, Sedimentary basins of Arizona and adjoining areas: Geol. Soc. America Bull., v. 62, p. 481-506.

Melton, F. A., 1925, The ancestral Rocky Mountains of Colorado and New Mexico: Jour. Geology, v. 33, p. 84-89.

Needham, C. E., 1937, Some New Mexico Fusulinidae: New Mexico Bur. Mines and Mineral Res. Bull. 14, 88 p.

..................., 1940, Correlation of Pennsylvanian rocks of New Mexico: Am. Assoc. Petroleum Geologists Bull., v. 24, p. 173-179.

Noble, E. A. 1950, Geology of the southern Ladron Mountains, Socorro County, New Mexico: Univ. New Mexico unpub. master's thesis, 81 p.

Northrop, S. A., and Wood, G. H., Jr., 1946, Geology of Nacimiento Mountains, San Pedro Mountain, and adjacent plateaus in parts of Sandoval and Rio Arriba Counties, New Mexico: U. S. Geol. Survey Oil and Gas Inv. Prelim. Map 57.

Read, C. B., and Andrews, D. A., 1944, Upper Pecos River and Rio Galisteo region, New Mexico: U. S. Geol. Survey Oil and Gas Inv. Prelim. Map 8.

Read, C. B., and Wood, G. H., Jr., 1947, Distribution and correlation of Pennsylvanian rocks in late Paleozoic sedimentary basins of northern New Mexico: Jour. Geology, v. 55, p. 220-236.

Read, C. B., and others, 1944, Geologic map and stratigraphic sections of Permian and Pennsylvanian rocks of parts of San Miguel, Santa Fe, Sandoval, Bernalillo, Torrance, and Valencia Counties, north-central New Mexico: U. S. Geol. Survey Oil and Gas Inv. Prelim. Map 21.

Renick, B. C., 1931, Geology and ground-water resources of western Sandoval County, New Mexico: U. S. Geol. Survey Water-Supply Paper 620, 117 p.

Smith, C. T., 1958, Geologic map of Inscription Rock fifteen-minute quadrangle: New Mexico Bur. Mines and Mineral Res. Geol. Map 4.

Smith, C. T., and others, 1959, Geologic map of Foster Canyon quadrangle, Valencia and McKinley Counties, New Mexico: New Mexico Bur. Mines and Mineral Res. Geol. Map 9.

Spiegel, Z. E., and Baldwin, W. B., 1956, Geology and water resources of the Santa Fe area, New Mexico, with contributions by F. E. Kottlowski and E. L. Barrows, and a part on geophysics by H. A. Winkler: U. S. Geol. Survey Water-Supply Paper (in manuscript).

Stark, J. T., and Dapples, E. C., 1946, Geology of the Los Pinos Mountains, New Mexico: Geol. Soc. America Bull., v. 57, p. 1121-1172.

Thompson, M. L., 1942, Pennsylvanian system in New Mexico: New Mexico Bur. Mines and Mineral Res. Bull. 17, 92 p.

Ver Wiebe, W. A., 1930, Ancestral Rocky Mountains: Am. Assoc. Petroleum Geologists Bull., v. 14, p. 765-788.

Wengerd, S. A., 1958a, Origin and habitat of oil in the San Juan Basin of New Mexico and Colorado, in Weeks, L. G., ed., Habitat of oil— a symposium: Am. Assoc. Petroleum Geologists, p. 366-394.

..................., 1958b, Lucero basin attracts wildcatters—New Mexico's newest prospect: Oil and Gas Jour., v. 56, p. 207-215.

..................., 1959, Regional geology as related to the petroleum potential of the Lucero region, west-central New Mexico, in New Mexico Geol. Soc. Guidebook of west-central New Mexico, 10th Field Conf.: p. 121-134.

Wengerd, S. A., and Matheny, M. L., 1958, Pennsylvanian system of Four Corners region: Am. Assoc. Petroleum Geologists Bull., v. 42, p. 2048-2106.

Wilpolt, R. H., and others, 1946, Geologic map and stratigraphic sections of Paleozoic rocks of Joyita Hills, Los Pinos Mountains, and northern Chupadera Mesa, Valencia, Torrance, and Socorro Counties, New Mexico: U. S. Geol. Survey Oil and Gas Inv. Prelim. Map 61.

MISSISSIPPIAN AND PENNSYLVANIAN FOSSILS OF THE ALBUQUERQUE COUNTRY

STUART A. NORTHROP
University of New Mexico

MISSISSIPPIAN FOSSILS

Prior to 1951, no diagnostic fossils—with the exception of a foraminifer, **Endothyra baileyi**—had been found in pre-Pennsylvanian strata in New Mexico north of Ladron Peak, between Socorro and Belen. More than a century ago Marcou (1856; 1858) misidentified Pennsylvanian fossils from Pecos, the Sandia Mountains, and Tijeras Canyon as Mississippian species. He concluded that the Madera or Magdalena limestone was "calcaire du carbonifere inferieure" or limestone of the Lower Carboniferous. Later he called it the "Mountain Limestone" and stated that the Sandia rim was "composed of **Carboniferous Limestone, which here merits most truly its name of Mountain Limestone,** for it is the only limestone of any importance met with in the Rocky Mountain region." Within a few years other workers assigned this limestone to the Upper Carboniferous or Pennsylvanian.

Apparently, the first recognition of pre-Pennsylvanian Paleozoic strata in New Mexico north of Ladron Peak was in 1940, when the 7,407-foot well in the Rattlesnake field was completed; Needham and Bates (1942) assigned 215 feet of strata in this well to the Mississippian. This same year Thompson (1942) found 106 feet of pre-Pennsylvanian rocks at the north end of the Sandia Mountains near Placitas. Above the Precambrian he measured 16 feet of conglomerate and sandstone overlain by 90 feet of unfossiliferous limestone and hazarded the opinion that these rocks might be "of lower Paleozoic age" (Thompson, 1942, p. 19). During the period 1942-1947 it was suggested by several members of the U. S. Geological Survey that such scattered remnants of pre-Pennsylvanian strata might be Mississippian or older (Read and Henbest, 1942; Henbest, Read, and others, 1944; Read and others, 1944; Henbest, 1946a, 1946b; Kelley and Wood, 1946; Northrop and Wood, 1946; Northrop and others, 1946; Read and Wood, 1947). On the basis of **Endothyra**, Henbest (1946a, 1946b) correlated this unit in the Sangre de Cristo and Sandia Mountains with the Leadville of Colorado.

It remained for A. K. Armstrong, an undergraduate student at U.N.M., to discover the first diagnostic megafossils in the pre-Pennsylvanian rocks. Early in 1951 Armstrong was engaged in a field problem under the direction of J. Paul Fitzsimmons. He was examining Precambrian rocks at the south end of the Nacimiento Mountains west of Jemez Pueblo, when he found fossils in small patches of limestone faulted down into the Precambrian basement. The first two slabs of this limestone Armstrong submitted to me early in 1951 contained **Conularia** sp. and **Eumetria** sp. Recognizing the latter as a Mississippian form, I suggested that Armstrong make further search for fossils. Fitzsimmons concurred and the emphasis of the problem shifted from Precambrian to Mississippian. Further collections were made by Armstrong and some were made by Fitzsimmons and myself. On May 21, 1951, I submitted to Armstrong a memorandum on all the material, tentatively identifying a variety of brachiopods and representatives of five other classes of invertebrates. I wrote as follows:

"The age of these fossils is Mississippian. I had anticipated that any Mississippian strata of northern New Mexico would prove to be older Mississippian, that is, Kinderhook or Osage, because these strata extend farther north in southern New Mexico than do younger Mississippian strata, such as Meramec and Chester. Again, in southern Colorado the Leadville or Madison limestone is chiefly Kinderhook or Osage in age.

"However, the **Eumetria** in your collections seems close to **Eumetria verneuiliana**, which is found in the Middle Mississippian Meramec of the Mississippi Valley region (Salem limestone and St. Louis limestone) and ranges up into the Upper Mississippian Chester series."

I suggested to Fitzsimmons that, because these were the first pre-Pennsylvanian megafossils ever found in northern New Mexico in a distance of 200 miles between Ladron Peak, New Mexico, and Piedra River Canyon, Colorado, the fossils should be submitted to Mackenzie Gordon, Jr., a Mississippian specialist of the U. S. Geological Survey.

It was decided to name the formation the Arroyo Penasco formation. Gordon's report on the fossils, listing 39 species, corroborated my determination of a Meramec, possibly St. Louis, age. A paper by Fitzsimmons, Armstrong, and Gordon (1956) was submitted in June 1955 and published in August 1956. Meanwhile Armstrong (1955) had published independently a report that included observations on Mississippian rocks in the Sangre de Cristo, Sandia, Manzano, and Ladron Mountains. Chiefly on the basis of microfossils, he concluded that the upper part of the "Arroyo Penasco" of the Sangre de Cristos is Meramec in age but that the lower unfossiliferous strata might be equivalent to the Leadville of Colorado or the Caloso of Ladron Peak. In this connection it may be noted that Baltz and Read (1960) collected Early Mississippian fossils at several localities in the Sangre de Cristos; they named two new formations, the Tererro of Early Mississippian (Kinderhook and Osage) age, and the Espiritu Santo of possible Devonian age. In view of the fact that the Meramec fossils of the Arroyo Penasco at the type locality of that formation occur in the upper part, it is possible that the unfossiliferous lower part of the Arroyo Penasco may be Lower Mississippian and equivalent to the Tererro formation.

Fossils of the Arroyo Penasco formation are listed below. Practically all of these are from the type locality of the formation in Penasco Canyon near the southern end of the Nacimiento Mountains, T. 16 N., R. 1 E., Jemez Indian Reservation, San Ysidro quadrangle. The identifications, unless otherwise noted, are by Mackenzie Gordon, Jr. (in Fitzsimmons, Armstrong, and Gordon, 1956). Generic assignments for several of the brachiopods have been changed by me. Names followed by (1) were cited by Armstrong (1955); names followed by (2) were cited by Armstrong (1958).

FORAMINIFERA
    Endothyra sp. aff. E. baileyi
    E.   macra (2)
    E.   prodigiosa (2)
    E.   sp. (1)
    E.   (planispiral type)
    Plectogyra sp. (1,2)
SCYPHOZOA
    Conularia sp. (1)
ANTHOZOA
    Homalophyllites? sp.
    Syringopora sp.
    Trochophyllum? sp.
    Zaphrentites? sp.
    Zaphrentoid coral fragments
BRYOZOA
    Archimedes? sp. (1)
    Fenestella spp. (1)
    Septopora sp.
    Stenoporoid, gen. indet.
    Sulcoretepora sp. aff. S. lineata group
BRACHIOPODA
    Brachythyris sp. aff. B. altonensis
    B.   sp.
    Composita sp. aff. C. lewisensis (1)
    C.   sp.
    C.?   sp.
    Dielasma cf. sinuatum
    Eumetria vera (1)
    E.   verneuiliana (1)
    E.   cf. verneuiliana
    Girtyella sp.
    Ovatia ovata (1)
    O.   pileiformis
    O.?   tenuicostus
    O.?   sp.
    "Productus (Pustula?) cf. indianensis"
    Protoniella? n. sp. aff. P.? parva
    Pugnoides cf. ottumwa
    Punctospirifer sp.
    Setigerites scitulus
    Spirifer cf. pellaensis
    S.   cf. subaequalis
    S.   sp. (1)
    Strophomenoid, gen. and sp. indet.
PELECYPODA
    Leptodesma sp. (1)
    Lithophagus? sp.
    Fragment, gen. and sp. indet.
GASTROPODA
    Bellerophon cf. sublaevis
    Euomphalus sp.
    Euphemites sp.
    Straparolus sp. (1)
    S.   sp. indet.
    Fragments, gen. and sp. indet.
OSTRACODA
    Ostracod molds, gen. and sp. indet.
CRINOIDEA
    Columnals and plates
INDETERMINATA
    Indet. fragments

In the Placitas area at the north end of the Sandia Mountains, Toomey (1953) measured ten sections of pre-Pennsylvanian strata, ranging from 20 to 81 feet in thickness. The only determinable fossils he found were poorly preserved **Euomphalus** sp., two high-spired gastropods, and a cephalopod. Later, in the Placitas area, Armstrong (1955) measured one section of 102 feet of pre-Pennsylvanian rock and cited poorly preserved **Straparolus?** [**Euomphalus?**] sp., **Stegocoelia?** sp., **Goniatites** sp., and **Plectogyra** sp. Subsequently Armstrong (1958) cited **Endothyra prodigiosa.**

At the south end of the Sandia Mountains in Tijeras Canyon, Szabo (1953) measured ten sections of the pre-Pennsylvanian sequence, ranging from 8 to 48 feet in thickness. However, in his thickest section, as much as 32 feet of red shale may be Pennsylvanian in age. If the questionable red shale that appears in most of his sections be assigned to the Pennsylvanian, the remaining pre-Pennsylvanian strata range from 8 to 27 feet in thickness. Armstrong (1955) measured only one section in Tijeras Canyon, 16 feet thick. Some of my colleagues hold the opinion that, in the absence of diagnostic fossil evidence, the so-called pre-Pennsylvanian rocks in Tijeras Canyon should be assigned to the Sandia formation. Certainly, along much of the Sandia crest, the pre-Pennsylvanian seems to be missing. On the other hand, Toomey (1953, p. 12) observed that the basal unit of the Sandia formation in the vicinity of the Sandia crest "contains numerous, large, reworked fragments of pre-Pennsylvanian limestone."

At Bosque Peak in the southern Manzano Mountains, east of Los Lunas and a few miles southwest of Mosca Peak, Armstrong (1958) found 22 feet of limestone that may be Mississippian. He observed also a few isolated remnants of limestone, 20-30 feet thick, at several places in the Manzanita and Manzano Mountains between Tijeras Canyon and Bosque Peak.

It now seems likely that all of the pre-Pennsylvanian rocks of the Sandia-Manzanita-Manzano area should be assigned to the Tererro (or Tererro and Espiritu Santo formations). As Baltz and Read (1960, p. 1768) have well said, "Further paleontologic studies and studies of the physical stratigraphy must precede correlation, firm assignments of age, and adjustments in the terminology of the Espiritu Santo, Tererro, and Arroyo Penasco formations."

PENNSYLVANIAN FOSSILS

The Pennsylvanian strata of north-central New Mexico, especially in the Albuquerque country, are abundantly fossiliferous at many localities. Good specimens of fossil plants are generally scarce, but marine invertebrates are common, diversified, and often well preserved. The total marine fauna probably numbers several hundred species. Excellent specimens can be collected at a number of localities in the Manzano-Manzanita-Sandia Mountains, in the Nacimiento Mountains, and especially in such canyons cutting the Jemez Plateau as Guadalupe Canyon (of the Rio de las Vacas) and San Diego Canyon (of Jemez River).

Fusulinids, brachiopods, bryozoans, and crinoids are perhaps most abundant; corals, pelecypods, gastropods, ostracods, and echinoids are common; other groups, such as sponges, conularids, nautiloid cephalopods, scaphopods, annelids, trilobites, and shark teeth, are less common and generally scarce at most localities. Groups not yet found or reported in the literature include blastoids, asteroids, crustaceans, insects, myriapods, scorpions, and eurypterids. Unfortunately there is no general report dealing with the paleontology of the Pennsylvanian of the State. Illustrations and descriptions of the fossils must be sought in many reference works and scattered papers in various technical journals dealing with the faunas of other regions.

Of possible interest to the professional as well as the amateur collector is the observation that, on the whole, better preserved fossils can be found in the Jemez-Nacimiento area than in the Sandia-Manzano area. At many places in the Jemez country, quantities of excellent fossils weather free from the matrix; with few exceptions, this is not true for the Sandia-Manzano country. Differences in ecology are apparent, also. For example, corals are generally small in size and relatively uncommon in the Jemez area, whereas they are larger and locally quite common in the Sandia Mountains. Their abundance here was

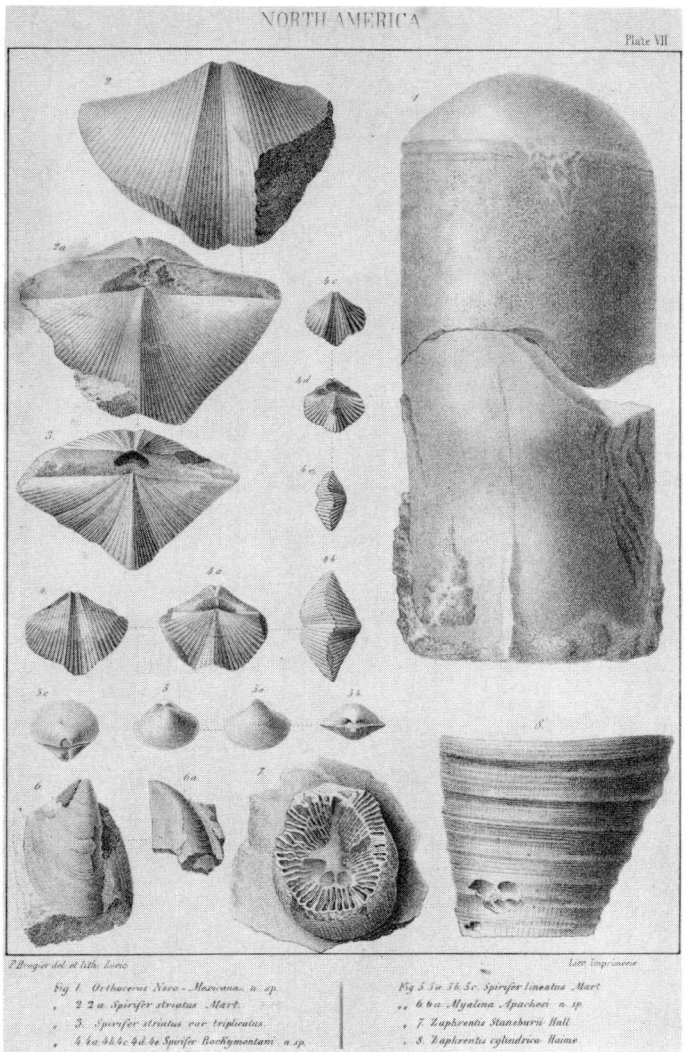

One of Marcou's plates (X ½) illustrating Pennsylvanian fossils from the Sandia Mountains. (Plate 7 of "Geology of North America," by Jules Marcou, published in Zurich, 1858; P. Brugier del. et lith. Zuric; lier Imprimerie.)

Figure 1. — **Orthoceras Nova-Mexicana**, n. sp. "I found only one specimen of this species; it was in a block of blue limestone, with several beautiful specimens of the **Productus semi-reticulatus**, in a deep ravine near the summit of the Sierra de Sandia, behind Albuquerque" (p. 44).

Figures 2, 2a. — **Spirifer striatus** Mart. [= Neospirifer] ". . . it forms a complete bed of limestone a foot thick, in the **Mountain Limestone** of Pecos village . . . . I found it also at the summit of the Sierra de Sandia, 12,000 feet above the sea-level, and also at the village of Tigeras, New Mexico" (p. 49). Figured specimen from Pecos village.

Figure 3. — **Spirifer striatus var. triplicatus.** [= Neospirifer dunbari] " . . . abundant in the Rocky mountains, especially at Pecos village, at Tigeras, on the summit of the Sierra de Sandia . . . " (p. 49-50). Figured specimen from Pecos village.

Figures 4, 4a, 4b, 4c, 4d, 4e. — **Spirifer Rockymontani**, n. sp. [4, 4a, 4b = **Spirifer matheri** Dunbar and Condra; 4c, 4d, 4e = **Spirifer rockymontanus** Marcou] "I found this beautiful species in the Mountain Limestone of Tigeras, Canon of San Antonio, New Mexico; where it is not rare" (p. 50).

Figures 5, 5a, 5b, 5c. — **Spirifer lineatus** Mart. [= **Phricodothyris perplexa**] "I found it at Pecos village and at Tigeras, where it is not very common" (p. 50). Figs. 5, 5a, 5b: "Different views of specimen from Pecos." Fig. 5c: "Specimen from Tigeras, showing to the naked eye the reticulation of its surface."

Figures 6, 6a. — **Myalina Apachesi**, n. sp. " . . . near the ranchos of Pecos village" (p. 44).

Figure 7. — **Zaphrentis Stansburii** Hall. In the text (p. 52-53) the spelling stansburyi is used. "I saw a great many at Tigeras, on the summit of the Sierra de Sandia, and at Pecos village." Figured specimen from Tijeras: "fragment showing the interior of the turbine."

Figure 8. — **Zaphrentis cylindrica** Haime. "I saw a great number of specimens in ascending the Sierra de Sandia from [San] Antonito, and several limestone beds were full of them. I also found it at Tigeras" (p. 53). Figured specimen from Sandia Mountains.

---

noted more than a century ago by Jules Marcou (1858, p. 53). In describing a horn coral that he misidentified as **Zaphrentis cylindrica**, he wrote:

"This gigantic species of coral ,so common in the Mountain Limestone of England, Belgium and France, had not been found previously in America. I saw a great number of specimens in ascending the Sierra de Sandia from [San] Antonito, and several limestone beds were full of them. I also found it at Tigeras [Tijeras]."

And, in describing another horn coral, **Zaphrentis stansburyi**, of which he "saw a great many at Tigeras, on the summit of the Sierra de Sandia, and at Pecos village," he observed that "the limestone in which it is found is so hard, that it is difficult to obtain well preserved and complete specimens."

Good specimens of brachiopods, bryozoans, and crinoid stems can be collected readily in the Jemez country. Such specimens occur in the Sandias and Manzanos but are usually more difficult to collect. Again, I have never observed any notable abundance of pelecypods or gastropods in the Sandia-Manzano area, such as may be found at several places in the Jemez country.

Two check lists of Pennsylvanian fossils are given below, one for the Jemez-Nacimiento Mountains area and one for the Sandia-Manzanita-Manzano Mountains area.

Pennsylvanian Fossils of the Jemez-Nacimiento Mountains Area

Unless otherwise indicated, these are from Northrop and Wood (1946), which included microfossils by Henbest, Read, and others (1944). Other citations are indicated by key numbers in parentheses, as follows:

1. Bisbee (1932)
2. Needham (1937)
3. Moore and Dudley (1944)
4. Northrop and Wood (1945)

5. Thompson (1948)
6. Armstrong (1955)
7. Lovejoy (1958)

FORAMINIFERA
　Bradyina 2 sp.
　B.? 　　　sp.
　Climacammina sp.
　Endothyra sp.
　E.? 　　　sp.
　Fusulina of F. cylindrica group
　　F. 　　sp. aff. F. euryteines
　　F. 　　leei
　　F. 　　sp. aff. F. leei
　　F. 　　tregoensis?
　　F. 　　sp.
　Fusulinella carmani?
　　F. 　　sp. aff. F. iowensis
　　F. 　　cf. juncea (5)
　　F. 　　stouti
　　F. 　　sp.
　　F.? 　　sp.
　Millerella sp.
　Spiroplectammina sp.
　Tetrataxis sp.
　Textulariidae
　Triticites irregularis
　　T. 　　irregularis var.
　　T. 　　jemezensis [syntypes] (2)
　　T. 　　kellyensis [syntypes] (2)
　　T. 　　kellyensis?
　　T. 　　nebraskensis
　　T. 　　sp. aff. T. nebraskensis
　　T. 　　sp. aff. T. plummeri
　　T. 　　cf. rhodesi (7)
　　T. 　　ventricosus (7)
　　T. 　　ventricosus var.
　　T. 　　sp.
　　T.? 　　sp.
　Wedekindellina euthysepta
　　W. 　　excentrica
　　W. 　　excentrica?
　　W. 　　minuta
　　W. 　　sp.

PORIFERA
　New genus, new species (red siliceous sponge)
　Spicules (7)
　Sponge(?) borings

ANTHOZOA
　Aulopora cf. prosseri
　　A. 　　sp. (4)
　Axophyllum? sp.
　Chaetetes milleporaceus
　　C. 　　sp.
　Cyathaxonia distorta?
　Lophophyllidium proliferum (1)
　　L. 　　proliferum?
　Neozaphrentis? sp.
　Pleurodictyum? sp.
　Undet. horn corals

BRYOZOA
　Bascomella sp. (7)
　Batostomellid
　Cyclotrypa pelagia [holotype and paratypes] (3)
　Fenestellids
　Heteronema? sp. (7)
　Prismopora sp.
　Rhombopora cf. lepidodendroides
　Septopora biserialis
　Undet. genera of massive, encrusting, and foliate forms

BRACHIOPODA
　Antiquatonia coloradoensis
　　A. 　　cf. hermosana
　　A. 　　portlockiana
　　A. 　　portlockiana crassicostata (7)
　　A. 　　sp.
　　A.? 　　sp.
　Beecheria bovidens
　Cancrinella boonensis
　Chonetes granulifer

　　C. 　　granulifer meekanus (7)
　　C. 　　sp.
　Chonetinella flemingi alata (7)
　　C.? 　　sp.
　Cleiothyridina orbicularis (7)
　Composita cf. elongata (7)
　　C. 　　cf. gibbosa
　　C. 　　cf. magna (7)
　　C. 　　ovata (7)
　　C. 　　subtilita
　　C. 　　trilobata (7)
　　C. 　　cf. trilobata
　　C. 　　sp.
　Crurithyris planoconvexa
　Derbyia bennetti
　　D. 　　cf. bennetti
　　D. 　　crassa
　　D. 　　crassa texana
　　D. 　　crassa cf. texana
　　D. 　　cymbula?
　　D. 　　cf. haesitans
　　D. 　　sp. aff. D. haesitans
　　D. 　　plattsmouthensis (7)
　　D. 　　sp.
　Desmoinesia cf. missouriensis
　Echinaria moorei
　　E. 　　cf. moorei (7)
　　E. 　　semipunctata
　　E. 　　cf. semipunctata
　　E. 　　sp.
　Hustedia cf. miseri
　　H. 　　mormoni
　　H. 　　sp. (4)
　Hystriculina wabashensis
　Juresania nebrascensis
　Kozlowskia splendens (1)
　Lingula sp.
　Linoproductus cf. oklahomae
　　L. 　　platyumbonus
　　L. 　　sp. aff. L. platyumbonus
　　L. 　　prattenianus
　　L. 　　cf. prattenianus
　　L. 　　sp.
　"Marginifera" sp. [probably most = Kozlowskia]
　Meekella striatocostata
　　M. 　　cf. striatocostata
　　M. 　　sp.
　Neospirifer alatus
　　N. 　　dunbari
　　N. 　　cf. dunbari
　　N. 　　gibbosus (7)
　　N. 　　sp.
　Orbiculoidea? sp. (7)
　Petrocrania modesta
　Phricodothyris perplexa
　Pulchratia cf. ovalis
　　P. 　　symmetrica? (7)
　Punctospirifer kentuckiensis
　　P. 　　kentuckiensis?
　Schizophoria oklahomae (6)
　　S. 　　cf. oklahomae
　Schuchertella? sp. (7)
　Spirifer occiduus [formerly S. occidentalis]
　　S. 　　cf. occiduus
　　S. 　　opimus
　　S. 　　rockymontanus
　　S. 　　cf. rockymontanus
　　S. 　　sp. A (7)
　　S. 　　spp. (6)
　Wellerella immatura
　　W. 　　osagensis
　Genus undet. (7)

PELECYPODA
　Acanthopecten carboniferus
　Allorisma terminale
　　A. 　　sp.
　Anthraconeilo? sp.
　Astartella vera (1)
　Aviculopecten occidentalis (1)
　　A. 　　sp.
　　A.? 　　sp.

Aviculopinna nebrascensis
A. peracuta
A. cf. peracuta
Edmondia aspinwallensis (1)
E. gibbosa
E. cf. gibbosa
E. nebrascensis
E. sp.
Limipecten? sp.
Myalina (Myalinella?) sp.
M. (Orthomyalina) cf. slocomi
M. (Orthomyalina) subquadrata
M. (Orthomyalina) sp.
M. sp.
Nuculana sp.
Pleurophorus sp. aff. P. tropidophorus
Pseudomonotis equistriata
P. robusta (1)
P. sp.
P.? sp.
Schizodus cuneatus
S. subcircularis? (1)
S. wheeleri (1)
S. sp. (1)
S.? sp.
Septimyalina sp.
Solenomya cf. trapezoides
S.? sp.
Streblochondria sp.
GASTROPODA
Amphiscapha catilloides
A. cf. subrugosa
A. sp.
Bellerophon cf. giganteus
B. sp.
Euomphalus sp.
E.? sp.
Euphemites nodocarinatus
Meekospira? sp. (1)
Naticopsis sp. (7)
Orthonychia parva
Pharkidonotus percarinatus (1)
Phymatopleura? sp. (1)
Shansiella carbonaria (1)
Straparolus sp.
Strobeus primogenius (1)
S. sp.
S.? sp.
Strophostylus remex (1)
S. sp.
Trepospira depressa (1)
T. discoidalis (7)
T. sp.
T.? sp.
Worthenia sp. (1)
Undet. large form
CEPHALOPODA
Dolorthoceras? sp.
Endolobus? sp.
Ephippioceras cf. ferratum
Mooreoceras? sp.
"Orthoceras" sp.
Tainoceras sp.
SCAPHOPODA
Dentalium? sp.
ANNELIDA
Spirorbis sp.
S.? sp.
Worm (?) borings
TRILOBITA
Ameura sp.
Ditomopyge parvula? (1)
D. new species (7)
D. sp.
Undet. pygidium
CRINOIDEA
Delocrinus sp. (1)
Hydreionocrinus sp. (1)
Undet. columnals and plates
ECHINOIDEA
Echinocrinus sp. (plates and spines)
VERTEBRATA
Shark teeth and a fin spine

Pennsylvanian Fossils of the Sandia-Manzanita-Manzano Mountains Area

Citations are indicated by key numbers in parentheses, as follows:
1. Marcou (1858)
2. White (1877)
3. Herrick (1900)
4. Herrick and Bendrat (1900)
5. Herrick and Johnson (1900)
6. Bisbee (1932)
7. Dunbar and Condra (1932)
8. Needham (1937)
9. Szabo (1953)
10. Toomey (1953)
11. Werrell (1961)
12. Read, C. B. (personal communication)

FORAMINIFERA
Fusulina euryteines (8,11)
F. rockymontana (11)
F. socorroensis (11)
F. sp. aff. F. taosensis (11)
F. sp. (9,11)
Triticites fresnalensis (8)
T. irregularis (9)
T. nebraskensis (11)
T. ventricosus (8,9)
T. ventricosus, 2 var. (11)
T. wellsi (8)
T. spp. (10,11)
Wedekindellina euthysepta (8)
W. excentrica (8,11)
W. sp. (9,10)
SCYPHOZOA
Conularia sp. (4)
ANTHOZOA
Amplexus coralloides? (1) [= an English species]
Aulopora? anna (9)
Caninia torquia (9)
C.? sp. (10)
Chaetetes milleporaceus (9,10)
C. cf. milleporaceus (6)
Dibunophyllum valeriae (9)
D. sp. (10)
Lophophyllidium proliferum (6,9)
Neozaphrentis sp. (10)
Pleurodictyum sp. (10)
Syringopora multattenuata (9)
S. cf. multattenuata (6)
S. sp. (10)
Zaphrentis cylindrica (1) [= an English species]
Z. stansburyi (1) [probably = Neozaphrentis]
BRYOZOA
Cystodictya sp. aff. C. carbonaria (4)
Fenestella albuquerqucana [syntypes] (4)
F. limbata (4)
F. norwoodiana (4)
F. spp. (9,10)
Fistulipora incrustans (9)
F. nodulifera (9)
Megacanthopora sp. (9)
Penniretepora trilineata (4)
P. cf. whitei (4)
P. spp. (9,10)
Polypora coyotensis [holotype] (4,5)
P. elliptica (9)
P. fastuosa (4)
P. sp. (10)
Prismopora sp. (9,10)
Rhombopora lepidodendroides (9)
R. sp. (10)
Septopora biserialis (4)
S. sp. (9)
Tabulipora heteropora (9)
T. sp. (10)
Undet. bryozoans (1)
BRACHIOPODA
Antiquatonia portlockiana (9,10)
A. portlockiana crassicostata (9,10)

Beecheria bovidens (6,9,10)
Cancrinella boonensis (4,9)
Chonetes granulifer (3,6,9,10)
Chonetinella flemingi (9)
C.   flemingi crassiradiata (10)
C.   verneuiliana (6,9)
Cleiothyridina orbicularis (9,10)
Composita argentea (9)
C.   elongata (9,10)
C.   magna (9,10)
C.   ovata (9,10)
C.   subtilita (1,4,6,9,10)
C.   trilobata (9,10)
Crurithyris planoconvexa (6,9)
Cryptacanthia compacta (7)
Derbyia crassa (4,6,9,10)
Desmoinesia missouriensis (9)
D.   muricatina (9,10)
Dictyoclostus americanus (10) [probably = Antiquatonia]
Echinaria semipunctata (6,9,10)
E.   semipunctata knighti (9)
Enteletes hemiplicatus (6,9)
E.   hemiplicatus plattsburgensis (9)
Hustedia mormoni (6,9,10)
Hystriculina wabashensis (9,10)
Juresania nebrascensis (4,6,9,10)
Kozlowskia splendens (6,9,10)
Lingula tighti (4)
Linoproductus insinuatus (9)
L.   oklahomae (9)
L.   platyumbonus (9)
L.   cf. platyumbonus (10)
L.   prattenianus (1,2,4,6,9,10)
Meekella striatocostata (6,9,10)
Mesolobus mesolobus (4,9,10)
M.   mesolobus decipiens (10)
Neospirifer alatus (10)
N.   cameratus (6,9)
N.   dunbari (1,9)
N.   gibbosus (9,10)
N.   latus (9)
Orbiculoidea capuliformis (3)
O.   missouriensis (9,10)
O.   ? nitida (4) [= an English species]
Phricodothyris perplexa (1,4,6,9,10)
Productus costatus (6) [probably = Antiquatonia]
P.   flemingi (1) [= an English species; probably Desmoinesia]
P.   punctatus (1) [see Echinaria]
P.   pustulosus (1) [= English Mississippian]
P.   pyxidiformis (1) [= English Mississippian]
P.   scabriculus (1) [= English Permian; Juresania]
P.   semireticulatus (1,4,6) [see Antiquatonia]
Punctospirifer kentuckiensis (6,9,10)
Retaria lasallensis (9,10)
Rhipidomella carbonaria (6) [formerly R. pecosi]
Rhynchonella sp. (4) [probably Rhynchopora]
Schizophoria cf. oklahomae (10)
S.   resupinoides (9)
Schuchertella pratteni (10)
Spirifer fultonensis? (4) [not recognizable]
S.   matheri (7,9)
S.   occiduus (9,10) [formerly S. occidentalis]
S.   occiduus, var. (9)
S.   opimus (4,9,10)
S.   rockymontanus [types] (1,9,10)
Terebratula plano-sulcata (1) [= Cleiothyridina]
Wellerella immatura (10)
W.   osagensis (6,9,10)

PELECYPODA
Acanthopecten carboniferus (9,10)
Allorisma terminale (9,10)
Annuliconcha interlineata (9)
Astartella concentrica (9)
A.   newberryi (4)
A.   varica (4)
Aviculopecten basilicus (10)
A.   occidentalis (9)
A.   occidentalis? (4)
A.   sp. (10)
Aviculopinna nebraskensis (9)
A.   peracuta (9)
Bakewellia parva (3)
Cypricardinia carbonaria (4)
Dunbarella knighti (9)
Edmondia aspinwallensis (9)
E.   gibbosa (9)
E.   nebrascensis (9)
E.   nebrascensis? (4)
E.   sp. (3)
Fasciculoconcha scalaris (4)
Lima retifera (4)
Myalina (Myalina) wyomingensis (9)
M.   (Orthomyalina) subquadrata (9)
M.   sp. (10)
M.?   sp. (3)
Nuculana bellistriata (9,10)
N.   bellistriata attenuata (9)
Parallelodon obsoletus (9)
P.   tenuistriatus (9)
Pleurophorus subcuneatus (3)
P.   tropidophorus (9)
Promytilus swallovi (3)
Pseudomonotis equistriata (9)
P.   hawni (9) [= Permian species]
Pteria? longa (3)
Schizodus wheeleri (9)
Septimyalina perattenuata (3)
Streblochondria? tenuilineata (4)
Yoldia glabra (9)

GASTROPODA
Amaurotoma? sp. (10)
Anomphalus rotulus (9)
Bellerophon crassus (9)
B.   crassus? (4)
B.?   sp. (10)
Cymatospira montfortiana (3,9)
Euconospira missouriensis (9)
E.   turbiniformis (9)
Euomphalus plummeri (9)
E.   reedsi (9)
Euphemites carbonarius (9)
E.   nodocarinatus (9)
E.   vittatus (10)
Goniasma lasallensis (9)
Meekospira? sp. (6)
Naticopsis remex (9)
N.   scintilla (9,10)
Orthonychia parva (9,10)
Pseudozygopleura perversa (9)
Strobeus primogenius (9)
Worthenia speciosa (9)
Yunnania subsinuata (9)

CEPHALOPODA
Metacoceras cornutum (9)
M.   perelegans (9)
Mooreoceras sp. (9)
"Orthoceras nova-mexicana" [holotype] (1)

SCAPHOPODA
Dentalium sp. (10)

TRILOBITA
Ameura major (5)
A.   sangamonensis (9)
A.   sangamonensis? (6)
Ditomopyge olsoni (9,10)
D.   parvula? (6)
D.   sp. (10)
"Phillipsia new species" A (5)
"P.   new species" B (5)
"P.   sp." (4)

OSTRACODA
Amphissites 2 sp. (11)
Bairdia chaseae (11)
B.   7 undet. spp. (11)
Bairdiacypris cf. acuminata (11)
Bythocypris procera (11)

B. sp. (11)
Cytherella sp. aff. C. footei (11)
C. sp. (11)
Kellettina binoda, 2 var. (11)
Kirkbya sp. aff. K. canyonensis (11)
K. sp. (11)
Paraparchites claytonensis (11)
Silenites sp. (11)
CRINOIDEA
Cibolocrinus punctatus (9)
C. tumidus (9)
Delocrinus cf. verus
D. n. sp.
Ulocrinus sp. (10)
Crinoids, gen. and sp. undet. (9)
ECHINOIDEA
Echinocrinus sp. (6,10)
VERTEBRATA
Shark teeth, undet. (9)
PLANTS
Asterophyllites equisetiformis (12)
Calamites sp. aff. C. suckowii (12)
Cardiocarpon sp. (9,10)
Cordaites sp. (9,10)
Lebachia sp. (9)
Neuropteris ovata (12)
N. scheuchzeri (9,10)
N. tenuifolia (9,10)
Pecopteris vestita (9)
Sigillaria sp. (9)

The first significant attempt to correlate the Pennsylvanian strata of New Mexico with standard sequences in other regions was by Needham (1937) in his bulletin on New Mexico fusulinids. In 1940 he published a short paper entitled "Correlation of Pennsylvanian rocks in New Mexico." Using about twenty-five species of fossils, chiefly brachiopods and a few fusulinids, he suggested that the oldest Pennsylvanian strata of central New Mexico are younger than Bend, Morrow, or lower Pottsville. Two years later, Thompson (1942) proposed the term Derry series for the essentially pre-Desmoinesian Pennsylvanian rocks of central to south-central New Mexico, and correlated the Derry with the Atoka of Oklahoma, Cheney's Lampasas of Texas, and the basal part of the Des Moines of some areas in the Mid-Continent region. He did not believe that the New Mexico Pennsylvanian sequence included any part of Morrowan time.

Thompson correlated the Sandia formation of the Sandia Mountains with his Elephant Butte formation of the Armendaris group of Desmoinesian age. According to him, a section at the northern end of the Sandia Mountains includes rocks of Desmoinesian, Missourian, and Virgilian age, while sections at Jemez Springs include rocks of Derryan age as well. However, in the same year, Read and Henbest (1942) stated that the Pennsylvanian of northern New Mexico includes rocks of Morrowan age. In 1944 Henbest and Read recognized the **Millerella** zone in the Jemez country near Jemez Pueblo and again at the Soda Dam, and concluded that it is of probable Morrowan age. (See also Read and Wood, 1947.) Northrop and Wood (1945; 1946) assigned a Morrowan age to certain strata in the Jemez country, citing especially the large and distinctive brachiopod **Schizophoria** cf. **oklahomae** (ranging up to 73 mm across), which occurs in the Wapanucka and Morrow of Oklahoma. We collected this striking brachiopod near the base of the Sandia formation at two localities in Guadalupe Canyon, about 7 and 9 miles, respectively, north of Jemez Pueblo. Later, Armstrong (1955) found an abundance of good specimens of this species in Penasco Canyon, about 7½ miles west of Jemez Pueblo.

In 1946 Northrop and Wood reported for the Jemez-Nacimiento area a total of about 185 species, based on a preliminary study of nearly 100 collections from 33 stratigraphic sections, and proposed five faunal zones—designated A, B, C, D, and E (from oldest to youngest)—"each of which is characterized either by species having short stratigraphic ranges, by the earliest appearance of longer-ranging species, by a notable abundance of certain long-ranging species which range through more than one zone, or by a combination of these." Faunal zone A = Morrowan; B = late Morrowan, Lampasan, and early Desmoinesian; C = late Desmoinesian and earliest Missourian; D = remainder of Missourian; and E = Virgilian.

In conclusion, it seems likely that the Pennsylvanian sequence in the Jemez country ranges from Morrowan to Virgilian, whereas the sequence in the Sandia country may lack representatives of Morrowan and Lampasan (Atokan) time.

REFERENCES CITED

Armstrong, A. K., 1955, Preliminary observations on the Mississippian system of northern New Mexico: New Mexico Bur. Mines and Mineral Res. Circ. 39, 42 p., illus.

────────, 1958, Meramecian (Mississippian) endothyrid fauna from the Arroyo Penasco formation, northern and central New Mexico: Jour. Paleontology, v. 32, p. 970-976, illus.

Baltz, E. H., and Read, C. B., 1960, Rocks of Mississippian and probable Devonian age in Sangre de Cristo Mountains, New Mexico: Am. Assoc. Petroleum Geologists Bull., v. 44, p. 1749-1774, illus.

Bisbee, W. A., 1932, The paleontology and stratigraphy of the Magdalena group of northern and central New Mexico: Univ. New Mexico unpub. master's thesis, 99 p., illus.

Dunbar, C. O., and Condra, G. E., 1932, Brachiopoda of the Pennsylvanian system in Nebraska: Nebraska Geol. Survey 2d ser. Bull. 5, 377 p., illus.

Fitzsimmons, J. P., Armstrong, A. K., and Gordon, Mackenzie, Jr., 1956, Arroyo Penasco formation, Mississippian, north-central New Mexico: Am. Assoc. Petroleum Geologists Bull., v. 40, p. 1935-1944, illus.

Henbest, L. G., 1946a, Stratigraphy of the Pennsylvanian in the west half of Colorado and in adjacent parts of New Mexico and Utah [abs.]: Am. Assoc. Petroleum Geologists Bull., v. 30, p. 750-751.

────────, 1946b, Correlation of the marine Pennsylvanian rocks of northern New Mexico and western Colorado [abs.]: Washington Acad. Sci. Jour., v. 36, p. 134.

Henbest, L. G., Read, C. B., and others, 1944, Stratigraphic distribution of the Pennsylvanian Fusulinidae in a part of the Sierra Nacimiento of Sandoval and Rio Arriba Counties, New Mexico: U. S. Geol. Survey Oil and Gas Inv. Prelim. Chart 2.

Herrick, C. L., 1900, The geology of the White Sands of New Mexico: Univ. New Mexico Bull., v. 2, fascicle 3, 17 p., illus.

Herrick, C. L., and Bendrat, T. A., 1900, Identification of an Ohio Coal Measures horizon in New Mexico: Univ. New Mexico Bull., v. 2, fasciculus 2, 10 p.

Herrick, C. L., and Johnson, D. W., 1900, The geology of the Albuquerque sheet: Univ. New Mexico Bull., v. 2, pt. 1, 67 p., illus.

Kelley, V. C., and Wood, G. H., Jr., 1946, Lucero uplift, Valencia, Socorro, and Bernalillo Counties, New Mexico: U. S. Geol. Survey Oil and Gas Inv. Prelim. Map 47.

Lovejoy, B. P., 1958, Paleontology and stratigraphy of the Jemez Springs area, Sandoval County, New Mexico: Univ. New Mexico unpub. master's thesis, 101 p., illus.

Marcou, Jules, 1856, Report on the geology of the route: No. 2, Resume and field notes . . . with a translation by William P. Blake [Whipple's reconnaissance near the 35th parallel], in Reports of explorations and surveys . . . : U. S. 33d Cong. 2d Sess. Senate Exec. Doc. 78 and House Exec. Doc. 91, v. 3, pt. 4, p. 121-164, illus.

────────, 1858, Geology of North America: Zurich, 144 p., illus.

Moore, R. C., and Dudley, R. M., 1944, Cheilotrypid bryozoans from Pennsylvanian and Permian rocks of the Midcontinent region: Kansas Geol. Survey Bull. 52, pt. 6, p. 229-408, illus.

Needham, C. E., 1937, Some New Mexico Fusulinidae: New Mexico Bur. Mines and Mineral Res. Bull. 14, 88 p., illus.

——————, 1940, Correlation of Pennsylvanian rocks of New Mexico: Am. Assoc. Petroleum Geologists Bull., v. 24, p. 173-179.

Needham, C. E., and Bates, R. L., 1942, Pre-Cretaceous, in Bates, R. L., The oil and gas resources of New Mexico, 2d ed.: New Mexico Bur. Mines and Mineral Res. Bull. 18, p. 117-121.

Northrop, S. A., and Wood, G. H., Jr., 1945, Large Schizophoria in the basal Pennsylvanian of New Mexico [abs.]: Geol. Soc. America Bull., v. 56, p. 1185.

——————, 1946, Geology of Nacimiento Mountains, San Pedro Mountain, and adjacent plateaus in parts of Sandoval and Rio Arriba Counties, New Mexico: U. S. Geol. Survey Oil and Gas Inv. Prelim. Map 57.

Northrop, S. A., and others, 1946, Geologic maps of a part of the Las Vegas basin and of the foothills of the Sangre de Cristo Mountains, San Miguel and Mora Counties, New Mexico: U. S. Geol. Survey Oil and Gas Inv. Prelim. Map 54.

Read, C. B. (personal communication), Memorandum of June 29, 1961; identification of fossil plants collected in Tijeras Canyon by W. W. Atkinson, Jr., Carol Bambrook, and S. P. Marsh during May 1954 and following months.

Read, C. B., and Henbest, L. G., 1942, Pennsylvanian and Permian stratigraphy of northern New Mexico [abs.]: Am. Assoc. Petroleum Geologists Bull., v. 26, p. 910.

Read, C. B., and Wood, G. H., Jr., 1947, Distribution and correlation of Pennsylvanian rocks in late Paleozoic sedimentary basins of northern New Mexico: Jour. Geology, v. 55, p. 220-236, illus.

Read, C. B., and others, 1944, Geologic map and stratigraphic sections of Permian and Pennsylvanian rocks of parts of San Miguel, Santa Fe, Sandoval, Bernalillo, Torrance, and Valencia Counties, north-central New Mexico: U. S. Geol. Survey Oil and Gas Inv. Prelim. Map 21.

Szabo, Ernest, 1953, Stratigraphy and paleontology of the Carboniferous rocks of the Cedro Canyon area, Manzanita Mountains, Bernalillo County, New Mexico: Univ. New Mexico unpub. master's thesis, 137 p., illus.

Thompson, M. L., 1942, Pennsylvanian system in New Mexico: New Mexico Bur. Mines and Mineral Res. Bull. 17, 90 p., illus.

——————, 1948, Studies of American fusulinids: Univ. Kansas Paleont. Contrib., Protozoa, Art. 1, 184 p., illus.

Toomey, D. F., 1953, Paleontology and stratigraphy of the Carboniferous rocks of the Placitas region, northern Sandia Mountains, Sandoval County, New Mexico: Univ. New Mexico unpub. master's thesis, 192 p., illus.

Werrell, W. L., 1961, Pennsylvanian ostracods and fusulinids of Tijeras and Cedro Canyons, Bernalillo County, New Mexico:· Univ. New Mexico unpub. master's thesis, 102 p., illus.

White, C. A., 1877, Report upon the invertebrate fossils . . . : U. S. Geog. Surveys West of the 100th Meridian (Wheeler), v 4, pt. 1.

PERMIAN STRATA OF CENTRAL NEW MEXICO

D. L. Baars
Shell Oil Company, Farmington, New Mexico

The Permian system of central New Mexico is a colorful sequence of red beds, massive light-colored sandstones, carbonate rocks, and evaporites that resulted from deposition in complexly interrelated marine and continental environments. The Permian rocks outcrop along the Lucero uplift southwest of Albuquerque, in the Zuni Mountains southeast of Gallup, along the east flank of the Manzano and Sandia Mountains, and are rather extensive along the Nacimiento Mountains as far north as San Pedro Mountain near Cuba, New Mexico. The section has been penetrated by several deep wells in the southern part of the San Juan Basin and along the flanks of the Zuni uplift. The nature and spacing of both the outcrop and subsurface control is adequate to readily correlate the Permian strata from one outcrop area to the next within the general area of the 1961 Field Conference (see Fig. 1), for the stratigraphic changes are relatively simple and natural. Regional correlations are not so well established, however, and are the subject of some controversy. While it is not within the scope of this paper to discuss the regional relationships, the terminology and correlations will here be modeled after a rather extensive study of the Permian stratigraphy of the Colorado Plateau by Baars (1961, in press) which deals with these problems at some length.

The Permian rocks of central New Mexico generally overlie the Pennsylvanian system conformably. Transitional beds are present in the southern part of the area that are termed the Bursum formation and Red Tanks member of the Madera formation. However, the Permian rests on older rocks in local areas of uplift. The basal Permian strata that overlie the Madera or Bursum formations are the red beds of the Abo formation. The Abo grades northward into the lower part of the Cutler formation of the Four Corners area, and interfingers toward the south with most of the Wolfcampian Hueco limestone (see Fig. 2). The Abo formation is overlain conformably by the orange-colored sandstones and siltstones of the De Chelly sandstone, until recently referred to the Meseta Blanca member of the Yeso formation (Baars, 1961). The De Chelly is in turn overlain by the red beds and evaporites of the Yeso formation, which formerly was termed the San Ysidro or Los Vallos member of the Yeso formation. As restricted by Baars (1961), the Meseta Blanca member was made a separate formation and correlated with the De Chelly sandstone, leaving only the upper evaporite red beds and thin dolomites in the Yeso formation. Light-colored Glorieta sandstones overlie the Yeso conformably, and interfinger or grade upward into the marine carbonates, clastics, and evaporites of the San Andres formation of probably uppermost Leonardian and/or lowermost Guadalupian age. This tightly interrelated sequence represents only about the early half of the Permian period, with late Permian time being represented by the erosional surface present everywhere on the Colorado Plateau between the Permian and Triassic rocks.

NATURE OF THE PERMO-PENNSYLVANIAN BOUNDARY

The Permo-Pennsylvanian boundary is probably represented by continuous sedimentation over most of central New Mexico. In the area south of Albuquerque, beds are present that are believed to be gradational between Pennsylvanian and Permian; these are known as the Bursum formation east of the Rio Grande and as the Red Tanks member of the Madera formation in the Lucero Mesa area (Kelley and Wood, 1946; and others). These units are largely red beds with thin interbedded limestones that overlie marine rocks of late Virgilian (uppermost Pennsylvanian) age, and at least locally contain early Wolfcampian fusulinids. Thus, if the section is not entirely conformable, very little time is available for a major hiatus. Although no known Bursum or Red Tanks beds are present north of Albuquerque, sedimentation was probably continuous across the temporal boundary throughout the southern San Juan Basin region. It is probable that basal red beds of the Abo formation are of Bursum age in the Zuni and Nacimiento Mountains and in the subsurface of the San Juan Basin, and these strata usually rest on Virgilian marine rocks of the Madera formation. The gradational Permo-Pennsylvanian boundary may continue as far north in the San Juan Basin as the Colorado border.

The major positive areas of Pennsylvanian age were not buried completely until Permian time, permitting the sedimentation of Lower Permian rocks on pre-Virgil units. Thus, the Abo red beds overlie Precambrian rocks on the Defiance, Zuni, and Penasco (Nacimiento Mountains) uplifts, and beds of early Missourian age in the Joyita Hills west of Socorro. There is little doubt that the red beds are post-Pennsylvanian on the Defiance, Penasco, and Joyita uplifts, but beds are present on the Zuni uplift that may be Upper Pennsylvanian in age. These marine beds contain a nondiagnostic megafauna that could be either uppermost Pennsylvanian or basal Permian in age, so that the exact date of complete burial of the Zuni positive element is in doubt.

ABO FORMATION

The Abo formation was named by Lee in 1909 (Jicha and Lochman-Balk, 1958) for exposures of red beds overlying the Madera and Bursum formations in Abo Canyon near Mountainair in the southern Manzano Mountains. The Abo consists of reddish brown shales, siltstones, and usually arkosic sandstones that become somewhat coarser in grain-size toward the Uncompahgre-San Luis uplift source area to the northeast. The formation is very similar lithologically to the lower Supai of eastern Arizona and the lower Cutler of the Four Corners region which are lateral equivalents of the Abo (Fig. 2). The very irregular and often lenticular bedding of the sandstones suggests a fluvial mode of deposition for much of the unit, and the occasional occurrences of vertebrate and plant fossils tend to verify a continental origin. However, the Abo interfingers toward the south with the marine Hueco limestone (Kottlowski and others, 1956; and others), which implies that sedimentation was probably on a broad coastal plain that may have been periodically flooded by marine waters in the southern part of the province. The Abo formation overlies Wolfcampian beds of the Bursum formation at the type section, dating the Abo as post-Pennsylvanian in that area. The southward interfingering of the Abo with the Hueco limestone dates the unit as mostly Wolfcampian, but there is a possibility that the uppermost part of the red beds may be Leonard in age.

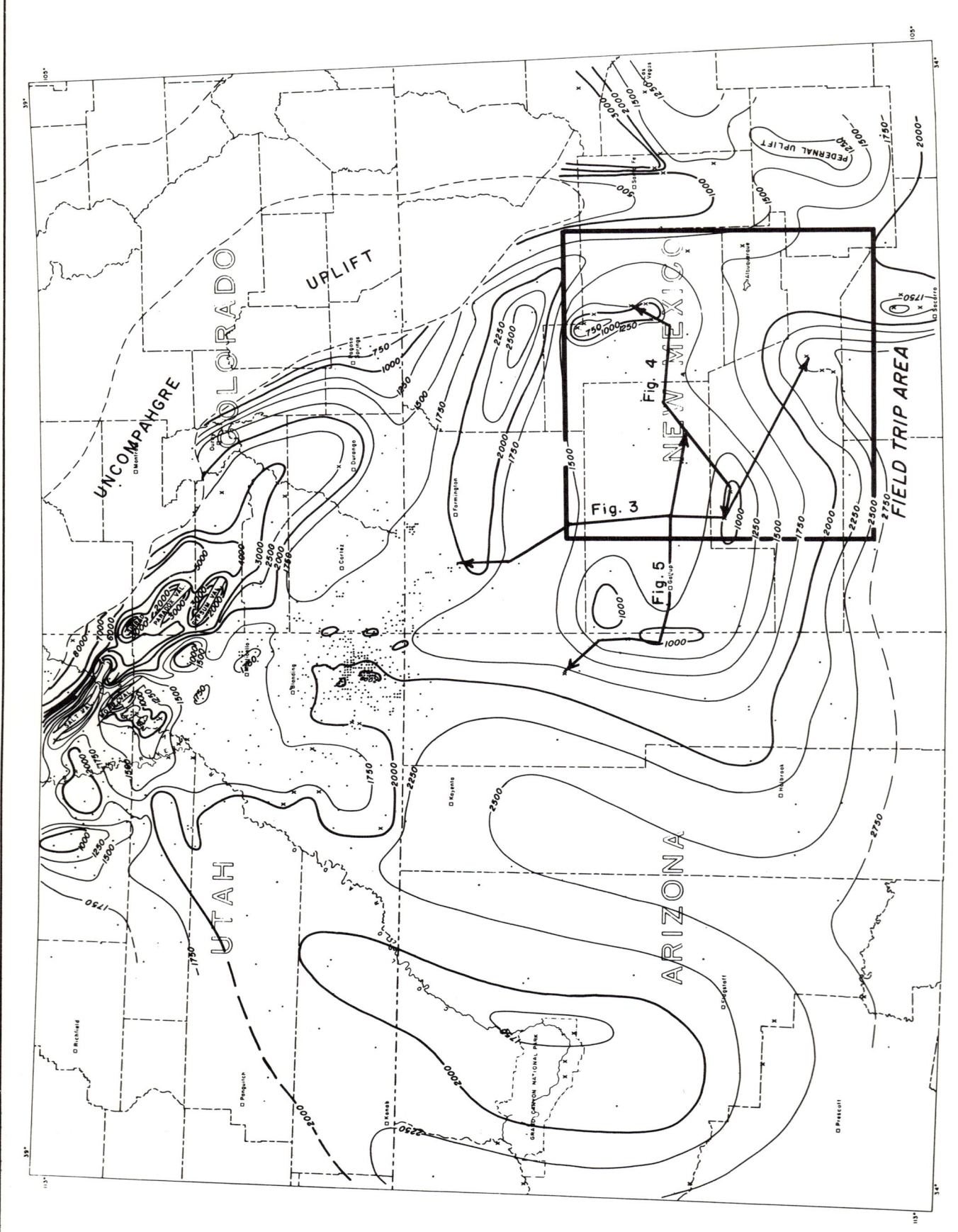

Figure 1

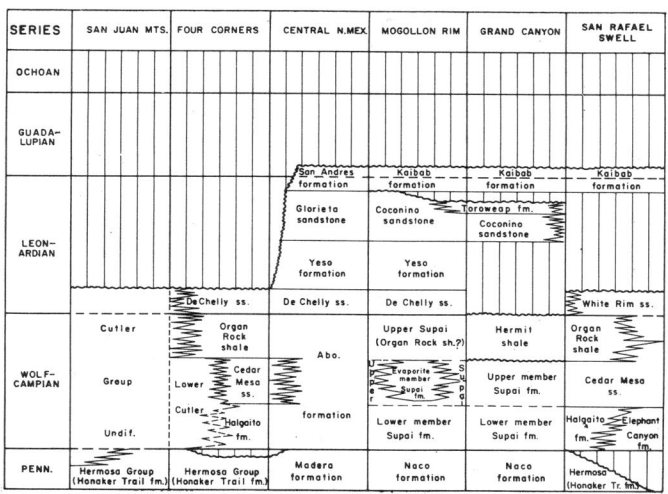

FIGURE 2

The Abo formation ranges from about 800 to 900 feet thick in the Lucero Mesa and Abo Canyon areas, but thins to less than 200 feet in the central Zuni Mountains (see Fig. 3). It averages 400-600 feet thick in the southern San Juan Basin and thins to less than 400 feet in the Nacimiento Mountains exposures. The Abo grades northward into the undifferentiated Cutler formation in the vicinity of San Pedro Mountain near Cuba, New Mexico (Wood and Northrop, 1946), and can be correlated through subsurface control into the Four Corners, Defiance uplift, and eastern Arizona areas (Figs. 4 and 5) (Baars, 1961). The red beds thicken eastward into the upper portion of the very thick Sangre de Cristo formation of the Rowe-Mora basin east of Santa Fe.

DE CHELLY SANDSTONE

The Abo red beds are overlain by orange-red sandstones and siltstones that were previously assigned to the basal Yeso formation, and were termed the Meseta Blanca member by Wood and Northrop (1946). The possibly eolian to shallow marine sandstone is very similar in lithology to the De Chelly sandstone of the Defiance uplift and Four Corners area, and was correlated with the De Chelly through subsurface and Defiance uplift studies by Baars (1961). As the result of that correlation, the Meseta Blanca member is referred to the De Chelly sandstone, and separated from the Yeso formation for ease and clarity of usage. The unit will therefore be termed the De Chelly sandstone in this paper.

The De Chelly sandstone was named for magnificent exposures of the unit in Canyon de Chelly on the Defiance uplift by Gregory (1917), and was subsequently correlated into central New Mexico into the "basal Yeso sandstone" by Baars (1961). It is an orange-red highly cross-stratified sandstone in its northern occurrences, but becomes finer grained and massive to thinly and horizontally bedded toward the south. In the Zuni Mountains and Lucero Mesa area, it is largely a flat-bedded siltstone that is undoubtedly subaqueous in origin, and possibly marine. In the southern Nacimiento Mountains, it is a highly cross-stratified fine-grained sandstone much like the Defiance uplift exposures that are generally believed to be eolian deposits. The De Chelly sandstones are usually fairly well sorted and well rounded, and are poorly cemented by ferruginous material toward the north, becoming harder and more calcareous southward. [Not all workers would agree.—Ed.] The formation cannot be accurately dated, but is probably early Leonardian because it overlies possible Leonardian Abo beds and is closely related to the definitely Leonardian Yeso formation which immediately overlies the De Chelly.

The De Chelly sandstone thickens eastward from less than 200 feet on the southern Defiance uplift to more than 300 feet in the Zuni Mountains and 600 feet in the southern San Juan Basin. The siltstones thin generally southward to 400 feet in the southern Lucero Mesa area and to about 200 feet in the vicinity of Socorro, New Mexico (Figs. 3, 4, and 5). South of this latitude, it becomes increasingly thinner and less distinctive (Kottlowski and others, 1956). The De Chelly thins to the north also, and is 200 to 300 feet thick in the Nacimiento Mountains south of its facies change into Cutler red beds near Cuba, New Mexico (Wood and Northrop, 1946). This belt of facies change (from the red cross-stratified sandstone to arkosic Cutler red beds in a northeasterly direction) extends toward the northwest into the Four Corners area in the subsurface, outcropping again on the Monument upwarp in southern Utah. It is probable that the sandstone was derived from contemporaneously deposited red clastics of the undifferentiated Cutler arkosic facies, and windblown toward the southwest into the southern San Juan Basin where marine environments were encountered.

YESO FORMATION

The Yeso formation, as herein restricted, is a mixture of red beds, evaporites, and thin beds of carbonate rocks that conformably overlie the De Chelly sandstone. Only the northern margin of the Yeso depositional basin is present in central New Mexico. The formation is composed largely of Cutler-like red beds in the Nacimiento Mountains, where the unit is probably truncated by pre-Triassic erosion in the northern part of the range (Wood and Northrop, 1946). Toward the south, the Yeso contains thin beds of dolomite and becomes lighter red in color in the Zuni Mountains, and contains gypsums along with the light red beds and dolomites in the eastern Zunis and in the Lucero Mesa area (Figs. 3, 4, and 5). The Yeso simultaneously thickens in a southerly direction from 0-100 feet in the Nacimientos to about 600 feet in the Lucero Mesa area (Kelley and Wood, 1946). The formation may be divided areally into a northerly dark red-bed facies termed the San Ysidro facies by Wood and Northrop (1946) and a southerly light red-bed and evaporite facies termed the Los Vallos facies by Kelley and Wood (1946). The terms were originally member names assigned to the Yeso, but they may be usefully applied as facies terms with the present terminology. The clastic content of the Yeso becomes more arkosic and coarse grained toward the north as the rocks become darker colored and less evaporitic, suggesting a northerly source for the clastics. Since it is very unlikely that the Uncompahgre-San Luis source area was active after about De Chelly time, it is probable that the Yeso red beds are derived from the reworking of Cutler arkosic red beds to the north. The general lithology of the Yeso suggests that the depositional environment was a shallow partially restricted sea which received red clastics from a ready supply in the north.

The Yeso type section is on Mesa del Yeso near Socorro, New Mexico, where the formation was named and described by Lee in 1909 (Jicha and Lochman-Balk, 1958). In that general area, the Yeso is divisible into a lower orange sandstone member, a lower evaporite member, the Canas gypsum member, and the Joyita sand-

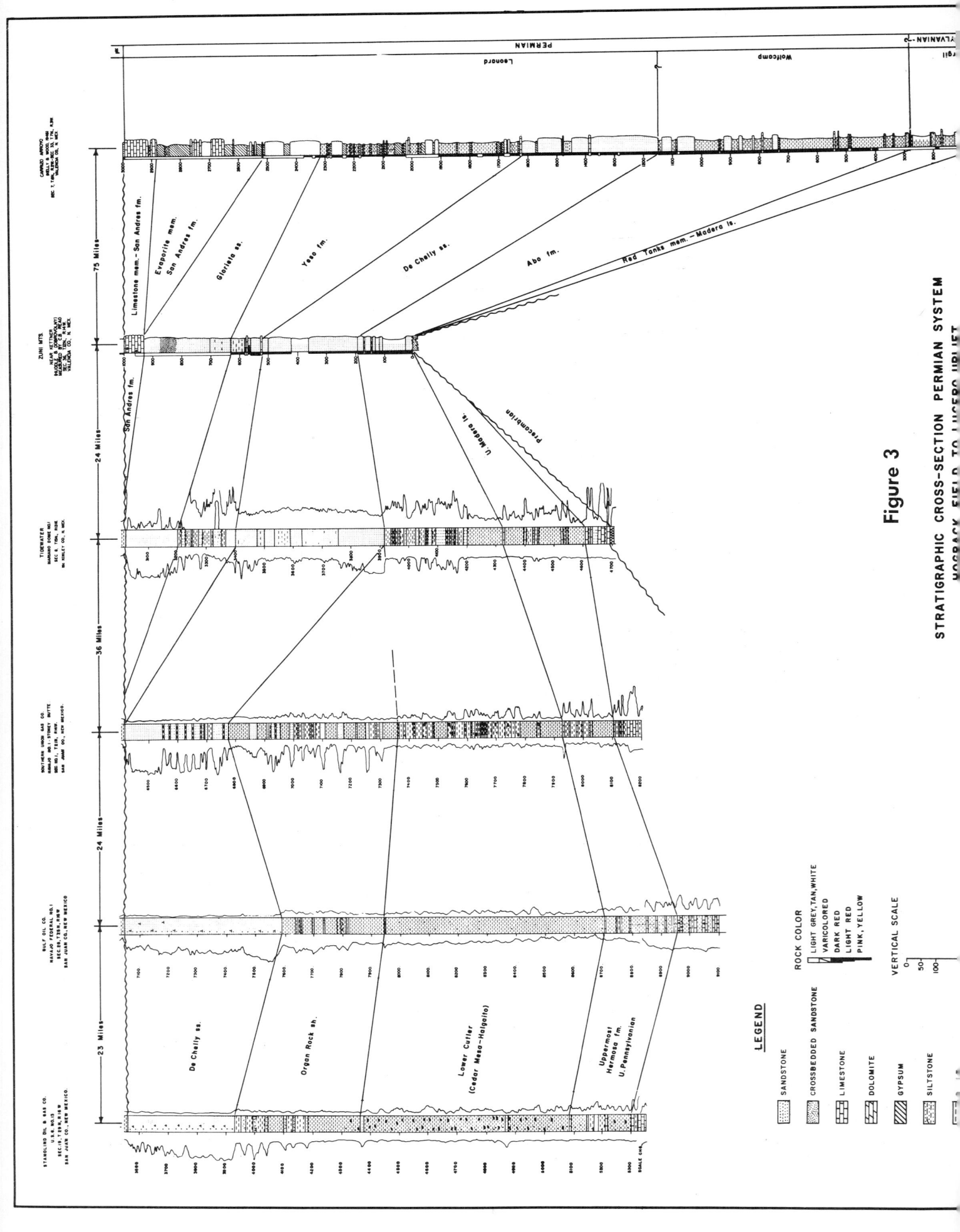

Figure 3

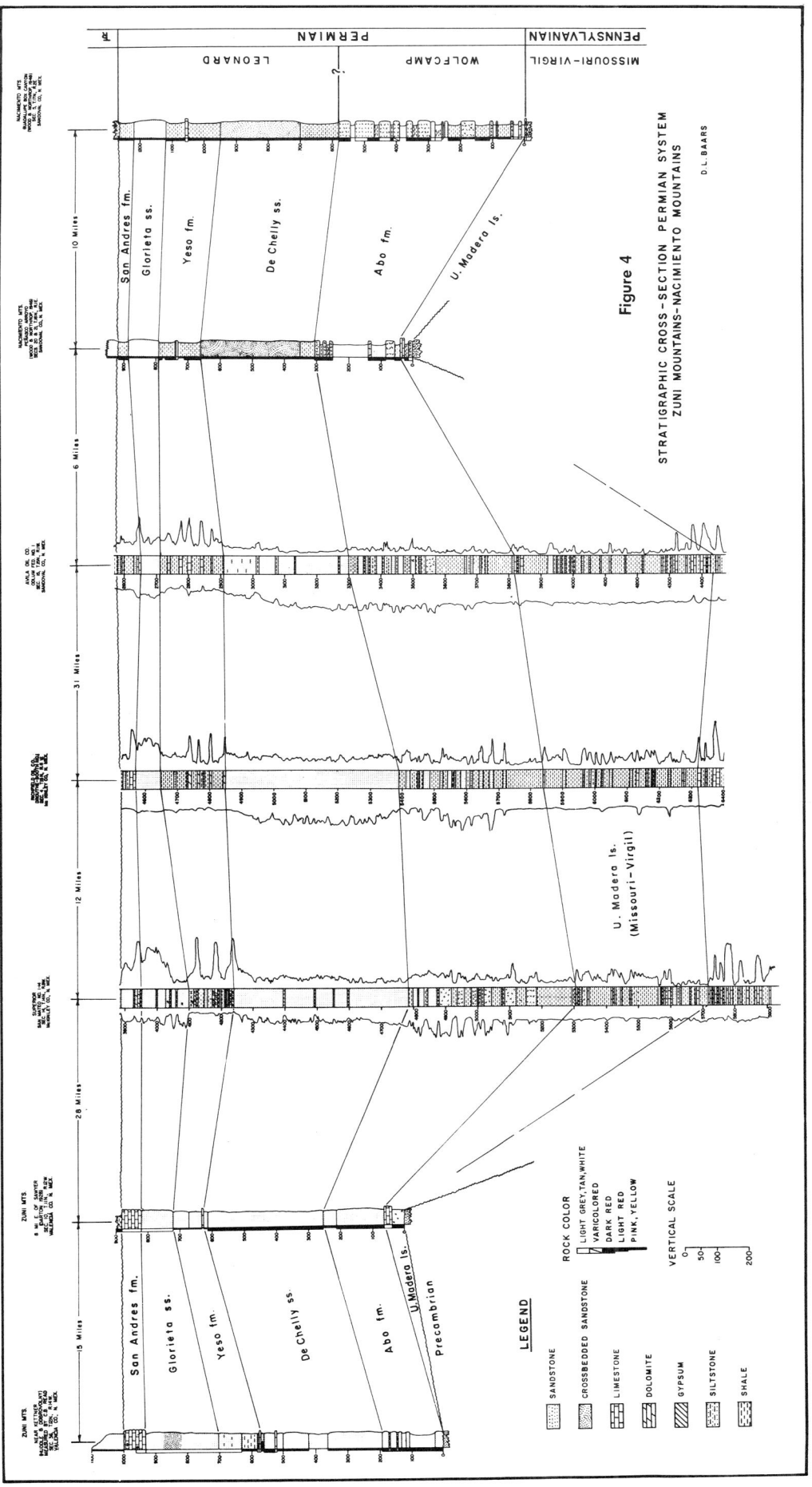

Figure 4

STRATIGRAPHIC CROSS-SECTION PERMIAN SYSTEM
ZUNI MOUNTAINS-NACIMIENTO MOUNTAINS

D. L. BAARS

stone member, in ascending order (Needham and Bates, 1943). The Yeso is dated mostly by work done in southern New Mexico, where it is considered to be Leonard in age on the basis of invertebrate megafossil and fusulinid studies. The formation is not present in the Four Corners area for it pinches out and is truncated by pre-Triassic erosion across the southern San Juan Basin, but it is present in eastern Arizona where it is the uppermost part of the Supai as previously used.

GLORIETA SANDSTONE

The term Glorieta sandstone has been used in a variety of ways since 1915, and was defined in its present usage by Needham and Bates (1943) who designated the type section at Glorieta Mesa near Rowe, New Mexico. The unit is a white fine- to medium-grained, siliceous sandstone that is typically cross-stratified. [In many places the cement is calcareous.—Ed.] The bedding is typified by cross-strata in two- to six-foot thick simple sets that are each bevelled to a plane at the upper surface. The primary dips of the cross-stratification average 10 to 20 degrees. The general impression is one of horizontal thin bedding, with massive large-scale cross-stratification confined to a few isolated occurrences in the Zuni Mountains. It is probable that the Glorieta sands were deposited in a high-energy littoral environment, with only local inclusion of offshore bar or eolian deposits. The equivalent Coconino sandstone in northern Arizona (Fig. 2) differs mainly in type of cross-stratification. The Coconino is composed of large-scale, randomly oriented wedge-shaped cross-stratification sets that are unmistakably of eolian origin. The Glorieta sandstone interfingers with both the underlying Yeso formation and the younger San Andres formation, placing it conformably between two marine deposits of Leonardian age.

The Glorieta sandstone is a relatively uniform deposit, striking approximately east-west and thickening gradually southward. The northward termination is one of depositional thinning complicated by later truncation. In the northern Nacimiento Mountains, the Glorieta is truncated by pre-Triassic erosion (Wood and Northrop, 1946), much as is the case in the subsurface of the southern San Juan Basin and on the Defiance uplift (Baars, 1961). The formation thickens southward to about 300 feet in both the Zuni Mountains and Lucero Mesa areas (Fig. 3). The Glorieta is very widespread to the south and east in New Mexico.

SAN ANDRES FORMATION

The uppermost Permian unit of central New Mexico is the San Andres formation named by Lee in 1909 (Jicha and Lochman-Balk, 1958) for exposures in the San Andres Mountains of central southern New Mexico. A type section was designated by Needham and Bates (1943) in Rhodes Canyon in the northern San Andres Range. The formation is composed largely of carbonate rocks and fine-grained clastics in the Zuni Mountains, but changes rapidly to red beds toward the north and evaporites toward the southeast. The San Andres formation has long been considered equivalent to the Kaibab formation of northern Arizona (Fig. 2).

The San Andres formation of the Zuni Mountains contains two distinctive units that weather to a lower ledgy slope and an upper massive cliff. The lower unit consists of a thin- to medium-bedded alternation of sucrosic dolomites, shales, siltstones, and sandstones that make up half or more of the formation. The upper cliff-forming unit of the San Andres is typically a massive limestone that is quite variable laterally. Most commonly it is a very dense carbonate mud deposit that contains large productid brachiopods and large cephalopods, but varies to local deposits of skeletal calcarenites that appear to be beach deposits that alternate with quartzose Glorieta-like sandstones. The upper San Andres also contains rare biohermal accumulations that are partially dolomitized. This upper unit was apparently deposited on a shallow marine shelf in tropical waters.

The shallow carbonate shelf assemblage grades rapidly to a shoreward red-bed facies in the subsurface north of the Zuni Mountains (Fig. 4). Thin carbonates are occasionally present, but they are only a minor constituent in the southern San Juan Basin. The sequence is similar in the southern Nacimiento Mountains where a single dolomite bed is present in a thin red-bed unit. The San Andres is truncated northward by pre-Triassic erosion in the northern Nacimientos (Wood and Northrop, 1946), as well as in the subsurface of the southern San Juan Basin and on the Defiance uplift. The present northern limits of the formation are probably not very different from the position of the shoreline, however, for the northern red-bed facies is interpreted as shoreward lagoonal and intertidal deposits.

The San Andres thickens rapidly toward the southeast into an evaporite basin that centers approximately in the Lucero Mesa area (Fig. 3). Kelley and Wood (1946) described the thick evaporites in outcrops along the Lucero uplift, which appear to be equivalent to the lower part of the Zuni Mountain sequence. The San Andres evaporites differ from the underlying Yeso evaporitic deposits in that red beds are not associated with the San Andres formation in the restricted basin. The association of evaporites with drab-colored related sediments may indicate deeper water and reducing bottom conditions in the San Andres basin.

The San Andres formation thickens gradually southward from a feather-edge in the central Nacimiento Mountains and southern San Juan Basin to about 100 feet in the Zuni Mountains. Its thickness increases to 400 feet in the evaporitic section along the Lucero uplift. The San Andres can be readily traced southward through good outcrops to the type section and the Guadalupe Reef country, where the formation is probably partly Leonardian and partly Guadalupian in age (Boyd, 1958). It is probable that only the lower Leonardian portion of the San Andres is present in the area of the Field Conference.

PERMIAN-TRIASSIC UNCONFORMITY

The contact between the Permian rocks and the overlying Triassic beds is everywhere unconformable in central New Mexico. The hiatus involved the last half of Permian and earliest Triassic time. Physical evidence of the unconformity is usually a low-relief erosional surface, but local areas display more profound erosional features. The surface in the Zuni Mountains is generally a rolling hill-and-valley topography with about 40 feet of relief, but in the vicinity of Ft. Wingate in the western part of the range steep valleys were cut 100 feet into the Permian rocks, removing all of the San Andres formation in local channels. The unconformity is slightly angular in the Nacimiento Mountains, for the Permian strata were truncated northward until the Triassic rests directly on the De Chelly sandstone near Cuba (Wood and Northrop, 1946). A similar northward truncation exists in the subsurface north of the Zuni Mountains, but since the upper formations are all

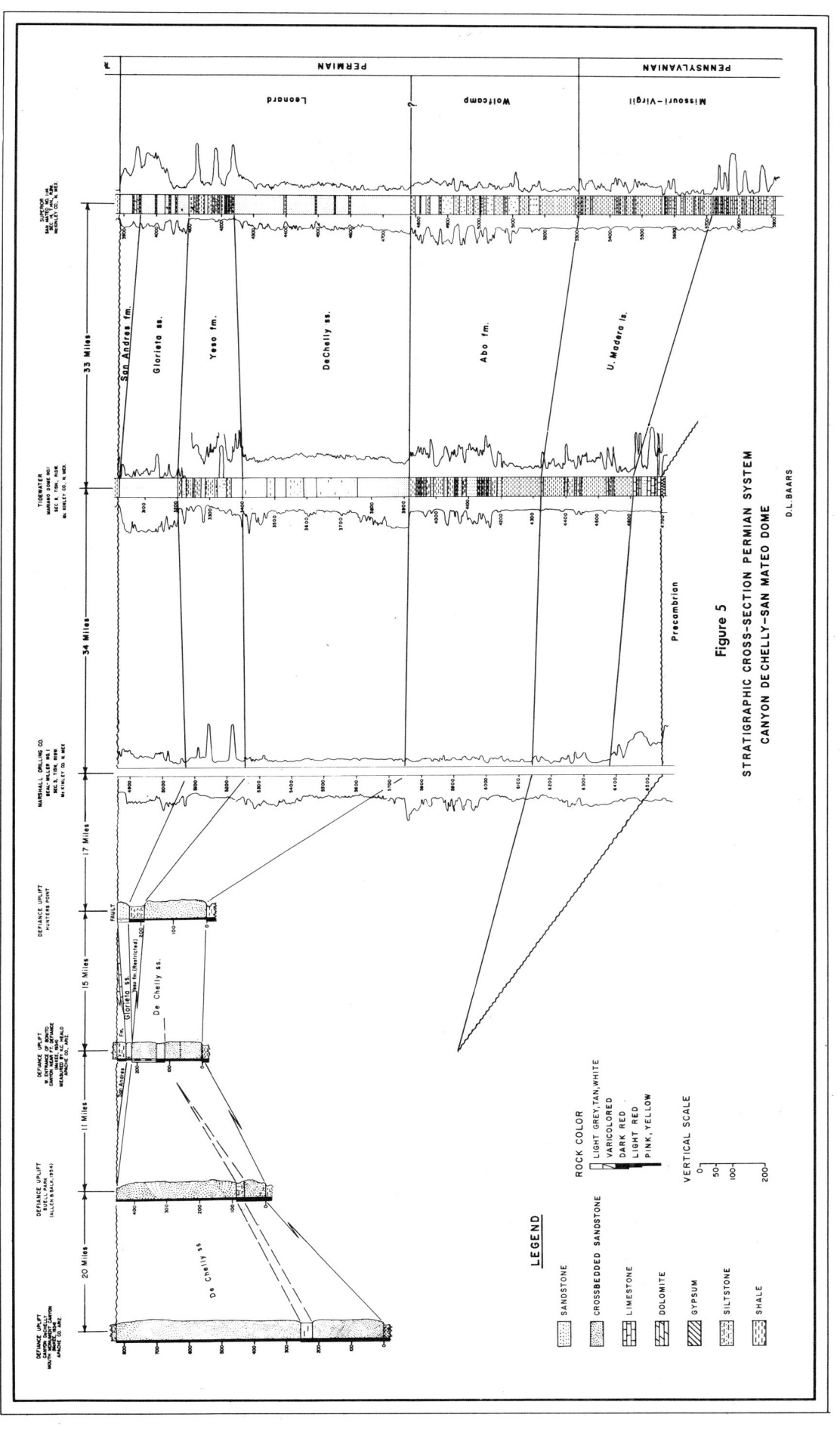

Figure 5

STRATIGRAPHIC CROSS-SECTION PERMIAN SYSTEM
CANYON DE CHELLY—SAN MATEO DOME

D.L. BAARS

near their depositional limits it is difficult to evaluate the effectiveness of the erosion. A similar northward removal of Permian rocks is evident along the Defiance uplift.

REFERENCES CITED

Baars, D. L., 1961, Permian system of the Colorado Plateau: Am. Assoc. Petroleum Geologists Bull. (in press).

Boyd, D. W., 1958, Permian sedimentary facies, central Guadalupe Mountains, New Mexico: New Mexico Bur. Mines and Mineral Res. Bull. 49.

Gregory, H. E., 1917, Geology of the Navajo country: U. S. Geol. Survey Prof. Paper 93.

Jicha, H. L., Jr., and Lochman-Balk, Christina, 1958, Lexicon of New Mexico geologic names: Precambrian through Paleozoic: New Mexico Bur. Mines and Mineral Res. Bull. 61.

Kelley, V. C., and Wood, G. H., Jr., 1946, Lucero uplift, Valencia, Socorro, and Bernalillo Counties, New Mexico: U. S. Geol. Survey Oil and Gas Inv. Prelim. Map 47.

Kottlowski, F. E., Flower, R. H., Thompson, M. L., and Foster, R. W., 1956, Stratigraphic studies of the San Andres Mountains, New Mexico: New Mexico Bur. Mines and Mineral Res. Mem. 1.

Needham, C. E., and Bates, R. L., 1943, Permian type sections in central New Mexico: Geol. Soc. America Bull., v. 54, p. 1653-1658.

Wood, G. H., Jr., and Northrop, S. A., 1946, Geology of Nacimiento Mountains, San Pedro Mountain, and adjacent plateaus in parts of Sandoval and Rio Arriba Counties, New Mexico: U. S. Geol. Survey Oil and Gas Inv. Prelim. Map 57.

[Note.—It is anticipated that this stimulating paper will evoke lively discussion.—Ed.]

TRIASSIC AND JURASSIC ROCKS OF THE ALBUQUERQUE AREA

CLAY T. SMITH
New Mexico Institute of Mining and Technology

The Albuquerque area may be defined as the Albuquerque-Belen basin of the Rio Grande depression (Kelley, 1952) and the adjacent associated platforms, uplifts, channels, and constrictions (see Fig. 1). The present configuration is chiefly the result of Tertiary and Quaternary diastrophism and bears little relation to the distribution of Triassic and Jurassic rocks except as it controls the outcrops of these beds.

Many of the units so well known in the classical sections of the Colorado Plateau region are either missing or have merged with other members until all become unrecognizable. The areas in which outcrops occur are widely scattered, commonly confined to the mountain blocks, or to isolated structural basins and complexly faulted zones along the margins of the Rio Grande depression.

TRIASSIC ROCKS

Traditionally, the Triassic system has been subdivided into tripartite units usually labeled lower, middle, and upper. As additional information has been collected it is obvious that such a separation is not everywhere applicable. McKee and others (1959) utilized three intervals, A, B, C, in ascending order, in their treatment of the Triassic rocks of the United States, although recognizing that interval B has a very restricted distribution. The intervals A, B, and C of their paper are correlative with the German tripartite division of the Triassic, as well as with accepted groupings of the Alpine European stages.

The classic Colorado Plateau section consisting of the Moenkopi, Shinarump, and Chinle formations is assigned to intervals A and C by McKee and others (1959) and has been enlarged through inclusion of the Wingate formation of the Glen Canyon group in the C interval by Harshbarger, Repenning, and Irwin (1957). The Dockum group of eastern New Mexico, West Texas, Oklahoma, and southwestern Colorado is apparently confined to the C interval and has not been as extensively subdivided as has the Colorado Plateau section.

In the Albuquerque area only rocks of the C interval are present, corresponding to the German Keuper or the combined Karnian, Norian, and Rhaetian stages of the European marine sequence. The Albuquerque area lay on a shelf between a western basin containing more than 2,000 feet of Chinle sediments in the Zuni Mountains-St. Johns area, and an eastern basin containing more than 2,000 feet of Dockum sediments in and near Lea County, New Mexico, and Yoakum County, Texas. Correlation between Chinle-type sediments west and north of Albuquerque, and Dockum-type sediments east and south of Albuquerque has been difficult because of the intervening present-day Rio Grande structural trough. The southerly depositional margin of the Triassic rocks induced facies changes that are rapid and unpredictable owing to local variations in tectonic activity. Local names have been introduced in several areas, including some originating in the Albuquerque area, and the relationships between such local units are not always clear (see Table 1).

The Triassic sediments of the Albuquerque area are predominantly fine-grained sandstone, siltstone, and mudstone with intercalated lenticular conglomerate and coarse-grained sandstone beds. In most places the lower part of the section contains more sandstone and is coarser grained than the upper part, although this is not the case in exposures in parts of the Lucero Mesa area (Kelley and Wood, 1946). Maroon, reddish purple, and brown colors are prominently developed and often serve as identifying features for this rock sequence. Locally the sandstones and conglomerates may be buff to nearly white in color and stand out sharply against the bright-red mudstone slopes. Bentonitic clays are abundant in the mudstone units and the alternate shrinking and swelling of the soil in the semi-arid southwestern climate results in characteristic "crazed" exposures. In the upper part of the lower sandy facies, petrified wood and chert pebbles are locally abundant.

The Chinle formation was named by Gregory (1917) from exposures in Chinle Valley, Arizona; Gregory's original description of the formation did not include the Shinarump conglomerate, which he considered a separate formation. McKee and others (1959) included the Shinarump as a lower member of the Chinle formation and indicated that it extends little if any distance east of the New Mexico-Arizona stateline. Other local members of the Chinle formation have been described in Arizona, such as the Petrified Forest member, Owl Rock member, and Sonsela sandstone member, but these cannot be extended very far to the east or north (Stewart, 1957). Wood and Northrop (1946) subdivided the Chinle formation in the Nacimiento uplift into four units, in ascending order: Agua Zarca sandstone, Salitral shale, Poleo sandstone, and the upper Chinle beds. These units are not readily recognizable away from the type localities northwest of the Jemez Mountains and were not individually delineated on the Nacimiento uplift map. Along the north flank of the Zuni Mountains, Smith (1954) mapped a lower member, a middle sandstone member, and an upper member of the Chinle formation; these beds had originally been erroneously described by Darton (1928) as Moenkopi, Shinarump, and Chinle formations. The lower and middle members in the Zuni Mountains suggest correlation with the lower Petrified Forest and the Sonsela sandstone members of the Arizona section while the upper member contains limestone layers and lenses similar to the Owl Rock member. In the Lucero Mesa area Kelley and Wood (1946) divided the Chinle formation into two units: a lower red shale member and the overlying Correo sandstone member; they also recognized a thick unit between the Chinle formation and the underlying Paleozoic limestones which they referred to the Shinarump conglomerate; however, it seems likely that these beds are merely the lower sandy facies of the Chinle formation and may correlate much more closely with the Santa Rosa sandstone member of the Dockum group to the east, or with the Agua Zarca, Salitral, and Poleo members farther north. The Correo sandstone member has a very local distribution and is not recognized away from Mesa Gigante in the northern part of the Lucero Mesa area.

West of the Albuquerque area, the Chinle formation is a thick mass of red mudstone, siltstone, and sandstone with marly beds and intercalated conglomerate lenses. A sandy facies occupies the lower one-third to one-half of the formation while mudstone and shale are predominant in the upper portion. The lower sandy facies averages 300 to 500 feet thick from the Lucero Mesa area to the New Mexico-Arizona stateline, whereas the upper shaly portion ranges

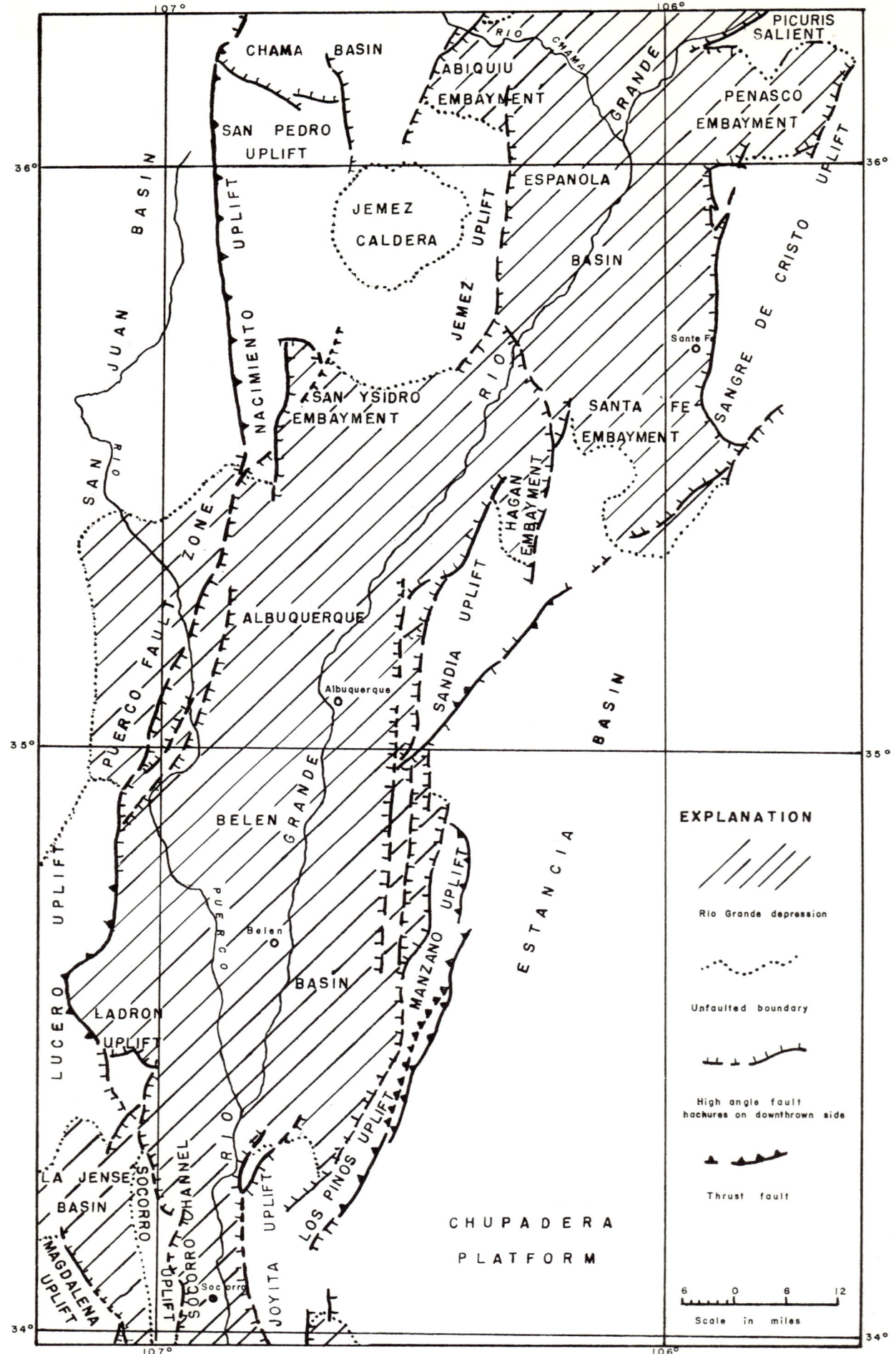

Figure 1. ALBUQUERQUE AREA (after Kelley, 1954)

from a few hundred feet to more than 1,500 feet in thickness. At least part of the variation in thickness of the upper member may be due to pre-Jurassic erosion. The appearance of coarser grained units in the upper parts of the formation to the south suggests also some depositional variation. A thickening of nearly 20 feet per mile occurs between the east end of Mesa Gigante and Ramah on the south side of the Zuni Mountains.

The Dockum beds were described by Cummins in 1890 as conglomerate, sandstone, and red clay, 150 feet thick, near Dockum, Texas (Wilmarth, 1938, p. 616). McKee and others (1959) showed thicknesses in excess of 2,000 feet along the southern part of the Texas-New Mexico stateline and thicknesses of 1,000 to 1,500 feet in east-central New Mexico. Southeast of the Albuquerque area considerable thicknesses of Triassic rocks have been removed by erosion. Locally, near Cerrito del Lobo, the Dockum rests upon Precambrian metamorphic rocks as a result of pre-Triassic erosion. Lithologically, the Dockum beds are similar to the Chinle units, although the bentonitic layers so common in the Arizona section are subordinate or lacking in the Texas and eastern New Mexico exposures. Several members, principally of local significance, were described east of the Albuquerque area. A lower sandy facies similar to the lower unit in the Nacimiento and Zuni Mountains sections is called the Santa Rosa sandstone member and an upper mudstone facies, the Redonda member. In Texas, the Camp Springs conglomerate, the Tecovas and Trujillo formations, and the Sloan Canyon formation have been assigned to the Dockum beds. McKee and others (1959) placed the Pierce Canyon red beds, which underlie the Santa Rosa sandstone in southeast New Mexico, in the Triassic (?) as the lowest unit in the Dockum group, although there is some evidences suggesting a Permian age for these rocks.

McKee and others (1959) estimated that the Triassic rocks in the Albuquerque area had an original thickness between 500 and 1,000 feet.[1] These thicknesses do not include any rocks correlated with the Wingate or Kayenta formations since these beds do not extend this far east. Outcrops to the north and south of the Albuquerque area show some thinning; north of the Jemez uplift Triassic rocks wedge out against the Precambrian core of the Brazos uplift. In the latitude of Socorro more than 400 feet of Triassic rocks are present with less than 100 feet of this thickness assignable to a lower sandy (Santa Rosa?) facies. Kelley and Silver (1952, p. 108) stated that Triassic rocks are absent in the Caballo Mountains 75 miles south of Socorro; it is not clear whether pre-Cretaceous erosion or Triassic non-deposition is indicated by such absence. The thinning of the lower sandy facies as compared with areas to the north, west, and east is suggestive of non-deposition.

Originally the Wingate sandstone was considered the lower member of the Glen Canyon group and placed in the Jurassic. However, Harshbarger, Repenning, and Irwin (1957) restricted the Wingate sandstone of Dutton (1885) to the lower half of the type section at Fort Wingate, New Mexico; they recognized two members, a lower Rock Point member and an upper Lukachukai member within the restricted Wingate over much of the Navajo Reservation of New Mexico and Arizona. Fossil evidence coupled with intertonguing between the underlying Chinle formation and the Rock Point member places all of the restricted Wingate sandstone in the Triassic. Although the Lukachukai member extends considerably farther east than the Rock Point member, neither of these units is present in the Albuquerque area; the Lukachukai member is reported to pinch out a few miles south and east of Laguna, New Mexico.

Faunal evidence suggests that deposition of Dockum beds began prior to the deposition of the Chinle formation. In Arizona and southern Utah no hiatus is present between the latest stages of Triassic deposition and the overlying Jurassic deposits. During Triassic time the locus of deposition appears to have shifted westward and sedimentation continued after deposition in eastern New Mexico and west Texas had ceased. Correlation is difficult because of the variable lithologies and the fact that fossils are scarce and poorly preserved. A continuous evolution from primitive phytosaurs in the Tecovas beds of west Texas through more advanced forms in the Petrified Forest member of the Arizona section to highly advanced types in the Redonda member of the Dockum group and the Rock Point member of the Wingate sandstone provides the framework on which Table 1 is based. The lower sandy facies in the Albuquerque area is represented by the Agua Zarca, Salitral, and Poleo members to the west, or the Santa Rosa sandstone to the east. It contains no diagnostic fossils and correlations within this part of the section are extremely tenuous. The large collections of vertebrate fossils described from the Ghost Ranch area north of the Albuquerque area are confined to the upper shaly member of the Chinle formation and merely provide an upper limit to the age of the lower sandy facies; the Ghost Ranch fauna is correlated with forms from the upper part of the Petrified Forest member and from shale units below the Redonda and Sloan Canyon members.

JURASSIC ROCKS

The Jurassic rocks of the Albuquerque area represent a complex series of marine (?) and non-marine units which, as they are traced toward the southern edge of the Albuquerque area, coalesce into a single inseparable mass of sandstone and finally wedge out by intraformational and interformational unconformities. The classic Jurassic section of the Colorado Plateau region contained the Glen Canyon group, the San Rafael group, and the Morrison formation. Local member and formational names have been applied and extended without benefit of faunal control and considerable nomenclatural confusion has resulted. McKee and others (1956) subdivided the Jurassic system into four units, in ascending order, A, B, C, and D. The unit boundaries do not necessarily coincide with time or formational planes but in a general way the four intervals can be correlated with the European stages. Rocks from the uppermost portion of interval B, most of interval C, and a part of interval D are exposed in the Albuquerque area. Table 2 illustrates the relationships between the units of the Albuquerque area and adjoining regions. Three units of the San Rafael group plus the Morrison formation have been recognized to the west and north of the Albuquerque area. Similar units also extend eastward at least to the Texas-New Mexico stateline, but all strata pinch out southward in response to a combination of pre-Cretaceous erosion and non-deposition.

The oldest Jurassic beds in the Albuquerque area are massive alternating evenly bedded and cross-bedded sand-

---

[1]This maximum appears to be low. In an unpublished thesis, Harrison (1949) reported about 2,100 feet in the Hagan basin—a figure generally believed to be excessive. —Ed.

Table 1. — Proposed Correlation of Triassic Rocks between the Albuquerque and adjacent Areas

U.S. Geol. Survey Paleotectonic Map Intervals	Eastern Arizona	Gregory Units	North Flank, Zuni Mtns., N. Mexico	Albuquerque Area — West	Albuquerque Area — East	Eastern New Mexico	N.E. New Mexico & Western Texas	European Stages — Alpine	European Stages — German
Interval C	Moenave formation							Rhaetian	Keuper
	Wingate sandstone — Lukachukai member		Wingate sandstone — Lukachukai member				Sheep Pen sandstone	Rhaetian	Keuper
	Chinle formation — Rock Point member	A	Chinle formation — Upper member	Chinle formation — Correo member	Dockum group — "Chinle" formation — Redondo member	Dockum group — "Chinle" formation — Redondo member	Dockum group — Sloan Canyon formation	Norian	Keuper
	Chinle formation — Owl Rock member	B	Chinle formation — Upper member	Chinle formation — Red Shale member	Dockum group — "Chinle" formation — Shale member	Dockum group — "Chinle" formation — Shale member	Dockum group — Trujillo formation	Norian	Keuper
	Chinle formation — Upper Part Petrified Forest member		Chinle formation — Middle member	Chinle formation — Poleo ss. / Salitral sh.			Dockum group — Tecovas formation	Norian	Keuper
	Chinle formation — Sonsela member	C	Chinle formation — Middle member	Chinle formation — Poleo ss. / Salitral sh.	Dockum group — Santa Rosa sandstone	Dockum group — Santa Rosa sandstone	Dockum group — Tecovas formation	Norian	Keuper
	Chinle formation — Lower Part Petrified Forest member		Chinle formation — Lower member	Chinle formation — Agua Zarca sandstone	Dockum group — Santa Rosa sandstone	Dockum group — Santa Rosa sandstone	Dockum group — Camp Springs conglomerate	Karnian	Keuper
	Chinle formation — Lower Sandstone member	D	Chinle formation — Lower member	Chinle formation — Agua Zarca sandstone			Dockum group — Basal Dockum beds	Karnian	Keuper
	Chinle formation — Shinarump member			—?—	—?—	Pierce Canyon redbeds		Karnian	Keuper
Interval B	Moenkopi formation							Ladinian / Anisian	Muschelkalk
Interval A								Scythian	Bunter

stone layers assigned to the Entrada formation. The Entrada formation disconformably overlies the Chinle or Dockum beds, although no angularity can be measured in individual outcrops. The Entrada formation was named by Gilluly and Reeside in joint conference with Moore and Gregory (Wilmarth, 1938) from exposures on Entrada Point in the San Rafael Swell, Utah. At the type locality the formation is alternating thin- and thick-bedded, red sandstone and siltstone grading upward into massive red-brown earthy sandstone. Traced eastward from the type locality, the Entrada sandstone develops an upper clean buff-white sandy facies often referred to as the slick-rim Entrada, and the red silty facies of the type locality becomes very thin. Harshbarger, Repenning, and Irwin (1957) describe a third facies that underlies the other two facies and is a clean sandy facies; its distribution is restricted to the northwestern part of the Navajo Reservation in Arizona. Harshbarger, Repenning, and Irwin's (1957) terminology is adopted for this paper: the lowest unit is the lower sandy facies; the typical unit of Entrada Point is the medial silty facies; and the slick-rim unit is the upper sandy facies. Only the medial silty facies and the upper sandy facies are present in the Albuquerque area. The medial silty facies is recognized only in the western portion, where it is 10 to 50 feet of even-bedded fine-grained buff to white sandstone in 1- to 2-foot layers interbedded with platy red mudstone and siltstone ranging from a few inches to 2 feet in thickness. The sandstone is stained red from the interbedded mudstone and the whole weathers to a steep slope or cliff. The medial silty member is overlain by the upper sandy facies which consists of buff to brown sandstone, predominantly evenly bedded at the base and grading upward into a mixture of small-scale, simple, and planar cross-stratification; the uppermost parts of the upper sandy facies are yellowish to white in color and contain even-bedded layers. Locally, the upper sandy facies intertongues with the overlying Todilto limestone, whereas a short distance away angularity of 10 to 15 degrees may be measured.

The Todilto limestone was originally described by Gregory (1917) from exposures at Todilto Park, New Mexico. Todilto Park is near the western margin of deposition of the Todilto limestone and the type section contains much clastic material which is not present in the Albuquerque area. The lower part of the formation is sandy, particularly in those areas where the formation intertongues with the underlying Entrada. Elsewhere the base of the unit is thin-bedded, platy, fetid gray limestone with intercalated layers of black or greenish mudstone and shale; limestone beds are from 2 to 12 inches in thickness and the shaly layers 4 inches or less. The basal limestone is usually from 12 to 15 feet thick, although extremes of less than 5 feet and more than 25 feet are known. The limestone grades upward into lenticular massive gypsum, locally very pure, that may reach thicknesses of more than 100 feet. The northern part of the Albuquerque area appears to have been the center of an evaporite basin during Todilto time because the gypsum deposits decrease in thickness and uniformity away from it.

The upper contact of the Todilto limestone exhibits considerable change from west to east across the Albuquerque area. On the eastern side the gypsum layers are overlain disconformably by sandstone and mudstone assigned to the lower part of the Morrison formation. On the western side several sandstone, siltstone, and mudstone facies intertongue and grade upward into recognizable Morrison beds. Farther west and to the south Harshbarger, Repenning, and Irwin (1957) have recognized the Cow Springs sandstone as a thick eolian sandstone unit which is equivalent to parts of the Entrada, Todilto, upper San Rafael group, and Morrison beds. Pre-Upper Cretaceous erosion has destroyed most of the evidence for such a unit in the Albuquerque area, but a southerly increase in sandstone in the Morrison formation as well as in the Todilto limestone and overlying upper San Rafael units along the western side of the Albuquerque area is very suggestive (Silver, 1948).

In the San Rafael Swell two formations comprise the upper part of the San Rafael group: the marine limestones and shales of the Curtis and the overlying Summerville siltstones, sandstones, and mudstones. The Curtis formation extends only a few miles south and east of the San Rafael Swell, but Harshbarger, Repenning, and Irwin (1957) recognize the Summerville formation as far south and east as Ft. Wingate, New Mexico, and correlate it with the "buff shale and brown-buff sandstone members of the Morrison formation" (Kelley and Wood, 1946) in the Lucero Mesa area. The Summerville formation was named by Gilluly and Reeside (1928) from exposures on Summerville Point in the San Rafael Swell. At the type locality the boundary between the underlying Curtis formation and the Summerville is arbitrary, but to the south and east Harshbarger, Repenning and Irwin (1957) recognize a lower silty facies and an upper sandy facies in the Summerville which they believe correspond to the Curtis and Summerville formations of the type localities. In the western part of the Albuquerque area the upper sandy facies of the Summerville is thought to be present, associated with tongues of the Cow Springs sandstone. The Summerville beds are distinguished from adjacent rocks by good sorting, fineness of grain, and even, thin bedding. Intraformational crumpling and slump structures are common, often bounded by undisturbed layers of essentially identical material. The layers are red to reddish brown and seldom vary in color throughout the entire range in grain size from sandstone to claystone. Some representatives of the Summerville formation may be present on the east side of the Albuquerque area, but they cannot be easily distinguished from the lower part of the Morrison formation.

The Morrison formation includes the youngest Jurassic rocks in the Albuquerque area. The name Morrison formation was first published by Cross (1894) for the exposures near the town of Morrison, Colorado. The formation has subsequently been extended over most of the Western Interior of the United States. Local facies names have been used extensively but McKee and others (1956) restricted these to seven fairly widespread units (see Table 2). In the Albuquerque area the principal unit is the Brushy Basin member, although a lower sandy facies in the Brushy Basin member to the east and north may represent equivalents of the Recapture, Westwater Canyon, or Salt Wash members. The white sandstone member in the Lucero Mesa area (Kelley and Wood, 1946) is interpreted as a tongue of the Cow Springs sandstone by Harshbarger, Repenning, and Irwin (1957). The Brushy Basin member of the Morrison formation is the most extensive unit as well as the most uniform. It consists of variegated, green, gray, buff, and pink mudstone and siltstone interbedded with buff to white, lenticular sandstone beds. The sandstone layers are

Table 2 – Proposed Correlation of Jurassic Rocks between the Albuquerque and adjacent Areas

U.S. Geol. Survey Paleotectonic Map Intervals	Eastern Utah	Northeastern Arizona	North Flank, Zuni Mtns, New Mexico	Albuquerque Area West	Albuquerque Area East	Eastern New Mexico	European Stages
Interval D	Morrison formation — Brushy Basin member; Lower sandy member	Morrison formation — Brushy Basin member, Westwater member, Recapture member, Salt Wash member	Morrison formation — Brushy Basin member, Prewitt member, Westwater member, Recapture member	Morrison formation — Brushy Basin member	Morrison formation — Brushy Basin member	Morrison formation — Brushy Basin member	Portlandian
					Lower member	Lower member	Kimmeridgian
Interval C	Curtis formation	Bluff sandstone; Summerville formation; Curtis formation; Upper sandy mem.	Bluff sandstone; Summerville; Upper member; Lower member	White Sandstone member; Brown buff sandstone member; Buff shale member; Upper sandy member; Medial silty m.	Summerville form.; Thoreau form.; Upper sandy member; Medial silty member	Entrada sandstone (Ocate ss., Exeter ss.)	Oxfordian
				Cow Springs ss. — San Rafael group	Entrada Sandstone		Callovian
Interval B	Preuss sandstone; Twin Creek formation	Carmel formation	Entrada; San Rafael group	Entrada			Bathonian
							Bajocian
							Toarcian
Interval A	Nugget sandstone	Navajo sandstone; Kayenta formation; Glen Canyon group	Navajo sandstone; Kayenta formation; Glen Canyon group				Pliensbachian
							Sinemurian
							Hettangian

often coarse grained and conglomeratic and some of the finer grained layers are marly. North of the Albuquerque area the Brushy Basin member contains bentonitic layers and glass shards indicative of volcanic activity during latest Jurassic time. To the south and west the sand content of the Brushy Basin member increases and the member cannot be distinguished from the upper part of the Cow Springs formation. Similar difficulties may arise to the west where the Westwater Canyon member can be separated from the upper part of the Cow Springs. Facies changes are very rapid in the Albuquerque area because of proximity to the southern depositional margin of the Jurassic rocks. Likewise, thicknesses vary greatly in relatively short distances because of pre-Upper Cretaceous erosion.

Correlation and relative ages of the Jurassic rocks are less certain than for the Triassic beds. Fossils have not been found in the Entrada sandstone, Summerville formation, or Cow Springs formation in this area. The Morrison formation has yielded fragmentary dinosaur remains. According to S. A. Northrop (personal communication, July 23, 1961), a few pieces of bone, some of which were radioactive, were collected by W. L. Chenoweth from the variegated member of the Morrison formation at several localities in Valencia County during the summer of 1952, notably in the Mesa Gigante-Suwanee Peak area. In his unpublished master's thesis, Chenoweth (1953) noted that although the variegated member of Kelley and Wood had been correlated by several workers with the Brushy Basin member, he believed it to be older and probably equivalent to the Chaves or Recapture member. Dinosaur bones collected by Chenoweth and a bone collected by J. E. Self during the summer of 1953 from the Morrison formation near Grants were submitted by Northrop to E. H. Colbert, of the American Museum of Natural History, who reported that three well-known dinosaur genera are represented, as follows:

Brontosaurus: near Grants
Allosaurus: near Acoma and also near Suwanee Peak
Stegosaurus: west side of Mesa Gigante

The Todilto limestone has yielded fresh- or brackish-water ostracods and a few fish with marine affinities, but none of the forms is particularly diagnostic. The Curtis formation in the San Rafael Swell has a characteristic marine fauna as does the Carmel formation immediately below the Entrada sandstone in the same locality. Practically all the dinosaur fauna reported from the Morrison formation comes from areas far to the north so that age assignments and correlations must rest largely upon lithologic grounds. Except for parts of the Todilto-Summerville sequence all the Jurassic rocks in the Albuquerque area are eolian or fluviatile floodplain deposits; the Todilto-Summerville sequence is thought to represent rather abnormal marine or tidal-flat [possibly lacustrine? Ed.] conditions. The uppermost parts of the Brushy Basin member may also contain units that may be Lower Cretaceous (Burro Canyon, Stokes and Phoenix, 1948) in age, although in the Albuquerque area evidence for this has been removed by pre-Upper Cretaceous erosion.

SEDIMENTATIONAL HISTORY

The early Mesozoic was an interval during which epeirogenic forces were active, but no major orogenies took place in the southwestern region. The extensive continental seas which had flooded the area during the Pennsylvanian and Permian periods did not reappear until the Cretaceous period. The Albuquerque area was a nearly flat, featureless plain which was bounded to the south by a gentle rise to a broad belt of low hills which extended across the southern part of New Mexico and Arizona (Mogollon Highlands of Harshbarger, Repenning, and Irwin, 1957); to the north, parts of the old Uncompahgre positive area were uplifted and intermittently shed sediment southward. Westward, the plain sloped very gently toward a marine shelf whose maximum eastward extent was in central Arizona and which in turn extended westward into a miogeosyncline whose trough occupied most of Nevada and western Utah. Deposition began in early Triassic time in the Nevada miogeosyncline and in the Arizona shelf area with limestone and fine-grained clastics. The older Defiance and Zuni positive areas, although greatly reduced, apparently marked the eastern limit of deposition of the early Triassic beds. The red mudstones and siltstones of the Moenkopi formation do not extend east of this area. In the Albuquerque area erosion was leveling the region, exhuming ancient positive elements (Pedernal high) to the southeast.

Erosion continued throughout early and middle Triassic time, but by the beginning of the late Triassic, gentle, irregular warping began to deform the region into local basins and uplifts. Deposition of Dockum beds began in central West Texas with a relatively fine-grained siltstone and mudstone but as warping continued conglomerate and sandstone were deposited particularly near the margins of the basins. The Albuquerque area developed as a low shelf separating basins to the southeast and west where more than 2,000 feet of terrestrial mudstone, siltstone, and sandstone accumulated. The late Triassic terrane was traversed by sluggish streams meandering generally westward and eventually reaching the marine waters in Arizona. The late Triassic deposits are all continental and contain some marl and limestone. Exterior drainage was maintained across the basins and evaporite sequences are lacking. By late Triassic time the Defiance and Zuni positive areas had disappeared, but the Uncompahgre uplift was still weakly active. Uplift of the Mogollon Highlands to the south of the Albuquerque area apparently kept pace with the sinking of the depositional area, because little change in the type sedimentation is visible throughout the Chinle and Dockum beds. Locally, conglomerate and sandstone layers suggest minor variations in uplift and erosion of the source areas.

By the end of the Triassic the source areas of sediment for the Albuquerque area had been leveled and deposition ceased. Orogenic movements were not a factor because farther west no hiatus occurs between Triassic and Jurassic sediments. However, the climate did become more arid and some erosion undoubtedly occurred during early Jurassic time in the Albuquerque area. Farther west the Lukachukai member of the Wingate sandstone was accumulating as extensive sand dunes, and broad upwarping to the north and east brought about changes in the drainage patterns. The Rock Point member of the Wingate sandstone accumulated in a basin whose axis trended northeast-southwest.

During early Jurassic time a gradual realignment of the depositional areas took place and marine waters invaded the Western Interior region from the north. The earliest Jurassic beds were the fluviatile and eolian deposits of the Kayenta, Navajo, and Nugget formations of Arizona and Utah, but in early middle Jurassic time abundant marine faunas in the Twin Creek formation of Utah, Idaho, and

Wyoming attest to the invasion of the boreal seas. During middle Jurassic time the seaway extended southward beyond the Arizona-Utah stateline, and tidal-flat and floodplain deposition extended considerably farther south and east. Rejuvenation of the low-lying Mogollon Highlands in southern Arizona and New Mexico blocked deposition to the south and provided a source of abundant sand from the earlier Navajo and Wingate accumulations. Harshbarger, Repenning, and Irwin (1957, p. 44) pointed out that an uplift to the southwest at the close of Kayenta time eliminated the gap between the old Cordilleran geanticline to the west and the Mogollon Highlands to the south and also provided much of the source area for the upper Jurassic sediments in the southern Cordilleran region. In the Albuquerque area deposition did not begin until late in middle Jurassic time. The medial silty member of the Entrada sandstone marked the easterly edge of tidal-flat and floodplain deposition. Above these layers was spread the fluviatile and eolian blanket of the upper sandy facies of the Entrada sandstone. The upper sandy facies of the Entrada sandstone was the first Mesozoic unit to spread eastward over the old Uncompahgre positive area and it had multiple sources. In the Albuquerque area most of the Entrada sandstone was derived from sources to the south and east.

Continued uplift of the Mogollon Highlands resulted in a restriction of the Entrada depositional basin and the limestone and evaporite deposits of the Todilto limestone began to form. The environment of deposition of the Todilto limestone is uncertain (Anderson and Kirkland, 1960). The scarcity of fossils and the fetid nature of the beds suggest an abnormal condition and yet desiccation was never complete enough to result in saline deposits. Harshbarger, Repenning, and Irwin (1957) postulated a gulf with a restricted channel which allowed alternating desiccation and renewal of marine waters. They proposed a connection just southwest of the Four Corners area. However, a northeasterly connection to the eastern Colorado evaporite basin, which in turn was connected to the Sundance sea to the north, is also a possibility. The thick gypsum deposits indicate that the central part of an essentially land-locked basin lay in the Albuquerque area. Following the withdrawal of the Todilto sea, erosion removed portions of the evaporite deposits, although deposition was still continuing farther west in the old marine basin.

Jurassic deposition in the Albuquerque area closed with the Morrison formation. The exact nature of the hiatus between the Todilto and Morrison is not known, because correlatives of the intervening units in the more complete plateau section cannot be recognized in the sandy facies below the typical Brushy Basin member. Relief on the contact between the units rarely exceeds a few tens of feet and is often less than one foot; layers above and below the boundary are essentially parallel. It seems likely that the Albuquerque area remained close to base level during the time represented by the Curtis, Summerville, Salt Wash, Recapture, and Westwater deposition farther west; certainly deposition and erosion were at a minimum.

The Brushy Basin member of the Morrison formation was a floodplain deposit of mudstone and siltstone with occasional channel-sandstone and conglomerate lenses. Petrified wood and bone fragments are common in the coarser grained portions of the member. It spread over the entire Rocky Mountain region grading abruptly into eolian sandstone along the southern margin of the depositional area. In the Albuquerque area the Mogollon Highland provided a local source for the eolian sands but most of the material was derived from far to the east and west of the area. Pre-Upper Cretaceous erosion has removed any very late Jurassic beds as well as Lower Cretaceous rocks that might have accumulated in the Albuquerque area, but the proximity of the Jurassic depositional margin to the south would seem to have precluded extensive deposition.

In summary, the Albuquerque area was a stable platform during most of Triassic and Jurassic time. A total of less than 2,000 feet of sediment was deposited and much of the material is fine-grained siltstone, sandstone, or mudstone. Minor downwarping and uplift are reflected in local sandstone and conglomerate layers, but no orogenic movements of any magnitude disturbed the stability of the platform. Subsequent structural complexity and extensive erosion hamper detailed correlation between various facies, but the stable nature of the area throughout the entire Mesozoic is unquestioned.

BIBLIOGRAPHY

Anderson, R. Y., and Kirkland, D. W., 1960, Origin, varves, and cycles of Jurassic Todilto formation, New Mexico: Am. Assoc. Petroleum Geologists Bull., v. 44, p. 37-52.

Chenoweth, W. L., 1953, The variegated member of the Morrison formation in the southeastern part of the San Juan Basin, Valencia County, New Mexico: Univ. New Mexico unpub. master's thesis, p. 30, 33-34, 62.

Cross, Whitman, 1894, Pikes Peak, Colorado: U. S. Geol. Survey Geol. Atlas, Folio 7.

Darton, N. H., 1928, "Red Beds" and associated formations in New Mexico: U. S. Geol. Survey Bull. 794 [1929].

Dutton, C. E., 1885, Mount Taylor and the Zuni Plateau: U. S. Geol. Survey 6th Ann. Rept., p. 105-198.

Gilluly, James, and Reeside, J. B., Jr., 1928, Sedimentary rocks of the San Rafael Swell and some adjacent areas in eastern Utah: U. S. Geol. Survey Prof. Paper 150-D.

Gregory, H. E., 1917, Geology of the Navajo country, a reconnaissance of parts of Arizona, New Mexico, and Utah: U. S. Geol. Survey Prof. Paper 93, p. 42.

Harrison, E. P., 1949, Geology of the Hagan coal basin: Univ. New Mexico unpub. master's thesis, 177 p.

Harshbarger, J. W., Repenning, C. A., and Irwin, J. H., 1957, Stratigraphy of the uppermost Triassic and the Jurassic rocks of the Navajo country: U. S. Geol. Survey Prof. Paper 291.

Kelley, V. C., 1952, Tectonics of the Rio Grande depression of central New Mexico, in New Mexico Geol. Soc. Guidebook of the Rio Grande country, 3d Field Conf.: p. 93-105.

................., 1954, Tectonic map of a part of the upper Rio Grande area, New Mexico: U. S. Geol. Survey Oil and Gas Inv. Map OM-157.

Kelley, V. C., and Silver, Caswell, 1952, Geology of the Caballo Mountains: Univ. New Mexico Pub. in Geol., No. 4, p. 108.

Kelley, V. C., and Wood, G. H., Jr., 1946, Lucero uplift, Valencia, Socorro, and Bernalillo Counties, New Mexico: U. S. Geol. Survey Oil and Gas Inv. Prelim. Map 47.

McKee, E. D., and others, 1956, Paleotectonic maps, Jurassic system: U. S. Geol. Survey Misc. Geol. Inv. Map 1-175.

McKee, E. D., and others, 1959, Paleotectonic maps, Triassic system: U. S. Geol. Survey Misc. Geol. Inv. Map 1-300.

Silver, Caswell, 1948, Jurassic overlap in western New Mexico: Am. Assoc. Petroleum Geologists Bull., v. 32, p. 69-81.

Smith, C. T., 1954, Geology of the Thoreau quadrangle, McKinley and Valencia Counties, New Mexico: New Mexico Bur. Mines and Mineral Res. Bull. 31.

Stewart, J. H., 1957, Proposed nomenclature of part of upper Triassic strata in southeastern Utah: Am. Assoc. Petroleum Geologists Bull., v. 41, p. 441-465.

Stokes, W. L., and Phoenix, D. A., 1948, Geology of the Egnar-Gypsum Valley area, San Miguel and Montrose Counties, Colorado: U. S. Geol. Survey Oil and Gas Inv. Prelim. Map 93.

Wilmarth, M. G., 1938, Lexicon of geologic names of the United States: U. S. Geol. Survey Bull. 896, p. 691.

Wood, G. H., Jr., and Northrop, S. A., 1946, Geology of the Nacimiento Mountains, San Pedro Mountain, and adjacent plateaus in parts of Sandoval and Rio Arriba Counties, New Mexico: U. S. Geol. Survey Oil and Gas Inv. Prelim. Map 57.

CRETACEOUS ROCKS OF THE ALBUQUERQUE COUNTRY

Attempts were made by the Field Conference Committee to obtain for this Guidebook at least two papers dealing with the Cretaceous stratigraphy of the Albuquerque country and a third dealing with the igneous geology of the Mount Taylor volcanic field and particularly its volcanic necks. Because of previous commitments, those approached were unable to prepare the solicited papers. In view of the economic significance of the Cretaceous stratigraphy, authors' abstracts of several published papers are reprinted here.

CHARLES B. HUNT, 1936, GEOLOGY AND FUEL RESOURCES OF THE SOUTHERN PART OF THE SAN JUAN BASIN, NEW MEXICO; PART 2, THE MOUNT TAYLOR COAL FIELD: U. S. GEOL. SURVEY BULL. 860-B, P. 31-80, ILLUS.

ABSTRACT (p. 31-32)

"**The Mount Taylor coal field was studied primarily to determine its coal and other fuel resources. The exposed rocks range in age from Jurassic to Recent. The Jurassic, cropping out only locally, is represented by the Morrison formation, of variegated shale and some sandstone. Its top is marked by an erosional unconformity. The overlying Upper Cretaceous covers most of the area and is represented by three formations—in ascending order the Dakota (?) sandstone, the Mancos shale, and the Mesaverde formation. The Dakota (?) sandstone is a lenticular clastic deposit and is locally absent. The Mancos consists mostly of marine shale; three sandstones found in the lower 350 feet in the area east of Mount Taylor thin out to the northeast. The relations between the Mancos and the next younger formation, the Mesaverde, are complex. In the southern part of the field the Mancos is only 1,000 feet thick and represents only the earlier part of Colorado time (Benton and earliest Niobrara). It is overlain by the predominantly continental, coal-bearing Mesaverde formation, which, however, includes in its lower part two thick zones of marine shale. In passing northward there is a marked and rapid change in the lower part of the Mesaverde; the continental beds and the nearshore sandstones become thinner and less conspicuous, and the two marine shale zones become correspondingly thicker. This transition continues until, at the north edge of the field, the sandstones and continental beds practically disappear and the two shale units merge with the older shale to form an expanded Mancos about 2,000 feet thick. The shale units within the Mesaverde at the south are thus seen to be tongues of the Mancos. In the northern part of the area the Mancos represents all of Colorado time and perhaps earliest Montana time as well. The main body of the Mesaverde continues northeastward as a coal-bearing formation. Late Tertiary clastic deposits are present in the eastern part of the area, and there are recent deposits of alluvium and gravel throughout the area.

"Intense volcanic activity occurred in this area in middle and late Tertiary time, beginning with the eruptions on Mount Taylor. The huge depression covering nearly 4 square miles at the head of Water Canyon and just east of Mount Taylor Peak marks the old crater, now enlarged by erosion. The eruptions began with rhyolitic tuff, followed by a series of porphyritic latite and trachyte, and ended with porphyritic andesite. The eruptions continued until a cone at least 2,000 feet high had been built. However, with the gradual lessening of the activity of Mount Taylor lava was erupted from vents that broke out on the periphery of the old crater. These vents are marked by lava cones and volcanic necks. They surround Mount Taylor but are most numerous northeast of the mountain. None of these later vents seem to have been very long-lived, each supplying one or at most very few sheets of a relatively nonporphyritic andesite or basalt. This later activity was extended far to the north and northeast. The basaltic lava flows in the San Jose Valley, along the south border of this area, and the Albuquerque volcanoes, 10 miles east of this area, are very recent and not directly related to the volcanism on and around Mount Taylor.

"Most of the field lies in the southeastern part of the San Juan Basin where a gentle northward dip generally prevails. However, there are several domes which locally have steep dips and numerous faults. The shallower zones have been tested for petroleum in most of the domes, but no production has yet been obtained. The eastern part of the field lies in the Basin and Range province and has been severely faulted. All the faults, so far as known, are normal and have nearly parallel trends at the surface. The displacements reach a maximum of about 3,500 feet. In general the major faults within this part of the field produce a stepdown to the west. The faulted blocks generally dip east, although the amount of dip has considerable range. The deformation probably began in middle Tertiary time and continued until after the basal beds of the Santa Fe formation had been deposited in the eastern part of the field.

"There is generally a sharp boundary separating the severely faulted eastward-tilted beds in the Basin and Range province and the slightly faulted northward-tilted beds of the San Juan Basin. The boundary lies chiefly along faults that have dropped the areas in the Basin and Range province with respect to those in the San Juan Basin.

"The coal beds of the Mount Taylor field are confined to the Mesaverde formation. The coal is of subbituminous rank, and many beds are present. The usual thickness of the coal beds is about 15 inches, but there are numerous exceptions, and some are as much as 6 feet thick. The lack of good roads over most of the field precludes commercial mining on a large scale at this time. However, the south side of Mount Taylor is near the Atchison, Topeka & Santa Fe Railway and United States Highway 66, and the northeast corner of the field is near a State highway, and several small mines are active in these two localities."

CARLE H. DANE, 1936, GEOLOGY AND FUEL RESOURCES OF THE SOUTHERN PART OF THE SAN JUAN BASIN, NEW MEXICO; PART 3, THE LA VENTANA-CHACRA MESA COAL FIELD: U. S. GEOL. SURVEY BULL. 860-C, P. 81-161, ILLUS.

ABSTRACT (p. 81-82)

"*** The exposed rocks are of Upper Cretaceous and Tertiary age. The Dakota (?) sandstone, at the base of the Upper Cretaceous series, and the overlying Mancos shale, of marine origin, crop out only in the eastern part of the area. Above the Mancos shale lies a varied assemblage of partly marine and partly continental beds, which are included in the Mesaverde formation but differentiated into five members — the marine Hosta sandstone at the base, the Gibson coal member above it, the Allison member still higher, the marine Chacra sandstone member at the top in the western part of the area, and the marine La Ventana sandstone at the top in the eastern part. The overlying formation, the Lewis shale, is thin where it lies above the Chacra sandstone but increases greatly in thickness eastward by the successive passing of all of the Chacra sandstone and the upper part of the La Ventana sandstone into gray marine shale. Above the Lewis lies the thin Pictured Cliffs sandstone, the highest marine formation of the Upper Cretaceous. The coal-bearing Fruitland formation, the Kirtland shale above it, and the conglomeratic Ojo Alamo sandstone are also included in the Upper Cretaceous series. Above the Ojo Alamo lie rocks of Eocene age—the banded drab clay and light-colored sandstone of the Puerco (?) and Torrejon formations, capped by the conglomeratic sandstone of the Wasatch formation.

"The area lies in the southeastern part of the San Juan Basin, in which the rocks are gently warped into the form of a great shallow bowl about 100 miles in diameter. The structure of the basin is mostly simple, showing low dips toward the center, with irregular low undulations but no pronounced folds. The rocks are broken by some normal faults of small throw. The western flank of the Nacimiento Mountain uplift forms the eastern margin of the basin along the eastern edge of this area, and here the rocks are steeply folded and even overturned toward the basin.

"The coal is of subbituminous rank and of fairly good grade, but the coal beds are very irregular and lenticular. Most of the coal beds are thin, but some beds are from 5 to 9 feet thick. Coal occurs in the Fruitland formation and in the Chacra, Allison, and Gibson members of the Mesaverde formation. Considerable prospecting and some commercial mining has been done on Allison and Gibson coals along the Rio Puerco in the eastern part of the area, where railroad transportation is available."

J. D. SEARS, C. B. HUNT, AND T. A. HENDRICKS, 1941, TRANSGRESSIVE AND REGRESSIVE CRETACEOUS DEPOSITS IN SOUTHERN SAN JUAN BASIN, NEW MEXICO: U. S. GEOL. SURVEY PROF. PAPER 193-F, P. 101-121, ILLUS.

ABSTRACT (p. 101)

"In explanation of the large-scale intertonguing of marine and continental deposits shown by the Mancos shale and the Mesaverde formation in the southern part of the San Juan Basin, New Mexico, and of the marked variations in the stratigraphic boundary between those formations, the paper offers views as to sedimentation processes that are believed not only to account for the features observed in this field but also to be applicable in the interpretation of similar deposits in many other fields. Three successive series of beds, each comprising a sequence of marine, near-shore, coastal, flood-plain, coastal, near-shore, and marine deposits, are evidence of three transgressions and regressions of the Upper Cretaceous sea. The writers have endeavored to visualize the conditions and processes of land and sea movement and of sedimentation that would bring about such repeated transgressions and regressions and the deposition and preservation of materials in such sequences.

"The paper is divided into three sections: First, a presentation of the depositional concept held by the writers, with reasons for its adoption; second, a description of the nature, relations, and variations of the Mancos and Mesaverde in the southern part of the San Juan Basin; and third, an outline of the inferred depositional history of these formations.

"According to the concept presented, deposition took place in a broad, shallow trough or geosyncline, the middle, deeper part of which was occupied by a shallow sea, which at times spread over the adjacent lowlands and at times withdrew to the middle zone. Those transgressions and regressions of the sea are recorded in the alternations of marine and continental deposits around the margins of the trough. The writers accept the usual view that the advances of the sea and the development of transgressive deposits were brought about by a sinking of the trough. They do not, however, accept as applicable in this and similar cases the frequently expressed view that retreats of the sea and the development of regressive deposits were brought about by a reversal of the movement—that is, by a rising of the trough. Instead, they believe that both the regressions and the regressive deposits were due to a process of trough filling that operated during periods when the rate of sinking of the trough was much reduced and when the supply of debris was sufficient to build the nearshore deposits upward to and above the water surface and also outward, thus forcing the sea to retreat. As the result of continued, though slower, subsidence there was room beneath the profile of equilibrium for the quiet, conformable deposition of thick near-shore sands upon the older off-shore muds without erosion of the older material through wave action. This is shown by the widespread occurrence of transition zones between shale and overlying regressive sandstone, and by the extent, thickness, and uniformity of such sandstones. With continued subsidence there would also be opportunity for the development of thick coal-bearing coastal-swamp deposits behind and encroaching upon the beach sands as the sands grew upward and seaward. On the contrary, a reversal of movement with rise of the trough would bring at least a part of the previous transgressive deposits up into the zone of subaerial and subaqueous erosion and would almost surely not permit thick and widespread regressive deposits to be laid down on them and preserved. Moreover, in a broad structural downfold or trough, the natural tendency of further epeirogenic movement would be in a continuous downward direction, and frequently repeated reversals or up-and-down movements of the trough would appear to be so unlikely that they should not be postulated unless unmistakably required by evidence in the rocks.

"In the southwestern part of the San Juan Basin, near Gallup, the Mancos shale is 725 feet thick and consists principally of more or less sandy shale with several subordinate sandstones. Overlying it is about 1,800 feet of the Mesaverde; the upper part of the formation has been removed by erosion. The Mesaverde comprises sandstones, clays, and coal beds, and is predominantly of continental origin. In this area it has been divided into five units, named in ascending order the Gallup sandstone member, the Dilco coal member, the Bartlett barren member, the Gibson coal member, and the Allison barren member. From the vicinity of Gallup eastward across the southern edge of the basin the lower thousand feet of the Mesaverde (representing the units from the Gallup sandstone member to the Gibson coal member, inclusive) show great progressive changes. At first, two new massive sandstones appear in the section; of these, the Dalton replaces the upper part of the Dilco coal member, and the Hosta splits the Gibson coal member into two parts. Moreover, the lower third of the Gallup is divided and in part replaced by wedges of

Mancos shale. Farther east, a tongue of shale, the Mulatto, comes in between the Dilco and the Dalton, and a higher tongue of shale, the Satan, splits the Hosta sandstone member. These two shale tongues thicken steadily eastward. Concurrently, the intervening units of the Mesaverde grow thinner, and some die out; in the southeastern part of the basin even their most persistent layers, two thin sandstones that represent, respectively, the Gallup and a union of the Dalton and lower Hosta, become nothing more than sandy zones in the midst of a great body of shale about 2,000 feet thick. That shale body, a union of the thin Mancos farther west with the greatly expanded Mulatto and Satan tongues, forms the Mancos of the southeastern and eastern parts of the basin. It is directly overlain by the upper part of the Hosta sandstone, which in that part of the field marks the base of the restricted Mesaverde. Thus the Mancos-Mesaverde boundary rises stratigraphically about 1,200 feet in a distance of 100 miles from west to east—a direction that is basinward but oblique to the trends of the ancient shore lines.

"The depositional history of the three transgressive and three regressive stages that are recorded in the rocks of the Mancos and Mesaverde is outlined in the concluding section of the paper, in accordance with the general concept of depositional processes herein presented."

——O——

There have been a number of revisions in the nomenclature since the last paper was published. Field conferences held by the New Mexico Geological Society in 1950, 1951, 1953, and 1959 passed through parts of the Albuquerque country and the guidebooks prepared for these conferences contain papers dealing with Cretaceous stratigraphy. Most such papers include selected bibliographies, and thus are highly useful as a starting point for bibliographic research.

——O——

NOTE ON CRETACEOUS FOSSILS BY EDITOR

Cretaceous rocks are exposed over extensive areas in the northern half of the State. At first, continental sedimentation predominated; this was followed by marine sedimentation and then alternating marine and continental sedimentation; finally, the seas withdrew from New Mexico and continental sedimentation prevailed.

Fossils of Cretaceous (predominantly Upper Cretaceous) age may be collected at a number of localities in the Albuquerque country, notably (1) in the Rio Puerco valley west of Albuquerque—all the way from Cuba and La Ventana southward to Correo, Suwanee, and the vicinity of Mount Taylor—and (2) in smaller areas east of the Rio Grande—such as the Tijeras coal basin, the Hagan-Tonque basin, and in the vicinity of Madrid and Cerrillos.

Marine strata yield abundant fossils, including oysters such as **Ostrea soleniscus**, as much as 24 inches in length; clams such as **Inoceramus**, nearly as large; snails; coiled ammonites 15 to 20 inches in diameter; and shark teeth of both flesh-cutting and shell-crushing types. Other groups of organisms, such as corals, brachiopods, scaphopods, worms, echinoids, and asteroids, are rare. Foraminifers are common but because of their small size not conspicuous.

The continental deposits of rivers, deltas, lakes, and swamps yield abundant leaves and silicified wood; land animals such as dinosaurs; and fresh-water clams, snails, fishes, turtles, and crocodiles. (Large septarian concretions are often mistaken by the uninitiated for fossil turtles!) Interesting specimens have been found in the Rio Puerco valley of logs riddled by the burrows of **Teredo**, the boring pelecypod, whose living descendants are known as "shipworms."

Relatively few reports have been published describing and illustrating these Cretaceous fossils, and, what is still more unfortunate, the reports are mostly from earlier years and now out-of-print.

——O——

LATE CENOZOIC SEDIMENTS OF THE LOWER JEMEZ RIVER REGION

Zane Spiegel
New Mexico Institute of Mining and Technology

INTRODUCTION

Mapping of several important areas of late Cenozoic sediments in the Rio Grande trough has been accomplished by recent workers. However, four units (see correlation chart, Figure 2) mapped by Bryan and McCann (1937) along the Rio Puerco had apparently not been restudied in sufficient detail to assure definite correlations with the sections observed elsewhere. Therefore, this work was undertaken by the writer in August, 1960[1], as part of a quantitative investigation of the relationships of aquifer systems in this area to streamflow in the Rio Grande drainage basin. A geologic map was made of the lower Jemez River basin proper (Fig. 1) but the "Lower Jemez River Region" as described herein extends from White Rock Canyon to Alameda.

Field work consisted primarily of reconnaissance traverses in a four-wheel-drive truck up each of the major arroyos that drain northward into the Jemez River or eastward into the Rio Grande in the reach from the vicinity of Zia Pueblo to Alameda. Many of the faults and contacts observed in the truck traverses were traced on foot across the narrow badland ridges separating the numerous arroyos, and all data were recorded directly on 7½-minute series topographic maps (scale 1:24,000). In part of the area north of Jemez River (see Fig. 1), a map by Soister (1952, scale 1 inch per mile) was adapted. This area had previously (1958) been reconnoitered by the writer and Bruce Maxwell, and the eastern edge of Santa Ana Mesa was mapped at that time. Conclusions concerning the geologic history of the region are based in great part on reconnaissance traverses made by the writer in the course of previous investigations of ground-water resources at various localities.

REGIONAL GEOLOGIC EVENTS IN EARLY TERTIARY TIME

During Cretaceous time, the lower Jemez River region had a relatively uniform environment that produced fine-grained clastic marine sediments. Much of New Mexico became tectonically very active in latest Cretaceous time, and by early Tertiary time some areas were uplifted greatly; intervening basinal areas were gradually filled with thick sections of fine-grained red fluviatile sediments. The rocks deposited in these basins, called the El Rito, Galisteo, and Baca formations, appear to reflect a common set of conditions in the respective areas of erosion and deposition. Known outcrops of these rocks are of such limited extent that details of the original shape, topography, and geology of the basins and source areas cannot presently be reconstructed with certainty.

However, the great thickness, good sorting, and fine-grained character of the westernmost outcrops of the Galisteo formation (near La Cienega, La Bajada, and Placitas) suggest that its depositional basin was common with that of the El Rito formation, which crops out less than 40 miles to the northwest. No evidence is known that suggests the alternative hypothesis—that a drainage divide (hence a common source area) existed between the outcrop regions of these two formations. The principal source areas for the Galisteo-El Rito basin were the southern Sangre de Cristo Mountains and eastern Rio Arriba County. On the other hand, the Baca formation in central and western Socorro County appears to have been derived from uplifts in the region of the Ladron and Los Pinos Mountains in northern Socorro County; thus an east-west drainage divide probably separated the Baca and Galisteo-El Rito depositional basins. The only outcrops of the Galisteo formation in the map area (Fig. 1) are red clays near Placitas (sec. 36, T. 13 N., R. 4 E., and in T. 13 N., R. 5 E.). These fine-grained deposits do not give any direct evidence of the location and nature of the source areas, but suggest that the southern edge of the basin was far to the south of Placitas.

The character of sedimentation changed markedly in both the Galisteo-El Rito and Baca basins, because shallow intrusives broke through to the surface at several local centers (for example, Cerrillos, Cienega, Hagan, and numerous localities in Socorro County). Lava flows, breccias, pyroclastics, and volcanic-derived sediments spread out over the fluviatile sediments, filled the basins, and were in turn intruded and locally domed up by later igneous masses. The extensive disruption of pre-existing drainage by these tectonic, volcanic, and intrusive events formed several large lake and playa basins and filled them with ash and fine-grained weathering products. The entire complex of post-Galisteo volcanics and associated sediments in and near the Hagan basin has been called the Espinaso volcanics, and a similar post-Baca igneous facies in Socorro County has been called the Datil formation. The Potosi volcanic series of the San Juan region, some volcanics and intrusives in the Sangre de Cristo Mountains near Questa and Costilla, and some of the older volcanics and intrusives of the Jemez region are also possible equivalents of the post-Galisteo igneous facies.

Most of the deformation during early Tertiary time seems to have been by broad folding and basin formation, although strong folding and thrusting occurred locally. Many of the intrusive masses caused severe local deformation, metamorphism, and alteration.

REGIONAL GEOLOGIC EVENTS IN MIDDLE AND LATE TERTIARY TIME

Volcanism apparently continued sporadically in many large areas of New Mexico, contemporaneously with renewed broad uplift and erosion of old positive areas such as the San Juan-Conejos, Nacimiento-San Pedro and Zuni Mountains on the west, and the Sangre de Cristo Mountains and Pedernal Hills on the east, during late Miocene(?) and Pliocene time.

As volcanism waned, the lava and pyroclastic piles were deeply weathered and eroded and the sediments derived from them and underlying rocks were deposited in a large, broad basin or complex of basins that was warped down slowly (locally on normal faults) between these eastern and western lines of uplifts. The succession of

---

[1]Geologic and hydrologic reconnaissance of the area shown in Figure 1 had recently been completed by Bruce Maxwell, Geologist, U. S. Geological Survey. Mr. Maxwell accompanied the writer in the field during most of this investigation.

basin deposits, as one would expect, generally has the inverse order of superposition of the older rocks present in a particular source area; that is, volcanic facies at the bottom, then reworked Galisteo-El Rito rocks, Cretaceous rocks, and so on through the section present at the inception of this depositional period. Locally, intense volcanism contributed lava beds and pyroclastic deposits, temporarily blocked streams, and created new sediment source areas. This entire sequence of clastic deposits and interbedded lava flows in the broad Rio Grande depression has been included in the Santa Fe group by Baldwin (1961). It should be noted that the Santa Fe group is arbitrarily limited geographically, by past usage and by Baldwin's redefinition, to deposits in the Rio Grande valley. Similar sediments in many parts of New Mexico and other western states bear various local names, but have essentially the same geologic age and mode of origin.

THE SANTA FE GROUP IN THE LOWER JEMEZ RIVER VALLEY

The Santa Fe group in the map area was divided into three formations (Fig. 1), which were further subdivided into members.

Lower Unnamed Formation

The oldest unit, called herein the lower unnamed formation, consists of two main members and a minor facies mappable only locally. The lower member (Tl on Fig. 1) consists of a thick light tan to gray sandstone that appears to be derived from sandstones of Cretaceous or lowermost Tertiary age. The sandstone is generally poorly cemented except where faulted. It is poorly exposed except where the upper red member is present above it, or where local cementation along faults is abundant (e.g., southwest part of T. 14 N., R. 3 E.). The upper part of the lower gray sandstone commonly contains interbedded pumice ash and granule beds south of Jemez River, but observed exposures were too few to map separately. A local volcanic-derived facies, apparently equivalent to these beds, was mapped by Soister (1952) as the Bodega Butte member on the west side of Santa Ana Mesa (T. 14 N., R. 3 E.).

The writer believes that sediments under the eastern and northeastern rim of Santa Ana Mesa (also mapped by Soister as Bodega Butte member) are much higher in the section than the sediments on the west side, and they are mapped separately herein. Further work should be done in the area north of Santa Ana Mesa in order to fully resolve this problem, as well as to trace the volcanic facies back to the source area.

The upper member of the lower unnamed formation consists of red mudstone, reddish brown sandstone, and red silty conglomerate that appears to be derived largely from the Abo-Cutler formation and other red beds to the north. It is on the order of 500 feet thick under and southwest of Santa Ana Mesa, and in the Rincones de Zia, but apparently thins to several thick red clay beds aggregating about 100 feet in thickness near sec. 26, T. 14 N., R. 2 E. The red beds clearly interfinger extensively with the underlying gray sandstone beds and are therefore included in the lower formation.

These two areas of greater thickness of the red member may represent two distinct basins of sedimentation. The source area of the eastern basin apparently was north of Santa Ana Mesa. In the region between these basins contributions of debris from the erosion of the volcanic rocks of the Jemez Mountains may have accompanied sediments derived from erosion of the pre-volcanic red-bed terrane. The source area of the western basin was in the early Santa Fe-age Nacimiento-San Pedro Mountain uplift, prior to the eruption of the basalts on San Pedro Mountain.

Inasmuch as the regional dip of the lower and upper unnamed formations of the Santa Fe group is eastward in the eastern part of the map area, and southward in the southern part, the lower formation crops out only in the northwestern part. There is no evidence that a single through-flowing stream was present during the deposition of the lower unnamed formation; instead, there is evidence (Wright, 1946) that these alluvial deposits ("Lower Gray and Middle Red members" of Wright's "Santa Fe formation") at that time were graded to a large playa in and near T. 6 N., R. 2 W. The fine-grained sediments reported in the lower part of the Norins Well in sec. 19, T. 11 N., R. 4 E. (see Stearns, 1953, p. 475) may represent an eastern area of playa deposits distinct from, but equivalent to, those described by Wright in the lower Rio Puerco area. These fine-grained deposits, together with those of the red member along the Rio Grande near Bernalillo and Sandia Pueblo, suggest that the Sandia Mountains were not uplifted very high in early Santa Fe time. The Abiquiu (?) formation of Stearns (1953) is interpreted herein as a sedimentary facies of the lower part of the Santa Fe group, derived principally from erosion of deeply weathered volcanic rocks (Stearn's Espinaso formation) in and around the Galisteo Creek valley and the foothills near Santa Fe. The lakes inferred by Stearns (1953) at La Bajada may have been part of a large playa area which was eventually filled and later covered by coarse-grained sediments of the upper unnamed formation of the Santa Fe group.

Upper Unnamed Formation

The upper unnamed formation consists of (a) a western facies (Tub) of alluvial fan sand and gravel containing many pebbles of red granite and boulders of basalt derived from the Nacimiento-San Pedro uplift; (b) an eastern facies (Tuc) derived from Paleozoic and Mesozoic rocks east of the Rio Grande; and (c) an axial gravel facies (Tug, Tugc) that represents the deposits of a very large river that flowed generally southward. Although the streams that deposited the coalescing alluvial fans of the western and eastern facies were tributaries of the axial river, the pebbles in the river channel deposits are principally quartzite resembling Precambrian rocks in north-central New Mexico. In as much as pebbles of andesite and rhyolite similar to flows resting on the Precambrian rocks are the second most common type in these river deposits, it is inferred that the principal headwater region of the ancient river was in the Conejos-San Juan and Questa regions. Occasional gray quartzite pebbles were observed that have a hard red ferruginous cement filling fractures and external pits, and these pebbles may be reworked from former outcrops of the El Rito formation north of El Rito. It is possible that most of the quartzite and volcanic pebbles were reworked from uplifted outcrops of alluvial fan deposits and interbedded lavas of early Santa Fe age in the Tusas-Tres Piedras region (see Butler, 1946).

West of the longitude of Zia Pueblo, the sequence of sediments from the lower to the upper formations of the Santa Fe group clearly represents the cycle of erosion of the section of older rocks from the Nacimiento-San Pedro and western Jemez Mountains. The presence of numerous basalt pebbles in the western facies of the upper formation indicates that extensive basalt flows were poured out

FIGURE I.
GEOLOGY OF THE LOWER JEMEZ RIVER AREA, NEW MEXICO.
by
Zane Spiegel

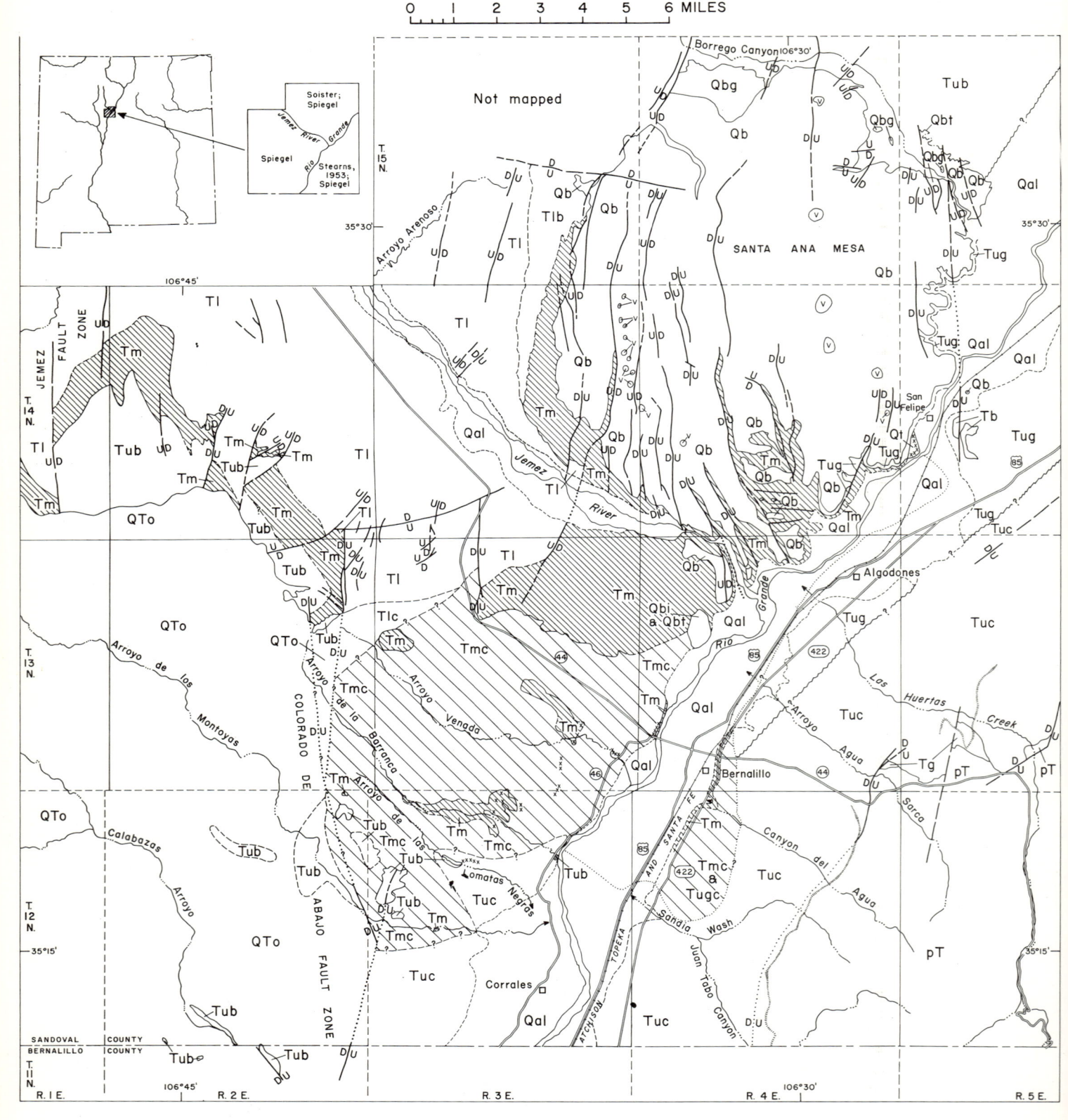

EXPLANATION

Recent — Quaternary

Qal
Alluvium
Channel deposits, low terraces, fans, and slopewash along Rio Grande and Jemez River

UNCONFORMITY

Qt
xx x xx
Terrace deposits
Gravel deposited by the late Pleistocene Rio Grande; X, selected outcrops only

Pleistocene

Qbg
Basalt gravels
Basalt boulders, gravel, and sand north of Santa Ana Mesa

Qb, Qbi
Qbt
Basalt
Qb, flows from Santa Ana Mesa; Qbi, dikes and neck; Qbt, cinders and vent-wall debris (also present nearly everywhere under the basalt on the east and northeast rims)

QTo
Uppermost gravel
Coarse sand and gravel capping high plain west of the Rio Grande

ANGULAR UNCONFORMITY

Santa Fe Group — Miocene (?) to Pliocene — Pliocene

Tub	Tug	Tuc
	Tugc	
	Tb	

Upper formation
Tub, western facies, sand and gravel fan deposits, locally pumiceous; Tug, axial river gravels (Tugc where covered); Tb, basalt flow interbedded in Tug; Tuc, eastern facies, undifferentiated, generally poorly exposed or covered

| Tm | Tmc |
| Tl | Tlb |

Lower formation
Tm, red member, mudstone, sandstone, and silty conglomerate; Tmc, covered area; Tl, lower member, light tan to gray sandstone; Tlb, pumiceous upper part of lower member

ANGULAR UNCONFORMITY

Eocene

Tg
Galisteo formation
Red mudstone

ANGULAR UNCONFORMITY

pT
Pre-Tertiary rocks

TERTIARY

———·····
Formation contact
Dashed where uncertain; dotted where covered

— — — — —
Contact of alluvium on older rocks

∼∼∼∼∼
Zone of interfingering

U
— — — ·····
D
Fault
Dashed where uncertain; dotted where covered

Ⓥ
Basalt cone

at this time, and in fact, basalt flows are interbedded in the western facies northwest of Santa Ana Mesa, and also rest on an erosion surface that bevels the Precambrian rocks of San Pedro Mountain.

The interfingering of the axial river gravels and the western facies is either missing by erosion or not clearly exposed in the map area. The interfingering with the eastern facies is exposd about 2 miles east of Algodones and the general easterly dip of the upper unnamed member reverses there so that a thick section of the eastern facies, consisting of alluvial fan deposits derived from uplifted Paleozoic rocks, is exposed locally. Coarse conglomerate beds that may be equivalent in age to the lower unnamed formation in the northwest part of the map area, and to the Tesuque formation of the Santa Fe area, are exposed locally on the upthrown side of northeast-trending faults near Placitas, but have not been differentiated on the geologic map (Fig. 1).

The axial river gravels in the upper unnamed formation of the Santa Fe group crop out, with eastward dip and thickness greater than 500 feet, almost continuously from San Felipe to the mouth of White Rock Canyon. White ash beds and pumice lenses derived from the Jemez region are interbedded with the river deposits and superjacent sediments at numerous localities, especially near Pena Blanca.

North of the latitude of Santo Domingo, and east of the Rio Grande, the axial gravels interfinger with, and are overlain by, fine-grained red sediments possibly derived from the Galisteo formation. The principal thalweg of the ancient river probably trended southwest from Otowi to near Cochiti, and trended southward from a point about 6 miles west of Cochiti to Algodones, thence just east of the present inner valley of the Rio Grande to San Acacia, and through Socorro valley just west of the present river. The band of coarse channel sediments deposited by the ancestral Rio Grande is 3 to 6 miles wide from Cochiti to Socorro, but may be very narrow in the White Rock Canyon reach.

A thick bed of tilted and faulted vent-wall debris and basalt cinders underlies, or possibly is interbedded with, the axial river gravels at Cochiti diversion dam, and this "pyroclastic" unit was probably a precursor of the thick basalt flow extruded from a vent exposed near the mouth of Bland Canyon, about 4 miles north of Cochiti. Boulder beds interbedded with younger basalt flows in lower White Rock Canyon (T. 17 N., R. 6 E.) probably represent channels of the ancestral Rio Grande after it overtopped the temporary dam caused by the underlying basalt flows.

Although the boulder beds were not traced continuously through the canyon, they appear to be equivalent to the river channel deposits (Denny, 1940) in the Santa Fe group near Otowi. The latter interfinger eastward with the Ancha formation and westward with coarse arroyo deposits derived from erosion of an uplift of older volcanic rocks of the Jemez Mountains, and are underlain by the Tesuque formation (Fig. 2).

Uppermost Gravels and Other Deposits

This classification tentatively includes all sediments and basalt flows capping high surfaces, except those that were obviously deposited on erosion surfaces cut by a stream system that had the form of the present drainage network. The high plain in the southwestern part of the map area is underlain by 10 to 30 feet of gravelly sand, herein called the uppermost gravels, in which pebbles of red granite and large basalt boulders are conspicuous. This unit is generally unconformable on the western facies of the upper formation (which it closely resembles) and on the red member of the lower formation, and slopes southeastward. It was probably derived in part from the bedrock of the San Pedro-Nacimiento highland mass, and in part by reworking of other units of the Santa Fe group that lapped up on the margins of the older and broader highlands of early and middle Santa Fe time.

The uppermost gravels are equivalent to the "Ortiz gravels" and related erosion surfaces of Bryan (see discussion of this problem in Baldwin, 1961). The unit consists of the deposits of arroyos draining the uplands that were created or renewed by greatly increased normal faulting in late Santa Fe time.

There was a great change from sedimentation in deep slowly subsiding basins interspersed among broad uplifts (Pliocene and early Pleistocene (?) time), to the deposition of relatively thin blankets graded to a master drainage system which in Pleistocene time developed into the present stream network by cyclic downcutting.

The uppermost gravels reflect rapid uplift of narrow fault blocks, superimposed on epeirogenic uplift of the entire region. In contrast, late Miocene and Pliocene time was characterized by great depression of the basins in an absolute sense, and concurrent uplift of adjacent broad upland regions.[2]

Santa Ana Mesa is a complex of basalt flows (Qb) and related vent debris (Qbt) erupted from north-trending lines of cones. The flow complex was erupted onto an eastward-sloping erosion surface of low relief. As in all the other basaltic centers in the Rio Grande depression, the first fissure or vent intrusions into saturated sediments of the Santa Fe group produced violent eruptions of basalt cinders mixed with sand torn from the vent walls. This material was deposited as a thin sheet of olive, gray-brown, or tan pyroclastic material with characteristic thin bedding caused by aerial sorting. The basalt eventually covered the pyroclastic beds in most areas, except north of lower Borrego Canyon in secs. 17, 18, and 20, T. 13 N., R. 5 E. About two miles south of Jemez Dam the core of a minor eruption center has been bared by erosion, and the complex of dikes (Qbi) and pyroclastic vent-well debris (Qbt) is well exposed. Boulder beds (Qbg) derived from older basalt flows form terraces cut into the north margin of Santa Ana Mesa.

TERRACE AND CHANNEL GRAVELS

Terraces cut by the Rio Grande and tributaries are difficult to map in most areas because the soft sediments into which they are cut are easily masked by slopewash. However, some conspicuous outcrops of terrace gravels were mapped, especially those in which the contact with underlying rocks was exposed (usually the red member of the lower unnamed formation). The pebbles are well rounded, principally of gray quartzite and volcanic rocks, and were probably derived principally from the axial gravels of the ancestral Rio Grande.

The inner valleys of the Rio Grande and Jemez River are erosional channels partially refilled with boulders,

[2]The most convincing evidence of the absolute direction of movement in the basins is the contrast of the thick basin-filling sediments of the Santa Fe group with the thin blanket-like deposits of corresponding age (Ogallala formation and equivalents) on the plains to the east.

FIGURE 2.-- CORRELATION OF CENOZOIC ROCKS IN PART OF THE RIO GRANDE DEPRESSION.

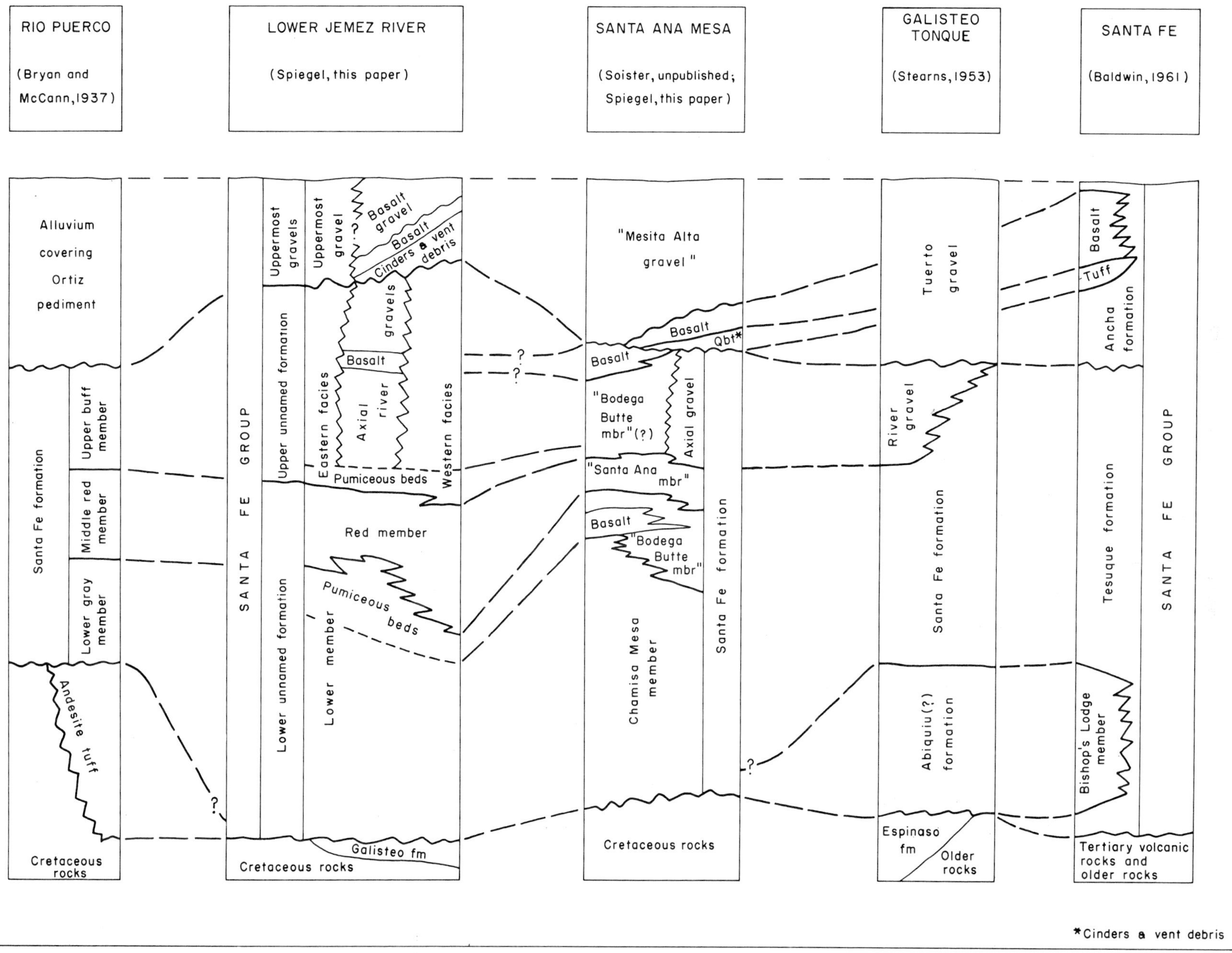

*Cinders & vent debris

gravel, and sand. The base of the channel fill is difficult to determine from well logs in most places, and the only reliable data obtained were the logs of test holes drilled at bridge or dam sites. The base of the channel fill is reported to be 56 feet below stream level (elev. 6278) at a bridge site 1½ miles above Jemez Springs and 65 feet deep at Jemez Dam. The base of the fill is about 70 feet below river level at the site of the proposed Cochiti Dam and 55 feet below the surface (elev. 5275) in the dry channel of Galisteo Creek at the site of the proposed Galisteo Dam (U. S. Army, 1958), in sec. 28, T. 15 N., R. 6 E.

ACKNOWLEDGMENT

This report was prepared as a phase of a research program carried out under a National Science Foundation Cooperative Fellowship at New Mexico Institute of Mining and Technology in 1960-61.

REFERENCES

Baldwin, Brewster, 1961, Part 2, Geology, in Spiegel, Zane, and Baldwin, Brewster, Geology and water resources of the Santa Fe area, New Mexico: U. S. Geol. Survey Water-Supply Paper 1525 (in press).

Bryan, Kirk, and McCann, F. T., 1937, The Ceja del Rio Puerco—A border feature of the Basin and Range province in New Mexico; Pt. 1, Stratigraphy and structure: Jour. Geology, v. 45, p. 801-828.

Butler, A. P., Jr., 1946, Tertiary and Quaternary geology of the Tusas-Tres Piedras area, New Mexico: Harvard Univ. unpub. doctoral dissertation; (Abs.), Geol. Soc. America Bull., v. 57, p. 1183.

Denny, C. S., 1940, Santa Fe formation in the Espanola valley, New Mexico: Geol. Soc. America Bull., v. 51, p. 677-693.

Soister, P. E., 1952, Geology of Santa Ana Mesa and adjoining areas, Sandoval County, New Mexico: Univ. New Mexico unpub. master's thesis.

Stearns, C. E., 1953, Tertiary geology of the Galisteo-Tonque area, New Mexico: Geol. Soc. America Bull., v. 64, p. 459-507.

U. S. Army, 1958, Review survey for flood control, interim report on main stem of the Rio Grande above Elephant Butte Dam: Corps of Engineers, U. S. Army Engineer District, Albuquerque, December, App. A, pls. 2, 5.

Wright, H. E., Jr. 1946, Tertiary and Quaternary geology of the lower Rio Puerco area, New Mexico: Geol. Soc. America Bull., v. 57, p. 383-456.

OUTLINE OF THE GEOLOGY OF THE JEMEZ MOUNTAINS, NEW MEXICO[1]

C. S. ROSS, R. L. SMITH, and R. A. BAILEY
U. S. Geological Survey
Washington 25, D. C.

INTRODUCTION

The Jemez Mountains have long been recognized as the site of the Valles caldera, popularly known as one of the largest volcanic "craters" in the world, and for this reason alone the mountains are of unusual interest geologically. They are in addition, however, important for the influence they have had locally on the structural and geomorphological development of the Rio Grande depression, a major structural feature of southern Colorado and New Mexico.

Little has been published concerning either the Valles caldera or the volcanic geology of the Jemez Mountains—although a number of geologists have mapped parts of the area or mentioned it incidentally in reports on adjacent areas (Newberry, 1876; Iddings, 1890; Reagan, 1903; Lindgren, Graton, and Gordon, 1910; Henderson, 1913; Ross, 1931, 1938; Bryan, 1938; Smith, 1938; Church and Hack, 1939; Denny, 1940; Wood and Northrop, 1946; Stearns, 1953; Kelley, 1956). This report constitutes a brief summary of the results of the authors' investigations in the area since 1946, and it is hoped that it will help fill a void that has persisted in the geologic literature of New Mexico for 50 years or more.

Physiographic and Geologic Setting

The Jemez Mountains are along the western margin of the Rio Grande depression and are bounded on the north by the Chama basin, the east by the Espanola-Santa Fe basin, the south by the Albuquerque-Belen basin, and the west by the Sierra Nacimiento. The Jemez Mountains constitute a complex volcanic pile of Tertiary and Quaternary age and consist geomorphologically of a maturely eroded, central mountainous mass surrounded by more youthfully dissected plateaus and mesas. In the midst of the mountains is the Valles caldera, a subcircular volcanic depression 12 to 15 miles in diameter, 500 to 2,000 feet deep, and surrounded by peaks that rise to altitudes exceeding 10,000 feet. Within this depression are the beautiful high-montane valleys for which the region is so well known and from which the mountains take their name [Sierra de los Valles or Valles Mountains]. Valle Grande is the largest and best known of these valleys, but Valle Toledo, Valle San Antonio, and several other valleys to the north and west are equally beautiful, though less accessible. Separating these valleys are a dozen or more dome-shaped mountains; the largest is Redondo, which rises to an altitude of 11,254 feet in the center of the caldera.

The volcanic rocks of the Jemez Mountains unconformably overlie igneous, metamorphic, and sedimentary rocks ranging in age from Precambrian through late Tertiary. On the west, they rest on dominantly Paleozoic and Mesozoic sedimentary rocks that form the eastward-dipping backslope of the Sierra Nacimiento (Wood and Northrop, 1946). On the north, east, and south they overlie middle and upper Tertiary sediments of the Santa Fe group: the Abiquiu tuff of Miocene age (Smith, 1938) and a sequence of arkosic sands and silts of late Miocene and Pliocene age—the Santa Fe formation of Hayden (1869) and as used by Cope (1877), Johnson (1903), Osborn (1909, 1918), Frick (1933, 1937), Bryan (1938), and Denny (1940).

Volcanic Stratigraphy

Volcanism in the Jemez Mountains probably began in early to middle Pliocene time with the eruption of basalt; it continued throughout the Pliocene with the successive eruption of andesite, dacite, quartz latite, and associated rhyolite; and it culminated in Pleistocene time with the catastrophic eruption of tremendous volumes of rhyolitic ash flows. As a result of this culminating series of outbursts, two calderas of slightly different ages formed: the younger and largest is the Valles caldera; the older, here unnamed, was truncated by the younger; the remaining segment is northeast of the Valles caldera near the head of Santa Clara Canyon. Subsequent activity was confined within the Valles caldera and included structural adjustments of the caldera floor and the eruption of rhyolitic domes and flows.

The following is a much simplified description of the stratigraphy of the Jemez Mountains volcanic rocks. The areal distribution and stratigraphic relations of the major units are generalized in Figures 1 and 2.

The earliest basaltic lavas of the Jemez Mountains erupted from numerous centers over a wide area. They formed a field of low coalesced shields, the remnants of which now form Borrego Mesa in the south and Lobato Mesa and Mesa de la Grulla in the north. In the vicinity of Bear Springs a group of rhyolites is interbedded with these early basalts, and on Borrego Mesa rhyolite tuffs associated with these centers are exposed between two sequences of basalt flows.

A thick sequence of andesitic tuffs, breccias, and flows overlies the basalts and rhyolites. These rocks crop out most extensively in the southern Jemez Mountains and are well exposed in Paliza, Peralta, and Cochiti Canyons, in the San Miguel Mountains, locally in Santa Clara Canyon, and in the walls of the Valles caldera. They represent the remnants of coalesced composite cones built upon the earlier basaltic shields.

Overlying but locally interbedded with the andesites is a thick sequence of dacites and quartz latites. These rocks locally attain a thickness of 2,000 feet and individual flows may be as thick as 800 feet. They occur mainly in the central and northern Jemez Mountains and make up most of the peaks surrounding the calderas. Excellent exposures occur in Guaje and Santa Clara Canyons and in upper Rio del Oso and Polvadera Creek. A number of well-preserved and relatively young centers of this group of rocks occurs on the western side of Lobato Mesa and on Mesa de la Grulla. Very late Pliocene or Pleistocene basalt flows are associated with some of these centers. The younger basalts of the Cerros del Rio, east of the Rio Grande, may also be contemporaneous.

---

[1] Publication authorized by the Director, U. S. Geological Survey. As submitted, this title read: "Outline of the geology of the Valles Mountains, New Mexico." The term "Valles Mountains" has been changed to "Jemez Mountains" throughout the paper. The term "Valles caldera" has not been changed. — **Ed.**

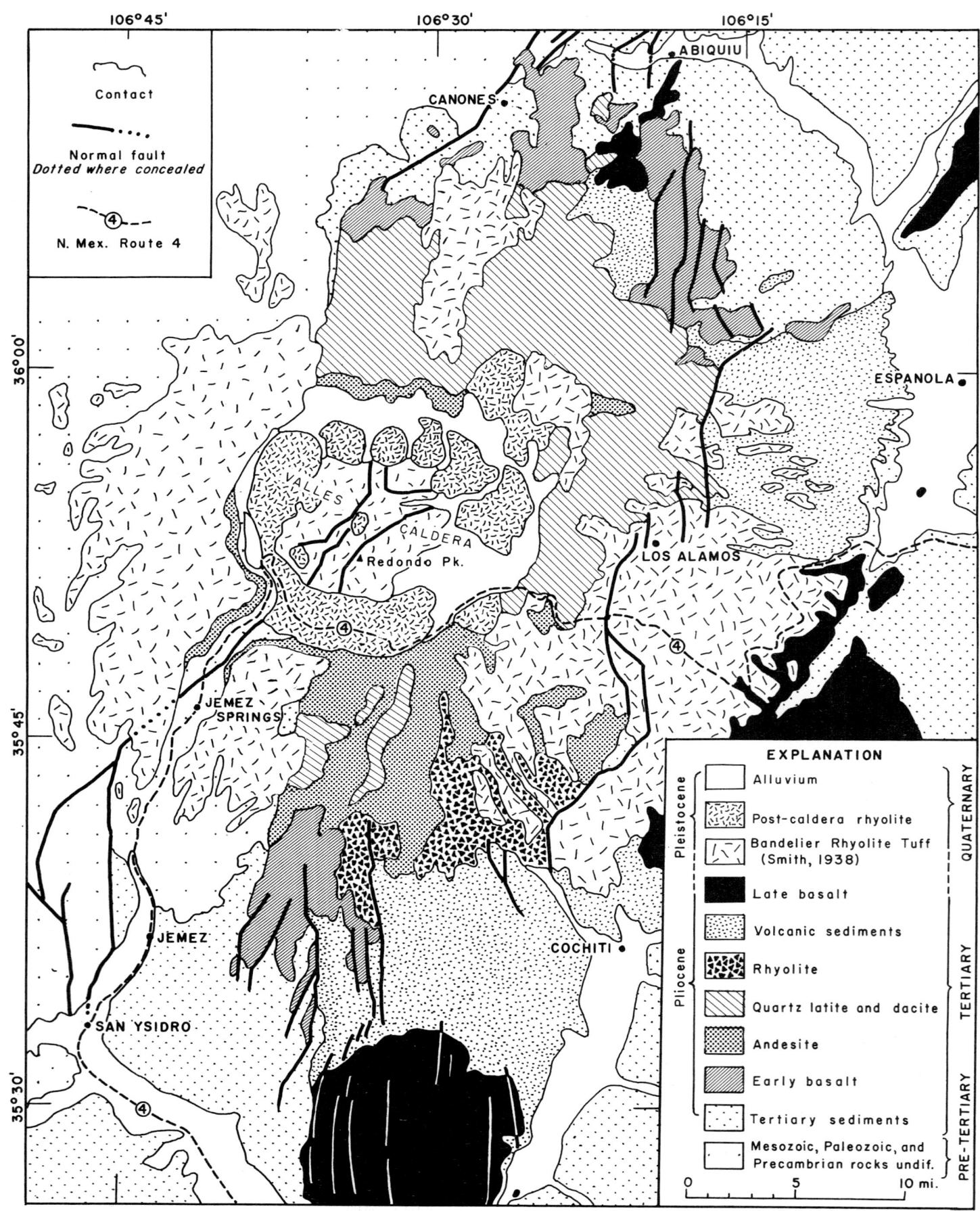

Figure 1. Generalized geologic map of the Jemez Mountains, New Mexico.

In the southern mountains a second group of pre-caldera rhyolites intrudes and overlies the andesites and older dacites. The largest center for these rocks is in the vicinity of Bearhead, where nearly 2,000 feet of rhyolitic tuffs, breccias, and flows occur. The Peralta tuff member (local usage) of Bryan and Upson (see Stearns, 1953, p. 499-500) exposed in lower Peralta Canyon is related to this center.

All the above-mentioned volcanic rocks are interbedded with thick sequences of volcanic sediments. These deposits, mainly fanglomerates, mud-flow deposits, and reworked pyroclastic materials, accumulated as broad fans on the eastern and southeastern flanks of the mountains. Typical of these deposits is the Puye gravel of H. T. U. Smith (1938) which is well exposed along the northeastern margin of the Pajarito Plateau. Genetically comparable but older deposits are exposed farther south in the vicinity of Cochiti Pueblo.

Unconformably overlying all these older volcanic rocks and sediments, which constitute the pre-caldera edifice of the Jemez Mountains volcanic pile, is the Bandelier rhyolite tuff (Smith, 1938). These tuffs are the deposits of hot, turbulent ash flows. They erupted from the crest of the Valles range from centers now obscured, poured down valleys in the higher mountainous terrain, and spread out as broad coalescing fans on the gentler surrounding slopes. These tuffs underlie the Pajarito and Jemez Plateaus on the east and west and Mesa del Medio on the north. They cover an area of nearly 400 square miles, locally attain a thickness of 1,000 feet, and represent the accumulation of more than 50 cubic miles of ash and pumice.

The Bandelier rhyolite tuff is composed of two distinct depositional sequences that are separated locally by a marked erosional disconformity. Each of these depositional sequences is correlative with one of the two calderas in the mountains, the lower sequence having its source in the older caldera at the head of Santa Clara Canyon, and the upper sequence having its source in the Valles caldera. Although the rocks in each of these sequences superficially resemble each other, they may be distinguished by means of a number of diagnostic criteria, the most conspicuous of which is the greater amount of accidental lithic inclusions in the lower sequence.

The youngest volcanic rocks in the Jemez Mountains are the Pleistocene rhyolites that fill the Valles caldera and constitute the volcanic domes of San Antonio Mountain, Cerro Santa Rosa, Cerro del Abrigo, Cerros de los Posos, Cerro del Medio, Cerro la Jara, and several other unnamed peaks, as well as the crater of El Cajete. These volcanic centers form a nearly complete ring within the Valles caldera and very probably correspond to a continuous rhyolite ring dike at depth. The youngest of these centers is El Cajete, and it is of particular interest because from it issued the welded tuff of Battleship Rock in upper San Diego Canyon, the "popcorn" pumice surrounding El Cajete crater, and the glass flow of Banco Bonito. These three deposits represent a related sequence of eruptions that record a continuous decrease in gas content during a waning stage of volcanism.

Interbedded with the caldera rhyolites are a variety of tuffaceous sediments that were deposited in lakes that formed at several stages during the history of the caldera.

VOLCANIC STRUCTURES

The Valles caldera formed as a consequence of collapse of the roof of the magma chamber following erup-

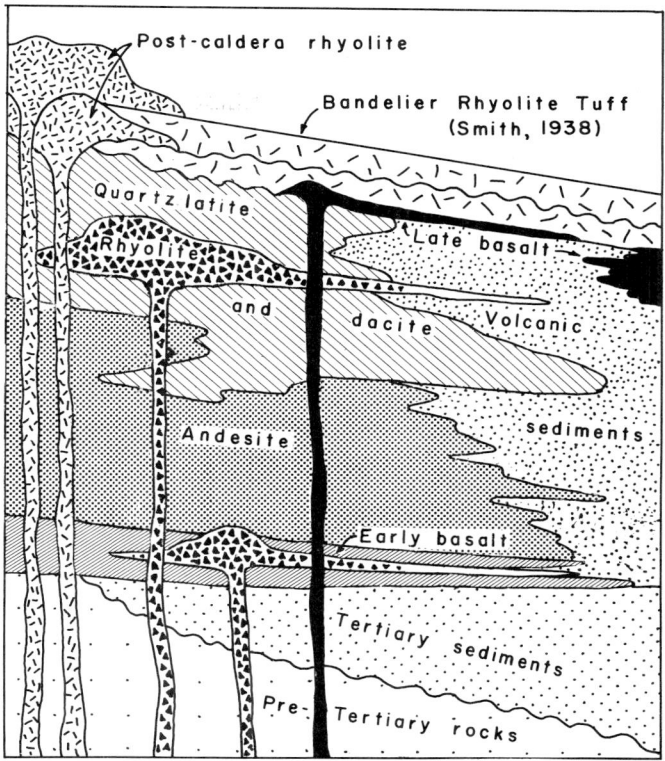

Figure 2. Schematic diagram showing the generalized stratigraphic relations of the Jemez Mountains volcanic rocks.

tion of Bandelier rhyolite tuff. (See Williams, 1941, p. 251-252.) The ring fault bounding the subsided caldera block is mostly covered by younger volcanics and alluvium, but existing exposures indicate that it constitutes a complex fracture zone two to three miles wide. Within this ring-fracture zone is a central, initially more or less intact block that is now arched into a steep-sided, slightly elongate structural dome. This dome is essentially a mosaic of radially dipping blocks broken by radial faults and bisected by a northeast-trending longitudinal graben. It is approximately eight miles in diameter and displays a structural and topographic relief of nearly 3,000 feet. The topographic elements comprising the dome are Redondo Border and Redondo (Mountain), the highest point of which is Redondo Peak (11,254 feet). The prominent position of Redondo, which rises 1,000 to 2,000 feet higher than the peaks on the caldera rim, is most striking when viewed from the vicinity of San Ysidro, 25 miles to the south-southwest.

The Redondo structural dome is not the result of differential collapse of the caldera block, but rather the result of post-collapse uplift of the caldera floor, probably consequent upon a resurgence of new magma from below with accompanying intrusion of a stock or laccolith, or possibly owing to hydrostatic readjustment of the viscous magma that remained in the chamber following eruption of the upper sequence of ash flows of the Bandelier.

During and following the gradual rise of this structural dome, large quantities of viscous rhyolite were extruded from the peripheral ring-fracture zone, giving rise to the ring of volcanic domes that surround Redondo. Because of the spatial and temporal relations of these ring extrusions, it has been suggested (Smith, Bailey, and Ross, 1960) that some ring dikes may be emplaced during post-collapse uplift and doming of the caldera floor rather than during subsidence of the caldera block as suggested by Clough, Maufe, and Bailey (1909) in their classic study of the ring intrusions of Scotland. More detailed evidence and explanation of the mechanics of this interpretation are presented by Smith, Bailey, and Ross (in press).

REGIONAL STRUCTURE

Bryan (1938, p. 204) and Smith (1938, p. 950 and 958) interpreted the older volcanic rocks of the Jemez Mountains (the Chicoma volcanic formation of Smith, 1938) as older than the Abiquiu tuff, and they thought that throughout Abiquiu time the mountains were a highland against which the Abiquiu tuff was deposited. They concluded that the mountains were subsequently buried by sediments of the Santa Fe formation and that the mountains owe their present relief to post-Pliocene uplift along normal faults. Stearns (1953, p. 496) has pointed out, however, that there is no evidence that highlands existed in either the Nacimiento or Valles areas during Abiquiu time and suggested that the Abiquiu tuff fan extended over much of the area now occupied by the Jemez Mountains. There is in fact considerable evidence indicating that volcanism in the Jemez Mountains did not begin until late Santa Fe time: 1) tuffaceous sediments tentatively correlated with the Abiquiu tuff are exposed beneath old volcanics in the west and northwest walls of the Valles caldera, 2) nowhere are the older sediments of the Santa Fe group known to contain volcanic rocks of the Jemez Mountains[2], and 3) wherever the oldest volcanic rocks of Jemez Mountains are exposed, they unconformably overlie faulted and eroded arkosic sediments of the Santa Fe group. This relation suggests that volcanism in the Jemez Mountains did not begin until commencement of the late Santa Fe faulting that determines the present outlines of the Rio Grande depression. Evidential in this respect is the location of the Jemez Mountains—that is, athwart the western margin of the depression at a point where its north-south trend is offset westward by a series of en echelon faults. The tensional environment associated with this offset may well have provided the zone of weakness for the locus of volcanism.

The extreme western margin of the Rio Grande depression in the Jemez area is delineated by a zone of northeast-trending faults that extends from just west of Jemez Pueblo in the south to beyond Canones in the north. The southern segment of this zone is defined primarily by the Jemez fault, which west of Jemez Pueblo brings sediments of the Santa Fe group in steep contact with pre-Tertiary rocks on the west. Northeastward the fault passes into pre-Tertiary rocks entirely and is partly covered by the Bandelier rhyolite tuff of the Jemez Plateau. In San Diego Canyon at Soda Dam, just north of Jemez Springs, the fault brings an isolated mass of Precambrian granite up against Permian sandstones of the Abo formation (Wood and Northrop, 1946). Thence it continues northeastward to the head of the canyon where it presumably intersects the caldera ring fracture zone. The Jemez fault cannot be traced into the caldera area, but the alignment of it with the post-caldera graben between Redondo and Redondo Border suggests that it may have continued into the caldera before dying out, and that it may have predetermined the position and orientation of the graben.

Northwest of the Valles caldera the western margin of the Rio Grande depression is covered by volcanics and is poorly defined. North of the mountains, in the vicinity of Canones, however, it is sharply delineated again by several northeast-striking faults that bring the Abiquiu tuff down to the southeast against older rocks.

Another major fault zone on the west side of the Rio Grande depression extends from Santa Ana Mesa north-northeastward along the eastern side of the Jemez Mountains to Abiquiu. This zone differs from the westernmost zone in that it consists of a series of north-striking faults arranged en echelon to the north-northeast. The southern end of this en echelon zone is delineated by the San Felipe fault zone (Kelley, 1954) which transects the Quaternary basaltic lavas of Santa Ana Mesa. The San Felipe zone continues northward into the southern Jemez Mountains, where it has been active for a considerably longer time and has tilted and displaced downward to the east the older rocks of the volcanic pile.

North of Cochiti the en echelon zone is expressed by the Pajarito fault zone, a series of arcuate faults that sweep around the east side of the San Miguel Mountains and pass northward through Los Alamos to Clara Peak, north of Santa Clara Canyon. The Pajarito fault zone displaces the Bandelier rhyolite tuff 300 feet or more, but displacements in the underlying dacitic rocks exceed 1,000 feet and indicate a long activity. North of Santa Clara Canyon the fault zone continues as a series of antithetic faults that displace the basalts along the eastern edge of Lobato Mesa. Near Abiquiu these north-trending faults meet the northeast-trending faults of the westernmost zone.

The character of faulting in the eastern and western fault zones differs in several important ways. The faults in the western zone generally show normal displacement downward to the east and bound blocks that are tilted westward. The faults in the eastern zone on the other hand commonly are antithetic and bound blocks that are tilted eastward. The faults of the eastern zone furthermore show considerably greater syn-volcanic and post-volcanic displacement than those in the western zone, and as a consequence the volcanic pile thickens markedly to the east. These relations suggest indirectly that volcanism in the Jemez Mountains is related to the initiation of faulting in the Rio Grande depression, and that it consequently postdates deposition of the Abiquiu tuff and probably most of the arkosic sediments of the Santa Fe group also.

Volcanic and Intrusive Rocks of the Bland Mining District

In the headwaters of Bland and Colle Canyons and extending north into Medio Dia Canyon and south into Peralta Canyon is a group of volcanic rocks intruded by monzonitic and dioritic dikes and sills. The volcanics range in composition from basalt to dacite, and associated with them are tuffaceous sediments and a problematical arkosic sandstone. These rocks are intensely faulted and considerably altered and mineralized. The ghost mining camps of Bland and Albemarle are located in the area (Lindgren, Graton, and Gordon, 1910; Bundy, 1958).

The precise stratigraphic position of this suite of rocks has not been established. They are the oldest volcanic rocks in the Jemez area and have been almost completely buried by younger rocks of the Jemez Mountains volcanic sequence. The intrusive rocks resemble those of the Ortiz Mountains and Cerrillos Hills, east of the Rio Grande, and possibly they are the same age. As such, they would be

---

[2]Pebbles of volcanic rocks do occur in Santa Fe beds on the east and north beneath the basalts of Lobato Mesa and the Puye gravel, but these rocks are unlike those in the Jemez volcanic pile and appear to have come from a more distant source.

Oligocene in age (Stearns, 1953; Jaffe and others, 1959) and the intruded arkosic sands would belong to the Galisteo formation of Eocene and Oligocene (?) age, or to one of several older formations. However, one inconclusive lead-alpha age determination made on zircons from a fine-grained granodiorite from the Bland area has yielded an approximate age of 19 million years (Jaffe and others, 1959). This middle Miocene age, if valid, would place the intrusives in early Santa Fe time, and the intruded sandstone could be correlative with the earliest sediments of the Santa Fe group.

Because of the uncertainty of the stratigraphic position of these rocks, they have been omitted from the general discussion in this paper.

SUMMARY

The following historical summary is based on the work of Bryan (1938), Smith (1938), and Stearns (1953), supplemented and modified by the authors' observations.

Stratigraphic and structural relations indicate that volcanism in the Jemez Mountains, exclusive of the Bland area, began in early to middle Pliocene time. The area now occupied by the Jemez Mountains was then a basin of sedimentation situated between the Sangre de Cristo Range on the east and the Nacimiento Mountains, probably a subdued upland, on the west. Volcanism commenced along the western slope of the basin and was shortly preceded and accompanied by faulting along a zone extending from the vicinity of Jemez Pueblo to Abiquiu.

It is probable that the ancestral Rio Grande was established as a through-flowing stream during and possibly as a consequence of this faulting. Bryan (1938, p. 207) postulated that this ancestral river flowed in a course west of its present position, and Stearns (1953, p. 501) suggested that it has since been diverted eastward by volcanic accumulation in the Jemez Mountains. This is well demonstrated by the manner in which the Rio Grande flows around the toe of the huge fan that constitutes the Puye gravel, which overlies quartzitic gravels presumed to be deposits of the ancestral Rio. Farther south in the vicinity of White Rock Canyon, the history of the Rio Grande is further complicated by basaltic eruptions of the Cerros del Rio, which temporarily dammed the river, forming a shallow lake in the vicinity of Buckman and Totavi. Drainage in this area was subsequently reestablished to the west. It was again dammed by the Bandelier rhyolite tuff and finally reestablished in its present course.

Volcanism in the Jemez area began with widespread eruption of basalts and continued with the successive effusion of andesites, dacites, quartz latites, and associated rhyolites. Of these older rocks, those in the north are generally younger than those in the south. In Pleistocene time, after a period of quiescence and erosion, catastrophic eruption of hot ash flows from the crest of the volcanic pile resulted in the deposition of the Bandelier rhyolite tuff and the formation of the Valles caldera and a slightly older and smaller caldera to the northeast. Subsequent activity, restricted within the Valles caldera, included structural doming of the caldera floor, producing the central mountains of Redondo and Redondo Border, and contemporaneous extrusion of a peripheral ring of rhyolite domes. Intermittently the caldera was filled by lakes which have since been drained by headward erosion of the Jemez River and San Antonio Creek. Solfataric and hot-spring activity, the vestiges of volcanism, continue today within the caldera, notably at Sulfur Springs, and outside the caldera at several localities in San Diego Canyon.

Although some regional doming probably accompanied intrusion of magma in the Jemez area, the mountains owe their present relief mainly to volcanic accumulation and differential subsidence of the Rio Grande depression.

REFERENCES CITED

Bryan, Kirk, 1938, Geology and ground-water conditions of the Rio Grande depression in Colorado and New Mexico, in Regional planning; Pt. 6, The Rio Grande joint investigation in the upper Rio Grande Basin in Colorado, New Mexico, and Texas, 1936-1937: [U. S.] National Resources Committee, v. 1, pt. 2, sec. 1, p. 197-225.

Bundy, W. M., 1958, Wall-rock alteration in the Cochiti mining district, New Mexico: New Mexico Bur. Mines and Mineral Res. Bull. 59, 71 p.

Church, F. S., and Hack, J. T., 1939, An exhumed erosion surface in the Jemez Mountains, New Mexico: Jour. Geology, v. 47, p. 613-629.

Clough, C. T., Maufe, H. B., and Bailey, E. B. 1909, The cauldron subsidence of Glen Coe and the associated igneous phenomena: Geol. Soc. London Quart. Jour., v. 65, p. 611-678.

Cope, E. D., 1877, Report upon the extinct Vertebrata obtained in New Mexico by parties of the expedition of 1874, in U. S. Geographical Surveys west of the 100th meridian [Wheeler]: v. 4, pt. 2, 371 p.

Denny, C. S., 1940, Santa Fe formation in the Espanola Valley, New Mexico: Geol. Soc. America Bull., v. 51, p. 677-693.

Frick, Childs, 1933, New remains of trilophodont-tetrabelodont mastodons: Am. Mus. Nat. History Bull., v. 59, p. 505-562.

—————, 1937, Horned ruminants of North America: Am. Mus. Nat. History Bull., v. 69, 669 p.

Hayden, F. V., 1869, Preliminary field report of the U. S. Geological Survey of Colorado and New Mexico: U. S. Geol. and Geogr. Surv. Terr. 3d Ann. Rept., p. 69-70.

Henderson, Junius, 1913, Geology and topography of the Rio Grande region in New Mexico, in Hewett, E. L., Henderson, Junius, and Robbins, W. W., The physiography of the Rio Grande valley, New Mexico, in relation to pueblo culture: Bur. Am. Ethnology Bull., v. 54, p. 23-39.

Iddings, J. P., 1890, On a group of volcanic rocks from the Tewan Mountains, New Mexico, and on the occurrence of primary quartz in certain basalts: U. S. Geol. Survey Bull. 66, 34 p.

Jaffe, H. W., Gottfried, David, Waring, C. L., and Worthing, H. W., 1959, Lead-alpha age determinations of accessory minerals of igneous rocks (1953-1957): U. S. Geol. Survey Bull. 1097-B, p. 65-148.

Johnson, D. W., 1903, The geology of the Cerrillos Hills, New Mexico: School of Mines (Columbia Univ.) Quart., v. 24, p. 304-350.

Kelley, V. C., 1954, Tectonic map of a part of the upper Rio Grande area, New Mexico: U. S. Geol. Survey Oil and Gas Inv. Map OM-157.

—————, 1956, The Rio Grande depression from Taos to Santa Fe, in New Mexico Geol. Soc. Guidebook of southeastern Sangre de Cristo Mountains, New Mexico, 7th Field Conf.: p. 109-114.

Lindgren, Waldemar, Graton, L. C., and Gordon, C. H., 1910, The ore deposits of New Mexico: U. S. Geol. Survey Prof. Paper 68, 361 p.

Newberry, J. S., 1876, Geological report, in Macomb, J. N., Report of the exploring expedition from Santa Fe, New Mexico, to the junction of the Grand and Green Rivers of the Great Colorado of the West in 1859: U. S. Army Engineer Dept.: p. 9-118.

Osborn, H. F., 1909, Cenozoic mammal horizons of western North America: U. S. Geol. Survey Bull. 361, 138 p.

—————, 1918, Equidae of Oligocene, Miocene, and Pliocene of North America, iconographic type revision: Am. Mus. Nat. Hist. Mem., n.s. 2, pt. 1, p. 1-330.

Reagan, A. B., 1903, Geology of the Jemez-Albuquerque region, New Mexico: Am. Geologist, v. 31, p. 67-111.

Ross, C. S., 1931, The Valles Mountains volcanic center of New Mexico [abs.]: Am. Geophys. Union Trans. 12th Ann. Mtg., p. 185-186.

—————, 1938, Valles volcano, New Mexico [abs.]: Washington Acad. Sci. Jour., v. 28, p. 417.

Smith, H. T. U., 1938, Tertiary geology of the Abiquiu quadrangle, New Mexico: Jour. Geology, v. 46, p. 933-965.

Smith, R. L., Bailey, R. A., and Ross, C. S., 1960, Calderas: aspects of their structural evolution and their relation to ring complexes [abs.]: Geol. Soc. America Bull., v. 71, p. 1981.

—————, in press, Structural evolution of the Valles caldera and its bearing on the emplacement of ring dikes, in U. S. Geological Survey, Short papers in the geologic and hydrologic sciences, U. S. Geol. Survey Prof. Paper 424-D (in press).

Stearns, C. E., 1953, Tertiary geology of the Galisteo-Tonque area, New Mexico: Geol. Soc. America Bull., v. 64, p. 459-507.

Williams, Howel, 1941, Calderas and their origin: Univ. California Pub. Dept. Geol. Sci. Bull., v. 25, p. 239-346.

Wood, G. H., Jr., and Northrop, S. A., 1946, Geology of Nacimiento Mountains, San Pedro Mountain, and adjacent plateaus in parts of Sandoval and Rio Arriba Counties, New Mexico: U. S. Geol. Survey Oil and Gas Inv. Prelim. Map 57.

STRUCTURAL PROBLEMS OF THE RIO GRANDE TROUGH IN THE ALBUQUERQUE COUNTRY

Anonymous

INTRODUCTION

In 1954 V. C. Kelley graphically summarized the results of geological mapping by many individuals in the upper Rio Grande area, New Mexico. However, because of lack of time it was impractical to write an accompanying text. In addition, it probably would have been unwise to have attempted to analyze and explain many of the puzzling structural features. Even now this is to a considerable extent still the case. Hence this title, "Structural Problems of the Rio Grande Trough in the Albuquerque Country."

MAJOR STRUCTURAL ELEMENTS

As shown on the tectonic map[1] in the pocket, the limits of the Albuquerque country are approximately defined by the 36° parallel on the north and the 34° 36' on the south. To the east the arbitrary boundary is quite irregular but in the vicinity of Albuquerque and Bernalillo and from there north it is approximately defined by the 105° 50' meridian, while to the west the limits of the map are 107° 10' on the southern margin and 107° on the northern margin. This area in fact emcompasses the broad valley of the Rio Grande and either all or marginal parts of the adjacent structural uplifts. This great valley, in this area, is a major and complex structural trough or graben. The marginal uplifts are also the margins of the trough and many of them are structurally very complex. Structural elements and major basins are enumerated and briefly described below.

The northernmost basin area (Fig. 1) has been referred to as the Espanola basin (Kelley, 1954). In or adjacent to it are the Penasco and Abiquiu embayments, only portions of which are included on the map, and the Santa Fe embayment. The northern margin is vague but as indicated on the small-scale tectonic map it is limited by the Embudo channel, a constriction between the Espanola and San Luis basins. Similarly much of the southern margin is vague but locally the La Bajada escarpment defines the margin on the southwest. On the east the margin is the great fault escarpment of the Sangre de Cristo uplift, while on the west the Espanola basin is limited by the Pajarito fault in an area considered in detail in this Guidebook.

The Espanola basin (Fig. 1) is a complex graben. Much of the evidence for its complexity lies in the vicinity of the Embudo channel where a series of Precambrian blocks constitutes an arcuate trend from the Picuris Mountains on the southeast to the Petaca and Ortega Mountains on the northwest. These Precambrian elements are horsts in the major graben.

Direct evidence of internal complexities in that part of the Espanola basin here discussed is primarily a series of inferences because of the difficulty of identifying structural features within the Rio Grande trough. However, some evidence of these may be seen along the eastern margin north of Santa Fe and in the area between Espanola and Los Alamos on the western margin. Adjacent to

[1]Tectonic map of a part of the upper Rio Grande area, New Mexico, by V. C. Kelley, 1961.

the Espanola basin is the eastwardly thrust and tilted Sangre de Cristo Mountains with a most complex fault zone along its western margin. The Jemez uplift, which is limited on the east by the Pajarito fault, is the western margin of the Espanola basin and is a volcanic plateau surmounted by the Jemez caldera. This topographically high feature is believed to be a part of the Rio Grande trough.

It seems most likely that the approximate western margin of the Rio Grande trough is in fact the Jemez fault zone and its possible continuation under the Jemez volcanic plateau. This fault zone, which approximately defines the eastern structural margin of Sierra Nacimiento, is a series of faults dominantly down to the east and appears to be en echelon with the Puerco fault zone which lies farther south.

Sierra Nacimiento (map in pocket) is a rather narrow but long uplift characterized by a rather steep thrust or reverse fault along its western margin.

Southwest of the large Espanola basin is the apparently en echelon Santo Domingo basin (Fig. 1). To the northeast its margin is the La Bajada fault escarpment while to the west it is limited by the San Felipe fault belt. Its southeastern margin is the Hagan fault. In consequence a feature that has been called the Hagan embayment has been recognized. The northern and northwestern margins of the Santo Domingo basin are the continuations of the Pajarito fault and farther southwest the approximate margin of the Jemez volcanic series is the Jemez Plateau.

Marginal uplifts are the domical northern part of the Ortiz porphyry belt and the relatively high Hagan basin in which pre-Tertiary rocks are exposed. The Ortiz porphyry belt actually extends from South Mountain north to the Cerrillos Hills, a short distance south of Santa Fe.

The Ortiz Mountains and Cerrillos Hills (map in pocket), which are the two intrusive features marginal to the Santo Domingo basin, are laccolithic and stocklike and were emplaced prior to deposition of the Santa Fe. The La Bajada fault escarpment is dominantly down to the west while the San Felipe fault belt consists of one or more grabens extending from the Jemez uplift south towards the Sandia Mountains.

The Albuquerque-Belen basin (Fig. 1), which by arbitrary definition includes the remainder of the Rio Grande trough in the Albuquerque country, extends as far south as approximately the 34° 15' parallel. However, only that portion of it that lies north of the approximate latitude of Belen is here discussed. This large late Tertiary sedimentary basin is limited on the east by the San Felipe fault belt, the fault margin of the eastwardly tilted Sandia uplift, and farther south by the fault margins of the eastwardly tilted Manzano and Los Pinos uplifts.

On the south the Albuquerque-Belen basin is terminated by a constriction that has been called the Socorro channel. On the west the margin of the Albuquerque-Belen basin is defined by the Puerco fault zone, the Lucero uplift, and in the extreme southwest by the Sierra Ladron.

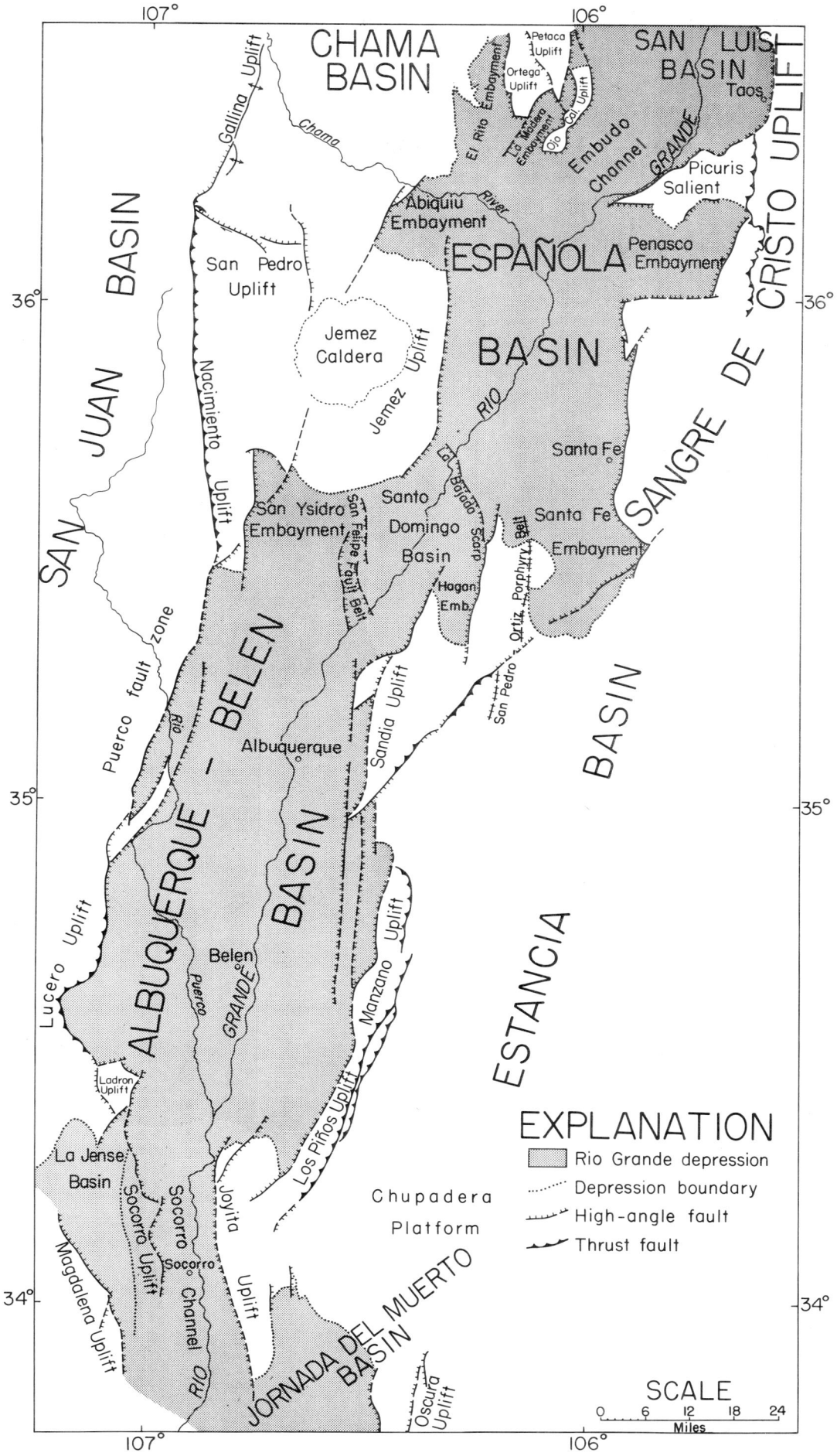

Figure 1. Tectonic map of the middle Rio Grande depression (modified from U. S. Geol. Survey Map OM-157 by V. C. Kelley)

The Puerco fault zone, as indicated on the maps (Fig. 1 and map in pocket), is a broad zone of complex normal faults. Some of these faults are structurally down to the east, others to the west. In consequence the belt is characterized by numerous grabens and horsts. However, despite these complications, the dominant deformation is down to the east.

The Lucero uplift (see maps), the eastern margin of which may be in part a continuation of the Puerco fault zone, is a feature that was upthrust from west to east in relatively early Tertiary time after which it sustained one or more episodes of normal faulting in later Tertiary time. Still farther south along the western margin of the Albuquerque-Belen basin is the Sierra Ladron. Although somewhat indecisive, data regarding the margins of this feature suggest that it is limited on all sides by supposedly normal faults. On the northwest and northern margins the Albuquerque-Belen basin and its San Ysidro embayment are limited by the Jemez fault and the erosional margin of the Jemez uplift or plateau.

MAJOR STRUCTURAL PROBLEMS

In the preceding discussion it has been established that the Rio Grande trough is believed to be a major downwarp or graben with many internal complications. However, the details of movement along the margins remain to be determined. Is the movement primarily vertical with only minor horizontal components or is it primarily horizontal with minor vertical components? Such features as the sawtooth-like fault near the mouth of Juan Tabo Canyon in the Sandia Mountains suggest vertical displacement. On the other hand, the stratigraphic dissimilarities of such features as formational thicknesses and facies on the two margins of the trough, together with local drag effects, suggest the possibility of major horizontal components with the possibility of horizontal shift of as much as several miles.

The apparent echelon relationships of major basins such as the Espanola and Albuquerque-Belen basins are not well understood. The terminations of some of these, such as the southern margin of the Espanola basin in the Santa Fe area, are very puzzling. The eastern margin, of course, is limited by the complex fault zone in front of the Sangre de Cristo Mountains. However, south of Lamy major faulting appears to end rather abruptly and apparently the Santa Fe laps across the older rocks as it thins. The same is true in the vicinity of Cerrillos where again the relationships appear to be simple and without the structural control farther north.

What is the pre-Santa Fe or early Tertiary history of the area? Locally, at least, the Galisteo formation and farther south the Baca formation which are believed to be mainly Eocene in age occupy parts of the trough and adjacent uplifts. The Galisteo formation is as much as 5,000 feet thick while the Baca is somewhat thinner. Therefore, there must have been one or more sedimentary basins during early Tertiary episodes of orogeny. In the general area of the Rio Grande trough does this basin or series of basins approximately conform to the present outline of the trough and its margins or has the present trough been superimposed only by accident upon earlier basins of deposition that had vastly different outlines?

How much thrusting was involved in the development of the early Tertiary orogenic belts along the margins of the present Rio Grande trough? The Lucero uplift is believed by some to be thrust to the east with later superposition of a normal fault system. By contrast, the Sierra Nacimiento, which would appear to be an approximate continuation of the Lucero uplift north of the Puerco fault zone, is thrust westward along a relatively steep fault. This westward thrusting is also believed to be early Tertiary in age. Why should there be this change in direction of thrusting? On the east side of the Rio Grande trough westward-dipping thrust faults have been mapped from the Los Pinos uplift northward through the Manzanos. These are also relatively steep faults. Is it possible that the interpretation of these as high-angle thrust faults is incorrect and that they are normal faults, the apparent reversal being due to eastward tilting of the blocks during the development of the Rio Grande trough?

What is the true nature of Tijeras fault? All available data suggest that it has substantial horizontal movement. Is it possible that this feature should be interpreted as a thrust fault?

In the vicinity of Socorro it is apparent that Paleozoic and Mesozoic rocks underlie the Tertiary sediments in much if not all of the trough. Similar relationships are suggested farther north in the vicinity of Belen where a drill hole is believed to have gone into Cretaceous rocks at a depth of approximately 9,000 feet. In the latitude of Albuquerque and farther north the presence of Mesozoic rocks at the surface in the broad Puerco fault zone suggests that pre-Tertiary sedimentary rocks underlie the Tertiary sequence of the Rio Grande trough. In the vicinity of Santa Fe, New Mexico, the Pennsylvanian rocks are locally exposed in the Santa Fe fault zone along the margin of the Rio Grande trough. This also suggests, but does not prove, the presence of a sedimentary sequence intervening between the Precambrian and the Tertiary strata in the trough at this latitude.

In the canyon of the Rio Grande from the vicinity of Dixon north to near Taos Junction, Precambrian rocks immediately underlie the Santa Fe formation. The existence of the Precambrian inlier at Cerro Azule nearly half way between the Dixon area and the margin of the Petaca and Ortega Mountains in the vicinity of Ojo Caliente suggests that the Precambrian immediately underlies the Santa Fe in the trough. Similar relationships are seen in the Picuris, Ortega, and Petaca Mountains and support this view.

If the assumption is correct that the Santa Fe formation rests on Precambrian rocks in the Dixon-Ojo Caliente area in the Rio Grande trough then there is a change that may be either abrupt or gradual in the sequence somewhere between the northern end of the Puerco fault zone and the latitude of Dixon. Where does this change take place and what is the nature of it?

The answers to many of the questions posed above should wait on considerably more detailed mapping and analysis of the local structures within the several basins as well as in the adjoining uplifts.

REFERENCES

Anderson, J. E., 1960, Geology and geomorphology of the Santo Domingo basin, Sandoval and Santa Fe Counties, New Mexico: Univ. New Mexico unpub. master's thesis, 110 p.

Baldwin, Brewster, Unpublished map of the Santa Fe area: New Mexico Inst. Min. Tech., State Bureau Mines and Mineral Res.

Bryan, Kirk, and McCann, F. T., 1938, The Ceja del Rio Puerco; a border feature of the Basin and Range province in New Mexico: Jour. Geology, v. 45, p. 808, fig. 4.

Cabot, E. C., 1938, Fault border of the Sangre de Cristo Mountains north of Santa Fe, New Mexico: Jour. Geology, v. 46, p. 92, fig. 2.

Disbrow, A. E., and Stoll, W. C., 1957, Geology of the Cerrillos area, Santa Fe County, New Mexico: New Mexico Bur. Mines and Mineral Res. Bull. 48.

Emerick, W. L., 1950, Geology of the Golden area, Santa Fe County, New Mexico: Univ. New Mexico unpub. master's thesis, 66 p.

Harrison, E. P., 1949, Geology of the Hagan coal basin: Univ. New Mexico, unpub. master's thesis, pl. 1.

Hunt, C. B., 1936, Geology and fuel resources of the southern part of the San Juan Basin, New Mexico; Pt. 2, The Mount Taylor coal field: U. S. Geol. Survey Bull. 860-B, pl. 19.

——————, 1938, Igneous geology and structure of the Mount Taylor volcanic field, New Mexico: U. S. Geol. Survey Prof. Paper 189-B, pl. 7.

Kelley, V. C., 1948, Geology and pumice deposits of the Pajarito Plateau, Sandoval, Santa Fe, and Rio Arriba Counties, New Mexico: Univ. New Mexico Los Alamos Proj.—Pumice Inv., 16 p.

——————, 1951, Tectonics of the San Juan Basin, in New Mexico Geol. Soc. Guidebook of the south and west sides of the San Juan Basin, New Mexico and Arizona, 2d Field Conf.: p. 128.

——————, 1952, Tectonics of the Rio Grande depression of central New Mexico, in New Mexico Geol. Soc. Guidebook of the Rio Grande country, central New Mexico, 3d Field Conf.: p. 93-105.

——————, 1954, Tectonic map of a part of the upper Rio Grande area, New Mexico: U. S. Geol. Survey Oil and Gas Inv. Map OM-157.

Kelley, V. C., and Wood, G. H., Jr., 1946, Lucero uplift, Valencia, Socorro, and Bernalillo Counties, New Mexico: U. S. Geol. Survey Oil and Gas Inv. Prelim. Map 47.

Northrop, S. A., and Wood, G. H., Jr., 1946, Geology of Nacimiento Mountains, San Pedro Mountain, and adjacent plateaus in parts of Sandoval and Rio Arriba Counties, New Mexico: U. S. Geol. Survey Oil and Gas Inv. Prelim. Map 57.

Read, C. B., and others, 1944, Geologic map and stratigraphic sections of Permian and Pennsylvanian rocks of parts of San Miguel, Santa Fe, Sandoval, Bernalillo, Torrance, and Valencia Counties, north-central New Mexico: U. S. Geol. Survey Oil and Gas Inv. Prelim. Map 21.

Reiche, Parry, 1949, Geology of the Manzanita and North Manzano Mountains, New Mexico: Geol. Soc. America Bull., v. 60, pl. 5.

Reynolds, C. B., 1954, Geology of the Hagan-La Madera area, Sandoval County, New Mexico: Univ. New Mexico unpub. master's thesis, 82 p.

Silver, Caswell, Unpublished map of the French Mesa area.

Soister, P. E., 1952, Geology of Santa Ana Mesa and adjoining areas, Sandoval County, New Mexico: Univ. New Mexico unpub. master's thesis, fig. 4.

Stark, J. T., 1956, Geology of the South Manzano Mountains, New Mexico: New Mexico Bur. Mines and Mineral Res. Bull. 34.

Stearns, C. E., 1943, The Galisteo formation of north central New Mexico: Jour. Geology, v. 51, p. 302, fig. 1.

——————, 1953, Tertiary geology of the Galisteo-Tonque area, New Mexico: Geol. Soc. America Bull., v. 64, pl. 1.

Sun, Ming-Shan, and Baldwin, Brewster, 1958, Volcanic rocks of the Cienega area, Santa Fe County, New Mexico: New Mexico Bur. Mines and Mineral Res. Bull. 54.

Wright, H. E., Jr., 1946, Tertiary and Quaternary geology of the lower Rio Puerco area, New Mexico: Geol. Soc. America Bull., v. 57, pl. 8.

THE RIO GRANDE TROUGH NEAR ALBUQUERQUE, NEW MEXICO[1]

H. R. JOESTING, J. E. CASE, and L. E. CORDELL
U. S. Geological Survey
Washington, D. C., Berkeley, California, and Albuquerque, New Mexico

Gravity and aeromagnetic surveys have been made of part of the Rio Grande trough and adjoining areas near Albuquerque, New Mexico, to learn more about the structural boundaries and configuration of the trough. The area covered by the gravity and aeromagnetic surveys is shown on Figure 1.

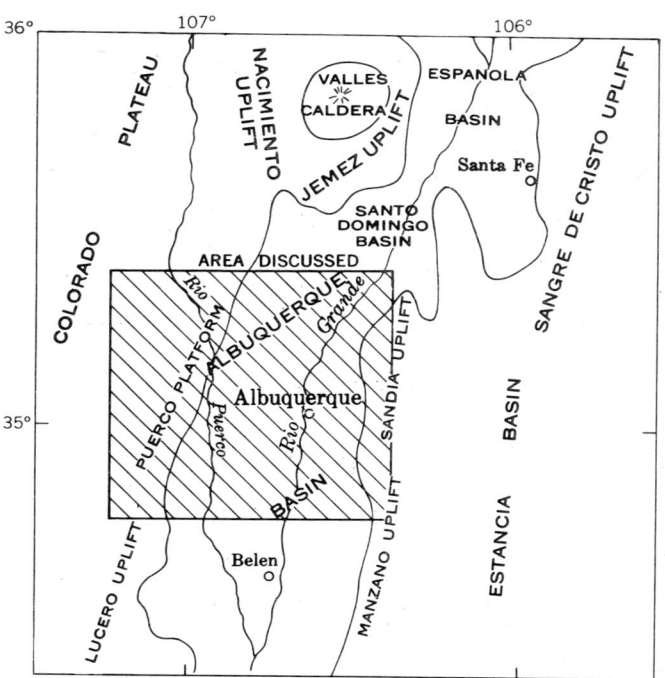

Figure 1.—Sketch map of part of Rio Grande trough and associated structures in north-central New Mexico. Area studied crosshatched; Rio Grande trough shown by stippled pattern. Structural boundaries from Kelley (1952).

The Rio Grande trough (Kelley, 1952, 1954; Fitzsimmons, 1959) is a series of complexly faulted troughs or basins, arranged en echelon. It extends from the northern end of the San Luis valley in Colorado, southward 450 miles along the course of the Rio Grande in New Mexico, to near El Paso, Texas. The trough is bounded on the west by the Colorado Plateau and on the east by uplifts of the southern Rocky Mountains.

The Albuquerque basin, the largest basin of the Rio Grande trough, is about 90 miles long and 30 miles wide. It is bounded by the Sandia, Manzanita, and Manzano uplifts on the east, by the Lucero uplift and Puerco platform on the west, and by the southern end of the Nacimiento uplift on the northwest. Small volcanoes and fissure flows mark the boundaries at several localities. The basin is filled with poorly consolidated Cenozoic deposits whose constituents were eroded from the uplands. Older sedimentary rocks doubtless underlie the valley fill. The

[1]Preprinted from U. S. Geological Survey Professional Paper 424-D.

thickness of sedimentary rocks is unknown, but Precambrian rocks may lie 10,000 feet below sea level in parts of the basin, whereas they are about 9,000 feet above sea level in the Sandia uplift and about sea level in the Puerco platform.

Gravity map. — A large gravity low shown on Figure 2 is associated with the valley fill (density about 2.3 g per cm^3), and prominent highs with the denser sedimentary

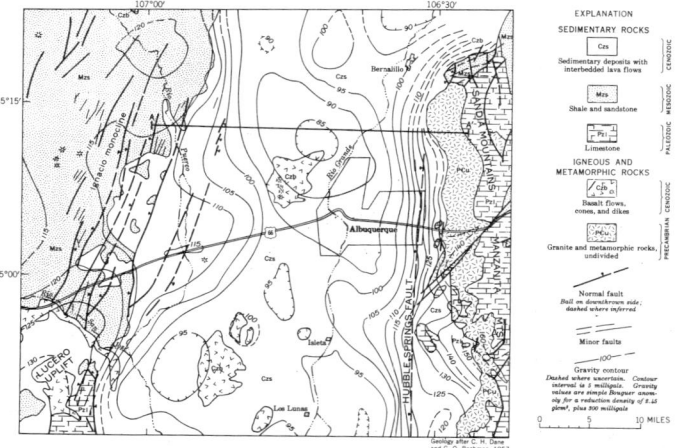

Figure 2—Preliminary gravity map and generalized geologic map of Rio Grande area near Albuquerque, New Mexico.

and crystalline rocks of the bordering uplifts (densities about 2.45 to 2.7 g per cm^3). Steep gradients between the low and the highs mark major bounding fault zones.

East of the trough, steep gravity gradients coincide in part with scarps along the mountain fronts, and with the projection of the Hubble Springs fault (Kelley, 1954). As some of the steeper gradients are several miles farther west, parts of the main fault zone are evidently covered by consolidated material.

A fault zone also bounds the west side of the trough, as shown by steepened gradients. They are less pronounced than on the east, because the comparatively dense Precambrian and Paleozoic rocks are covered by several thousand feet of less dense Mesozoic rocks; in addition, the fault zone may be wider or may dip less steeply. To the south steep gradients coincide with the faulted eastern flank of the Lucero uplift. At U. S. Highway 66 the contours bulge northeastward, indicating a buried extension of the Lucero uplift. A similar bulge on the eastern side constricts the trough. North of U. S. Highway 66 the west margin of the trough trends north, about parallel to observed and inferred faults. The Ignacio monocline is marked by a broad gravity high.

Some of the closed gravity lows within the trough may coincide with comparatively great thicknesses of low-density valley fill. If so, the ancient drainage may have been west of the present Rio Grande, except to the south near Los Lunas. Conversely, some of the prominent highs may represent uplifted blocks of the denser Paleozoic and Precambrian rocks and thinner valley fill. The most prominent high, in addition to the positive bulges already mentioned, is west of Bernalillo.

An analysis of the gravity anomaly across the Rio Grande trough is shown on Figure 3. A residual gravity low of about 45 milligals is superimposed on an assumed

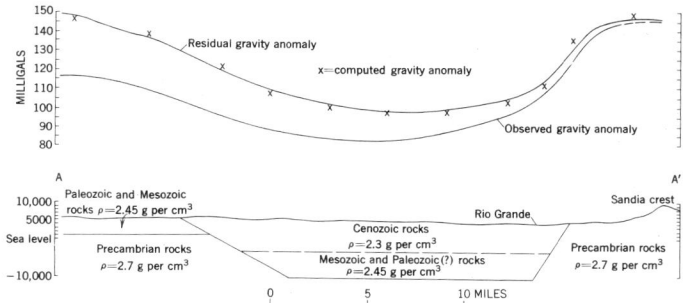

Figure 3.—An interpretation of the gravity anomaly across the Rio Grande trough north of Albuquerque, New Mexico.

linear regional gradient. The density of the Cenozoic fill probably increases with depth, but the depth at which this becomes significant is unknown. The assigned density of the Mesozoic and Paleozoic rocks (2.45 g per cm^3) may be somewhat low, especially for the deeply buried rocks in the trough.

Based on densities shown on Figure 3, the total thickness of sedimentary rocks in the trough is about 15,000 feet, and the total relief of the Precambrian basement along the Sandia front is about 20,000 feet. These values are approximations only, as they depend in part on estimated rock densities. Single fault planes were assumed along the margins of the trough, although displacement probably occurred along many steeply dipping step faults.

Aeromagnetic profiles.—Aeromagnetic profiles across the Rio Grande trough are shown on Figure 4. The large magnetic highs are associated with the uplifted, comparatively magnetic crystalline rocks bordering the trough; smaller, local highs are associated with volcanic rocks. The sedimentary rocks are virtually nonmagnetic. In general, the profiles and gravity map are in agreement.

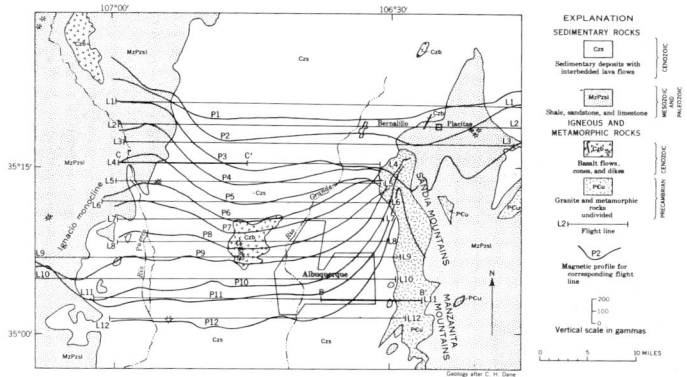

Figure 4.—Magnetic profiles, flight lines, and generalized geologic map of Rio Grande area near Albuquerque, New Mexico.

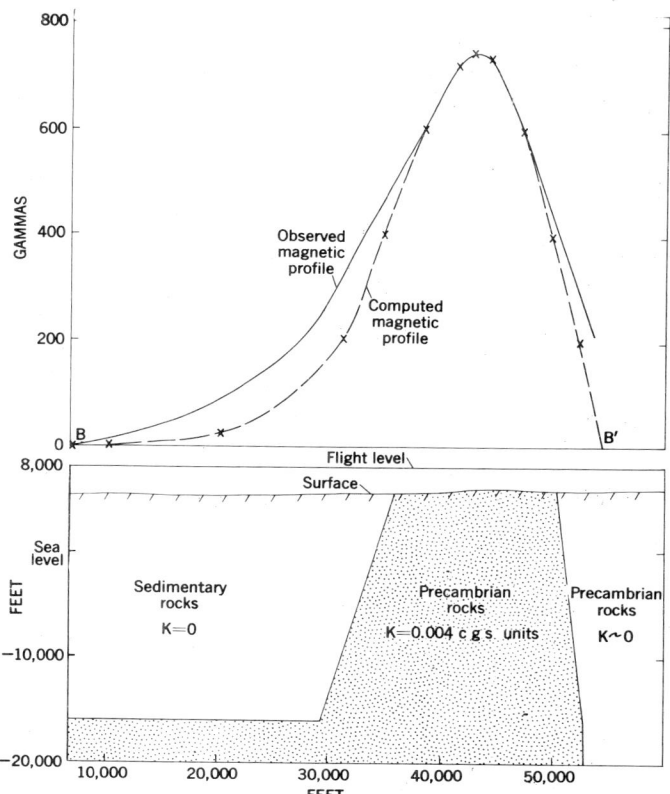

Figure 5.—An interpretation of the magnetic anomaly across the eastern boundary of the Rio Grande trough, southeast of Albuquerque, New Mexico.

The magnetic anomalies are related to variations in both the magnetization and uplift of the Precambrian rocks. For example, the magnetic susceptibility of the eastern part of the exposed Precambrian rocks near Albuquerque is quite low, whereas along the western edge it is moderately high (about 0.004 cgs units). The remanent magnetization is generally low throughout. The magnetic contrast is reflected in the peak and the sharp eastward decrease of profiles 11 and 12. The profiles also show that the more magnetic rocks continue westward some 2 miles from the mountains under outwash material. The main fault zone near Albuquerque therefore coincides approximately with the Hubble Springs fault (shown on Figure 2).

At the north end of the Sandia uplift the smaller amplitude of the profiles is probably related primarily to lower magnetization of the Precambrian rocks. Still farther north they reflect the apparent right-lateral offset of the Rio Grande trough, which is shown more clearly by the gravity contours.

At the west ends of lines 9 to 12 there is little magnetic expression of the buried structural boundary of the trough. The small anomalies on profiles 10 and 12, southwest of the large area of volcanic rock, agree in position with the bordering gravity anomalies, but they may be caused by shallow volcanic rocks rather than displacement of the basement. Volcanoes, however, are commonly alined along the borders of the trough. North of line 9 the basement rocks are more magnetic and appear to

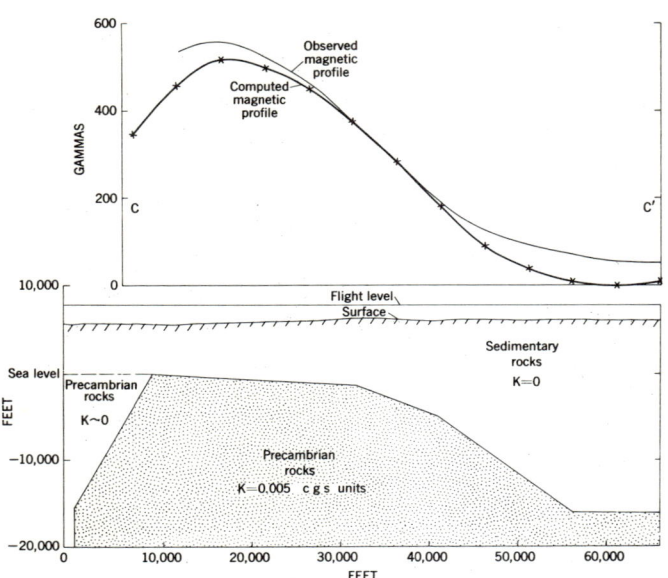

Figure 6.—An interpretation of the magnetic anomaly across the western boundary of the Rio Grande trough, northwest of Albuquerque, New Mexico.

delineate clearly the western edge of the trough. The fault zone is probably defined by the inflection points on the profiles.

Analyses of two aeromagnetic profiles based on the polar chart of Pirson (1935) are shown on Figures 5 and 6. The shapes and magnetic susceptibilities of the Precambrian rocks were arbitrarily chosen so that the computed and observed effects are in reasonable agreement. Reasonable fits were obtained when the Precambrian rock in the trough was placed at -16,000 feet, sea level datum. Assuming a lesser depth would have required flattening of the fault planes, or assigning more than one susceptibility. On Figure 5 the departure of computed and observed profiles along their west flank indicates that either the susceptibility of the down-faulted basement increases westward, or the slope of the fault decreases, perhaps step-fashion. The indicated displacement of the basement is nearly 22,000 feet along the Sandia front, and 16,000 feet on the west side. These estimates are in reasonable agreement with those based on gravity interpretations; but the correctness of both depends on the degree of correctness of the assigned magnetic susceptibilities and densities.

REFERENCES

Dane, C. H., and Bachman, G. O., 1957, Preliminary geologic map of the northwestern part of New Mexico: U. S. Geol. Survey Misc. Geol. Inv. Map I-224.

Fitzsimmons, J. P., 1959, The structure and geomorphology of west-central New Mexico: a regional setting, in New Mexico Geol. Soc. Guidebook of west-central New Mexico, 10th Field Conf.: p. 112-116.

Kelley, V. C., 1952, Tectonics of the Rio Grande depression of central New Mexico, in New Mexico Geol. Soc. Guidebook of the Rio Grande country, 3d Field Conf.: p. 93-105.

────────── 1954, Tectonic map of part of the upper Rio Grande area, New Mexico: U. S. Geol. Survey Oil and Gas Inv. Map OM-157.

Pirson, S. J., 1935, Polar charts for interpreting magnetic anomalies: Am. Inst. Min. Metall. Engineers Contr. 91.

EARTHQUAKES OF CENTRAL NEW MEXICO

STUART A. NORTHROP
University of New Mexico

After experiencing several earthquakes in Albuquerque in 1930 and 1931, and especially the Belen swarm of 1935-36, I became interested and in 1941, as State Collaborator for New Mexico, Seismological Field Survey, U. S. Coast and Geodetic Survey, I began to participate in gathering noninstrumental information by the questionnaire-card method. (New Mexico did not have a seismological station until 1959.)

A study of available information, chiefly old newspaper files, shows that more than 600 earthquakes have been definitely felt in New Mexico between 1855 and the present. For several years it was thought that the earliest quake was one in 1868, but the diary of a soldier stationed at Socorro refers to one there in 1855 (apparently the earliest in the Rocky Mountain region except for one recorded in Montana by the Lewis and Clark expedition in 1805).

About 95 percent of the State's quakes have originated in a narrow belt along the Rio Grande depression between Socorro and Albuquerque; the majority of these have been concentrated in the southern part of the belt between Belen and Socorro. Shocks have been felt in the Socorro-Albuquerque belt in at least 30 different years from 1855 to the present. About half of the 600 shocks were recorded vaguely, the other half more definitely. There have been several of intensity VII to VIII on the Rossi-Forel scale. This scale, ranging from I (least) to X (greatest), has been replaced in this country by the Modified Mercalli Intensity (Damage) Scale of 1931,[1] which ranges from I (least) to XII (greatest).

Notable features of the Rio Grande earthquakes include: (1) occurrence in swarms (daily for 3 weeks in 1935, almost daily for 3 months in 1893, almost daily for 6 months in 1906); (2) maximum nocturnal frequency (more people notice them while in bed); (3) maximum annual frequency (82 percent) in the July-December period; (4) numerous strong to moderately strong shocks; (5) generally small areas affected by most of the shocks although a few extended beyond the State's borders; and (6) occasional property damage, but no loss of life.

In connection with items 2 and 3, it may be noted that, according to Davison's hypothesis, in continental interiors there is a nocturnal maximum along with a winter maximum and shocks tend to be of moderate intensity, whereas along continental borders there is a day-time maximum along with a summer maximum and shocks are often of destructive intensity. Along the Rio Grande the maximum monthly frequency is in July, but December ranks second, and September, third.

It is interesting, but perhaps not significant, that our maximum seismicity in July coincides with maximum precipitation. Furthermore, the maximum seismicity of the last six months of the year coincides with maximum precipitation during these same months (amounting to about two-thirds of the annual amount at Socorro). A further curious fact is that the 1906 swarm of quakes was preceded in 1905 by the heaviest annual precipitation (22 inches) recorded in half a century for Socorro. I am not much impressed by these coincidences, for, as G. K. Gilbert astutely remarked long ago, many attempts at working out the periodicity of earthquakes are apparently successful because the great frequency of earthquakes on this planet furnishes examples for almost any time-system postulated.

Many of our shocks have been felt over small areas, ranging from less than 3,000 to about 7,000 square miles. Some have been felt over much larger areas. For example, one shock of the 1906 series was felt over an area of 75,000 square miles; another, over 95,000 square miles; and one over 180,000 square miles—from Raton, New Mexico, to El Paso, Texas, and Douglas, Arizona.

Property damage has occasionally been fairly heavy. Practically all the towns, villages, and farms are located on the floodplain of the Rio Grande and alluvium enhances the amplitude of motion. Also, the widespread use of adobe-brick construction accounts for much of the damage to buildings. An adobe building, of course, like one of brick, tile, or block, does not have the resilience of, and is not as earthquake-resistive as, a wood-frame or reinforced concrete building.

In the past, a number of explanations for the Rio Grande quakes have been offered by laymen, journalists, mining engineers, mathematicians, and even a few geologists. The quakes have been attributed to landslides in the mountains to the east or west of the valley; to faulting of bedrock in these mountains; to volcanic activity (fears have been expressed on several occasions that volcanoes near Socorro and those near Albuquerque might come to life and start spurting lava again). In 1906 the opinion was held by some that the Socorro series was caused by the San Francisco quake. And in 1931 a journalist thought one of the Albuquerque quakes was "the tail end of a shock" registered by instruments and known to have originated several thousand miles away in the Pacific. Apparently, no one ever considered the possibility that some of the earthquakes might be originating in the Rio Grande valley itself, that is, beneath the floodplain. Slow drifting, perhaps laterally in the bedrock beneath the valley fill at depths of several miles, may be in progress; occasionally a slight slip along a fault may occur, followed by elastic rebound to a position of no strain.

Earthquakes have been felt in Albuquerque on at least 26 different days in 11 different years from 1893 to 1956. Some of these originated near Socorro; some were near Belen; one was at Cerrillos; two were in the Sandia Mountains. But thirteen of them apparently originated beneath Albuquerque.

---

[1] Used in the quarterly "Abstracts of Earthquake Reports for the Pacific Coast and the Western Mountain Region," issued by the U. S. Coast and Geodetic Survey.

LIST OF EARTHQUAKES FELT IN OR NEAR ALBUQUERQUE
(Rossi-Forel Intensity Scale)

1893, April 8. A Belen shock (intensity VII) was felt in Albuquerque.
July 12. Three shocks at Albuquerque, one of Intensity VI.
1906, July 16. A Socorro shock (VIII at Socorro?) was felt here.
Nov. 15. Another Socorro shock (VII to VIII?) felt here.
1918, May 28. Severe shock of shallow focus at Cerrillos (possibly VIII to IX there) was felt here (IV).
1930, Mar. 23. Slight.
Dec. 3. About VI.
Dec. 4. Slight.
1931, Jan. 27. III.
Feb. 3. V.
Feb. 4. VI to VII.
1935, Dec. 12 to 1936, Jan. 4. The Belen swarm, with 81 shocks on 24 different days at or near Belen. Of these, seven were felt at Albuquerque, as follows:
Dec. 17   Dec. 28
Dec. 18   Dec. 30—most severe one felt here
Dec. 19   Jan. 4 (1936)
Dec. 21
1936, Sept. 9. IV to possibly V.
Sept. 11. Three shocks of about III each.
1938, April 15. Slight.
April 16. Slight.
1947, Nov. 6. Slight, in Sandia Mountains.
1954, Nov. 2. IV.
Nov. 3. V.
1956, April 25. Slight, in Sandia Mountains.

Sanford and Holmes (1961) have reported on an instrumental study of the July 1960 swarm of earthquakes at Bernardo and La Joya, between Belen and Socorro. See also their article in this Guidebook.

REFERENCES

Northrop, S. A., 1945, Earthquake history of central New Mexico [abs.]: Geol. Soc. America Bull., v. 56, p. 1185.

—————, 1947, Seismology in New Mexico [abs.]: Geol. Soc. America Bull., v. 58, p. 1268.

Sanford, A. R., and Holmes, C. R., 1961, Note on the July 1960 earthquakes in central New Mexico: Seimol. Soc. America Bull., v. 51, p. 311-314, 3 figs.

EARTHQUAKE RESEARCH AT NEW MEXICO INSTITUTE OF MINING AND TECHNOLOGY

A. R. SANFORD and C. R. HOLMES
New Mexico Institute of Mining and Technology

INTRODUCTION

The Rio Grande valley between Socorro and Albuquerque is historically the region of highest seismicity in New Mexico. Numerous earthquakes have been felt along the valley, particularly at Socorro and Albuquerque. Prior to 1959, however, no serious instrumental studies of earthquakes in this region had been attempted. In the fall of 1959, Carnegie Institution, Washington, D. C., loaned New Mexico Institute of Mining and Technology a high-magnification seismograph. During a trial period of 650 hours of operation, 49 very small earthquakes were recorded. Eighty percent of these shocks originated within 10 miles of Socorro.

The large number of quakes recorded indicated that high-magnification instruments could give a large amount of information on earthquakes in New Mexico, particularly those quakes originating near Socorro. In the summer of 1960, two high-magnification seismographs were permanently installed in two abandoned mines located two miles west of the main NMIMT campus. These instruments have been in nearly constant operation since that time.

INSTRUMENTATION

The two seismographs being used for earthquake studies at NMIMT are: (1) a single-channel seismograph recording continuously at a slow rate (3.5 mm/sec), and (2) a three-channel seismograph recording intermittently at a high rate (30 mm/sec and 60 mm/sec). The seismograph used for continuous recording consists of a vertical transducer (Willmore seismometer with natural frequency of 1 cps), a high-gain transistor amplifier, and a drum recorder with pen and ink registration. The magnification of this instrument is about eight million at a frequency of 20 cps.

The three-channel seismograph used for high resolution recording consists of three transducers (Willmore seismometers), three high-gain amplifiers, and a high-speed (30 or 60 mm/sec) strip chart recorder with pen and ink registration. The magnification of this instrument is variable with a maximum of about ten million at a frequency of 20 cps. An example of a three-component seismogram for this instrument is shown in Figure 1.

EARTHQUAKE STATISTICS

Most of the earthquake research at NMIMT has been concentrated on the shocks originating within 10 miles of Socorro. The number of quakes with epicenters near Socorro is impressive. In the period from September 15, 1960 to March 20, 1961, 207 of these quakes (with S-phase peak to peak amplitude exceeding 8 mm on the twenty-four hour records) were recorded. Fifty percent of these events occurred within the month of October, 1960. Three of the quakes recorded in the six-month period were sufficiently strong to be felt in Socorro: October 25, 1960, 12:21 MST, intensity III (modified Mercalli Intensity Scale); December 19, 1960, 16:28 MST, intensity IV-V; and January 27, 1961, 23:33 MST, intensity III-IV.

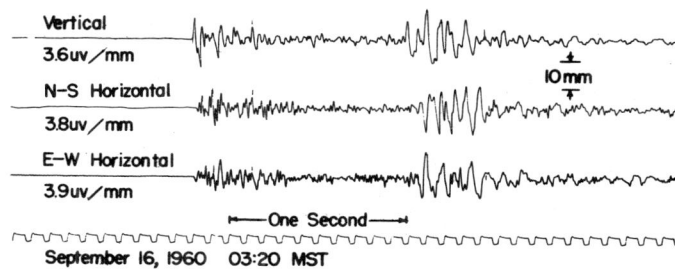

Figure 1. Three-component seismogram for an earthquake with an epicenter five miles southwest of the NMIMT recording station. The energy release for this quake is about 100 million ergs and the magnitude about negative 2 on the Richter scale.

High-speed (30 mm/sec and 60 mm/sec) three-component and tripartite recording on the three-channel seismograph has shown that ninety percent of the close quakes, including the three felt in Socorro, originated in a 50-square-mile area southwest of Socorro. This area is part of the narrow elevated fault block which borders the western margin of the Rio Grande valley at Socorro. Preliminary work with the high resolution records also indicates that these quakes had abnormally shallow foci. Depths of focus for nine quakes ranged from 9,000 to 20,000 feet and averaged 12,000 feet.

No lower limit to the magnitude of an earthquake has been detected in the recording to date. The number of earthquakes increases regularly with decreasing energy release down to the limit of recognition of earthquakes on the seismograms. For each one-tenth reduction in energy release, the number of quakes increases by a factor of about five. The energy release for the smallest quakes recorded is less than 10 million ergs which corresponds to a quake of negative 2.9 magnitude on the Richter Magnitude Scale.

Areas with the same degree of seismic activity as Socorro may exist elsewhere between Socorro and Albuquerque. The large number of shocks that originated from the southeast end of the Ladron Mountains in July and August of 1960 (Sanford and Holmes, 1961) suggests that other active areas do exist.

REFERENCE

Sanford, A. R., and Holmes, C. R., 1961, Note on the July 1960 earthquakes in central New Mexico: Seismol. Soc. America Bull., v. 51, p. 311-314.

The New U. S. Coast and Geodetic Survey Seismological Laboratory at Albuquerque

The following press releases issued by the U. S. Department of Commerce have been furnished by Herman J. Wirz, Jr., technical director of the new seismological laboratory.

New World-Wide Network Will Improve Detecting of Earthquakes and Monitoring of Earth Vibrations
(Complete text of press release for May 26, 1961)

A modern network of earthquake recording stations, spanning six continents, will be instrumented by the Coast and Geodetic Survey beginning in mid-1961, it was announced today by Secretary of Commerce Luther H. Hodges.

Information gathered from this improved world-wide network will provide data on the nature, location, and frequency of world earthquakes that might ultimately lead to prediction of destructive shocks.

With financial support of the Advanced Research Projects Agency (ARPA), of the Department of Defense, Coast and Geodetic Survey technicians will be sent to 65 countries and islands to install modern seismic equipment at 125 existing earthquake recording stations.

The major objective of this modernization program, the Secretary said, is to provide sensitive standardized instrumentation capable of furnishing uniform quantitative data for the study of earthquakes, earthquake mechanisms, seismic wave propagation, and energy determinations.

Each station will be equipped with three-component short-period and long-period electromagnetic seismographs capable of recording seismic waves from nearby and distant earthquakes with wide-period ranges (about 0.1 to 100 seconds). Time control for each station is furnished by an electronic clock, accurate to 1 second in 40 days, which also regulates the power supply to the recorders, thereby providing a very uniform rate of rotation of the recording drum. Time signals, detected by high-quality radios, are automatically impressed on the records.

The entire program is focused on a precise, uniform method of recording and reporting earth vibrations. The Advanced Research Projects Agency is supporting this effort, which is one part of ARPA's project Vela-Uniform, the national program of research in seismic phenomena. The modern seismic instrumentation to be installed by the Coast and Geodetic Survey aims to upgrade seismic research throughout the world and permit scientists to learn more about thousands of minor earthquakes that occur each year.

By mutual agreement, records made at the 125 stations will be forwarded to the Coast and Geodetic Survey, U. S. Department of Commerce, in Washington. The Coast and Geodetic Survey is establishing an analysis center in the Washington, D. C., area where the seismograms from all participating stations will be available for examination and study by competent researchers of all nationalities.

The Vela-Uniform Program will develop improved knowledge of the world's crust and mantle, particularly with regard to the number, thickness, and nature of the major layers. It will improve world knowledge of wave propagation characteristics through the earth, including a thorough study of regional travel time anomalies, and it will provide improved data for comparison of all types of seismic waves from earthquakes.

U. S. Coast and Geodetic Survey seismologists will begin installing the instruments at universities and scientific institutions around the world about August 15, 1961. In many instances the Survey will provide the respective institutions with modern earthquake recording equipment which it could not otherwise obtain. Installation is scheduled for completion late in 1962.

New Laboratory Built for Earthquake Studies
(Excerpts from press release for June 29, 1961)

Construction of the Nation's newest and most modern seismological laboratory has been completed by the Coast and Geodetic Survey on [a 673-acre tract of] land owned by the Isleta Indians near Albuquerque, New Mexico. The laboratory will serve as the principal research and development center for earthquake studies and instrumentation in the Survey, an agency of the U. S. Department of Commerce, and provide a vital link in the Agency's vast program of locating earthquakes throughout the world.

Rear Admiral H. Arnold Karo, Director of the Coast and Geodetic Survey, announced that the laboratory will play an important role in the development of seismic instrumentation, particularly strong motion equipment which is extremely important in engineering seismology and, in turn, gives data from which codes for the safe construction of buildings in earthquake areas are formulated. Experimental work to be done at the New Mexico site could prove to be very valuable in the perfection of a system for detecting artificial explosions, Admiral Karo said.

The facility, which will cost approximately $340,000 when fully equipped, is made up of seven buildings and two specially constructed vaults. The three principal buildings contain the instrumental research laboratory, the office, and the instrument shop—all fully air conditioned. The two vaults are about one-quarter mile distant from the buildings and located inside the granite mountain at the end of 40-foot tunnels. Within these vaults some of the most sensitive seismographic equipment in the world will operate. The entire construction program was carried out under the technical direction of the Bureau of Indian Affairs at Albuquerque, New Mexico.

A highly trained staff of seismologists and instrument makers will man the laboratory under the direction of Mr. Herman J. Wirz, Jr., of Tulsa, Oklahoma. Personnel will commute from Albuquerque to the laboratory, a distance of approximately 15 miles.

Further information may be obtained from Mr. Herman J. Wirz, Jr., Technical Director, Coast and Geodetic Survey, Seismological Laboratory, Sandia Base Branch Post Office, Albuquerque, New Mexico.

Mineral Resources of Bernalillo, Sandoval, and Santa Fe Counties, New Mexico (Exclusive of Oil and Gas)

WOLFGANG E. ELSTON
University of New Mexico

INTRODUCTION

This article is a preliminary report, part of a larger study sponsored by the New Mexico Bureau of Mines and Mineral Resources. It is a summary of the literature, supplemented by brief field checks.

HISTORY OF MINING

First Period: Beginning to 1880

From the beginning of the industry in prehistoric days to the arrival of the A., T. & S. F. Railway in 1880, mining was confined to two types of products: those used locally and those of small bulk and high value, such as precious metals and turquoise,[1] that could be carried on the backs of humans or animals to outside markets.

Among materials used locally were turquoise, pottery clay, mineral pigments, adobe, gypsum, and stone, worked by the Indians for centuries. The Spaniards introduced metals in the 16th century. At least one small mine, The Mina del Tiro (or Mina del Tierra) was worked by the Spaniards in the Cerrillos district, Santa Fe County. However, most stories of fabulously rich Spanish mines, filled in by Indians after the 1680 pueblo revolt, have been manufactured in recent years by promoters who "rediscovered" them. In the last couple of years I have been able to trace two of these stories (both of which made the Albuquerque newspapers) to their fraudulent sources.

Systematic mining for precious metals began only with the discovery of the Old Placers in 1828, followed by the discovery of gold-bearing quartz veins in the Ortiz Mountains in 1833, and of the New Placers in the San Pedro Mountains in 1839. In 1845 the combined gold production of the Old and New Placers is said to have reached $250,000 (Northrop, 1959).

More modern mining methods were introduced after the American occupation in 1846. By 1869 the 40-stamp mill of the Ortiz mine (Old Placers district) impressed the much-travelled F. V. Hayden, geologist of the U. S. Geological and Geographical Survey of the Territories, as the most substantial he had seen in the West. The stamps were powered by a steam engine fired by coal from the Cerrillos field (Jones, 1904).

Second Period: 1880-1945

The arrival of the Santa Fe Railroad revolutionized the mining industry in New Mexico. Now base-metal ores and coal could be carried cheaply to smelters and other markets, and low-grade precious metal deposits could be worked at a profit. The emphasis quickly shifted from placer mining to lode mining. In rapid order came the development of the lead-zinc veins of the Cerrillos district (1879), the sandstone copper deposits of the Nacimiento Mountains (1880), the San Pedro contact-metamorphic copper deposit (1884), and the low-grade gold-silver veins of the Cochiti (Bland) district in the Jemez Mountains (1893). Beginning in 1890, the ancient turquoise industry was put on a modern basis by the American Turquoise Co. Coal output of Santa Fe County rose from 3,600 tons in 1882 (the first year of accurate records) to 252,731 tons in 1900. A host of small and short-lived mills and smelters was active.

All this activity may give the impression of a flourishing mineral industry, but this would be misleading. Most mining enterprises during this period were able to operate only in times of high metal prices. Not a single metal mine in the three-county area was able to operate continuously for the 10 to 15 years ordinarily considered the minimum period for a profitable undertaking. Placer workings were plagued by lack of water. This problem stumped even Thomas A. Edison, who unsuccessfully attempted to work the Old Placers by a dry method in 1900. In consequence, the total metal production of Bernalillo, Sandoval, and Santa Fe Counties, from 1828 to the present, has been only a little under $11 million. By way of contrast, the Chino copper mine at Santa Rita, Grant County, has at times yielded that much in less than three months. Coal, the mainstay of mining during the entire period from 1880 to 1945, declined after 1929, first through competition with other coal fields and later through competition with oil and natural gas.

Third Period: 1945 to Present

The end of World War II brought radical changes into the mineral economy of north-central New Mexico, most of them adverse to existing producers. While the cost of mining, especially labor, doubled and tripled in the general inflation, gold prices remained fixed at pre-war levels. The rise in silver and base-metal prices lagged behind the rise in production costs. New pipelines brought petroleum products to consumers who had previously relied on coal, and the railroads switched to diesel fuel. To survive, the mineral industry switched to industrial non-metals and became a supplier to the booming construction industry (Table 1). Among the three counties, Santa Fe lost the leadership it held in mineral production since earliest days; its place was taken by Bernalillo County. Cement, gypsum wallboard, sand, gravel, and pumice blocks may lack the glamour of Indian turquoise and Spanish silver, but they provide the basis for a stable mineral industry.

METALS

From 1828 to 1959, Bernalillo, Sandoval, and Santa Fe Counties have produced metals valued at over $10,700,000 (Table 2). During the 19th century the total was a little over $6,000,000, about two-thirds of which can be credited to placer gold from the Old and New Placers in Santa Fe County before 1880. During the 20th century the yield has been about $4,500,000. Of this, about four-fifths came from two mines in the San Pedro (New Placers) district, Santa Fe County: the San Pedro copper-gold-silver mine, and the Lincoln-Lucky (Carnahan) lead-zinc-silver mine.

---

[1] This spelling is preferred by most dictionaries; Dana's System gives it as turquois.—Ed.

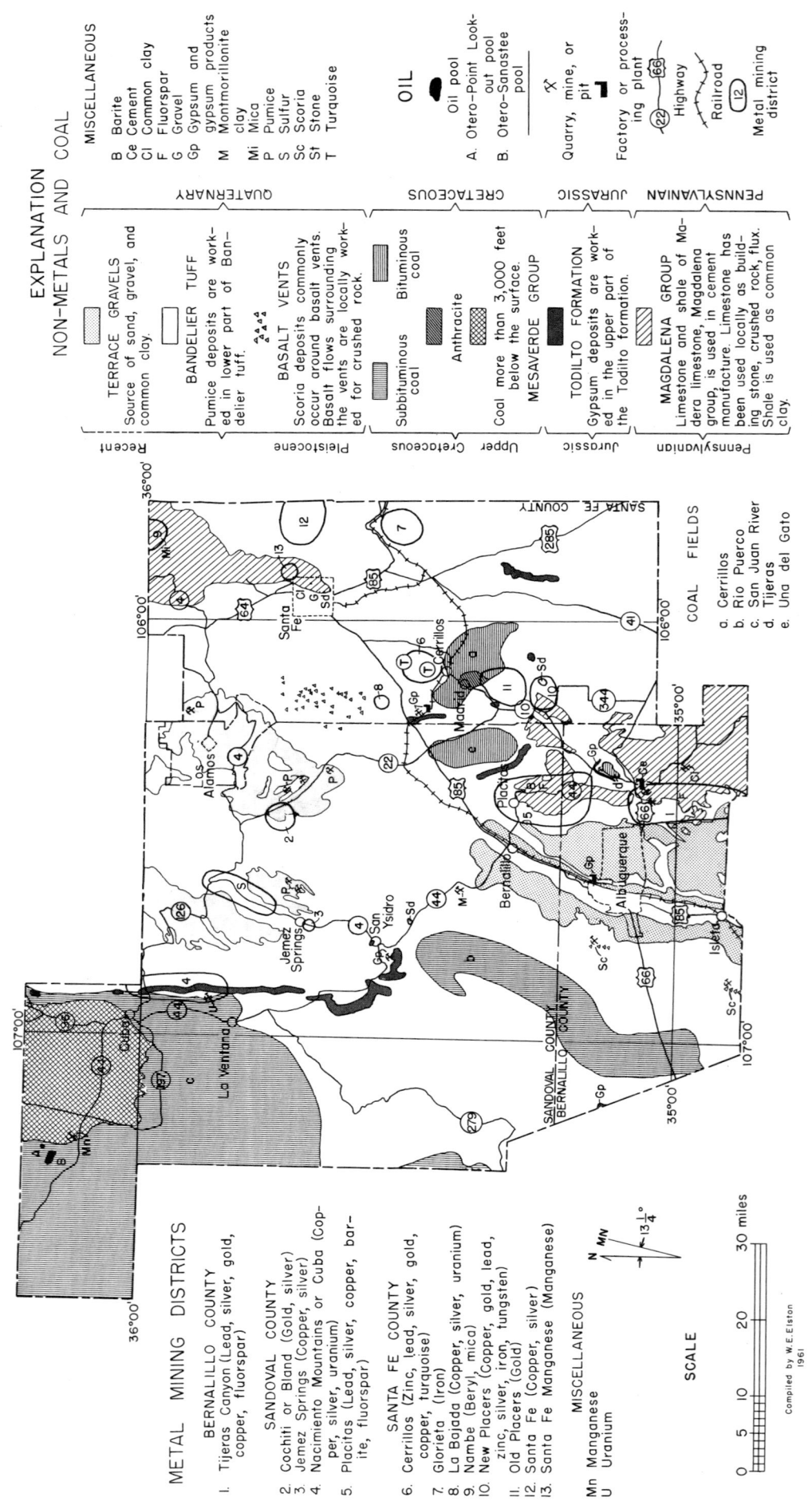

FIG. 1 ECONOMIC GEOLOGY OF BERNALILLO, LOS ALAMOS, SANDOVAL, AND SANTA FE COUNTIES, NEW MEXICO

Table 1. Value in Dollars of Mineral Production of Bernalillo, Sandoval, and Santa Fe Counties, New Mexico, Fiscal Years 1949 to 1960.

County	Metals	Pumice & Scoria	Sand Gravel, Clay	Coal	Other	Total
Bernalillo	–	559,410[1]	12,986,988	32,628	98,463[2]	13,677,489
Sandoval	22,154	1,669,564	3,573	206,987	–	1,902,278
Santa Fe	196,606	872,280	1,506,330	1,333,518	20,326[3]	3,925,060
Totals	214,760	3,101,254	14,496,891	1,573,133	118,789	19,504,827

[1] Estimated in part. Figure is for 1950 to 1960 only. [2] Mainly cement materials. [3] Mainly gypsum.

Source of data: State (of New Mexico) Inspector of Mines, Annual Reports, 1949 to 1960. The figures in the Annual Reports are consistently lower than those given by the U. S. Department of the Interior Minerals Yearbooks because of differences in estimating the value of minerals processed by the producer (e.g., pumice, scoria, and cement materials).

Note: This table does not yet include the cement and gypsum industry for a full working year, since the plants did not go into full production until late in 1960.

Bernalillo County

Tijeras Canyon (Soda Springs, Hell Canyon, Coyote Canyon) District

The Tijeras Canyon mining district includes the southern end of the Sandia Mountains, the Manzanita Mountains, and the Manzano Mountains as far south as the Torrance County line. It has yielded negligible amounts of fluorspar, gold, lead, and silver, and there has been some prospecting for copper. Metal production in this century has been worth only $4,100. Ross (1909) described most of the metal mines of the Coyote Canyon area during their most active period of development.

The rocks of the district consist of Precambrian gneiss, schist, slate, quartzite, and granite, capped by the Pennsylvanian Magdalena group on the higher mountains. The veins are post-Pennsylvanian, probably Tertiary. Most of them occupy north-trending high-angle faults, but some of them have a northeasterly trend. Their mineralogy seems to be controlled by distance from the Precambrian-Pennsylvanian contact. All shoots that have been mined since 1910 lie in Precambrian rocks directly or a short distance below Pennsylvanian limestone. The veins consist of brecciated fragments of wall rock cemented by fluorite and lesser amounts of barite, galena, quartz, and calcite. At depth, away from the limestone contacts, quartz increases at the expense of other minerals, copper minerals make their appearance, and gold values rise slightly. All ore shoots discovered up to now are small. The largest one is at the Blackbird fluorspar mine in SW¼ sec. 16, T. 9 N., R. 5 E. It is a few inches to 5 feet wide, 130 feet long, and has been stoped from the 42-foot level to the surface. The average fluorite content is a little less than 60 percent.

A few small deposits between Coyote Canyon and Tijeras Canyon belong to the "fahlband" type and were probably formed in Precambrian time. They consist of small lenses of fine-grained quartz, specularite, chalcopyrite, sphalerite, auriferous pyrite, and their oxidation products, oriented parallel to the northeastward trend of the enclosing greenstone schist.

The future of the Tijeras Canyon district looks no more promising than its past. The main product, fluorspar, has had no market in New Mexico since 1953. Some of the district lies on Sandia Base or in the Isleta Pueblo grant and is not open to the prospector.

Sandoval County

Cochiti (Bland) District

The Cochiti or Bland mining district is on the eastern side of the Jemez Mountains in western Sandoval County, about 30 miles west of Santa Fe and 15 miles northwest of the A., T. & S. F. Railway at Santo Domingo Pueblo. The more important mines are located in two separate areas where canyons have cut into mineralized andesite and monzonite below the Bandelier rhyolite tuff (Quaternary). The most important mine, the Albemarle, is in Colla Canyon in sec. 35 (unsurveyed), T. 18 N., R. 4 E.; most of the other mines are in Bland (or Pino) Canyon in secs. 24, 25, and 31, T. 18 N., R. 4 E. Between 1894 and 1948 the low-grade epithermal quartz veins of the district produced gold worth $861,983 and silver worth $457,034, making a total of $1,321,582. About four-fifths of this was mined in the boom years between 1894 and 1903. The district has been idle since 1948. All of the claims are now owned by Miss Effie Jenks of Santa Fe, New Mexico.

According to Bundy (1958), the oldest rocks in the district are a group of andesite flows and associated pyroclastic rocks and arkosic sandstones. The age is unknown, but is probably no older than late Cretaceous

Table 2. Metal Production of Bernalillo, Sandoval, and Santa Fe Counties, 1828 to 1959

County	District	Metal	Estimated Production in Dollars[1]	Geologic Type
Bernalillo	Tijeras	Gold, lead, silver	10,000	Telethermal veins, fahlbands
Sandoval	Cochiti (Bland)	Gold, silver	1,320,000	Epithermal veins
"	Nacimiento	Copper, silver	800,000[2]	"Redbeds"
"	Jemez Springs	Copper, silver	10,000	"Redbeds"
"	Placitas	Lead		Telethermal veins and replacement deposits
Santa Fe	Cerrillos	Lead, zinc, silver, copper	620,000	Veins
"	Old Placers (Ortiz)	Gold	2,200,000	Placers, quartz veins
"	New Placers (San Pedro, Golden)	Gold, copper, lead, zinc, silver	5,750,000	Pyrometasomatic, limestone replacement pipes, quartz veins, placers
"	Santa Fe Manganese	Manganese	10,000	Epithermal replacement
"	La Bajada	Copper, silver, uranium		Epithermal veins
"	Santa Fe (Pecos, Cooper)	Copper, silver		High-temperature veins
"	Glorieta	Iron		Supergene replacement
"	Nambe			Pegmatites
		Total	$ 10,720,000	

[1] Rounded off to the nearest $10,000.   [2] Sandoval County only.

Sources: Jones (1904; Lindgren, Graton, and Gordon (1910); Lasky and Wootton (1933); Anderson (1957); Northrop (1959); U. S. Department of the Interior annual Mineral Resources of the United States (1882 to 1931); U. S. Department of the Interior annual Minerals Yearbook (1932 to 1959).

and not younger than early Tertiary. They were intruded and arched by a monzonite stock. Fracturing accompanied intrusion of monzonite and was followed, successively, by emplacement of andesite porphyry dikes, gold- and silver-bearing quartz veins with small amounts of base-metal sulfides, rhyolite dikes, and barren quartz veins with small amounts of pyrite. Later, erosion produced an irregular surface which was covered in mid-Pleistocene time by pumiceous and welded rhyolite tuff beds of the Bandelier formation.

Most of the veins in and around Bland Canyon have a northerly trend. The Albemarle vein and other veins in and around Colla Canyon trend to the northeast. All veins dip steeply (50° to 85°), some east, some west.

The veins consist largely of quartz and chalcedony and were formed by replacement of wall rock. They are as much as 1,500 feet long. Like most replacement veins, they are highly irregular in width, but in places they are as much as 150 feet wide (Graton, in Lindgren, Graton, and Gordon, 1910). Some of the gold and silver were found in rich streaks of shipping-grade ore, usually $30-50 per ton, but ore mined before 1904 probably averaged only about $6 per ton, and ore mined since then (some of it sorted) averaged only $8 per ton. Some parts of the veins are barren.

Bundy (1958) described the paragenesis as follows. First calcite was emplaced along faults. Most of the calcite was then replaced by quartz. A period of brecciation was followed by the emplacement of pyrite, minor chalcopyrite, sphalerite (up to 3 percent of the veins), a minute amount of galena, quartz, gold-bearing pyrite, and argentite, in that order. All of the sulfides are in minute grains. The post-rhyolite phase of mineralization consisted of quartz and some pyrite, barren of precious metals. The veins are drusy, vuggy, and contain abundant inclusions of wall rock, sometimes surrounded by haloes of metallic minerals. Hydrothermal alteration, according to Bundy (1958), has taken the form of regional propylitization and more local argillization and silicification. All veins are oxidized from the outcrop down to a variable depth. The oxidized zone was leached of base-metal sulfides but enriched in residual gold. Silver remained roughly constant. Gold can be extracted by amalgamation from oxidized ore and by cyanidation from primary ore.

The largest mine in the district was the Albemarle, in Colla Canyon, credited with an output of $667,500 (Jones, 1904). The Lone Star—Iron King—Crown Point group of claims in Bland Canyon is next in importance. They were at different times worked separately or as a group. Since 1904 they have been the scene of sporadic unsuccessful attempts to revive the district. Cossak Mining Co. operated the Lone Star—Iron King—Crown Point group from 1914 to 1916 and treated the ores by cyanidation. Some shipments were recorded during the 1930's. A post-war attempt to revive the Iron King mine ended when mine and mill were attached by the Sandoval County sheriff in 1947.

The decline and fall of the Cochiti district was caused by: (1) low grade of ore; (2) decline in width and tenor of veins at depth; no minable ore was found deeper than 585 feet; (3) high transportation costs; (4) lack of water; (5) mismanagement; (6) litigation; and (7) declining silver prices after 1893. Only after 1897, when a ruling of the U. S. Supreme Court against the absentee owners of the Canada de Cochiti grant placed the district in the public domain, did outside capital become available. The Cochiti Gold Mining Co. and its successor, the Navajo Gold Mining Co. of Boston, finished the Albemarle mill in 1899 and acquired other major mines in the district by 1900. In February 1902 it went into receivership.

As far as known, all ore shoots in the Albemarle mine were mined out, but a considerable tonnage of low-grade material remains in some other mines. A revival of mining could occur only if the government should raise gold and silver prices appreciably. Ores average 85 to 95 percent SiO_2 (Wynkoop, 1900) and could be sold as siliceous flux, but transportation to a smelter would be expensive.

Nacimiento (Cuba) District

The Nacimiento district is in northeastern Sandoval County and southwestern Rio Arriba County, on the western face of the Nacimiento Mountains. Most of the mines are 3 to 5½ miles southeast of Cuba, but one mine, the San Miguel, lies about 6 miles south of the others. Between 1881 and 1960 the district produced about 7,500,000 pounds of copper and several tens of thousands of ounces of silver, valued at over $1,100,000. The deposits are of the "redbeds" or sandstone type.

The rocks of the district range from Precambrian to Tertiary, but commercial mineralization is confined to the Agua Zarca sandstone member of the Chinle formation (Triassic). Noncommercial showings occur in the Cutler formation (Permian) and the Poleo sandstone member of the Chinle formation (Triassic).

The dominant structure of the region is a large westward-directed reverse fault, the Nacimiento fault. The rocks near the fault are steeply tilted to the west, or are overturned, for about a mile west of the fault and for a few hundred yards east of it. Farther west they dip gently westward into the San Juan Basin, and farther east they are nearly horizontal (Wood and Northrop, 1946).

The Eureka and Cliff mines are in nearly horizontal sandstone and conglomerate beds of the Agua Zarca member east of the Nacimiento fault in sec. 32 (unsurveyed), T. 21 N., R. 1 E., and in sec. 6, T. 20 N., R. 1 E., respectively. All other mines in the district seem to be in steeply dipping Agua Zarca sandstone near the Nacimiento fault. One group is east of Copper City, in and around sec. 1, T. 20 N., R. 1 W. Schrader (in Lindgren, Graton, and Gordon, 1910) mentioned the Copper Glance and Kelley mines; of these two the Copper Glance was the more important. Another mine, the Bluebird, is about 1½ miles farther south, near Senorito, in sec. 11, T. 20 N., R. 1 W. Finally, the San Miguel mine is in NW¼ sec. 24, T. 19 N., R. 1 W., about 5½ miles northeast of La Ventana.

All of the mines have the same type of mineralization. The primary ore mineral is chalcocite, formed by replacement of fossil wood and carbonaceous trash. Malachite, azurite, and chrysocolla, formed by oxidation of chalcocite, occur in an irregular halo dispersed around accumulations of organic material, as well as in the organic material itself. Most of the ore assays less than 3 percent copper, but hand sorting raised the grade of material smelted before 1900 to 25-65 percent. The silver content is 0.5 to 2 ounces for every 100 pounds of copper, and there is almost no gold.

The copper deposits form small, discontinuous lenticular bodies in several stratigraphic horizons. Most of them are in cross-bedded coarse fluvial sandstone or conglomerate. Although the enclosing rocks may be red the mineralized rocks usually are not. Since the uranium boom of the mid-1950's the behavior of ore deposits in ancient stream channels has been better understood than formerly, and there has been a slight revival of interest in sandstone copper deposits.

In the Chalcocite prospect, about three-fourths of a mile north of the Copper Glance mine, malachite and chalcocite occur in a 35-foot band of Precambrian schist contained in granite. Since low-grade copper deposits in Precambrian basement rocks have been postulated as the ultimate source of copper in the sandstone deposits, this occurrence is of theoretical interest.

The Nacimiento copper deposits were known as early as 1859 (Newberry, 1876). Systematic mining did not begin until the early 1880's and ended around 1900. During this period the mines yielded about 6,300,000 pounds of copper and several tens of thousands of ounces of silver, valued at about $700,000. Of this, 5,000,000 pounds came from San Miguel mine and about 1,250,000 pounds from the Copper Glance (Lindgren, Graton, and Gordon, 1910). Hand-sorted high-grade ore was hauled by wagon to a 30-ton smelter at Copper City or a 25-ton smelter at Senorito, and matte was hauled by wagon 60 miles to the railroad at Bernalillo. Mining was done in open pits and shallow underground workings at low cost.

Since 1900 there have been two short-lived attempts to revive the district, the first from 1916 to 1920, the second from 1955 to 1957. The dollar value of production in 1956, $231,831, was probably the highest in the history of the district. Most of it can be credited to the Eureka mine in Rio Arriba County.

The known deposits were thoroughly high-graded by the oldtimers, but considerable reserves of low-grade material, containing 0.75 to 3 percent copper, remain. The Eureka, Copper City, and San Miguel areas could each probably yield several tens of thousands of tons of low-grade ore. The high cost of transportation remains a severe handicap.

Jemez Springs District

The Jemez Springs district consists of only one insignificant mine, the Spanish Queen, which is at the bottom of Jemez Canyon, 2.7 miles south of Jemez Springs. It formerly worked a low-grade copper deposit of the sandstone type. Geologically it is similar to the copper deposits of the Nacimiento district, except that the host rock consists of nearly horizontal beds of the Abo formation (Permian). Since 1904 the mine has produced copper and silver worth $3,138, from 233 tons of ore.

Placitas District

The Placitas district includes the northern end of the Sandia Mountains in Bernalillo and Sandoval Counties. Its fluorspar-barite-galena veins resemble those of the Tijeras Canyon district in mineralogy, texture, size, and geologic setting. Being close to Albuquerque and Santa Fe, the district has attracted more than its share of promoters, but actual production since 1904 has been only 35 tons of ore valued at $848. The district had a minor boom around 1880, but it soon died down.

Santa Fe County
Cerrillos District

The Cerrillos district covers Los Cerrillos, a group of low hills 15 miles southwest of Santa Fe. The main line of the A., T. & S. F. Railway skirts the southern edge of the hills. The district is best known for its turquoise deposits, but has also yielded zinc, lead, silver, copper, and gold worth $620,000.

According to Disbrow and Stoll (1957) the mineralized rocks of the district are the Jurassic Morrison formation, the Cretaceous Dakota sandstone, Mancos shale, and Mesaverde group, the Eocene Galisteo formation, and a group of intrusive Oligocene (?) monzonites with their extrusive equivalents, the Espinaso volcanics. Four distinct phases of monzonite have been recognized. All except the first have volcanic equivalents and have the form of central plugs or stocks, surrounded by dikes and swarms of sills and laccoliths spread out in the incompetent Mancos shale. The intruded rocks have been arched into a steep-sided dome. Following intrusion of the monzonites the rocks were fractured and mineralized. Most veins have a northerly or northeasterly trend.

The major metal mines are grouped in three distinct areas. Monzonite forms most of the bedrock in all three. The first is in SE¼ sec. 5, T. 14 N., R. 8 E., the second is in and around S½ sec. 30, T. 15 N., R. 8 E., and the third is in secs. 19 and 20, T. 15 N., R. 8 E. The veins are controlled by shear zones and are usually 1 to 6 feet wide and a few hundred feet long. A few are as much as 16 feet wide and 2,500 feet long. Only a fraction of the shear zones is filled with vein matter.

Commercial ore occurs in definite shoots, but their structural control is not known. The two largest shoots discovered up to now are in the Pennsylvania and Tom Payne mines, both probably on different segments of the same north-trending vein in sec. 30, T. 15 N., R. 8 E. Each contained a few thousand tons of ore.

Disbrow and Stoll (1957) described the veins as follows:

> "In the Pennsylvania mine, ore occurs as thin tabular seams of coarse interlocking sphalerite and galena crystals, or as similar seams of crustified ore in which sphalerite, galena, quartz, and pyrite occur in parallel bands of almost pure mineral. The Tom Payne ore is similar but contains more quartz. In the Mina del Tiro deposit the ore shoot is an elongate lens of vuggy quartz, containing disseminations and thick streaks of galena and sphalerite. In the Franklin mine, galena and sphalerite occur without gangue as small masses and disseminations in a thin zone of highly sericitized monzonite porphyry. The other shoots probably originated largely by filling of narrow openings, to judge from the crustification, but ore in the Franklin mine has formed by replacement of the rock."

The rocks are usually altered to sericite and smaller amounts of pyrite, carbonates, quartz, and tourmaline. To a distance of 1 to 10 feet on either side of the veins, chlorite has locally formed beyond the sericite zone. Oxidation has affected all veins down to the water table, 50 to 150 feet below the surface. Zinc has been leached from the upper part of the oxidized zone and added to the lower part; other metals are present in about the same amounts as in primary ore. The rich silver strikes reported from the early days of mining probably were made in small oxidized pockets.

The district was known in Spanish colonial days, but went through its boom only after 1879. By 1890 mining had switched to turquoise, having resulted in production of lead and silver "not likely to exceed a few hundred thousand dollars" (Lindgren, in Lindgren, Graton, and Gordon, 1910). Turquoise mining declined sharply between 1904 and 1906. From 1904 through 1959 there has been some metal production in 30 years out of 56, but the output has exceeded 1,000 tons in only 7 or 8 years, when lead and zinc prices were unusually high. No mine has operated continuously for more than 5 years. The output since 1904 has been 26,816 tons of milling-grade ore, containing 735 ounces of gold, 27,884 ounces of silver, 181,824 pounds of copper, 1,578,340 pounds of lead and 1,935,727 pounds of zinc, valued at $422,743.

In 1959 Bear Creek Mining Co., a subsidiary of Kennecott Copper Corp., began an intensive exploration campaign, but the results have not been announced. According to newspaper stories the main target was a low-grade copper deposit disseminated in monzonite porphyry. Signs of low-grade disseminated copper ores are abundant, especially in the southern end of the district, northeast of the Mina del Tiro, where dumps show small grains of pyrite and chalcopyrite in altered monzonite. The Evelyn mine, at the northern end of the district, formerly produced low-grade oxidized copper-gold ores disseminated in monzonite.

Glorieta District

The Glorieta district covers a large area near Glorieta pass, 15 miles southeast of Santa Fe. The only recorded shipments have been a few thousand tons of supergene limonitic iron ore from clastic beds of the San Andres formation (Permian) on the rim of Glorieta Mesa. Most of the ore was used as flux in lead smelters, but some was used in paint factories and steel mills. The remaining reserves are small (Kelley, 1949). Copper occurs in several small sandstone and vein deposits.

La Bajada District

The La Bajada district consists of only one mine, also called La Bajada. It lies in La Bajada Canyon, at the foot of La Bajada Hill, about 2 miles north of U. S. Highway 85. The ore body follows a north-trending fault cutting Miocene (?) Cieneguilla limburgite.

Mineralization probably occurred in Pliocene or Pleistocene time, under near-surface conditions. Lustig (1957) described 17 minerals from the deposit and 6 from an oxidized dump. The chief hypogene metallic minerals are pyrite, sphalerite, marcasite, colusite, chalcopyrite, and bornite, formed in that order. Brannerite has been reported and its uranium content is said to account for the anomalous radioactivity of the deposit. Colloform textures characterize the ore minerals and indicate a low temperature of formation.

The deposit was developed by La Bajada Mining Co. in the 1920's, but total production came to only 8 tons of copper-silver ore valued at $363. In the 1950's the discovery of uranium in the deposit caused a renewal of interest. A small shipment of uranium by Lone Star Mining Co. was recorded in 1957.

Nambe District

The name Nambe district was assigned by Northrop (1959) to an area of granite pegmatites in the Sangre de Cristo Mountains east of Cordova, along the Santa Fe—Rio Arriba County line. The bedrock consists of Precambrian mica schist, granite gneiss, and migmatite, all trending northeastward and containing small lenses of granite pegmatite. The largest known pegmatite body is on the Rocking Chair claim, which was prospected for feldspar, mica, and beryl. Only a few pounds of beryl have been found.

Concentrations of scrap mica, usually only a few inches wide, occur around the contacts of pegmatites and mica schist and in small irregular (hydrothermal?) albite-quartz-muscovite replacement veins that cut across the earlier microcline-quartz phase of the pegmatites. Books of sheet mica are present here and there, but only in small amounts. Santa Fe County has since 1949 produced muscovite mica worth only $550. In addition, mica from Rio Arriba County has been processed at Santa Fe.

New Placers (San Pedro, Golden, Tuerto) District

The New Placers district is in southern Santa Fe County, in T. 12 N., R. 12 E., directly southeast of the village of Golden. It includes the San Pedro or Tuerto Mountains, a low range formed by the intrusion of early Tertiary stocks and laccoliths. The igneous intrusions are part of a north-trending porphyry belt that also includes Los Cerrillos, Ortiz Mountain, and South Mountain. Production of copper, gold, silver, lead, and zinc since 1904 has been worth $3,694,431.

According to Atkinson (1960), the sedimentary rocks of the district include the Madera limestone (Pennsylvanian), the Abo, Yeso, and San Andres formations (Permian), and the Dockum group (Triassic). The prevailing dip is to the east. The sedimentary rocks were arched, irregularly fractured, and metamorphosed in early Tertiary (?) time by a variety of igneous intrusions. First came a few diabase porphyry dikes, then five small monzonite stocks, then rhyolite porphyry dikes and sills, and finally two monzonite porphyry laccoliths and a large number of monzonite porphyry and latite porphyry dikes and sills. Of the five monzonite stocks, four are in the eastern end of the range. One stock and both monzonite porphyry laccoliths are in the western end, in the neighborhood of the San Pedro and Lincoln-Lucky mines.

The district has six types of ore deposits. (1) Pyrometasomatic copper-gold-silver-tungsten deposits. Chalcopyrite is the chief ore mineral; the tungsten is in scheelite. An example is the San Pedro mine. (2) Replacement pipes and veins of sphalerite and argentiferous galena in limestone. An example is the Lincoln-Lucky mine. (3) Iron veins and bedded replacement deposits containing magnetite, specularite, or both. These are economically unimportant, although formerly they were worked for flux and the Oro Quay mine made small shipments in 1958. (4) Small shear zones and fissures filled with quartz and auriferous pyrite. In the oxidized zone, usually within 100 feet of the surface, they contain free gold. There are many deposits of this type, but none has produced more than $30,000. (5) Small pockets of auriferous pyrite disseminated in tactite, containing free gold in the oxidized zone. These are economically unimportant. (6) Placers derived from types 4 and 5. Before 1880 they probably yielded between $1,000,000 and $2,000,000 in gold; since 1880 they have been relatively unimportant.

Atkinson (1960) demonstrated the existence of hypogene zoning in the lode deposits. Copper occurs in contact-metamorphosed limestone, not far from igneous rocks. The controlling structure is a highly irregular "marble line." On the southeastern side of the "marble line", limestone that has undergone contact metasomatism has turned into garnet tactite, and on the northwestern side limestone that has undergone only thermal metamorphism has turned into marble. Lead and zinc are found farther away from igneous rocks, replacing unmetamorphosed limestone. Of the iron minerals, Atkinson (1960) wrote:

"Deposits containing magnetite alone are generally

closer to the stock than those containing specularite alone, while those containing both magnetite and specularite occupy an intermediate position."

The gold-bearing veins do not seem to have a zonal distribution.

The pyrometasomatic San Pedro deposit is by far the most important in the district. It is on the southern end of a belt of garnet tactite, 150 feet thick, that runs for about 1½ miles along the western side of San Pedro Mountain, from SW¼ sec. 15 (unsurveyed), T. 12 N., R. 7 E. to NW¼ sec. 27, T. 12 N., R. 7 E. The replaced beds are in the upper part of the Madera limestone. The tactite lies directly below a rhyolite porphyry sill and 50 to 150 feet above a monzonite porphyry laccolith. The best ore irregularly replaces marble beds at the crest of a small anticline, 75 to 90 feet below the rhyolite porphyry sill. The ore body is cut by several post-ore faults, one of which seems to terminate it on its eastern end.

The San Pedro mine dates back to the middle of the 19th century. From 1889 until 1938 the mine was operated intermittently by the Santa Fe Gold and Copper Co. During the 1890's a small smelter treated the ore at the village of San Pedro; from 1900 to 1919 a 125-ton smelter stood near the mine. In 1938 the mine was purchased by Raskob Mining Interests, Inc. and was worked by 70 men at the rate of 110 tons per day in 1940 and 1941. The ore was concentrated by a 150-ton flotation mill on the property. The present owner is C. F. Williams of Santa Fe, the present lessee Tom B. Scartaccini.

In spite of the relatively high grade of ore, the mine has never been profitable for long. Distance from the railroad, smelter, and refinery, high exploration and mining costs, and metallurgical problems are to blame. The mine was worked on a large scale only in times of unusually favorable copper prices. A total output of 250,000 to 300,000 tons of ore, yielding about 15,000,000 pounds of copper, 15,000 ounces of gold, and 200,000 ounces of silver, seems reasonable. The ore mined during 1940 and 1941 averaged 3.54 percent copper, 0.056 ounce of gold, and 0.81 ounce of silver per ton. During World War II the presence of tungsten in the San Pedro mine was brought to the attention of the U. S. Geological Survey by V. C. Kelley. Detailed mapping by Smith and others (1945) established the fact that significant amounts of low-grade copper and tungsten ores remained in the mine.

The Lincoln-Lucky (Carnahan) lead-zinc-silver mine is in NW¼ sec. 28, T. 12 N., R. 7 E., half a mile southwest of the San Pedro mine and part of the same property. It is a limestone-replacement deposit of pipelike shape that plunges about 15° E. The pipe is elliptical in cross-section, measuring about 60 feet across in the widest places. It follows the intersection of a steeply dipping, eastward-trending fault and a particular bed of the Madera limestone down-dip for about 3,600 feet. The primary minerals are coarsely crystalline sphalerite and argentiferous galena, a little pyrite, chalcopyrite, and alabandite, in a quartz-calcite gangue. A complex gossan was found near the surface. The deposit was mined out for a length of 2,300 feet in the 1880's. A second period of operation was from 1919 to 1928, first by Collier Mines Co. (1919 to 1926) and then by Carnahan Mines Co. (1926 to 1928). From 1925 to 1928 a 50-ton selective flotation mill milled 27,377 tons of ore, containing 380 ounces of gold, 97,972 ounces of silver, 15,973 pounds of copper, 3,540,515 pounds of lead, and 3,995,000 pounds of zinc. The drop in metal prices during the Great Depression discouraged a search for additional ore after 1928.

Placer gold of 920 fineness occurs in unconsolidated eluvial and alluvial deposits in many places. The most important ones are the San Lazarus placer on the southern edge of the range, and the Golden placer off the northwestern end of the range. The tenor ranges from 10 cents to $1.75 per cubic yard. Placer gold also occurs in consolidated gravels (the so-called "cement beds") halfway between Golden and the Una del Gato coal field. All large-scale modern placer operations have failed because there is insufficient water for wet methods of extraction and the ground is too wet for dry methods.

Old Placers (Ortiz, Dolores) District

The Old Placers district covers the Ortiz or Placer Mountains, 7 miles south of Cerrillos and 3 miles northeast of Golden. The district has yielded about $2,200,000, almost all of it from gold. Placers have been more important than lode mines. The entire district lies within the Ortiz Mine grant, owned by Potter and Sims Mining Co. of Joplin, Missouri. In recent years G. R. Griswold of Albuquerque has been in charge of mineral exploration.

The geology of the Ortiz Mountains has many similarities with the geology of Los Cerrillos and San Pedro Mountain. In the Ortiz Mountains the intruded sedimentary rocks are almost entirely Cretaceous (Dakota sandstone, Mancos shale, Mesaverde group). Only in the southwestern tip of the range do pre-Cretaceous rocks crop out. The regional dip is 10° to 30° E. The Cretaceous rocks were intruded by two stocks of nepheline-bearing augite monzonite, two small stocks of quartz monzonite, and a swarm of laccoliths, sills, and plugs of latite-andesite porphyry. A hydrothermally altered body of trachyte-latite with brecciated border was interpreted as a volcanic vent by Peterson (1958) and McRae (1958). It occupies both sides of Cunningham Gulch in the western part of the range, and the most important lode mines of the district are in its brecciated border zones.

The district has four types of ore deposits. (1) Gold in quartz fissure veins in the brecciated border zone of the Cunningham Gulch vent. Examples are the Ortiz, Benton, and Liveoak mines, which produced several hundred thousand dollars in gold in the 19th century. (2) Gold and scheelite disseminated in the brecciated border zone, near the southeastern end of the Cunningham Gulch vent. Production has been small. (3) Contact pyrometasomatic auriferous pyrite and chalcopyrite disseminated in garnet tactite at the southern tip of the mountains. The Greenhorn limestone member of the Mancos shale is the replaced horizon. Production has been small. (4) Placers, which have accounted for 80 to 90 percent of the total output. The most important placers are at the mouth of Cunningham Gulch, near the Dolores ranch. Modern attempts at exploitation have been frustrated by the same difficulties as at the New Placers. The unsuccessful attempt of Universal Placer Mining Corp. to work the gravels in 1939 and 1940 accounted for $38,000 of the $53,000 produced by the district in this century.

Santa Fe District

The Santa Fe district covers a large and ill-defined area of Precambrian granite, schist, and diabase in the southern end of the Sangre de Cristo Mountains, east of Santa Fe. It has showings of placer gold and base-metal sulfides, but has never produced ore commercially. Its proximity to the important Willow Creek district in San Miguel County has stimulated intensive prospecting.

Santa Fe Manganese District

The Santa Fe Manganese district was described by Wells (1918) as being 4 miles northeast of Santa Fe. Pyrolusite and psilomelane partially replace Pennsylvanian shale along bedding planes; the ore occurs in nodules and small irregular pockets. The district was worked on a very small scale during World Wars I and II, and the years during and since the Korean War. Total manganese production of Santa Fe County (including gossan material from the Lincoln-Lucky mine and other deposits in the New Placers district) has amounted to only a few thousand dollars, and ceased entirely with the termination of the U. S. Government carlot purchasing program in August, 1959.

Miscellaneous Metal Deposits

Small amounts of various metals have come from places not included under the several mining districts. Bernalillo, Sandoval, and Santa Fe Counties were caught up in the prospecting fever for uranium and "rare metals" that gripped the entire country a few years ago, but the results were negligible. Mesozoic and early Cenozoic sandstones in the foothills of the Nacimiento Mountains and the Hagan basin, both in Sandoval County, were the rocks most favored by prospectors.

Manganese has come from the Lander and Jicarilla mines, on Jicarilla tribal lands in sec. 21, T. 22 N., R. 4 W., Sandoval County, about 17 miles northwest of Cuba. The San Jose formation (Eocene) is the bedrock of the area.

INDUSTRIAL NON-METALS

Barite and Fluorspar

Barite and fluorspar deposits are discussed under Metals, Tijeras Canyon district (Bernalillo County) and Placitas district (Sandoval County). The deposits are very small.

Cement

The Ideal Cement Co. plant at Tijeras, 8 miles east of Albuquerque, is the largest single operation in the mineral industries of the three-county area and the only cement plant in New Mexico. Limestone and shale of the lower gray limestone member of the Madera formation (Pennsylvanian) are quarried next to the plant. In the fiscal year 1959-1960 the plant consumed 289,060 tons of limestone and dolomite, 42,266 cubic yards of shale, and 10,385 tons of gypsum. Natural gas brought in from Albuquerque by Southern Union Gas Co. is used as fuel. The plant cost $19,000,000 and has a capacity of 2,500,000 bbls. per year. It employs 100 men, including 8 or 9 in the quarry. The product is a complete line of Portland and masonry cements, sold all over New Mexico and southern Colorado.

Common Clay

Kinney Brick Co. of Albuquerque is at present the only large producer and consumer of common clay in the area. Its plant on South Second Street has a capacity of 1 million bricks per month, and employs 40 men. A pit in the Manzano Mountains just west of State Highway 10, about 8 miles south of Tijeras, supplies the plant with 90 to 95 percent of its raw material—shale from the Magdalena group (Pennsylvanian). The rest is Mancos shale (Cretaceous) from a small pit west of Cerrillos, on the north side of the A., T. & S. F. railroad tracks. The Pennsylvanian shale burns light coral-red; the Cretaceous shale is used for lighter shades. Before 1946 the company used Recent alluvial clay from a pit next to its plant, but shale has been found to be a superior material. In recent years the plant has run at 60 to 95 percent of capacity, using on the average 4,000 tons of clay per month. Brick and tile are trucked to all major cities in northern and central New Mexico, within a 200-mile radius of Albuquerque.

Brick and tile were made at the old State Penitentiary at Santa Fe from about 1884 to 1957. The raw material was shale of the Magdalena group (Pennsylvanian) obtained from a pit on leased land east of Palace Avenue (Talmage and Wootton, 1937).

A small brick plant was formerly located near Tonque, north of Hagan, Sandoval County. It used Mancos shale (Cretaceous).

Gemstones

Turquoise has been the outstanding gemstone produced in the area since the 8th century A. D. (Northrop, 1959). It occurs in two localities in the Cerrillos mining district, Santa Fe County: (1) Mt. Chalchihuitl, near the center of sec. 5, T. 14 N., R. 8 E., and (2) Turquoise Hill, near the center of sec. 31, T. 15 N., R. 8 E. In modern times the most important operation was by American Turquoise Co., which worked the Turquoise Hill deposits from 1890 to about 1904. Estimates of production vary from $2,000,000 to $9,000,000. George F. Kunz, the famous gemologist, described the turquoise in 1893 as sky-blue, resistant to fading, and equal or superior to Persian material. Stones up to 60 carats were found, which sold for as much as $4,000. Mining was by surface and underground workings. In recent years the production has been negligible.

Turquoise occurs in irregular narrow veinlets and stringers cutting altered monzonite porphyry. Its origin is the subject of dispute, one school holding that it is hydrothermal, and another that it is supergene.

Precious opal has been reported from the Cochiti mining district (Wynkoop, 1900). Petrified wood is abundant in the Galisteo formation on Sweet's Ranch, 3 miles east of Cerrillos.

Gravel and Sand

At present 14 sand and gravel companies are active in the Albuquerque area, employing 98 men. The largest operations are by Springer Transfer Co. and Albuquerque Gravel Co. The only sand and gravel producer in the three-county area outside Greater Albuquerque is Kauffman Trucking Co. at Santa Fe.

All of the sand and gravel in Bernalillo County comes from Quaternary terraces of the Rio Grande, especially the lowest terrace above the present floodplain. This terrace is made up of well-sorted and well-rounded axial gravels. Figure 1 shows that terrace gravels are scarce north of Bernalillo, although small deposits have been used locally in construction work.

Gypsum

Aside from the new cement industry in Tijeras Canyon, the most important development in the mineral industries of the three-county area in the last few years has been the emergence of a sizeable gypsum products industry. Three quarries and two manufacturing plants are now active.

The gypsum resources of New Mexico have recently been described by Weber and Kottlowski (1959). Virtually all the gypsum in Bernalillo, Sandoval, and Santa Fe Counties occurs in the Todilto formation (Jurassic), which consists of thinly laminated limestone, 2 to 10 feet thick, overlain by 50 to 100 feet of gypsum 95 to 99 percent pure. Its outcrops are shown on Figure 1.

In June 1960 Kaiser Gypsum Co. began production at its quarry and plant at Rosario, Santa Fe County. Here the A., T. & S. F. Railway crosses the outcrop of the Todilto gypsum on the western side of the Galisteo monocline, 5 miles northwest of Cerrillos. At present the plant turns out plaster board, a fireproof 5/8-inch board made of plaster and fiberglass, plain and impregnated gypsum sheathing, and gypsum lath. When operating at capacity, the plant will require more than 100,000 tons of gypsum annually. At present, the company has 110 employees at the plant site, including 5 men in the quarry. The sales territory of the Kaiser plant includes southern Wyoming, western Louisiana, and all of Missouri, Kansas, Oklahoma, Texas, Colorado, and New Mexico.

American Gypsum Co. is quarrying gypsum at White Mesa, south of San Ysidro, Sandoval County, and trucking it to its plant north of Albuquerque. The plant began production on November 2, 1960, and is now operating four 24-hour days per week. The raw gypsum consumption is 252 tons per working day, the output 300,000 square feet of ½-inch plaster board per day. The company employs 85 to 90 men, including 5 men at the open-pit quarry. Its largest markets are in Phoenix and Los Angeles, but shipments are also made to Denver, Oklahoma City, El Paso, Lubbock, and Amarillo.

A small quarry supplies gypsum to the Ideal Cement Co. plant in Tijeras Canyon. It is 5 miles northeast of the cement plant, at the point where State Highway 10 crosses the steeply dipping Todilto formation on the western limb of the Tijeras basin. The quarry is operated by Duke City Gravel Products Co. In the fiscal year 1959-60 it quarried 10,385 tons of gypsum valued at $18,692.

The reserves of gypsum in the three-county area are virtually inexhaustible. Weber and Kottlowski (1959) estimated that the 1,180-acre site owned by American Gypsm Co. on White Mesa alone contains 98,000,000 tons under a 5- to 8-foot overburden of unusable gypsite. An additional 123,000,000 tons are present under thin overburden of Morrison sandstone. The Kaiser quarry has open-pit reserves sufficient for at least 50 years, and large additional reserves could be developed within a few miles.

Marble
All American Marble Co. of Albuquerque recently announced plans to exploit a deposit of banded travertine on the Laguna Indian Reservation in Valencia County. Similar deposits, formed by Pleistocene to Recent mineral and thermal springs, occur in many places along the Rio Puerco-Nacimiento fault zone in western Bernalillo and Sandoval Counties, especially near San Ysidro. Nothing is known about their commercial possibilities. While not true marble in the sense in which geologists use the term, the travertine would be considered marble by the building trade.

True marble occurs in the San Pedro Mountains, Santa Fe County, where Madera limestone (Pennsylvanian) and San Andres limestone (Permian) have been recrystallized by thermal metamorphism near igneous contacts.

Mica
The mica deposits of the Nambe district, Santa Fe County, have already been described in connection with the metal-mining districts.

Montmorillonite Clay
Montmorillonite clay (including bentonite) has not been produced in the three-county area, but at least two occurrences have been reported. One deposit lies just south of Santa Ana Pueblo, near State Highway 44, in secs. 30 and 31, T. 15 N., R. 3 E., Sandoval County. The deposit was recently explored by New Mexico Quartz Manufacturing Co., Inc. Talmage and Wootton (1937) mentioned a deposit of bentonite near Waldo, Santa Fe County, but gave no details. Both deposits appear to be part of the late Tertiary Santa Fe formation.

Pumice and Scoria
Pumice and scoria are both used in light-weight aggregate, especially in the manufacture of building blocks. The largest producer is the Pyramid pumice mine near Cochiti, Sandoval County. The annual report of the State Inspector of Mines for the fiscal year 1959-60 lists seven producing companies, two each in Bernalillo and Santa Fe Counties, and three in Sandoval County. Although it was a poor year in the building trade, they produced 94,651 cubic yards of raw pumice and scoria, valued at $129,979, and employed 35 men, not counting those engaged in manufacturing blocks.

Scoria is obtained from the swarm of small Quaternary basalt volcanoes on the western side of the Rio Grande (Fig. 1). In many volcanoes the eruptions began with an explosive outpouring of scoriaceous lapilli tuff, followed later by quiet lava flow eruptions. Even where no scoriaceous tuff is exposed at the surface near a volcanic vent, it may yet be found under a thin crust of flow rock. Pumice comes from the basal member of the middle Pleistocene Bandelier tuff in the Jemez Mountains. The upper part of the Bandelier formation is a cliff-forming welded rhyolite tuff, unsuitable for use as aggregate, but the lower member is an unconsolidated slope-forming pumiceous lapilli tuff. Many active and abandoned pumice quarries lie on the edge of the outcrop area of the Bandelier tuff (Fig. 1).

The reserves of pumice in the Bandelier tuff are inexhaustible. The reserves of scoria are more limited but are sufficient for the foreseeable future.

Specialty Sand and Sandstone
Wind-blown dune sand occurs along Jemez River near Santa Ana Pueblo in secs. 20 and 21, T. 14 N., R. 3 E., Sandoval County. It is sold to Marvel Roofing Co., Albuquerque, for use as roofing sand.

New Mexico Quartz Manufacturing Co., Inc., of Albuquerque, has recently explored the Glorieta sandstone (Permian) in secs. 23 and 26, T. 12 N., R. 7 E., in the eastern end of the San Pedro Mountains, Santa Fe County. The Glorieta sandstone here is a nearly pure quartz sand, poorly aggregated. Elsewhere it has a calcareous or ferruginous cement.

Stone
Building stone and flagstone have been quarried for local use in many places. They include Precambrian granite, Pennsylvanian limestone, and several types of sandstone from Mesozoic formations. Recently, angular talus blocks of Precambrian quartzite, obtained from the Great Combination gold mining claim in NE¼ sec. 12, T. 9 N., R. 4½ E., Tijeras Canyon district, have become popular in Albuquerque.

Crushed stone of many types has been used for construction work. An attempt has been made recently to

Table 3. Total Original Coal Reserves of Bernalillo, Sandoval, and Santa Fe Counties, New Mexico

County and Field	Geologic Formation	Reserves in Millions of Short Tons					
		Measured	Indicated	Inferred	Inferred on Coal Zone Basis	Total	Rank
Bernalillo							
Tijeras	Mesaverde	0.4	1.2	-	-	1.6	Bituminous
Rio Puerco	Mesaverde	1.0	-	-	-	1.0	Subbituminous
Sandoval							
San Juan River	Mesaverde	67.3	320.9	547.9	2,399.1	3,335.2	Subbituminous
San Juan River	Fruitland	0.2	0.5	-	1,609.6	1,610.3	Subbituminous
Una del Gato	Mesaverde	0.6	15.9	0.8	-	17.3	
Santa Fe							
Cerrillos	Mesaverde	6.6	14.6	26.3	-	47.5	Bituminous
Cerrillos	Mesaverde	2.8	2.9	-	-	5.7	Anthracite
Totals		78.9	356.0	575.0	4,008.7	5,018.6	

This table includes all anthracite and bituminous coal beds more than 14 inches thick, less than 3,000 feet deep, and all subbituminous coal beds more than 30 inches thick, less than 3,000 feet deep.
Source of data: Read and others (1950).

develop a large vein of white bull quartz on Sandia Pueblo land, in the Sandia Mountains near Juan Tabo Canyon, for use as roofing granule. Similar veins are known also in the Manzano Mountains.

Sulfur

Sulfur occurs in two areas of active solfataras in Jemez Canyon, Sandoval County. The deposits were discovered by Spaniards in the 16th century and worked on a small scale into the 20th century. The larger locality, called Jemez Sulphur Springs, covers about 10 acres, 11 miles north-northeast of Jemez Springs. The second locality covers about an acre, 4½ miles north-northeast of Jemez Springs. It contains 15 to 39 percent free sulfur and 6 to 8 percent sulfur combined as sulfate. In 1933 New Mexico Acid Co. built a 150-ton plant at this deposit but it was never operated successfully (Talmage and Wootton, 1937).

COAL

Bernalillo, Sandoval, and Santa Fe Counties contain measured, indicated, and inferred reserves of coal amounting to nearly 5,300,000,000 tons, or 8.6 percent of the entire reserves of the State of New Mexico (Read and others, 1950). Most of the reserves are in relatively inaccessible parts of Sandoval County. The bulk of production has come from the Cerrillos district, Santa Fe County, where the coals are high-grade anthracite and bituminous coking coal and lie near the main line of the A., T. & S. F. Railway. Total production in the three counties has been more than 7,000,000 tons. Most of the coal beds are part of the Mesaverde group of late Cretaceous age, but about one-third of the reserves of Sandoval County are in the Fruitland formation, which is late Cretaceous also, but younger than the Mesaverde group. Coal beds are present in other formations, ranging in age from Pennsylvanian to Tertiary, but have no economic value.

In the western parts of Bernalillo and Sandoval Counties, which are within the relatively undeformed Colorado Plateau province, the coals are subbituminous. Bituminous coals occur in the structurally complex intermontane basins of Santa Fe County and eastern Bernalillo and Sandoval Counties. Thermal metamorphism near the contacts of a monzonite sill has raised parts of the uppermost coal beds in the Cerrillos field to anthracite rank. The Cerrillos field is one of the few areas in the United States outside eastern Pennsylvania where anthracite has been mined in significant amounts.

The thickness of coal beds in the region ranges from

a feather edge to more than 5 feet. Commercial beds are 3 feet or more thick, although thinner beds have been worked from time to time for local markets. Cretaceous coals are notoriously discontinuous. They pinch out laterally because of non-deposition, erosion beneath minor unconformities, or facies changes.

Coal mining began in the Cerrillos region around 1835 (Lee, 1913), but only about 10,000 tons was produced before 1880. Commercial mining began in the late 1880's and was greatly expanded after a railroad spur was built to Madrid in 1895. Production reached its peak between the end of World War I and the beginning of the Great Depression in 1929, when the annual output was about 250,000 tons, valued at $1,000,000. The decline that began in 1929 became precipitous after World War II and finally led to the virtual extinction of the industry by 1960. The annual report of the State Inspector of Mines for the fiscal year 1959-60 lists only two small coal mines as active in the entire three-county area: the Padilla No. 2 mine near La Ventana, Sandoval County, and the Tabor No. 2 mine at Madrid, Santa Fe County.

Bernalillo County

Bernalillo County has two coal fields, neither of them important. The small Tijeras field is about 20 miles east of Albuquerque, just north of U. S. Highway 66. The coal measures of the Mesaverde group are preserved over an area of 2½ square miles in the core of a syncline on the east side of the Sandia Mountains. Beds dip steeply on the sides of the syncline but are nearly horizontal in the middle. Small amounts of bituminous coal have been mined in the past for consumption in Albuquerque (Lee, 1912). The beds are thin and badly fractured.

Subbituminous coal occurs in the Rio Puerco valley of western Bernalillo County. Small coal mines and prospects were formerly worked on the Canoncito Navajo Indian Reservation, but have never had commercial importance.

Sandoval County

Sandoval County has two coal fields, the La Ventana-Chacra Mesa section of the San Juan River field in the western part of the County, and the Una del Gato or Hagan field in the southeastern part.

The San Juan River field contains 89 percent of the total coal reserves of New Mexico. The La Ventana-Chacra Mesa area is on its southeastern and eastern border, where the coal measures are turned up steeply along the front of the Nacimiento Mountains and then dip gently westward into the San Juan Basin. A number of subbituminous coal beds are present at two stratigraphic levels: the Creary coal member of the Menefee formation of the Mesaverde group (Beaumont, Dane, and Sears, 1956), and the Fruitland formation. The geology has been described in detail by Dane (1936). The field is far from rail transportation and has never been exploited on a large scale. In the past, coal from the La Ventana-Chacra Mesa field supplied the copper smelters at Copper City and Senorito, near Cuba.

The Una del Gato field is a faulted eastward-dipping homocline in the southeastern part of Sandoval County, between the Sandia and Ortiz Mountains. Several beds of high-quality bituminous coal occur in an area of 30 square miles (Read and others, 1950; Harrison, 1949). The beds may correlate with those in the Cerrillos field. At the Hagan mine, in the center of sec. 33, T. 13 N., R. 6 E., the main coal bed—the Hopewell bed—is a constant 48-52 inches thick, folded but not faulted, has a strong sandstone roof and floor, and dips from 15° N. to 15° E. (Campbell, 1907). Mining conditions are not everywhere as favorable as the Hagan mine; locally the coal is faulted or contains shaly partings.

Santa Fe County

Santa Fe County has only one coal field, the Cerrillos field, about 25 miles southeast of Santa Fe. The main line of the A., T. & S. F. Railway skirts the northern edge of the field; Cerrilios is the nearest shipping point. The Cerrillos field has produced approximately 7,000,000 tons.

The Cerrillos coal field is a structural basin, bordered on the northwestern and southwestern edges by igneous rocks of Los Cerrillos and the Ortiz Mountains. Almost all production has come from its western edge, where the beds dip 7° to 15° E. The extent of the field has been estimated at between 30 square miles (Lee, 1913) and 80 square miles (Read and others, 1950). On the northern and northeastern side of the basin, all or part of the Mesaverde group was removed by erosion prior to deposition of the early Tertiary Galisteo formation (Lee, 1913; Stearns, 1953), but the exact extent of the unconformity is unknown. There are indications that the two most productive beds in the field are cut out by the pre-Galisteo unconformity a few miles north, and possibly east, of the outcrop at Madrid.

Read and others (1950) computed the reserves of the field on the basis of the three minable beds in the Cerrillos-Waldo-Madrid area: the Miller Gulch bed, 190 feet above the base of the Mesaverde group, the Cook and White bed, about 465 feet higher in the section, and the White Ash bed, 100 feet above the Cook and White bed. A thick monzonite sill lies between the Miller Gulch and Cook and White beds, and another lies above the White Ash bed.

The Miller Gulch bed was described by Turnbull and others (1951) as high-volatile bright banded bituminous coal, producing coke not quite so good as coke from the Sunnyside bed, Carbon County, Utah, which is used as a standard for western coking coal. They also showed by four diamond-drill holes that the bed does not continue far downdip in minable thickness. The Miller Gulch bed has not been traced southward into the area west of Madrid.

The Cook and White bed, and its northward continuation—the Waldo bed—has yielded large quantities of bituminous coal in the Madrid area. It is 3 to 4½ feet thick, but locally has shaly partings. Turnbull and others (1951) classified it as high-volatile bright banded bituminous coal, producing coke definitely stronger than coke from the Sunnyside bed in Utah. Mine workings and a drill hole have shown that the coal changes laterally into carbonaceous shale 1½ to 2 miles north of Madrid. At its northernmost surface exposure, a mile south of Waldo, the Galisteo formation lies directly on the Cook and White (or Waldo) bed, and the fuel value of the coal was destroyed by pre-Galisteo weathering. The southern and eastern limits of the Cook and White bed have not been determined. The Jones and Cook & White mines were among the important ones working this bed.

The White Ash bed is coking bituminous coal at the White Ash mine, about a quarter of a mile northeast of Madrid. Farther south it changes into anthracite and thins from about 5½ feet to about 3 feet. The change from bituminous coal to anthracite via semianthracite takes place within a few hundred feet opposite the town of Madrid.

The rank of coal possibly depends on the distance between the coal bed and the overlying monzonite sill. At the White Ash mine, chief producer of bituminous coal from this bed, the sill is 30 to 50 feet above the coal; at the Lucas mine, chief and northernmost producer of anthracite, the sill is 8-9 feet above the coal, and at the Anthracite No. 4 mine, a quarter of a mile south of Madrid, only a few inches of shale separate the sill from the coal. The White Ash bed has been traced from a locality about three-fourths of a mile north of Madrid into a faulted area three-fourths of a mile south of Madrid.

Several other coal beds are known in the Madrid area, but have not yet proved to be commercial. Outside the Madrid area, the Cerrillos field has produced coal in only one place—the Omera or Block mine in sec. 32, T. 13 N., R. 9 E. The coal here is in two beds, 40 and 36 inches thick, separated by a 9-foot bed of sandstone. The coal is bituminous in rank (Gardner, 1910) and was formerly used at the copper mine and smelter at San Pedro. The coal at the Omera mine is stratigraphically lower than the Cook and White and White Ash beds at Madrid, and is unconformably overlain by the Galisteo formation.

Outside the Cerrillos field, thin and impure Pennsylvanian coals are known at the southern end of the Sangre de Cristo Mountains.

REFERENCES CITED

Anderson, E. C., 1957, The metal resources of New Mexico and their economic features through 1954: New Mexico Bur. Mines and Mineral Res. Bull. 39, 183 p., 5 pls., 3 figs.

Atkinson, W. W., Jr., 1960, Geology of the San Pedro Mountains, Santa Fe County, New Mexico: Univ. New Mexico unpub. master's thesis, 81 p., 3 pls., 8 figs.

Beaumont, E. C., Dane, C. H., and Sears, J. D., 1956, Revised nomenclature of Mesaverde group in San Juan Basin, New Mexico: Am. Assoc. Petroleum Geologists Bull., v. 40, p. 2149-2162.

Bundy, W. M., 1958, Wall-rock alteration in the Cochiti mining district, New Mexico: New Mexico Bur. Mines and Mineral Res. Bull. 59, 71 p., 2 pls., 31 figs.

Campbell, M. R., 1907, Una del Gato coal field, Sandoval County, New Mexico: U. S. Geol. Survey Bull. 316-F, p. 427-430.

Dane, C. H., 1937, Geology and fuel resources of the southern part of the San Juan Basin, New Mexico; Pt. 3, the La Ventana-Chacra Mesa coal field: U. S. Geol. Survey Bull. 860-C, p. 81-161.

Disbrow, A. E., and Stoll, W. C., 1957, Geology of the Cerrillos area, Santa Fe County, New Mexico: New Mexico Bur. Mines and Mineral Res. Bull. 48, 73 p., 5 pls., 3 figs.

Harrison, E. P., 1949, Geology of the Hagan coal basin: Univ. New Mexico unpub. master's thesis, 177 p., 1 pl., 5 figs.

Hayden, F. V., 1869, Santa Fe to Placiere Mountain and return: U. S. Geol. and Geog. Survey Terr. 3d Ann. Rept., p. 166-168.

Jones, F. A., 1904, New Mexico mines and minerals: Santa Fe, 349 p.

Kelley, V. C., 1949, Geology and economics of New Mexico iron-ore deposits: Univ. New Mexico Pub. in Geol. No. 2, 246 p., 16 pls., 46 figs.

Kunz, G. F., 1893, Precious stones: U. S. Geol. Survey Mineral Resources U. S. 1892, p. 756-781

Lasky, S. G., and Wootton, T. P., 1933, The metal resources of New Mexico and their economic features: New Mexico Bur. Mines and Mineral Res. Bull. 7, 178 p., 2 pls.

Lee, W. T., 1912, The Tijeras coal field, Bernalillo County, New Mexico: U. S. Geol. Survey Bull. 471-H, p. 575-578.

──────, 1913, The Cerrillos coal field, Santa Fe County, New Mexico: U. S. Geol. Survey Bull. 531-J, p. 285-312.

Lindgren, Waldemar, Graton, L. C., and Gordon, C. H., 1910, The ore deposits of New Mexico: U. S. Geol. Survey Prof. Paper 68, 361 p., 22 pls., 33 figs.

Lustig, L. K., 1957, The mineralogy and paragenesis of the Lone Star deposit, Santa Fe County, New Mexico: Univ. New Mexico unpub. master's thesis, 55 p., 13 figs.

McRae, O. M., 1958, Geology of the northern part of the Ortiz Mountains, Santa Fe County, New Mexico: Univ. New Mexico unpub. master's thesis, 112 p., 13 figs.

Newberry, J. S., 1876, Geological report, in Macomb, J. N., Report of the exploring expedition from Santa Fe .... in 1859: U. S. Army Engineer Dept., p. 9-118.

Northrop, S. A., 1959, Minerals of New Mexico, rev. ed.: Albuquerque, Univ. New Mexico Press, xvi, 665 p., map.

Peterson, J. W., 1958, Geology of the southern part of the Ortiz Mountains, Santa Fe County, New Mexico: Univ. New Mexico unpub. master's thesis, 115 p., 11 figs.

Read, C. B., Duffner, R. T., Wood, G. H., Jr., and Zapp, A.D., 1950, Coal resources of New Mexico: U. S. Geol. Survey Circ. 89, 24 p., 1 pl.

Reiche, Parry, 1949, Geology of the Manzanita and North Manzano Mountains, New Mexico: Geol. Soc. America Bull., v. 60, p. 1183-1212, 5 pls., 5 figs.

Ross, Edmund, 1909, A report on a portion of the Soda Springs mining district in Bernalillo County, New Mexico: Univ. New Mexico unpub. senior thesis, 20 p., illus.

Rothrock, H. E., Johnson, C. H., and Hahn, A. D., 1946, Fluorspar resources of New Mexico: New Mexico Bur. Mines and Mineral Res. Bull. 21, 239 p., 23 pls., 15 figs.

Smith, J. F., Jr., Wadsworth, A. H., Cooper, J. R., Farwell, F. W., and Weissenborn, A. E., 1945, San Pedro and Carnahan mines, New Placers mining district, Santa Fe County, New Mexico: U. S. Geol. Survey unpub. open-file rept., 49 p., 12 pls., 2 figs.

State (of New Mexico) Inspector of Mines, 1912 to 1960, Annual Reports.

Stearns, C. E., 1953, Tertiary geology of the Galisteo-Tonque area, New Mexico: Geol. Soc. America Bull., v. 64, p. 459-507, 3 pls., 10 figs.

Talmage, S. B., and Wootton, T. P., 1937, The non-metallic mineral resources of New Mexico and their economic features (exclusive of fuels): New Mexico Bur. Mines and Mineral Res. Bull. 12, 159 p., 2 pls., 4 figs.

U. S. Dept. Interior, 1882 to 1932, Mineral Resources U. S. (annual); 1932 to 1959, Minerals Yearbook (annual).

Weber, R. H., and Kottlowski, F. E., 1959, Gypsum resources of New Mexico: New Mexico Bur. Mines and Mineral Res. Bull. 68, 68 p., 6 pls., 5 figs.

Wells, E. H., 1918, Manganese in New Mexico: New Mexico Mineral Res. Survey Bull. 2, 85 p.

Wood, G. H., Jr., and Northrop, S. A., 1946, Geology of the Nacimiento Mountains, San Pedro Mountain, and adjacent plateaus in parts of Sandoval and Rio Arriba Counties, New Mexico: U. S. Geol. Survey Oil and Gas Inv. Prelim. Map 57.

Wynkoop, W. C., 1900, The Cochiti district, New Mexico: Eng. and Min. Jour., v. 70, p. 215-217, 4 figs.

MINERALOGICAL NOTES ON THE URANIUM DEPOSITS OF THE GRANTS AND LAGUNA DISTRICTS

ABRAHAM ROSENZWEIG
University of New Mexico

INTRODUCTION

In the eleven years since the uranium deposits in the vicinity of Haystack Butte first attracted attention, the Grants and Laguna districts have developed into major uranium-producing areas of the United States. A single deposit in the Laguna district, the Jackpile mine, represents about one-third of the total uranium reserves of New Mexico. In addition to their great economic significance, these deposits have shed considerable light on the geochemistry and mineralogy of uranium deposits in sedimentary rocks. Several new minerals have been discovered in the area, which, though not spectacular, are of considerable scientific interest. The mineral collector may find here outstanding specimens of uraninite and some of its alteration products.

Most of the deposits in the two districts are in Jurassic rocks. Those in the Laguna district are in the sandy facies of the Brushy Basin member of the Morrison formation, and those of the Grants district are in the Westwater Canyon member of the Morrison formation and in the Todilto limestone. Several minor deposits occur in other Jurassic rocks and in the Dakota sandstone. The nature of the host rock, limestone or sandstone, provides a convenient as well as economically significant classification of the ore types. A more fundamental scheme of classification can be established on the basis of the oxidation state of the uranium and vanadium and the ratio of these elements to one another (Weeks and others, 1959), thereby separating the ores into unoxidized and oxidized types. A genetic classification, though very desirable, is as yet impractical, for ten years of intensive research has failed to resolve the question of origin of these deposits.

Todilto limestone ores. The Todilto limestone of the Grants district is typically gray in color and has a distinctly fetid odor. It varies from thin bedded in the lower part to massive in the upper part. The mineralized zones are irregular tabular bodies several feet thick and up to several tens of thousands of square feet in area. Mineralization is generally concentrated in areas of small-scale intraformational folding and faulting. The ores are generally of the unoxidized type, and have been subdivided into uranium, uranium-fluorine (fluorite), and uranium-vanadium ores (Truesdell and Weeks, 1960). This subdivision is not practical in a general discussion, for the ore varies rapidly from one type to another within a single small deposit. Hematite staining of the limestone is common in the higher grade ores. Fracture zones and vugs are commonly coated with oxidized uranium and vanadium minerals.

Sandstone ores of the Grants district. The Poison Canyon deposit is typical of the deposits in the Morrison formation in this district. The ore body is in the Poison Canyon sandstone (local usage), a tongue of the Westwater Canyon member extending into the Brushy Basin member. The deposit is tabular, consisting of several nearly parallel layers as much as 20 feet thick. The greatest concentration of mineralization is near the base of the host unit and directly above thin mudstone beds within the sandstone. The ore is primarily black and unoxidized with a concentration of oxidized minerals near the surface and along faults which are younger than the deposit. Minor amounts of sulfides, primarily pyrite and marcasite, but containing significant amounts of molybdenum and selenium, are characteristic of this deposit.

Sandstone ores of the Laguna district. The Jackpile deposit is characteristic of deposits in the Laguna district. The host rock is the Jackpile sandstone (local usage) in the upper part of the Brushy Basin member of the Morrison formation. The largest of the ore bodies, the North ore body, consists of two subparallel layers whose total thickness averages 20 feet. The ore body is about 1,300 feet wide and several thousand feet long. In the lower grade parts of the ore layers, and especially in the zone between the two layers, there are concentrations of uranium associated with carbonaceous material in rod-like vertical bodies. The ore is primarily of the unoxidized type, but a wide variety of oxidized minerals is also present.

The Woodrow deposit, about one mile east of the Jackpile mine, is unique in the area, it being the only deposit in a sandstone pipe. Several similar structures are known in the Laguna district but none of them is significantly mineralized. The pipe is nearly vertical, extends to a known depth of 230 feet, and is approximately 35 feet in diameter. The pipe cuts the Brushy Basin member of the Morrison formation and is separated from it by a complex, branching ring fault. The average tenor of the ore is about two percent uranium, the highest concentration being in the upper part of the pipe and along the bounding ring fault. The core of the pipe is essentially barren. The ore minerals are primarily of the unoxidized type, but many secondary minerals are also present, especially near the surface.

THE MAJOR ORE MINERALS

The terms primary and secondary have frequently been used in referring to the minerals of these and other Colorado Plateau uranium deposits. In view of the controversy regarding the origin of the deposits, the terms primary and secondary should be replaced by unoxidized and oxidized, respectively. The oxidized minerals are in fact secondary in a genetic sense in that they are derived from the unoxidized minerals, primarily through the action of ground water. The unoxidized minerals, however, are primary only in the sense that they are the source of material for the oxidized minerals. In the unoxidized ores the uranium is ideally in the tetravalent state and the vanadium is in the trivalent or tetravalent state. In the oxidized ores the uranium is hexavalent, usually as the uranyl $(UO_2)^{+2}$ ion, and the vanadium is almost always pentavalent. In general the unoxidized minerals are of the greatest economic importance, but the oxidized minerals are locally important, especially in the Todilto limestone. The great permeability of the sandstones may account for the removal of the highly soluble uranyl ion.

Uraninite. Uraninite or pitchblende is the major unoxidized uranium mineral in the Todilto limestone deposits and is an important constituent of the sandstone ores.

Ideally it has the composition UO_2, but partial oxidation will have frequently taken place so that the U:O ratio may range from 1:2 to 1:2.6. In none of the ores do we find the cubic crystal habit, the form generally being as small masses, blebs, and seams in the host rock, or as coatings on the sedimentary grains. The mineral is black, has a submetallic to pitchlike luster (limestone ores), or may be dull and earthy (sandstone ores). In the Todilto limestone, the uraninite content may be quite high, and where this is true the limestone may be heavily stained with hematite. The dark streaks of uraninite, often surrounded by yellow oxidation products, in a reddish limestone give the highest grade ores a distinctive, crudely banded appearance. The discovery of uraninite in the Todilto limestone was one of the first reported occurrences of tetravalent uranium in a deposit of the Colorado Plateau type.

Coffinite. The elements zirconium and thorium are found in nature as the orthosilicates zircon ($ZrSiO_4$) and thorite $ThSiO_4$). The chemical similarity of uranium and thorium would lead one to expect a similar uranium silicate. As early as 1953, John W. Gruner noted that some of the asphaltic materials of certain Colorado Plateau uranium ores gave X-ray diffraction patterns that resembled those of zircon. The phase producing the pattern was not isolated and its chemical nature was not ascertained. The problem was pursued by several investigators, and several years later the mineral was isolated and given the name coffinite (Stieff, and others, 1956). As expected, the mineral is a uranous orthosilicate, but the orthosilicate group is in part replaced by hydroxyl ions. The substitution is in the ratio of four hydroxyl ions per orthosilicate, giving a general formula $U(SiO_4)_{1-x}(OH)_{4x}$. Coffinite is almost invariably associated with some organic matter, especially asphaltite, which it closely resembles both as to color and luster. For this reason the mineral is often very difficult to recognize. In the Grants and Laguna districts, coffinite is one of the most important ore minerals in the sandstone ores and a minor one in the limestone ores.

Vanadium oxides and hydroxides. In the unoxidized ores the uranium and vanadium occur in separate minerals. The vanadium minerals are black, as are those of uranium, but they are generally somewhat fibrous or bladed in habit. The oxidation state varies from trivalent to tetravalent, both ions being present in some of the minerals. Truesdell and Weeks (1960) have studied the paragenesis of the Todilto limestone ores, and have found that the vanadium mineralization is usually earlier than the uranium mineralization. They found some early vanadium-bearing clay, but most of the unoxidized vanadium is present as the hydroxides and oxides haggite, paramontroseite, and possibly montroseite. Haggite, a new mineral, contains both tri- and tetravalent vanadium and is generally earlier than the uraninite, but may itself be a replacement of montroseite which contains only trivalent vanadium. Paramontroseite contains only tetravalent vanadium and is an alteration product of haggite. The vanadium mineralization of the sandstone ores has not been so thoroughly investigated, but probably involves similar minerals as well as the vanadium mica roscoelite.

The uranyl vanadates. Oxidation of ores containing both uranium and vanadium commonly yields double salts containing the uranyl ion and pentavalent uranium. The most familiar of these minerals are carnotite, tyuyamunite, and metatyuyamunite. Carnotite, a hydrous potassium uranyl vanadate, is known from all ore types in the area, but is probably not present in sufficient quantities to be important economically. The analagous calcium compounds, tyuyamunite and metatyuyamunite (differing only in the hydration state), are far more important, making up a significant part of the ore in some of the Todilto limestone deposits. All three minerals are bright yellow, powdery or scaly in habit, and form incrustations on the unoxidized minerals or coat fractures and bedding planes in the limestone. When associated with recrystallized calcite they may be found in rather spectacular specimens.

Uranophane. The calcium uranyl silicate, uranophane, is occasionally referred to as an ore mineral in the Todilto limestone deposits. It is probably of only minor economic significance, but the specimens are of such exceptional quality and beauty as to warrant a brief comment. The mineral occurs as rosettes and radiating clusters of bright yellow acicular crystals coating fractures or filling vugs. Vugs several inches in diameter are sometimes completely lined with these radiating clusters. Such specimens are amongst the finest known of this mineral.

NON-URANIUM MINERALS OF SPECIAL INTEREST

Fluorite. Locally the Todilto limestone contains considerable amounts of fluorite. The fluorite is present as small, irregular dark purple grains scattered through the limestone, giving it a speckled appearance. In some cases the concentration of fluorite is so great as to give a uniform dark purple color to the limestone. Truesdell and Weeks (1960) state that uraninite and fluorite are not necessarily associated, being found as separate masses as often as they are intergrown. Laverty and Gross (1956), however, note intimate intergrowths of the two minerals on a microscopic scale. I have observed that all specimens of fluorite which were available to me were radioactive to a degree significantly above background, but that in some instances no uranium mineral could be detected. Microscopically (magnifications of near 1000x), the dark purple color may be seen as very small, intense color patches in a nearly colorless fluorite. The purple color is permanently destroyed on heating for several hours at 500°C. Late-formed veinlets of calcite cutting the fluorite-rich limestones often have microscopic colorless cubes of fluorite at the veinlet wall, apparently in crystallographic continuity with the purple fluorite. These observations suggest to me that the purple color may be due to radiation damage in the fluorite lattice caused by submicroscopic areas of uraninite within the fluorite, with which uraninite is isostructural.

Molybdenum minerals. At the Poison Canyon deposit one often finds specimens of heavily mineralized, black, friable sandstone with a bright blue staining. The stain is caused by the hydrous molybdenum sulfate, ilsemannite. The blue-stained specimens are most common near the surface or in ore which has been lying on the surface for some time. Undoubtedly the ilsemannite is formed by oxidation of sulfide minerals. The molybdenum sulfides jordisite and molybdenite have been found in the ore from this and other localities, but they are not visible to the naked eye.

Selenium minerals. One of the common plants in the vicinity of the Poison Canyon and other deposits in the Morrison formation is **Astragalus pattersoni** or rattle weed. The plants of this genus utilize selenium in their metabolic processes and consequently may be used as "selenium indicator plants". The common association of minor amounts of selenium with uranium in many of the Colorado

Plateau deposits makes possible the use of these plants as prospecting guides. The unoxidized sandstone ores of the Grants district contain small amounts of marcasite and pyrite which have been shown to contain minor amounts of selenium in substitution for the sulfur. Native selenium has been found at several localities in the area (Sun, 1959). The selenium occurs as incrustations consisting of steel-gray, metallic, acicular crystals. Some of the specimens are of exceptionally fine quality.

CHECK LIST OF URANIUM AND VANADIUM MINERALS

Following is a list of minerals containing uranium, vanadium, or both which have been reported from the Grants and Laguna districts. The minerals are grouped according to the oxidation state of the uranium and vanadium, and may accordingly be assigned to the unoxidized or oxidized ore types. Literature references are given for the new and less familiar minerals wherever possible. New minerals for which the Grants district is the type locality, or which were discovered here shortly after the initial discovery at some other locality are underlined. Minerals whose occurrence is questionable are enclosed in parentheses.

BIBLIOGRAPHY

Appleman, D. E., and Evans, H. T., Jr., 1957, The crystal structure of carnotite [abs.]: Acta Crystallographica, v. 10, p. 765.

Barnes, W. H., 1955, "Hewettite" and "metahewettite": Am. Mineralogist, v. 40, p. 689-691.

Evans, H. T., Jr., and Frondel, Clifford, 1950, Studies of uranium minerals (II); Liebigite and uranothallite: Am. Mineralogist, v. 35, p. 251-254.

Evans, H. T., Jr., and Mrose, M. E., 1955, A crystal chemical study of montroseite and paramontroseite: Am. Mineralogist, v. 40, p. 861-875.

.............., 1958, The crystal structures of three new vanadium oxide minerals: Acta Crystallographica, v. 11, p. 56-58.

Frondel, Clifford, 1950, Studies of uranium minerals (V); Phosphuranylite: Am. Mineralogist, v. 35, p. 756-763.

.............., 1951, Studies of uranium minerals (IX); Saleeite and novacekite: Am. Mineralogist, v. 36, p. 680-686.

.............., 1952, Studies of uranium minerals (X); Uranopilite: Am. Mineralogist, v. 37, p. 950-959.

.............., 1958, Systematic mineralogy of uranium and thorium: U. S. Geol. Survey Bull. 1064, 400 p.

Frondel, Clifford, and Meyrowitz, Robert, 1956, Studies of uranium minerals (XIX); Rutherfordine, diderichite, and clarkeite: Am. Mineralogist, v. 41, p. 127-133.

Frondel, J. W., and Cuttitta, Frank, 1953, Studies of uranium minerals (XII); The status of billietite and becquerelite: Am. Mineralogist, v. 38, p. 1019-1024.

Gorman, D. H., 1952, Studies of radioactive compounds; V—Soddyite: Am. Mineralogist, v. 37, p. 386-393.

Hurlbut, C. S., Jr., 1950, Studies of uranium minerals (IV); Johannite: Am. Mineralogist, v. 35, p. 531-535.

.............., 1954, Studies of uranium minerals (XV); Schroeckingerite: Am. Mineralogist, v. 39, p. 901-907.

Laverty, R. A., and Gross, E. B., 1956, Paragenetic studies of uranium deposits of the Colorado Plateau, in Geology of uranium and thorium: United Nations Proc. Internat. Conf. Peaceful Uses Atomic Energy, Geneva, 1955, v. 6, p. 533-539.

Northrop, S. A., 1959, Minerals of New Mexico, rev. ed.: Albuquerque, Univ. New Mexico Press, 665 p.

Outerbridge, W. F., Staatz, M. H., Meyrowitz, Robert, and Pommer, A. M., 1960, Weeksite, a new uranium silicate from the Thomas Range, Juab County, Utah: Am. Mineralogist, v. 45, p. 39-51.

Smith, D. K., Jr., Gruner, J. W., and Lipscomb, W. N., Jr., 1957, The crystal structure of uranophane: Am. Mineralogist, v. 42, p. 594-618.

Stern, T. W., Stieff, L. R., Evans, H. T., Jr., and Sherwood, A. M., 1957, Doloresite, a new vanadium oxide mineral from the Colorado Plateau: Am. Mineralogist, v. 42, p. 587-593.

U^{+4} MINERALS

Uraninite - UO_2 to $UO_{2.6}$

<u>Coffinite</u> - $U(SiO_4)_{1-x}(OH)_{4x}$ (Stieff and others, 1956)

V^{+3} AND V^{+4} MINERALS

<u>Doloresite</u> - $3V_2O_4 \cdot 4H_2O$ (Stern and others, 1957)

<u>Häggite</u> - $V_2O_2(OH)_3$ (Evans and Mrose, 1958)

Montroseite - $VO(OH)$ (Weeks and others, 1953)

<u>Paramontroseite</u> - VO_2 (Evans and Mrose, 1955)

Roscoelite - $K(Al,V)_2(Al,Si_3)O_{10}(OH)_2$

Vanadium clay

V^{+4} - V^{+5} MINERALS

Corvusite - $V_2O_4 \cdot 6V_2O_5 \cdot nH_2O$

<u>Grantsite</u> - $Na_4CaV_{12}O_{32} \cdot 8H_2O$

U^{+6} AND V^{+5} MINERALS

Autunite - $Ca(UO_2)_2(PO_4)_2 \cdot 10\text{-}12H_2O$

Becquerelite - $2UO_3 \cdot 3H_2O$ (Frondel and Cuttitta, 1953)

Beta-uranophane - (see uranophane)

Carnotite - $K_2(UO_2)_2(VO_4)_2 \cdot 1\text{-}3H_2O$ (Appleman and Evans, 1957)

Cuprosklodowskite - possibly a copper analog of uranophane

Gummite - a mixture of hydrous uranium oxides

Hewettite - $CaV_6O_{16} \cdot 9H_2O$ (Barnes, 1955)

Johannite - $Cu(UO_2)_2(SO_4)_2(OH)_2 \cdot 6H_2O$ (Hurlbut, 1950)

Meta-autunite - $Ca(UO_2)_2(PO_4)_2 \cdot 8H_2O$

Metatyuyamunite - $Ca(UO_2)_2(VO_4)_2 \cdot 3\text{-}5H_2O$ (Stern and others, 1956)

Novacekite - $Mg(UO_2)_2(AsO_4)_2 \cdot 8\text{-}10H_2O$ (Frondel, 1951)

Pascoite - $Ca_3V_{10}O_{28} \cdot 16H_2O$

(Rauvite) - $CaO \cdot 2UO_3 \cdot 5V_2O_5 \cdot 16H_2O$

Rutherfordine - $(UO_2)CO_3$ (Frondel and Meyrowitz, 1956)

Saléeite - $Mg(UO_2)_2(PO_4)_2 \cdot 8H_2O$ (Frondel, 1951)

<u>Santafeite</u> - $Na_2O \cdot 3MnO_2 \cdot 6(Mn,Ca,Sr)O \cdot 3(V,As)_2O_5 \cdot 8H_2O$ (Sun and Weber, 1957)

Schroeckingerite - $NaCa_3(UO_2)(CO_3)_3(SO_4)F \cdot 10H_2O$ (Hurlbut, 1954)

Sklodowskite - possibly a magnesium analog of uranophane

Soddyite - $(UO_2)_5(SiO_4)_2(OH)_2 \cdot 5H_2O$ (Gorman, 1952)

Tyuyamunite - $Ca(UO_2)_2(VO_4)_2 \cdot 5\text{-}8H_2O$ (Stern and others, 1956)

Uranophane - $Ca(H_3O)_2(UO_2)_2(SiO_4)_2 \cdot 3H_2O$ (Smith and others, 1957)

Uranopilite - $(UO_2)_6SO_4(OH)_{10} \cdot 12H_2O$ (Frondel, 1952)

(Uvanite) - $2UO_3 \cdot 3V_2O_5 \cdot 15H_2O$

<u>Weeksite</u> - $K_2(UO_2)_2(Si_2O_5)_3 \cdot 4H_2O$ (Outerbridge and others, 1960)

Zippeite - $K_4(UO_2)_6(SO_4)_3(OH)_{10} \cdot H_2O$

Stern, T. W., Stieff, L. R., Girhard, M. N., and Meyrowitz, Robert, 1956; The occurrence and properties of metatyuyamunite: Am. Mineralogist, v. 41, p. 187-201.

Stieff, L. R., Stern, T. W., and Sherwood, A. M., 1956, Coffinite a uranous silicate with hydroxyl substitution—a new mineral: Am. Mineralogist, v. 41, p. 675-688.

Sun, Ming-Shan, 1959, Native selenium from Grants, New Mexico: Am. Mineralogist, v. 44, p. 1309-1311.

Sun, Ming-Shan, and Weber, R. H., 1957, Santafeite, a new hydrated vanadate from New Mexico [abs.]: Geol. Soc. America Bull., v. 68, p. 1802.

Truesdell, A. H., and Weeks, A. D., 1960, Paragenesis of uranium ores in Todilto limestone near Grants, New Mexico: U. S. Geol. Survey Prof. Paper 400-B, p. 52-53.

Weeks, A. D., Cisney, E. A., and Sherwood, A. M., 1953, Montroseite, a new vanadium oxide from the Colorado Plateaus: Am. Mineralogist, v. 38, p. 1235-1241.

Weeks, A. D., Coleman, R. G., and Thompson, M. E., 1959, Summary of the ore mineralogy, in Garrels, R. M., and Larsen, E. S., 3rd, editors, Geochemistry and mineralogy of the Colorado Plateau uranium ores: U. S. Geol. Survey Prof. Paper 320, p. 65-80.

Weeks, A. D., and Thompson, M. E., 1954, Identification and occurrence of uranium and vanadium minerals from the Colorado Plateaus: U. S. Geol. Survey Bull. 1009-B, p. 13-62.

Check Lists of Minerals for Mining Districts and Other Localities Near Albuquerque

STUART A. NORTHROP
University of New Mexico

Most of these records of occurrence are taken from the writer's (1959) "Minerals of New Mexico." Mineral occurrences of unusual interest are indicated by an exclamation mark (!); exceptional occurrences are indicated by two such marks (!!).

BERNALILLO COUNTY
Tijeras Canyon Mining District

This is a large district located in the southern Sandia Mountains, Manzanita Mountains, and northern Manzano Mountains. Subdistricts and synonyms include Carnuel, Coyote, Coyote Basin, Coyote Canyon, Coyote Springs, Hell Canyon, Soda Springs, Sandia (in part), Star, and Star Canyon.

Anglesite
Anhydrite
Argentite
Azurite
Barite!
Biotite
Bornite
Calcite
   Tufa
Chalcocite
Chalcopyrite
Chlorite
Copper
Cuprite
Descloizite, var.
   Cuprodescloizite
Epidote!
Feldspar
Fluorite!!
Galena
Garnet
Gold
   Placer gold
Graphite
Gypsum
Hematite
Hornblende
Ilmenite!
"Limonite"
   Ocher
Magnetite
Malachite
Microcline
Molybdenite
Mottramite (?)
Muscovite
   Sericite
Nickel minerals
Orthoclase
Plagioclase
   Labradorite
Pyrite
Pyromorphite
Pyroxene
Quartz
   Chalcedony
   Flint and chert
   Jasper
Siderite
Sillimanite
Silver (?)
Silver minerals
Smithsonite
Sphalerite
Sphene
Strontianite
Tin minerals
Tourmaline
Uranium minerals
Witherite (?)
Zircon

In addition to the minerals listed above, recent petrographic work on the Precambrian rocks of the Tijeras Canyon area (Bruns, 1959; Lodewick, 1960; accompanying Guidebook paper by J. P. Fitzsimmons) has yielded the following minerals:

Actinolite
Amphibole
Apatite
Augite
Diopside
Kaolinite
Kyanite
Penninite
Plagioclase
   Albite
   Andesine
   Oligoclase
Rutile
Tremolite
Zoisite, var.
   Saussurite

Juan Tabo Area

In northern Sandia Mountains, northeast of Alameda; has been included in the Placitas district (of Sandoval County).

Anthophyllite
Biotite
Chalcopyrite
Chlorite
Chrysocolla
Enstatite
Epidote
Garnet
Hornblende
Kaolinite
Magnetite
Microcline
Muscovite
   Sericite
Orthoclase
Plagioclase
   Albite
   Oligoclase
Pyroxene
Quartz
Sillimanite
Sphene
Tenorite
Tourmaline
Zircon
Zoisite

Cerro Colorado

This is a small volcano west of Albuquerque near U. S. Highway 66 bridges across the Rio Puerco.

Barite
Biotite
Carnotite (?)
Chlorite
Cristobalite
Hematite
Hornblende
Magnetite
Muscovite
   Sericite
Orthoclase
   Sanidine
Plagioclase
   Labradorite
Pyroxene
Quartz
   Agate
   Chalcedony
Uranium minerals

Modern Sands of the Rio Grande Valley

The following minerals occur in modern river sands of the Rio Grande valley in Bernalillo, Sandoval, Socorro, and Valencia Counties.

Andalusite
Apatite
Barite
Biotite
Calcite
Diopside
Enstatite
Epidote
Feldspar
Garnet
Hornblende
Hypersthene
Ilmenite
Kyanite
"Leucoxene"
Magnetite
Monazite
Muscovite
Pyroxene
Quartz
Rutile
Sillimanite
Sphene
Spinel
Staurolite
Topaz
Tourmaline
Zircon
Zoisite

Miscellaneous Localities

Barite
Calcite!
Celestite
Clinochlore
Clinozoisite
Cummingtonite (?)
Epidote
Fluorite
Garnet
Gold
Gypsum
   Selenite
Hematite
Hornblende
Kaolinite
Lepidomelene
"Leucoxene"
"Limonite"
   Ocher
Magnesite
Muscovite!
   Sericite
Olivine
Opal, var.
   Wood-opal
Orthoclase
   Microperthite
Penninite
Plagioclase
   Labradorite
Quartz
   Agatized wood
   Flint and chert
   Jasper
Resin
Riebeckite
Rutile
Serpentine, var.
   Antigorite
Silver minerals
Sphene
Tellurium (?)
Tourmaline
Zircon
Zoisite

For Placitas mining district, see under Sandoval County.

LOS ALAMOS COUNTY

- Augite
- Biotite
- Celadonite
- Cristobalite
- Hornblende
- Hypersthene
- "Iddingsite"
- Orthoclase
  - Sanidine!
- Plagioclase
- Quartz
- Saponite
- Tridymite

McKINLEY COUNTY

For uranium minerals of the Grants district of McKinley and Valencia Counties, see paper by A. Rosenzweig, this Guidebook.

SANDOVAL COUNTY
Cochiti Mining District

Also known as Albemarle, Bland, and Peralta Canyon.

- Argentite
- Arsenopyrite(?)
- Augite
- Biotite
- Bromyrite
- Carnotite
- Chalcopyrite
- Chlorite
- Cuprite
- Dickite
- Dufrenite(?)
- Euclase(?)
- Galena
- Gold
- Hematite
  - Specularite
- Hornblende
- "Limonite"
- Magnetite
- Malachite
- Muscovite, var.
  - Sericite
- Opal
  - Hyalite
  - Precious opal
  - Wood-opal
- Orthoclase
  - Sanidine!
- Plagioclase
  - Oligoclase
- Pyrite
- Quartz
  - Chalcedony
- Siderite
- Sphalerite
- Sphene
- Stevensite
- Stibnite(?)
- Tellurium minerals
- Tourmaline
- "Wad"
- Zircon

Jemez Springs Mining District
Includes the Spanish Queen mine and Soda Dam.

- Azurite
- Barite
- Calcite!
  - Tufa and travertine!
  - Oolites and pisolites!!
- Chabazite
- Chalcocite
- Copper
- Covellite
- Feldspar
- Gold
- Gypsum, var.
  - Selenite
- Hematite
- "Limonite"
- Malachite!
- Muscovite
- Pyrite
- Quartz
  - Agatized wood
  - Flint and chert
- Tenorite, var.
  - Melaconite(?)
- Uranium minerals

Jemez Sulfur Mining District

Also known as Otero Sulphur Springs, San Diego Sulphur, Sulfur Springs, Sulphur Springs; includes a small area near Battleship Rock.

- Calcite
  - Tufa
- Cristobalite
- Dufrenite
- Hornblende
- Opal
  - Hyalite
  - Wood-opal!
- Quartz
  - Flint and chert
- Sulfur!!

Nacimiento Mountains Mining District

Subdistricts and synonyms include Copper City, Cuba, Nacimiento, San Miguel, Senorito, Sierra Nacimiento.

- Azurite
- Bornite
- Cerussite
- Chalcocite!
- Chrysocolla
- Copper
- Covellite
- Cuprite
- Feldspar
- Gypsum!
  - Selenite
- Hematite
- Hornblende
- Jarosite
- "Limonite"
- Malachite!
- Pyrite
- Quartz
  - Agate
  - Flint and chert
- Sphalerite
- Tenorite, var.
  - Melaconite
- Uranium minerals
- Vivianite, var.
  - Odontolite(?)

Placitas Mining District

Subdistricts and synonyms include Algodones, Bernalillo, Capulin Peak, La Madera, Las Placitas, Montezuma, and Sandia (in part).

- Anglesite
- Azurite
- Barite
- Calcite
  - Tufa and travertine
  - Dripstone, Mexican onyx
- Cerargyrite(?)
- Chalcopyrite
- Fluorite
- Galena!
- Garnet (in sand)
- Gold
  - Placer gold
- Gypsum
  - Selenite
- Hematite
  - Specularite
- Ilmenite
- "Limonite"
- Magnetite (in sand)
- Malachite
- Pyrite
- Quartz
  - Flint and chert
- Silver
- Silver minerals
- Zircon (in sand)

Cabezon Area

- Aragonite
- Augite!
- Calcite!
- Diopside
- Dolomite
- Enstatite
- Olivine!
- Plagioclase
  - Labradorite!
- Quartz
- Serpentine
  - Antigorite(?)
  - Bastite
- Spinel

Miscellaneous Localities

Especially in the Jemez Plateau or the San Juan Basin.

- Alunogen
- Analcime
- Apatite
- Aragonite!
- Autunite
- Biotite
- Calcite
  - Anthraconite
  - Tufa and travertine!
- Carnotite
- Celadonite
- Chabazite
- Coffinite
- Cristobalite
- Gypsum
  - Satin spar
  - Selenite
- Hornblende
- Hypersthene
- "Iddingsite"
- Kaolinite
- Magnetite!
  - Manganoan magnetite
- Manganese minerals
- Natrolite
- Olivine
- Opal
  - Diatomite
  - Wood-opal
- Orthoclase
  - Moonstone!
- Plagioclase
  - Albite
  - Anorthite
  - Bytownite
  - Labradorite!
  - Oligoclase
- Psilomelane!
- Pyrite
- Quartz
  - Agatized wood!
  - Flint and chert
  - Jasper
- Resin
- Saponite
- Serpentine(?)
- Siderite
- Tridymite
- Uranium minerals
- "Wad"!
- Wheelerite (type)!!
- Zircon

SANTA FE COUNTY
Cerrillos Mining District

Subdistricts and synonyms include Bonanza City, Carbonateville, Galisteo, Galisteo Creek, Hungry Gulch, Los Cerrillos, Mount Chalchihuitl, Turquesa, Turquois, and Turquoise (City, Hill).

- Allanite
- Analcime
- Ankerite
- Apatite
- Argentite
- Augite
- Azurite
- Barite
- Biotite
- Bournonite
- Bromyrite
- Calcite
  - Manganoan calcite
- Cerargyrite
- Cerussite
- Chalcanthite
- Chalcocite
- Chalcopyrite
- Chlorite
- Chrysocolla(?)
- Covellite
- Dolomite
- Epidote
- Feldspar
- Fluorite
- Gahnite
- Galena!
- Gold
  - Placer gold
- Gypsum
  - Selenite
- Halloysite
- Hematite
  - Specularite
- Hornblende
- Ilmenite

Kaolinite
"Limonite"!
Magnetite
Malachite
Melanterite
Muscovite
  Sericite
Nepheline
Olivine
Opal
Orthoclase
  Microperthite
  Sanidine
Plagioclase
Proustite(?)
Pyrargyrite(?)
Pyrite
Pyroxene
Quartz
  Amethyst
  Chalcedony

Jasper
Rutile
Serpentine
Siderite
  Spherosiderite
Silver
Smithsonite!
Sodalite
Sphalerite!!
Sphene
Stibnite
Talc
Tetrahedrite
Tourmaline!
Turquois!!!
Uranium minerals
Vanadinite
"Wad"
Wulfenite
Xanthoconite
Zircon

In addition to the minerals listed above, Disbrow and Stoll (1957) recorded the following:

Montmorillonite,
  as Bentonite
Plagioclase
  Andesine

Psilomelane
Rhodochrosite
"Wad", as
  Manganese oxides

La Bajada Mining District

Analcime
Augite
Autunite
Asphaltite!
Azurite
Barite
Biotite
Bornite
Brannerite
Butlerite
Calcite
  Mexican onyx
Chalcocite
Chalcopyrite!
Colusite
Copiapite
Crednerite
Halotrichite
Hydronephelite
"Iddingsite"
Malachite

Marcasite!
Melanterite!
"Mineral gel"
Nepheline
Olivine
Opal
Orthoclase
Plagioclase
Pyrite
Pyroxene
Quartz
  Chalcedony
Serpentine
Siderite
Sphalerite
Sulfur
Thorium minerals
Uranium minerals
Voltaite
Wurtzilite(?)
Zeolites

New Placers Mining District

This district, located in the San Pedro Mountains, has a large number of subdistricts and synonyms, such as Carnahan, Golden, Lazarus Gulch, Placer del Tuerto, Real de San Francisco, San Isidro, San Lazaro, San Pedro, San Ysidro Mountains, San Zaro, Silver Butte, Tuerto Mountain, and Tuertos Range.

Alabandite
Anglesite!
Argentite
Aurichalcite *
Azurite!
Barite
Biotite
Bornite!
Calcite!
  Papierspath
Cerargyrite
Cerussite!
Chalcanthite!
Chalcocite
Chalcopyrite!!
Chlorite
Chrysocolla
Cuprite
Diopside
Epidote
  Bucklandite
Feldspar!
Fluorite
Galena!
Garnet
  Almandite
  Andradite!!

Grossularite
Gold!
  Placer gold!
Goslarite
Gypsum
Hematite
  Specularite!
Hornblende
Idocrase
Kaolinite
"Limonite"
Ocher
Magnetite
Malachite!!
Marcasite
Melanterite
Minium
Molybdenite
Muscovite
  Sericite
Orthoclase
  Adularia!
Plagioclase
  Albite
Pyrite!
Pyrolusite
Polianite

Pyrrhotite
Quartz!!
  Flint and chert
Rosasite *
Scheelite
Siderite
Silver
Smithsonite
Sphalerite
Talc

Tellurium minerals
Tenorite, var.
  Melaconite
Tetrahedrite
Tourmaline
Tremolite
"Wad"
Wolframite
Wollastonite
Zoisite

* Specimen from the Carnahan mine donated by Sherman P. Marsh, June, 1960.

In addition to the minerals listed above, the following are cited by Atkinson (1960):

Apatite
Augite
Copper
Goethite
Hemimorphite

Plagioclase
  Andesine
  Labradorite
Quartz
  Amethyst
Serpentine
Sphene

Old Placers Mining District

This district, located in the Ortiz Mountains, has been known as Dolores, El Real de Dolores, Lone Mountain, Ortiz, Ortiz Mountain, Rio Galisteo (in part), Sierra del Oro, Sierra Obscura, and The Placer.

Aegirite(?)
Apatite
Argentite
Arsenopyrite
Augite
Bornite!
Calcite
Chalcopyrite
Chlorite
Copper
Epidote
Feldspar
Galena
Garnet
  Pyrope
Gold
  Placer gold!
Hematite
  Specularite

Hornblende
Idocrase
Ilmenite
Kaolinite
"Limonite"
Magnetite
Malachite
Molybdenite
Muscovite
  Sericite
Nepheline
Olivine
Pyrite
Quartz
Scheelite!
Siderite!
Sphene
Talc
Wollastonite

In addition to the minerals listed above, recent petrographic work on the rocks of the Ortiz Mountains (McRae, 1958; Peterson, 1958) has yielded the following:

Actinolite
  Uralite
Allanite(?)
Biotite
Calcite
  Travertine
Diopside(?)
Leucite(?)
"Leucoxene"
Orthoclase

Penninite
Plagioclase
  Andesine
  Labradorite
Quartz
  Chert
Tremolite
Zircon
Zoisite
Saussurite

VALENCIA COUNTY

For uranium minerals of the Grants and Laguna mining districts, see paper by A. Rosenzweig, this Guidebook.

REFERENCES

Atkinson, W. W., Jr., 1960, Geology of the San Pedro Mountains, Santa Fe County, New Mexico: Univ. New Mexico unpub. master's thesis, 81 p.

Bruns, J. J., 1959, Petrology of the Tijeras greenstone, Bernalillo County, New Mexico: Univ. New Mexico unpub. master's thesis, 119 p.

Disbrow, A. E., and Stoll, W. C., 1957, Geology of the Cerrillos area, Santa Fe County, New Mexico: New Mexico Bur. Mines and Mineral Res. Bull. 48, 73 p.

Lodewick, R. B., 1960, Geology and petrography of the Tijeras gneiss, Bernalillo County, New Mexico: Univ. New Mexico unpub. master's thesis, 63 p.

McRae, O. M., 1958, Geology of the northern part of the Ortiz Mountains, Santa Fe County, New Mexico: Univ. New Mexico unpub. master's thesis, 112 p.

Northrop, S. A., 1959, Minerals of New Mexico, rev. ed.: Albuquerque, Univ. New Mexico Press, xvi, 665 p.

Peterson, J. W., 1958, Geology of the southern part of the Ortiz Mountains, Santa Fe County, New Mexico: Univ. New Mexico unpub. master's thesis, 115 p.

PETROLEUM EXPLORATION IN A PART OF NORTH-CENTRAL NEW MEXICO

EDWARD C. BEAUMONT
Consultant, Albuquerque, New Mexico

The area shown on the accompanying maps (Figs. 1 and 2) comprises about 9,000 square miles which amounts to about 7 per cent of the area of New Mexico. It is difficult to conceive of another map of similar dimensions which might embrace a greater diversity of geologic conditions. The northwestern part of the map includes a portion of the San Juan Basin of the Colorado Plateau province whereas the east-central and southeastern parts of the map include most of the Estancia basin and the west flank of the Pedernal uplift—units sometimes assigned to the Great Plains province, but by Fenneman (1930) to the Basin and Range province. Separating segments of the Rocky Mountain province in the northern part of the map-area and lying between the Colorado Plateau and Great Plains (or Basin and Range) provinces farther south there is the Rio Grande trough and its flanking uplifts—an area of debatable major province association.

The problems and challenges presented to those searching for oil and gas are commensurate with the geologic variation. Although touching to the northwest on the prolific oil- and gas-producing region of the San Juan Basin and lying between that area and the area of even greater production in southeastern New Mexico, the area of this report remains, as of this writing, essentially nonproductive. Nevertheless, the wide range of geologic prospects continues to attract the petroleum industry, and in a period of more than 40 years almost 200 tests have been drilled. Only about a dozen of these tests have become commercially productive of either oil or gas and all of these are in the San Juan Basin (Fig. 2). Encouragement has been derived from numerous reports of shows of either oil or gas or both, as well as several other natural resources that have been encountered in commercial or potentially commercial quantities.

Just about half of the 199 wells shown on the maps (Figs. 1 and 2) and listed in Table 1 are within or on the margin of the San Juan Basin—an area amounting to less than one-tenth of the total map area. The other half are distributed through the remaining area of the map, but about 80 percent of the extra-San Juan Basin tests lie in the southern third of the map area. The northern two-thirds of the map area east of the San Juan Basin has had but a few scattered tests, and quite naturally some of the higher uplifts in which Precambrian rocks are exposed have gone untested.

If it were not for the delineation of the Rio Grande trough, a cursory examination of Figure 1 might lead one to conclude that the narrow band of tests across the lower part of the map is alined along some east-west-trending geologic feature. This band reaches from the Lucero uplift region of the Colorado Plateau across the Rio Grande trough and through the Estancia basin segment of the Great Plains (or Basin and Range) province. Although the present geologic divisions are based principally upon Laramide structural developments, and pre-Laramide trends might well cross these boundaries, it is likely that the apparent alinement is coincidental.

The Rio Grande trough probably represents the area of least knowledge with respect to oil and gas potential within the area of interest—despite having been the site of considerable exploratory activity. The abruptness and magnitude of this depression is illustrated by the deepest test in the map area, Humble #1 Santa Fe Pacific test (Ref. no. 12), which is located about six miles east of exposures of Mesozoic and Paleozoic strata along the western margin of the trough. This test penetrated nearly 10,000 feet of Quaternary and Tertiary sediments before entering Cretaceous strata and is presumed to have bottomed in Cretaceous rocks at 12,691 feet. Just north of Albuquerque the Norrins Realty No. 2 fee test bottomed in Tertiary sediments at 5,024 feet from a surface elevation of 4,950 feet—about five miles west of the Sandia Mountains where Precambrian rocks attain an elevation of over 9,000 feet. A remote wildcat test in the Rio Grande trough east of Espanola, the Castle and Wigzell No. 1 Federal (Ref. no. 199), has been spudded and promises to shed some light on this structural feature should it be drilled to its anticipated total depth.

Oil and gas have been discovered and produced from three small fields in Sandoval County, but two of the fields, the Torreon-Mesaverde in T. 19 N., R. 4 W. and the Media-Entrada in T. 19 N., R. 3 W. have been abandoned. Production is still being obtained from the San Luis-Mesaverde field in T. 18 N., R. 3 W., and many wells are being drilled or are nearing completion in that township.

Discovery of carbon dioxide as early as 1926 led to the development of New Mexico's first carbon-dioxide plant in 1934 north of Estancia. Natural depletion, water encroachment, and changing economic conditions brought this once-flourishing industry to a conclusion. The reported discovery of sizable quantities of steam in the Westates Petroleum Company's No. 1 Bond et al. test, which is located within the Jemez caldera in northern Sandoval County (Ref. no. 198), caused considerable speculation as to the commercial possibilities of this potential source of energy. The development of ground water is a natural product of unsuccessful petroleum exploration and many of the tests shown have been completed as water wells.

Space and time will not permit even the broadest discussion of the many intriguing tests drilled in the various parts of the map area. The accompanying table is intended to present the factual data concerning all oil and gas (including carbon-dioxide) tests known to have been drilled or currently being drilled within the area. The data assembled in Table 1 are drawn from many sources, but principally from U. S. Geological Survey Circular 333 (Dixon and others, 1954), New Mexico Bureau of Mines and Mineral Resources petroleum exploration maps of the various counties, and various commercial reports.

The tabular information is not consistent throughout. The completeness of the available data varies considerably from well to well. The writer also found numerous discrepancies in the information pertaining to many of the tests as obtained from the various sources, and it was impossible to reconcile many of these. Therefore the data in the table are not purported to be completely accurate, but the writer hopes that it represents an improvement on previous compilations.

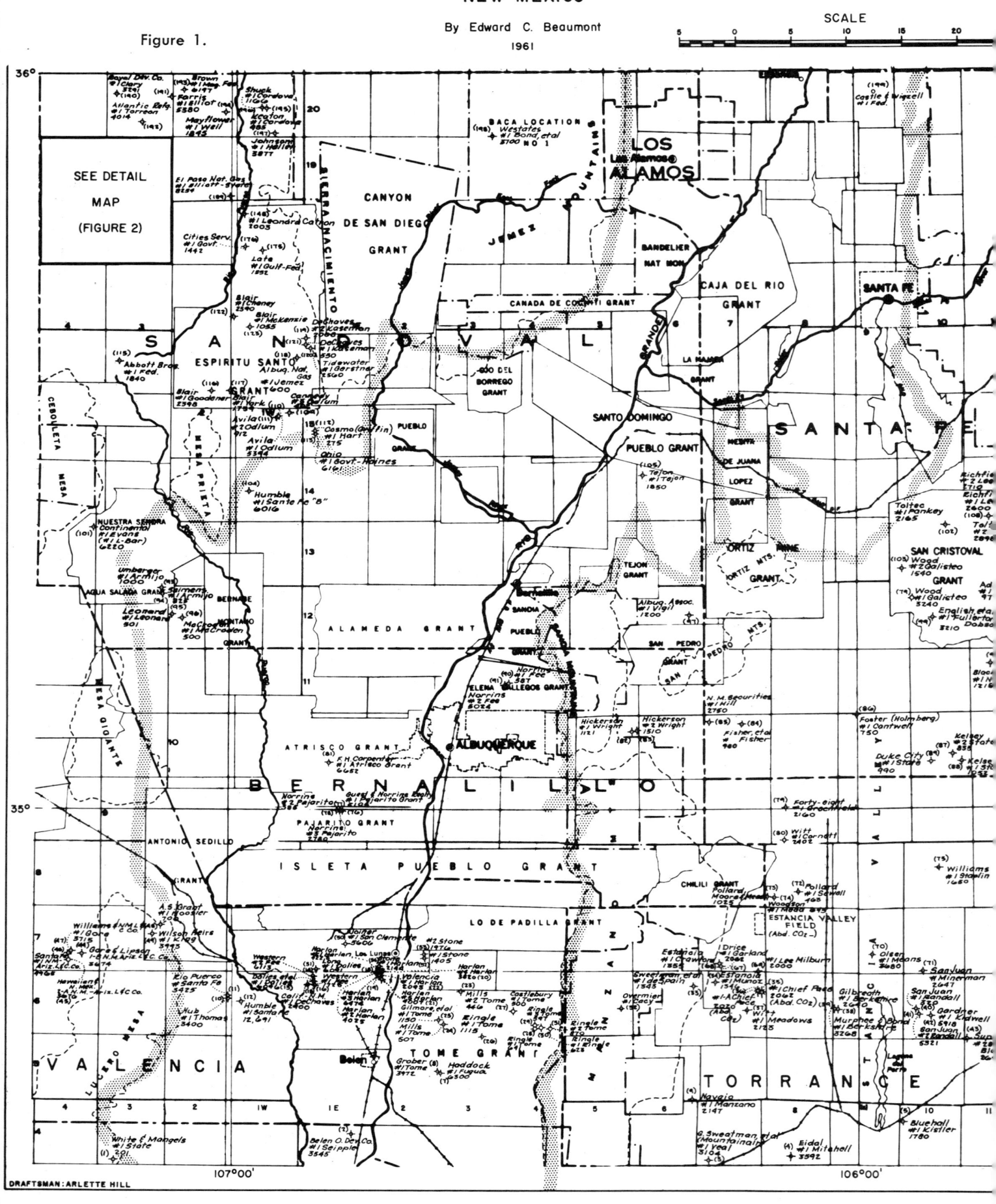

DRY-HOLE MAP OF A PART OF CENTRAL NEW MEXICO

By Edward C. Beaumont
1961

Figure 1.

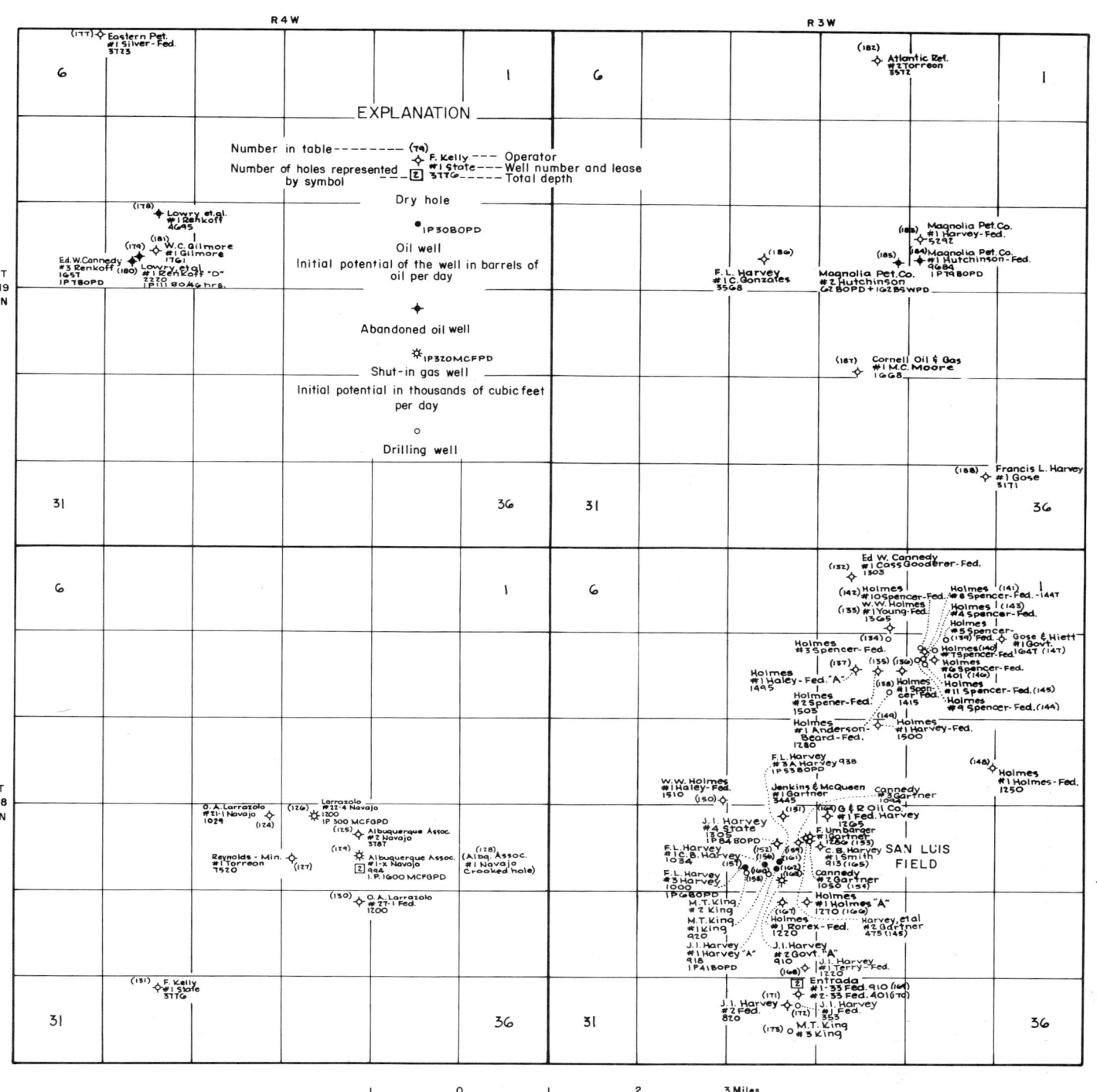

Figure 2. — Map showing area of production and greatest exploration activity, Sandoval County. See northwest corner of Figure 1 for location.

Table 1. Oil and gas tests drilled in a part of north-central New Mexico.

REF. NO.	Twp.	Rge.	Section	County	OPERATOR, LEASE, AND WELL NUMBER	STATUS AND DATE	ELEV.	TOTAL DEPTH	BOTTOM FM.	PRODUCTION, SHOWS, TESTS, AND TOPS
1	4N	3W	SENW 32	Socorro	F. B. White & G. T. Mangels, 1 State	A 1947	6200	201	pє?	
2	4N	1E	NENENE 23	Torrance	Belen Oil & Devel. Co., Seipple 1	A 1931		3545	Pa	SO 2375
3	4N	7E	NMSW 32	"	G. Sweatman et al., J. E. Veal & W. M. Parnell 1	A 1952	6540	3104	P?	SO 2190, 2600, 2835
4	4N	8E	SWNNE 33	"	Eidal Mfg. Co., B. L. Mitchell 1	A 1947	6350	3592	pє	SG 3460, T/Pa 851, IP 2090
5	4N	10E	CNWSW 7	"	Bluehall Oil & Gas Co., Kistler 1	A 1931	6258	1785	P	SG (CO$_2$) 1400
6	5N	2E		Valencia	C. S. Ringle, L. Gabaldone 1	A 1936		750		(Not on map)
7	5N	3E	NENE 19	"	Haddock Construction Co., Wm Fugua 1	A 1946		6300		
8	5N	3E	NWNE 19	"	Grober, Tome Grant 1	A 1940	6500	3972		SO 3928; SG 900
9	5N	6E	SWSWSW 36	Torrance	Navajo Oil, Manzano 1	A 1931		2147	IP?	SO 1104, 1208
10	6N	2W	NESENE 13	Valencia	Hubb Oil Co., Thomas 1	A 1931		3400	Jm	
11	6N	2W	SWNENE 13	"	Rio Puerco Oil Co., Re: Hubb Oil Co. Ball 1	A 1931		3425		
12	6N	1W	CSESE 18	"	Humble Oil & Ref., 1 Santa Fe & Pacific	A 1953	5092 DF	12,691	K?	SO 3350, 4600
13	6N	1E	CSWSE 5	"	Dalies and von Glahn, E. Y. Sketchley 1 Dalies	A 1949	5298	6096	Kd?	
14	6N	1E	SWSWNE 5	"	West Natl. Res. Corp., re: Big Three Oil Co., De Chavez 2	A 1939		6113	Kd?	
15	6N	1E	NWNWNW 8	"	Navajo Pet. Co., re: Calif.-N. Mex. Oil Synd. 1 De Chavez	A 1931		2900	IP	
16	6N	1E	SENWNE 8	"	West Natl. Res. Corp., N. Duran- De Chavez Grant 1	A 1932		1725	Tsf	
17	6N	2E	NWNWNE 5	"	Harlan et al., Harlan 1	A 1931	4841	4223		SG 2510
18	6N	2E	NWNWNE 5	"	Harlan et al., Harlan 2	A 1931	4841	4025	Kmv?	
19	6N	2E	NWNWNE 5	"	Harlan et al., Harlan 3	A 1931	4841	6900?		TD may be 4021
20	6N	2E	NNWNE 5	"	Harlan et al., Harlan 4	A 1931	4841	3820		
21	6N	2E	NSWSE 5	"	Harlan et al., Harlan 5	A 1932	4841	4007		
22	6N	2E	SWNE 5	"	Valencia Pet. Co., Harlan 1	A		2039		
23	6N	3E	SESE 9	"	Homer C. Mills, 2 Tome Grant	A		446		
24	6N	3E	SWSWNW 29	"	H. C. Mills, Inc., Tome Grant 1	A 1933		507		
25	6N	3E	NENE 30	"	Gilmore and Sheldon, Tome Grant 1	A 1931	4877	1180		
26	6N	3E	CSESE 35	"	Ringle Devel. Co., Tome Grant 1	A 1936	4800	1115		

REF. NO.	LOCATION Twp.	Rge.	Section	County	OPERATOR, LEASE, AND WELL NUMBER	STATUS AND DATE	ELEV.	TOTAL DEPTH	BOTTOM FM.	PRODUCTION, SHOWS, TESTS AND TOPS
27	6N	4E	SENWSW 20	Valencia	S. M. Castleberry, 1 Tome Grant	A 1948	5140	500		
28	6N	4E	SWNENW 34	"	C. S. Ringle, Tome Grant 1	A 1946		641		
29	6N	4E	NNENW 34	"	C. S. Ringle, Tome 3	A 1948	5600	597		
30	6N	4E	SWNENE 34	"	C. S. Ringle, Ringle 1	1947	6150	623		
31	6N	4E	SENWNE 35	"	C. S. Ringle, Tome Grant 2	A 1947		870		SO 530-60
32	6N	5E	SENE 23	Torrance	C. L. Overmire & W. L. Cacy, 1 Cacy	TA 1958	7501 Gr	955		Reported good SO 885-911; reported swbd 70 BO/48 hrs
33	6N	6E	CSENW 12	"	Sweetman, Parnell & Aday, 1 de Spain	1954		1343	pЄ?	SOG 1027
34	6N	6E	NESW 5	"	Munoz Oil Co., Strong 1	A 1931	6800	1346	pЄ	
35	6N	7E	WSE 12	"	Chief Oil and Gas, 1 Pace	A 1940		2062		Abandoned CO_2 well
36	6N	7E	NWSW 12	"	Chief Oil and Gas, 1-A Pace (2 Pace)	A 1940		2020		Abandoned CO_2 well
37	6N	7E	NSWNE 23	"	Witt Ice and Gas Co., F. T. Meadows 1	A 1945		2123	pЄ	
38	6N	9E	CNENW 19	"	F. E. Gilbreath, Berkshire 1	A 1950		2640	IP	T/ IP 1588
39	6N	9E	NWNENW 19	"	Murphee & Bond Drlg. Co., 1 Berkshire	A 1948	6101	3268	pЄ	
40	6N	10E	NWNW 19	"	San Juan Coal & Oil Co., 1 Randell			320		
41	6N	10E	NESW 20	"	San Juan Coal & Oil Co., Randell 2	A 1931	6100	5321	pЄ	SO 3537
42	6N	10E	SESESW 21	"	Gardner Petroleum Co., Ed Kidwell 1	A 1954	6177 DF	5918	pЄ	T/IP 1865, pЄ 5900
43	6N	11E	SESWSW 31	"	Superior Oil Co., 28-31 Blackwell	A 1954	6136 DF	2646	pЄ	T/Abo 940, IP 1410, pЄ 2590
44	7N	4W	SENW 26	Valencia	Gore & Lipson, 1-B N.Mex. Ariz. L.&C.	A 1958	6052 Gr	3674	pЄ	T/Py 398, Pa 1435, **IP** 2645
45	7N	4W	NESWNW 27	"	Hawaiian & N.Mex. Oil Ventures, 2-A N.Mex.-Ariz. L. & C. Co.	TA 1959	6061 DF	3676	IP?	
46	7N	4W	WSWNW 27	"	Acme Oil Co., N.M.-Ariz. L. & C. Co. 1	A 1935		4965	pЄ	
47	7N	4W	CNWSW 27	"	Williams & Gore, 1 N.M.-Ariz. L. & C.Co. A	1957	5958 Gr	3663	**P**?	T/Psa 120, Psg 270, Py 430, Pa 1435, IP 2700
48	7N	3W	SENWSE 12	"	Hoosier Oil Co., Valley 1	A 1932		700		
49	7N	3W	NENESE 14	"	Richard King, Jr., 1 Wilson Heirs Unit	A 1958	5884 Gr	3993	pЄ	T/Pa 1076, IP 2000, pЄ 3944, pЄ gr 3990
50	7N	1E	NESENW 23	"	Joiner Oil Corp., San Clemente Grant 1	A 1939		5606		SG 4202-4306
51	7N	1E	CSESE 32	"	H. C. Long, Dalies 1	A 1952		6091		
52	7N	2E	SENWNW 25	"	A. W. Stone et al., 1	A 1931		1405		SO 902
53	7N	2E	SENWNW 25	"	Swisher & Wallace, re: A. W. Stone et al., 2	A 1931		1976		

REF. NO.	Twp.	Rge.	Section	County	OPERATOR, LEASE, AND WELL NUMBER	STATUS AND DATE	ELEV.	TOTAL DEPTH	BOTTOM FM.	PRODUCTION, SHOWS, TESTS, AND TOPS
54	7N	2E	NENESW 32	Valencia	A. W. Stone, Harlan 1	A 1931		2144		
55	7N	7E	SWSE 1	Torrance	Estancia Valley CO_2 Devel. Co., Kellog 2	A 1936	6552	1415	IP?	IP 679,000 CF CO_2 PD
56	7N	7E	CSENW 12	"	Estancia Valley CO_2 Co., DeHart 2	1934	6526 DF	1545		
57	7N	7E	SESWNE 12	"	Estancia Valley CO_2 Co., DeHart 3	1936	6540 DF	1264		
58	7N	7E	SESWNE 12	"	Estancia Valley CO_2 Co., DeHart 4			1236		
59	7N	7E	SESWNE 12	"	Estancia Valley CO_2 Co., DeHart 5	1937	6534 DF	1258		
60	7N	7E	NWNE 12	"	Estancia Valley CO_2 Co., Kellogg 1	1935	6550 DF	1268		
61	7N	7E	CSESE 12	"	Estancia Valley CO_2 Devel. Co., C. B. Roland 1	A 1934		1359		SG 168, 1214, 1267
62	7N	7E	NENW? 12	"	Estancia Valley CO_2 Co., Wilcox 4			1050?		
63	7N	7E	SWSESE 12	"	Sinoco Oil, DeHart 1	A 1931		765	IP	SG 208
64	7N	7E	NESESW 12	"	Sinoco Oil Co., DeHart 2	1931	6151 Gr	1440		IP 140,000 CF CO_2 PD from 1270'
65	7N	7E	NWNENW 13	"	Estancia Valley CO_2 Co., Kutchin 1	1937	6644 Gr	1428		
66	7N	7E	CNENW 13	"	Sinoco Oil Co., Kutchin 1	1929		299		
67	7N	7E	NESENE 32	"	The Drice Co., Garland 1	A 1941	6280?	2062	p€	
68	7N	7E	SENENE 32	"	Estancia Valley CO_2 Devel. Co., Crawford 1	A 1939		1355		
69	7N	7E	SWSW 36	"	Orville J. Lee, Milburn 1	A 1941		2000	p€	SG 1717-22, 1769, 1792, SO 368
70	7N	9E	CNMNW 27	"	R. Olsen Oil Co., H. Means, Jr. 1	A 1950	6000	3680	p€	
71	7N	10E	SWSE 32	"	San Juan Coal & Oil, Minerman 1	A 1931	6132	2647	P	
72	8N	8E	CNENE 28	"	Pollard Bros., 1 H. J. Sewell	1956		463		
73	8N	8E	CSWSW 30	"	Pollard Bros., 1 Moore & Mead	1956		1025		
74	8N	8E	SWSWSE 30	"	Woodson, 1 Moore-Mead	1956		645		
75	8N	10E	NENENE 16	"	H. L. Williams, Staplin 1	A 1931	6350	1650	P	
76	9N	1E	NWNE 22	Bernalillo	E. B. Guest & Norrins Realty Co., Pajarito Grant 1	A 1946		5104	P?	Reported in sh., red ss., and ls. below 4906
77	9N	1E	NWMNE 22	"	Norrins Realty Co., Norrins Realty Co. 3	A 1946	5300	2780		
78	9N	1E	NENE 22	"	Norrins Realty, Pajarito Grant 2			385		
79	9N	8E	CNMSW 17	Torrance	Forty-eight Prod. Co., Greenfield 1	A 1937	6100	2160	p€?	SG 530, 1500

REF. NO.	Twp.	Rge.	Section	County	OPERATOR, LEASE, AND WELL NUMBER	STATUS AND DATE	ELEV.	TOTAL DEPTH	BOTTOM FM.	PRODUCTION, SHOWS, TESTS, AND TOPS
80	9N	8E	CNESW 32	Torrance	Witt Ice & Gas Co., Cornett 1	A 1944		2402		
81	10N	1E	CSESE 28	Bernalillo	F. H. Carpenter, Atrisco Grant 1	A 1942	5772	6652	Tsf?	SO 3350-60
82	10N	5E	SESENW 12	"	L. O. Hickerson, Wright 1	A 1947		1121	Km	
83	10N	5E	SWSWNE 12	"	L. O. Hickerson, Wright 2	A 1948	6554	1510	Jm	
84	10N	7E	SW 3	Santa Fe	Fisher & Wolcott, Fisher	A 1931		980		
85	10N	7E	NENESW 6	"	N. Mex. Securities Co., Hill 1	A 1935	7000	2750	pЄ	SO 1365, 1850, 2585; SG 850, 1050
86	10N	9E	NWNNW 5	"	Sam Foster, Cantwell 1	A 1935		750		
87	10N	10E	22	"	Kelsey Clients Co., State 2	A 1937	6638	835	P	
88	10N	10E	SWSWNE 26	"	Kelsey Clients Devel. Co., State 1	A 1933		1052	P	
89	10N	10E	NESE 29	"	Duke City Pet., State 1	A 1931		990	Tsf	
90	11N	4E	SENNNW 19	Bernalillo	Norrins Realty Co., Norrins Realty Co. 1	A 1936	4950	587	Tsf	
91	11N	4E	SENNNW 19	"	Norrins Realty Co., Norrins Realty Co. 2	A 1940	4950	5024	Pa?	
92	11N	11E	SMNNW 9	Santa Fe	J. H. Blackstone, Neville 1	A 1950	5900	1215	Jm	T/Pa 65, T/IP 520
93	12N	3W	SENNNW 1	Sandoval	P. B. Umbarger, Armijo 1	A 1946	6000	1000	Km?	
94	12N	3W	SESW 1	"	Siemens & Boyd, D. Armijo 1	A 1941	5700	325	Km	T/IP 2490, pЄ 3200
95	12N	2W	SESWSE 18	"	H. Leonard, H. Leonard 1	A 1934	5700	501	Km	
96	12N	2W	NWNNNW 20	"	N. G. McCrodan, N. G. McCrodan 1	A 1934		500	IP	
97	12N	6E	NWSE 14	Santa Fe	Albuquerque Associates, 1 Vigil	TA 1954	6561	1200	IP	
98	12N	10E	NENENE 7	"	Wood et al., Galisteo (Pan Key) 1	A 1931	6444 Gr	3240	pЄ	
99	12N	10E	SSESE 16	"	P. B. English, Fullerton Dobson 1	A 1945	7120	3210	pЄ	
100	12N	11E	SWNNW 23	"	E. S. Adkins, H. H. Basher 1	A 1945	6265	977	pЄ	
101	13N	4W	SESENE 2	Sandoval	Continental Oil Co., L Bar Cattle 1 Evans	A 1935	6149 DF	6220	pЄ	Kd 258, Jm 290, Trc 1330, Psa 2765, Pg 2865, Pa 3630, IP 4815, pЄ 6134
102	13N	10E	SW 2	Santa Fe	Toltec Oil Co., Panky (Eaton) 1	A 1918	6900	2165	pЄ	
103	13N	10E	SW 30	"	Wood et al., 2 Galisteo	A 1931		1540		
104	14N	1W	NMNNW 20	Sandoval	Humble Oil & Ref., 1 Santa Fe Pac. "B"	A 1954		6016	pЄ	Sa T/IP 4930, T/pЄ 6008 (El Psa 2730, Py 3492)
105	14N	6E	7	"	Tejon Oil Co., 1	A 1914		1850		SO 1000
106	14N	11E	14	Santa Fe	Richfield Oil Corp., Lee 2	A 1945		2725	pЄ	

REF. NO.	Twp.	Rge.	LOCATION Section	County	OPERATOR, LEASE, AND WELL NUMBER	STATUS AND DATE	ELEV.	TOTAL DEPTH	BOTTOM FM.	PRODUCTION, SHOWS, TESTS, AND TOPS
107	14N	11E	CSWNW 25	Santa Fe	Richfield Oil Corp., Lee 1	A 1945	7098	2588	pɛ	
108	14N	11E	NWSESW 33	"	Toltec Oil Co., Panky 2	1919		2898		
109	15N	1W	NESESE 11	Sandoval	Cannedy & Larrazolo, 3 Odlum	A 1955	5710 Gr	402	Je	T/Jt 270, T/Je 396
110	15N	1W	NNENE 15	"	Avila Oil Co., 1 Odlum	A 1953	5963 KB	5394	pɛ	T/Jt 742, Je 858, Trc 1043, Psa 2151, Psg 2308, Pa 3693, IP 4551, pɛq 5250
111	15N	1W	NNENE 15	"	Avila Oil Co., 2 Odlum	A 1954	5944 Gr	912	Je	T/Je 860
112	15N	1E	SWNW 20	"	Percy Griffin, 1 Federal (Hart)	A 1954	5726 Gr	275	Trw	
113	15N	1E	NESWSW 20	"	Ohio Oil Co., 1 Ohio-Govt. Haines	A 1960	5761 Gr	6161	pɛ?	T/Trc 300, Traz 2250, Py 2422, Pa 3950
114	15N	5E		"	Anschutz & Guest, Tejon Spanish Grant 1	A 1931		550	Kd	Not shown on map
115	16N	3W	CSWSW 17	"	Abbott Bros., 1 Fed.	TA 1959	6100 DF	1840	Kd?	
116	16N	2W	SWNESE 34	"	Blair & Price, 1 Goodener	A 1955	6292 Gr	2398	Je	T/Kd 1300, T/Je 2333
117	16N	2W	CNWSE 36	"	Blair & Price, 1 Jess York	A 1955	6050 Gr	1759	Je	
118	16N	1W	13	"	Albuquerque Nat. Gas Co., Jemez 1	A 1931		600		
119	16N	1E	SW 6	"	De Chavez Pet. Co., Kaseman 2	A 1932		2008	P	T/P 1911, pɛ gr. 2480
120	16N	1E	NENWSE 7	"	Tide Water Assoc. Oil Co., Gerstner 1	A 1949	6220	2560	pɛ	
121	16N	1E	7	"	De Chavez Pet. Co., Kaseman 1	A 1925		550		
122	17N	2W	SENWSE 25	"	Jack N. Blair, 1 Cheney	A 1955	6362 Gr	2390	Je	T/Kd 1395, T/Jm 1810, T/Je 2359
123	17N	1W	SWNESE 32	"	Blair & Price, 1 McKenzie	A 1955	6051 Gr	1055	Je	T/Je 1049
124	18N	4W	NENE 21	"	O. A. Larrazolo, 22-1 Navajo	A 1959	6405 Gr	1200	Kmv	PB 973, Perf. 878-904 Compl.as W
125	18N	4W	NWSENE 22	"	Albuquerque Assoc., 2 Navajo	A 1953	6348 DF	3787	Jm?	T/Kd 3450, Jm 3662, Kd 4208
126	18N	4W	NENW 22	"	O. A. Larrazolo, 22-4 Navajo	Gas 1959	6429 Gr	1200		IP 300 MCFPD 1056-1109 Kmv
127	18N	4W	CNWSW 22	"	Reynolds Mining, 1 Torreon	A 1956	6388 DF	7520		T/Kd 3471, Jm 3738, Je 4585, Trc 4792, Pc 5891
128	18N	4W	CNESE 22	"	Albuquerque Assoc., 1 Navajo	A 1953		100		Crooked hole, skidded rig
129	18N	4W	NWNESE 22	"	Albuquerque Assoc., 1-X Navajo	Gas 1953	6290 Gr	994	Kmv	IP: 594, MCF 3 hrs from Kmf
130	18N	4W	NENE 27	"	O. A. Larrazolo, 27-1 Fed.	A 1959	6329 Gr	1200	Kmv	SG 490-500, 645-660, 880-950, 1090-1100
131	18N	4W	CNWNE 32	"	F. F. Kelly, State 1	A 1953	6490 DF	3776	Jm	PB 1025 T/Kd 3380
132	18N	3W	NSENW 3	"	Ed W. Cannedy (John Fidel), 1 Cass Goodener Fed.	TA 1955	6619 Gr	1303	Kmv?	T/Kmf 681
133	18N	3W	CSWSESE 3	"	W. W. Holmes, 1 Young-Fed.	A 1961	6683 Gr	1365	Kmv	
134	18N	3W	NWNENE 10	"	W. W. Holmes, 3 Spencer-Fed.	Loc. 1961	6678 Gr			

REF. NO.	LOCATION Twp.	Rge	Section	County	OPERATOR, LEASE, AND WELL NUMBER	STATUS AND DATE		ELEV.	TOTAL DEPTH	BOT-TOM FM.	PRODUCTION, SHOWS, TESTS, AND TOPS
135	18N	3W	SESWNE 10	Sandoval	W. W. Holmes, 2 Spencer-Fed.		1961	6741 Gr	1503		T/Kpl 1375
136	18N	3W	SESENE 10	"	W. W. Holmes, 1 Spencer-Fed.	A	1961	6696 Gr	1415	Kmv	
137	18N	3W	SESENW 10	"	W. W. Holmes, 1 Haley-Fed. "A"	A	1959	6644 Gr	1495	Kmv	Several slight shows of oil in cores
138	18N	3W	SWNESE 10	"	W. W. Holmes, 1 Anderson Beard-Fed.	Dlg.	1961	6715 Gr	1280	Kmv	Spud 6/3/61
139	18N	3W	NENENW 11	"	W. W. Holmes, 5 Spencer-Fed.			6775 Gr			Loc. 7/12/61
140	18N	3W	SWNENW 11	"	W. W. Holmes, 7 Spencer-Fed.			6755 Gr			Loc. 7/12/61
141	18N	3W	SENWNW 11	"	W. W. Holmes, 8 Spencer-Fed.		1961	6750 Gr	1447		
142	18N	3W	SENWNW 11	"	W. W. Holmes, 10 Spencer-Fed.			6692 Gr			Loc. 7/12/61
143	18N	3W	NESWNW 11	"	W. W. Holmes, 4 Spencer-Fed.			6708 Gr	1145		Rec. 3' sd w/ bleeding oil from core #2 1139-45; 120 fillup oil; testing 7/12/61
144	18N	3W	SWNW 11	"	W. W. Holmes, 9 Spencer-Fed.	A	1961		1470		
145	18N	3W	NESWNW 11	"	W. W. Holmes, 11 Spencer-Fed.	Dlg.	1961	6709 Gr	1401		Spud 6/26/61
146	18N	3W	NWSENW 11	"	W. W. Holmes, 6 Spencer-Fed.		1961	6714 Gr			
147	18N	3W	NWNWNW 12	"	F. H. Gose & C. Hiett, 1 Govt.	TA	1955	6680 Gr	1647	Km?	
148	18N	3W	NENESE 14	"	W. W. Holmes, 1 Holmes-Fed.	A	1961	6660 Gr	1250	Kmv	
149	18N	3W	NENNWE 15	"	W. W. Holmes, 1 Fed.-Harvey	A	1961	6682 Gr	1500	Kmv	
150	18N	3W	SESESE 17	"	W. W. Holmes, 1 Haley-Federal	A	1959	6673 Gr	1510	Kmv	
151	18N	3W	CNWNE 21	"	Jenkins & McQueen, Gartner 1	A	1948	6885	3445	Kd	
152	18N	3W	SWSENE 21	"	J. I. Harvey, 4 Harvey-Fed.	A	1959	6679 DF	1305	Kmv	Several shows of oil and gas
153	18N	3W	ESENE 21	"	F. B. Umbarger, C. B. Gartner 1	A	1950	6397	1287	Km	Completed as water well
154	18N	3W	CSENE 21	"	F. B. Umbarger, C. B. Gartner 2	A	1949	6623	1050	K	PB 811
155	18N	3W	SENE 21	"	Harvey et al., 2 Gartner		1949		475		
156	18N	3W	NESW 21	"	Francis L. Harvey, 1 Clyde Harvey Fed.	Dis	1960	6740 Gr	1024	Kmv	IP: 84 BOPD & 12 BWPD from 992-1000' in Kmv
157	18N	3W	SENWSW 21	"	F. L. Harvey, 3 Harvey	Oil	1961	6687 Gr	1000		IP 6 BOPD
158	18N	3W	NESWSW 21	"	Myron T. King, 2 King			6673 Gr			Loc. 7/12/61
159	18N	3W	SWSENE 21	"	E. W. Cannedy, 3 Gartner	TA	1955	6626 DF	1094		P.B. 932, SG 861-81
160	18N	3W	NESESW 21	"	Myron T. King, 1 King	WOO	1961	6650 Gr	920		Spud 7/2/61
161	18N	3W	SWNWSE 21	"	F. L. Harvey, 3-A Fed.	Oil	1961	6685 Gr	935		IP 53 BOPD/908-935' in Kmv
162	18N	3W	SWNWSE 21	"	J. I. Harvey, 1 Harvey-Fed. "A"	Oil	1959	6663 Gr	918	Kmv	IP: 41 BOPD from 891-918' (est. 200 MCFGPD)

REF. NO.	LOCATION				OPERATOR, LEASE, AND WELL NUMBER	STATUS AND DATE		ELEV.	TOTAL DEPTH	BOT-TOM FM.	PRODUCTION, SHOWS, TESTS, AND TOPS
	Twp.	Rge.	Section	County							
163	18N	3W	SWSE 21	Sandoval	J. I. Harvey, 2-A Federal	Gas	1959	6604 DF	910	Kmv	Gas Disc.
164	18N	3W	NWNW 22	"	G & R Oil Co., 1 Fed. Harvey		1950	6143 Gr	1265		
165	18N	3W	SWSWNW 22	"	Clyde B. Harvey, 1 Smith	A	1958	6605 Gr	913	Kmv	SO 502-525 & 565-70; T/Kpl 805
166	18N	3W	NENE 30	"	W. W. Holmes, 1 Holmes "A"	A	1961	6549 Gr	1270	Kmv	
167	18N	3W	NWNE 28	"	W. W. Holmes, 1 Rorex	A	1959	6695 DF	1215	Kmv	Slight SO 410-20, 594-609, 895
168	18N	3W	SESE 28	"	J. I. Harvey, 1 Terry-Fed.	A	1960	6477 Gr	1220		
169	18N	3W	SWNENE 33	"	Entrada Corp., 1-33 Fed.	A	1958	6464 Gr	910	Kmv	Slight SO 292-300, 314-19; wtr at 865
170	18N	3W	SWNENE 33	"	Entrada Corp., 2-33 Fed.	A	1958	6590 Gr	401	Kmv	Slight SO 292-328, sulfur wtr at TD
171	18N	3W	NESWNE 33	"	J. I. Harvey, 2 Fed.	A	1959	6462 Gr	820		
172	18N	3W	NWSENE 33	"	J. I. Harvey, 1 Fed.	A	1959	6540 Gr	353		Flowed 5 BO + 5 BWPD from 338-353
173	18N	3W	NENNWSE 33	"	Myron T. King, 3 King			6434			Loc. 7/12/61
174	18N	1W	CNNNE 7	"	H. Leonard et al., Catron Grant 1	A	1931	6774 Gr	2003	Jm	T/Ksa 760, T/Kd 1210, T/Jm 1555
175	18N	1W	NWSESW 28	"	Late Oil Co., 1 Gulf-Federal	A	1958	6460 Gr	1552	Jm	T/Kd 1264
176	18N	1W	NESWNE 30	"	Cities Service Oil Co., 1 Govt.	A	1953	6650 Gr	1442	Kd?	
177	19N	4W	NENE 6	"	Eastern Petroleum Co., 1 Silver-Fed.	A	1957	6643 Gr	3729	Km	DST 2164-2214 rec 60' free oil, 160' MCO, 107' mud; T/Kch 834, Kmf 1475, Kpl 2350, Km 2480, Kgs 3460
178	19N	4W	SWNNNE 17	"	Lowry et al., 1 Renkoff	A	1953	6647 Gr	4695	Jm	Rec. shows at sev. depths on DST's; PB 2212 T/Kd 4380
179	19N	4W	NESW 17	"	Lowry Oil, 1 "D" Renkoff	A	1954	6774 Gr	2220		Pumped 61 BO, 3 BW in 48 hrs from Kmv; respudded 1954 and drilled to TD.
180	19N	4W	SWNESW 17	"	Ed W. Cannedy, 3 Renkoff	TA	1957	6638 DF	1657	Kgs	Pumped 7 BOPD, SI
181	19N	4W	NWNWSE 17	"	W. C. Gilmore, 1 Gilmore	A	1957	6675 Gr	1761		
182	19N	3W	SENE 3	"	Atlantic Refining, 2 Torreon	A	1961	6806 DF	3572		Strat test; no information released
183	19N	3W	CSWNW 14	"	Magnolia Petroleum, 1 Harvey-Fed.	A	1954	6841 DF	5292	Je	T/Kd 4205, Je 5215, Je 5231; DST 5217-32 Rec. 90' sli O&CM, 90' sli O&WCM
184	19N	3W	CNWSW 14	"	Magnolia Petroleum, 1 Hutchison-Fed.	Oil	1953	6841 DF	9684	pE	T/Km 2114, Je 5215, Je 5197; IP: 62 BO & 162 BSW in 24 hrs from 5200-02
185	19N	3W	CNESE 15	"	Magnolia Petroleum, 2 Hutchison	Oil	1954	6868 DF	5202	Je	T/Kd 4172, Je 5197; IP: 62 BO & 162 BSW in 24 hrs from 5200-02
186	19N	3W	CNESE 16	"	F. L. Harvey, 1 C. Gonzales	A	1956	6868 DF	3568	Km	P.B. 900', sold as wtr well
187	19N	3W	SESESW 22	"	Cornell O & G Corp., M.C. Moore 1	A	1952	6635	1668		
188	19N	3W	SENENE 35	"	Francis L. Harvey, 1 Gose	A	1956	6740 KB	3171	Km	

REF. NO.	Twp.	Rge.	Section	County	OPERATOR, LEASE, AND WELL NUMBER	STATUS AND DATE	ELEV.	TOTAL DEPTH	BOTTOM FM.	PRODUCTION, SHOWS, TESTS, AND TOPS
189	19N	2W	NWSENW 36	Sandoval	El Paso Natural Gas Co., 1 Elliott-State	A 1953	6668 DF	8254	pЄ	T/Kd 2825, Je 3925, Psa 5394, IP 7049, pЄ 8237
190	20N	3W	CSESE 7	"	Royal Dev. Co., 1 P. Clary	TA 1954	6885 DF	3291	Km	T/Kpc 965, Kl 1044, Kch 1634, Klv 1930, Km 3260
191	20N	3W	CNENE 13	"	Joe D. Farris, 1 Elliott	A 1957	7141 Gr	5380	Jm	T/Kpc 570, Kch 985, Km 2940, Kgs 3690, Kd 5080, Jm 5355
192	20N	3W	CNESW 27	"	Atlantic Refining Co., 1 Torreon	A 1961	6799 Gr	4014		Strat test; no information released
193	20N	2W	NWSW 8	"	A. N. Brown, 1 Magnolia-Fed.	A 1959	6875 Gr	6197	Je	T/Kpc 520, Kch 2025, Kpl 2706, Km 2910, Kd 5023, Jm 5215, Je 6055
194	20N	2W	SNESE 23	"	Mayflower O & G Co., Weil 1	A 1931		1845	Km	
195	20N	1W	NWNE 21	"	Keaton, 1 Cordova			985		
196	20N	1W	NWNWNW 21	"	Schuck, 1 Cordova	A 1953	6833 DF	1166		T/Kch 675, Kpl 1002
197	20N	1W	NESW 34	"	S. D. Johnson, 1 Heller		6923 KB	3877		T/Km 410, Kgl 1430, Kd 2706
198	20N	3E	CSESE 35	"	Westates Pet. Co., 1 Bond et al.	A 1960	8697 Gr	3700		Reported to have flowed 3-5,000 MCF steam PD
199	20N	9E	SWSWSW 11	Santa Fe	Castle & Wigzell, 1 Federal	Dlg 1961	6032 DF			Spudded 8/61

Abbreviations and symbols used in table:

Stratigraphic Units
K - Cretaceous rocks
Kl - Lewis shale
Kmv - Mesaverde group
Kch - Cliff House sandstone
Kmf - Menefee formation
Kpl - Point Lookout sandstone
Klv - La Ventana sandstone
Km - Mancos shale
Kgs - Gallup sandstone
Ksa - Sanostee formation
Kd - Dakota sandstone
Jm - Morrison formation
Jt - Todilto limestone
Je - Entrada sandstone
Tr - Triassic rocks
Trc - Chinle formation
Traz - Agua Zarca sandstone
Trs - Shinarump conglomerate
P - Permian rocks
Pc - Cutler formation
Psa - San Andres formation
Psg - Glorieta sandstone
Py - Yeso formation
Pa - Abo formation
IP - Pennsylvanian rocks
pЄ - Precambrian rocks
pЄg - Precambrian granite
pЄq - Precambrian quartzite

Other Symbols
A - Dry and abandoned
BOPD - Barrels of oil per day
BSW - Barrels of salt water
BWPD - Barrels of water per day
DF - Derrick floor
Dis. - Discovery
Dlg. - Drilling
DST - Drill-stem test
El T/ - Formation top from electric log
Gr - Ground
KB - Kelly bushing
Loc. - Location
MCFPD - Thousand cubic feet per day
MCO - Mud-cut oil
OCM - Oil-cut mud
O&WCM - Oil-and water-cut mud
Sa T/ - Formation top from samples
SG - Show of gas
SI - Shut-in
SO - Show of oil
SOG - Show of oil and gas
T/ - Formation top
TA - Temporarily abandoned
TD - Total depth
WOO - Waiting on orders
Wtr - Water
WW - Water Well

GROUND-WATER GEOLOGY OF THE RIO GRANDE TROUGH IN NORTH-CENTRAL NEW MEXICO, WITH SECTIONS ON THE JEMEZ CALDERA AND THE LUCERO UPLIFT[1]

Frank B. Titus, Jr.
U. S. Geological Survey, Albuquerque, New Mexico

INTRODUCTION

The Rio Grande structural trough in north-central New Mexico contains a thick section of Tertiary and Quaternary rocks that serves as an underground reservoir for an immense volume of water. This paper briefly describes the interrelationship between geology and the occurrence of ground water in that part of the trough extending from Espanola southward to the Valencia County line a few miles south of Belen. The Ground Water Branch of the U. S. Geological Survey has been studying, since about 1949, the hydrologic conditions and the related geology in this area in cooperation with the New Mexico State Engineer Office, the State Bureau of Mines and Mineral Resources Division of the New Mexico Institute of Mining and Technology, the City of Albuquerque, and the Atomic Energy Commission at Los Alamos. This report is essentially a compilation of the published and publishable data and conclusions arrived at as a result of these projects. The area described in each of the several reports is shown on the source map for Figure 1. Bjorklund and Maxwell's report (1961) is the only one of the group to have been published to date. The work by Spiegel and Baldwin in the Santa Fe area (1958), Theis and Conover in the Los Alamos area (1961), and Theis, Conover, and Griggs in the Valle Grande and Valle Toledo area (1961) is presently available only in open-file reports of the Geological Survey, but each is in the process of publication. A report on eastern Valencia County is in preparation by the writer. In the remainder of the area, mostly in eastern Sandoval County, limited data on file in the Ground Water Branch office in Albuquerque were compiled to obtain the contours on the water-table and artesian-pressure surface shown on Figure 1.

AQUIFERS—THEIR GEOLOGY AND HYDROLOGY

All of the sedimentary rocks and some of the igneous rocks that crop out in the Rio Grande trough yield water to wells at one place or another. Generally, however, the sedimentary rocks of early and middle Tertiary age, which include the Galisteo formation, and the Espinaso volcanics and Cieneguilla limburgite of Stearns (1953), have low permeabilities and are capable of yielding only very small quantities of water. Ground water is obtained from these rocks locally where they crop out south and southwest of Santa Fe. The intrusive and extrusive rocks in this part of the area also produce small quantities of ground water locally. The important water-bearing and water-yielding stratigraphic units in the Rio Grande trough are the Santa Fe group and the Quaternary alluvium. These units have hydrologic characteristics that differ sharply from the early and middle Tertiary rocks upon which they rest and from the pre-Tertiary rocks that bound the trough on both sides. The relatively high porosity, permeability, and great combined thickness of the units result in the Rio Grande structural trough being a huge conduit through which ground water moves with relative ease.

Santa Fe Group

The Santa Fe group consists of several thousand feet of terrestrial sediments that were deposited in the subsiding Rio Grande trough between middle(?) Miocene time and Pleistocene(?) time. The group is composed mainly of interbedded silt, sand, and gravel. In general it is poorly indurated. However, the beds range from noncoherent to tightly cemented and highly compacted. Clay is present only in minor amounts in most of the Santa Fe. Terrace deposits in the incised valley occupied by the Rio Grande and elsewhere in the trough, which are sometimes lumped with the Santa Fe, often contain large amounts of this constituent. Spiegel and Baldwin (1958, p. 71-81), working in the Santa Fe area, recognized an underlying Tesuque formation consisting principally of pinkish tan silty sandstone, which forms the bulk of the Santa Fe group, and an overlying Ancha formation which consists of sand and gravel. They estimated the maximum thickness of the Ancha formation to be at least 300 feet. Most of the Santa Fe throughout its area of occurrence is lithologically similar to the Tesuque formation; gravel beds are subordinate constituents.

The thickness of the Santa Fe group has been reported at only a few locations. Spiegel and Baldwin estimated a thickness of several thousand feet in the vicinity of Santa Fe. Stearns (1953, p. 475) concluded from the driller's log of a deep test hole that the Santa Fe was about 2,150 feet thick at a point 9 miles northeast of Albuquerque. R. L. Bates (in Reiche, 1949, p. 1204), after studying the samples from an oil test located about 6 miles east of Belen, concluded that the thickness of the Santa Fe here was 4,550 feet. The maximum thickness of the Santa Fe recorded by Bjorklund and Maxwell (1961, p. 21) is 6,100 feet at a location about 12 miles west of Albuquerque.

Ground water has been obtained from the Santa Fe group wherever the unit has been tested within the Rio Grande trough. Pumping yields reported from the aquifer range from a few gallons per minute to several thousand gallons per minute. Care must be taken in interpreting these data, however, because the yields depend to a large extent upon the total thickness of saturated permeable beds penetrated by the well, and upon the construction of the well itself. Large-diameter wells, and wells that have been subjected to adequate well-completion procedures, remove water from the aquifer with relatively low pumping drawdown. Recognizing the limitations, it is still interesting to note some of the yields reported from the Santa Fe. In the vicinity of the city of Santa Fe and to the west of the city, maximum yields recorded by Spiegel (in Spiegel and Baldwin, 1958, figs. 38A, 38B) are on the order of 500 to 700 gpm (gallons per minute). The wells penetrate a few hundred feet of saturated Tesuque formation. A small

[1] Publication authorized by the Director, U. S. Geological Survey.

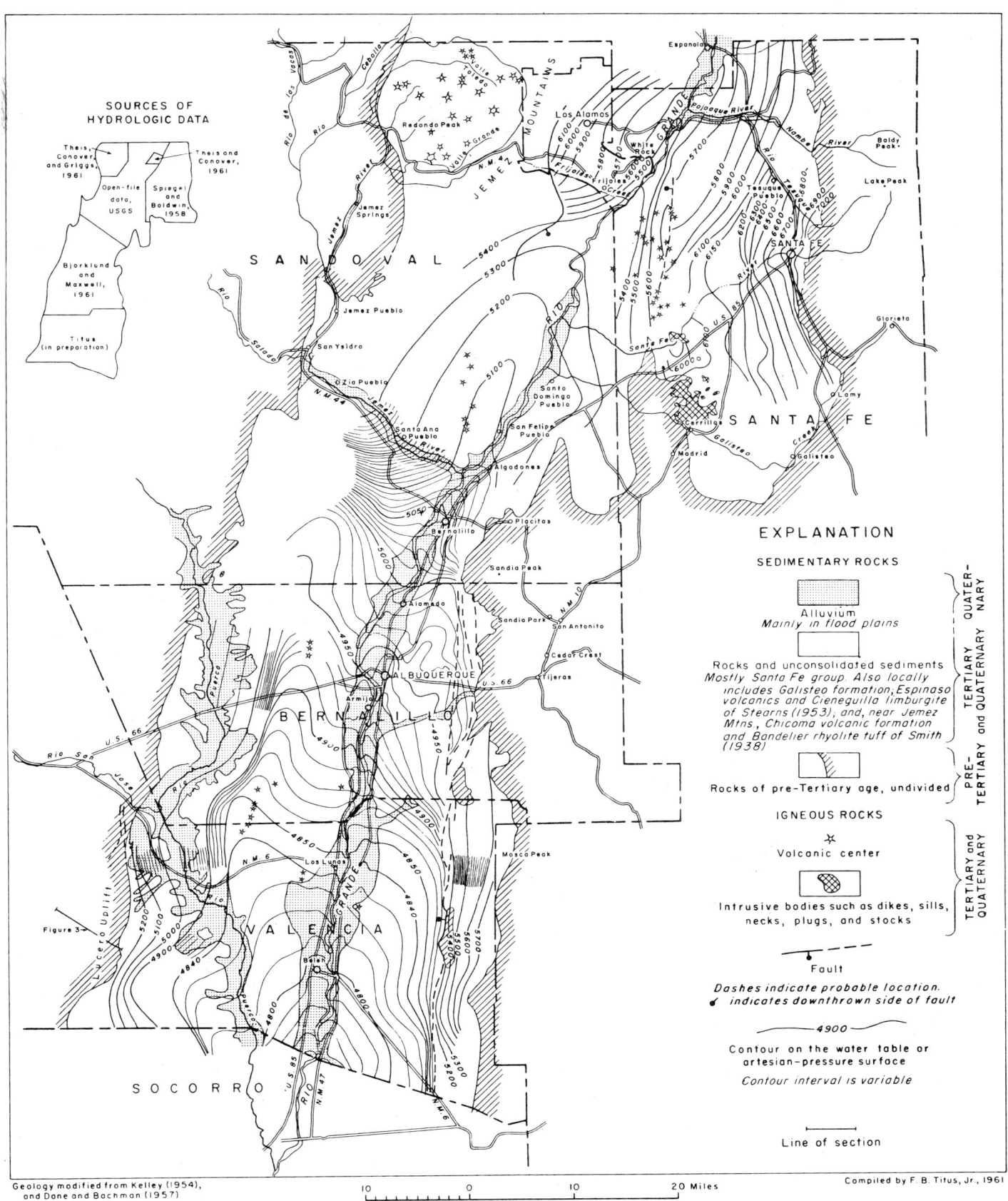

Figure 1. -- Water-table and artesian-pressure-surface contours for ground water in the Rio Grande trough in Santa Fe, Sandoval, Bernalillo, and Valencia Counties, New Mexico.

part of the discharge may come from the lower part of the Ancha formation. In the city of Albuquerque well fields the maximum yield is 3,360 gpm from a municipal well in the Rio Grande valley. The well penetrates almost 950 feet of saturated aquifer. Part of the discharge may come from the Quaternary alluvium. A well located about 5½ miles northeast of downtown Albuquerque produces 2,475 gpm from about 680 feet of saturated Santa Fe. The city of Belen pumps nearly 900 gpm from a well penetrating about 400 feet of saturated Santa Fe.

Very few data are available that would indicate potential pumping yields outside of populated areas in the Rio Grande trough. Water requirements here are not large, and most of the wells are pumped with windmills. The few available data suggest that, with aquifer penetration of a few hundred feet, only a few 10's of gallons per minute may be expected from wells in the Santa Fe a few miles or more west of the Rio Grande valley in Valencia, Bernalillo, and southern Sandoval Counties. Between the valley and the normal faults several miles east of the valley in Bernalillo County (Fig. 1) large potential yields are indicated by existing wells in the Albuquerque area. To the south in Valencia County potential yields may be somewhat lower.

The average temperature of ground water in the Albuquerque area is 64°F. Ground water pumped in 1960 from a new 1,180-foot municipal well 5 miles west of downtown Albuquerque had a temperature of 90°F. The unusually warm water may be the result of the volcanism that formed the Albuquerque volcanoes located about 4 miles northwest of the well.

Artesian conditions in the Santa Fe occur in parts of Sandoval and Santa Fe Counties. Wells in the Los Alamos Canyon well field, lying from 1 mile to about 4 miles west of the Rio Grande along New Mexico Highway 4 near Los Alamos, obtain water from an artesian aquifer, and in 1950 were pumped at rates ranging from about 250 to 650 gpm. A few miles north of Santa Ana Pueblo, water was reported to have risen 45 feet during drilling of a new well after the confining bed over the aquifer was penetrated. Across the Rio Grande from White Rock, in the northeast corner of Santa Fe County, two "artesian" wells are shown on the Geological Survey's 7½' topographic map. Artesian conditions would not be surprising in the area northwest of the city of Santa Fe. Spiegel has stated that, "As the Tesuque formation dips westward and northwestward to areas of discharge along the Rio Grande, more steeply than the slope of the piezometric surface, water must move across the dipping beds in order to discharge, even though the permeability across beds of the Tesuque formation is low" (Spiegel and Baldwin, 1958, p. 222).

Alluvium

Unconsolidated alluvium of Recent age underlies the floodplains of the major streams in the area. The alluvium consists mainly of thin to medium beds of clay, silt, sand, and fine gravel. In the Rio Grande valley in Valencia County, and possibly elsewhere, gravel is most common in the lower part of the unit. The alluvium under the valley floor of the Rio Grande resembles the Santa Fe because of the predominance of silt in both units and because of similarities in bedding and color; but it differs from the Santa Fe in that it contains larger amounts of gravel, clay, and organic material. Terrace deposits along the sides of the Rio Grande valley south of the mouth of the Jemez River closely resemble the alluvium.

The maximum thickness of the alluvium in the Rio Grande valley is about 120 feet. The thickness of the alluvium in the Rio Puerco valley is not known. It is greater, however, than the approximate 40 feet that the Rio Puerco has been incised within historic time.

The alluvium in the Rio Grande valley is the most prolific aquifer in the area because of its high permeability and because in most places nearly the entire thickness is saturated. The depth of the water table almost everywhere in the valley is less than 10 feet. The maximum reported yield from the alluvium is about 3,000 gpm. Irrigation wells with capacities ranging from 200 to 2,000 gpm number about 200 in Valencia, Bernalillo, and southern Sandoval Counties. These wells mostly supplement the surface water that is the main source of supply for irrigation. Bjorklund and Maxwell (1961, p. 34) estimate that there are between 1,000 and 2,000 small-yield wells also used for irrigation. The number of wells supplying domestic water is of the same order of magnitude.

SHAPE OF THE WATER TABLE AND DEPTH TO WATER

The contour lines on Figure 1 are drawn on the water table or on the artesian-pressure surface where the ground-water body is confined. (The artesian-pressure surface indicates the altitude to which pressure in a confined aquifer at any location would raise water if the confining bed were penetrated by a well.) The general slope of the water table and artesian-pressure surface in the Tertiary and Quaternary aquifers is southward at an average angle equal to the slope of the Rio Grande. Superimposed on the over-all southward slope is a component of slope toward the central part of the aquifer from either side. The result is a trough in the water table or artesian-pressure surface, the axis of which, as seen from Figure 1, is coincident with the alignment of the Rio Grande in some places and in other places is roughly parallel to the alignment but situated to one side.

A sloping water table or artesian-pressure surface indicates the existence of a pressure gradient in the ground-water body and, therefore, implies movement of the ground water. The movement at any point must be normal to the contour lines and down the slope of the surface.

The continued existence of a natural ground-water trough depends upon water being transmitted more readily down the central part of the trough than toward the axis from both sides. Ground-water movement parallel to the trough axis is in response to a lower pressure gradient than is movement toward the axis from the sides. In addition, the volume of water moving parallel to the axis is the sum of the volume already in the central part of the trough and that being added from the sides. Thus, a ground-water trough indicates a lineal drain for the ground-water body. In the northern and southern parts of the map area (Fig. 1), where the axis of the ground-water trough coincides with the Rio Grande valley, draining is due to the combined effect of the Quaternary alluvium, which is more permeable than the Santa Fe, and to the Rio Grande and a system of drainage ditches, which remove ground water from the alluvium and carry it off as surface flow.

Where the ground-water trough lies to the west of the Rio Grande valley and the water table is at great depth, as in much of the central part of the area, the necessary lineal drain results either from anomalously high permeability of the Santa Fe along the axis or from greater thickness of the Santa Fe along the axis than on either side. The few wells along the ground-water trough in Bernalillo and Valencia Counties do not show an anomalously high permeability in the upper part of the saturated zone of the Santa Fe. Numerous small volcanic centers lying in a discontinuous line along the axis of the trough might be related to fractures which could increase the transmissibility of the aquifer. (Transmissibility is the transmitting capacity of the entire thickness of the aquifer.) The trough in Sandoval County also has volcanic centers nearby, although they lie to the west of the trough axis. Several small faults which could increase transmissibility have been mapped along this axis (Dane and Bachman, 1957). There is some evidence that the Santa Fe is relatively thick in the vicinity of the Bernalillo County trough. Thus, great aquifer thickness and high permeability may both be factors in the existence of the ground-water troughs. The steep slope on the west side of the Bernalillo County trough suggests that the Santa Fe thins rapidly to the west of the trough axis.

The depth of water below land surface in the Rio Grande structural trough ranges from zero at springs to more than a thousand feet under the upland west of Albuquerque and under the plateaus and mesas northeast of the Jemez River. At Santa Fe, the depth to water is a few 10's of feet. Locally there are perched bodies of water at very shallow depths. West and northwest of Santa Fe the depth to water is generally between 200 and 600 feet. In the Los Alamos Canyon well field, though the artesian-pressure surface is shallow, the wells are 870 to more than 1,900 feet deep, suggesting that the water-yielding beds are well below the artesian-pressure surface.

In the alluvium of the Rio Grande valley the water table generally is less than 10 feet below the surface. On either side of the valley the land surface rises at a steeper angle than the water table. East of the Rio Grande in Bernalillo and Valencia Counties the maximum depth to the water table is 400 to 500 feet immediately west of the faults shown on Figure 1. In Valencia County ground water moving toward the fault from the east flows through the Santa Fe on top of an uplifted block of pre-Tertiary rocks. At the fault it cascades several hundred feet to a lower level in the thick Santa Fe on the downthrown western block. Several springs occur along the fault.

RECHARGE

Some recharge to the Santa Fe must take place along both the east and west margins of the structural trough since the water-table contours invariably show movement toward the center of the trough from either side. The mountains that bound the trough on both sides throughout most of the area generally have higher precipitation rates than the lowlands in the structural trough. Recharge to the Santa Fe probably occurs both from ground water percolating through interstices and fractures in the pre-Tertiary rocks and from surface runoff to the lowlands, most of which infiltrates in the alluvial fans at the foot of the mountains.

In the vicinity of Los Alamos the thick Bandelier rhyolite tuff of Smith (1938) overlies the Santa Fe above the zone of saturation. Little information is available on hydrologic characteristics of the Bandelier. Since the artesian-pressure surface slopes toward the Rio Grande, there must be recharge to the aquifer from the Jemez Mountains. The welded tuff of the Bandelier might prevent or reduce recharge to the Santa Fe in the area between the Jemez Mountains and the canyon through which the Rio Grande flows in the vicinity of White Rock.

The amount of recharge to the Santa Fe from infiltration of precipitation and infiltration of arroyo flow has not been determined. When conditions are such that this water percolates to a depth below the zone of root interception and the zone in which circulation of air can evaporate water in the interstices of the rock, even where the water table lies considerably below the bases of these zones, the water may ultimately recharge the aquifer. The time interval between infiltration and recharge is much shorter than that required for a given drop of water to move the distance from the land surface to the water table. One drop of water infiltrating below the zone of evapotranspiration may quickly release one drop of water to the water table by a sort of chain reaction. The frequency with which water infiltrates below the zone of evapotranspiration needs investigation.

THE EFFECT OF THE RIO GRANDE

The depth of the water table under the floodplain of the Rio Grande south of Algodones is in most places 7 to 10 feet. A depression in the water table under downtown Albuquerque, developed by extensive pumping and lack of natural recharge, has a maximum depth of almost 30 feet. Under most of the floodplain the depth to water is maintained at a minimum of about 5 feet by a system of drainage ditches incised in the floodplain. The drains intercept shallow ground water, carry it off as surface flow, and eventually dump it into the river. Prior to the construction of the drainage-ditch system, which took place about 1930, the water table stood several feet higher than at present, and a large part of the floodplain was a marsh.

The elevation of the bed of the Rio Grande is in many places slightly above the elevation of the natural floodplain outside of the main levees. This has been caused by alluviation in the channel since the channel was confined by levees. Because the bed of the river is generally several feet above the level of the water table, seepage loss from the river is a potential source of recharge to the alluvium. Riverside drains on each side of the river immediately outside of the levees are designed to pick up this seepage to prevent its raising the water table under the floodplain on either side of the river channel.

Surface water diverted from the Rio Grande into a complex network of distribution ditches is used extensively for irrigation purposes during the growing season. A significant portion of this water seeps to the water table, and this recharge tends to raise the water table. Interior drains, which follow natural low places in the valley floor, are designed to remove excess ground water recharged from irrigation, as well as from precipitation and subsurface inflow from the Santa Fe.

The elevation of the water table throughout most of the valley is thus fixed rather closely by the discharging effect of the drainage ditches and the recharging effect of the river and irrigation.

Transpiration by plants and direct evaporation cause large losses from the combined ground- and surface-water reservoir in the Rio Grande valley and elsewhere where the water table is shallow. The shallow water table is conducive to the growth of a group of plants called phreatophytes which will thrive when their roots are below the water table or within the capillary fringe immediately above the water table. Included in this group are willows, cottonwoods, saltcedar, and alfalfa. Bjorklund and Maxwell (1961, p. 56) estimate that where the valley is covered by dense growth of cottonwood, willow, and saltcedar, the amount of water transpired annually is about

4 acre-feet per acre. Transpiration by alfalfa where the plant is cultivated and irrigated might be greater than this.

CHEMICAL QUALITY OF WATER

The chemical quality of ground water throughout most of the area considered in this report is such that the water may be used for drinking purposes. This applies to the part of Santa Fe County for which water-table contours are shown on Figure 1, Sandoval County north of the Jemez River and west of the Rio Grande, Bernalillo County east of the valley of the Rio Puerco, and Valencia County east of the axis of the ground-water trough. Recharge from storm runoff in the Jemez River and the Rio Puerco generally contains large amounts of dissolved material. Wells located near these two rivers usually produce water too high in dissolved solids, particularly in sulfate, to be potable. In Valencia County a significant amount of recharge to the Santa Fe comes from springs and seeps along the fault zone on the east side of the Lucero uplift. Water from the springs contains a maximum recorded dissolved-solids content of 33,900 ppm (parts per million), with a chloride content of more than 9,000 ppm. This water moves generally southeastward in the subsurface to the axis of the ground-water trough which, south of Belen, is coincident with the alignment of the Rio Grande. The dissolved-solids content of the water in the Santa Fe east of the fault zone generally decreases with distance from the faults, which suggests some recharge from precipitation. The concentration of dissolved solids does not decrease to the point of potability until the water reaches the Rio Grande valley.

Ground water from the alluvial aquifer in the Rio Grande valley is somewhat more highly mineralized than water in the adjacent Santa Fe aquifer, but chemically potable water can be obtained from the alluvium throughout the valley. The concentration of dissolved solids appears to be highest at the water table, diminishes rapidly in the uppermost few feet of aquifer, and then diminishes slowly to the base of the aquifer, where it is about the same as water in the Santa Fe. It is inferred from ground-water relationships in Valencia County that the high concentration of dissolved material near the water table is caused by phreatophyte transpiration. These plants remove water from the top of the ground-water body leaving the dissolved solids behind. This process has resulted in high concentrations within the root zone, and, because of periodic flushing by irrigation and floods, has probably contributed to the content of dissolved solids lower in the alluvium.

GEOLOGY AND HYDROLOGY OF VALLE GRANDE AND VALLE TOLEDO, SANDOVAL COUNTY[2]

A large volcanic depression [Valles or Jemez caldera] in the Jemez Mountains of north-central New Mexico was studied for its potential as a source of water for the town of Los Alamos, New Mexico. The depression is bowl shaped and is roughly 12 miles in diameter. The floor of the depression is divided into a network of valleys by numerous domes of rhyolite. Two valleys in the eastern half of the depression, Valle Grande and Valle Toledo, comprise the area investigated.

[2] This section is taken entirely from the open-file report by Theis, Conover, and Griggs (1961), and consists of a condensation of the abstract with a few additional notations from the text of the report.

The Jemez Mountains primarily consist of a volcanic caldera and an encircling apron of consolidated volcanic ash and pumice. Rhyolite domes were extruded in the caldera, and the lowland area remaining between the rhyolite domes and the caldera rim was, for a time, a lake. The lake gradually filled with debris derived largely from the rhyolite domes and, in part, from rocks of the caldera rim.

The rocks that crop out in the area are volcanic and sedimentary. An older sequence of flow rocks (Chicoma volcanic formation of Smith, 1938) is of probable Pliocene and Pleistocene age; a younger series of extrusive domes and tuff (Bandelier rhyolite tuff of Smith, 1938) is of probable Pleistocene age. The sedimentary rocks are lacustrine deposits of Pleistocene age and surface alluvium consisting of terrace, fan, and channel deposits, all younger than the volcanic rocks.

The Chicoma volcanic formation of Smith (1938) and the Bandelier rhyolite tuff of Smith (1938) do not contain important aquifers in the area. The same is true of the rhyolite domes, but the blocky crust and the porous rhyolite of the domes make them important as areas of recharge for the sedimentary rocks of the caldera fill (Fig. 2). Probably little if any water flows off the domes; it percolates downward through the porous rhyolite and into the porous strata in the lake beds and perhaps the alluvial fan material on the edges of the valleys.

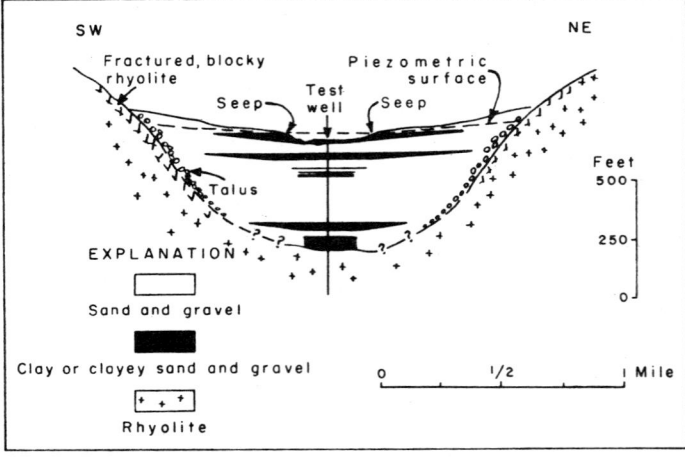

Figure 2.—Generalized section across Valle Toledo, Sandoval County, New Mexico. Modified from Theis, Conover, and Griggs (1961, fig. 4).

Several clayey members interfinger with the pumiceous sand and gravel of the caldera fill. Test drilling indicated that individual clay members are as much as 20 feet thick in the Valle Toledo; however, at places in that valley, the clayey members unite to form a clayey zone as much as 80 feet thick. In the Valle Grande, a thick zone of clay overlies a thicker zone of pumiceous sand and gravel. The maximum known thickness of the upper clay and underlying sand and gravel are 295 feet and 880 feet, respectively. The underlying sand and gravel unit was not completely penetrated by the well in which this thickness was measured. The pumiceous sand and gravel of the lake sediments form the principal aquifers in the Valle Toledo and Valle Grande, and ground water in these aquifers is confined under pressure by clay zones.

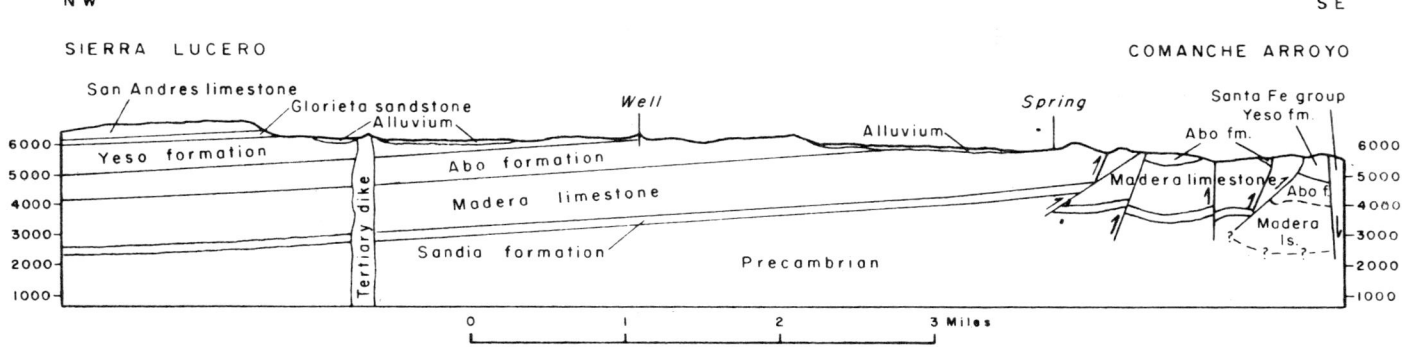

Figure 3. — Generalized section across the Lucero uplift in Valencia County, New Mexico, showing well and spring locations discussed in text. Modified from Kelley and Wood (1946, section E - E').

Properly constructed wells in the lake deposits might be expected to yield more than 1,000 gpm each. Large-discharge wells should be spaced far enough apart to avoid undue interference among the wells.

Considerable water could be pumped from storage, but the amount of water perennially available to wells in each valley would be the amount of water issuing from springs in their respective valleys — about 2,200 acre-feet in the Valle Grande and about 1,600 acre-feet in the Valle Toledo. Pumping from wells would deplete the flow of the springs, some of which now flow nearly 1,000 gpm, and thereby interfere with surface-water rights downstream.

Water from the lake deposits is high in silica content but low in total dissolved solids. The water is soft. Water in the Valle Toledo is relatively high in fluoride content and would have to be mixed with low-fluoride water before using in a municipal system.

GROUND-WATER CONDITIONS ON THE EAST SIDE OF THE LUCERO UPLIFT, VALENCIA COUNTY

Numerous springs discharge highly mineralized water to the surface along the fault zone on the east side of the Lucero uplift. In the northern part of the fault zone the water comes from rocks ranging in age from Pennsylvanian to Cretaceous that crop out on the sloping east side of the uplift. In the southern part of the fault zone, in southern Valencia County and northern Socorro County, the springs are restricted to water gaps through a hogback formed by tilted strata of the Madera limestone of Pennsylvanian age (Fig. 3; the well and spring locations in Figure 3 have been projected to the line of the cross section from nearby arroyos). The water discharging from the several springs contains from 15,000 to nearly 34,000 ppm dissolved solids, yet the ratios between individual chemical constituents strongly suggest a common source for all of the water. Apparently, dilution with water low in dissolved solids takes place locally near some of the springs. The water is very salty, having a high concentration of sodium and chloride ions, and it has a moderately high concentration of sulfate ions.

In the southern part of the area, erosion has produced strike valleys west of the fault zone. Several stock wells tap water in sandstones in the upper part of the Abo and the lower part of the Yeso formation. This water differs considerably from water discharging at the springs. It has a dissolved-solids content of roughly 4,000 to 5,000 ppm, and is predominantly a calcium-sulfate water with a low concentration of chloride ions. Water contained in this aquifer was probably recharged on the nearby Sierra Lucero and in the strike valleys, and the calcium sulfate was dissolved from gypsum beds in the San Andres limestone, the Glorieta sandstone, and the Yeso formation.

The two bodies of ground water having distinctly different chemical characteristics are separated by shales in the lower part of the Abo formation. Since both surface and subsurface drainage from the strike valleys must be eastward across the fault zone, and the only path across the hogback is through the gaps, water discharged at the southern springs is potentially a mixture from both ground-water bodies. Water from the upper aquifer is inferred to move across the Abo outcrop to the springs as underflow through arroyo channels. The underflow in the arroyos probably also includes water low in dissolved solids that is derived from local runoff.

Ground water discharging from the springs in the northern part of the Lucero fault zone on the average has a slightly higher ratio of sulfate to chloride than the water from the springs to the south. This suggests that more water is contributed to the springs from aquifers in the Abo and Yeso formations in the north. The Abo and Yeso here are mostly in the subsurface and are cut by faults.

Persistent reports have been heard from oldtimers in the area that some of the springs in gaps across the hogback yielded potable water "many years ago." Extended periods of high rainfall should increase the amount of water contributed to the springs by the upper aquifer but should not affect the contribution from the lower aquifer.

Furthermore, during these periods, ground water should be flushed more rapidly through the upper aquifer and thus have less time to pick up dissolved solids from the rock. Even so, it is a reasonable guess that what these old-time cowboys and sheepherders considered to be potable water might not meet the recommendations of the U. S. Public Health Service (1946).

REFERENCES CITED

Bjorklund, L. J., and Maxwell, B. W., 1961, Availability of ground water in the Albuquerque area, Bernalillo and Sandoval Counties, New Mexico: New Mexico State Engr. Tech. Rept. 21, 117 p.

Dane, C. H., and Bachman, G. O., 1957, Preliminary geologic map of the northwestern part of New Mexico: U. S. Geol. Survey Misc. Geol. Inv. Map I-224.

Kelley, V. C., 1954, Tectonic map of a part of the Rio Grande area, New Mexico: U. S. Geol. Survey Oil and Gas Inv. Map OM-157.

Kelley, V. C., and Wood, G. H., Jr., 1946, Lucero uplift, Valencia, Socorro, and Bernalillo Counties, New Mexico: U. S. Geol. Survey Oil and Gas Inv. Prelim. Map 47.

Maxwell, B. W., 1960, Availability of ground water for irrigation near Zia Pueblo, Sandoval County, New Mexico: U. S. Geol. Survey open-file report, 18 p.

Reiche, Parry, 1949, Geology of the Manzanita and North Manzano Mountains, New Mexico: Geol. Soc. America Bull., v. 60, p. 1183-1212.

Smith, H. T. U., 1938, Tertiary geology of the Abiquiu quadrangle, New Mexico: Jour. Geology, v. 46, p. 933-965.

Spiegel, Zane, and Baldwin, Brewster, 1958, Geology and water resources of the Santa Fe area, New Mexico: U. S. Geol. Survey open-file report, 403 p.

Stearns, C. E., 1953, Tertiary geology of the Galisteo-Tonque area, New Mexico: Geol. Soc. America Bull., v. 64, p. 459-508.

Theis, C. V., and Conover, C. S., 1961, Pumping tests in the Los Alamos Canyon well field near Los Alamos, New Mexico: U. S. Geol. Survey open-file report, 42 p.

Theis, C. V., Conover, C. S., and Griggs, R. L., 1961, Geology and hydrology of Valle Grande and Valle Toledo, Sandoval County, New Mexico: U. S. Geol. Survey open-file report, 73 p.

U. S. Public Health Service, 1946, Public Health Service drinking water standards, 1946: Public Health Reports, v. 61, p. 371-384; also available as U. S. Public Health Service reprint no. 2697.

ABSTRACTS OF TECHNICAL PAPERS
Presented at the 14th Annual Meeting
Socorro, April 22, 1960

This set of abstracts was inadvertently omitted from last year's Guidebook.

A STUDY OF THE APPARENT VARIATION IN COMPOSITION OF PHENOCRYST OLIVINE IN THE MESA PAREA FLOW, BERNALILLO COUNTY, NEW MEXICO

John H. Carman

New Mexico Institute of Mining and Technology,
Socorro, New Mexico

Samples were obtained from the flow outcrop over a length of approximately 15,000 feet. At each sample locality chip samples were taken at 6-inch intervals from the base to the top of the flow and these were combined into a single composite sample for the respective locality. In addition, grab samples of about 1 to 2 pounds each were taken from the top, middle, and bottom of the flow.

Each sample was examined in the laboratory and a portion of the phenocryst olivine was selected for x-ray analysis. Olivine compositions were determined using the method of Yoder and Sahama (1957).

The statistical range in apparent olivine composition was 72.0 to 82.0 percent forsterite, while the average for all samples was 77.4 (+ or - 1.8) percent forsterite. The distribution of olivine compositions will be discussed.

Appreciation is expressed to the New Mexico Geological Society for financial assistance.

UPPER CRETACEOUS VOLCANISM AND MINERALIZATION IN STEEPLE ROCK MINING DISTRICT, GRANT COUNTY, NEW MEXICO

Wolfgang E. Elston

University of New Mexico, Albuquerque, New Mexico

The complex Au-Ag-Pb-Zn-Cu veins of the $6 million Steeple Rock district were formerly considered epithermal and associated with Tertiary volcanic rocks. New evidence shows that volcanism and mineralization are late Cretaceous.

The rocks of the district are: Precambrian granite; Upper Cretaceous Beartooth quartzite (60 feet), Colorado shale (800 feet), pre-Datil formation dacite-rhyolite-andesite sequence (0-4,000+ feet), Virden formation (clastic sedimentary rocks, 0-4,000 feet); Tertiary Datil formation (rhyolite and latite, 2,000+ feet). No intrusive "porphyry" is known.

Pre-Datil volcanic rocks are hosts to rhyolite dikes, mineralization, and wide-spread hydrothermal alteration. They are dated as late Cretaceous by Carlile marine invertebrates in underlying Colorado shale, and Montana-Lance terrestrial plant fossils in overlying Virden sandstone. Boulders of hydrothermally altered volcanic rocks in the Virden formation date mineralization as late Cretaceous also.

Mineralization follows major NW-trending faults for over 10 miles, toward the Morenci, Arizona mining district. Like Morenci, Steeple Rock probably belongs to the Laramide ("porphyry") base-metal province, not the Tertiary ("volcanic") gold-silver province.

Favorable factors in prospecting are:
1. Laramide base-metal veins tend to persist deeper than Tertiary gold-silver veins.
2. A buried intrusive "porphyry" may be present, and could possibly be located by studies of hydrothermal alteration, hypogene zoning, and geologic thermometry.

Unfavorable factors are:
1. A buried "porphyry", intrusive into pre-Datil volcanic rocks, was probably never subjected to pre-Datil weathering and supergene enrichment, as at Morenci and Santa Rita.
2. Paleozoic limestone may be absent; hidden pyrometasomatic deposits are therefore unlikely.

Future exploration should be directed toward finding new shoots along faults and extensions of known shoots at depth. Morenci-like "disseminated porphyries" and pyrometasomatic deposits are less likely to be discovered.

COLONIAL CORALS OF THE MONTOYA GROUP

Rousseau H. Flower

State Bureau of Mines and Mineral Resources Division,
New Mexico Institute of Mining and Technology,
Socorro, New Mexico

Colonial corals of the Montoya group include 29 species in 14 genera. Those of the different formations are very distinct; in ascending order, the Second Value contains 17 species in a fauna of Red River affinities; the Aleman has yielded 9 species of Richmond and Stony Mountain aspect; and the Cutter has only 4 species, showing late Richmond and Stonewall affinities. The species in the successive faunas are readily recognized; more difficult was their correlation with forms from previously described faunas. One of the chief difficulties was the general recognition of very poorly and inadequately known species. Such problems could not be carried to completion without undertaking a general revision of the North American Ordovician corals; the results will aid in regional correlations of the New Mexico sections with those of other areas.

Some new morphological facts were found concerning the nature of the wall structure, including a previously unrecognized type of deposit; some suggestions as to the relationships of the corals resulted.

Most surprising of the present findings is a series of organic bodies attached to the corals that are unlike anything previously noted. They are described and illustrated, but their taxonomic position, even as to phylum, remains as yet highly uncertain.

PRECAMBRIAN ROCKS AT NORTH FRANKLIN MOUNTAIN, TEXAS

Robert L. Harbour

U. S. Geological Survey, Denver, Colorado

At North Franklin Mountain, in the western tip of Texas, more than 5,000 feet of sedimentary and volcanic rocks lie unconformably beneath the Bliss sandstone (Upper Cambrian?). Except for algal mounds, the older rocks are unfossiliferous and are thought to be Precambrian in age. Granite, probably Precambrian, is intrusive into the sequence.

In ascending order the Precambrian rocks consist of a limestone formation, a breccia formation, the Lanoria quartzite, and a rhyolite unit. The limestone formation, 1,100 feet thick, includes limestone, hornfels, and chert, as well as diabase sills. It contains mound-like algal structures near the base and rests on intrusive granite. The breccia, as much as 250 feet thick, consists of basalt rubble of unknown source resting unconformably upon the limestone. The Lanoria quartzite, 2,600 feet thick, is composed of fine-grained sandstone, siltstone, and shale; all are metamorphosed. It is divided into three members by a middle unit of massive quartzite. The rhyolite unit contains rounded pebbles of Lanoria quartzite at its base and attains its maximum known thickness, 1,400 feet, at North Franklin Mountain.

The limestone formation may be equivalent to the Allamoore limestone of the Van Horn area, 100 miles to the east. The other Precambrian formations in the two areas are so dissimilar that positive correlation can not be made.

PETROLEUM EXPLORATION IN SOUTHEASTERN NEW MEXICO

Phil D. Helmig

Hondo Oil and Gas Company, Roswell, New Mexico

A review of individual cases of oil exploration in southeastern New Mexico is made to determine how some of the discoveries have occurred. The story of the first oil discovered in New Mexico is reviewed and carried up to the present discovery of the 100,000,000-barrel Empire Abo Oil Field in an attempt to point out salient features of the geological and exploration processes involved.

Exploration histories of Artesia, Hobbs, Maljamar, Vacuum, Eunice, Lovington, Monument, Crossroads, Bough, Bagley, Anderson Ranch, Chalk Bluff, and Empire Abo fields are given in relationship to southeastern New Mexico geology. Finally, exploration methods and trends are discussed and extended into the future of the southeastern New Mexico oil province.

VIRDEN FORMATION AND FLORA, HIDALGO COUNTY, NEW MEXICO

Biswa M. Pradhan and Yogendra L. Singh

University of New Mexico, Albuquerque, New Mexico

Virden formation is a new name proposed for a late Cretaceous nonmarine sequence, more than 1,000 feet thick, of tuffaceous sandstone, shale, fanglomerate, and conglomerate with boulders of rounded to angular dacite, andesite, and granite. The type locality lies about six miles northeast of Virden, Hidalgo County, New Mexico.

The Virden formation lies unconformably above Coloradoan shale (Carlile) in the southeastern part of its outcrop belt, and above a thick group of volcanic rocks in the northwestern part. It is overlain unconformably by Datil formation rhyolite and latite.

No animal fossils were found in the Virden formation. On the basis of plant fossils, it was dated as late Montanan to early Lancean. Of the plants, fragments of **Araucarites longifolia** (Lesquereux) Dorf are dominant and diagnostic as to age. Other species include **Salix(?) sp., Juglans leconteana, Viburnum sp., Canna(?) magnifolia, Cinnamomum sp.**

The discovery of these fossils is significant because they are the first of Montanan to Lancean age recognized in the southwestern corner of New Mexico and because they date associated volcanic rocks.

THE GROWTH PRESSURE OF FIBROUS SODIUM CHLORIDE

Jacques R. Renault

Bear Creek Mining Company, Santa Fe, New Mexico

The effects of a so-called growth pressure or force of crystallization have frequently been observed by geologists. In particular, efflorescent crystal growths in mines sometimes dislodge portions of the wall rock, and cross-fiber asbestos may have dilated the fractures in which it grows. The growth pressure of fibrous sodium chloride was investigated in the laboratory in order to gain some insight into these phenomena.

Direct measurement of the growth pressure shows that fibrous NaCl can exert a force of 24.6 bars against a static load. Calculation of growth pressure from growth rate measurements at varying loads gives an average value of 25.5 bars. The maximum calculated growth pressure is 42.4 bars, but this probably represents a metastable condition.

The magnitude of the growth pressures of fibrous NaCl is comparable with the tensile strengths of many rocks and is therefore of geologic significance. Evidence gained from examination of rocks at Zuni Salt Lake, New Mexico, indicates that under surface conditions, the crystallization of halite in fractures can be important in the disintegration of rocks at the margins of salt lakes. The fibrous habit as produced in the laboratory, however, was not found to occur at Zuni Salt Lake.

A portion of this investigation was supported by a grant from the New Mexico Geological Society.

OPTICAL AND TWIN ORIENTATION OF SPURRITE

Abraham Rosenzweig

University of New Mexico, Albuquerque, New Mexico

Contact-metamorphosed limestone on the east flank of the Tres Hermanas Mountains, Luna County, New Mexico, contains considerable amounts of anhedral, twinned spurrite crystals. Although the crystals have no planar boundaries, plane-bounded zonal growths are common. Two laws which produce 30-degree wedge-shaped segments have been noted. Previous descriptions of spurrite from Scawt Hill, Ireland, Velardena, Mexico, and Crestmore, California, all refer to two twin planes at approximately 60 degrees, but much confusion and inconsistency is apparent in these descriptions.

Suitably oriented twins of spurrite several millimeters in diameter were removed from thin sections after determining their optical orientation, and X-ray diffraction patterns of the several twin segments were obtained by the precession method. This technique permits the determination of cleavage, optical, and lattice orientation on the same sample. The diffraction patterns display pseudo-orthorhombic and pseudo-hexagonal symmetry. A prominent cleavage appears parallel to (001) and a poor one parallel to (100). The zonal growth boundaries correspond to the planes (001), (100), (201), (20$\bar{1}$), and (20$\bar{7}$). The optical orientation is X $=$ b, Z $\wedge$ c $=$ 59° to 67°. Simple and polysynthetic twinning occur with the composition planes (20$\bar{5}$) and (001), respectively. In a few instances simple twinning occurs alternately on each law, producing sixlings which appear in thin section as twelve 30-degree segments.

LANDSCAPES AND SOILS IN THE SOUTHERN NEW MEXICO DESERT: ORGAN PEAK AND LAS CRUCES QUADRANGLES AND ADJACENT AREAS, DONA ANA COUNTY*

Robert V. Ruhe

Soil Conservation Service, U. S. Department of Agriculture, University Park, New Mexico

Ten major geomorphic surfaces have been delineated which, in order of increasing age, are:
1. Mountain slopes and summits, undifferentiated.
2. Rio Grande floodplain and tributary arroyos (modern).
3. White Bottom surface (modern): a scarplet erosion surface bordering the Jornada lake plain and cut into the Organ surface.
4. Fort Selden surface (Recent: 2,620 + or - 200 years): an erosion surface and alluvial-fan piedmont on the inner valley slope of the Rio Grande.
5. Organ surface (Recent): an alluvial fan apron bordering the mountain ranges which is cut into and below, but also deposited on, the Jornada-La Mesa surface.
6. Lake Tank surface (late Pleistocene-Recent): lake plain of Jornada Basin.
7. Picacho surface (late Pleistocene): an erosion surface and remnantal alluvial-fan piedmont on the inner valley slope of the Rio Grande: locally a rock pediment.
8. Tortugas surface (mid-late Pleistocene): a remnantal erosion surface bordering the Rio Grande and just below the outer valley rim; adjacent to the Dona Ana Mountains, in part, a rock pediment.
9. Jornada-La Mesa surface (mid-Pleistocene): an alluvial-fan piedmont from mountains to outer valley rim of Rio Grande; adjacent to mountains, in part, a rock pediment.
10. Dona Ana surface (early Pleistocene?): remnantal rock pediment and alluvial fan.

Bedrock distribution in the Organ to San Andres Mountains is: rhyolite northward to Fillmore Canyon; monzonite mountain cores with flanking, dipping Paleozoic limestones and shales with andesite and basalt sills and dikes northward to Baylor Canyon; monzonite northward to Lohman Canyon; and Paleozoic quartzite, limestone, shale, and sandstone with minor andesite to the north of Lohman Canyon.

In the Dona Ana Mountains and adjacent areas of rock pediment the bedrock is monzonite mountain cores with flanking rhyolite and latite-andesite breccias, conglomerates, and flows. Paleozoic limestone, sandstone, and shale occur also. Tortugas Mountain is dolomitic limestone.

These rocks served as the source of the sediments of the alluvial-fan piedmont (Jornada-La Mesa surface) and the mountain-front fan apron (Organ surface). Composition of the fan sediments changes northward along the Organ-San Andres front from south to north in the order of:
1. Dominantly rhyolite.
2. Rhyolite with mixtures of andesite, basalt, monzonite, and limestone.
3. Monzonite with mixtures of andesite, basalt, limestone, and rhyolite.
4. Dominantly monzonite.
5. Monzonite with mixtures of limestone and sandstone.
6. Limestone, sandstone, and shale with mixtures of monzonite and andesite.

Composition of the alluvial fans clockwise around the Dona Ana Mountains from the east is:
1. Mixture of monzonite and volcanics (rhyolite, latite, andesite).
2. Dominantly volcanics.
3. Mixture of volcanics and limestone.
4. Dominantly limestone.
5. Mixture of volcanics and monzonite.
6. Dominantly monzonite.

The Tortugas surface is cut into and below the fan piedmont gravels of the Jornada-La Mesa surface, and into mixed, rounded gravels that contain erratic cobbles. The gravels also contained the jawbones of **Cuvieronius** and teeth of **Equus**. According to Hibbard, "the **Equus** tooth associated with the mastodon jawbone based on present knowledge indicates a Kansas (Pleistocene) age". The mixed, rounded gravels are separated stratigraphically from the overlying gravels of Jornada-La Mesa surface by sands containing at least three well-developed paleosols. Thus, the mixed, rounded gravels probably are early mid-Pleistocene, and the Jornada-La Mesa surface is mid- to late Pleistocene in age. The Dona Ana surface that stands above the Jornada-La Mesa surface may be early Pleistocene in age.

The Picacho surface is cut into and below the Tortugas and older surfaces and is considered late Pleistocene in age. The Fort Selden surface is cut into and below the Picacho and older surfaces and is Recent in age. It has been dated by a buried hearth site along Fillmore Arroyo at 2,620 + or - 200 years B. P. (U. S. Geol. Survey Radiocarbon Laboratory, W-819). The Organ surface is believed to be the mountain front analogue of the Fort Selden surface.

The White Bottom surface is cut into and below the Organ surface and sediment thereby derived has been deposited in places on the lower adjacent Lake Tank surface. Thus, these surfaces are younger than several millennia. Probably both are historic or modern. The Lake Tank surface in part may date from late Pleistocene.

All sediments on which the Picacho and younger surfaces occur are local mixtures of materials derived headward toward the periphery of any source watershed.

The stage of development of surficial soils in general correlates with the sequence of geomorphic surfaces from youngest to oldest. Regosols or less intensively developed calcisols occur on the youngest surfaces. On the oldest surfaces are Red Desert soils with relatively strong textural B horizons over subjacent horizons of carbonate accumulation.
*Contribution of Soil Survey Investigations, Soil Conservation Service, U. S. Department of Agriculture.

PROGRESS REPORT ON A GRAVITY SURVEY IN THE VICINITY OF SOCORRO, NEW MEXICO

Allan R. Sanford

Research and Development Division, New Mexico Institute of Mining and Technology, Socorro, New Mexico

Eight hundred gravity observations have been made over a 400-square-mile area in the vicinity of Socorro, New Mexico. The area covered includes: (1) the Rio Grande valley from Polvadera to San Antonio, (2) the valley lying between the Magdalena and Socorro Mountains, and (3) a small area on the western edge of the Jornada del Muerto.

Although a detailed interpretation of the gravity data has not been made, some important structural features are apparent on a Bouguer anomaly map of the area. The Rio Grande graben consists of at least three linked structural depressions between Polvadera and San Antonio. Where data are available, these depressions are sharply faulted on the western margin and step-faulted on the eastern margin. The valley between the Magdalena and Socorro Mountains is a northwest-trending graben which appears to be down-dropped very nearly the same amount as the Rio Grande graben. The Jornada del Muerto in the region covered is a west-trending structural depression nearly equal in depth to the Rio Grande depression.

GEOLOGY AND URANIUM MINERALIZATION OF THE TODILTO LIMESTONE IN THE GRANTS MINERAL BELT

William D. Tipton

U. S. Atomic Energy Commission, Grants, New Mexico

In the Grants uranium district, the Todilto limestone crops out along the Todilto bench, which is the prominent erosional feature on the southwestern edge of the uranium belt. It was along this bench that uranium minerals were first discovered in the Grants area.

The Todilto limestone is a dark gray, mostly fine-grained, dense, varved, thin-bedded limestone, crinkly in the upper part and platy in the lower part. Where mineralization occurred, the character of this limestone is changed markedly; it is metamorphosed to a recrystallized, bleached, porous limestone in the upper part and a softened, partially argillized, brown-, black-, red-, and buff-colored, porous limestone in the lower part. The Todilto rests disconformably on the Entrada sandstone, and the upper part apparently intertongues with the basal silty member of the overlying Summerville formation. The uppermost Todilto unit appears to be gradational into the basal Summerville, indicating a transitional facies which is herein designated the transitional horizon or the interface horizon of the Todilto lmestone and the Summerville formation.

The intrinsic features of uranium-ore localization in the Todilto are small-magnitude anticlinal, domal, and nose structures. These structures occur as isolated features and in major structural trends that are approximately parallel in orientation with respect to one another. Moreover, some of the major structural trends seem to occur in a somewhat rhythmic pattern spaced approximately 1,000 to 1,200 feet apart. This spacing indicates an apparent periodicity of fold trends which, if it exists (is a fact), means that subsurface structural trends in a specific locality could be predicted.

The folds range in size from small crenulations to relatively large structures that are more than 60 feet across. The vertical magnitude varies from slightly perceptible to very tight, narrow recumbent folds that may attain as much as 30 feet of structural relief. Most of the anticlinal folds are very low angle to almost flat near the base of the Todilto and sharply folded to recumbent in the upper part, including the transitional horizon.

The Todilto folds are complex structures that appear to be in part intraformational structures and superimposed compressional structures. However, most of the deformation appears to have been the result of slippage between the underlying Entrada and the overlying sedimentary sequence that ranged from the Summerville to include some of the Mesaverde formation. The intermediate plastic Todilto limestone and the incompetent transitional horizon responded by flowage to differential stress generated during structural movements in the Zuni uplift. Flowage is indicated in the folds by the Todilto being thicker at the crests and near the troughs and thinned on the flanks of folds.

Uranium minerals are associated with altered rock. The alteration is characterized by bleached siltstone and bleached recrystallized limestone in the transitional horizon and the upper part of the Todilto with softening (mild to moderate argillization) and strong coloration (brown, black, red, yellow, and buff) in the lower part. The transitional horizon and the upper part of the Todilto are more strongly altered than is the lower part of the formation. A larger volume of rock is affected where strong mineralization and uranium ore bodies occur. Alteration is not continuous along the Todilto bench; it appears to be confined to belts where solutions moved. These may have been controlled by shallow sags or synclinal features. In general, the alteration is more intense in and surrounding those positive structures where uranium mineralization is localized.

The mineralizing solutions were introduced laterally into the Todilto. Those solutions evidently permeated the transitional (interface) horizon and were transmitted areally along the horizon adjacent to and along the top of the Todilto. It seems reasonable to postulate that those solutions originated as meteoric water on a Todilto bench somewhere upslope from the present Todilto bench. This water dissolved uranium minerals and other minerals and transported them, as mineralized solutions, into the sub-surface through the interface horizon.

It is suggested that the source of mineralization in the Todilto limestone was formerly existing orebodies in the Poison Canyon and Westwater sandstone of the Morrison formation. These are now ghost orebodies in space somewhere up the Zuni slope. In time, weathering and geochemical processes converted uranium deposited in the Morrison into supergene uraniferous solutions. These solutions penetrated the subsurface through the interface horizon to eventually be redeposited in favorable structural locales along the transitional horizon and in the Todilto limestone.

Uranium ore deposits of commercial significance in the Todilto have not been found in geometrically planar strata where there has been no structural disturbance. Uranium ore, insofar as is known, is always associated in some way with structure and most of the known occurrences are in anticlinal structures. Small orebodies usually are associated with small structures and the larger orebodies are usually associated with the larger structures.

The primary ore minerals are uraninite and pitchblende, associated with manganese minerals, fluorite, calcite, pyrite, barite, and hematite. Megascopically, the black uranium and fluorite appear to be closely associated. These minerals may be mixed or they may be in an intermolecular combination, with manganese being the minor constituent of the combination. The secondary minerals (oxidation products) are tyuyamunite, carnotite, uranophane, metatyuyamunite, limonite, and black manganese. These secondary minerals fill joints and vugs, and coat bedding, joint, and fracture surfaces, as mineral paint.

ABSTRACTS OF TECHNICAL PAPERS
Presented at the 15th Annual Meeting
Roswell, May 5, 1961

PERMIAN SYSTEM OF THE COLORADO PLATEAU

D. L. Baars

Shell Oil Company, Farmington, New Mexico

The Permian system of the Colorado Plateau contains a variety of marine and continental sedimentary rocks deposited during Wolfcampian and Leonardian time. In southwestern Colorado and southwestern Utah the system is largely arkosic red beds which become finer grained and segregated into distinctive units southwestward from the source area of the Uncompahgre uplift. The red beds were deposited on arid coastal plains intimately related to shallow marine environments along the southern and western margins of the province. The removal of clastics from the source area was almost complete by the close of Wolfcamp time, for Leonardian deposits consist of eolian sandstone of wide lateral extent in the Four Corners region and marine sandstones, carbonates, and evaporites along the southern and western Plateau.

Continuous sedimentation probably occurred across the Pennsylvanian-Permian temporal boundary along the margin of the Uncompahgre source area and in the San Juan and Black Mesa Basins of New Mexico and Arizona. Many local areas were positive during Pennsylvanian time, but were buried by early Permian or slightly older sedimentation. Most of southeastern Utah was subjected to late Pennsylvanian or early Permian erosion that was related to intense bevelling of the Emery and Defiance uplifts where the Pennsylvanian was entirely removed. A previously used term "Rico formation" is abandoned because it is neither useful nor mappable.

Coarse clastics of the undifferentiated Cutler group were derived entirely from the Uncompahgre uplift, and grade laterally into the finer grained lower Cutler in the Four Corners area, the Abo formation of central New Mexico, and the Supai formation of northern Arizona. The lower Cutler red beds grade westward into the lower Halgaito red beds, and interfinger with the overlying near-shore marine Cedar Mesa sandstone. The lower Cutler and Halgaito clastics interfinger with marine carbonates toward the northwest. The Wolfcampian carbonates are designated the Elephant Canyon formation in this report. The Supai formation of the Grand Canyon represents the Halgaito and Cedar Mesa formations, but the twofold distinction in the Supai (restricted) of east-central Arizona is not apparent. The equivalent Supai and Abo formations interfinger with marine carbonates toward the south and west.

Lateral equivalents of the upper Cutler are the Organ Rock-Hermit red beds, and the overlying eolian to marine De Chelly sandstone. The Organ Rock-Hermit shales are restricted to the Four Corners—Monument Valley—Grand Canyon areas. The De Chelly sandstone, the youngest Permian deposit of the central Colorado Plateau, is eolian over most of the province, but grades to marine sandstone along the southern extremes of the Plateau. It is recommended that equivalent sandstones in east-central Arizona (formerly the upper Supai formation) and central New Mexico (formerly the Meseta Blanca member of the Yeso formation) be referred to the De Chelly sandstone of Leonardian (?) age.

Post-Cutler (post-De Chelly) sedimentation was restricted to the southern and western margins of the Plateau. The oldest of these deposits, the Yeso formation (restricted), is a mixed marine association of carbonates, evaporites, and clastics that extend across the southern part of the Colorado Plateau. The overlying Coconino-Glorieta sandstone is a shallow marine deposit in central New Mexico (Glorieta) that grades westward into thick eolian deposits (Coconino). The youngest Permian deposits on the Plateau are the San Andres formation of central New Mexico, and the equivalent Kaibab-Toroweap formations of northern Arizona and the western margin of the province in Utah. These sediments are largely shallow marine carbonates and clastics, with local occurrences of evaporites.

An epeirogenic uplift occurred during late Permian or early Triassic time, but the amount and time of uplift was not great, for only relatively minor erosional features are known. The time lapse represented by the disconformity is the upper half of the Permian and the lowermost Triassic, but erosion took place late enough to allow thorough lithification of Permian sediments.

The climate of the province was arid or semi-arid during Permian time, as shown by the preservation of red beds and fresh feldspar detritus, and the presence of vast dune deserts and extensive evaporite deposits throughout the system.

THE INVESTIGATION AND INTERPRETATION OF THE NIOBIUM-BEARING SANOSTEE HEAVY MINERAL DEPOSIT, SAN JUAN BASIN, NORTHWESTERN NEW MEXICO

Edward C. Bingler

New Mexico Institute of Mining and Technology, Socorro, New Mexico

The sedimentary sequence exposed near Sanostee, New Mexico includes undifferentiated Jurassic rocks; Upper Cretaceous Dakota (?) sandstone, lower Mancos shale, Gallup sandstone, and upper Mancos shale; and Tertiary Chuska sandstone. Heavy mineral and clay mineral zones in the section are correlated with similar zones at Todilto Park, New Mexico.

Littoral marine, lagoonal, and nonmarine facies are represented in the Gallup sandstone. Mineralogic composition, grain morphology, and inclusions in quartz indicate that during deposition of the Gallup sandstone sediments the source area contained both crystalline and sedimentary rocks with the latter predominating.

Six en echelon heavy mineral lenses occur within the littoral marine unit of the Gallup sandstone. The principal mineral constituents are quartz, ilmenite, zircon, tourmaline, leucoxene, and brookite. Both the heavy mineral lenses and the normal Gallup sandstone contain niobium-bearing heavy minerals and similar mineral suites. It is concluded that the heavy mineral lenses were formed by local concentrations of heavy minerals during deposition of the Gallup sandstone sediments.

Niobium-bearing ilmenite, leucoxene, anatase, and brookite impart a high niobium content to the deposit. Twenty-seven quantitative X-ray fluorescent analyses of three heavy mineral lenses reveal a range of 0.17 to 0.30 weight percent niobium. The deposit is also estimated to contain 9-weight percent zircon and 10-weight percent titanium. Probable (790 tons), possible (5,241 tons), and maximum possible (33,410 tons) tonnage estimates are made.

GEOHYDROLOGY OF THE SAN ANDRES LIMESTONE, ROSWELL BASIN

Robert L. Borton

New Mexico State Engineer Office, Roswell, New Mexico

The San Andres limestone, of Permian age, is the most important aquifer in the Roswell basin, furnishing more than half of the ground water pumped in the basin in addition to being the main source of recharge to the Chalk Bluff formation and the Quaternary valley fill. In the Roswell basin, which roughly lies between Vaughn and the Seven Rivers Hills, and between the crest of the Sacramento Mountains and the Pecos River, the San Andres limestone consists of a thick sequence of limestones, dolomitic limestones, and dolomites with minor amounts of gypsum or anhydrite and limy shale. It is underlain by the Glorieta sandstone and separated from the overlying Chalk Bluff formation or the Quaternary valley fill by an erosional unconformity. The San Andres limestone has a maximum thickness of about 1,000 feet in the southern part of the basin. The upper portion, in particular, is cavernous and contains many types, sizes, and shapes of solution openings. Permeable zones in the San Andres limestone are very erratic and vary in extent both laterally and vertically. General zones of greater permeability exist in the vicinity of tributaries to the Pecos River.

Outcropping in a broad belt on the west and north sides of the Roswell basin, the San Andres limestone dips southeastward at about 50 feet per mile with progressively younger beds being exposed to the south and east. In the southern part of the basin the regional dip is interrupted by three long narrow northeast-trending structural zones which serve to facilitate recharge to the San Andres limestone. With the possible exception of the Y-O structural zone, they apparently have little effect on ground-water conditions in the basin.

The San Andres limestone is recharged mainly by precipitation falling on a 7,000-square-mile outcrop area extending from the latitude of Vaughn southward to the latitude of Lake McMillan. The amount of average annual recharge has been estimated and computed to be 235,000 and 266,000 acre feet, respectively. Ground-water movement in the southern part of the basin is from the recharge area eastward and in the northern part of the basin it is southward and southeastward. Ground water in the outcrop area of the San Andres limestone is under water-table conditions; it is confined under pressure where the limestone is completely saturated and is overlain by relatively impermeable beds in the eastern part of the basin. Artesian heads of more than 75 feet above land surface have been observed in local areas near the Pecos River.

Records of observation wells finished in the San Andres limestone reveal secular, seasonal, and diurnal fluctuations of artesian water levels in response to recharge and discharge. Before the construction of artesian wells the bulk of natural discharge of water from the San Andres limestone was through large artesian springs near Roswell and by upward leakage into the Chalk Bluff formation and the Quaternary valley fill. Since the early 1900's the large-scale development of artesian water by wells has intercepted much of the artesian water that would otherwise move to former areas of natural discharge. Aquifer tests of the San Andres limestone in the irrigated part of the Roswell basin by Hantush in 1955 indicate that the coefficient of transmissibility ranges from 66,000 to 1,400,000 gpd/ft. and the coefficient of storage ranges from 0.00001 to about 0.0001. In the recharge area he computed these values to be 75,000 gpd/ft. and somewhat less than 0.01.

Quality of water studies in the Roswell basin have been limited essentially to the Roswell area where the westward encroachment of saline ground water in the San Andres limestone threatens the irrigation economy of the area and the city water supply of Roswell. Drought and heavy pumpage in the Roswell area have reduced artesian pressures, thereby facilitating movement of saline water from the vicinity of the Pecos River. Seasonal fluctuations in chloride content as large as 1,500 parts per million have been observed.

The first artesian well of record in the Roswell basin was drilled in 1891. Development of artesian water by large-diameter irrigation wells began in 1903 and continued until 1931 when the State Engineer declared and closed the Roswell Artesian Basin to further appropriations of artesian water for purposes other than domestic or livestock uses. The boundaries of the declared basin have been extended until they now encompass approximately 4,000 square miles in Chaves, Eddy, Lincoln, and Otero Counties.

SAN ANDRES LIMESTONE IN THE GUADALUPE MOUNTAINS

Philip T. Hayes

U. S. Geological Survey, Denver, Colorado
No abstract available at this time.

PETROLEUM GEOLOGY OF THE SAN ANDRES FORMATION, SOUTHEAST NEW MEXICO

Edward E. Kinney

Petroleum Consultant, Artesia, New Mexico

The San Andres formation of upper Permian age is a dolomitic limestone which covers a large portion of the State of New Mexico. In the subsurface of southeastern New Mexico, the San Andres is 1,500 feet thick. The formation is made of thin to medium-thick beds of tan to dark brown crystalline and oolitic dolomite.

The Goat Seep reef of white to blue-gray limestone forms a barrier reef between the San Andres and the lower Delaware sand.

Completion in January, 1930, of a 7275 BOPD well from the white crystalline reef zone in the Hobbs pool started the real oil development of southeastern New Mexico. The San Andres along the reef front is a good oil reservoir. Production through 1960 has exceeded 500 million barrels of oil. The San Andres has been productive from four zones: (1) between the top of the San Andres and 100 feet down, (2) 25 feet above to 25 feet below the Lovington, (3) 300 to 400 feet below the top of the formation, and (4) 500 to 700 feet below the top in the Keely section.

TYPE SECTION OF THE SAN ANDRES LIMESTONE—TYPICAL OR NOT?

Frank E. Kottlowski

New Mexico Bureau of Mines and Mineral Resources, Socorro, New Mexico

The type section of the San Andres limestone, as designated by Lee and Girty (1909) and more accurately remeasured by Needham and Bates (1943), is near Rhodes Pass in the north-central San Andres Mountains. The basal 30-foot-thick Glorieta (?) sandstone member is gradational downward into reddish sandstones of the underlying Yeso formation, and grades upward, as intercalated arenaceous dolomitic limestone and yellowish silty calcareous sandstone, into a lower light-gray limestone unit, about 95 feet thick, which includes dolomitic limestones and lenses of limy sandstone and arenaceous limestone. Above is about 220 feet of dark-gray massive limestone; the upper 255 feet is of light-gray dolomitic limestone, massive to thin bedded, with some interbedded argillaceous limestone and many porous petroliferous coquinoid beds.

This type San Andres limestone contains a very large fauna, largely undescribed, and because it occurs in hard limestone and is not often silicified, the fauna is rarely collected. Brachiopods, chiefly those once known as **Dictyoclostus ivesi, D. bassi,** and **D. indicus,** characterize the lower beds; upper dolomitic limestones are dominated by a varied molluscan assemblage including many nautiloids, the ammonoids **Perrinites** and **Pseudogastrioceras,** and numerous undescribed gastropods and pelecypods. No fusulinids have been found in central New Mexico. The fauna is of Leonardian aspect.

The type San Andres limestone is about 600 feet thick but its top is recent air. Triassic (?) red beds relatively conformably overlie the limestone northwest of Rhodes Pass; in nearby oil tests, the San Andres limestone is only 650-700 feet thick beneath these red beds. Southward in the San Andres Mountains the Dakota (?) sandstone is unconformable on the limestone, and near Ash Canyon pre-Dakota Lower (?) Cretaceous strata rest on a thinned San Andres limestone, or perhaps even on the underlying Yeso formation.

The thick San Andres unit of southeastern New Mexico is dated by fusulinids as chiefly Guadalupian in age, with perhaps a lower part of upper Leonardian age. Is the type limestone merely the lower part of the southeastern San Andres unit? Is the molluscan fauna of the type limestone a relic Leonardian fauna in early Guadalupian rocks? Or is there an almost imperceptible southeastward facies change, across the buried Pedernal landmass, with the type San Andres limestone being a time equivalent of the upper Yeso-lower San Andres dolomites of the southeast?

NEW MEXICO'S FOSSIL RECORD

Stuart A. Northrop

University of New Mexico, Albuquerque, New Mexico

In 1928 N. H. Darton stated that the composite maximum thickness of Paleozoic, Mesozoic, and Cenozoic sediments in New Mexico was about 16,000 feet. Today, a third of a century later, this figure has been increased to 75,000 feet.

New Mexico's stratigraphic record for the last 500 million years from Cambrian to present is reviewed. Time and rock thickness have been plotted on a chart, together with environment of deposition. This chart emphasizes the well-known fact, on the one hand, that there are long spans of time not represented by sediments and, on the other hand, that great thicknesses of sediments were deposited in certain relatively short spans of time. The early history of notable discoveries of fossils, starting in 1844, is summarized briefly.

Floral and faunal assemblages are reviewed and analyzed. A census of New Mexico fossils from Cambrian through Eocene has been compiled. At least 2,000 species have been reported from the Paleozoic, more than 900 from the Mesozoic, and more than 400 from the early Cenozoic. A biologic breakdown shows that invertebrates (chiefly marine) lead with nearly 2,500 species, followed by more than 500 plants, and more than 300 vertebrates.

New Mexico has yielded more than 600 new species of plants and animals and several scores of new genera. In a few cases, higher taxonomic units, such as families and even a suborder, have been founded on New Mexico types.

The system yielding the largest number of species of plants and animals is the Cretaceous; second is the Pennsylvanian; and third, the Mississippian. The Jurassic has yielded very few fossils. Greatest diversity of sponges, trilobites, and conodonts is found in the Ordovician; of corals, brachiopods and echinoderms, in the Mississippian; of foraminifers, bryozoans, and ostracods, in the Pennsylvanian; of amphibians, in the Permian; of pelecypods, gastropods, cephalopods, and plants, in the Upper Cretaceous; of reptiles and mammals, in the Cenozoic.

Illustrations of actual specimens and numerous restorations will be presented.

THE STRATIGRAPHIC SIGNIFICANCE OF THE FOSSIL FERN **TEMPSKYA** IN THE WESTERN STATES

Charles B. Read and Sidney R. Ash

U. S. Geological Survey, Albuquerque, New Mexico

The extinct fern genus **Tempskya** has been found in Cretaceous rocks at numerous localities in the Western States and is of particular interest because of its limited stratigraphic range. The only known remains of the species of **Tempskya** are silicified masses of stems and roots that are organized into a composite or so-called false stem. The individual stems of the composite structure are the dichotomous branches of a single plant. The roots are small and masses of them constituted a felt-like matrix in which the branching stem system was embedded. During life some species may have had sufficient rigidity to stand erect, whereas in other species it is possible that the growth form was that of a vine. Six species of **Tempskya** have been described from the Cretaceous rocks in the Western States and material which appears to represent two new species has recently been found in rocks of Cretaceous age in southwestern New Mexico. On the bases of associated marine invertebrate fossils and physical stratigraphy it is believed that all unreworked occurrences of **Tempskya** in the Western States are of Albian or uppermost early Cretaceous age.

PERMIAN STRATIGRAPHY OF NORTHWESTERN NEW MEXICO AND ADJACENT PARTS OF ARIZONA AND UTAH

Charles B. Read and A. A. Wanek

U. S. Geological Survey, Albuquerque, New Mexico and Menlo Park, California

The Permian strata of northwestern New Mexico and adjacent parts of Arizona and Utah are dominantly clastic, although a minor amount of dolomite and limestone is present. In most of the uplifts where the strata can be examined at the outcrops the sequences are characterized by a lower suite of dominantly nonmarine red beds variously referred to as the Abo formation, the lower part or lower member of the Supai formation, the Halgaito tongue of the Cutler formation, and the lower part of the Cutler formation. Although mainly Wolfcamp in age, the uppermost part of each of these intervals is believed to be Leonard on the basis of rather meager paleontologic evidence.

In much of the area thick cross-bedded sandstones overlie these continental strata. The sandstone beds have been called the Meseta Blanca sandstone member of the Yeso formation in New Mexico, the middle member of the Supai formation on the Mogollon Rim, Arizona, the lower member of the De Chelly sandstone on the Defiance uplift, Arizona, and the Cedar Mesa sandstone member of the Cutler formation in Monument Valley, Arizona and Utah. These strata are believed to be Leonard in age.

The succeeding correlative strata are even-bedded fine-grained clastic rocks called the San Ysidro member of the Yeso formation in New Mexico, the upper member of the Supai formation on the Mogollon Rim, the upper part of the Supai in the southern part of the Defiance uplift, and Organ Rock tongue of the Cutler formation in Monument Valley. Paleontologic data indicate that these strata are also Leonard in age.

The Glorieta sandstone, the upper member of the De Chelly sandstone, or the Coconino sandstone, which constitute a second correlative interval of thick cross-bedded sandstones, succeed the underlying evenly bedded fine-grained red beds. In New Mexico the San Andres limestone usually overlies the second sandstone interval but locally it interfingers with the Glorieta sandstone. Carbonate rocks are absent above the Coconino and De Chelly and probably were never deposited in much of northwestern Arizona as well as in adjacent parts of Utah.

GEOLOGY OF THE SOUTHERN PART OF THE FRA CRISTOBAL RANGE, SIERRA COUNTY, NEW MEXICO

Sam Thompson III
Humble Oil and Refining Company, Roswell, New Mexico

Permian rocks of the Abo, Yeso, and San Andres formations are exposed in the southern part of the Fra Cristobal Range. The Abo is a typical "red bed" section. Clastic, carbonate, and evaporite units are present within the Yeso. Most of the San Andres is limestone.

To the south in the Cutter sag are the Upper Cretaceous Dakota, Mancos, Mesaverde, and McRae formations. The Mesaverde is further subdivided into an unnamed main body and the Ash Canyon member, and the McRae into the Jose Creek and the Hall Lake members. All are clastic, but the Dakota and Mancos are marine in origin, whereas the Mesaverde and McRae are continental.

The Fra Cristobal uplift trends north-south and separates the Jornada del Muerto from the Rio Grande depression. North of the uplift is the San Pascual platform. The Cutter sag joins with the Caballo uplift to the south.

Laramide (?) overturned folds and thrusts (to east) are mapped within the range proper. Upper Tertiary normal faults on the west side of the uplift trend northwest and are down to the west. Those on the east side generally trend northwest and are down to the east.

In the Cutter sag, normal faults trend northeast and are down to the west. A few north-trending, open folds are present. Important right-lateral drag folds are mapped along the faults. Some left-lateral movement is indicated on the Hot Springs fault. Strike-slip faulting may have been an important mechanism in the formation of the Rio Grande depression.

———O———

ERRATA

Page

79, column 2, paragraph 2, line 4, for "of pueblo", read "of a pueblo"

94, column 1, line 7 from bottom of page, for "rogenesis", read "orogenesis"

99, column 2, under AREAL DESCRIPTIONS . . . . . , paragraph 2, line 6, for "Pennsylvanian and Desmoinesian", read "Pennsylvanian with Desmoinesian"

102, column 2, paragraph 1, line 7, for "590 feet, sections", read "590 feet) sections"

paragraph 2, line 3, for "argoses", read "arkoses"

103, column 1, line 14 from bottom of page, for "(146)", read "(1946)"

123, column 1, paragraph 1, line 2 from bottom of paragraph, for "evidences", read "evidence"

128, column 2, last line, for "Oiland", read "Oil and"

148, column 1, title of Figure 1, delete "Rio Grande trough shown by stippled pattern"

163, column 1, subhead "Miscellaneous Metal Deposits" should be in boldface type

Albuquerque's Three Leading Downtown Hotels Are Your Hosts For Your 1961 N. M. G. S. Conference

The Alvarado
ALBUQUERQUE, NEW MEXICO
110 First Street SW, at Central Avenue

Air-Conditioned
118 Rooms with Tub and Shower
Radio and TV in All Rooms
Dining Room, Coffee Shop
Spot Light Room
Free Parking for Overnight Guests

PHONE: CHAPEL 7-0711
TELETYPE AQ 62

A *Fred Harvey* HOTEL

A new concept in modern living combined with traditional Southwestern hospitality

The Lamplighter Room and Bird Cage Lounge offers the nostalgic atmosphere of the Gay Nineties . . . roast beef a specialty! Dancing Nightly.

COMPLETELY AIR-CONDITIONED

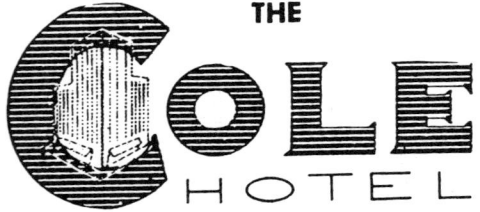

THE **COLE** HOTEL

- Spacious modern Lobby
- Downtown Location
- Free Parking
- TV in all rooms

200 Comfortable Rooms

20 minutes from airport by limousine!
Near Rail and Bus Depots
In the center of Albuquerque

TELEPHONE: CHAPEL 3-5561
TELETYPE: AQ 267

enjoy the unusual

El Seville

YEAR ROUND AIR CONDITIONING AND DRIVE-IN ENTRANCE FOR YOUR COMFORT AND CONVENIENCE

LUNCHEON
DINNER
COCKTAILS

the **Hilton** Hotel

Business and Professional Directory

**SAN JUAN BASIN
LEASE OWNERSHIP MAPS
SCALE 2" = 1 MILE**

FREE BROCHURE — WRITE

ROSWELL MAP AND BLUEPRINT CO.
"Your Oil Information Headquarters"
307 N. Penn. St., Roswell, New Mexico

LEONARD'S RESTAURANT

Best of Food — Finest in Drinks
Music Nightly — Dancing

6616 CENTRAL S.E.

**West Texas Electrical Log Service
Rocky Mountain Well Log Service
Panhandle Electrical Log Service
North Texas Well Log Service
Bess Mason Log Service**

all divisions of

Electrical Log Services, Inc.

Offices in:

DALLAS • MIDLAND • DENVER • AMARILLO
ABILENE • WICHITA FALLS • DURANGO
CASPER • BILLINGS • SALT LAKE CITY

Consider This a Personal Invitation to...

Drop in and See Us
Whenever You're
in Albuquerque

ALBUQUERQUE NATIONAL BANK
Albuquerque's oldest and largest

HEAD OFFICE—SECOND AND CENTRAL
E. CENTRAL OFFICE—4401 CENTRAL AVE. NE
N. FOURTH OFFICE—1610 FOURTH ST. NW
SIMMS BLDG. OFFICE—FOURTH AND GOLD
MENAUL OFFICE—5400 MENAUL BLVD. NE
WINROCK OFFICE—115 WINROCK CENTER
DRIVE-IN—SECOND AND COPPER
MEMBER FDIC

Business and Professional Directory

Natural Gas Producer   **Oilfield Engineers**

KINNEY ENGINEERING CO.

204 N. Orchard   Farmington, New Mexico

 **AKE MOTEL**

PHONE 376

HIGHWAY 85 & 60   SOCORRO, N. M.

There is no substitute for "know-how"

**UTLEDGE DRILLING COMPANY**

General Offices: Petroleum Building, Santa Fe, N. M.
Paul F. Rutledge, President

LIQUID CARBON DIOXIDE

delivered anywhere in the Southwest from our plant at Solano, New Mexico. Now delivering.

CARBONIC CHEMICALS CORP.
Albuquerque, New Mexico

Edward Edmunds, Jr., executive vice president

Riding Watch On Your Banking Needs Since 1890

As Roswell has grown . . . as the community has grown . . . so has this home-owned institution progressed. For 71 years we have been anticipating the ever-increasing and changing needs of our Southwest, and meeting these needs with new services to contribute more convenience and security to you.

The First National Bank of Roswell

Roswell, New Mexico

Member—Federal Deposit Insurance Corp.

QUINN & CO.
Members
New York Stock Exchange
American Stock Exchange Associate

200 SECOND STREET, N.W.
ALBUQUERQUE, NEW MEXICO

DENVER, COLORADO   EL PASO, TEXAS
FARMINGTON, NEW MEXICO   SANTA FE, NEW MEXICO

TELEPHONES   MEMBER   REFRIGERATED AIR
HEATED POOL   BEST WESTERN MOTELS   STEAM HEAT

 "Fit for a King"

U. S. HIGHWAY 70 AND 285   PHONE MA 2-0110
2001 N. MAIN ST.
ROSWELL, NEW MEXICO
C. M. MAUS   H. C. HOGAN

Business and Professional Directory

DESERT INN
DOWNTOWN MOTOR HOTEL
918 CENTRAL AVE. S.W.
ON HIGHWAY 66
ALBUQUERQUE, NEW MEXICO

Phone CH 3-1773 TWX AQ 163

Dick Kent Photography

Commercial   Industrial
Aerial   Illustrative

Photo Murals of the Southwest for home or office.

3705 Central Ave., N.E.   Ph. AL 5-4540
Albuquerque, New Mexico

PUEBLO MOTOR LODGE
Socorro, New Mexico

first in the field — foremost in research

When Schlumberger introduced the Electrical Log, new horizons were opened in the search for oil and gas. Since that time, Schlumberger research has led the way in developing better methods—better tools— for scientific, economical subsurface evaluation.

THE **EYES** OF THE OIL INDUSTRY
SCHLUMBERGER

All your money matters handled efficiently!

BANK ON US TO HELP *YOU*

We are qualified through years of experience and training to manage all your financial matters... real estate, securities, investment, taxes, etc. No matter what your problem, you may find this service most beneficial. Talk it over with us.

FIRST NATIONAL BANK 1st IN ALBUQUERQUE

Central at Third Downtown
Auto Bank Third at Copper

North Fourth at Candelaria
North Fourth.........Auto Bank

Hoffmantown Shopping Center

East Central at San Mateo
East Central..........Auto Bank

828 Bridge Boulevard SW
Bridge Boulevard..Auto Bank

Winrock Shopping Center

Member Federal Deposit Insurance Corporation

Business and Professional Directory

Happy Motoring!

on your

FIELD TRIP

HUMBLE OIL & REFINING CO.

America's Leading
ENergy COmpany

VAL R. REESE
AND ASSOCIATES, INC.
CONSULTING GEOLOGISTS

Oil & Gas Consulting For
THE FOUR CORNERS AREA

Well Drilling and Completions
Reserve Calculations and Economic Evaluations

LOBBY OF SIMMS BUILDING   **CH 3-3569**

ALBUQUERQUE, NEW MEXICO

Val R. Reese, 609 Alvarado Dr., N.E.; AL 5-9749
Lewis C. Jameson, 9811 Snow Heights Blvd., N.E.; AX 9-1561

EL RIO MOTEL
RESTAURANT
BAR

Socorro   Phone 300   New Mexico

FIFTH AND MAIN • MAin 3-3501

MEMBER FEDERAL DEPOSIT INSURANCE CORPORATION

CASE THOMPSON PRINTING CO.
1516 Fifth St., N.W. - P. O. Box 172
Albuquerque, New Mexico

Printers of the Guidebook

PI WELL LOGS
ELECTRIC & RADIOACTIVITY LOGS
Scale 1" to 100'

P. I. REGULAR LOG printed on 24 lb. rag content stock.

P. I. TRANSPRINT LOG is a reproducible log printed on 14 lb. quality rag content stock.

P. I. TRANSFILM LOGS are reproduced on CRONAR FILM (clear or matte). With Transfilm you need order only the footage sections of any wells... and scale desired. Tailor made for cross-section work.

D-J BASIN "SPECIAL" LOGS

This D-J Basin economy log, scaled 1" to 100', is on 8½x14" paper and shows Niobrara through the J sand, detail section of the Bentonite, D & J sands, microlog and caliper survey.

OTHER P. I. SERVICES

Daily Oil & Gas Reporting Services.
Up-to-Date Oil & Gas Maps in the Rocky Mountain Region.
Oil in the Rockies-Monthly wildcat map and activity summary.
Resume-annual review of Oil and Gas operations in the Rocky Mountain Region.
Production & Disposition Reports & Well Completion Cards

PETROLEUM INFORMATION
CORPORATION
DENVER, COLORADO, 1640 Grant St., Phone: TA 5-2181, TWX: DN-327
CASPER · BILLINGS · DURANGO · BISMARCK · SALT LAKE CITY

KNOX • BERGMAN • SHEARER
Consulting Photogeologists
1600 OGDEN STREET   TAbor 5-4795   DENVER 18, COLORADO

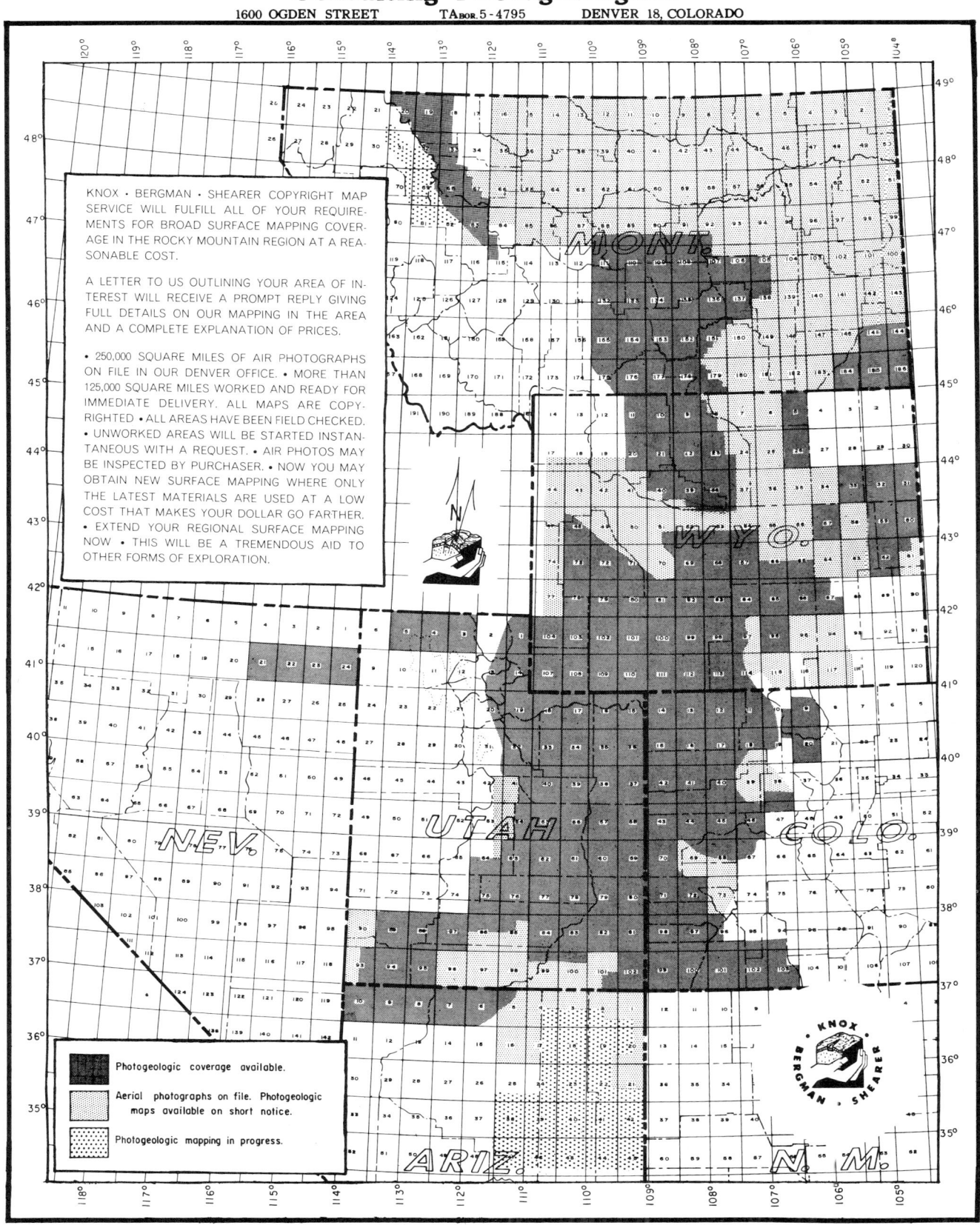

Business and Professional Directory

THE LEADERS IN
QUALITY
PHOTOGEOLOGY

Doeringsfeld, Amuedo and Ivey

240 Washington   Denver, Colorado

Tel. SHerman 4-3147

Bankers to the New Mexico Geological Society

FIRST STATE BANK
Member F.D.I.C.

Socorro, New Mexico

RESOURCES ARE OUR BUSINESS

SHIRLEY'S CAFE

Mr. & Mrs. Davy Jones and Staff

SOCORRO, NEW MEXICO

RETAILERS OF:
MAPS, GLOBES, ATLASES, BOOKS
DRAFTING ACCESSORIES &
EQUIPMENT
TELESCOPES & BINOCULARS

AUTHORIZED AGENTS FOR SALE OF:
USGS MAPS
USC & GS AVIATION CHARTS
US GOV'T. PRINTING OFFICE
PUBLICATIONS

MAPS – TECHNICAL BOOKS   DRAFTING SUPPLIES

HOLMAN'S
The House of Maps
401 WYOMING BLVD. NE
ALBUQUERQUE, NEW MEXICO
PHONE AL 5-0171

Your Host From Coast To Coast

HOLIDAY INN
of America

THE NATION'S INNKEEPER

The New Mexico Geological Society's
"Home" in Roswell

CECIL'S DINING ROOM & COCKTAIL LOUNGE   ROSWELL, NEW MEXICO

Business and Professional Directory

American Stratigraphic Company
1820 BROADWAY • DENVER, COLORADO

CASPER, WYOMING
524 EAST YELLOWSTONE

DURANGO, COLORADO
P.O. BOX 1089

BILLINGS, MONTANA
17 NORTH 31ST STREET

ANCHORAGE, ALASKA
1829 E. FIFTH AVENUE

CANADIAN STRATIGRAPHIC SERVICE, LTD.
705 11TH AVENUE WEST
CALGARY, ALBERTA

- STRATIGRAPHIC STUDIES
- SAMPLE LIBRARIES
- WELL-SITE CONSULTING

CENTRAL CANADIAN STRATIGRAPHIC SERVICE, LTD.
2027 BROAD STREET
REGINA, SASKATCHEWAN

NOTES

NOTES

NOTES